This book is an extraordinary collaboration between monastics, military chaplains, experts in international humanitarian law, and elite scholars of Buddhist ethics from diverse cultural contexts. As such, it is a valuable primary text that documents the current range of thinking about Buddhist conduct during warfare. The project produced broad intercultural and multi-perspectival cross pollination on this vital current topic, and it is essential reading for anyone working in this area. As in classical Buddhist texts, these rich studies recognise that the ethical conduct of war is as important to address as its prevention.

Stephen Jenkins, Professor Emeritus, Humboldt State University

Though both Buddhism and international humanitarian law have exactly the same intention to reduce human suffering, this ICRC-supported book represents the first concerted effort to bring them together. Internationally well-known scholars of both Buddhism and IHL have now started to engage in open and enlightening dialogue between the two domains, and this breakthrough work shows what they have revealed so far.

Oxford Sayadaw Venerable Professor Khammai Dhammasami,
Rector of Shan State Buddhist University and Executive
Secretary of the International Association of Buddhist Universities

International humanitarian law (IHL) speaks profoundly to ideas of common humanity and the need for restraint during war. These concepts are found in religious and cultural teachings across the globe. 'Buddhism and International Humanitarian Law' is a unique, necessary and timely contribution to scholarship aiming to find stronger traction between religious principles, humanitarian norms and rules of IHL. In examining the interface between Buddhism and IHL, reflecting on warfare in Buddhist history, and looking at ways to explain and teach IHL differently, this important book adds weight to the aspiration of reducing suffering during times of armed conflict.

Helen Durham AO, Board Member of Geneva Call,
Senior Fellow of the Lieber Institute, Capita Selecta Scholar,
and former Director of International Law and Policy at
the International Committee of the Red Cross

As a religion of peace, there is a conundrum concerning whether Buddhism also has a message for the conduct of war. The rich panoply of articles in this volume shows that it does. Notions of compassion, kindness and tolerance emanating from Buddhist roots all help to undergird core IHL principles such as distinction, military necessity, proportionality and precaution, thereby helping to protect those not directly involved in hostilities. This pioneering book illustrates how the Buddhist middle-way and its mindfulness techniques can nurture the self-control and sense of moderation necessary to humanise war and prevent its worst excesses.

Vitit Muntarbhorn, Professor Emeritus at Chulalongkorn University,
former UN Independent Expert and Member of UN
Commissions of Inquiry on Human Rights, current UN
Special Rapporteur, UN Human Rights Council, Geneva

Buddhism and International Humanitarian Law

What guidance can Buddhism provide to those involved in armed conflict and to belligerents who must perhaps kill or be killed or defend their families, communities or countries from attack? How, moreover, does Buddhism compare with international humanitarian law (IHL) – otherwise known as the law of armed conflict – which protects non-combatants and restricts the means and methods of warfare to limit the suffering it causes?

Despite the prevalence of armed conflict in parts of the Buddhist world, few contemporary studies have addressed these questions. While there is a wealth of material on Buddhist conflict prevention and resolution, remarkably little attention has been paid to what Buddhism says about the actual conduct of war. IHL is also still relatively little known in the Buddhist world and might not therefore influence the behaviour of belligerents who self-identify as Buddhists and are perhaps more likely to be guided by Buddhist principles. This ground-breaking volume is part of an International Committee of the Red Cross project, which seeks to fill this gap by exploring correspondences between Buddhist and IHL principles and by identifying Buddhist resources to improve compliance with IHL and equivalent Buddhist or humanitarian norms.

This book will be of much interest to students and researchers of International Law, Buddhism, Ethics as well as War and Conflict studies. The chapters in this book were originally published as a special issue of *Contemporary Buddhism*.

Andrew Bartles-Smith has many years of experience engaging with religious circles and non-state armed groups in Asia. He has pioneered ICRC efforts to promote research and debate on IHL and religious teachings and leads this project on Buddhism and IHL. He holds an MA in War Studies from King's College London.

Kate Crosby is Numata Professor of Buddhist Studies at Oxford University, UK. Her books include Santideva's *Bodhicaryavatara* with Andrew Skilton (1995), the *Mahabharata's The Dead of Night & The Women* (2009), *Theravada Buddhism: Continuity, Identity, Diversity* (2014) and *Esoteric Theravada: The Story of the Forgotten Meditation Tradition of Southeast Asia* (2020).

Peter Harvey is Emeritus Professor of Buddhist studies at the University of Sunderland, UK. His books include *The Selfless Mind: Personality, Consciousness and Nirvana in Early Buddhism* (1995), *An Introduction to Buddhism: Teachings, History and Practices* (1990, 2013) and *An Introduction to Buddhist Ethics: Foundations, Values and Issues* (2000).

Asanga Tilakaratne is Emeritus Professor of Pali and Buddhist Studies at the University of Colombo, Sri Lanka, and Founding Chairman of the Damrivi Foundation. He has published extensively on Buddhist philosophy, practical ethics and Buddhist epistemology, among other subjects. He is Editor-in-Chief of the *Encyclopaedia of Buddhism*, Government of Sri Lanka.

Daniel Ratheiser is a regional advisor for the ICRC. He studied economics and religious sciences at George Washington University and the Universities of Heidelberg and Maastricht, held consulting roles in India and China and taught at the Max Mueller Bhawan. His research focuses on cultural relations between China and India.

Noel Maurer Trew is an international law adviser for the British Red Cross, a former US Air Force research psychologist and instructor and a former volunteer for the Buddhist chapel at the USAF Academy. He holds a PhD in Strategy and Security Studies from the University of Exeter, UK.

Stefania Travagnin is Reader in Chinese Buddhism at SOAS University of London, UK. Her publications include the volume *Religion and Media in China* (2016) and three co-edited volumes on *Concepts and Methods for the Study of Chinese Religions* (2019–2020). She is Co-director of the research project *Mapping Religious Diversity in Modern Sichuan* (CCKF funding; 2017–2023).

Elizabeth J. Harris is an honorary senior research fellow within the Cadbury Centre for the Public Understanding of Religion at the University of Birmingham, UK, and President of the UK Association for Buddhist Studies, on which she writes. Her latest monograph is *Religion, Space and Conflict in Sri Lanka: Colonial and Postcolonial Contexts* (2018).

Ven Mahinda Deegalle is Emeritus Professor of Religions, Philosophies and Ethics at Bath Spa University, UK; Visiting Scholar at the University of Cambridge, UK; and Executive Director of the Research Centre for Buddhist Studies, Kandy, Sri Lanka. He is the author of *Popularizing Buddhism* and editor of several other volumes.

Christina A. Kilby is Associate Professor of Religion at James Madison University, Harrisonburg, USA. She earned her Master of Theological Studies from Harvard University, Cambridge, USA, and her PhD in History of Religions from the University of Virginia, Charlottesville, USA. She has conducted extensive fieldwork among Tibetan communities, and her current research focuses on Buddhism and displacement.

Buddhism and International Humanitarian Law

Edited by
Andrew Bartles-Smith, Kate Crosby, Peter Harvey, Asanga Tilakaratne, Daniel Ratheiser, Noel Maurer Trew, Stefania Travagnin, Elizabeth J. Harris, Mahinda Deegalle, and Christina A. Kilby

Routledge
Taylor & Francis Group
LONDON AND NEW YORK

First published 2024
by Routledge
4 Park Square, Milton Park, Abingdon, Oxon, OX14 4RN

and by Routledge
605 Third Avenue, New York, NY 10158

Routledge is an imprint of the Taylor & Francis Group, an informa business

Funded by International Committee of the Red Cross (ICRC).

British Library Cataloguing-in-Publication Data
A catalogue record for this book is available from the British Library

ISBN13: 978-1-032-57549-0 (hbk)
ISBN13: 978-1-032-57550-6 (pbk)
ISBN13: 978-1-003-43982-0 (ebk)

DOI: 10.4324/9781003439820

Typeset in Myriad Pro
by codeMantra

Publisher's Note
The publisher accepts responsibility for any inconsistencies that may have arisen during the conversion of this book from journal articles to book chapters, namely the inclusion of journal terminology.

Disclaimer
Every effort has been made to contact copyright holders for their permission to reprint material in this book. The publishers would be grateful to hear from any copyright holder who is not here acknowledged and will undertake to rectify any errors or omissions in future editions of this book.

Contents

Citation Information *x*
Notes on Contributors *xiv*

Preface 1
Andrew Bartles-Smith

Introduction: How Does Buddhism Compare with International Humanitarian Law, and Can It Contribute to Humanising War? 8
Andrew Bartles-Smith

PART I
Situating Buddhism in Relation to IHL **53**

1 Buddhist Motivation to Support IHL, From Concern to Minimise Harms Inflicted by Military Action to Both Those Who Suffer Them and Those Who Inflict Them 55
Peter Harvey

2 Implications of Buddhist Political Ethics for the Minimisation of Suffering in Situations of Armed Conflict 76
P. D. Premasiri

3 Two Dimensions of Buddhist Practice and Their Implications on Statecraft 91
Asanga Tilakaratne

4 The Paradox of the Buddhist Soldier 105
Daniel Ratheiser and Sunil Kariyakarawana

5 Buddhist Empirical Realism and the Conduct of Armed Conflict 147
Elizabeth J. Harris

6 Fundamental Intelligence, A Buddhist Justification for the Universal Principles Underlying IHL 167
Diane Denis

PART II
The Military and the Conduct of War 193

7 The Buddhist Soldier: A Madhyamaka Inquiry 195
Dharmacārin Siṃhanāda

8 Limiting the Risk to Combatant Lives: Confluences Between International Humanitarian Law and Buddhism 213
Vishakha Wijenayake

9 'Not Knowing Is Most Intimate': Koan Practice and the Fog of War 228
Noel Maurer Trew

10 Siege Warfare and the Prohibition of Intentional Starvation of Civilians: The Convergence of IHL and Buddhist Ethics 257
Nishara Mendis

PART III
Minimising Harm and Practical Values 287

11 'Freedom From Hatred': The Role of *Khanti* in Complementing the Work of International Humanitarian Law (IHL) 289
Alex Wakefield

12 Restraint in Warfare and Appamāda: The Concept of Collateral Damage in International Humanitarian Law in Light of the Buddha's Last Words 307
Bhagya Samarakoon

13 The Gift of Fearlessness: A Buddhist Framework for the Protection of Vulnerable Populations Under International Humanitarian Law 330
Christina A. Kilby

Citation Information

The chapters in this book were originally published in the journal *Contemporary Buddhism*, volume 22, issue 1–2 (2021). When citing this material, please use the original page numbering for each article, as follows:

Preface
Andrew Bartles-Smith
Contemporary Buddhism, volume 22, issue 1–2 (2021) pp. 1–7

Introduction
How Does Buddhism Compare with International Humanitarian Law, and Can It Contribute to Humanising War?
Andrew Bartles-Smith
Contemporary Buddhism, volume 22, issue 1–2 (2021) pp. 8–51

Chapter 1
Buddhist Motivation to Support IHL, From Concern to Minimise Harms Inflicted by Military Action to Both Those Who Suffer Them and Those Who Inflict Them
Peter Harvey
Contemporary Buddhism, volume 22, issue 1–2 (2021) pp. 52–72

Chapter 2
Implications of Buddhist Political Ethics for the Minimisation of Suffering in Situations of Armed Conflict
P. D. Premasiri
Contemporary Buddhism, volume 22, issue 1–2 (2021) pp. 73–87

Chapter 3
Two Dimensions of Buddhist Practice and Their Implications on Statecraft
Asanga Tilakaratne
Contemporary Buddhism, volume 22, issue 1–2 (2021) pp. 88–101

Chapter 4
The Paradox of the Buddhist Soldier
Daniel Ratheiser and Sunil Kariyakarawana
Contemporary Buddhism, volume 22, issue 1–2 (2021) pp. 102–143

Chapter 5
Buddhist Empirical Realism and the Conduct of Armed Conflict
Elizabeth J. Harris
Contemporary Buddhism, volume 22, issue 1–2 (2021) pp. 144–163

Chapter 6
Fundamental Intelligence, A Buddhist Justification for the Universal Principles Underlying IHL
Diane Denis
Contemporary Buddhism, volume 22, issue 1–2 (2021) pp. 164–189

Chapter 7
The Buddhist Soldier: A Madhyamaka Inquiry
Dharmacārin Siṃhanāda
Contemporary Buddhism, volume 22, issue 1–2 (2021) pp. 190–207

Chapter 8
Limiting the Risk to Combatant Lives: Confluences Between International Humanitarian Law and Buddhism
Vishakha Wijenayake
Contemporary Buddhism, volume 22, issue 1–2 (2021) pp. 208–222

Chapter 9
'Not Knowing Is Most Intimate': Koan Practice and the Fog of War
Noel Maurer Trew
Contemporary Buddhism, volume 22, issue 1–2 (2021) pp. 223–251

Chapter 10
Siege Warfare and the Prohibition of Intentional Starvation of Civilians: The Convergence of IHL and Buddhist Ethics
Nishara Mendis
Contemporary Buddhism, volume 22, issue 1–2 (2021) pp. 252–280

Chapter 11
'Freedom From Hatred': The Role of Khanti *in Complementing the Work of International Humanitarian Law (IHL)*
Alex Wakefield
Contemporary Buddhism, volume 22, issue 1–2 (2021) pp. 281–298

Chapter 12

Restraint In Warfare and Appamāda: The Concept of Collateral Damage in International Humanitarian Law in Light of the Buddha's Last Words
Bhagya Samarakoon
Contemporary Buddhism, volume 22, issue 1–2 (2021) pp. 299–321

Chapter 13

The Gift of Fearlessness: A Buddhist Framework for the Protection of Vulnerable Populations Under International Humanitarian Law
Christina A. Kilby
Contemporary Buddhism, volume 22, issue 1–2 (2021) pp. 322–334

Chapter 14

Addressing the Causes of Conflict-Related Sexual Violence with the Buddhist Doctrine of Lack of a Permanent Self and Meditation Training
Charya Samarakoon
Contemporary Buddhism, volume 22, issue 1–2 (2021) pp. 335–354

Chapter 15

How Buddhist Principles Can Help the Practical Implementation of IHL Values During War with Respect to Non-Combatants
Ven Kosgama Muditha, Ven Koralegama Gnanawasa and Ven Kirindiwela Pagngnawansa
Contemporary Buddhism, volume 22, issue 1–2 (2021) pp. 355–366

Chapter 16

Buddhism, the Royal Imaginary and Limits in Warfare: The Moderating Influence of Precolonial Myanmar Royal Campaigns on Everyday Warriors
Michael W. Charney
Contemporary Buddhism, volume 22, issue 1–2 (2021) pp. 367–379

Chapter 17

Between Common Humanity and Partiality: The Chogye Buddhist Chaplaincy Manual of the South Korean Military and Its Relevance to International Humanitarian Law
Hyein Lee
Contemporary Buddhism, volume 22, issue 1–2 (2021) pp. 380–397

Chapter 18

International Humanitarian Law and Nichiren Buddhism
Daiki Kinoshita
Contemporary Buddhism, volume 22, issue 1–2 (2021) pp. 398–413

Chapter 19

Socially Engaged Buddhism and Principled Humanitarian Action During Armed Conflict
Ha Vinh Tho, Edith Favoreu and Noel Maurer Trew
Contemporary Buddhism, volume 22, issue 1–2 (2021) pp. 414–436

For any permission-related enquiries please visit:
http://www.tandfonline.com/page/help/permissions

Notes on Contributors

Andrew Bartles-Smith has many years of experience engaging with religious circles and non-state armed groups in Asia. He has pioneered ICRC efforts to promote research and debate on IHL and religious teachings and leads this project on Buddhism and IHL. He holds an MA in War Studies from King's College London.

Michael W. Charney is a military and imperial historian specialising in Southeast Asia in both the premodern and modern periods. He received his PhD at the University of Michigan, Ann Arbor, USA, in 1999. After two years as a postdoctoral research fellow with the Centre for Advanced Studies at the National University of Singapore (1999–2001), Singapore, he joined the School of African and Oriental Studies at the University of London, UK.

Kate Crosby is Numata Professor of Buddhist Studies at Oxford University, UK. Her books include Santideva's *Bodhicaryavatara* with Andrew Skilton (1995), the *Mahabharata's The Dead of Night & The Women* (2009), *Theravada Buddhism: Continuity, Identity, Diversity* (2014) and *Esoteric Theravada: The Story of the Forgotten Meditation Tradition of Southeast Asia* (2020).

Ven Mahinda Deegalle is Emeritus Professor of Religions, Philosophies and Ethics at Bath Spa University, UK; Visiting Scholar at the University of Cambridge, UK; and Executive Director of the Research Centre for Buddhist Studies, Kandy, Sri Lanka. He is the author of *Popularizing Buddhism* and editor of several other volumes.

Diane Denis is Assistant Professor of Buddhist studies and languages at Kathmandu University, Nepal. She is an active scholar, translator, philosopher and socially concerned individual. Her research interests include Indian and Tibetan Buddhist philosophy, in particular the works of Maitreya and their practical application to today's world. She has a long experience of fieldwork in Nepal, India and Tibet and shares her actual teaching time between Nepal, France and Quebec.

Edith Favoreu is a co-coordinator of the Certificate of Advanced Studies 'Happiness in Organisations' at the Geneva Management School and head of the

'Happy Schools' programme in Switzerland. She is also a senior programme advisor, trainer and facilitator at the Eurasia Learning Institute for Happiness and Wellbeing. She has worked in development aid in fragile contexts and post-conflict areas for over 16 years, operating in field and headquarters roles for national and international NGOs and for UNESCO.

Ven Koralegama Gnanawasa earned his BA degree in Buddhist studies from the University of Peradeniya (2018) and is currently reading for his master's of philosophy in the Postgraduate Institute of Humanities and Social Sciences at the University of Peradeniya, Sri Lanka.

Elizabeth J. Harris is an honorary senior research fellow within the Cadbury Centre for the Public Understanding of Religion at the University of Birmingham, UK, and President of the UK Association for Buddhist Studies, on which she writes. Her latest monograph is *Religion, Space and Conflict in Sri Lanka: Colonial and Postcolonial Contexts* (2018).

Peter Harvey is Emeritus Professor of Buddhist studies at the University of Sunderland, UK. His books include *The Selfless Mind: Personality, Consciousness and Nirvana in Early Buddhism* (1995), *An Introduction to Buddhism: Teachings, History and Practices* (1990, 2013) and *An Introduction to Buddhist Ethics: Foundations, Values and Issues* (2000).

Sunil Kariyakarawana has been lecturing on Buddhism, philosophy, theoretical linguistics and cognitive science for over 20 years at several universities including the University of Kelaniya, Sri Lanka; City, University of London, UK; Cardiff University in Wales, UK; University College London, UK; Cornell University, USA; and Rikkyo University, Tokyo, Japan. He provides spiritual/pastoral advice and guidance to the Ministry of Defence and other government departments in the United Kingdom.

Christina A. Kilby is Associate Professor of Religion at James Madison University, Harrisonburg, USA. She earned her Master of Theological Studies from Harvard University, Cambridge, USA, and her PhD in History of Religions from the University of Virginia, Charlottesville, USA. She has conducted extensive fieldwork among Tibetan communities, and her current research focuses on Buddhism and displacement.

Daiki Kinoshita works for the Public Relations Office of the Soka Gakkai and is responsible for academic affairs. He has been an associate member of the Japanese Association for the Study of Religion and Society since 2012, a member of the Research Institute for Indo-Pacific Affairs since 2019 and a member of the International Human Rights Law Association since 2021.

Hyein Lee is a doctoral candidate at the Graduate School of East Asian Studies at Freie Universitat Berlin, Germany, and holds a master of arts from the Graduate School of Korean Studies at the Academy of Korean Studies and a bachelor of education from the Seoul National University of Education,

South Korea. Her research interests include Buddhist military chaplaincy, Buddhist militia and institutionalisation processes of Buddhist concepts in contemporary society.

Nishara Mendis is Senior Lecturer in the Department of Public and International Law at the Faculty of Law at the University of Colombo, Sri Lanka, and an attorney-at-law. She is the academic co-ordinator of the E-Diploma in Human Rights for the Center for the Study of Human Rights. She has a keen interest in the interface of religion and literature with law and ethics and has taught and been a research adviser for members of the armed forces and police on human rights and humanitarian law.

Ven Kosgama Muditha earned his BA degree in Pali studies from the University of Peradeniya (2018), Sri Lanka; was a temporary lecturer (2020–2021) in the Department of Pali and Buddhist Studies at the University of Peradeniya, Sri Lanka; and is currently reading for his master's degree at the Centre of Buddhist Studies at the University of Hong Kong, Hong Kong.

Ven Kirindiwela Pagngnawansa earned his BA degree in Buddhist studies from the University of Peradeniya, Sri Lanka (2018), and is currently reading for his master's of philosophy in the Postgraduate Institute of Humanities and Social Sciences at the University of Peradeniya, Sri Lanka.

P. D. Premasiri is Emeritus Professor of Pali and Buddhist studies at the University of Peradeniya, Sri Lanka. He is still affiliated with its Postgraduate Institute of Social Sciences and Humanities and with the Sri Lanka International Buddhist Academy (SIBA). He has published extensively in the areas of Buddhist philosophy, Buddhist ethics, Buddhist psychology and comparative philosophy.

Daniel Ratheiser is a regional advisor for the ICRC. He studied economics and religious sciences at George Washington University and the Universities of Heidelberg and Maastricht, held consulting roles in India and China and taught at the Max Mueller Bhawan. His research focuses on cultural relations between China and India.

Bhagya Samarakoon is a researcher attached to the Centre for Policy Alternatives, Colombo, Sri Lanka. She obtained her LLB from the Faculty of Law at the University of Colombo in 2020. As a student at the Faculty of Law, she was a member of the semi-finalist team at the Jean Pictet Competition on International Humanitarian Law (IHL) (34th Edition) in Denpasar, Bali, in 2020 and was also Editorial Assistant for the *Colombo Law Review* (2019) at the Faculty of Law at the University of Colombo, Sri Lanka. Her publications include articles in the *Colombo Law Review* and the *Colombo Law Journal.*

Charya Samarakoon holds a bachelor of laws degree from the Faculty of Law at the University of Colombo, Sri Lanka, and is a researcher for the Research and Advocacy Team at the Centre for Policy Alternatives.

Dharmacārin Siṃhanāda is a Buddhist practitioner and teacher. His principal interests are dialectics, Madhyamaka as anti-philosophy and the Yogacara-Madhyamaka synthesis. As a secular professional, he has broad cross-sector experience over 40+ years as a researcher, psychometrician, teacher, trainer of trainers, business school lecturer, group facilitator, activist, change agent and management consultant in the field of organisational development (OD). His efforts to cross-fertilise these fields with traditional Buddhist practice include harnessing Madhyamaka as a problem-solving technology.

Asanga Tilakaratne is Emeritus Professor of Pali and Buddhist Studies at the University of Colombo, Sri Lanka, and Founding Chairman of the Damrivi Foundation. He has published extensively on Buddhist philosophy, practical ethics and Buddhist epistemology, among other subjects. He is Editor-in-Chief of the *Encyclopaedia of Buddhism*, Government of Sri Lanka.

Stefania Travagnin is Reader in Chinese Buddhism at SOAS University of London, UK. Her publications include the volume *Religion and Media in China* (2016) and three co-edited volumes on *Concepts and Methods for the Study of Chinese Religions* (2019–2020). She is Co-director of the research project *Mapping Religious Diversity in Modern Sichuan* (CCKF funding; 2017–2023).

Noel Maurer Trew is an international law adviser for the British Red Cross, a former US Air Force research psychologist and instructor and a former volunteer for the Buddhist chapel at the USAF Academy. He holds a PhD in Strategy and Security Studies from the University of Exeter, UK.

Ha Vinh Tho is Founder of the Eurasia Learning Institute for Happiness and Wellbeing and Chairman of the Eurasia Foundation. He was Program Director of the Gross National Happiness (GNH) Center Bhutan and is the former Head of Training, Learning and Development at the International Committee of the Red Cross. He is a lay Buddhist teacher in the Vietnamese Zen Tradition (Thich Nhat Hanh).

Alex Wakefield is a writer and researcher. He holds a master's degree in Buddhist studies from SOAS University of London, UK, with research focusing on Buddhist and ancient Indian cosmology. He has worked as Visiting Lecturer at the University of Greenwich, UK, and currently develops educational programmes for Buddhist centres in the UK.

Vishakha Wijenayake is a doctoral candidate at McGill University's Faculty of Law, Montreal, Canada, specialising in international humanitarian law. At McGill, she is also an O'Brien fellow attached to the Center for Human Rights and Pluralism and a recipient of a grant by Fonds de recherche du Québec. Her publications include peer-reviewed articles in journals such as the *International Review of the Red Cross*. She has also contributed to research for the ICRC-updated commentaries to the Four Geneva Conventions and the Customary IHL study of the ICRC. Her research interests include international humanitarian law, international human rights law, gender studies and legal pluralism.

ICRC

PREFACE

Andrew Bartles-Smith

What guidance can Buddhism provide to those involved in armed conflict, and to belligerents who must perhaps kill or be killed, or defend their families, communities or countries from attack? How, moreover, does Buddhism compare with international humanitarian law (IHL) – otherwise known as the law of armed conflict – which protects non-combatants and restricts the means and methods of warfare in order to limit the suffering it causes?

Despite the prevalence of armed conflict in parts of the Buddhist world, few contemporary studies have addressed these questions. While there is a wealth of material on Buddhist conflict prevention and resolution, remarkably little attention has been paid to what Buddhism says about the actual conduct of war. IHL is also still relatively little known in the Buddhist world, and might not therefore influence the behaviour of belligerents who self-identify as Buddhists and are perhaps more likely to be guided by Buddhist principles.

It was for these reasons that in 2017 the International Committee of the Red Cross (ICRC), whose mandate is to assist and protect victims of armed conflict and to promote respect for IHL, launched a project on Buddhism and IHL. Having reached out to Buddhist clergy, scholars, legal experts, and military and humanitarian actors around the world, the first phase of the project culminated in an international conference titled 'Reducing Suffering During Armed Conflict: The Interface Between Buddhism and International Humanitarian Law' in Dambulla, Sri Lanka, in 2019. It was here that the first drafts of the articles that comprise this volume were presented.[1] A substantial co-written article with the same name (Bartles-Smith et al. 2020), an early draft of which served as the position paper for the conference, was also published in the previous volume of *Contemporary Buddhism* (21: 1–2), staking out the territory with regard to the study of both Buddhism and IHL and its potential practical applications.[2]

DOI: 10.4324/9781003439820-1

This volume and the project of which it is a part has a number of aims. Firstly, it identifies correspondences between Buddhism and IHL by examining Buddhist teachings and concepts relevant to the conduct of war with which Buddhist belligerents might be more familiar. Insofar as Buddhism and IHL align, and Buddhist principles correspond with IHL rules, this should help to legitimise and improve compliance with IHL in Buddhist-majority contexts, and might be integrated into IHL education and military training programmes. While militaries in Buddhist-majority countries have often adopted Western training models, this project offers the possibility that Buddhist combatants might also draw on a Buddhist legacy of restraint in war. Moreover, Buddhist clergy in many countries are often highly respected by their communities, governments, military personnel and non-state armed group members, and Buddhist guidance with respect to conduct of hostilities, and by extension IHL, can therefore be significantly enhanced through them.

Beyond correspondences between IHL and Buddhist principles, this volume also explores how Buddhist practices and psychological resources might be directed to improve voluntary compliance with IHL and equivalent Buddhist or humanitarian norms, thereby bridging the disconnect between IHL and its implementation to some degree. The Buddhist focus on the training of the mind, and its remarkable mindfulness techniques, hold out the possibility that military training might be enhanced to heighten resilience, self-control and situational awareness of the battlespace in high-stress conflict situations, better equipping combatants to act with precision and restraint.

A first milestone was achieved when Professor Peter Harvey, Professor P. D. Premasiri and Professor Asanga Tilakaratne wrote the initial drafts of position papers on the subject. This established a framework for research as it subsequently developed, and which informed the position paper and call for papers for the Dambulla conference.[3] The articles in this volume have been reviewed and refined over the intervening period by project working group members, the editorial team of *Contemporary Buddhism* and IHL experts. Apart from Buddhist and legal scholars, they include contributions from humanitarian and other practitioners, and are not an exclusively academic endeavour.

The volume opens with an introductory article on Buddhism and IHL by Andrew Bartles-Smith, which outlines much of the rationale for the project and compares and contrasts the normative systems of Buddhism and IHL, including the just war roots from which IHL emerged. The article then identifies aspects of Buddhism most pertinent to the regulation of armed conflict, including the training of military personnel, and explores the degree to which Buddhism and IHL might complement and reinforce one another to humanise the conduct of war.

The first section of the volume, *Situating Buddhism in Relation to IHL*, contains articles that lay down some of the groundwork on the topic. It opens with an article by Peter Harvey, who argues that Buddhist compassion and concern to limit the bad karmic consequences of one's actions mean that it is in the interest of Buddhist combatants to regulate their intention and minimise the harm they inflict during armed conflict strictly in accordance with IHL principles of humanity, military necessity, distinction, proportionality and precaution. Harvey explains that while IHL lays down rules to be followed, Buddhism emphasises broader ethical principles and motivations that can be incorporated into military training and contribute to better IHL compliance.

P. D. Premasiri concurs that the fundamental principles of Buddhist ethics underline the minimisation of suffering during war, and reflects on the inner roots of armed conflict. Focusing on the realm of political ethics, Premasiri examines Buddhist ideals of statecraft with respect to the conduct of war in Pali texts, and highlights examples of Buddhist restraint in the *jātaka* tales and stories about the god Sakka, as well as the edicts of emperor Ashoka and the Sri Lankan *Mahāvaṃsa* chronicle.

Asanga Tilakaratne argues that in the context of war, as elsewhere, ethical expectations for monastics aiming to achieve enlightenment or liberation from *saṃsāra* should be distinguished from those of lay Buddhist belligerents with the lesser ambition of achieving better rebirths within it. Lay Buddhists must pragmatically balance Buddhist ideals with their worldly responsibilities, not least to defend their loved ones, communities and countries from attack. Tilakaratne argues that acts that are 'meritorious' (*puñña*) by worldly standards, although skilful (*kusala*) to a degree, are not therefore the same as a nirvana-seeker's *kusala* acts. Buddhism therefore understands that defensive or protective war, while unfortunate, is sometimes necessary, and that lay Buddhist belligerents must balance Buddhist and humanitarian ideals with military goals, in line with IHL.

Daniel Ratheiser and Sunil Kariyakarawana examine the apparent paradox between Buddhism and the military. By drawing on canonical Buddhist teachings as well as voices from the Sangha and Buddhist military practitioners, they challenge the idea that serving in the military is necessarily at odds with Buddhist ideas of ahiṃsā, karma and skilful (*kusala*) action. They then explore what guidance Buddhist teachings provide to soldiers and its implications for military training, arguing that Buddhism endorses the maintenance of disciplined, virtuous and skilled military forces to defend what is good.

Drawing on examples from the *Sutta Piṭaka*, Elizabeth Harris shows that, contrary to popular perception, the Pali texts of early Buddhism such as the *Cakkavatti-sīhanāda Sutta* (Dn.26), *Mahā-dukkha-kkhandha Sutta* (Mn.13) and

Mahā-nidāna Sutta (Dn.15) are characterised by an empirical realism that is deeply acquainted with the grim realities of war. They also contain a sophisticated analysis of the psychological and societal causes of armed conflict and its intractable nature, and how greed, hatred and delusion produce different constructions of reality in human communities that are fed by *papañca*, or proliferating thought. Harris shows how these constructions exacerbate the bitterness of armed conflict and increase the likelihood that parties to conflict might resist compliance with IHL or hamper the work of humanitarian actors.

Diane Denis's article explores the interface of IHL with the *Dharma-dharmatā-vibhāga* (DDV), an ancient North Indian Mahāyāna Buddhist text often associated with the Yogācāra school. It explores how such texts can provide insight into the nature of the universal principles that IHL is said to embody, and how they might relate to the inner workings of the individual consciousness in relation to armed conflict, informing both the individual and collective concerns of IHL. According to the DDV, the nature of all living organisms is fundamental wisdom or intelligence which is inseparable from compassion, and Denis explores how these ideas might develop individual willingness to care for others and behave ethically even during armed conflict.

The second section of the volume, *The Military and the Conduct of War*, focuses on Buddhist guidance for combatants in particular, and how Buddhism might contribute to improving the conduct of hostilities. It opens with an article by Dharmacārin Siṃhanāda, who examines the idea of the Buddhist Soldier, viewed by some as something of a contradiction given the centrality of non-violence or non-harming (ahiṃsā) to Buddhism. Rather than look to examples of how Buddhist principles might apply within the military context, Siṃhanāda adopts a Madhyamaka approach to seek an understanding of what it might mean to be a Buddhist soldier using Buddhist conceptual tools.

Vishakha Wijenayake examines how both Buddhism and IHL encourage reciprocal restraint during armed conflict, not least to protect the lives of combatants themselves. She examines Buddhist teachings in this regard alongside IHL, particularly the narratives of the *jātaka* stories, and looks in particular at how unnecessary risk to combatants is mitigated through the IHL rule of surrender, which is endorsed in the *Seyya Jātaka* (no. 282).

Noel Trew investigates how Zen kōan practice, a form of meditation involving short stories or riddles to focus attention, might help alleviate the notoriously difficult problem of applying IHL to targeting in practice, since compliance requires combatants to correctly understand what is happening in the battlespace. He argues that kōan practice can better prepare combatants to make important decisions based on ambiguous information, and to correct errors in their thinking or perception, thereby helping them to cut through the fog of war.

Siege warfare is as old as civilisation and still a depressingly frequent feature of contemporary warfare. Nishara Mendis draws on the *Ummagga Jātaka* (no. 546) and *Asātarūpa Jātaka* (no. 100) to examine how Buddhist ethics might support IHL to regulate siege warfare and prevent the intentional starvation of civilians, and argues that the complexity of these ancient case studies suggests their potential use in legal or military training and education.

The third section of the volume, *Minimising Harm and Practical Values*, focuses on specific Buddhist qualities, concepts and practices relevant to the practical minimisation of harm during armed conflict. Alex Wakefield first explores how the Buddhist quality of *khanti/kṣānti* – patience, forbearance or tolerance – can support IHL by reducing unskilful behaviour during war. Since *khanti* is the opposite of hatred and anger, and encompasses non-retaliation and forgiveness, it is particularly relevant to the conduct of war, negating anger and the consequent loss of self-control that can lead to the use of excessive force, including atrocities motivated by victimhood and revenge. Wakefield argues that *brahma-vihāra* meditations can be used to develop *khanti*, and can be combined with *mettā* practice and *anattā* analysis to reinforce military training and IHL compliance.

Bhagya Samarakoon examines how the Buddhist quality of *appamāda* or 'heedfulness', mentioned several times in the Buddha's sermons and in his last words, can contribute to restraint in warfare and reduction of collateral damage. This is particularly important since the decision to proceed with an attack that could cause harm to civilians is dependent on the perceptions, values and good faith of the military commander in the specific instance, and is highly relevant to the IHL principle of precaution. She argues that the concept has a moral dimension that is useful in decision-making for Buddhists engaged in warfare, and can be transmitted through both sermons and meditation.

Christina Kilby presents *abhaya-dāna*, 'the gift of fearlessness', as a Buddhist framework for the protection of populations who are vulnerable to violence, terror or displacement during times of armed conflict. Although it is an ancient Indian idea rarely invoked by Buddhists today, she argues that *abhaya-dāna* is a vital Buddhist principle of protection that complements and reinforces principles of protection enshrined in IHL, and reminds governments and parties to conflict of their duty to protect those they purport to govern.

Conflict-related sexual violence remains prevalent in warfare despite global efforts to address it. Charya Samarakoon examines how Buddhist teachings and practices might complement IHL to help address this problem. She focuses in particular on the use of meditation training for combatants, and the importance of the Buddhist doctrine of a lack of a permanent self as expounded in the *Anattalakkhaṇa Sutta* (Sam.22.59), thereby increasing their capacity for empathy and compassion. Samarakoon argues that these Buddhist resources are a practical means of dispelling the toxic conceptions of power and gender that exacerbate sexual violence in armed conflict situations.

Ven. Kosgama Muditha, Ven. Koralegama Gnanawasa and Ven. Kirindiwela Pagngnawansa then examine how Buddhism can facilitate the practical application of IHL and reduce suffering in war by increasing awareness of the mental defilements at the root of conflicts. They argue that Buddhist teachings can help belligerents to develop the necessary self-control, discipline and responsibility for the humane and impartial treatment of all those caught up in war, with particular reference to the *Vepacitti Sutta* (Sam.11.4), and suggest that a formula provided in the *Mahācattārīsaka Sutta* (Mn.117) can aid in the practical application of these qualities.

The fourth and final section of the volume, *Buddhist Historical and Humanitarian Dimensions*, focuses on historical examples in which Buddhist principles have been put into practice in relation to war, and on Buddhist humanitarian responses to armed conflict. Michael Charney argues that while IHL rules for the protection of non-combatants are often attributed to Western origins, restraint in the conduct of war was pursued by many non-Western societies, and shows how the court of pre-colonial Myanmar developed its own Buddhist-inspired limits on warfare. He goes on to explain how this model was forgotten due to the British removal of the Burmese king, disintegration of the standing army and the brutal Pacification Campaign that followed, erasing the memory of earlier Buddhist-inspired restraint.

Hyein Lee examines a manual for Buddhist chaplains called *Kukkun pŏbyo chip, Essential Buddhist Teachings for the Armed Forces*, which was compiled by the Chogye Order of Korean Buddhism and is distributed in the military camps of South Korea. She describes how the manual draws on Buddhist classical texts and teachings to provide chaplains both with doctrinal and practical information, as well as guidance for performing funerals and other important rites. Combining Buddhist ideas with Korean nationalism, it reflects a tension between Buddhism and military necessity that chimes with IHL, even though IHL is not explicitly referred to. Lee suggests that there is therefore potential for developing education on complementary Buddhist and IHL values into Korean military chaplaincy.

Daiki Kinoshita explores how Mahāyāna interpretations of the *Lotus Sūtra* in China by Zhiyi, and in Japan by Nichiren and the Soka Gakkai, relate to core IHL principles. He examines three key Soka Gakkai doctrines in this regard, and analyses how Buddhist organisations can promote respect for IHL today, specifically with regard to the prohibition on nuclear weapons.

The volume closes with an article by Ha Vinh Tho, Edith Favoreu and Noel Trew highlighting the correspondences between Socially Engaged Buddhism and the core principles of humanity, impartiality, neutrality and independence originally adopted by the International Red Cross and Red Crescent Movement. While not part of IHL, these fundamental principles underpin the neutral, impartial and independent approach to humanitarian action in armed conflict situations where IHL applies, and also guide the work of many other humanitarian actors.

The list of people to thank for their invaluable contributions to this Buddhism and IHL project is too long to include here. Apart from the authors and editors of this volume and those involved in the Dambulla conference, the project would not have been possible without a host of collaborators and ICRC colleagues who have contributed to its arrangement. Information on many more Buddhism and IHL articles and events, as well as similar ICRC projects with other religions, can be found on the ICRC's *Religion and Humanitarian Principles* website: https://blogs.icrc.org/religion-humanitarianprinciples.

Notes

1. See https://blogs.icrc.org/religion-humanitarianprinciples/project-on-the-interface-between-buddhism-and-ihl/.
2. See https://blogs.icrc.org/religion-humanitarianprinciples/contemporary-buddhism-publishes-icrc-article-exploring-interface-between-buddhism-and-ihl/.
3. See the Buddhism and IHL Project webpage: https://blogs.icrc.org/religion-humanitarianprinciples/project-on-the-interface-between-buddhism-and-ihl/.

Abbreviations

References to Pali texts using these abbreviations are to PTS editions of the Pali texts. References to other texts are to the editions or translations given here.

Dn. *Dīgha Nikāya*. Translated by M. Walshe. [1987] 1995. *The Long Discourses of the Buddha: A Translation of the Dīgha Nikāya*. Boston: Wisdom.
Mn. *Majjhima Nikāya*. Translated by Bhikkhu Ñāṇamoli and Bhikkhu Bodhi. 1995. *The Middle Length Discourses of the Buddha: A Translation of the Majjhima Nikāya*. Boston: Wisdom.
Sam. *Saṃyutta Nikāya*. Translated by Bhikkhu Bodhi. 2000. *The Connected Discourses of the Buddha: A Translation of the Saṃyutta Nikāya*. Boston: Wisdom.

Disclosure Statement

This article has been supported by the International Committee of the Red Cross (ICRC).

ICRC

INTRODUCTION:HOW DOES BUDDHISM COMPARE WITH INTERNATIONAL HUMANITARIAN LAW, AND CAN IT CONTRIBUTE TO HUMANISING WAR?

Andrew Bartles-Smith

ABSTRACT

This article examines Buddhist teachings relevant to the regulation of war and compares them with international humanitarian law (IHL) and the just war tradition by which it has been informed. It argues that Buddhist ethics broadly align with IHL rules to minimise harm inflicted during war, and that Buddhism's psychological resources can help support IHL to improve compliance with common humanitarian norms. Indeed, Buddhist mindfulness techniques can support even non-Buddhist combatants by enhancing their psychological resilience and capacity to fight with skill and restraint. While IHL is a legal regime that legitimises violence under certain conditions, and lays down clear universally ratified rules, Buddhism is primarily an ethical and psychological system that addresses the motivations and inner roots of behaviour and can be understood and interpreted in different ways. In this respect, Buddhism overlaps with the field of military ethics, and can contribute much to enhance military training. However, while the centrality of non-harming (*ahiṃsā*) to Buddhism dictates that extraordinary efforts should be made to prevent war or otherwise minimise the harm inflicted – thereby checking interpretations of IHL that are overly permissive – Buddhism's consequent reluctance to legitimise and thereby institutionalise war, and the ambiguity of its teachings in this regard, have generally precluded it from developing clear just war guidelines for belligerents to follow, and Buddhist resources to improve the conduct of hostilities have remained largely untapped. Mainstream traditions of Buddhist ethics must also be distinguished from more esoteric and localised beliefs and practices, and from the lived Buddhisms with which most lay Buddhists are more familiar, which do not necessarily embody the same degree of restraint. Belligerents might therefore have different conceptions or expectations of Buddhism depending on their culture and particular circumstances, or be unclear about what it says on the conduct of war.

DOI: 10.4324/9781003439820-2

Introduction

International humanitarian law (IHL), now synonymous for many with *jus in bello*, is the branch of international law that governs the conduct of war. Even though the main instruments of IHL have been universally ratified, however, and IHL is perhaps the most effective means so far developed to limit the effects of war, it is notoriously difficult to implement and enforce (Sassòli 2007, 46–47; Bartles-Smith 2022, 1726). The extreme conditions of armed conflict are inherently anarchic, and diminish, furthermore, the resolve and ability of belligerents to regulate themselves (Sassòli 2007; Pfanner 2009, 280). While the law is a necessary condition for regulating armed conflict, it is not therefore always sufficient, and extra-legal means must be sought to improve compliance with it (Sassòli 2007; 52, 73; Bartles-Smith 2022, 1727).

In recent years organisations like the International Committee of the Red Cross (ICRC) have opened up debate on correspondences between IHL and religious traditions to promote compliance with common humanitarian norms (ICRC 2021a; Bartles-Smith et al. 2020). Given that serious violations of IHL continue to occur in parts of the Buddhist world, and Buddhists are included in the armed forces of many other nations, the ICRC launched a project on Buddhism and IHL in 2017 (ICRC 2019a). Surprisingly little attention had hitherto been paid to Buddhism's potential to inform the conduct of contemporary war (Bartles-Smith et al. 2020, 370–372). Although Buddhists have been fighting wars for two and a half millennia, Buddhism and war are commonly regarded as incompatible, and Buddhist resources to restrain war are often therefore unexplored (Harris 2003, 93–94).

This article compares Buddhism with IHL and the Western just war tradition by which it has been informed, and explores whether Buddhism can support IHL to humanise the conduct of war. It argues that Buddhism is in broad alignment with IHL, and that the fundamental principles of Buddhist ethics mean that it is in the interest of belligerents to minimise the harm they inflict on others, and the karmic consequences to themselves, very much in line with IHL principles (Harvey 2021, in this volume). Many Buddhist teachings therefore correspond with IHL rules and contain stories and anecdotes of exemplary restraint (Bartles-Smith et al. 2020).

Comparing Buddhism with IHL is not, however, to compare like with like, and means examining the relative strengths and weaknesses of two very different normative systems. Indeed, these differences are as revealing as their similarities, and can throw fresh light on how the conduct of war might be improved. Although the content and jurisdiction of IHL are intended to be universal, it is nevertheless Western in design, and engagement with Buddhism can make it more accessible to many Asian constituencies in particular (Caserta 2021; Kinsella and Mantilla 2020; Bartles-Smith 2022, 1731).

Whereas IHL is a secular international legal regime that lays down clearly codified rules for belligerents to follow, Buddhism is at once a religion, philosophy and practical path to human development, encompassing diverse traditions that interpret it in different ways (Gethin 1998, 1; Jerryson 2010, 5). Many scholars prefer for this reason to speak of Buddhisms in the plural (Gethin 1998, 1). The main schools nevertheless tend to converge upon the central tenets of Buddhist teaching, and it is primarily this ethical and psychological core from which the article will draw (Keown 2005, 3).

Like other religious and philosophical systems, on the topic of war Buddhism is concerned not just with the conduct of hostilities, but whether the recourse to war is justified. This is governed by another branch of international law, *jus ad bellum*, now embodied in the United Nations (UN) Charter of 1945, which prohibits war except in self-defence or when authorised by the UN Security Council (Melzer 2016, 27). Moreover, Buddhism extends beyond the realm of law to the ethical and motivational frameworks that underpin it (Harvey 2021, in this volume). In both these respects, Buddhism contains analogues of the Western just war tradition from which the core ideas contained in *jus ad bellum* and *jus in bello* ultimately derive, and which is similarly concerned with the intentions and inner life of belligerents (Whetham 2011b, 71–72). Indeed, given the importance of Christianity to the Western tradition, and the influence of Stoic philosophy and Roman law, meaningful parallels can be drawn between the radical non-violence of early canonical Pali Buddhist texts and the New Testament, and between the concepts of Buddhist Dharma and natural law (Neff 2005, 54). The contribution of monastics such as St Thomas Aquinas to the development of the just war tradition is also pertinent considering the centrality of the monastic community, the Sangha, to Buddhism, and in framing its response to war.

At its core, Buddhism is an ethical and psychological system that addresses the inner roots of behaviour, so that good conduct is internalised and supported while reducing the need for external sanctions (Keown 2005, 31; Gethin 2004, 190). This orientation would appear to complement IHL rules which are difficult to enforce, and the potential role that Buddhism can play in improving voluntary compliance with IHL or equivalent Buddhist norms is therefore crucial (Terry and McQuinn 2018; Bartles-Smith et al. 2020, 388). According to Buddhism, the root causes and manifestations of conflict can only be permanently changed by some degree of introspection and the disciplining and control of the mind. Time and again Buddhist teachings reiterate the importance of restraint in thought, word and deed (Dhp.234; Sam.I.168–169). Indeed, the best soldiers combine an almost monastic discipline with the highest ideals of restraint and self-sacrifice (Jenkins 2010a, 67; Sugiki 2020a, 1; Thomas 2019, 544).

Amidst the complexity, confusion and trauma of war, when fatigue, stress and strong emotions can debilitate belligerents' cognitive, affective and moral faculties, such self-regulation and capacity for ethical thinking are essential (van Baarda 2011, 157; Mallon and Nichols 2010; Whetham 2011a). Buddhist mindfulness techniques are proven, moreover, to enhance the resilience and mental functioning of even non-Buddhist combatants, and their capacity to act with precision and restraint (Stanley et al. 2011; Jha et al. 2015). In these respects, Buddhism overlaps with the field of military ethics, and can contribute much to military training.

Above all, Buddhism understands that war is a psychological or subjective phenomenon as much as an external reality, and that while there are bright and positive features within us, we are all in some sense at war within ourselves (Sinclair 2014, 160; Harris 2021, in this volume). The language of Buddhism includes military metaphors and analogies to describe the inner conflict within every sentient being (Kosuta 1997). The archetypal battle in Buddhism is fought between the meditating Siddhārtha and Māra the Tempter, a personification of negative emotions, under the Bodhi Tree. Siddhārtha's victory, achieved by mindfully recognising and thereby undermining these negative emotions, leads to his enlightenment as the Buddha (Dn.II.104; Whitaker and Smith 2017, 70; Singh 2017, 261). Mahāyāna Buddhism is replete, furthermore, with violent weapon-wielding depictions of *bodhisattvas* (beings on the path to enlightenment), and all traditions include benevolent deities who protect practitioners from Māra's armies, the negative mental qualities which assail them (Jerryson 2017, 58). Whether wars are won or lost, and how they are fought, depends as much on the protagonists' state of mind as on external factors, just as morale is often more important than the material result of any particular battle.

But while non-violence or non-harming (*ahiṃsā*) is axiomatic to Buddhism and dictates that extraordinary efforts should be made to avoid harm, Buddhism's consequent reluctance to endorse war, reflected in the ambiguity and multivocality of its teachings in this regard, has also tended to undercut its potential to humanise war in practice (Frydenlund 2013, 2017b, 209; Bartles-Smith et al. 2020, 420).

While IHL evolved from a just war tradition that sets out criteria according to which states may legitimately resort to war and how it should be conducted, Buddhism hesitates to justify and thereby institutionalise even defensive war (Harris 2003, 93; Bartles-Smith et al. 2020, 420). There is therefore no developed just war tradition in Buddhism, although the lineaments of one have sometimes been traced out (Frydenlund 2017b, 206; Harris 2003).

This lack of a clear just war framework has both pros and cons. On the one hand, Buddhist qualms about the legitimacy of even 'just' or defensive war mean that it is doctrinally more intent than other traditions to minimise the harm inflicted should war break out, thereby checking interpretations of IHL that are overly permissive. On the other hand, this has forestalled the development of practical just war guidelines for belligerents to follow, and Buddhist resources to support them in their role are often largely untapped (Bartles-Smith et al. 2020, 420). This can suggest to some belligerents that war is beyond the pale of Buddhism, potentially leaving a vacuum in which no principles are thought to apply at all. Although historically Buddhism has sometimes been applied to restrain the conduct of war, it has also therefore been instrumentalised on occasion to enable uninhibited violence (Jayatilleke 1967, 555–557; Charney 2021, in this volume; Schmithausen 1999, 52, 63; Victoria 2022).

Differences between mainstream traditions of Buddhist ethics, more esoteric and localised beliefs and practices, and the 'lived' Buddhism of the majority of lay Buddhists, also mean that belligerents might not understand or practise Buddhism in the same way (Stanford and Jong 2019; van Schaik 2020; Spiro 1970). Indeed, there sometimes appears to be a disconnect between various conceptions or expectations of Buddhism and the realities of war in the Buddhist world (Schmithausen 1999, 53). While some Buddhists adopt variations on a pacifist position, and there are those who concede, like the Dalai Lama, that limited just wars might be possible if motivated by compassion and for the benefit of many people, others have harnessed Buddhism to support wars in which grave violations of Buddhist and IHL norms have been committed (Scorsine 2014, 118).

However much individual Buddhist belligerents attempt to limit the violence they inflict in line with Buddhist precepts, war is a collective undertaking, and Buddhist ethics must also therefore be integrated into military doctrines and training programmes to effectively influence their group behaviour (Muñoz-Rojas and Frésard 2004). Although Buddhism is part of military life in some contexts, however, and clergy often play an important role in bolstering the morale and spiritual welfare of troops, the actual content of military training is overwhelmingly secular, and Buddhist ethics do not generally feature at all (Selth 2021; Kent 2008; ICRC 2021c). The idea that Buddhism might align with IHL, or be practically applied to restrain the conduct of hostilities, has not therefore been deeply institutionalised.

While there is growing consensus that Buddhism can help legitimise, enhance and complement IHL, and that IHL can reinvigorate Buddhist resources relevant to the regulation of contemporary war, this potential is still largely unrealised (ICRC 2019b, 2020, 2021b).

Content and structure

This introductory article is chiefly an investigation into Buddhist resources to restrain the conduct of war, using IHL and the Western just war tradition as springboards. The article draws primarily on early Indian Buddhist teachings, which are regarded as particularly authoritative. These include the Pali canon of the Theravāda ('Teaching of the Elders') school that now predominates in Sri Lanka and mainland Southeast Asia, and key teachings from the

Mahāyāna ('Greater Vehicle') and Vajrayāna ('Thunderbolt Vehicle') Buddhist schools that now predominate in East and Inner Asia. The article also incorporates commentaries from respected contemporary clerics.

Part 1 of the article examines IHL and its limitations, and discusses how reengagement with its religious roots can improve compliance with common humanitarian norms. The article then introduces the Western just war tradition and the Indian traditions from which Buddhism emerged, and which it broke from in important respects. Part 2 reviews the relationship between Buddhism and war since its inception, and digs down into the psychological nature and functioning of Buddhist ethics relevant to its conduct. Part 3 describes how this translates into Buddhist statecraft to prevent war and minimise its suffering, and explains how the lineaments of just war have developed in some Buddhist traditions. Part 4 then examines how Buddhism and IHL might complement one another to restrain the actual conduct of war, and how Buddhist ethics and mindfulness techniques can enhance military training. Finally, Part 5 explains how Buddhist belligerents have nevertheless sometimes failed to apply Buddhist ethics in practice, or have misrepresented its teachings to transgress humanitarian norms.

Part 1: IHL, religion and just war

IHL and its limits

The main instruments of IHL are the four Geneva Conventions of 1949, which have been universally ratified, and their Additional Protocols (AP I and II) of 1977. As well as a large body of such treaty law, customary IHL (CIHL) enshrines humanitarian norms against the use of unlawful force during armed conflict across cultures. Some of these are peremptory *jus cogens* ('compelling law') norms, regarded as fundamental principles of international law from which no derogation is permitted (Melzer 2016, 22; Henckaerts and Doswald-Beck 2005; Khen 2016, 34).

IHL embodies a balance between humanity and military necessity. It is based on the understanding, set out in the St Petersburg Declaration of 1868, that 'the only legitimate object which States should endeavour to accomplish during war is to weaken the military forces of the enemy' and that '[t]he civilian population and individual civilians shall enjoy general protection against dangers arising from military operations' (Melzer 2016, 18). IHL therefore imposes restrictions on the means and methods of warfare, prohibiting those that are indiscriminate, cause unnecessary injury and suffering, severe harm to the natural environment, or a combination thereof (ICRC 2022, 5–6). IHL also protects the lives and dignity of those who do not, or no longer, engage in hostilities, including wounded and sick combatants, civilians and those deprived of their freedom during armed conflict (ICRC 2022).

In regulating the conduct of hostilities, IHL endeavours to limit the suffering and destruction of war for non-combatants based on three core principles: *distinction*, *proportionality* and *precaution* (ICRC 2022, 5–6). The principle of distinction requires that parties to armed conflict 'at all times distinguish between the civilian population and combatants and between civilian objects and military objectives and accordingly shall direct their operations only against military objectives' (AP I, Art. 48; CIHL, Rules 1 and 7; Melzer 2016, 18). Attacks in which incidental harm to civilians or civilian objects cannot be avoided are subject to the principle of proportionality, according to which parties to conflict should refrain from 'any attack which may be expected to cause incidental loss of civilian life, injury to civilians, damage to civilian objects, or a combination thereof, which would be excessive in relation to the concrete and direct military advantage anticipated' (AP I, Arts 51[5][b] and 57[2][a][iii] and [b]; CIHL, Rules 14, 18 and 19; Melzer 2016, 19). Similarly, the principle of precaution requires that 'constant care shall be taken to spare the civilian population, civilians and civilian objects' and that all feasible measures must therefore be taken by both attacking forces and those under attack to ensure that incidental civilian death and injury is minimised (AP I, Arts 57[1] and 58; CIHL, Rule 15 and 22; Melzer 2016, 18–19).

The legal framework of IHL has expanded rapidly since the adoption of the first Geneva Convention in 1864 into an impressive body of international law. But while governments are increasingly fulfilling their responsibilities to integrate IHL into domestic legislation, educational and military training programmes, its effectiveness in regulating the behaviour of belligerents is frequently called into question. Apart from the lack of a strong enforcement regime, the international consensus on which IHL otherwise depends for its implementation often breaks down (Sassòli 2007, 52). Although laudable efforts have been made to promote IHL in recent years, it is still relatively little known compared to human rights law, for example, and more work needs to be done to increase societal understanding and acceptance of IHL across cultures (Sassòli 2007, 47; Kaplan 2013; Bartles-Smith 2022, 1756).

Belligerents and those to whom they are accountable might not always therefore be sufficiently knowledgeable or heedful of IHL rules, and are frequently incentivised to deliberately transgress them. Despite weak IHL enforcement, there is also a general lack of effective military ethics training to enhance voluntary compliance and help belligerents to apply the rules in difficult and complex wartime scenarios (Williams 2015; Wolfendale 2008).

Religion and just war

While international law must be secular to be universally accepted, positivist and secularising tendencies in legal studies have tended to underplay the connections between religion and law, and the idea of law as culture, and this risks detaching law from its moral and cultural underpinnings (French and Nathan 2014, 15; Stephens 2014).

Religions have traditionally been the glue that bind people together into moral communities, promoting cooperation within groups while helping to mobilise them against external threats (Haidt 2012, 246–273; Martin 2018, 8). They therefore provide a potent motivational framework for the conduct of war, and their power to encourage combatants to fight and die for their religion, nation or some other 'just' cause has long been harnessed (Haidt 2012, 312; Fiske and Rai 2014, 93; Hassner 2016, 8–11, 87–89). Although religions have sometimes incentivised the infliction of unlimited violence against enemy others, they have also pioneered the universal principles, concepts and rules of war from which the modern edifice of IHL has evolved (Bryant 2021; Juergensmeyer, Kitts, and Jerryson 2017, 6). Either way their force-multiplying potential can be channelled to incentivise restraint in support of IHL, while checking their potential for victimisation (Bartles-Smith 2022, 1735–1736). Research has shown that moral values are often more powerful than legal rules in motivating behaviour, and that belligerents are more likely to comply with IHL if it chimes with their identities and moral codes, and is therefore socialised or internalised by them to some degree (Terry and McQuinn 2018; Koh 2005; Kaplan 2013).

IHL is deeply influenced by the Western just war tradition, which originated in the deliberations of St Augustine of Hippo (354–430) about Christianity and war (Bryant 2021, 88; Neff 2005). Confronted by existential threats posed to Christian civilisation by barbarian invasions and a proliferation of 'heretical' sects, Augustine reconciled the non-violence of the gospels with the obligation of the Roman Empire to defend the innocent from attack (Whetham 2011b, 71; Neff 2005, 46–47). A succession of theologians and jurists including St Thomas Aquinas (1225–1274) and Hugo Grotius (1583–1645) developed the just war tradition into essentially its modern form, thereby laying the foundations of modern international law (Whetham 2011b, 71; Bryant 2021, 88; Neff 2005, 46–48). Classical conceptions of natural law were pivotal to this evolution, influencing first Christian and then Enlightenment ideas, due to their premise that humans possess a shared moral conscience that transcends cultures and the authority of any single state (Boyle and Meyer 1998, 214–216; Neff 2005, 45; Traven 2021, 16).

According to the Western just war tradition, wars are considered just only if they fulfil certain criteria. While authorities differ, essential *jus ad bellum* criteria to resort to war are that there should be: 'a just cause; legitimate authority; a right intention; a reasonable chance of success; and all other reasonable alternatives have been exhausted', such that war is a last resort (Robinson 2003, 1). Essential *jus in bello* criteria for the conduct of war are that discrimination should be exercised as to who is targeted, and that the amount of violence used should be proportionate to the ends sought (1). It is upon these foundations that the IHL principles of distinction and proportionality have developed.

But IHL and just war rules can be found in many other religions and cultures (Bryant 2021; Fox and Sandler 2004, 167). The ancient Indian traditions from which Buddhism evolved were particularly highly developed in this regard, and challenge assumptions about what is acceptable in war still today (Penna 1989; Draper 1995).

Righteous war in ancient India

War was endemic in ancient India, and although there was no single coherent theory of warfare, it was institutionalised to a remarkable degree (Singh 2017, 245, 468; Brekke 2006; Armour 1922). The concept of Dharma in Brahmanical or Hindu traditions embodies a cosmic order according to which each caste (*varṇa*) or birth group (*jāti*) has its own dharma (law or duty) and place in the social order. *Dharma-yuddha* or 'righteous war', fought in accordance with Dharma, is an Indian equivalent to just war, and was the raison d'être of the *kṣatriya* or warrior caste (Penna 1989, 338; Bryant 2021, 39). *Dharma-yuddha* is permitted only as a last resort, when the aim of fighting is righteous, and the appropriate rules for waging war are observed, with no prohibited weapons or tactics used by either side (Bryant 2021, 39; Penna 1989).

Accordingly, war epics such as the *Mahābhārata* (c. 400 BCE–300 CE) and *Rāmāyaṇa* (c. 700 BCE–300 CE), and treatises on law or statecraft like the *Dharma-sūtra*s (c. 600–100 BCE), *Manu-smṛti* (c. 200 BCE–300 CE) and *Arthaśāstra* (c. 200 BCE–300 CE) describe remarkably detailed and humane rules of conduct that match or exceed those of IHL (Penna 1989; Balkaran and Dorn 2022). These include, for example, rules to protect civilians and warriors who are *hors de combat*, incapacitated or otherwise unable to defend themselves (Balkaran and Dorn 2022). Similarly, there were also prohibitions on the use of hyper-destructive weapons, as well as provisions for medical corps personnel to take care of enemy wounded (Penna 1989, 340, 345). While there is little evidence of the degree to which these rules were actually followed, early foreign observers such as the Greek Megasthenes (c. 350–290 BCE) remarked on the unusual level of restraint that characterised warfare at the time of the Mauryas, for example, commenting that peasants were able to cultivate the land even as battles raged nearby, since soldiers had been ordered not to molest them (Roy 2012, 50; Singh 2017, 266–67; Salomon 2007).

Although war fought according to the various conceptions of *dharma-yuddha* was legitimate, and texts such as the *Mahābhārata* and *Manu-smṛti* saw no evil in killing enemies, non-violence and the renunciant ideal nevertheless preoccupied rulers and combatants to an extraordinary degree (Singh 2017, 279). This is reflected in the anguish expressed by kings and warriors such as Yudhiṣṭhira in the *Mahābhārata* at the seemingly senseless slaughter (Singh 2017, 279; Brekke 2006, 114).

This tension between violence and non-violence (*ahiṃsā*) has been a staple of Indian religious and political discourse throughout its history and reflects a dichotomy between the world-affirming warrior ethos of the Vedas, the earliest texts of Hinduism, according to which those who died in battle went to heaven, and the non-violent renunciant ideals first found in the *Upaniṣads* (from c. 800 BCE) and later developed in Buddhism and Jainism (Singh 2017, 480; Balkaran and Dorn 2022, 1766–1767). Texts such as the *Mahābhārata* and *Rāmāyaṇa* embody a synthesis between these two streams (Balkaran and Dorn 2022, 1766–1767).

Part 2: Buddhist ethics in relation to war

The emergence of Buddhism in part as a response to war

Buddhism therefore arose amidst armed conflicts in the subcontinent, and early Buddhist scriptures contain graphic descriptions of war and its consequences (Harris 2021, in this volume). The century before the Buddha's birth, traditionally thought to be c. 563 BCE or 480 BCE, appears to have been particularly turbulent, with tribal states gradually overtaken by competing monarchies, and military organisation becoming more systematised (Singh 2017, 248; Bodhi 2014). The Shakyan republic to which the Buddha was said to have belonged experienced war during his lifetime, becoming a vassal of Kosala (Bodhi 2014). According to legend, when the Buddha was old, the Kosalan king Viḍūḍabha massacred the Shakyans, 'beginning with babes at the breast', a genocidal act of violence reminiscent of more recent war crimes (Jat.IV.91–98; Bodhi 2014).

It was in response to this background of escalating of war and violence, and Brahmanical animal sacrifice, that the Buddha and his contemporary Mahāvīra, the founder of Jainism, developed their non-violent ethics of renunciation and self-control (Singh 2017, 248). Since both were said to belong to the *kṣatriya* caste, they expressed these ideas in the language of the warrior ethos in which they were steeped (Singh 2017, 248; Jerryson 2010, 10). War was more than a metaphor for both men, who in some respects never ceased to be warriors, redirecting their energies from external battles to the cultivation of their inner selves (Jenkins 2017).

The Buddha rejected *dharma-yuddha* and the traditional warrior idea that war was righteous or meritorious. Buddhism therefore critiqued Brahmanical or Hindu rules of war, moderating and adapting their provisions to prevent war or restrain its violence still further, and textual references suggest that this had a significant, if sporadic, humanising effect (Jayatilleke 1967, 544–557; Sugiki 2020b).

Crucially, the Buddha also rejected the Brahmanical caste system as an indicator of spiritual purity (An.VIII.19; Gombrich 2006, 30). His conversion of Dharma into a universal law or truth that applies equally to all sentient beings, and regulates the natural and moral order of the cosmos, was an historic humanitarian breakthrough, illustrated most famously in his expression of the golden rule: 'All beings tremble at the rod; all are afraid of death. Seeing their likeness to yourself, you should neither kill nor cause to kill' (Dhp.129). Buddhist Dharma is also therefore an equivalent to natural law, so pivotal to the development of international law in the West (Keown 2005, 3). Recognition of our common humanity and human dignity is fundamental to both Buddhism and IHL, and underlines belligerents' duty of respect towards one another, and of impartial care towards war's victims (Bartles-Smith et al. 2020, 382–384).

Buddhism's radical empathy with all beings still feels seminal to this day, and its recognition of 'common sentience' beyond the confines of our species exposes humanitarianism for its chauvinism (Bartles-Smith et al. 2020, 384). While Buddhism privileges humanity, since a human rebirth affords a rare chance for spiritual development, it nevertheless stresses the interrelatedness of all beings, which are continuously reborn in new forms (Mn. III.169; Harvey 2000, 30). This is reinforced by Buddhist doctrines such as lack of a permanent self (Pali *anattā*, Sanskrit *anātman*), according to which beings have no fixed identity, impermanence (Pali *anicca*, Sanskrit *anitya*), and equality (*samatā*) (Bartles-Smith et al. 2020, 382–383). In contrast, IHL provisions to safeguard the natural environment are only a recent add-on, prompted by the United States' extensive use of herbicides during the Vietnam War (Murphy and Gieseken 2021).

The psychological core of Buddhist ethics

Although Buddhism frequently exhibits a culturally adapted polytheism, and gods, demons and other supernatural beings feature in its cosmologies, it is in essential respects non-theistic. Buddhism has no creator or law-giving god, and no divine commandments to be enforced (Skilton 2013, 341–342). Indeed, Buddhist training precepts (Pali *sikkhapada*, Sanskrit *śikṣapada*) are voluntary beneficial commitments. While those who choose to enter the monastic life must adhere to the strict discipline of monastic codes (*vinaya*) which might contain over 200 training precepts – sometimes referred to as 'Buddhist law' in its narrower jurisprudential sense – in several traditions they can nevertheless choose to disrobe at any time. Buddhism is generally therefore characterised as an ethical or psychological rather than rule-based normative system, focused on transforming the consciousness of its practitioners rather than regimenting their behaviour (Cozort and Shields 2017; Keown 2005, 13). In comparison with Western traditions, Buddhism perhaps most closely resembles a form of Aristotelian virtue ethics, which puts a similar emphasis on skill and training to internalise virtues that are their own reward, and also underpins most Western writing on military virtues (Olsthoorn 2019, 38; Keown 2005, 23–25; Gethin 1998, 36).

Alongside its idealism and belief in human perfectibility, Buddhism shares with realist political thinkers a sober assessment of the human condition, and incorporates a sophisticated analysis of the psychological and societal causes of conflict and how to mitigate them. Life is impermanent and full of suffering, pain and dissatisfaction (Pali *dukkha*, Sanskrit *duḥkha*), which enmesh sentient beings in a continuous cycle of becoming (*saṃsāra*) in which they are born, suffer, die, and are reborn again. While physical pain and discomfort are important components of *dukkha*, it is primarily psychological in nature, and is caused by craving (Pali *taṇhā*, Sanskrit *tṛṣṇā*). The three poisons or unwholesome roots of greed/lust (Pali *lobha*), anger/hatred (Pali *dosa*, Sanskrit *dveṣa*) and ignorance/delusion (*moha*) are at the root of craving and the cause of conflict, violence and all other unwholesome actions (Harvey 2018). It follows that these poisons are the root cause of wars and the atrocities committed within them, the prevention of which depends on training the mind to counter them with their respective antidotes of generosity, loving-kindness and wisdom (Harvey 2018, 13).

The Noble Eightfold Path summarises the means by which Buddhists can reduce and ultimately eliminate suffering and conflict to achieve nirvana or liberation from *saṃsāra*. It combines morality (Pali *sīla*, Sanskrit *śīla*) or the following of Buddhist training precepts, with the practice of meditation (*samādhi*) and the cultivation of wisdom (Pali *paññā*, Sanskrit *prajñā*) to generate the requisite discipline, self-awareness and insight to transform behaviour (Whitaker and Smith 2017, 51).

The moral dimension of Dharma incorporates ideas of justice and virtue, and is manifest in the law of karma (Pali *kamma*) or intentional action (Harvey 2000, 251). Skilful or wholesome (*kusala*) intentions and actions are in accord with Dharma and sow beneficial karmic seeds that lead to happiness, fulfilment and, if sustained and developed, ever higher or more auspicious rebirths until liberation from *saṃsāra* is achieved. Unskilful (*akusala*) intentions and actions are not in accord with Dharma and, if sustained, lead to ever less auspicious rebirths.

The intention or volition (*cetanā*) behind an action *is* karma, and determines the karmic consequences (Harvey 2018, 8). Importantly, *cetanā* refers to the immediate impulse that triggers action, and the states of mind that feed into and accompany this, and must therefore be distinguished from motivations or plans that have a longer duration (Harvey 2018, 9; Kent 2008, 117). In Buddhism, intentionally causing harm to others is morally wrong not only in a conventional sense but because it is caused by, and itself causes, unskilful mental states (Gethin 2004, 190). Indeed, Buddhist ethics is as much a description of how the mind works, and the psychological phenomena that motivate us to act, as an ethical system (Gethin 2004, 190).

Buddhism has interrogated the psychological, indeed biological, basis of our common humanity with a rigour not dissimilar to that of modern psychology and neuroscience (Wallace 2007). Buddhism's acute awareness of the relative and subjective nature of our thoughts and emotions is highly pertinent both to the prevention of war and to the motivations of belligerents and their behaviour (Harris 2021, in this volume). Indeed, the canonical Theravāda *Abhidhamma* (Sanskrit *Abhidharma*) texts of Buddhist psychology chime with critical theory and constructivism in their attempt to deconstruct the perceived realities and assumptions which contribute to war and its excesses, and their descriptions of cognitive processes, afflictive mental states (Pali *kilesa*, Sanskrit *kleśa*), aggregates (Pali *khandha*, Sanskrit *skandha*) and mental constructs (Pali *saṅkhāra*, Sanskrit *saṃskāra*) overlap with the latest psychological research (Lancaster 1997; Harvey 2018; Ronkin 2018).

Buddhist non-violence and the reality of war

However, despite the fact that Buddhism possesses sophisticated psychological resources relevant to the conduct of hostilities, the centrality of non-harming (*ahiṃsā*) means that it is uniquely conflicted with regard to the legitimacy of war under any circumstances (Harris 2003, 93–94; Premasiri 2006, 81). Canonical Theravāda texts, for example, contain no endorsement for any kind of violence, and the Buddha's take on the futility of war is encapsulated in his reply to King Pasenadi after the latter's defeat by his nephew Ajātasattu: 'Victory breeds enmity; the defeated one sleeps badly. The peaceful one sleeps at ease, having abandoned victory and defeat' (Dhp.201; Sam.I.83; Harvey 2000, 255; Bartles-Smith et al. 2020, 397–398).

Apart from practical measures such as the carrying of a stick or clubbing together to provide a minimal defence or deterrent against attackers, Buddhist monastics are otherwise enjoined not even to kill an ant (Vin.I.97; Vin.IV.124–125; Bartles-Smith et al. 2020, 380). The Buddha warned that they should avoid talk of low or unedifying matters, including 'kings, robbers, ministers, armies, dangers and wars', and according to the Theravāda *vinaya* or monastic code they are prohibited from visiting military installations or observing battles and military training, except under exceptional circumstances (Dn.I.7–8; Vin.IV.104–107; Florida 2013, 332). The Mahāyāna *Brahmajāla Sūtra* for monastic and lay Buddhists similarly states that those who take *bodhisattva* vows should not participate in or support war in any way (Harvey 2000, 254).

But the Buddha did not proscribe war or tell rulers to disband their armies (Keown 2014, 668; Yu 2013, 195). He emphasised, moreover, that rulers are duty-bound to protect their people and maintain law and order (An.III.149;

Dn.III.58–79; Bartles-Smith et al. 2020, 393; Jayatilleke 1967, 540; Keown 2014, 668). Nor is soldiering included among the seven types of wrong livelihood or forms of commerce, even though trading in weapons is, and the Buddha did not encourage soldiers to leave their profession (An.III.208; Bartles-Smith et al. 2020, 412; Jerryson 2010, 11; Keown 2014, 669). Indeed, many canonical texts compare monastic with military virtues which were clearly admired (An. IV.181; Keown 2014, 669). While wars of aggression are generally anathema to Buddhism, it concedes for the most part that defensive wars might sometimes be necessary to prevent greater suffering, and the best that Buddhists can hope for is to limit its horrors (Bodhi 2014).

The confusion generated by these seemingly mixed messages is compounded by the fact that many Buddhists understandably distance themselves from military affairs, and do not necessarily get to the heart of what the texts have to say (Jenkins 2015). Indeed, Buddhists often tend to be more preoccupied with achieving inner peace than confronting the reality of war, or otherwise tend to compartmentalise it from their regular Buddhist practice (Salomon 2007, 57; Schmithausen 1999; Fuller 2021).

Monastic versus lay ethics

Crucially in this regard, Buddhism makes a distinction between the non-violent idealism of the Sangha and the more common-sense pragmatism of its lay followers, who must balance this with their worldly duties and responsibilities (Tilakaratne 2021, in this volume; Bodhi 2014). While monastics on their path towards enlightenment must generally adhere to strict non-violence, lay Buddhists are not on the same fast track to liberation, and essentially choose for themselves how many precepts they can realistically follow given their circumstances and spiritual ambition (Lammerts 2018; Tilakaratne 2021, in this volume).

The Five Precepts (Pali *pañcasīla*, Sanskrit *pañcaśīla*) against misconduct are the core of Buddhist ethics that all lay Buddhists strive to follow. While the first precept against killing will likely be broken during war, Buddhism accepts that lay people must sometimes use force or violence to protect themselves or others from attack – but that they will suffer the karmic consequences in proportion to the harm that they might therefore inflict. In this respect Buddhism empowers individuals to take control of their own fate, and the Buddhist ideal remains pristine just as most Buddhists fail to achieve it.

Buddhist ethics therefore has a gradualist quality, envisaging a gradation of behaviour from the monastic exemplar of complete non-violence to the karmic balance between Buddhist ideals and pragmatic compromises that lay Buddhist belligerents must make to adjust to the realities of politics and (national) security. As Peter Harvey states, 'if violence is then used, it is something that Buddhism may *understand* but not actually *approve of*' (Harvey 2000, 252).

Indeed, the stated goal of Buddhism is to reduce suffering, and *ahiṃsā* encompasses not merely the negation of violence but the energetic cultivation of compassion for all sentient beings, and it does not stop where war begins. The Buddha himself mediated disputes between warring kings and counted soldiers among his lay disciples (Sn.935–954; Florida 2013, 331). He was pragmatic about balancing Buddhist ideals with the social and political realities of his day, and understood that not everyone would be uniformly capable or disposed to follow his teachings (Tilakaratne 2021, in this volume). This is especially the case for Buddhist belligerents who must balance Buddhist ideals with the grim realities of war.

Part 3: Preventing violence before and after war breaks out

Buddhist statecraft and the prevention of war

In order to apprehend how Buddhism might help regulate the conduct of war, it is first important to understand what Buddhism says about the recourse to it. Indeed, Buddhism is primarily concerned with conflict prevention.

The Buddha was frank in his assessment of the spiritual precariousness of rulers and combatants, whose duties to govern and protect their people sometimes entail going to war (Jenkins 2017, 161). This predicament is encapsulated in the *Seyya Jātaka* when a *bodhisattva* ruler orders the gates of his capital to be thrown open to an invading army, stating 'I want no kingdom that must be kept by doing harm' (Jat.II.273–274).

The main and most illustrative sources of Buddhist statecraft within early Buddhism are the *jātaka* tales found in all traditions, and which are also the most popular and accessible Theravāda canonical texts (Jenkins 2017, 162; Premasiri 2021, in this volume). These contain stories of the previous rebirths of the Buddha when he was enmeshed in the duties and concerns of lay Buddhists. Since he is frequently reborn as a king, minister or warrior, the *jātakas* suggest how war can be creatively prevented, or its violence minimised, in even the direst circumstances (Jenkins 2017, 166–167; Premasiri 2021, in this volume; Mendis 2021, in this volume).

Much of the early Buddhist conception of statecraft is encapsulated in the Theravāda idea of the first king of our world age, the *Mahā-sammata*, the 'Great Elect', which details the rights of citizens and their rulers (Dn.III.93; Jerryson and Juergensmeyer 2010, 11–12). The Buddhist ideal of rulership is the righteous 'wheel-turning king' (Sanskrit *cakravartin*, Pali *cakkavatti*), and the Buddha claimed to have been a *cakravartin* in previous rebirths (An.IV.89–90, cf. Dn.I.88–89; Dn.III.59; Harvey 2000, 252). Sovereignty does not ultimately reside in the ruler, but is subject to the ethical principles of Dharma, which bind the ruler into a social contract to provide 'righteous care, ward and protection to all citizens', care extended moreover to the 'birds and beasts' (An.III.149; Dn.III.58–79; Bartles-Smith et al. 2020, 393; Jayatilleke 1967, 540).

Buddhism first provides guidance to rulers about how to govern justly and develop good relations with others, thereby cauterising the potential for internal and external unrest. The duty of the ruler to provide security to his citizens in the broadest sense was also expressed as the 'gift of fearlessness' (*abhaya-dāna*, a concept common to several Indian traditions) that a ruler gives to his people, said to be greater even than peace (Kilby 2021, in this volume). At the state and societal level, war is attributed to the failure of rulers to provide this. Unchecked poverty, corruption and exploitation are identified as among the main causes of the crime and social discord that can fuel conflict, and one mythical story in the *Cakkavatti-sīhanāda Sutta* (Dn.26) illustrates how neglect of just one of a ruler's responsibilities – thereby allowing poverty to develop – creates a domino effect that leads to war (Dn.III.64; Harris 2021, in this volume).

In foreign affairs, the ruler is duty bound to cooperate with neighbouring states for the common good, and not to launch aggressive attacks, reminiscent of today's UN Charter (Jayatilleke 1967; 557; Dias and Gamble 2010, 18). The perfect *cakravartin* monarch, though commanding a powerful fourfold army, abandons conquest and wins over potential adversaries not by violence but by the persuasive soft power of righteousness (Dn.III.58–79; Bartles-Smith et al. 2020, 393–394). However, Buddhism concedes that this mythical ideal was only achievable in a prior golden age when all people behaved righteously, and not in the debased age of declining Dharma we inhabit (Sugiki 2020a, 5; Nattier 1991). Buddhism therefore understands that rulers must sometimes use judicious force or violence, or the threat of it, to protect their people, and are expected to maintain a standing army as both a deterrent and a last resort (Jenkins 2017, 162; Keown 2014, 666). Thus, while offensive war was condemned, a defensive military capability was expected. In addition, Gethin identifies ten virtues of a good king found in Theravāda sutras which have a bearing on conduct of war: 'charity, moral restraint, generosity, honesty, gentleness, religious practice, good temper, mercy, patience, and cooperativeness' (Gethin 2014, 73).

Should tensions escalate, one striking feature of Buddhism, and ancient Indian statecraft in general, is their relative reluctance to risk war in the first place (Jenkins 2017, 161; Singh 2017, 321), showcasing a broad palette of options to avoid war as far as possible. Kautilya's *Arthaśāstra* helpfully categorises these into four types of expedients (*upāyas*) for dealing with interstate tensions, only one of which involves the use of force: conciliation (*sāma*), gifts (*dāna*), force (*daṇḍa*) and subversion (*bheda*) (Singh 2017, 310;

Sugiki 2020b, 15). Together they encompass a range of methods, including diplomacy and espionage, to solve problems short of armed conflict, some of which anticipate the hybrid or new-generation warfare pursued by a number of states today.

Buddhist texts modify and repurpose these expedients to showcase how compassion and intellect can be employed to achieve objectives without resort to violence, both before and after a state of war exists (Sugiki 2020b, 17). In order to avoid war, the ruler might become a monk, or choose to flee or surrender to avoid battle (Sugiki 2020b, 4; Jenkins 2010a, 65; Jat.II.224–226). Less drastic options include befriending the enemy, placating them with gifts, and intimidating them with a powerful army or strong alliances with other states (Jenkins 2010a, 66). The glory of the ruler's righteousness can similarly overawe the enemy and dissuade them from attacking, or rally supernatural forces to his aid, and the righteous king might even preach to his opponent to show him the error of his ways (Sugiki 2020b, 6–8).

The example of Ashoka

Some rulers strove harder than others to emulate the *cakravartin* ideal, or be seen to do so. Ashoka Maurya (Pali Asoka, Sanskrit Aśoka, c. 304–232 BCE), the great third-century BCE propagator of Buddhism, is widely regarded as the outstanding historical exemplar of Buddhist kingship (Harvey 2000, 253). After a victorious conquest of Kaliṅga (modern Orissa) in 262 BCE in which over 100,000 people were killed and 150,000 displaced, Ashoka publicly renounced further conquest, and his famous Thirteenth Rock Edict concerns his remorse over the disastrous humanitarian consequences (Roy 2012, 50; Singh 2017, 268–270).

Ashoka's renunciation of war was not absolute. He reserved the right to maintain a powerful standing army, and gave an ominous warning to the forest peoples not to cause trouble lest he retaliate (Singh 2017, 270). Moreover, his establishment as a benign tyrant appears to have been made possible only by his previous military campaigns and the overwhelming military force that he commanded, which brought almost the entire subcontinent under his control (Jenkins 2017, 172–173).

Ashoka's rock edicts also show remarkable religious tolerance and sensitivity to the suffering of other humans and animals (Draper 1995, 196–197). He codified Buddhist and broader Indian ethics into imperial laws which, though short-lived, governed foreign and domestic relations, and required respect for the sanctity of human and animal life, and humane and just treatment for all (197). While Ashoka's edicts contain no rules on the conduct of war, he therefore stands out as a pioneering state practitioner of Buddhism and the universal principles of humanity and impartiality on which the modern regimes of IHL and human rights are built, and he remains relevant in countries across Asia, and indeed the world, to this day (205–206).

Since states are primarily responsible for the ratification, promotion and implementation of IHL rules to which they themselves are subject, the role of Buddhism in Asian state formation, and its incorporation into their legal systems, is also highly relevant, as is the fact that Buddhism continues to have an important influence on many governments and non-state armed groups (French 2015; 838; Jayatilleke 1967, 544–548). Indeed, the Buddhist Sangha is perhaps the world's oldest and most enduring international society (Jayatilleke 1967, 451). Just as the Catholic church, including monastic orders like the Dominicans, helped to lay down the foundations of international law and the just war principles embodied in IHL, the Sangha pioneered an earlier phase of globalisation in which Buddhist principles of statecraft were internationalised (Jayatilleke 1967, 549, 557; Dias and Gamble 2010, 16).

Greater accommodation for war in some Buddhist schools

As Buddhism expanded from its Indian renunciant origins to become the most important religion in Asia, it evolved from the kernel of early teachings found in the Theravāda Pali canon, and the texts of parallel early schools, into numerous Mahāyāna and Vajrayāna streams with various religious, philosophical and cultural inflections (French 2015, 835–836). Mahāyāna and Vajrayāna Buddhism became in some respects more socially and politically oriented than Theravāda Buddhism, thereby resolving the tension between non-violent monastic ideals and military necessities within a single value system (Schmithausen 1999, 62; Sinclair 2014, 152). Lay Buddhists, and rulers in particular, were thereby given a more active religious role, investing military activities with more forthright legitimisation (Schmithausen 1999, 62). In Korea, for instance, the monk Won Gwang (c. 541–630) provided five military-related precepts for lay people: 'First, serve the king with loyalty, ... fourth, do not retreat in battle, and fifth, do not kill indiscriminately' (Ahn 1989, 19; Schmithausen 1999, 54–55).

Some monastic orders even engaged in war and pioneered the development of the martial arts (Lorge 2011). Monastic fighting forces emerged in response to invasion, war and banditry in medieval China, Japan, Korea and Tibet, for example, and more recently during the Sino–Japanese war (Jerryson 2017, 60; Yu 2013; Schmithausen 1999, 52).

While the Western just war tradition, and latterly IHL, have evolved over time to become generally less permissive, Buddhism has sometimes become more open to the use of military force, and to some just war ideas.

Lineaments of just war in Buddhism

The lineaments of Buddhist just war thinking have developed where Buddhism has become closer to the state or the Buddhist majority (Jerryson 2010; Frydenlund 2017c, 27). This has often tended to occur where Buddhists have perceived themselves, like the Christians of Augustine's day, to be under existential threat, whether from foreign invasion or colonial encroachment, and seek religious legitimation for the use of military force (Frydenlund 2017c, 29). This led to a greater emphasis on prescriptions to compensate for the negative karmic effects of breaking the first precept, as well to the relativisation of the precept itself (Schmithausen 1999, 56–57).

Early justifications for war were developed in the *Mahāvaṃsa*, a non-canonical fifth-century CE text that chronicles the Sinhalese Buddhist hero King Duṭṭhagāmaṇi's (161–137 BCE) war against the Tamil King Eḷāra, said to be to protect Buddhism (Harvey 2000, 255–256). Duṭṭhagāmaṇi is described, for example, as marching his army to Anuradhapura with a Buddhist relic in his spear and accompanied by 500 monks (Singh 2017, 469).

Mahāyāna and Vajrayāna Buddhism are doctrinally more permissive regarding the use of violence than Theravāda Buddhism, since they encourage a more contingent and utilitarian interpretation of Buddhist precepts (Keown 2005, 18). This includes the idea of compassionate or altruistic killing by *bodhisattvas* in service of the greater good, reminiscent of early Catholic just war thinking which argued that love for one's neighbour might justify the use of lethal force against wrongdoers (Jayasuriya 2009, 424).

Compassionate killing is most famously illustrated by the influential early Mahāyāna *Upāya-kauśalya Sūtra* ('Skill-in-Means Sutra') about a *bodhisattva* sea captain who kills a would-be murderer of the passengers and crew of a ship, thereby taking upon himself the karmic penalty and saving the would-be murderer from a far worse karmic fate (Harvey 2021, in this volume). Because the sea captain accepts the possibility of hell for himself in order to save others, and his mind is therefore free from negative mental states, he is not in fact reborn there, or only for a brief time.

Other Mahāyāna texts have been more forthright (Schmithausen 1999, 57–59). The influential *Mahāparinirvāṇa Sūtra* (c. fourth century CE), for example, states that followers of Mahāyāna can override the moral precepts in defence of Buddhism, even if it means using weapons and killing (Schmithausen 1999, 57–58; Victoria 2022).

Perhaps the clearest and most succinct exposition of just war thinking in Buddhism is found in the Mahāyāna *Ārya-satyaka-parivarta* ('Noble Discourse of the Truth-Teller') written in India between the fourth and sixth centuries CE (Sugiki 2020a, 2; Bartles-Smith et al. 2020, 374). Whereas most Buddhist guidance on war is scattered across a vast and unwieldy corpus of texts, the *Ārya-satyaka-parivarta* advises rulers on how to deal with the approach of a hostile foreign army in the equivalent of a few short paragraphs. To prevent war, and in line with the *jātakas* and other canonical texts, the righteous ruler is advised to befriend the adversary, give them gifts or intimidate them by strong alliances (Sugiki 2020a, 11; Zimmermann 2000, 190–191).

The Vajrayāna *Kālacakra-tantra* also evinces some just war thinking. Written in India in the eleventh century when Buddhism was under threat from Muslim invaders, it prophesies an invasion of the mythical Himalayan kingdom of Shambhala by a foreign (*mleccha*) army, and tells how its *cakravartin* ruler will defeat the invaders and safeguard Buddhism (Sinclair 2014, 158; Schmithausen 1999, 58). The tantra contains preconditions for the use of military force similar to those in the *jātakas* and *Ārya-satyaka-parivarta*. War must be fought only as a last resort against an intractably violent opponent, and should be motivated solely by the desire to protect the country, and not by hatred towards the enemy or desire to plunder their wealth (Sinclair 2014, 160). Mahāyāna and Vajrayāna scriptures have therefore been more accommodating to the preoccupations of Buddhist belligerents.

Buddhist resources to prevent war extend into a range of esoteric beliefs and practices. War-related material in Indian Vajrayāna, for example, far outstrips that in non-tantric Buddhist discourses, and one Tibetan adept, Lodrö Gyeltsen (1552–1624), was known as Sokdokpa ('Mongol Repeller') because he performed elaborate rituals to repulse Mongol threats (Sinclair 2014, 150; Dalton 2011, 133–134). The use of such non-violent means is especially attractive for Buddhists, since it is compatible with Buddhist precepts, and expedients to prevent war include the deployment of magical or supernatural powers (Debreczeny 2019; van Schaik 2020, 89).

Part 4: Minimising violence during war according to Buddhism and IHL

Karma and intention during war

Having examined what Buddhism says about the prevention of war, and the resort to it (*jus ad bellum*), the second half of this article investigates what Buddhism says about the conduct of war (*jus in bello* or IHL) and the predicament in which belligerents find themselves.

A central concern of Buddhist belligerents is the negative karma they might accrue during war. The size of the karmic harm caused by harming or killing depends both upon the nature of the action, including the intensity of the desire to harm and the amount of effort used, and the nature of the victim of the action (Singh 2017, 254). In very broad terms, it is worse to harm a good as opposed to a bad person, a human as opposed to an animal, and a large as opposed to a small animal, due to the greater effort and therefore intention required (Harvey 2021, in this volume). The real or perceived moral status of the enemy is of course highly relevant in war, and the lack of concern for the killing of ogres or demons in the *jātaka*s would appear to reflect their very low moral status, suggesting that Buddhists might sometimes be as prone as others to demonise or dehumanise enemies in real life to enable violence against them (Jenkins 2017, 163–164).

Crucially, the karmic consequences for belligerents hinge on both their motivations to fight and their precise intention at the moment they use force – whether to incapacitate or kill the enemy, for example. Similarly, as the Buddha stated, the dying thought (*maraṇa-citta*) of a combatant has a crucial bearing on their next life (Jenkins 2017, 164). If combatants do have to kill or harm a living being during war, they must do so with as pure and altruistic intentions as possible, and this is difficult in conflict situations where combatants must cope with limited options, extreme stress and strong emotions.

Famously, when asked by a *yodhājīva* foot soldier or mercenary if he would go to heaven should he die in battle, the traditional Hindu idea, the Buddha replied reluctantly that he would be reborn in the battle-slain hell if his mind was 'inferior, depraved, and misdirected [with the thought] "Let these sentient beings be killed, bound, annihilated, perished, or never exist"' (Sam. IV.308–9; Sugiki 2020a, 8).

There are differing Buddhist perspectives on the degree to which belligerents can realistically prevent their minds from entering an unskilful state during war, and thus allay the negative karmic consequences (Keown 2014, 657, 670–671). According to Theravāda *Abhidhamma* texts, it is not psychologically possible to kill someone with entirely wholesome intentions, since even the most altruistic scenarios contain an underlying negative component (Gethin 2004, 190). However, a number of Mahāyāna texts maintain that belligerents can sometimes kill with a neutral or good state of mind (Sugiki 2020a, 6–8). Either way, it is clearly in the interest of Buddhist belligerents to minimise the amount of harm they inflict as far as possible in line with IHL.

Belligerents are individually responsible for their karma just as they are individually responsible for their actions under IHL, and obeying illegal orders is not an excuse (AP I, Art.86[1]). Since karma is intention, those who order the breaking of Buddhist precepts are as liable for the karmic results, or more so, than the troops who actually carry it out, implicating all those in a chain of command (Mn.II.188; Harvey 1999, 280). Indeed, according to the fourth-century Gandharan monk Vasubandhu, all soldiers in an army share responsibility for killing, such that they have a group karma (Harvey 2000, 254; Bartles-Smith et al. 2020, 401).

Buddhism's introspective focus on the intentions of belligerents is characteristic of other religions and ethical systems, including the Western just war tradition (Whetham 2011b, 71–72; Bartles-Smith 2022, 1745). Aquinas understood that rules will not necessarily be adhered to if the underlying intentions of belligerents are wrong, and this may partly explain why, like Buddhism, his just war theory provides only general principles rather than detailed *jus in bello* rules, since it is the motivation or intention behind an act that is the most important determinant and predictor of behaviour (Whetham 2011b, 71–72).

Applying Buddhism and IHL to the conduct of war

In addition to ruses and stratagems to prevent war, Buddhist texts such as the *jātaka* stories also show how violence might be creatively minimised should war break out. The Buddha is frequently reborn as a wartime king, minister or warrior in human or animal form – as a war horse, for example – combining intellect with heroic compassion and self-sacrifice (Jenkins 2017, 166–167). As a *bodhisattva* in these previous lives, his endeavours to curtail war's violence provide case studies of exemplary restraint that real belligerents might strive to emulate. The fact that these lively tales are carved on temples and monasteries, and are known and beloved by Buddhists throughout the world, suggests, moreover, how IHL rules might be disseminated (Mendis 2021, in this volume; Wijenayake 2021, in this volume).

One graphic, if unrealistic, example of Buddhist restraint in war is the canonical story of the Buddhist god Sakka, who when retreating from the *asura* (demi-god) army ordered his own army to turn and confront the enemy rather than risk his carriage poles striking the nests of some birds (Sam.I.224). While the balance here between compassion and military necessity has perhaps tipped too far towards the former, concern for innocent life is in accord with IHL, and has a practical military and strategic purpose (Jenkins 2017, 171). Indeed, the cultivation of compassion can help belligerents to refrain from inflicting unnecessary harm, since the compassionate use of force is not only better intended but more heedful (165). It is therefore more likely to be carefully calibrated and targeted.

Buddhist texts contain stories of warriors who avoid killing enemy forces even at war. These include capturing the enemy alive, then making them swear an oath to end their animosity before releasing them (Sugiki 2020b, 17). Similarly, the Mahāyāna *Mahāparinirvāna Sūtra* advocates the use of weapons to stop enemy attacks without killing (Sugiki 2020b, 12–13; Jenkins 2010a, 67). Less recommended is the use of siege blockades to avoid battle. Although used by a prince and his mother in the *Asātarūpa Jātaka* to cut off the city of Bārānasī from food and fuel, neither was a past rebirth of the Buddha, and they suffered the karmic consequences (Jat.I.242–43; Sugiki 2020b, 11).

Somewhat more realistic guidance is provided in the *Ārya-satyaka-parivarta*, which also describes how troops can most effectively be arrayed (Jamspal and Hackett 2010, 61). It instructs the righteous ruler to keep three thoughts in mind when readying for war: the complete protection of his people, defeat of the enemy, and the capture of the enemy alive (Sugiki 2020a, 14; Jenkins 2010a, 67).

Unusually, the *Ārya-satyaka-parivarta* states more clearly than in other texts that a righteous ruler can avoid the karmic consequences of killing and wounding enemy forces, and gain immeasurable merit, under the following conditions: he has previously made every possible effort to avoid war; he is motivated by compassion and heedfulness; and he is ready to sacrifice himself and his wealth for the protection of his people (Sugiki 2020a, 14; Jenkins 2017, 173). This is nevertheless an outlier for Buddhism, which generally refuses to let belligerents off the hook for their harmful actions in war, however well-intentioned in the conventional sense.

Separate from its discussion of war, though relevant to it, the *Ārya-satyaka-parivarta* also describes how a righteous ruler should 'protect sentient beings and their surroundings', broadly in line with IHL provisions:

> . . . a ruler should protect sentient beings without burning their surroundings or ruining it, etc. A ruler should not vent his anger through cities or villages, ruining reservoirs, wrecking dwelling places, cutting down fruit trees, or destroying harvests, etc. In short, it is not right to destroy any well-prepared, well-constructed, and well-extended regions. How is this? These are sources of life commonly used by many sentient beings who have not produced any faults. (Jamspal and Hackett 2010, 56)

The five precepts are fundamental for lay Buddhist ethics, and also therefore for the conduct of war. Although Buddhist belligerents understandably risk breaking the first precept against killing, it is nevertheless important for them to continuously reaffirm the precept, even when it seems impossible to uphold (Trew 2021, in this volume). Of course, there is no pretext for them to break the remaining four, all of which endorse IHL. The second precept against stealing aligns with IHL prohibitions on pillage and the confiscation of civilian property, and the third precept against sexual misconduct aligns with IHL prohibitions of rape and other forms of sexual violence (CIHL, Rule 51 and 52; Bartles-Smith et al. 2020, 414–415). The fourth precept against wrong speech or falsehood, is relevant to the IHL prohibition on perfidy (the abuse of IHL protections), as well as to malicious or abusive speech that might constitute cruel, inhuman and degrading treatment (CIHL, Rule 65 and Rule 90), and the fifth precept against partaking of intoxicants is conducive to the mental clarity required to adhere to IHL rules (Kilby 2021, in this volume).

Buddhist chanting, rituals and meditation techniques have also been variously deployed as forms of non-lethal spiritual warfare to overcome enemy forces (Sinclair 2014). Vajrayāna ritual manuals or *kriya-tantras*, for example, include detailed instructions on mantras, visualisations and yoga to stun, stop, freeze or disperse hostile armies, or cause them to surrender

(Sinclair 2014, 152–153). While the effectiveness of some these measures might be questioned, their intent is absolutely in line with Buddhist precepts and IHL.

Similar means have been used to protect combatants and non-combatants. The wearing of protective amulets and chanting of protective canonical verses and scriptures (*paritta*) in anticipation of military operations are also common practices in the Theravāda Buddhist world (Frydenlund 2017c, 37). Likewise, compassion is commonly considered to have an almost supernatural power to protect (Jenkins 2010a, 65). Such beliefs and practices reflect the important psychological dimension of warfare, and overlap with Buddhist practices such as meditation, whose beneficial effects are scientifically proven (Dalton 2011, 137).

Buddhist and IHL principles

The fundamental principles of Buddhist ethics therefore dictate that it is in the interest of those engaged in war to minimise the harm they inflict in accordance with core IHL principles of distinction, proportionality and precaution (Harvey 2021, in this volume). Explicit Buddhist teachings also correspond with IHL rules, regarding the protection of non-combatants, care for the wounded and humane treatment of prisoners or defeated enemies (Tilakaratne et al. 2021; Bartles-Smith et al. 2020, 405).

Just as IHL embodies a balance between humanity and military necessity, Buddhism interrogates whether each and every military action is necessary at all in the light of alternative, including non-military, options. The Buddhist determination of military necessity is clearly very exacting. Starting from the earliest military planning, options other than the infliction of harm should first be explored. Failing this, the use of force should be as restrained and directed as possible, targeting only those combatants or military objects that pose an immediate threat. Whenever feasible, enemy combatants should be neutralised or incapacitated rather than harmed or killed, which also dictates the military tactics and the choice of weapons used.

Destruction of civilian objects, infrastructure, means of livelihood, animals and the natural environment should be minimised, and the maximum effort made to repair the damage that has been done (Scorsine 2014, 123). While mistakes, such as the killing of non-combatants, might not be deliberate, they might nevertheless be critiqued for lack of heedfulness (*appamāda*) or mindfulness, in line with the IHL principle of precaution (Samarakoon 2021, in this volume). This degree of restraint in such high-stress combat situations also requires a high degree of personal bravery and willingness to put one's life on the line for the sake of others, and the level of self-sacrifice required of Buddhist combatants is particularly high (Jenkins 2010a, 67).

Ideas of military necessity and proportionality are central to IHL's practical application. While not infinitely elastic, they give commanders a wide margin of discretion, since the determination of the importance of a military objective, and the amount of collateral killing of non-combatants that is acceptable, relies on their own subjective assessment (Khen 2016 36; Gisel 2016, 23). Although solutions such as the 'reasonable military commander' standard have been proposed to get around this problem (essentially what a 'reasonable' commander would do in a particular circumstance), this raises the obvious question of how 'reasonable' might be defined in different operational circumstances and between commanders who have different doctrinal backgrounds (Henderson and Reece 2018).[1] The Buddhist focus on the intention of belligerents might help prevent these IHL principles from being too loosely interpreted, so that they prevent or minimise collateral damage more energetically. Judging from Buddhist texts, a Buddhist 'reasonable commander' would be highly restrictive in the use of military force, and would require the compassion, intellect and strategic vision – and indeed the mandate – to deploy non-harming, including non-military, means whenever possible. In modern military parlance, this would perhaps correspond more to an unconventional hearts-and-minds approach, in which military capability is just one element of an otherwise non-violent response, employed primarily as a deterrent or last resort. For this deterrent to be effective, as Thich Nhat Hanh has suggested, it is preferable to maintain a strong military force like the *cakravartin*'s fourfold army (Keown 2014, 675).

Since a fundamental part of a belligerent's role is to protect people, they are also in a privileged position to alleviate suffering (Harvey 2021, in this volume; Ratheiser and Kariyakarawana 2021, in this volume). IHL rules are intended not only to limit the harm inflicted in war, but to ensure care and support for its victims. Belligerents therefore have an opportunity to improve their karma by assisting the wounded, sick, captured, displaced and other victims of armed conflict.

Merit-making acts are still carried out by Buddhist belligerents to compensate for the negative karma they accrue in war, and though good karma does not prevent bad karma coming to fruition, its positive effects can nevertheless compensate to some degree (Schmithausen 1999, 53; Bartles-Smith et al. 2020, 393). Merit-making normally involves gift-giving (*dāna*) of food or other necessities to the Sangha, but can also take the form of government largesse to temples, for example, and might justifiably be viewed with cynicism when performed by those known to have carried out war crimes. But it might equally be performed by those who have followed the rules of war and are aware of the karmic penalty they have nevertheless incurred, much as medieval Christian knights performed penances after returning from battle (Verkamp 1988). Merit-making might also take the form of humanitarian care and assistance for war victims, in accordance with IHL (Harvey 2021, in this volume).

Buddhism and military ethics

Knowledge of IHL rules and Buddhist principles must be complemented by the skills to interpret and apply them in highly complex and stressful war situations, and these should ideally be rehearsed in advance of hostilities (Whetham 2011a). The Buddhist perspective on ethics as skilful or unskilful behaviour, and its emphasis on training and disciplining the mind in this regard, is therefore highly pertinent.

The parallels between military and monastic discipline and training have long been noted, and are a theme in early Buddhist texts (An.IV.181; Sam.I.98–99; Kent 2008, 98). Just as military virtues have been emulated by Buddhist practitioners seeking to conquer their inner demons, so can Buddhist virtues or mental attitudes benefit military personnel (Roebuck 2010, xlix). Buddhism's emphasis on character formation is well adapted to military training, and its psychological resources can interrogate the emotional, perception and attention factors behind belligerents' behaviour to provide insight into why they sometimes break the rules (Olsthoorn 2019, 38–39). The question for soldiers therefore becomes not simply 'What should I do?' but 'How can I become the kind of soldier who can do it?'

Buddhism takes seriously the power of emotions to affect our behaviour (McCrae 2017, 336). Like the battle against Māra, the final battle in the *Kālacakra-tantra* is fought simultaneously against the belligerent's inner defilements, and Buddhism recognises that just conduct in war is as dependent on the mental state of its protagonists as external conditions (Sinclair 2014, 160).

According to the great fourth- to fifth-century CE scholars Buddhaghosa and Vasabandhu, the etymology of the Pali term for morality in Buddhism, '*sīla*', more accurately translated as self-restraint, includes the meaning 'head' and 'cool' or 'refreshing', such that ethical conduct in Buddhism is associated with a cool or calm head (Whitaker and Smith 2017, 54). This is the antidote to the transcultural association of heat with the physiology of anger and hatred, the control of which is crucially important in the heat of battle (54).

When asked about the one thing he approved of killing, the Buddha replied the killing of anger 'with its honeyed crest and poison root' (Sam. I.41). Ashoka Maurya also understood the practical importance of non-anger, calm and patience to cultivate an impartial mental attitude and prevent the infliction of harm upon innocents, as he said in Kaliṅga Rock Edit 1:

> While being completely law-abiding, some people are imprisoned, treated harshly and even killed without cause .... Therefore your aim should be to

> act with impartiality. It is because of these things – envy, anger, cruelty, hate, indifference, laziness or tiredness – that such a thing does not happen. Therefore your aim should be: 'May these things not be in me'. And the root of this is non-anger and patience. (Dhammika 1993, 30)

The cultivation of positive affective states such as the Four Immeasurables (*brahmavihāras*) of loving-kindness (Pali *mettā*, Sanskrit *maitrī*), compassion (*karuṇā*), empathetic joy (*muditā*) and equanimity (Pali *upekkhā*, Sanskrit *upekṣā*) can help combatants to counter afflictive mental states such as anger or hatred and the violence they generate, and are highly relevant for restrained conduct in war (Gethin 1998; Bartles-Smith et al. 2020, 385). Patience or forbearance (Pali *khanti*, Sanskrit *kṣānti*) is also highly prized, as are qualities that correspond to more conventional military virtues, such as energy, perseverance and courage (Pali *viriya*, Sanskrit *vīrya*), and self-sacrifice (*tyāga*) (Wakefield 2021, in this volume; Bartles-Smith et al. 2020, 404–405).

Mindfulness and military training

Buddhist mindfulness techniques undergird its ethical content and have the potential, furthermore, to enhance combatant performance. Psychological and neuroscience research has proven that meditation can improve the resilience and mental functioning of combatants and reduce impairment of their cognitive faculties in high-stress battle situations, thereby enabling them to fight with greater self-control (Stanley et al. 2011; Jha et al. 2015; Braboszcz, Hahusseau, and Delorme 2010; Trew 2021, in this volume; Bartles-Smith et al. 2020, 408). This includes enhancement of mental skills such as concentration, situational awareness and working memory capacity, as well as handling ambiguity and complexity. More research must be done on exactly how effective these various techniques are in promoting adherence to IHL rules, but the United States Medical Health Advisory Team IV report showed that military personnel with higher levels of anger or stress, or with mental health issues, were twice as likely to mistreat non-combatants in Iraq (2006, 3–4).

According to United States combat veteran Elizabeth Stanley, who worked with neuroscientist Amishi Jha on Mindfulness-based Mind Fitness Training for the US military, 'resilience depends on a well-regulated autonomic nervous system ... which means that it can function more effectively during a stressful experience without either acting out against one's goals or values, or dissociating along the "freeze" spectrum', and is therefore important for enabling combatants to adhere to IHL norms (Stanley 2014). Buddhism also understands the importance of resilience for military personnel. The *Akkhama Sutta*, for example, describes how monks must be as resilient as a king's elephant who steels himself to the fearful sights, sounds, smells and tactile sensations of battle, such as piercing by arrows, in order to fight effectively (An.V.139).

Combatants must first protect themselves before they can effectively protect others, and Jha describes these mindfulness techniques as a form of 'mental armour' for combatants (Senauke and Gates 2014; French 2017, 8, 12). The need for such protection has been highlighted by psychological research into moral injury, a set of shame and guilt-based disturbances caused by perpetrating, failing to prevent or witnessing transgressive acts that violate one's deeply held moral or ethical beliefs (Hamrick, Kelley, and Bravo 2020, 109; Frankfurt and Frazier 2016; Bartles-Smith 2022, 1755). In the military context, such experiences include killing, injuring, excessive retribution, failure of leadership and ambiguity in the rules of engagement, which might also constitute violations of IHL (Hamrick, Kelley, and Bravo 2020, 109). Symptoms of moral injury range from difficulty to forgive oneself or others, anger, social withdrawal and demoralisation, through to depression, post-traumatic stress disorder (PTSD) and suicide (Hamrick, Kelley, and Bravo 2020, 110; Shay 2010, 115). For many belligerents the consequences of their transgressions, whether seen in karmic or purely psychological terms, are all too real.

Shame over wrongdoing (Pali *hiri*, Sanskrit *hirī*) and concern for its consequences (Pali *ottappa*, Sanskrit *apatrapya*) are also cherished Buddhist qualities (Bodhi 1993). The first is about guarding, not compromising, an individual's moral integrity and sense of self-worth, and the second is about avoiding repercussions such as remorseful self-blame, the blame of others, and other future karmic harms, including through legal sanctions: so, more powerful deterrents to bad behaviour than the threat of legal sanctions alone (Grasmick, Bursik, and Kinsey 1991; Bartles-Smith 2022, 1755–1756).

Buddhists understand the need for inner armour, and that its effectiveness is dependent upon one's conduct, as this excerpt from the Theravāda canon shows:

> Those who engage in misconduct of body, speech, and mind .... Even though a company of elephant troops may protect them, or a company of cavalry ... still they leave themselves unprotected. For what reason? Because that protection is external, not internal .... But those who engage in good conduct of body, speech, and mind protect themselves .... Because that protection is internal, not external ....
>
> ...
>
> Conscientious, everywhere restrained,
>
> One is said to be protected. (Sam.I.168–9)

The potential to draw on Buddhist-inspired martial arts, which emphasise mindfulness and self-discipline, has yet to be properly explored. Their characteristic emphasis on self-defence, restraint and the skilful control of physical force would seem, however, to be in accord with IHL (Lorge 2011; Bartles-Smith et al. 2020, 410–411). Indeed, research has shown that they can reduce aggression in young people (Harwood, Lavidor, and Rassovsky 2017). A number of martial arts are used as both meditation and fighting tools, and the Buddhist connection is particularly important in the Mahāyāna Chan (Zen) school where the Shaolin monastery, for example, was famous for the skilfulness of its warrior monks (Shahar 2008). Martial arts can also, of course, be utilised to simply produce better fighters, and Japanese samurai used Zen Buddhism to dissolve fear and concentrate the mind on the present moment for this very purpose (Soho 2012; Mann 2012; Victoria 2022). But this increased fighting efficiency must also incorporate restraint, just as mindfulness should be combined with other components of Buddhist ethics. Martial arts have also traditionally played a recreational role, whether for exercise or entertainment, and the degree to which they have previously been practically applied to enhance restraint in war is unclear (Lorge 2011, 3; Bartles-Smith 2022, 1748).

Clerical support to belligerents

Just as the Buddha and his disciples counselled kings and warriors, so monastics continue to counsel governments, militaries or non-state armed groups to this day, as well as presiding over religious ceremonies and providing them with spiritual support (Kent 2008; Frydenlund 2017a, 18). Military personnel often attend nearby temples, and Buddhist clergy preach sermons to them on special occasions (Kent 2008; Frydenlund 2017a, 18). Some militaries also employ Buddhist chaplains (Bosco 2014; Lee 2021, in this volume).

Studies carried out in Sri Lanka during the civil war have shown that, as in the Buddha's day, many Buddhist soldiers are concerned about the negative karma they might accrue (Kent 2008, 3–4). Clergy are therefore well placed to remind them that their own welfare is contingent on minimising the suffering they inflict on others, and much of the thrust of their sermons is to avoid anger and stay calm and mindful of their actions even in battle (Kent 2008, 131–158, 202). Monks also advise soldiers to take every opportunity to accumulate merit through good deeds. While some scholars have argued that Sri Lankan monks engage in just war thinking, for most of the clergy interviewed the terms of debate were different (Bartholomeusz 2005; Kent 2008, 200–201). They did not attempt to justify war but concerned themselves with the welfare and mental state of combatants, and therefore their karma (Kent 2008, 200–201; Frydenlund 2017c, 29).

One crucial element of belligerents' motivation is that they must reconcile themselves to the possibility of being killed. The psychological support provided by Buddhist clergy is crucial in this regard, and can enable combatants to remain mentally and spiritually intact. The fact that they also preside over the funerals of fallen combatants is also important, and can help mourners to come to terms with their untimely death (Kent 2008; Hassner 2016, 86–87). The Buddhist belief in rebirth is likely to reassure belligerents in this respect, and studies in Sri Lanka have shown that it has helped to prevent further traumatisation among veterans with combat trauma (Hassner 2016, 124–125).

Part 5: Failures to apply Buddhist and IHL norms in practice

Historical misrepresentation of Buddhism to enable unrestrained violence

Historically, despite the range of Buddhist teachings and resources to promote restraint, Buddhists have sometimes been responsible for wartime atrocities (Jerryson 2010). There are therefore fundamental questions about the degree to which Buddhist teachings have actually been applied to war situations, or even properly understood. Indeed, some Buddhist teachings have been so distorted on occasion as to *enable* unrestrained violence against enemy groups (Victoria 2022).

Like members of other communities, Buddhists have also sometimes been prone to discount the lives of non-Buddhists. In the Sri Lankan *Mahāvaṃsa* chronicle, one notorious verse relates how King Duṭṭhagāmaṇi, distressed at the number of deaths he had caused in his victory over King Elāra, is reassured by a group of supposed Arhats that he had done no wrong in waging the war because killing wicked people with wrong views was morally equivalent to killing animals (Gombrich 2006, 141; Singh 2017, 469). Though regarded as implausible by most serious scholars (Harvey 2021, in this volume), this verse has nevertheless been recycled by some contemporary Buddhists, including some high-profile monks (Fuller 2017).

A passage in the Mahāyāna *Mahāparinirvāṇa Sūtra* states that the killing of *icchantikas*, deluded beings who reject Mahāyāna in favour of unwholesome doctrines, is equivalent to 'felling ... trees, mowing grass, or dissecting a corpse', and the Vajrayāna *Sarva-durgati-pariśodhana-tantra* states that those 'who hate the Three Jewels ... have a wrong attitude to the Buddha's teachings ... or disparage the [Vajrayāna] masters' should be killed wherever they are found (Schmithausen 1999, 58). Lacking the Buddha nature intrinsic to other sentient beings, and therefore barred from enlightenment, their lives are essentially meaningless (Victoria 2022; Jerryson 2017, 50; Singh 2017, 256; Jenkins 2017, 164; Yu 2013, 204–205). Twentieth-century Zen Buddhist militarists maintained on this basis that that the killing of 'inferior' enemy beings was a compassionate act, since their Buddha nature would be revived in a more favourable rebirth, buttressing an imperial ideology which incited numerous war crimes (Demiéville 2010, 44–45).

Core Buddhist concepts of karma and rebirth have therefore been misrepresented to encourage a fatalistic approach to deaths in battle, which are seen as unavoidable karmic retribution, and this attitude has also encouraged Buddhist combatants to be less heedful of their own lives, as witnessed in the suicidal bravery of some Japanese soldiers during World War II, particularly kamikaze pilots (Victoria 2022).

While Māra is a demonic representation of undesirable inner qualities and temptations over which the Buddhist practitioner must triumph, it has sometimes been projected onto real adversaries who are literally demonised or dehumanised to enable violence against them (Victoria 2022; Jenkins 2017, 163–164; French and Jack 2015). The idea of the future Buddha Maitreya (Pali Metteya), foretold to re-establish Buddhism, has inspired several violent millenarian revolts against non-Buddhists, or the wrong kind of Buddhists. In sixth-century CE China, for example, the monk Faqing used drugs to send his followers into a killing frenzy, telling them they would attain high *bodhisattva* status if they killed ten enemies each in a cosmic battle against Māra (Jerryson 2017, 60; Victoria 2022).

Aspects of Vajrayāna Buddhism involve the deliberate transgression of Buddhist precepts by religious adepts, and perfect practitioners (*siddhas*) are considered to be above conventional moral norms (Schmithausen 1999, 61). Although many tantric texts describe symbolic rather than real violence, and include injunctions to minimise the use of lethal force, its practices were also intended for less inhibited killing (Sinclair 2014, 161; Dalton 2011, 133–138). The eighth-century CE *Hevajra-tantra*, for example, contains detailed rituals to destroy entire enemy armies, as well as their gods (Debreczeny 2019). Indeed, the Mongols employed Buddhist adepts to help them defeat real armies, and the Tibetan preceptor of Kublai Khan reportedly secured a magical victory over China's Southern Song (Debreczeny 2019; Dalton 2011, 136).

Although the *Kālacakra-tantra* is set in a mythical realm, and describes a psychological as much as a future physical battle, the king of Shambhala is nevertheless prophesied to annihilate barbarian forces and destroy their religion (though one commentary states that he shall not take enemy lives) and was one inspiration behind Aum Shinrikyo's 1995 Sarin gas attack in the Tokyo subway (Jerryson 2010, 8; Sinclair 2014, 159–60; Schmithausen 1999, 61–62).

Certain practices, such as sorcery and the propitiation of local spirits, are believed by some powerful Buddhists – including military and armed group members – to enable them to manipulate karma through supernatural means, thereby avoiding the karmic consequences of transgressive violence (Pranke 2010; van Schaik 2020, 98).

More permissive interpretations of Buddhism have tended to be more prevalent in the Mahāyāna and Vajrayāna Buddhist worlds, where concepts such as skill-in-means and compassionate violence have sometimes been weaponised and abused (Schmithausen 1999, 46; Jenkins 2010b, 308–310). Only advanced *bodhisattvas* are generally thought to possess the wherewithal to kill altruistically, but this stipulation was not, of course, always followed (Schmithausen 1999, 46; Jenkins 2010b, 308–310). When combined, furthermore, with Buddhist teachings on the lack of a permanent self, impermanence and the Mahāyāna concept of śūnyatā, according to which all things are empty of intrinsic existence, human life, and therefore the act of killing, has sometimes been relegated to something of almost trivial importance. As the Rinzai Zen Master Takuan wrote in the seventeenth century:

> The uplifted sword has no will of its own, it is all of emptiness . . . . The man who is about to be struck down is also of emptiness, and so is the one who wields the sword. . . . the 'I' who is about to be struck down is like the splitting of the spring breeze in a flash of lightning. (Victoria 2003, 26)

According to Japanese Imperial Army Major Ōkubo Kōichi, lack of a permanent self also means that '[t]he soldier must become one with his superior . . .. he must become the order he receives' (Victoria [1997] 2006, 103). While an aid to strict discipline, this clashes with core Buddhist teachings that each individual is responsible for their own karma, and with IHL rules according to which combatants have a responsibility not to obey illegal orders (Melzer 2016, 286).

The danger of misinterpreting and perverting some Buddhist teachings to justify violations of IHL is abundantly clear.

Contemporary failures to apply IHL and Buddhist ethics

Clearly, belligerents who self-identify as Buddhists do not necessarily practice its core teachings. Given the relevance of meditation to Buddhist ethics, for example, the question as to whether they meditate (most do not) is particularly pertinent (Richmond 2012). Moreover, the civil religion of the state and the lived Buddhisms of the majority of lay Buddhists tend to focus on the making of merit (Pali *puñña*, Sanskrit *puṇya*) – good karma – to address immediate worldly concerns, and are less preoccupied with higher Buddhist teachings to transform the consciousness of individuals (Stanford and Jong 2019; Frydenlund 2017a; Bellah 1967).

Serious violations of Buddhist and IHL norms continue to blight parts of the contemporary Buddhist world, and much has been made of the contradiction between the behaviour of some Buddhist-majority militaries and Buddhist ethics (Selth 2021; Deegalle 2006). Indeed, some Buddhist military personnel do appear to believe that merit-making donations can compensate for the negative karma of war crimes, or that they can kill their enemies with no karmic repercussions.

Despite the well-publicised interactions of some militaries with Buddhist clergy, however, it is worth bearing in mind that the nature and content of their formal military training is predominantly, if not exclusively, secular, and Buddhist ethics are not generally included at all (Frydenlund 2017a, 14–15; ICRC 2021c). Although a number of militaries employ Buddhist chaplains, relations between the Sangha and the military are not generally close, and their secular ethos is reinforced in some contexts by *vinaya* injunctions that separate monastic from military affairs, such that monks risk losing credibility if they become too involved with the military (Kent 2008, 42–43, 78; Frydenlund 2017a; ICRC 2021b). These restrictions are reciprocated by militaries themselves, which likewise discourage the presence of Buddhist and other clerics in military training (ICRC 2021c). Although some monks do informally counsel and support military personnel in relation to their conduct in battle, most also lack the knowledge of IHL to relate it to Buddhist teachings (Kent 2008; Bartles-Smith et al. 2020).

Factors such as the brutalisation of recruits and inculcation of strict unthinking discipline in some militaries are also likely to have a significant impact on their behaviour. Indeed, some contemporary military training is designed to dehumanise combatants and inculcate an 'us versus them' mentality that can separate military personnel from societal norms and heighten their aggression and enmity towards other groups (Grossman 2014; French and Jack 2015; Inspector-General of the Australian Defence Force 2020). This makes it easier for them to override inhibitions against killing.

While Buddhist ethics still have a powerful hold over many individual military personnel, sometimes inspiring exemplary restraint, they are less commonly integrated into the regimes of entire military units, and might therefore have less impact on their collective behaviour (ICRC 2019b, 2021b, 2021c). This can lead some belligerents to believe that the military is a separate sphere where Buddhist ethics do not apply, even though they accord with IHL, and leaves scope for others to misrepresent Buddhism as legitimising the use of unrestrained force (ICRC 2021b; Kariyakarawana 2011; Victoria [1997] 2006).

While there are indications in Buddhist texts and the historical record that Buddhism has contributed to humanising the conduct of war in the past, awareness of this legacy has also perhaps diminished, and the adoption of Western-inspired military methods and doctrines might sometimes have displaced Buddhist-inspired norms of restraint (Jayatilleke 1967, 555–557; Charney 2021, in this volume).

Nevertheless, concise, user-friendly compilations of war-related guidance like the *Ārya-satyaka-parivarta* still appear to have been the exception rather than the rule in Buddhism. Indeed, there is much to be said be said for codifying and adapting Buddhist teachings to provide practical and authoritative Buddhist advice for modern belligerents, with reference to IHL. In the meantime, some Buddhist soldiers have started to informally do this themselves (Little 2011; Peto 2014).

Conclusion

Despite expanding research into other traditions, and increased ownership of IHL by non-Western constituencies, IHL and war studies remain Western-dominated fields, and there is still much to learn about 'the wisdom of restraint' in warfare that was pioneered in the East (Keegan 1994, 392).

Buddhism shows how non-Western and decidedly non-military perspectives can shed fresh light on the regulation of war. Indeed, only by embracing both the differences and similarities between Buddhism and IHL can their full potential to complement and support one another be revealed. Insofar as Buddhism and IHL become more mutually intelligible, this should also have a positive impact on the perception and implementation of IHL in the Buddhist world, just as Buddhist resources are now starting to be applied by some Western militaries (Stanley 2014; ICRC 2021b).

Relatively unencumbered by notions of military glory, or that war is acceptable, Buddhism makes clear that however 'just' the cause in a conventional sense, war is inherently wrong. Since violence is never fully legitimised, belligerents therefore have an added incentive to act with restraint in accord with IHL rules. In this respect, Buddhism is attuned to modern sensibilities that are increasingly less tolerant of even war's legal horrors.

Putting these principles into practice is another matter, and Buddhist belligerents have sometimes failed to adhere to Buddhist and IHL principles of restraint. The Buddha baulked at codifying rules of war, apparently satisfied to outline only foundational ethical principles to guide belligerents should war be unavoidable, and there are question marks about the extent to which Buddhist principles and resources can be realistically integrated into military training (Harvey 2021, in this volume). Whether preventing war or limiting its horrors is better achieved by adhering – however imperfectly – to the categorical non-violence of the core of the Theravāda Buddhist canon, or the more contingent pragmatism of some *jātaka* stories and skill-in-means teachings of Mahāyāna and Vajrayāna Buddhism, is also unclear. To whatever degree war is accommodated in various Buddhist traditions, however, all are in broad agreement with IHL that the harm inflicted should be minimised once war breaks out.

Simply instructing belligerents to follow IHL rules is not enough. The extreme conditions of war and lack of effective IHL enforcement mean that they must develop the mental awareness and capacity to regulate themselves. This is a role that Buddhism is particularly well adapted to play, since it contains within itself the psychological insights and resources to understand why belligerents sometimes misbehave (Harris 2021, in this volume). To paraphrase Rupert Gethin, if we want to know how to act in accordance with Dharma – and with IHL – we must first know our own minds (Gethin 2004, 72).

Note

1. However, the 'reasonable commander' standard was expressly rejected as unworkable during the negotiation of Additional Protocol I.

Abbreviations

Primary Buddhist Texts

An. *Aṅguttara Nikāya*. Translated by Bhikkhu Bodhi. 2012. *The Numerical Discourses of the Buddha: A Translation of the Aṅguttara Nikāya*. Boston: Wisdom.

Dhp. *Dhammapada*. Translated by Valerie J. Roebuck. 2010. *The Dhammapada*. London: Penguin. See also, translated by Acharya Buddharakkhita. 1996. *The Dhammapada: The Buddha's Path of Wisdom*. https://www.accesstoinsight.org/tipitaka/kn/dhp/index.html

Dn. *Dīgha Nikāya*. Translated by Maurice Walshe. [1987] 1995. *The Long Discourses of the Buddha: A Translation of the Dīgha Nikāya*. Boston: Wisdom.

Jat. *Jātaka*. Translated by various hands under Edward Byles Cowell. 1895-1907. *The Jātaka or Stories of the Buddha's Former Births*, 6 vols. London: Pali Text Society. References by volume and page number.

Mn. *Majjhima Nikāya*. Translated by Bhikkhu Ñāṇamoli and Bhikkhu Bodhi. 1995. *The Middle Length Discourses of the Buddha: A Translation of the Majjhima Nikāya*. Boston: Wisdom.

Sam. *Saṃyutta Nikāya*. Translated by Bhikkhu Bodhi. 2000. *The Connected Discourses of the Buddha. A Translation of the Saṃyutta Nikāya*. Boston: Wisdom.

Sn. *Sutta Nipāta*. Translated by Kenneth Roy Norman. 1984. *The Group of Discourses (Sutta–Nipāta) Vol. 1, with alternative translations by IB Horner and Walpola Rahula*. London: Pali Text Society. Also, translated by Kenneth Roy Norman. 1992. *The Group of Discourses (Sutta-Nipātā) Vol. II, Revised Translation with Introduction and Notes*. London: Pali Text Society.

Vin. *Vinaya Piṭaka*. Translated by Isaline Blew Horner. 1938-1966. *The Book of the Discipline (Vinaya-pitaka)*, 6 vols. London: Pali Text Society. References by volume and page number.

IHL Texts

AP I (Additional Protocol I) Protocol additional to the Geneva Conventions of 12 August 1949, and relating to the Protection of Victims of International Armed Conflicts, 8 June 1977.

AP II (Additional Protocol II) Protocol additional to the Geneva Conventions of 12 August 1949, and relating to the Protection of Victims of Non-International Armed Conflicts, 8 June 1977.

Common Article 3 Article 3 common to the Geneva Conventions of 12 August 1949.

CIHL Customary International Humanitarian Law, according to the ICRC study. https://ihl-databases.icrc.org/customary-ihl/eng/docs/home

St Petersburg Declaration Declaration Renouncing the Use, in Time of War, of Explosive Projectiles Under 400 Grammes Weight, 29 November / 11 December 1868.

Acknowledgements

The author thanks Dr Stefania Travagnin, Professor Peter Harvey, Dr Elizabeth Harris, Professor Kate Crosby, Dr Noel Trew and Daniel Ratheiser for their helpful comments on the various drafts of this paper.

Disclosure statement

This article has been supported by the International Committee of the Red Cross (ICRC).

References

Ahn, K. H. 1989. "A Short History of Ancient Korean Buddhism." In *Introduction of Buddhism to Korea: New Cultural Patterns*, edited by L. R. Lancaster and C. S. Yu, 1–27. Berkeley: Asian Humanities Press.

Armour, W. S. 1922. "Customs of Warfare in Ancient India." *Transactions of the Grotius Society* 8: 71–88.

Balkaran, R., and W. Dorn. 2022. "Charting Hinduism's Rules of Armed Conflict: International Humanitarian Law in Indian Sacred Texts." *International Review of the Red Cross* 104 (920–921): 1762–1797. doi:10.1017/S181638312200056X.

Bartholomeusz, T. J. 2005. *In Defense of Dharma: Just-War Ideology in Buddhist Sri Lanka*. London: Routledge.

Bartles-Smith, A. 2022. "Religion and International Humanitarian Law." *International Review of the Red Cross* 104 (920–921): 1725–1761. doi:10.1017/S1816383122000376.

Bartles-Smith, A., K. Crosby, P. Harvey, P. D. Premasiri, A. Tilakaratne, D. Ratheiser, M. Deegalle, N. M. Trew, S. Travagnin, and E. J. Harris. 2020. "Reducing Suffering During Conflict: The Interface Between Buddhism and International Humanitarian Law." *Contemporary Buddhism* 21 (1–2): 369–435.

Bellah, R. N. 1967. "Civil Religion in America." *Journal of the American Academy of Arts and Sciences* 96 (1): 1–21.

Bodhi, B. 1993. "The Guardians of the World." *BPS Newsletter*, Cover Essay No. 23. Reprint Access to Insight (BCBS Edition). http://www.accesstoinsight.org/lib/authors/bodhi/bps-essay_23.html

Bodhi, B. 2014. "War and Peace: A Buddhist Perspective." *Inquiring Mind,* Spring 30: 2. https://www.inquiringmind.com/article/3002_5_bhodi-war-and-peace-a-buddhist-perspective/

Bosco, R. M. 2014. "Battlefield Dharma: American Buddhists in American Wars." *Journal of Buddhist Ethics* 21: 827–849.

Boyle, E. H., and J. W. Meyer. 1998. "Modern Law as a Secularized and Global Model: Implications for the Sociology of Law." *Soziale Welt* 49 (3): 213–232.

Braboszcz, C., S. Hahusseau, and A. Delorme. 2010. "Meditation and Neuroscience: From Basic Research to Clinical Practice." In *Integrative Clinical Psychology, Psychiatry and Behavioral Medicine: Perspectives, Practices and Research*, edited by R. Carlstedt, 755–778. New York: Springer.

Brekke, T. 2006. "Between Prudence and Heroism: Ethics of War in the Hindu Tradition." In *The Ethics of War in Asian Civilization: A Comparative Perspective*, edited by T. Brekke, 113–144. London: Routledge.

Bryant, M. S. 2021. *A World History of War Crimes: From Antiquity to the Present*. 2nd ed. London: Bloomsbury.

Caserta, S. 2021. "Western Centrism, Contemporary International Law, and International Courts." *Leiden Journal of International Law* 34 (2): 321–342.

Charney, M. W. 2021. "Buddhism, the Royal Imaginary and Limits in Warfare: The Moderating Influence of Precolonial Myanmar Royal Campaigns on Everyday Warriors." *Contemporary Buddhism* 22. doi:10.1080/14639947.2022.2038029.

Cozort, D., and J. M. Shields. 2017. "Introduction." In *The Oxford Handbook of Buddhist Ethics*, edited by D. Cozort and J. M. Shields, 1–4. Oxford: Oxford University Press.

Dalton, J. P. 2011. *The Taming of the Demons: Violence and Liberation in Tibetan Buddhism*. New Haven: Yale University Press.

Debreczeny, K. 2019. "War Magic: The Wizarding World of Tibetan Sorcery." *The Rubin*. https://rubinmuseum.org/spiral/war-magic-the-wizarding-world-of-tibetan-sorcery

Deegalle, M. 2006. "Introduction." In *Buddhism, Conflict and Violence in Modern Sri Lanka*, edited by M. Deegalle. London: Routledge.

Demiéville, P. 2010. "Buddhism and War." In *Buddhist Warfare*, Translated by M. Kendall, edited by M. Jerryson and M. Juergensmeyer, 17–58. Oxford: Oxford University Press.

Dhammika, S. 1993. *The Edicts of King Asoka: An English Rendering*. Wheel Publication No. 386/387. Kandy: Buddhist Publication Society.

Dias, N., and R. Gamble. 2010. "Buddhism and Its Relationship with International Law." *Law & Justice - The Christian Law Review* 164: 3–26.

Draper, G. I. A. D. 1995. "The Contribution of the Emperor Asoka Maurya to the Development of the Humanitarian Ideal in Warfare." *International Review of the Red Cross* 35 (305): 192–206.

Fiske, A. P., and T. S. Rai. 2014. *Virtuous Violence: Hurting and Killing to Create, Sustain, End, and Honor Social Relationships*. Cambridge: Cambridge University Press.

Florida, R. 2013. "State, Society, and the Buddhist Order." In *Human Rights and the World's Major Religions: Condensed and Updated Edition*, edited by W. H. Brackney. Westport: Praeger.

Fox, J., and S. Sandler. 2004. *Bringing Religion into International Relations*. New York: Palgrave Macmillan.

Frankfurt, S., and P. Frazier. 2016. "A Review of Research on Moral Injury in Combat Veterans." *Military Psychology* 28 (5): 318–330.

French, R. R. 2015. "What is Buddhist Law: Opening Ideas." *Buffalo Law Review* 63 (4): 833–880.

French, S. E. 2017. *The Code of the Warrior: Exploring Warrior Values Past and Present*. Lanham: Rowman & Littlefield.

French, S. E., and A. I. Jack. 2015. "Dehumanizing the Enemy: The Intersection of Neuroethics and Bioethics." In *Responsibilities to Protect: Perspectives in Theory and Practice*, edited by D. Whetham and B. Strawser, 169–195. Leiden: Brill Nijhoff.

French, R. R., and M. A. Nathan. 2014. "Introducing Buddhism and Law." In *Buddhism and Law: An Introduction*, edited by R. R. French and M. A. Nathan, 1–28. Cambridge: Cambridge University Press.

Frydenlund, I. 2013. "Canonical Ambiguity and Differential Practices: Buddhism and Militarism in Contemporary Sri Lanka." In *Buddhism and Violence: Militarism and Buddhism in Modern Asia*, edited by T. Brekke and V. Tikhonov, 95–119. New York: Routledge.

Frydenlund, I. 2017a. "'Operation Dhamma': The Sri Lankan Armed Forces as an Instrument of Buddhist Nationalism." In *Military Chaplaincy in an Era of Religious Pluralism: Military-Religious Nexus in Asia, Europe, and USA*, edited by T. Brekke and V. Tikhonov, 81–103. New Delhi: Oxford University Press.

Frydenlund, I. 2017b. "'Buddhism Has Made Asia Mild': The Modernist Construction of Buddhism as Pacifism." In *Buddhist Modernities: Re-Inventing Tradition in the Globalizing Modern World*, edited by H. Havnevik, U. Hüsken, M. Teeuwen, V. Tikhonov, and K. Wellens, 204–221. Abingdon: Routledge.

Frydenlund, I. 2017c. "Buddhist Militarism Beyond Texts: The Importance of Ritual During the Sri Lankan Civil War." *Journal of Religion and Violence* 5 (1): 27–48.

Fuller, P. 2017. "Sitagu Sayadaw and Justifiable Evils in Buddhism." *New Mandala*, November 13. https://www.newmandala.org/sitagu-sayadaw-justifiable-evils-buddhism/

Fuller, P. 2021. *An Introduction to Engaged Buddhism*. London: Bloomsbury.

Gethin, R. 1998. *The Foundations of Buddhism*. Oxford: Oxford University Press.

Gethin, R. 2004. "Can Killing a Living Being Ever Be an Act of Compassion? The Analysis of the Act of Killing in the Abhidhamma and Pāli Commentaries." *Journal of Buddhist Ethics* 11: 166–202.

Gethin, R. 2014. "Keeping the Buddha's Rules: The View from the Sutra Pitaka." In *Buddhism and Law*, edited by R. R. French and M. A. Nathan, 63–77. Cambridge: Cambridge University Press.

Gisel, L. 2016. "The Principle of Proportionality in the Rules Governing the Conduct of Hostilities Under International Humanitarian Law." International Expert Meeting, Quebec, June 22–23. https://www.icrc.org/en/document/international-expert-meeting-report-principle-proportionality

Gombrich, R. F. 2006. *Theravāda Buddhism*. 2nd ed. London and New York: Routledge.

Grasmick, H. G., R. J. Bursik, and K. A. Kinsey. 1991. "Shame and Embarrassment as Deterrents to Noncompliance with the Law: The Case of an Antilittering Campaign." *Environment and Behavior* 23 (2): 233–251.

Grossman, D. 2014. *On Killing: The Psychological Cost of Learning to Kill in War and Society*. New York: Open Road Media.

Haidt, J. 2012. *The Righteous Mind: Why Good People are Divided by Politics and Religion*. New York: Vintage Books.

Hamrick, H. C., M. L. Kelley, and A. J. Bravo. 2020. "Morally Injurious Events, Moral Injury, and Suicidality Among Recent-Era Veterans: The Moderating Effects of Rumination and Mindfulness." *Military Behavioral Health* 8 (1): 109–120.

Harris, E. J. 2003. "Buddhism and the Justification of War: A Case Study from Sri Lanka." In *Just War in Comparative Perspective*, edited by P. Robinson, 93–108. Abingdon: Ashgate.

Harris, E. J. 2021. "Buddhist Empirical Realism and the Conduct of Armed Conflict." *Contemporary Buddhism* 22. doi:10.1080/14639947.2022.2038025.

Harvey, P. 2000. *An Introduction to Buddhist Ethics: Foundations, Values and Issues*. Cambridge: Cambridge University Press.

Harvey, P. 2018. "Karma." In *Oxford Handbook of Buddhist Ethics*, edited by D. Cozort and J. M. Shields, 7–28. Oxford: Oxford University Press.

Harvey, P. 2021. "Buddhist Motivation to Support IHL, from Concern to Minimise Harms Inflicted by Military Action to Both Those Who Suffer Them and Those Who Inflict Them." *Contemporary Buddhism* 22. doi:10.1080/14639947.2021.2037892.

Harwood, A., M. Lavidor, and Y. Rassovsky. 2017. "Reducing Aggression with Martial Arts: A Meta-Analysis of Child and Youth Studies." *Aggression and Violent Behavior* 34: 96–101.

Hassner, R. E. 2016. *Religion on the Battlefield*. Ithaca: Cornell University Press.

Henckaerts, J. M., and L. Doswald-Beck, ed. 2005. *Customary International Humanitarian Law, Vol. 1: Rules*. Cambridge: Cambridge University Press.

Henderson, I., and K. Reece. 2018. "Proportionality Under International Humanitarian Law: The Reasonable Military Commander Standard and Reverberating Effects." *Vanderbilt Journal of Transnational Law* 51: 835.

ICRC. 2019a. "Reducing Suffering During Armed Conflict: The Interface Between Buddhism and International Humanitarian Law (IHL)." ICRC Conference, Dambulla, Sri Lanka, September 4-6. https://www.icrc.org/en/document/reducing-suffering-during-conflict-interface-between-buddhism-and-international

ICRC. 2019b. "Videos from the Buddhism and IHL Conference - Presentations." *ICRC Religion and Humanitarian Principles Blog*, November 1. https://blogs.icrc.org/religion-humanitarianprinciples/videos-from-the-buddhism-and-ihl-conference-presentations/

ICRC. 2020. "Project on the Interface Between Buddhism and IHL." *ICRC Religion and Humanitarian Principles Blog*, March 3. https://blogs.icrc.org/religion-humanitarianprinciples/project-on-the-interface-between-buddhism-and-ihl/

ICRC. 2021a. "Introduction." *ICRC Religion and Humanitarian Principles Blog*. https://blogs.icrc.org/religion-humanitarianprinciples/about/

ICRC. 2021b. "Interview with the Buddhist Chaplain to Her Majesty's (British) Armed Forces." *ICRC Religion and Humanitarian Principles Blog*, April 5. https://blogs.icrc.org/religion-humanitarianprinciples/interview-with-the-first-buddhist-chaplain-to-the-her-majesty-s-british-armed-forces/

ICRC. 2021c. "Sri Lanka: Discussions on Buddhism and IHL with the Security Forces." *ICRC Religion and Humanitarian Principles Blog*, September 14. https://blogs.icrc.org/religion-humanitarianprinciples/sri-lanka-discussions-on-buddhism-and-ihl-with-the-security-forces/

ICRC. 2022. *What is International Humanitarian Law*. Geneva: ICRC. https://www.icrc.org/en/document/what-international-humanitarian-law

Inspector-General of the Australian Defence Force. 2020. *The Inspector-General of the Australian Defence Force Afghanistan Inquiry Report*. Canberra: Department of Defence. https://www.defence.gov.au/sites/default/files/2021-10/IGADF-Afghanistan-Inquiry-Public-Release-Version.pdf

Jamspal, L., trans. 2010. The Range of the Bodhisattva, a Mahāyānasūtra (Ārya-bodhisattva-gocara): The Teachings of the Nigrantha Satyaka, edited by P. G. Hackett. New York: American Institute of Buddhist Studies.

Jayasuriya, L. 2009. "Just War Tradition and Buddhism." *International Studies* 46 (4): 423–438.

Jayatilleke, K. N. 1967. "The Principles of International Law in Buddhist Doctrine." *Académie de droit international: Recueil des cours* 120 (1967–I): 441–567.

Jenkins, S. 2010a. "Making Merit Through Warfare and Torture According to the Ārya-Bodhisattva-gocara-upāyaviṣaya-vikurvaṇa-nirdeśa Sūtra." In *Buddhist Warfare*, edited by M. Jerryson and M. Juergensmeyer, 59–75. Oxford: Oxford University Press.

Jenkins, S. 2010b. "On the Auspiciousness of Compassionate Violence." *Journal of the International Association of Buddhist Studies* 33 (1–2): 299–331.

Jenkins, S. 2015. "Of Demon Kings and Protestant Yakṣas." *Religious Studies Project*, May 21. https://www.religiousstudiesproject.com/response/of-demon-kings-and-protestant-yak%e1%b9%a3as/

Jenkins, S. 2017. "Once the Buddha Was a Warrior: Buddhist Pragmatism in the Ethics of Peace and Armed Conflict." In *The Nature of Peace and the Morality of Armed Conflict*, edited by F. Demont-Biaggi, 159–178. London: Palgrave Macmillan.

Jerryson, M. 2010. "Introduction." In *Buddhist Warfare*, edited by M. Jerryson and M. Juergensmeyer, 3–16. Oxford: Oxford University Press.

Jerryson, M. 2017. "Buddhist Traditions and Violence." In *Violence and the World's Religious Traditions*, edited by M. Juergensmeyer, M. Kitts, and M. Jerryson, 37–69. Oxford: Oxford University Press.

Jerryson, M., and M. Juergensmeyer, ed. 2010. *Buddhist Warfare*. Oxford: Oxford University Press.

Jha, A. P., A. B. Morrison, J. Dainer-Best, S. Parker, N. Rostrup, and E. A. Stanley. 2015. "Minds 'At Attention': Mindfulness Training Curbs Attentional Lapses in Military Cohorts." *Plos One* 10 (2): e0116889.

Juergensmeyer, M., M. Kitts, and M. Jerryson. 2017. "Introduction: The Enduring Relationship of Religion and Violence." In *Violence and the World's Religious Traditions*, edited by M. Juergensmeyer, M. Kitts, and M. Jerryson, 1–6. Oxford: Oxford University Press.

Kaplan, O. 2013. "Nudging Armed Groups: How Civilians Transmit Norms of Protection." *Stability: International Journal of Security and Development* 2 (3): 1–18.

Kariyakarawana, S. 2011. "Military Careers and Buddhist Ethics." *International Journal of Leadership in Public Services* 7 (2): 99–108.

Keegan, J. 1994. *A History of Warfare*. London: Victoria Books.

Kent, D. 2008. "Shelter for You, Nirvana for Our Sons: Buddhist Belief and Practice in the Sri Lankan Army." PhD diss., Department of Religious Studies, University of Virginia. https://thecarthaginiansolution.files.wordpress.com/2011/08/buddhist-belief-practise-in-sl-army.pdf

Keown, D. 2005. *Buddhist Ethics: A Very Short Introduction*. Oxford: Oxford University Press.

Keown, D. 2014. "The Role of Deterrence in Buddhist Peace-Building." *Journal of Buddhist Ethics* 21: 655–678.

Khen, H. M. E. 2016. "Aidōs and Dikē in International Humanitarian Law: Is IHL a Legal or a Moral System?" *The Monist* 99 (1): 26–39.

Kilby, C. 2021. "The Gift of Fearlessness: A Buddhist Framework for the Protection of Vulnerable Populations Under International Humanitarian Law." *Contemporary Buddhism* 22. doi:10.1080/14639947.2022.2038027.

Kinsella, H. M., and G. Mantilla. 2020. "Contestation Before Compliance: History, Politics, and Power in International Humanitarian Law." *International Studies Quarterly* 64 (3): 649–656.

Koh, H. H. 2005. "Internalization Through Socialization." *Duke Law Journal* 54 (4): 975–982.

Kosuta, M. 1997. "The Buddha and the Four-Limbed Army: The Military in the Pali Canon." *Religiologiques, Rituels Sauvages* 16 (automne 1997): 105–112.

Lammerts, D. C. 2018. *Buddhist Law in Burma: A History of the Dhammasattha Texts and Jurisprudence, 1250-1850*. Honolulu: University of Hawaii Press.

Lancaster, B. L. 1997. "On the Stages of Perception: Towards a Synthesis of Cognitive Neuroscience and the Buddhist Abhidhamma Tradition." *Journal of Consciousness Studies* 4 (2): 122–142.

Lee, H. 2021. "Between Common Humanity and Partiality: The Chogye Buddhist Chaplaincy Manual of the South Korean Military and Its Relevance to International Humanitarian Law." *Contemporary Buddhism* 22. doi:10.1080/14639947.2021.2089426.

Little, V. 2011. "Army's First Buddhist Chaplain Serving 11th Engineer Bn." *US Army*, December 15. https://www.army.mil/article/70976/armys_first_buddhist_chaplain_serving_11th_engineer_bn

Lorge, P. A. 2011. *Chinese Martial Arts: From Antiquity to the Twenty-First Century*. New York: Cambridge University Press.

Mallon, R., and S. Nichols. 2010. "Rules." In *The Moral Psychology Handbook*, edited by J. M. Doris and The Moral Psychology Research Group, 297–298. Oxford: Oxford University Press.

Mann, J. 2012. *When Buddhists Attack: The Curious Relationship Between Zen and the Martial Arts*. Rutland: Tuttle.

Martin, M. 2018. *Why We Fight*. Oxford: Oxford University Press.

McCrae, E. 2017. "The Psychology of Moral Judgement and Perception in Indo-Tibetan Buddhist Ethics." In *The Oxford Handbook of Buddhist Ethics*, edited by D. Cozort and J. M. Shields, 335–358. Oxford: Oxford University Press.

Melzer, N. 2016. *International Humanitarian Law: A Comprehensive Introduction*. Geneva: ICRC. https://www.icrc.org/en/publication/4231-international-humanitarian-law-comprehensive-introduction/

Mendis, N. 2021. "Siege Warfare and the Prohibition of Intentional Starvation of Civilians: The Convergence of IHL and Buddhist Ethics." *Contemporary Buddhism* 22. doi:10.1080/14639947.2022.2080362.

Muñoz-Rojas, D., and J.-J. Frésard. 2004. *The Roots of Behaviour in War: Understanding and Preventing IHL Violations*. Geneva: ICRC. https://www.icrc.org/en/publication/0853-roots-behaviour-war-understanding-and-preventing-ihl-violations

Murphy, V., and H. O. Gieseken. 2021. "Fighting Without a Planet B: How IHL Protects the Natural Environment in Armed Conflict." *ICRC Law & Policy Blog*, May 15. https://blogs.icrc.org/law-and-policy/2021/05/25/fighting-without-planet-b/

Nattier, J. 1991. *Once Upon a Future Time: Studies in a Buddhist Prophecy of Decline*. Nanzan Studies in Asian Religions, No. 1. Berkeley: Asian Humanities Press.

Neff, S. C. 2005. *War and the Law of Nations: A General History*. Cambridge: Cambridge University Press.
Olsthoorn, P. 2019. "Military Virtues and Moral Relativism." In *Military Virtues*, edited by M. Skerker, D. Whetham, and D. Carrick, 38–39. Havant: Howgate.
Penna, L. R. 1989. "Written and Customary Provisions Relating to the Conduct of Hostilities and Treatment of Victims of Armed Conflicts in Ancient India." *International Review of the Red Cross* 29 (271): 333–348.
Peto, A. 2014. "The Buddhist Solider." *Alan Peto*, June 22. https://alanpeto.com/buddhism/buddhist-soldier-military/
Pfanner, T. 2009. "Various Mechanisms and Approaches for Implementing International Humanitarian Law and Protecting and Assisting War Victims." *International Review of the Red Cross* 91 (874): 279–328.
Pranke, P. 2010. "On Saints and Wizards – Ideals of Human Perfection and Power in Contemporary Burmese Buddhism." *Journal of the International Association of Buddhist Studies* 33 (1–2): 453–488.
Premasiri, P. D. 2006. "A 'Righteous War' in Buddhism?" In *Buddhism, Conflict and Violence in Modern Sri Lanka*, edited by M. Deegalle, 78–85. London and New York: Routledge.
Premasiri, P. D. 2021. "Implications of Buddhist Political Ethics for the Minimisation of Suffering in Situations of Armed Conflict." *Contemporary Buddhism* 22. doi:10.1080/14639947.2021.2037893.
Ratheiser, D., and S. Kariyakarawana. 2021. "The Paradox of the Buddhist Soldier." *Contemporary Buddhism* 22.
Richmond, L. 2012. "Buddhism and Meditation: Why Most Buddhists in the World Don't Meditate." *HuffPost*, May 2. https://www.huffpost.com/entry/most-buddhists-dont-medit_b_1461821
Robinson, P. 2003. *Just War in Comparative Perspective*, edited by P. Robinson. London: Routledge.
Roebuck, V. J. 2010. "Introduction." In *The Dhammapada*, translated and edited by V. J. Roebuck, xiv–lxv. London: Penguin Classics.
Ronkin, N. 2018. "Abhidharma." In *Stanford Encyclopedia of Philosophy*. Summer 2018 ed., edited by E. N. Zalta. Stanford: Metaphysics Research Lab, Stanford University. https://plato.stanford.edu/archives/sum2018/entries/abhidharma/
Roy, K. 2012. *Hinduism and the Ethics of Warfare in South Asia: From Antiquity to the Present*. Cambridge: Cambridge University Press.
Salomon, R. 2007. "Ancient India: Peace Within and War Without." In *War and Peace in the Ancient World*, edited by K. A. Raaflaub, 52–64. Malden: Blackwell.
Samarakoon, B. 2021. "Restraint in Warfare and Appamāda: The Concept of Collateral Damage in International Humanitarian Law in Light of the Buddha's Last Words." *Contemporary Buddhism* 22. doi:10.1080/14639947.2021.2083397.
Sassòli, M. 2007. "The Implementation of International Humanitarian Law: Current and Inherent Challenges." *Yearbook of International Humanitarian Law* 10: 45–73.
Schmithausen, L. 1999. "Aspects of the Buddhist Attitude to War." In *Violence Denied: Violence, Non-Violence and the Rationalization of Violence in South Asian Cultural History*, edited by J. E. M. Houben and K. R. van Kooij, 45–67. Leiden: Brill.
Scorsine, J. M. 2014. "Reconciliation and Postbellum Restoration: The Buddhist Perspective." In *Buddhist Contribution to Global Peace-Building*, edited by T. N. Tu and T. D. Thien, 117–131. Vietnam: Religion Press.
Selth, A. 2021. *Myanmar's Military Mindset: An Exploratory Survey*. Griffith Asia Institute. https://blogs.griffith.edu.au/asiainsights/myanmars-military-mindset/

Senauke, A., and B. Gates. 2014. "Interview with Neuroscientist Amishi Jha: Mental Armor." *Inquiring Mind* 30: 2. https://www.inquiringmind.com/article/3002_18_w_jah-interview-with-neuroscientist-amishi-jha-mental-armor/

Shahar, M. 2008. *The Shaolin Monastery. History, Religion, and the Chinese Martial Arts*. Honolulu: University of Hawaii Press.

Shay, J. 2010. *Achilles in Vietnam: Combat Trauma and the Undoing of Character*. New York: Simon & Schuster.

Sinclair, I. 2014. "War Magic and Just War in Indian Tantric Buddhism." In *War Magic: Religion, Sorcery and Performance*, edited by D. S. Farrer, 149–164. New York: Berghahn.

Singh, U. 2017. *Political Violence in Ancient India*. Cambridge: Harvard University Press.

Skilton, A. 2013. "Buddhism." In *The Oxford Handbook of Atheism*, edited by S. Bullivant and M. Ruse, 337–350. Oxford: Oxford University Press.

Soho, T. 2012. *The Unfettered Mind: Writings from a Zen Master to a Master Swordsman*. Translated by W. S. Wilson. Berkeley: Shambhala Publications.

Spiro, M. E. 1970. *Buddhism and Society: A Great Tradition and Its Burmese Vicissitudes*. New York: Harper & Row.

Stanford, M., and J. Jong. 2019. "Beyond Buddhism and Animism: A Psychometric Test of the Structure of Burmese Theravada Buddhism." *Plos One* 14 (12): e0226414.

Stanley, E. A. 2014. "Cultivating the Mind of a Warrior." *Inquiring Mind* 30 (2): 16–31. https://www.inquiringmind.com/article/3001_16_stanley-cultivating-the-mind-of-a-warrior/

Stanley, E. A., J. M. Schaldach, A. Kiyonaga, and A. P. Jha. 2011. "Mindfulness-Based Mind Fitness Training: A Case Study of a High-Stress Predeployment Military Cohort." *Cognitive and Behavioral Practice* 18 (4): 566–576.

Stephens, D. 2014. "Behaviour in War: The Place of Law, Moral Inquiry and Self-Identity." *International Review of the Red Cross* 96 (895–896): 751–773.

Sugiki, T. 2020a. "Compassion, Self-Sacrifice, and Karma in Warfare: Buddhist Discourse on Warfare as an Ethical and Soteriological Instruction for Warriors." *Religions* 11 (2): item 66.

Sugiki, T. 2020b. "Warriors Who Do Not Kill in War: A Buddhist Interpretation of the Warrior's Role in Relation to the Precept Against Killing." *Religions* 11 (10): item 530.

Terry, F., and B. McQuinn. 2018. *The Roots of Restraint in War*. Geneva: ICRC. https://www.icrc.org/en/publication/4352-roots-restraint-war

Thomas, J. 2019. "Case Study: Professionalism in the Military." In *Military Virtues*, edited by M. Skerker, D. Whetham, and D. Carrick, 538–562. Havant: Howgate.

Tilakaratne, A. 2021. "Two Dimensions of Buddhist Practice and Their Implications on Statecraft." *Contemporary Buddhism* 22. doi:10.1080/14639947.2022.2038024.

Tilakaratne, A., P. Harvey, S. Kariyakarawana, and A. Bartles-Smith. 2021. "GCIII Commentary: A Buddhist Perspective on the Treatment of Prisoners of War." *ICRC Law and Policy Blog*, January 19. https://blogs.icrc.org/law-and-policy/2021/01/19/gciii-commentary-buddhist/

Traven, D. 2021. *Law and Sentiment in International Politics: Ethics, Emotions, and the Evolution of the Laws of War*. Cambridge and New York: Cambridge University Press.

Trew, N. M. 2021. "'Not Knowing is Most Intimate': Koan Practice and the Fog of War." *Contemporary Buddhism* 22. doi:10.1080/14639947.2022.2038026.

van Baarda, T. 2011. "The Ethical Challenges of a Complex Security Environment." In *Ethics, Law and Military Operations*, edited by D. Whetham, 148–172. London: Palgrave Macmillan.

van Schaik, S. 2020. *Buddhist Magic: Divination, Healing, and Enchantment Through the Ages*. Boulder: Shambala.

Verkamp, B. J. 1988. "Moral Treatment of Returning Warriors in the Early Middle Ages." *The Journal of Religious Ethics* 16 (2): 223–249.

Victoria, B. D. [1997] 2006. *Zen at War*. 2nd ed. Boulder: Rowman and Littlefield.

Victoria, B. D. 2003. *Zen War Stories*. London: Routledge Curzon.

Victoria, B. D. 2022. "Does Buddhism Hold the Instincts for War?" *Buddhistdoor Global*, May 18. https://www.buddhistdoor.net/features/does-buddhism-hold-the-instincts-for-war/

Wakefield, A. 2021. "'Freedom from Hatred': The Role of Khanti in Complementing the Work of International Humanitarian Law (IHL)." *Contemporary Buddhism* 22. doi:10.1080/14639947.2022.2038030.

Wallace, B. A. 2007. *Contemplative Science: Where Buddhism and Neuroscience Converge*. New York: Columbia University Press.

Whetham, D. 2011a. "Ethics, Law and Conflict." In *Ethics, Law and Military Operations*, edited by D. Whetham, 10–28. London: Palgrave Macmillan.

Whetham, D. 2011b. "The Just War Tradition: A Pragmatic Compromise." In *Ethics, Law and Military Operations*, edited by D. Whetham, 65–89. London: Palgrave Macmillan.

Whitaker, J. S., and D. Smith. 2017. "Ethics, Meditation, and Wisdom." In *The Oxford Handbook of Buddhist Ethics*, edited by D. Cozort and J. M. Shields, 51–73. Oxford: Oxford University Press.

Wijenayake, V. 2021. "Limiting the Risk to Combatants Lives: Confluences Between International Humanitarian Law and Buddhism." *Contemporary Buddhism* 22.

Williams, G. 2015. "Seeing Through the Fog of War: The Need for Professional Military Ethics Education." *Strife*, September 24. https://www.strifeblog.org/2015/09/24/seeing-through-the-fog-of-war-the-need-for-professional-military-ethics-education/

Wolfendale, J. 2008. "What is the Point of Teaching Ethics in the Military?" In *Ethics Education in the Military*, edited by P. Robinson, N. de Lee, and D. Carrick, 175–188. Abingdon: Ashgate.

Yu, X. 2013. *Buddhism, War, and Nationalism: Chinese Monks in the Struggle Against Japanese Aggression 1931-1945*. London: Routledge.

Yu, X. 2013. "Buddhism and the Justification of War with Focus on Chinese Buddhist History." In *Buddhism and Violence: Militarism and Buddhism in Modern Asia*, edited by T. Brekke and V. Tikhonov, 194–208. New York: Routledge.

Zimmermann, M. 2000. "A Mahāyānist Criticism of Arthaśāstra: The Chapter on Royal Ethics in the Bodhisattva-Gocaropāya-Viśaya-Vikurvaṇanirdeśa-Sūtra". In *Annual Report of the International Research Institute for Advanced Buddhology at Soka University for the Academic Year 1999*, 177–211. Tokyo: Soka University.

Part I

Situating Buddhism in Relation to IHL

ICRC

BUDDHIST MOTIVATION TO SUPPORT IHL, FROM CONCERN TO MINIMISE HARMS INFLICTED BY MILITARY ACTION TO BOTH THOSE WHO SUFFER THEM AND THOSE WHO INFLICT THEM

Peter Harvey

ABSTRACT

This article focuses on how Buddhist ethics contains ideas and principles that would urge those in a combat situation to minimise the harm they do to others, within the requirements of their military goal. This international humanitarian law principle is in line with both compassion for others and a concern to limit the bad karmic results to the combatant of their intentional killing and maiming. The motive for an act of killing can worsen or lessen its karmic results, and non-combat actions such as helping the wounded can generate good karmic results which can dilute, though not cancel, the bad karma of killing. Harm to both humans and non-humans is to be avoided wherever possible, but killing a human is worse than killing an animal. The *Mahāvaṃsa* passage on combatants killed by King Duṭṭhagāmaṇi's army as mostly being less than human, such that killing them produced little or no bad karma, is a totally implausible statement to put in the mouths of monks whom the text says were *Arahat*s, spiritually enlightened ones.

Buddhism and international humanitarian law (IHL)[1]

Given that a key principle of Buddhism is non-violence, and that violence – deliberately killing or injuring – is seen to bring bad karmic results to the perpetrator of it, then Buddhist combatants surely have a strong motive to limit the effects of their military violence in accord with IHL principles of distinction, proportionality and precaution. Both Buddhism and IHL aim to minimise harm and suffering, and while armed conflict will of course bring some of these, both Buddhist principles and IHL surely agree: the less, the better. This is strongly illustrated, for example, by a story of the Buddha-admiring god Sakka, who in warring conflict with the *asura* demi-gods, seeks to avoid his passing chariots even accidentally killing birds in their nests (S.I.224).[2]

DOI: 10.4324/9781003439820-4

While IHL spells out the specifics, which are then codified by states, Buddhism emphasises broader ethical principles, and a motivational framework. That said, there is a broad functional parallel between the life of a member of the armed forces and the life of a monk. Both live a disciplined life whose members are committed to the shared goals of their organisation. In the life of a monk, the general ethical principles of Buddhism are elaborated, extended and codified in detail. For a member of the armed forces, there are the general rules of military discipline, but in addition, knowledge of, training in and requirement to follow the rules of IHL support the relevant ethical norms that prevent 'might should be rightly exercised' from becoming 'might is right'.

Moreover, for Buddhism, whether one is a lay person living by the five precepts or a monastic living by over 200, practice includes regular recitation of the precepts, so as to bring them actively to mind with a positive resolve to follow them. This same practice may also be helpful with IHL rules, at least for Buddhists used to chanting precepts. At least for Theravāda Buddhism, it is better to know and seek to follow an ethical principle, even when one sometimes lapses from adhering to it, than to act badly without even trying not to. Some other schools, though, held that as precept-taking is a serious matter, it is better not to take a particular precept until one thinks one will be able to keep it (Harvey 2000, 82–87). One can certainly recognise that the positive resolve of precept-taking is good in itself and also makes bad behaviour less likely. The same surely applies to IHL rules. Alertness to rules and repercussions if they are broken helps guard behavioural standards from gradually deteriorating in an organisation. As expressed in the International Committee of the Red Cross (ICRC)'s *The Roots of Restraint in War* (2018, 9):

> An exclusive focus on the law is not as effective at influencing behaviour as a combination of the law and the values underpinning it. Linking the law to local norms and values gives it greater traction. The role of law is vital in setting standards, but encouraging individuals to internalize the values it represents through socialization is a more durable way of promoting restraint.

That said, armed forces and their governments should not seek to protect their reputations by *hiding* any IHL contraventions done by them. Transparency in admitting fault is actually a better way to protect an organisation's reputation, as when hidden faults become known, the previous hiding of them adds to the loss of reputation. One can see this, for example, in religious organisations that have tried to hide instances of sexual wrongdoing amongst their clergy, which then later became publicly known.

Buddhism and killing

Buddhist members of the armed forces are always open to the possibility that they will kill or injure one or more human beings, or support others in doing so. As Buddhists, the first of the five ethical precepts is: 'I undertake the training-precept (*sikkhā-padaṃ*) to abstain from striking down (*atipātā*) living beings (*pāṇā*; literally "breathers")' (Khp.1), which is based on the description of how a person accomplished in ethical discipline (*sīla*) behaves (e.g. A. IV.284). Vibh-a.381 explains 'from striking down a living being' as 'from destruction of a living being; "from killing" is the meaning'. As otherwise expressed:

> Abandoning the striking down of living beings, he abstains from this; without stick or sword, scrupulous, compassionate, trembling for the welfare of all living beings. (M.I.345; cf. D.I.4)

> One should not kill (*na hāne*) a living being ... (A.I.214 and 254)

> Laying aside violence (*daṇḍaṃ*) in respect of all beings, towards those in the world both firm and frail, he should not kill (*na hane*) living beings, or cause to kill, or approve of others killing (*hanataṃ*). (Sn.394)

The first precept is a commitment to avoid deliberate killing of any human or animal, which is a fundamental principle that should guide all behaviour. Lapses will occur, but a person should recognise and acknowledge these as lapses, while re-affirming their commitment to the precept. Injuring but not killing a being is clearly against the spirit of the precept, but does not fully break it – though a verse form of the precept at A.III.213 expresses it simply in terms of non-injury: 'To the utmost of one's ability, one should not injure living beings (*na hiṃse pāṇa-bhūtāni*) ... '. The first precept is broken even if a being is killed by someone else being ordered by one to do this, when both the orderer and the agent break the precept, unless the agent mistakenly kills a being other than the intended one, when only he or she is responsible (Khp-a.29–30). Overall, the first precept expresses the value of non-injury: *ahiṃsā* in Sanskrit, *avihiṃsā* in Pali (M.III.73), with the resolve for this being an aspect of right resolve, the second factor of the Noble Eight-factored Path.

Breaking the first precept is seen to naturally lead to unpleasant results due to the ripening of karma:

> Monks, killing living beings, if practised, cultivated, and repeated, leads to the hells, leads to an animal womb, leads to the world of ghosts. The slightest karmic result of killing living beings leads to shortness of life as a human being. (A.IV.247)

> Some man or woman kills living beings and is murderous, bloody-handed, given to blows and violence, merciless to living beings. Because of performing and undertaking such action, on the dissolution of the body, after death, he reappears in a state of deprivation, in an unhappy destination, a state of affliction, hell. . . . [or] wherever he is reborn, he is short-lived. (M.III.203).

Hence, killing in war is clearly seen as having bad karmic consequences. Once the Buddha was asked by a person who made his living as a warrior (*yodhājīva*) – it is unclear whether this means a professional soldier or a mercenary – whether one such as him who dies in battle is reborn in a special heaven. In response, the Buddha is silent, but when the man twice more repeats the question, he explains that such a person is actually reborn in a hell or as an animal, especially insofar as he dies with his mind in a misdirected state, wishing the death of others:

> When, headman, a *yodhājīva* is one who strives and exerts himself in battle, his mind is already low, depraved and misdirected by the thought: 'Let these beings be slain, slaughtered, annihilated, destroyed and exterminated'. If others then slay him and finish him off while he is striving and exerting himself in battle, then, with the breakup of the body, after death, he is reborn in the 'Battle-Slain Hell'.[3]

The passage continues on the *view* that a warrior is reborn in the heaven of the battle-slain *deva*s after dying with such a 'mind . . . depraved and misdirected by the thought . . . '. Here, the Buddha says that holding such a wrong view itself leads to being reborn in hell or as an animal. Michael Jerryson (2018, 466) reads this as meaning that 'Yodhājīva is cautioned to avoid debased thought at the time of death but not to avoid the act of killing'. This is clearly a misreading, as the Buddha is replying to the question of whether a warrior who dies in battle is reborn in a heaven. The question is not, as such, about his state of mind when dying. That said, it makes sense to say that the state of mind at death will have *some* effect on the nature of the entailed bad rebirth.

Buddhist-related concern at the havoc caused by war is shown in two examples (cf. Gethin 2007, 74–78). The Indian emperor Asoka (268–239 BCE) is widely revered by Buddhists as a great exemplar of Buddhist social ethics. In the early part of his reign, prior to becoming a committed Buddhist, he had conquered the Kaliṅga region, but his Kaliṅga Rock Edict[4] expressed horror at the carnage that this had caused. In ancient Ceylon (now Sri Lanka) it is said that the Buddhist King Duṭṭhagāmaṇi (Sinhala Duṭugämuṇu, 101–77 BCE), after defeating a South Indian Tamil ruler in the north of the Island, expressed distressed concern at having caused the deaths of a 'very large number/ complete army' (*akkhohiṇī*) (*Mahāvaṃsa* ch. XXV.103, 108; see Geiger 1912).

The value of human life, and the degree to which this is variable

In war, abuses of IHL are more likely to occur if the 'enemy' is seen as radically *different* from one, an alien 'other' with no shared common human interests, and indeed as less than human. This can contribute to 'moral disengagement', as described in the ICRC's *The Roots of Behaviour in War* (2004, 10):

> Whether insidiously or directly, the enemy is demonized and considered as vermin. And vermin have to be exterminated. Sometimes, the enemy is compared with a disease which needs to be eradicated. Once politicians, journalists, scientists, judges and intellectuals equate the enemy with vermin or viruses, combatants find it easier not only to attack them but also to rationalize the most extreme kinds of behaviour and to convince themselves that they are justified and necessary.

As there is a minority theme in Buddhist history which seems to echo such an idea, it needs examining and critically exploring. The classic expression of it again relates to King Duṭṭhagāmaṇi.[5] In response to his above concern, the *Mahāvaṃsa*, a late fifth-century CE chronicle of Ceylon claims (XXV.109–111) that eight enlightened monks (*Arahat*s) fly through the air to reassure the king that:

> That deed presents no obstacle on your path to heaven. You caused the death of just one and a half people [*manujā*], O king. One had taken the refuges [i.e. were Buddhist], the other the Five Precepts as well. The rest were wicked men of wrong view [*micchādiṭṭhī ca dussīlā*] who died like (or: as considered as) beasts [*pasu*[6]*-samā*]. You will in many ways illuminate the Buddha's teaching, so stop worrying. (Transl. Gombrich 2006, 141, with Pali added[7])

This was written many centuries after the events it purports to describe, at a time of renewed threat from South India; indeed, H. L. Seneviratne (1999, 21) says, 'the entire story is probably fictional', while Rupert Gethin describes it as 'largely legendary' (2007, 75). The surprising nature of the claim, put in the mouth of supposed *Arahat*s – saints who are incapable of lying[8] – strongly indicates that if this was said, it was *not* by any *Arahat*. Gethin comments on these '*Arahats*', or rather on Mahānāma, the text's author, 'How did these ... come to get their Buddhism so wrong?' (2007, 63 and 76–77). Now, it would have been appropriate for King Duṭṭhagāmaṇi to regret the deaths he and his army had caused, but the actual issue here is this surprising claim: that most of the people killed were not *really*, or not *fully*, human, so that there was little problem in killing them. True, the *Mahākammavibhaṅga Sutta* says that one who does bad action *may* still be reborn in a heaven in their next life, before their bad karma later catches up with them (M.III.209–215; Harvey 2000, 24–25). Nevertheless, other authoritative Buddhist texts strongly suggest that it is always worse to kill a human than to kill an animal – and even killing an animal has bad karmic consequences.

The first lay precept covers killing a human or an animal: it is against the intentional killing of any 'breather' or living being, but in the monastic code a monk or nun who deliberately kills a human is 'defeated' in the monastic life (Vin.III.73), whereas killing an animal, down to an ant, is a lesser offence (Vin. IV.124–125). Any human, belonging to any population, must have the past good karma to have been reborn a human, whereas an animal rebirth is a lower one, based on less good past karma. Moreover, being born as a human is a rare and precious opportunity for spiritual improvement. To gain a human or divine rebirth, or have two in a row, is said to be rare (S.V.75–76; cf. Dhp.182). As against the number of beings born in other realms, those reborn as humans are like a pinch of sand compared to the size of the Earth (S. II.263), or the number of India's pleasant groves compared to its rough terrain (A.I.35). The chance for a being in a hell to be reborn as a human is less than that of a blind turtle, surfacing once a century, to happen to put its head through a ring moved by the winds across the surface of the sea (M.II.169; Bca. IV.20). Tibetan Buddhists thus talk of having attained a 'precious human rebirth' (Guenther 1959, 14–21); a marvellous opportunity for spiritual growth that should be used wisely and respected in others.

That said, some early schools other than the Theravāda seem to have accepted that, sometimes, killing an animal could be worse than killing a human. Ann Heirman (2020, especially 31–34) discusses the views of Chinese *vinaya* master Daoxuan 道宣 (596–667), who drew on some Indian *vinaya* commentaries and treatises. In his discussion on killing (T40 no. 1804, 49a9–14), Daoxuan cites the *Lü ershier mingliao lun*[9] a *vinaya* commentary by the Indian monk *Buddhatrāta (?–?), a member of the Sāṃmitīya school:

> As mentioned in the *Mingliao lun* ... [i]f one acts intentionally, one experiences a heavy karmic effect. As this text explains, since there is no shame and not even a beginning of repentance, this is a non-benevolent state of mind. Therefore, the *Chengshi lun* [T32 no. 1646, 291a11–13] says that killing an ant with an evil state of mind is worse than killing a person with a compassionate state of mind. Since the karmic effect will be heavy, one certainly receives retribution, even if one expiates the *pācittika* offence[10] ... (cited by Heirman 2020, 32)

Daoxuan (T40 no. 1804, 92c22–24) himself cites the *Chengshi lun* (T32 no. 1646, 318c12–14), the translation of the **Tattvasiddhi-śāstra* compiled by the Indian monk Harivarman in the middle of the third century CE:

> As said in the *Ṣaṭpādābhidharma* [*liu zu pitan* 六足毘曇] texts [of the Sarvāstivāda *abhidharma*] killing a perverted person is a lighter [offence] than killing an insect or an ant. The reason for this is that such a person is polluting the world and causing a lot of damage.

Daoxuan 'concludes that killing even an ant with evil intent (*hai xin* 害心) is worse than killing a human being with compassion (*ci xin* 慈心)' (Heirman 2020, 32). The above quote seems to indicate that by killing with compassion,

Daoxuan probably had in mind the killing of an *evil* human being. For him, irrespective of the lesser *vinaya* offence, the karmic consequences of intentionally killing even an ant are severe. As to whether they can be more severe than killing a bad person, Heirman says, 'in this instance he goes very far, and I am not so sure that if one would confront him with what he is actually saying, he would go as far. On the other hand, intention (including careless behaviour) is primordial' (Heirman 2020, 32).

That said, the Mahāyāna *Mahā-parinirvāṇa Sūtra* (composed around the fourth century CE in India or Central Asia) explicitly says: 'Sentient beings possess the five good roots such as faith, but the *icchaāntika* has eternally severed those roots. Thus, while it is a fault to kill an ant, it is not a fault to kill an *icchāntika*' (Taishō 1, 562b). The idea of an *icchāntika* is that of a person who is an evil-doer incapable of salvation: one who 'slanders the true *Dharma*' repeatedly and without any signs of remorse; or breaks some of the most serious monastic rules, entailing defeat; or does one of the five deadly actions, such as killing a parent, without contrition (Taishō 374, xvi, 459a–460b, as cited in Demiéville 1957, 368; Welch 1972, 281).

That it is worse to kill an ant than a serious evil-doer is not found in the Pali Canon, but it is agreed amongst the schools that it is worse to kill some humans than to kill others. The most heinous actions, which are seen to definitely lead to hell in one's next rebirth, include intentionally killing one's mother, father or an *Arahat* (Vibh.378, M-a.IV.109–110). This implies that it is very bad to harm those one should have positive regard for, or who are of great ethical and spiritual worth.[11] More generally, the great Theravāda commentator Buddhaghosa (fifth century CE) says on the first precept:

> 'Striking down of a living being' is, as regards a living being that one perceives as living, the will to kill it (*vadha-cetanā*), expressed through body or speech, occasioning an attack which cuts off its life-faculty. That action, in regard to those without good qualities (*guṇa-*) – animals etc. – is of lesser fault (*appa-sāvajjo*) when they are small, greater fault when they have a large physical frame. Why? Because of the greater effort involved. Where the effort is the same, (it is greater) because of the object (*vatthu-*) (of the act) being greater. *In regard to those with good qualities – humans etc. – the action is of lesser fault when they are of few good qualities, greater fault when they are of many good qualities. But when size or good qualities are equal, the fault of the action is lesser due to the (relative) mildness of the mental defilements and of the attack, and greater due to their intensity*. Five factors are involved: a living being, the actual perceiving of a living being, a thought of killing, the attack, and death as a result of it. (M-a. I.198, cf. Khp-a.28–9 and As.97; and see Gethin 2004, 71–2)

Note, for later, that this also sees the state of mind of a killer as affecting the degree of unwholesomeness of the act of killing, and the intensity of the action.

That it is worse to kill a human than an animal, and a more virtuous human than a less virtuous one, seems to be a mirror image of the *sutta* idea there is more good karma in giving to a human than an animal, and to a more virtuous human than a less virtuous one. The *Dakkhiṇā-vibhaṅga Sutta*, at M. III.255, gives a list of beings and the relative amount of good karma that comes from giving to them: (a) to an animal, giving repays × 100 (in terms of various good qualities and benefits); (b) to an ordinary person (*puthujjana*)[12] who is unvirtuous, × 1000; to a virtuous ordinary person, 100 × 1000; to a non-Buddhist who is free from lust for sense-pleasures, × 100,000 × 100,000; to one practising for realisation of the fruit that is stream-entry, the result is incalculable, immeasurable, with this being even greater for the other kinds of spiritually noble persons, up to the *Arahat*. This implies that the bad karma of harming such beings might vary on a similar scale.

Indeed, this implication is spelled out in the *Vibhaṅga* commentary (Vibh-a.382–383). This says that the fault (*vajja*) in an act of killing an animal increases based on the size of the animal, giving as examples a small ant, large ant, small bird, large bird, iguana, hare, deer, ox, horse and elephant. It is worse again to kill a human, with the fault increasing in this order: one of bad conduct (*dussīla*); one of 'cattle-like virtue (*gorūpa-sīlaka*), which the sub-commentary explains as 'naturally good' (*pakati-bhaddo*), perhaps meaning one whose virtuous behaviour comes from dull, unthinking routine; one who has gone for refuge to the Buddha, Dhamma and Saṅgha; one who keeps the five precepts; a novice; an ordinary (*puthujjana*-) monk; a Stream-enterer; a Once-returner; a Non-returner; an *Arahant*. This is echoed in the twelfth-century *Upāsaka-janālaṅkāra* (Upj.206) of Ānanda, which then adds, 'However, all (types of) killing living beings entails a great fault (*pāṇātipāto pi mahā-sāvajjo va*)'. The text later refers to the story (Dhp-a.III.41–42) of woman reborn in a low hell due to drowning a dog (Upj.209).

So in a war situation, while it is appropriate to avoid killing animals if this can be avoided, it is even more important to avoid, or at least minimise, killing humans. It is of course hard to know of the level of virtue among 'enemies', but any population will certainly include people of developed virtue. And the Theravāda, at least, holds that one does not need to *know* a person is more virtuous for it to be worse to kill them (see note 11). So if one is taken in by wrong speech in the form of divisive false smears and propaganda about the 'evil' enemy community – nowadays aided by such as Facebook – this is no excuse. The more virtuous, though, will certainly be found among medical staff dedicated to helping others, while combatants are allied to the non-virtue of killing, and so in that respect are less virtuous. Children, of course, are generally more innocent than adults. Verses that imply violence towards the defenceless is particularly bad are:

> He who does harm with violence to non-violent innocent people, goes very soon indeed to one of these ten states: sharp pain, or disaster, bodily injury, serious illness, or derangement of mind, trouble from the king, or grave charges, loss of relatives, or loss of wealth, or houses destroyed by ravaging fire; upon dissolution of the body that ignorant man is born in hell. (Dhp.137–140)

As regards those who need medical attention and care, the Buddha said, 'whoever wishes to take care of me should take care of the sick' (Vin.I.301).

Besides the level of virtue, there is also the aspect of human connection and returning kindnesses. People of a different nation, ethnic group, culture and/or religion may be seen as in some ways 'other' or 'alien'; yet Buddhist teachings hold that, due to the countless past lives that we have all had, it is difficult to find a person (or animal) that in some past life has not been a close relative or friend and been very good to one (S.II.189–190). And of course, a person may in future be reborn as a member of the community he or she is currently fighting.

In IHL, while there is no reference to it being worse to kill or harm *more virtuous* people, its rules do *not* accept the targeting of either wounded or captured combatants, medical staff or civilians not directly participating in hostilities, but *do* tolerate – or at least are reconciled to – the targeting of able-bodied, non-surrendering enemy combatants and civilians directly participating in hostilities.[13] This might be seen to imply that IHL sees the killing and disablement of the former as worse than the killing and disablement of the latter. So Buddhist concerns, though sometimes articulated based on differing principles, seem to align with the IHL principle of *distinction.*

Minimising harm to others and oneself in a combat situation

For a combatant in a situation of armed conflict, some breaking of the first Buddhist precept is likely. But the precept should nevertheless be lived up to as far, and as often, as possible. This accords with the IHL principles of: *military necessity* – the parties to an armed conflict may only use 'that degree and kind of force required to achieve the legitimate purpose of a conflict';[14] *proportionality* – 'a military objective may be attacked only after [first concluding] that civilian losses are not expected to outweigh the military advantage foreseen';[15] and *precautions* – 'a party to an armed conflict must take constant care to spare civilians or civilian objects when carrying out military operations'.[16] This will mean that there is (1) minimum death and injury inflicted, and (2) minimum karmic harm to the precept-breaking combatant.

Buddhist ethics sees intentionally harming others as bringing harm to oneself, through the karmic results of the action. Hence it is said that one should reflect before (as well as during and after) a bodily action:

> Would this action that I wish to do with the body lead to my own affliction (-*attabyābādhāya*), or to the affliction of others, or to the affliction of both? Is it an unwholesome bodily action with painful consequences (*dukkhudraya-*), with painful ripening (*dukkhavipāka-*)? (*Ambalaṭṭhikārāhulovāda Sutta*, M.I.415)

If so, such an action is of the kind to avoid, due to the physical harm or mental hurt to others, and the psycho-ethical harm to oneself. Hence it is said that being mindful helps one take true care of oneself in a way that also cares for others. The cultivation of wholesome states of mind in oneself means that one treats others better; and by patient acceptance, harmlessness and kindness and compassion to others, while this directly benefits them, it also benefits oneself (S.V.169).

Knowledge of and alertness to IHL principles, and their emphasis within the relevant armed force, will be vital in relation to reducing harm to others. But the degree to which IHL norms affect the actual behaviour of a Buddhist combatant will be enhanced by their commitment to and mindful bearing in mind Buddhist ethical norms, and also that karmic self-harm will increase with the degree to which these are broken. While being mindful of values and norms is an individual practice, it can certainly be enhanced by the example of those one associates with. Relevant here is the role of socialisation. As the ICRC's *The Roots of Restraint in War* (2018, 25) says:

> There are three types of socialization identified that are of interest to us here. The first (Type 0) involves no internalization of norms, just temporary norm adoption following instrumental calculations of punishment or reward. The other two types involve differing degrees of internalization: learning and following a norm in order to conform to group expectations and behaviour (Type 1); and fully internalizing the norm, so that it becomes part of the individual's identity – the 'right thing to do' (Type 2).

Here it is worth reflecting on a key emphasis in Asanga Tilakaratne's article in this volume. He points out that the ethics of the monastic and lay Nirvana-seeker has no place for any kind of violence and killing, but that there is some place for limited violence within the ethics of the general Buddhist laity, who seek a happier state within *saṃsāra*, the conditioned realm of rebirths. In fact, a Buddhist whose focus is on happier future experiences in *saṃsāra* has a very strong motive, if a combatant, to avoid performing the evil actions involved in breaking IHL principles, as these will bring bad karmic results. The kinds of actions that violate IHL principles will be both unskilful/unwholesome (*akusala*) and 'demeritorious' (*apuñña*), evil (*pāpa*).

While I would not personally agree with Tilakaratne that 'meritorious' (*puñña*) actions are generally *akusala*/unskilful/unwholesome, I recognise that the attitude people may hold in seeking to do some *puñña* actions can have some *akusala* elements, e.g. 'I am going to give so that I can benefit from the good karmic results of this act'. Ironically, though, the lower the motive for a good action, the less good karma will come from it (A.IV.60–63; Harvey 2000, 19–21). Similarly, avoiding a bad action that breaks IHL out of compassion is a higher motive than doing so simply to avoid the bad karmic results of carrying it out, but it is a motivational factor that is surely relevant to many in a Buddhist context.

Minimising death and injury to the 'enemy'

Anger and fear are key states of mind that might make a combatant use more lethal force than is necessary, such as when a wounded enemy is killed or otherwise mistreated, or when non-combatants who directly or indirectly support them are harmed. Here, the calm and mental discipline that Buddhist practices enhance can play a beneficial role. Buddhism is very critical of anger and hatred, and we see above that Buddhaghosa says 'the fault of the action is lesser due to the (relative) mildness of the mental defilements and of the attack, and greater due to their intensity'.

Being more mindful aids self-discipline and not being carried away by one's emotions, and also aids both alertness and concentration. These qualities should help in avoiding or reducing 'collateral damage' to non-combatants through carelessness in targeting, which might arise due to a willingness to rely on poor intelligence, or being too gung-ho. Good concentration can aid precise targeting – though *during* the firing of a weapon aimed at killing or injuring, it will be unmindful *wrong* concentration[17] – while mindfulness should aid in bearing in mind IHL norms and that certain people should *not* be targeted.

Mental alertness may also bring the benefit of thinking of clever stratagems for gaining a military objective with minimum loss of life on both sides. The *(Mahā)-Ummagga Jātaka*[18] has the Buddha in a past life, as the advisor to a king, using spies, skilful devices and even deceptions to ensure that an impending armed conflict is avoided.

Minimising karmic harm to combatants themselves

As regards minimising karmic harm to the combatant, the associated mental state should be such as to minimise unwholesome, 'demeritorious' (*apuñña*) qualities, such as anger/hatred. The karmic harm from an action such as killing is also said to be lesser for someone with an overall well-developed moral and mental discipline than for a person in whom these are less developed. At A. I.249–250 (Threes, *sutta* 100, 'A Lump of Salt'), the Buddha says that, for a person whose mindfulness of the body,[19] ethical discipline (*sīla*), heart/mind (*citta*) and wisdom (*paññā*) are undeveloped, a small evil deed may lead to rebirth in a hell, just as a pinch of salt in a cup of water makes it undrinkable. For a person with developed mindfulness of the body, ethical discipline, heart/mind and wisdom, though, the same action will produce its karmic results in the present life, with little, if any, in a future life, just as a pinch of salt does not make the River Ganges undrinkable. This seems to imply that, in a spiritually developed person, a small moral slip will have less effect, as it will be 'diluted' by his or her generally moral nature. For a spiritually undeveloped person, described here as 'limited and small-minded (*paritta appātumo*), he dwells in suffering', the same act has a greater impact. It 'flavours' a person's character more, so to speak, setting up greater reverberations within it, in tune with other such reverberations. The good person suffers less from his or her bad action, though as most of the karmic results come in *this* life for him or her, this may not be immediately apparent. Such this-life results may perhaps include painful regret.

While this *sutta* passage concerns a small bad action, not one such as killing in war, the implication is that having a good character generally lessens the karmic effect of a precept-breaking action. So one in the armed forces should aim to be well developed in these qualities, so that the bad karma of any killing or wounding that they do will be relatively diluted, though not cancelled, by the good karma of their good qualities. Such good qualities can of course be cultivated as part of military life. This certainly includes IHL-related actions such as ensuring care for wounded combatants and non-combatants, from either side, and ensuring that they have food and shelter. Other such actions are peacekeeping activities, which may include preventing members of one ethnic group attacking members of another, so as to protect one group from physical harm and the other from generating bad karma by harming them. Other such actions are delivering help at times of disasters, voluntary charitable activities and generosity to the Saṅgha. Also, letting go of hatred, anger and distorted views about former enemies will be of benefit both for social harmony and inner calm.

The roots of unwholesome action are said in Buddhism to be greed, hatred and delusion (M.I.47). One expression of delusion is adherence to a wrong view, such as that there is nothing wrong with killing, and that an enemy is not to be respected as a human being with similar concerns and interests to oneself. This means that a combatant who acts from such a view will be likely not only to bring more harm to others, and break IHL, but also to generate more karmic harm to himself. To denigrate the humanity of an 'enemy' ignores that any human must have a good karmic past to have been reborn a human.

The basis of Buddhist ethics is a version of the golden rule: do not inflict on another being what you would not want done to you (*Veḷudvāreyyā Sutta*, S. V.353–356). Thus it is wrong to dismiss or completely override the interests of someone else. Buddhist precepts do get broken by Buddhists, but this should always be acknowledged by the precept-breaker, and not minimised as unimportant. There is a need to remain *mindful* of them, to bear them in mind. To deny that others have interests that should be respected as far as possible is delusion and wrong view.

At *Milindapañha* 84, it is said that if an evil action is done 'unknowingly (*ajānato*)', it has a worse karmic effect than if it is done 'knowingly'. This is illustrated by saying that a person taking hold of a red-hot iron ball is more severely burnt if he does so unknowingly. This suggests that an evil action – such as killing (Mil.158) – is worse if it is done without restraint or compunction. This will be the case if an action is not seen as at all wrong, as there will be no holding back on the volitional force put into the action. The commentary (29) on Mil.158 talks of the 'non-knowing of evil (*pāpa-ajānana-*)'. Such a mode of action can be seen to include indiscriminate attacks and superfluous injury, which are prohibited in IHL. Even when this is done in obedience to an order, this should make no difference, whether in Buddhist ethics or IHL.

The interplay of intentions and motives

The administration of law in courts often refers to motive, in deciding what a person is charged with or guilty of, but also in deciding the degree of penalty. In IHL, considerations of an act's intention are found in the articles of the conventions that deal with what are known as 'grave breaches': violations that are meant to incur criminal penalties. Here, use of the word 'wilful' shows the importance of the perpetrator's mental state (for example Geneva Convention I Art 50, Geneva Convention II Art 51 and Geneva Convention III 130[20]). Further, motivational factors in the mind of a combatant and/or his/her commander may make an IHL infringement less or more likely to occur.

For Buddhism, the key feature of an action, in terms of its ethical/unethical nature and its consequent karmic results, is its *cetanā*, the volition expressed in the action. 'It is volition (*cetanā*), O monks, that I call karma; having willed (*cetayitvā*), one acts through body, speech or mind' (A.III.415). *Cetanā* includes the motive for which an action is done, but particularly its immediate intention and the related immediate mental impulse which sets it going and sustains it. Note that the *intention* involved in killing may arise from differing *motives*, for example greed for an inheritance or the desire to protect someone else from harm. 'Karma' (Pāli *kamma*, Sanskrit *karma*), literally 'action', is the overall psychological impulse behind an action, that which plants a karmic 'seed' and sets in motion a chain of causes culminating in a karmic fruit. Actions, then, must be intentional if they are to generate karmic fruits: accidentally treading on an insect does not have such an effect, as the Jains believe, though reckless carelessness includes its own kind of bad intention (Harvey 1999, 276–278).

Reckless or negligent behaviour in war (e.g. by failing to take all feasible precautions in setting up an attack) can lead to indiscriminate killing or harming; this would tend to come from delusion and lack of concern for the consequences of one's actions on others and oneself. An uncaring attitude in war can also lead to immense suffering for the civilian population, for example when a commander proceeds with an attack even when it becomes clear that the killing or harming of civilians would be excessive compared to the military advantage gained by striking the target. This would tend to come from attachment to one's own goals and a degree of indifference to the fate of the civilian population. From a Buddhist perspective, repeated negligent indifference would tend to be the worst of these two, but reckless attachment could be worse if it arose from strong delusion.

Actions that are unskillful/unwholesome (*akusala*) are seen as ones that are rooted in greed, hatred/aversion (*dosa*) and/or delusion, and such actions bring unpleasant karmic fruits (M.I.47[21]). Those that are skilful/wholesome (*kusala*) are seen as ones that are rooted in non-greed (generosity, renunciation), non-hatred (kindness, compassion) and/or non-delusion (clarity of mind, wisdom), with such actions bringing pleasant karmic fruits. The karmic effects of an act will thus vary according to the nature of the roots of its volition.

As regards killing, Rupert Gethin comments:

> the possibility that an act of killing a living being can be motivated by wholesome (*kusala*) states of mind is simply not allowed in Abhidhamma Buddhist psychology; the intention to kill another being always crucially involves hatred or aversion (Gethin 2004). While certain acts of killing may be manifestations of stronger and more intense instances of anger, hatred or aversion, no act of killing can be entirely free of these. There can be no justification of any act of killing as entirely blameless, as entirely free of the taint of aversion or hatred. In Abhidhamma terms, acts of killing can only ever be justified as more or less *akusala*, never as purely *kusala* ... there is no possibility of killing in war being *kusala*. (Gethin 2007, 70–71)

The karmic results of intentional killing will be worse when the roots are mainly (for example) anger, revenge or deluded prejudice than if there is an associated motive of protecting others. In such cases, the motive of protecting others will have its own, positive fruits, alongside the negative fruits of an act of killing. Indeed, given that a combatant will generate bad karmic result from some of their actions, their *willingness to do this, out of a desire to defend others from harm*, can itself be seen as a positive mental action.

Some Mahāyāna texts actually justify killing a human being on the grounds of compassion in dire circumstances (Harvey 2000, 15–38). The *Upāya-kauśalya Sūtra* tells of the Buddha in a past life as a Bodhisattva sea captain who knows that a thief on his ship is planning to kill the 500 passengers, who are all Bodhisattvas of some level. To save them, *and* to save the thief from the bad karma from killing the 500, *and* to save the passengers the bad karma that would come from angrily killing the thief themselves, if they knew of the plot, he chooses to kill the man himself (Tatz 1994, 73–76). While he knows that his killing the thief may lead to his being reborn in hell for 'a hundred thousand aeons', he is willing to endure this for the sake of preventing suffering to the others, his act being done 'with great compassion and skill in means'. Consequently, the round of rebirths was 'curtailed' for him by 'a hundred thousand aeons', though in a later life, he, as the Buddha, treads on a thorn as 'the residue of the fruition of that deed' (Tatz 1994, 76). The implication seems to be, then, that the act had various bad karmic consequences, though not as bad as if it had been done without such a compassionate motivation. If the captain had not acknowledged that the deed could lead to many rebirths in hell, and not been *willing* to suffer accordingly, compassion (and wisdom) would have been lacking, and he *would* have suffered long in hell. That is, a long stretch in hell is only avoided here by willingly risking it in helping others. Even so, according to John Dunne,[22] most contemporary Tibetans assert that the *Bodhisattva* in the above story 'was reborn in hell because he took a life, but did not remain there long because the attitude behind the act was based on compassion'.

detailed study of the idea of compassionate killing in Indian Mayāyāna writings, Stephen Jenkins remarks on 'how broadly influential' the *Upāyakauśalya Sūtra* has been (Jenkins [2010] 2011, 299), and that many great Indian Mahāyāna thinkers have cited it and shared a 'general agreement that compassionate violence can be an auspicious merit-making opportunity without negative karmic consequences' (Jenkins [2010] 2011, 300). He notes that the writings of Asaṅga (fourth century) are an influential source, here. The latter talks of a Bodhisattva killing a thief about to kill many people of high spiritual development (Jenkins [2010] 2011, 301):

> The bodhisattva, seeing this imminent tragedy, realises that if he kills the thief then he himself may go to hell. But he decides that it is better that he go to hell than allow this person to suffer such a fate.
>
> > With this attitude, the *bodhisattva*, having discerned either a neutral or auspicious mind[23] [*kuśalacitto*]; regretting [*ṛtīyamānaḥ*] and employing a mind of empathy [*anukampācittam*] alone, then takes that living being's life. [That *bodhisattva*] becomes blameless [*anāpattiko*] and produces abundant merit [*puṇyaṃ*]. [*Bodhisattvabhūmi* 113.24–114.2]

Jenkins also reports a story, from the *Mahā-upāyakauśalya Sūtra*,[24] of a man in a caravan of 500 travellers, who kills the scout of 500 threatening bandits, even though he is his friend, to prevent the bandits killing the travellers or the latter killing the scout, with himself taking on the bad karma of killing (Jenkins [2010] 2011, 314). He points to 'a general pattern in Mahāyāna thought wherein the more pure a bodhisattva's intention is to go to hell, the less likely she is to do it. ... those who intend to endure hell realms do not, precisely because they are willing to do so' (Jenkins [2010] 2011, 319).

He says that 'I have not yet located an example where a compassionate killer suffers negative karmic consequences' (Jenkins [2010] 2011, 320), and points out (Jenkins [2010] 2011, 317) that the Buddha only treads on a thorn to teach others that bad actions have karmic consequences, though it was not itself a consequence of his own bad karma (Tatz 1994, 77). But this seems to be about portraying the Buddha as beyond all karmic results, which still apply even to *Arahats*. Jenkins himself cites Bhāviveka (490–570) (Eckel 2008, 185) as referring to those who turned from great evil to good, such as the mass murderer Aṅgulimāla, the patricidal King Ajātaśatru and the wicked King

Aśoka, as only spending a fleeting amount of time in hell. On the compassionate captain in the *Upāyakauśalya Sūtra*, Bhāviveka says that he certainly knew he would be reborn in hell, but only for a short time (Jenkins [2010] 2011, 320, citing Eckel 2008, 188). In line with this, contemporary Tibetan scholars see compassionate killers as spending an extremely brief period in hell (Jenkins [2010] 2011, 321).

This is all very well, but there is a problem: might this 'get-out-of-jail-free' card stop working once it becomes widely known? To escape rebirth in hell by compassionately risking such a rebirth in helping others, one must believe that there is a genuine risk. But one familiar with the above ideas might well doubt that there *is* a genuine risk. But then, there is now a risk again, so a compassionate killer can again avoid hell, from compassionately risking it! But this is all very risky. And as Jenkins points out (Jenkins [2010] 2011, 322–324), the *Upāyakauśalya Sūtra* passage is to discourage killing by emphasising how bad its karmic results can be (at least for the non-compassionate killer in very constrained circumstances).

Given that Buddhism holds that an action can be physical, verbal *or mental*, then the intentional thought to later do a physical or verbal action is itself a kind of action.[25] On the negative side, for a combatant this includes a resolve to kill if necessary in an upcoming combat event; at a lesser level, it would include the acceptance of the general possibility of future killing when joining the army.[26] But on the positive side, it would include hoping to avoid the need to kill, and regret at having done so. It also includes the aspiration to defend one's community, one's comrades and indeed oneself, and also non-combatants on either or no side in a conflict. Note that it is said that the duties of the ideal kind of ruler– for Buddhism, a *Cakka-vatti* – include that he 'arrange rightful (*dhammika*) shelter, protection and defense for ... brahmin householders, for town-dwellers and countryfolk, for ascetics and brahmin(-renouncer)s, for animals and birds'. (D.III.61). Such duties are also surely applicable to a member of the armed forces.

Nevertheless, when it comes to firing a weapon at someone, the immediate intention or volitional impulse will include physically harming them, which is an unwholesome intention. While in general all a combatant really needs to do in combat is to *incapacitate* an enemy, so that they can no longer contribute to actions that bring military harm to one's own side, sometimes the situation requires an action that is highly likely to kill or maim an enemy, which then becomes part of the intended result. Moreover, if the background motive, or the dominating state of mind when acting, is revenge, or a wish to show off – or to prevent enemies from a different country, ethnic group or religion from being able to survive and flourish as human beings, even if they do not bring any real harm to one's own side – this is more unwholesome and karmically harmful in Buddhist terms. For IHL, the intention behind an act can be relevant, as pointed out above. Nevertheless, it does not seem concerned about deeper background motivation. If a combatant's conduct is lawful – for instance, lawfully killing an enemy combatant – it is irrelevant whether his behaviour was motivated by revenge, wanting to show off or wanting to prevent the enemy from flourishing. So here, law and ethics/morality part ways. Consequently, wholesome states of mind certainly help to undergird compliance with the law, but they are not a necessary pre-condition for legitimate action under IHL.

Conclusion

So, we see that the outlook and values of Buddhism provide many factors that should help motivate Buddhist members of an armed force to act in accord with IHL, as in doing so they will also be acting in accord with Buddhist values. While their job means that they may well break the first ethical precept of Buddhism, against killing, they can still seek to *minimise* the harm to others of their military actions, and consequently reduce the karmic harm to themselves. Buddhist concerns should also motivate them to be as ethically disciplined, generous and helpful as they can be, in protecting and aiding their own community and those beyond it, whether human or animal.

Notes

1. For a brief introduction to IHL, see the introduction to this volume.
2. See Premasiri in this volume and cf. Dhp-a.I.279, Jat.I.202–03.
3. *Yodhājiva Sutta*, S.V.308–09. The Buddha then says the same when questioned by an elephant warrior (*hattāroha*) and a cavalry warrior (*assāroha*).
4. Nikam and McKeon (1959), 27–30.
5. For a different perspective on this passage, see Tilakaratne in this volume. See also the discussion in Premasiri.
6. *Pasu* generally means cattle.
7. See Deegalle (2002); Gombrich (1971, 257–258) discusses the views of some Sri Lankan village monks on this passage.
8. Though they might have the meditative power to be able to know the degree of virtue of each member of a defeated army!
9. 律二十二明了論 (*Treatise on the Elucidation of 22[Verses] on Vinaya*), T24 no. 1461.
10. An offence that, in *Vinaya* terms, is never as serious as killing a human.
11. The terrible results of killing a parent do not occur if the act was unintentional (Kv.593), but Theravādin texts (Vin-a.444–445 and Upj.315; Harvey 1999, 275) hold that the result is entailed even if the intended victim was an animal or another person (the Sārvāstivādin AKB.iv.103d differs on this), or if the parent is not known to be a parent (the Mahāyāna Uss.179 differs on this). Vin-a.444–445 explains this as being because of the intention to kill; that there was ignorance of what kind of being would be the victim is seen as irrelevant.

12. That is, a person who has not attained any of the levels of enlightenment: as a Stream-enterer, Once-returner, Non-returner, or a fully enlightened person, an *Arahat*, or one firmly established on the path to any of these four states.
13. ICRC (2014, 6–7, 46–49).
14. ICRC (2014, 6).
15. ICRC (2014, 47).
16. ICRC (2014, 48).
17. As, in Theravāda Abhidhamma theory, mindfulness is only present in wholesome mind-states (Bodhi 1993, 83–86), there can be no actual mindfulness at the moment of firing. Some other Buddhist traditions have lower standards for true mindfulness, such that it can occur in unwholesome mind states. The Theravāda sees reference to 'wrong mindfulness' in the *suttas* as really a form of misremembering or calling to mind in a wrong way (As.250; Gethin 2001, 42–44).
18. No. 546, Jat.VI.329–478, also known as the *Mahosadha Jātaka*; newly translated in Appleton and Shaw (2012, 187–333). See Premasiri in this volume.
19. *Kāya* – literally, simply 'body', but explained in the commentary (A-a.II.361) as mindful contemplation of the body.
20. GCI Art 50: Convention (I) for the Amelioration of the Condition of the Wounded and Sick in Armed Forces in the Field. Geneva, 12 August 1949: Commentary of 2016, Article 50: Grave Breaches: https://ihl-databases.icrc.org/applic/ihl/ihl.nsf/Comment.xsp?action=openDocument&documentId=21B052420B219A72C1257F7D00587FC3

    GCII Art 51: Convention (II) for the Amelioration of the Condition of Wounded, Sick and Shipwrecked Members of Armed Forces at Sea. Geneva, 12 August 1949: Commentary of 2017, Article 51: Grave Breaches: https://ihl-databases.icrc.org/applic/ihl/ihl.nsf/Comment.xsp?action=openDocument&documentId=51B3435E776E06CEC1258115003EC277

    GCIII 130: Convention (III) relative to the Treatment of Prisoners of War. Geneva, 12 August 1949: Commentary of 2020 Article 130: Grave Breaches: https://ihl-databases.icrc.org/applic/ihl/ihl.nsf/Comment.xsp?action=openDocument&documentId=B0BAF7DBF7E5B3FAC1258584004494BF
21. Harvey (1995, 2010, and 2000, 42–43, 46–49).
22. John Dunne, 'Precept Keeping' posting to 'Buddha-L' Internet discussion forum, 26 July 1995, and 'Killing Hitler' posting, 21 March 1996.
23. There is debate over whether this means the mind of the killer or killed; either is plausible, but Jenkins favours the view of the commentator Jinaputra that it concerns the mind of the killer (Jenkins [2010] 2011, 303–304).
24. Demiéville (1957, 379), citing Taishō (156, vii, 161b–162a).
25. Specifically cited examples of unwholesome mental action are covetousness, ill will and wrong view (M.I.47). Heim (2014, 72, 41) explains that such mental actions are fully developed active mind states, which go beyond the general motivational roots of greed, hatred and delusion, with the covetousness and ill will actually planning a specific future action. Similarly, As.77 explains that there is a mental act of giving when one resolves to make a particular gift in the future.
26. Vasubandhu, giving the Sarvāstivāda view, says that if a person is conscripted into an army, then unless he has previously resolved 'Even in order to save my life, I shall not kill a living being', he will share in the guilt of any killing done by others in the army, as all members share a common goal, and thus mutually incite one another (AKB.iv 72c–d).

Abbreviations

A — *Aṅguttara Nikāya*; tr. Bhikkhu Bodhi, *The Incremental Discourses of the Buddha*, Wisdom in 2012.
A-a — Untranslated commentary on A: *Manorathapūraṇī*.
AK — *Abhidharmakośa-bhāsyam* (of Vasubandhu – mostly Sarvāstivāda); tr. L. M. Pruden (from L. de La Valleé Poussin's French translation), *Abhidharmakośabhāṣyam*, 4 vols., Berkeley, Asian Humanities Press, 1991.
As — *Aṭṭhasālinī*; (tr. Pe Maung Tin), *The Expositor*, 2 vols., London, PTS, 1920 and 1921.
Bca — *Bodhicaryāvatāra* of Śāntideva; tr. K. Crosby and A. Skilton, *Śāntideva: The Bodhicaryāvatāra*, Oxford and New York, Oxford University Press, 1995.
D — *Dīgha Nikāya;* tr. M. Walshe, *Long Discourses of the Buddha*, 2nd revised edition, Boston, Wisdom, 1996, one vol.
Dhp — *Dhammapada*; tr. K. R. Norman, *The Word of the Doctrine*, London, PTS, 1997; tr. V. Roebuck, *The Dhammapada*, London, Penguin, 2010. Buddharakkhita and Ṭhānissaro translations on Access to Insight website.
Dhp-a — *Dhammapada Aṭṭhakathā*, commentary on Dhp; tr. E. W. Burlingame, *Buddhist Legends*, 3 vols., Harvard Oriental Series, Harvard University Press, 1921; repr. London, PTS, 1995.
Jat — *Jātaka with Commentary*; tr. by various hands under E. B. Cowell, *The Jātaka or Stories of the Buddha's Former Births*, 6 vols., London, PTS, 1895–1907. S. Shaw, *The Jātakas: Birth Stories of the Bodhisatta*, New Delhi: Penguin, 2006, translates 26 of the *Jātakas*.
Khp — *Khuddaka-pātha*; tr. with its commentary, Bhikkhu Ñāṇamoli, *Minor Readings and Illustrator*, London, PTS, 1960.
Khp-a — Commentary on Khp: see last item for translation.
Kv — *Kathāvatthu*; tr. S. Z. Aung and C. A. F. Rhys Davids, *Points of Controversy*, London, PTS, 1915.
M — *Majjhima Nikāya;* tr. Bhikkhu Ñāṇamoli and Bhikkhu Bodhi, *The Middle Length Discourses of the Buddha*, Boston, Wisdom, 1995.
M-a — Untranslated commentary on M: *Papañcasūdanī*.
Mil — *Milindapañha*; tr. I. B. Horner, *Milinda's Questions*, 2 vols., London, PTS, 1963 and 1964.
PTS — Pali Text Society.
S — *Saṃyutta Nikāya;* tr. Bhikkhu Bodhi, *The Connected Discourses of the Buddha*, Boston, Wisdom, 2005, one vol.
Sn — *Sutta-nipāta*; tr. K. R. Norman, *The Group of Discourses*, in paperback *The Rhinoceros Horn and Other Early Buddhist Poems*, London, PTS, 1984; tr. K. R. Norman, *The Group of Discourses* Vol.II, London, PTS, 1992, revised translation with introduction and notes.
Upj — *Upāsaka-janālaṅkāra*; tr. Giulio Agostini, *The Ornament of Lay Followers: Upāsakajanālaṅkāra*, Bristol, Pali Text Society, 2015.
Uss — *Upāsaka-śīla Sūtra*; tr. Heng-ching Shih, *The Sutra on Upāsaka Precepts*, Berkeley, Numata Center for Buddhist Translation and Research, Bukkyō Dendō Kyōkai, 1994 (translation from Chinese of Taishō, vol. 24, text 1488). References are to translation pagination.
Vibh — *Vibhaṅga*; tr. U. Thittila, *The Book of Analysis*, London, PTS, 1969.
Vibh-a — Commentary on Vibh., *Sammohavinodanī*; tr. Bhikkhu Ñāṇamoli, *The Dispeller of Delusion*, 2 vols., Oxford, PTS, 1996.
Vin — *Vinaya Piṭaka;* tr. I. B. Horner, *The Book of the Discipline*, 6 vols., London, PTS, 1938–1966. Vin III and IV are translated respectively as *Book of the Discipline*, vols. I plus II (1-163), and II (164-416) plus III, with Vin. I and II as *Book of the Discipline*, vols. IV and V, and Vin V is *Book of the Discipline* VI.
Vin-a — Untranslated commentary on Vin: *Samantapāsādikā*.

Disclosure statement

This article has been supported by the International Committee of the Red Cross (ICRC).

ORCID

Peter Harvey http://orcid.org/0000-0002-4696-0379

References

Appleton, N., and S. Shaw. 2012. *The Ten Great Birth Stories of the Buddha: The Mahānipāta of the Jātakavaṇṇanā*. Vol. 2. Chiang Mai: Silkworm.

Bodhi, B. 1993. *A Comprehensive Manual of Abhidhamma: The Abhidhammattha Sangaha*. Kandy: Buddhist Publication Society.

Deegalle, M. 2002. "Is Violence Justified in Theravada?" Current Dialogue 39: 8–17.

Demiéville, P. 1957. "Le Bouddhisme et la guerre: Postscriptum a L'Histoire des moines guerriers du Japon de G. Renondeau." *Melanges publiés par L'Institut des Hautes Etudes Chinoises* 1, 347–385. Reprinted in his 1973 *Choix d'etudes bouddhiques (1929–1970)*, 261–299. Leiden: E. J. Brill. Translated as "Buddhism and War" by M. Kendall, in *Buddhist Warfare*, ed. M. K. Jerryson and M. Juergensmeyer, 17–57. Oxford: Oxford University Press.

Eckel, M. 2008. *Bhāviveka and His Buddhist Opponents*. Cambridge: Harvard University Press.

Geiger, W. 1912. *The Mahāvaṃsa or Great Chronicle of Ceylon*. London: Pali Text Society.

Gethin, R. 2001. *The Buddhist Path to Awakening*. Oxford: Oneworld.

Gethin, R. 2004. "Can Killing a Living Being Ever Be an Act of Compassion? The Analysis of the Act of Killing in the Abhidhamma and Pāli Commentaries." *Journal of Buddhist Ethics* 11: 166–202. http://blogs.dickinson.edu/buddhistethics/files/2010/04/geth0401.pdf

Gethin, R. 2007. "Buddhist Monks, Buddhist Kings, Buddhist Violence." In *Religion and Violence in South Asia: Theory and Practice*, edited by J. R. Hinnells and R. King, 62–82. London: Routledge.

Gombrich, R. 1971. *Precept and Practice: Traditional Buddhism in the Rural Highlands of Ceylon*. Oxford: Clarendon Press.

Gombrich, R. 2006. *Theravāda Buddhism*. 2nd ed. London and New York: Routledge.

Guenther, H. V. 1959. *The Jewel Ornament of Liberation: SGam-po-pa*. London: Rider.
Harvey, P. 1995. "Criteria for Judging the Unwholesomeness of Actions in the Texts of Theravāda Buddhism." *Journal of Buddhist Ethics* 2: 140–151. http://www.buddhistethics.org/2/harvey.txt
Harvey, P. 1999. "Vinaya Principles for Assigning Degrees of Culpability." *Journal of Buddhist Ethics* 6: 271–291. http://www.buddhistethics.org/6/harvey991.pdf
Harvey, P. 2000. *An Introduction to Buddhist Ethics: Foundations, Values and Issues*. Cambridge: Cambridge University Press.
Harvey, P. 2010. "An Analysis of Factors Related to the *Kusala/Akusala* Quality of Actions in the Pāli Tradition." *Journal of the International Association of Buddhist Studies* 33 (1–2): 175–209. https://www.academia.edu/21057483/An_analysis_
Heim, M. 2014. *The Forerunner of All Things: Buddhaghosa on Mind, Intention, and Agency*. Oxford: Oxford University Press.
Heirman, A. 2020. "Protecting Insects in Medieval Chinese Buddhism: Daoxuan's *Vinaya* Commentaries." *Buddhist Studies Review* 37 (1): 27–52. doi:10.1558/bsrv.18495.
ICRC. 2004. *The Roots of Behaviour in War: Understanding and Preventing IHL Violations*. Edited by D. Muñoz-Rojas and J. Frésard. Geneva: ICRC. https://www.icrc.org/en/publication/0853-roots-behaviour-war-understanding-and-preventing-ihl-violations
ICRC. 2014. *International Humanitarian Law: Answers to Your Questions*, 6–7, 46–49. Geneva: ICRC. https://www.icrc.org/en/publication/0703-international-humanitarian-law-answers-your-questions
ICRC. 2018. *The Roots of Restraint in War*. Geneva: ICRC. https://www.icrc.org/en/publication/roots-restraint-war
Jenkins, S. [2010] 2011. "On the Auspiciousness of Compassionate Violence." *Journal of the International Association of Buddhist Studies* 33 (1–2): 299–331.
Jerryson, M. 2018. "Buddhism, War and Violence." In *Oxford Handbook of Buddhist Ethics*, edited by D. Cozort and J. M. Shields, 453–477. Oxford: Oxford University Press.
Nikam, N. A., and R. McKeon. 1959. *The Edicts of Aśoka*. Chicago and London: University of Chicago Press.
Seneviratne, H. L. 1999. *The Work of Kings: The New Buddhism in Sri Lanka*. Chicago and London: Chicago University Press.
Tatz, M. 1994. *Skill in Means: Upāyakauśalya, Sūtra*. Delhi: Motilal Banarsidass.
Welch, H. 1972. *The Practice of Chinese Buddhism, 1900–1950*. Cambridge: Harvard University Press.

ICRC

IMPLICATIONS OF BUDDHIST POLITICAL ETHICS FOR THE MINIMISATION OF SUFFERING IN SITUATIONS OF ARMED CONFLICT

P. D. Premasiri

ABSTRACT
This article, drawing on Pali materials, highlights the Buddhist emphasis on minimising suffering, even in the conduct of war, in line with principles of international humanitarian law (IHL). It reflects on the inner roots of conflict and explores ideals of governance and the conduct of war, especially as explored in the *Jātaka* stories and stories about the god Sakka, and then as reflected in the Edicts of emperor Asoka and the *Mahāvaṃsa* chronicle.

Introduction

It is evident that the two world wars of the past century have left bitter memories of the kind of suffering brought about by modern warfare. A considerable part of such suffering could be seen as the consequence of disregarding the humanitarian principles that should govern social behaviour even in the context of a conflict. Warfare has generally been subject to certain principles and customs; even ancient civilisations had explicitly or implicitly recognised humanitarian laws or principles to be followed in situations of armed conflict. Although in the remote past they were not always codified as universally agreed upon sets of laws, parties to conflict had generally respected such principles and customs, recognising them as a necessary requirement of social and political ethics. It was only as recently as the nineteenth century that attempts were made at the universal codification of humanitarian law. Resorting to war to resolve problems appears to have been recognised as unavoidable, especially in the context of international relationships. The industrialisation of war, which has increasingly made

DOI: 10.4324/9781003439820-5

weapons of great – indeed mass – destruction available, has increased the suffering of war, both for combatants and civilians; hence the necessity of a set of humanitarian laws that can win international approval, adoption and application in practice.

The two main concerns of international humanitarian law (IHL) relating to situations of armed conflict are the protection of those who are not, or no longer, taking part in fighting, and restrictions on the means of warfare, particularly the kinds of weapons used and the tactics of war resorted to. The intended consequence of these concerns is the minimisation of suffering. There is a rich body of ethical principles and conventions related to the conduct of war preserved in the Buddhist tradition, especially in its body of canonical and commentarial literature, and also reflected in the historical practices of those who have professed to be Buddhists. Although they were not codified as laws in the history of Buddhism, they can be recognised as extremely significant ethical principles that could have an impact on any attempt to develop a system of IHL that is intended to minimise human suffering in situations of war, whether international or civil. The following is an attempt to clarify those principles by examining narratives from the form of the early Buddhist canon preserved by the Theravāda school, along with its commentaries and the school's chronicles, and by considering principles found in the edicts of the mid-third century BCE Buddhist king Asoka (Pali, Sanskrit Aśoka).

Reflections on war and conflict in the *Sutta*s, discourses of the Buddha

In the canonical sources referring to the biography of the Buddha, it is mentioned that the motivation of the Buddha as a young prince, before his enlightenment, was to leave the ephemeral pleasures of the household life, and strive to find a way to supreme peace (*anuttaraṃ santivarapadaṃ*; M. I.163). After his enlightenment, when asked about the purpose of his teaching, he explained that it was for avoiding conflict (*viggaha*) with anyone in the world, and to end all tendencies in the human mind to engage in behaviour productive of quarrels that may eventually grow into wars or major forms of armed conflict (*kalaha-viggaha-vivāda … daṇḍādāna satthādāna*. M.I.108 f.). According to the Buddha's teaching, an unavoidable consequence of wars and conflicts is horrific suffering to humans as well as other living beings through human violence and cruelty. Human suffering that is brought about in situations of violent armed conflict is amply illustrated in the *Mahā-dukkha-kkhandha Sutta*, where a vivid description of the mutual sufferings inflicted on the battlefield by opposing combatants in situations of war is given (M. I.86). The Buddha repeatedly maintained that his teaching has always been for the elimination of all *dukkha*: suffering (M.I.140). His teaching was meant to overcome suffering at the holistic level, ensuring, for those who could commit themselves to fully practising it, a final end to all suffering, whether gross and obvious, or subtle.

Suffering is considered in Buddhism to be intrinsically bad, and therefore, at every possible level, it advocates the avoidance, prevention or minimisation of it. This does not mean that Buddhism avoids the kind of suffering involved in the sometimes challenging process of training that one must undergo to achieve a noble and worthy goal. Undergoing such suffering – for example, bodily discomfort at certain times in meditation – is a side effect in the process of working towards the elimination of the psychological roots of all unwholesome traits and actions that produce suffering for oneself and others. The suffering of the path of practice is not valued as an end in itself, but as part of the way to the elimination of all suffering at the individual level. Acting from the roots of greed, hatred and delusion brings suffering to a person themselves and leads to harmful actions towards others. On the other hand, imbuing one's life with the divine abidings (*brahma-vihāras*) of loving-kindness, compassion, empathetic joy and equanimity means that one ceases to inflict suffering on others.

Suffering is brought about by natural disasters such as earthquakes, storms and tsunamis as well as the natural processes of ageing, sickness and death. Besides this suffering, which is necessarily associated with the common predicament of living beings, there is suffering that is brought about by what Buddhism sees as the unwholesome conduct of human beings themselves. The Buddhist teaching deals primarily with the kind of suffering that humans inflict upon themselves as well as others due to not having insight into the unwholesome motivational roots of human conduct: greed (*lobha*) and hatred (*dosa*) conjoined with delusion (*moha*), which can be seen as the perverted cognitive ground for the arising of the first two. Of course, there is a wide variation in the maturity of insight and the level of transformation of the baser emotions that people are willing and able to achieve through the cultivation of calm and insight. Considering this, the Buddha was not so unrealistic as to imagine that all humans are capable of living in the world in perfect peace, and overcoming all the psychological sources of suffering. He recognised the fact that, given the nature of living beings, even though they may desire to live in harmony and peace, they are unable to do so due to being fettered by the two most potent causes of conflict: envy (*issā*) and miserliness (*macchariya*) (D.II.276). As previously noted, the worst kinds of suffering inflicted by humans upon themselves as well as others occur in situations of war.

Interstate war was not a rare phenomenon during the time of the Buddha. Even kings who were his close associates, constantly seeking his advice and guidance on matters connected with the principles of the ethical life, are known to have fought wars. The canonical sources recount how, while engaged in solitary contemplation, the following question occurred to the Buddha: Is it possible to perform the role of state governance adhering strictly to ethical principles, without engaging in killing, causing to engage in killing, without engaging in military conquest and causing others to engage in military conquest, without engaging in the infliction of sorrow, and causing others to engage in the infliction of sorrow (*sakkā nu kho rajjaṃ kāretuṃ ahanaṃ aghātayaṃ ajinaṃ ajāpayaṃ asocaṃ asocāpayaṃ dhammenāti*, S. I.116)? The text does not provide a definite answer to the question, perhaps because acting in this way was seen to be extremely difficult.

Although, in the past, aggressive wars were frequently fought with the intention of achieving territorial expansion or over resources, in the modern world threats to peace are more complex, not emanating, at least overtly, from such intentions but from other causes. True, the global superpowers constantly suffer from mutual suspicion, often due to competition for the limited material resources of the world. Yet apart from this major cause for conflict, there are also numerous others such as religious or ethnic identities, disputes relating to territorial limits, and disagreements about political ideologies that could threaten peaceful co-existence in the global context. An invariable tendency in situations of conflict is for each party to firmly assert the moral justification for its own stance. It follows that, despite many commendable achievements of modern humanity, the possibility of destructive wars cannot altogether be ruled out. Although Buddhism considers war an expression of the three roots of evil – namely greed, hatred and delusion – the possibility appears to have been admitted of even a just party being drawn into armed resistance in order to defend itself against unjust aggression. All human societies have ethical values, but have also been involved in wars, international and civil; so they need to reflect on any armed conflict in which they are involved in the light of their values. In the face of admission of the fact that the threat of war is constantly present in the contemporary global context, the ethical issues relating to the conduct of war can and must be raised. There is sufficient reason to say that in this respect the Buddhist religious tradition is in a position to make a valuable contribution.

The Buddhist teaching introduced the concept of an ethical ruler (*dhamma-rājā*), a 'Wheel-turning' (*Cakka-vatti*) universal ruler who is supposed to appear in the world from time to time to uphold an ethical system of governance within which the ruler abstains from the use of weapons of war for the establishment of his state authority and carrying out the functions of governance. However, even such a ruler is supposed to have maintained a powerful army consisting of the fourfold armed regiments and over a thousand warriors who are referred to as his own progeny capable of vanquishing enemy forces (D.III.59). This implies that war may not be altogether avoidable in state governance. Buddhism considered wars of aggression utterly unethical, being an obvious expression of greed and/or hatred. However, as noted above, the state has to safeguard its citizens from aggressive enemy forces, and the need could on occasion arise when the state has to resist unjustified aggression.

The *Jātaka* stories on conduct in armed conflict

In recognition of such situations, Buddhism has dealt with ethical issues relating to the conduct of war, sometimes through the introduction of mythical episodes as in the case of its description of the god Sakka, seen as a devout follower of the Buddha, engaging in war, but acting in ways that could minimise suffering. The large body of what I would call Buddhist fictional literature, the *Jātakas*, is supposed to contain stories of the past lives of the Buddha while he was engaging in the fulfilment of the perfections for attaining the goal of Buddhahood. They represent 'the Buddha to be' (*bodhisatta*), sometimes as a witness to situations of war, and sometimes as a direct participant in fighting. Several narratives from this body of literature relevant to the present discussion are introduced below. There are also instances in Buddhist history in which those who professed Buddhism as their faith have directly participated in war, though paying heed to the implicit ethical principles that should be adhered to as Buddhists in such situations. These instances reflect the ethical norms applicable to situations of war, especially relating to matters concerning the treatment of the innocent victims of war, the avoidance of extremely cruel methods of warfare, and the compassionate treatment of defeated and subdued enemies. The fundamental ethical doctrines enunciated in the Buddhist canonical sources such as the *Dhammapada*, which insist on the conquest of enmity through non-enmity, and hatred through compassion, are clearly reflected in such instances. They are relevant particularly to war situations where hatred and enmity play quite a prominent role.

In any situation where ethics matter, a fundamental question arises regarding the grounds for ethical evaluation. Since ethics deal with what is right or wrong, good or bad, what ought or ought not to be done, the grounds on which such determinations could be made need clarification. According to Buddhism, ethical judgements cannot be reasonably grounded on authority or tradition. Buddhism does not favour any form of commandment theory for making ethical decisions, even in terms of what is supposed to be commanded by God, though what the Buddha taught is certainly seen as very worthy of reflecting on for consideration. From the Buddhist point of view, ultimately humans themselves have to determine what is ethically good. The important issue is not (as a theist might see it) whether 'what is commanded by God' is good, but whether 'God commands' what is good, and for Buddhism the good can be determined only through autonomous human reflection about the matter. It becomes clear from an examination of the

Buddhist teachings that to be judged as universally valid, any ethical norm must take account of the happiness or suffering that human behaviour is likely to produce.

In all situations where ethical considerations matter, Buddhism insists that minimisation of suffering and maximisation of happiness are our foremost moral responsibilities. This Buddhist ethical ideal is reflected in its definition of the terms *kusala* and *akusala* – generally translated as wholesome or skilful and unwholesome or unskilful – which can respectively be said to be the closest equivalents to the terms 'ethical' or 'moral' and 'unethical' or 'immoral' in usual English usage. Unethical (*akusala*) action is that which brings about the long-term suffering (*dukkh'udrayaṃ dukkha-vipākaṃ*) of oneself and others, while ethical action is that which conduces to the long-term happiness (*sukh'udrayaṃ sukha-vipākaṃ*) of oneself and others (M.II.114–115). The humanitarian principle that in all circumstances it is a human responsibility to minimise suffering is evidently recognised in the Buddhist ethical system. No other criterion, such as divine commandment, is prioritised over the principle of minimisation of suffering. Therefore, this principle has its implications for the conduct of war within which infliction of suffering becomes a causally necessary consequence.

During the latter part of the canonical period of its literature, Buddhism formulated a code of political ethics referred to as the 10 principles of state governance (*dasa-rāja-dhamma*), which have quite obvious implications for the subject of our discussion. The most serious violations of ethical conduct in situations of war occur under regimes that act with the motive of seeking vengeance on a defeated enemy, and showing callous disregard for the suffering of the innocent. The Buddhist tradition has been aware of this, and has made a genuine attempt to prevent such actions, in accordance with its advocacy of compassion and forgiveness, by formulating ethical principles to which those exercising state authority ought to subscribe. Buddhist fiction represents the social reality of the cruelties and excesses associated with the abuse of state power by autocratic and tyrannical rulers. Recognising this tendency to the abuse of state power on the part of authoritarian regimes that followed the principle that might is right, the Buddhist tradition appears to have put together these 10 ethical principles to be followed in the exercise of state power as safeguards against acts of oppression and cruelty.

We find these 10 principles listed in the *Nandiyamiga Jātaka* (no.385) in which the Bodhisatta, said to have been born as the leader of a herd of deer, is represented as using his selfless bravery to prevent a king, who engaged in hunting deer for sport, from firing the arrow he was aiming at him. He was then able to exhort the king about the morality to be practised by people with his responsibilities. In this instance it is pointed out that kings should rule without falling into the four modes of unjust behaviour (*agati*) and adhering strictly to the 10 ethical principles of kingship (*dasa-rāja-dhamma*, Jat.III.274). These – (1) *dāna* (charitability), (2) *sīla* (virtuous conduct), (3) *pariccāga* (sacrifice), (4) *ajjava* (uprightness), (5) *maddava* (mildness), (6) *tapa* (austerity), (7) *akkodha* (absence of anger), (8) *avihiṃsā* (non-injury), (9) *khanti* (patience) and (10) *avirodhana* (non-retaliation) – each have direct implications for the minimisation of suffering in situations of armed conflict. The fictional literature of Buddhism can obviously be interpreted as a Buddhist device to inculcate certain ethical norms, including for the guidance of those who exercise state power in armed conflict. It should also be noted that the ethical ideal represented in those principles came to be adopted even in certain actual historical situations in which Buddhist heads of state had engaged in war.

A story widely known in several Buddhist traditions, which is likely to have had a considerable element of historical reality, makes reference to the wars fought between King Ajātasattu of Magadha and King Pasenadi of Kosala (Jat. II.243, Jat.IV.343).[1] Ajātasattu is represented as a patricide king who had cruel tendencies from the early stage of his life, and was exposed to the evil influence of Devadatta, a monk who happened to be a rival of the Buddha. According to these accounts, the sister of King Pasenadi was the chief queen of King Bimbisāra, who was Ajātasattu's father. After Ajātasattu's cruel act of starving his father to death, the queen died from grief. The revenue of a village, amounting to a hundred thousand *kahāpana*s, had been assigned to the queen as part of the dowry to be paid by her brother, King Pasenadi. After the death of his sister, Pasenadi refused to make that payment. War broke out repeatedly between the two parties over the issue. Pasenadi, after receiving some advice on war strategy that had inadvertently come from the monk Dhanuggahatissa Thera, a former combatant in war, was able to finally emerge victorious. Ajātasattu was taken prisoner and bound in chains. Since King Pasenadi happened to be a person who came under the direct influence of the Buddha's ethical teachings, Ajātasattu was punished with imprisonment for a few days, but later reconciliation was reached. Pasenadi ended up giving his own daughter, Vajirā, in marriage to Ajātasattu, restoring even the revenue of the disputed village as her 'bath-money'. This can be seen an instance illustrative of a number of principles coming under the 10 royal virtues, such as mildness, absence of anger and non-retaliation.

The restraint in conflict of the god Sakka

In Buddhist mythology the god Sakka is represented as an ethical model to be emulated in situations where the victorious party in war is in a position of strength. The collection of texts called the *Sakka-saṃyutta*, which refers to the wars fought between Sakka and Vepacitti, illustrates in this mythical context how some of the royal ethical virtues such as mildness, absence of anger, non-injury, patience and non-retaliation can be practised even in the face of severe provocation by the captured enemy. According to the story, the *devas* (gods) under the leadership of Sakka emerge victorious over the *asuras* (a group of evil-minded celestial beings) led by Vepacitti, and Vepacitti is brought to Sakka's territory bound in chains. Vepacitti, being imprisoned in a cell close to Sakka's assembly hall, happens to insult Sakka with harsh and abusive words as he goes in and out of his assembly hall. Mātalī, driver of Sakka's chariot, calls upon Sakka to retaliate. In this instance Sakka keeps his calm, and even contests Mātalī's view that one who is in a position of strength should show no mercy to the captured enemy. Sakka points out that the practice of restraint and patience while being in a position of strength is the most commendable kind of patience. The Buddha relates this story and states with appreciation that even when Sakka was exercising his sole royal authority over the Tāvatiṃsa *devas*, he extolled the value of patience (S.I.121–122).

In the same mythological context of the *Sakka-saṃyutta* there is an illustration of the Buddhist virtue of the protection of the life of the innocent and refraining from acting in a way that would endanger their lives even at the cost of adverse consequences to an embattled army. As related by the Buddha, on one occasion the *asuras* defeat the *devas*, and the *devas*, led by Sakka, flee from the battleground for the protection of their own lives. As they do so, their chariot poles hit some nests of the Supaṇṇa birds and kill some infant Supaṇṇas. Learning of this, Sakka orders his army to turn back, despite the imminent threat to his warriors' lives from the pursuing enemies. However, Vepacitti's army, suspecting that Sakka must have turned back with reinforcements to fight them, flees in fear. The Buddha then says that Sakka had become victorious because of his righteous conduct (*dhammeneva jayo*, S.I.225). An allusion to this story is given in the *Kulāvaka Jātaka* (no.31), where in the introduction to the story the Buddha says:

> In the past, even the wise rulers of gods, when defeated in war and fleeing over the ocean, resolved that the destruction of life (*pāṇavadhaṃ*) for the sake of maintaining one's power was unjustified. To this end, risking their great reputation, they brought their chariot to a stop, saving the life of the fledgeling Supaṇṇas.[2] (Jat.I.198).

This represents especially the royal virtue of self-sacrifice (*pariccāga*), along with others such as non-injury (*avihiṃsā*).

More from the *Jātakas*

The *Jātaka* commentary consists of many stories that contain substantial material reflecting Buddhist war ethics. As pointed out above, it is in this body of literature that the 10 royal virtues came to be formulated. There are several *Jātaka* stories that make reference to wars fought between rival kings where the Bodhisatta is represented as the key character exemplifying Buddhist virtues. In some instances, kings are addressed by wise animals (in some cases the animal in question happens to be the Bodhisatta himself) giving them instruction regarding the ethical norms that they should not violate when they participate in battles. The *Bhojājānīya Jātaka* (no.23) is one such instance. There the Bodhisatta is represented in his past life as a well-trained horse belonging to King Brahmadatta of Benares. Brahmadatta faced the threat of war from seven neighbouring kings, and was under siege by their joint forces. The horse is chosen by a knight to lead a charge. Despite the horse being fatally injured, he enables the knight to defeat the armies of the seven kings. The horse, approaching death, instructs King Brahmadatta not to kill the defeated kings but to release them after making them commit a binding oath of allegiance (Jat.I.180).

The *Mahāsīlava Jātaka* (no.51) narrates the story of the Bodhisatta born in a previous life as King Mahāsīlava (Immensely Virtuous), who ruled the kingdom of Benares practising patience (*khanti*), loving-kindness (*mettā*) and sympathetic concern (*anuddayā*) (Jat.I.261). He treats even criminals with sympathy. Plunderers are given gifts so that they will transform themselves once they have acquired wealth with which to make a living. A certain person is expelled for his wrongdoing by Mahāsīlava, and then incites the king of Kosala to conquer his kingdom. Mahāsīlava, although he has sufficient strength to easily defeat the Kosala king, orders his powerful army not to fight due to his dislike for harming human life. The king of Kosala takes over the kingdom, but Mahāsīlava through the power of his virtue and goodness, and using strategies that do not harm life, makes the usurper regret his misdeed and so return his kingdom to him.

The *Asātarūpa Jātaka* (no.100) is a good example of the Buddhist disapproval of unethical war strategies such as starving a civilian population in order to gain military objectives. It narrates the story of a king of Kosala who slew the virtuous king of Benares, the then Bodhisatta. The slain king's son escapes and after a time, having gathered a mighty army, challenges the usurper. The mother of the young prince advices the latter to adopt the strategy of blockading the rival king's territory, depriving the civilian population of all the requisites of life such as firewood, water and food, so that the war could be won even without a battle. After seven days' blockade the starving populace revolt against the king, killing him and bringing his head to the prince. On the face of it, this story seems to recommend siege practice, until we learn that the Buddha narrated this story with reference to Suppavāsā, a female lay disciple of his who is said to have remained pregnant for seven years, going through acute labour pains over seven days, unable to deliver the child. The acute suffering of both mother and child is explained by the Buddha as a consequence of the bad karma of the past resulting from adopting an unethical war strategy involving the starvation of the civilian population (Jat.I.409). (The pregnancy ends well, according to the commentary, after she sends a message to the Buddha regarding her faith in him and the Buddha wishes her well in response.)

A similar message is found in the *Dhonasākha Jātaka* (no.153), which narrates the story of a cruel king, Brahmadatta Kumāra, who performs torturous acts and suffers the consequences of his cruelty. On ascending the throne, he thinks of committing aggression against all neighbouring states. He then succeeds in capturing a thousand kings, after which he tries to seize the kingdom of Takkasilā as well. When he fails in this endeavour he is advised by his cruel family priest to perform a ritual sacrifice, pulling out the eyes of the already captured kings and using their flesh to make sacrificial offerings. According to the narrative, he had finally to succumb to the law of karma and was reborn in hell (Jat.III.157).

In the *Asadisa Jātaka* (no.181), the Bodhisatta is a king of Benares who is very skilled in warfare, and able to defeat an enemy with practically no damage to life. Although he was the older prince in the family, he renounced kingship in favour of his younger brother, who believed in the words of conspirators and betrayed him. However, when his brother came under attack surrounded by 10 kings who wanted to capture the city of Benares, the Bodhisatta, who happened to be an extremely skilled archer, dismissed the enemy armies just by warning them of his prowess. The intention in this case was to avoid bloodshed in war. Power was used in the most skilled manner to bring about minimum harm. The Bodhisatta in this instance did not mind his brother's betrayal, helping him in a time of need (Jat.II.87).

The *Kusa Jātaka* (no.531) narrates the story of Kusa, the Bodhisatta born as an extremely ugly looking prince. Kusa, somehow concealing his looks, wins the most beautiful princess of the time, Pabhāvatī, as his wife. When she becomes aware of the looks of her newly obtained husband, however, she becomes resentful and abandons Kusa, going back to the home of her father, King Madda. When seven neighbouring kings then go forth to battle against King Madda, each one demanding to have Pabhāvatī as his wife, King Madda is compelled to seek the help of Kusa to defeat them. Kusa, a valiant fighter, defeats all seven in battle and thereby wins over Pabhāvatī. Although King Madda permits Kusa to slay the seven kings, Kusa, being the virtuous Bodhisatta, seeks reconciliation and proposes instead that they give in marriage to each one of the defeated kings one of the seven other daughters of King Madda, each almost equal in beauty to Pabhāvatī (Jat.V.278).

The *Ummagga Jātaka* (no.546) excels among Buddhist fiction that illustrates the ethical virtue of minimising harm in situations of war. It narrates the story of the Bodhisatta as Mahosadha, the wise advisor to the king of Videha. According to this narrative, Mahosadha is hated by the other four advisors to the king due to their feelings of jealousy. They attempt several times to create a rift between the king and Mahosadha. On one occasion, the king realises that the advisers are giving him false information in order to bring about a conflict with Mahosadha. The king wishes to punish the four advisers by executing them. Mahosadha, however, pleads with the king not to impose such harsh punishment and persuades him to give them only mild punishment. After the king proposes milder forms of punishment, finally Mahosadha persuades the king to forgive them and reinstate them in their original ministerial positions (Jat.VI.389).

The *Ummagga Jātaka* also includes the story of a king called Brahmadatta and his chief adviser, Kevaṭṭa. Kevaṭṭa hatches a plan for the king to conquer his neighbouring countries in order to become king of all Jambudīpa (India). Kevaṭṭa plans to get the less powerful kings out of the way first, plotting to poison all 100 of them as a first step in a larger military venture against the king of Videha. The latter king's adviser, the *bodhisatta* Mahosadha, foils the plot through skilled espionage. He intervenes to prevent the cruel death of the 100 kings, even though they had been aligning themselves with Brahmadatta to attack the king of Videha. After this setback, Brahmadatta remains determined to defeat the king of Videha despite being cautioned against it by Kevaṭṭa, and he goes to war. Mahosadha then succeeds in trapping Brahmadatta, but spares his life and avoids a battle that could have brought about immense destruction of life. Finally, he reveals his skills to Brahmadatta, and tells him that if he so wished he could become king of the whole of Jambudīpa, but that wise people do not approve of gaining kingship by killing others. Mahosadha reconciles all the kings, and they all become happily united (Jat.VI.460).

The conduct of King Asoka, from his edicts

Apart from the Buddhist fiction discussed above, there are impressive real and historical events that illustrate the influence of Buddhist principles on the ethics of war. The finest example is of King Asoka of India (268–39 BCE), who renounced his earlier violent and militaristic mentality after he became a devout Buddhist. After establishing his empire through violent military conquest including a massacre in the war in Kāliṅga (modern-day Orissa), Asoka became extremely remorseful about the suffering he had inflicted on people during the battles.

In Rock edict XIII, Asoka expresses his remorse and greatly regrets the sorrows and sufferings he had caused:

(1) The Kalinga country was conquered by King Priyadarśin [Asoka] ... when he had been consecrated eight years. One hundred and fifty thousand persons were carried away as captives and one hundred thousand slain and many times that number died.
(2) After that ... Devānāmpriya [Asoka] is intensely devoted to Dharmapālana (the protection of Dharma) ...
(3) Devānāmpriya, the conquerer of Kaliṅga has remorse now, because of the thought that the conquest is no conquest, for there was killing, death or banishment of the people ... That is keenly felt with profound sorrow and regret ...
(6) Now, even the loss of a hundredth or even a thousandth part of all the lives that were killed or died or carried away captive at the time when Kāliṅgas were conquered – is considered deplorable by Devānāmpriya. (Murti and Aiyangar 1951, 39ff.)

In Kalinga Edict I, Asoka says:

> ... All people are my children. Just as I desire on behalf of my own children that they should be fully provided with all kinds of comfort and enjoyment in this as well as in the other world, similarly, I desire the same (happiness and enjoyment in this world and in the next) on behalf of all people. (Murti and Aiyangar 1951, 53–55)

In Rock Edict II, it is said that in the conquered territories as well as the borderlands Asoka initiated a number of benevolent measures, such as the establishment of medical services for both humans and animals (Murti and Aiyangar 1951, 5). Rock Edict V refers to the appointment of officers called Great Ministers of *Dharma* to look into the needs of the people and to see that they are instructed properly regarding the principles of ethical living (Murti and Aiyangar 1951, 15). The sentiments expressed in the above edicts undoubtedly reflect the influence of the ideal of the ethical ruler (*dhammiko dhamma-rājā*) in the Buddhist canonical teachings with which Asoka appears to show familiarity. Although the term *Dharma* was in common use in the context of political doctrine in almost all Indian systems of political thought, the Buddhist concept of *Dharma* was characteristically different. In Buddhism, *Dharma* was not interpreted merely as 'Law' divested of its ethical connotation. This becomes clear from the fact that where Buddhism speaks of *Dharma* in relation to state governance, it is supposed to exclude the infliction of any suffering through the use of weapons of war. A king committed to *Dharma* engages not in armed conquest, but in conquest through the exclusion of the use of armaments (*adaṇḍena asatthena dhammena abhivijiya*). Asoka's edicts also reflect to a considerable extent conformity with the royal ethical principles implicit in the standard list of 10 that came to be established in the later period of Buddhism. Conformity to such principles on his part was probably a result of the transformation of his character through the influence of Buddhism.

The *Mahāvaṃsa* chronicle of Sri Lanka on conduct during war

Buddhism was introduced to Sri Lanka during the reign of King Asoka, and according to the Sri Lankan chronicles and commentaries to the Buddhist canon, from its introduction it was established as the dominant or state religion. Subsequently, through a gradual process, a distinct ethno-religious identity that came to be referred to as 'Sinhala Buddhist' developed in the country. The Sri Lankan chronicles give the impression that during the formative period of this identity Sri Lanka confronted the threat of continuing military aggression from her southern Indian neighbour, inhabited by people having a different ethnic and religious identity.[3] The *Mahāvaṃsa*, the chronicle that has played a prominent role in creating the distinct Sinhala Buddhist ethno-religious identity, gives an account of what it conceived as a major threat of that kind that occurred around two centuries after the introduction of Buddhism to Sri Lanka. According to this account, the main capital city of the country was conquered by a powerful ruler of South Indian descent. This resulted in resistance from those who gave primacy to the preservation of Sinhala Buddhist identity, resulting in what is historically known as the battle between Duṭugämuṇu and Eḷāra. In this battle Duṭugämuṇu (Pali Duṭṭhagāmaṇi, 101–77 BCE) is said to have fought a fierce war against Eḷāra, with the *Mahāvaṃsa* proclaiming that the former fought not to gain political power for himself, but for the glory of the Buddha-*dhamma* (Geiger, 1912 *Mahāvaṃsa*, XXV, vv.2–3, 111), hence the protection of Buddhism in the country.

There has been much contemporary discussion about the problem of justification of such violence in terms of Buddhist ethical principles. In the discussion above, it was noted that in Buddhist literature the Bodhisatta himself is represented as a combatant in situations of war. The crucial point here is not about the justification of war, for Buddhism recognises the fact that in secular social relationships there could be situations when war becomes unavoidable. The relevant issue here is about the ethical principles to be followed in the conduct of war itself, which is the principal question addressed in this article. There are indications in the account given in the *Mahāvaṃsa*, regarding the war between Duṭugämuṇu and Eḷāra, that certain Buddhist ethical principles like non-hatred (*akkodha*) were observed by the victorious Duṭugämuṇu. The remorse that he is supposed to have felt after his victory reflects the Buddhist ethical concern about destruction of human life and the ethical value of non-injury (*avihiṃsā*). This situation is described in the *Mahāvaṃsa* thus:

> Sitting then on the terrace of the royal palace, adorned, lighted with fragrant lamps and filled with many a perfume, magnificent with nymphs in the guise of dancing-girls, while he rested on his soft and fair couch, covered with costly draperies, he, looking back upon his glorious victory, great though it was, knew no joy, remembering that thereby was wrought the destruction of millions (of beings). (Geiger, 1912, *Mahāvaṃsa*, XXV, vv.101–103)[4]

Another notable event associated with the Chronicler's account of the war was Duṭugämuṇu's response to the defeated enemy. It is said that upon his victory, he paid respect to the fallen enemy:

> When he had thus been victorious in battle and had united Laṅkā under one rule he marched, with chariots, troops and beasts for riders, into the capital. In the city he caused the drum to be beaten, and when he had summoned the people from a yojana around he celebrated the funeral rites for king Eḷāra. On the spot where his body had fallen he burned it with the catafalque, and there did he build a monument and ordain worship. And even to this day the princes of Laṅkā, when they draw near to this place are wont to silence their music because of this worship (Geiger, 1912, *Mahāvaṃsa*, XXV, vv.71–74).

Conclusion

In concluding this discussion, it could be maintained as a general observation with adequate support from historical evidence that instances of military aggression on the part of Buddhist communities with imperialist motives have been extremely rare in India and Sri Lanka. Such an attitude can be attributed to the emphasis in Buddhist teachings on the ethically defiled psychological sources of such conduct, as well as the priority given in the system to love and compassion. As we have noted above, the criterion that is prioritised in Buddhism in determining the ethical quality of human conduct is the long-term happiness or suffering produced by any mode of behaviour. Accordingly, even in situations where the use of violence is necessitated for achieving what may be called just ends, Buddhism has called upon persons who wield power and authority to act in such a way that they minimise suffering. Moreover, many examples of such behaviour can be found in the Buddhist teachings and history.

Notes

1. Cf. Harris' article in this volume.
2. Translation adjusted for modern readership.
3. Sri Lankan scholars in the 1990s were able to show that this is a retrospective interpretation. After all, there were Tamil Buddhists, and Tamil is often mentioned by the commentator Buddhaghosa as one of the languages that might be the mother tongue of a candidate for Buddhist ordination. Analysis also indicated that different ethnicities were fighting in Duṭugämuṇu's army.
4. The 'millions' translates *akkhohiṇī*, which Cone (2001, 7–8) explains as 'a complete army (or ... millions)'.

Abbreviations

D. *Dīgha-nikāya*, edited by T. W. Rhys Davids and J. Estlin Carpenter, in 3 vols. London, Luzac and Co., 1890–1911. Reprinted, London: Pali Text Society.

Jat *The Jātaka, Together with its Commentary*, edited by V. Fausboll, 6 vols. London, Luzac and Co. (vol.1), & Tibner and Co. (vols. 2–6), 1877–1896. The Pali, and English translations of all of them, are available at: https://jatakastories.div.ed.ac.uk. The translations are those done by various hands under E. B. Cowell, *The Jātaka or Stories of the Buddha's Former Births*, 6 vols., London: Pali Text Society, 1895–1907. Newer translations are the following: Naomi Appleton and Sarah Shaw, *The Ten Great Birth Stories of the Buddha; The Mahānipāta of the Jātakavaṇṇanā*, Chiang Mai: Silkworm, 2 volumes, 2015; this translates the final 10, and longest *Jātakas*: nos. 538–547. Sarah Shaw, *The Jātakas: Birth Stories of the Bodhisatta*, New Delhi: Penguin, 2006, translates 26 of the *Jātaka*s: nos. 1, 9, 20, 37, 48, 55, 75, 94, 95, 99, 106, 108, 121, 128, 248, 273, 313, 316, 385, 402, 407, 476, 506, 538, 539, and 540. Nos. 385 and 546 are discussed above.

M. *Majjhima-nikāya*, edited by V. Trenkner and Robert Chalmers, 3 vols. London, Luzac and Co., 1888–1899. Reprinted, London: Pali Text Society.

S. *Saṃyutta-nikāya*, edited by Leon Feer, 5 vols. London, Luzac and Co., 1884–1898. Reprinted, London: Pali Text Society.

Disclosure statement

This article has been supported by the International Committee of the Red Cross (ICRC).

References

Cone, M. 2001. *Dictionary of Pāli*. Vol. 1. Oxford: Pali Text Society.

Geiger, W. 1912. *The Mahāvaṃsa, or the Great Chronicle of Ceylon*. London: Pali Text Society.

Murti, G. S., and A. N. K. Aiyangar. 1951. *Edicts of Aśoka (Priyadarśin), with English Translation*. Adyar: Adyar Library.

ICRC

TWO DIMENSIONS OF BUDDHIST PRACTICE AND THEIR IMPLICATIONS ON STATECRAFT

Asanga Tilakaratne

ABSTRACT
This article argues that within Buddhism, the ethical principles of those aiming at better rebirths within the round of rebirths (*saṃsāra*), and those aiming at nirvana, the transcending of this, should be clearly distinguished. The ethics of the nirvana seeker, mostly monks and nuns, has no place for war and violence, while the more worldly concerns of other Buddhists allow some engagement in defensive wars while seeking to minimise suffering, in line with international humanitarian law. It is argued that the lay Buddhist's emphasis is on avoiding evil (*pāpa*) and doing what is 'meritorious' (*puñña*), i.e. bringing happy results within this and future lives. 'Meritorious' acts are 'good' by worldly standards but are not the same as a nirvana-seeker's 'skilful' (*kusala*) action, which should always be non-violent. This is not to say, however, that a lay Buddhist may not also perform some genuinely skilful actions.

Introduction

The thesis of this article is that in Buddhist practice there are two dimensions carrying different implications for statecraft in general, and for war as an aspect of statecraft in particular. This study further suggests that not making a clear distinction between these two dimensions – concerning what is worldly and what is beyond the worldly – has resulted in misunderstanding of the Buddhist position on war. This misunderstanding needs to be exposed as such for it adversely affects the applicability of the Buddha's teaching to a world that is beset with attachment, aversion and delusion (*lobha, dosa, moha*), three fundamental traits of the human mind that lie at the root of misery and suffering, including all types of conflicts and wars.

The matter that this article seeks to address is the interface between international humanitarian law (IHL) and Buddhism. IHL is the modern 'rules of war' (i.e. *jus in bello*), which aim to regulate its conduct and thereby minimise the suffering involved. As such, IHL is concerned only with what constitutes lawful conduct during war, and it does not comment either on the

DOI: 10.4324/9781003439820-6

legitimacy of war in general as a means for resolving political disputes, or on the legality or otherwise of any decision to go to war – or the aims for doing so (i.e. *jus ad bellum*). As a matter of modern international law, the legality of the reasons for resorting to armed conflict is covered by the United Nations Charter. Thus, IHL assumes and accepts the possibility of war without either condoning or condemning it, or taking any position on the justness or legality of the aims of any particular armed conflict.[1] However, as discussed below, Buddhism's stance on *jus ad bellum* is necessarily relevant because it affects how it views the legitimacy of *jus in bello*/IHL.

In an effort to discover an interface between IHL and Buddhism, it is crucial at the very beginning to be clear about the Buddhist position on war. On this, there is a position held by some, which I would call 'the ideal position', according to which Buddhism is unconditionally pacifist and hence there is absolutely no room for war in Buddhism.[2] If this position is correct then the discussion between IHL and Buddhism becomes one between two groups that share no common ground on the most fundamental issue of the discussion. I think, therefore, that it is important that we have a clear understanding of this issue as a prerequisite for broader deliberations concerning the interface between IHL and Buddhism. In this article I hope to show that there is ground shared by IHL and Buddhism on war, and hence that the proposed discussion is justified.

The ideal position

What I would call the ideal position may have arisen from not understanding properly the situation mentioned in the discourses such as *Raṭṭhapāla-sutta* (M *sutta* 82). Raṭṭhapāla, a young and wealthy householder, having listened to the Buddha, decides to leave his luxury household life to follow the Dhamma fully. When all the other listeners have left, he approaches the Buddha and says the following to him:

> Venerable sir, as I understand the Dhamma taught by the Blessed One, it is not easy while living in a home to lead the holy life, utterly perfect and pure as a polished shell. Venerable sir, I wish to shave off my hair and beard, put on the yellow robe, and go forth from the home life into homelessness. I would receive the going forth under the Blessed One, I would receive full admission. (M.II.55)

The case of Raṭṭhapāla exemplifies what is applicable to those who leave the household life in order to attain the ultimate liberation from *saṃsāra*.[3] It is reasonable to imagine that this was not the case with all those who listened to the Buddha and opted to follow him. Some, like Raṭṭhapāla, became renunciants (male *bhikkhu*, female *bhikkhunī*, as they are called in the Buddhist tradition), whereas many others opted to follow him as 'lay' followers (*upāsaka, upāsikā*). Of these four groups of followers, Raṭṭhapālā's story suggests that the two former groups were less in number relative to the latter two groups.[4] It provides a good example of as to how this was the case: Raṭṭhapāla approached the Buddha only when all those who were listening to him left at the end of the sermon. This suggests that on this particular day it was only Raṭṭhapāla who opted to become a monastic follower, whereas there may have been others who 'took refuge' in the Buddha, Dhamma and the Sangha and became lay followers.

It appears that, in addition to these four groups, there was presumably another much larger group which did not become even *upāsaka* or *upāsikā* but listened to the Buddha, received some guidance from him and supported the Sangha as ordinary householders. In the broader classification of householders (*gahaṭṭha*) and renunciants (*pabbajita*), found often in the discourses, this third group constituted householders as a whole among whom was the sub-group of *upāsaka*s and *upāsikā*s. The householders as a whole are the people who are described in the discourses as laymen enjoying sensual pleasures, living at home in a house full of children, using sandalwood from Kāsi, wearing garlands, scents and unguents, and receiving gold and silver (A. IV.281).

Two dimensions of Buddhist practice

The difference between the ideal position, meant for the renunciants, and the way of life of the lay followers may be illustrated with reference to several factors such as the Buddha's method of instruction, the gradually deepening character of the Dhamma, and the distinction between what is 'meritorious' (*puñña*) and what is 'skilful' (*kusala*), two broad concepts of good found in Buddhism.

It is said that the Buddha presented his teaching in a gradual manner and that the practice of the teaching itself was gradual. This gradual way of presenting the Dhamma is called 'progressive instruction' (*ānupubbī-kathā*) and, according to Buddhaghosa, the leading commentator on the Theravāda Buddhist canonical texts, is the exposition of giving, virtue, heaven and the path (*dāna, sīla, sagga, magga*) in that order (D-a.I.277). One among many instances of the Buddha's giving instruction in this manner is found in the 'Discourse to Upāli' (M. *sutta* 56):

> Then the Blessed One gave the householder Upāli progressive instruction, that is, talk on giving, talk on virtue, talk on the heavens; he explained the danger, degradation, and defilement in sensual pleasures and the blessing of renunciation. When he knew that the householder Upāli's mind was ready, receptive, free from hindrances, elated, and confident, he expounded to him the teaching special to [*sāmukkaṃsikā*] the Buddhas: suffering, its origin, its cessation, and the path. (M.I.379–380)

According to this statement, the Buddha would start with instruction meant for the ordinary people who are attuned to samsaric concerns, who would do good things in the hope of gaining heavenly pleasures in return. It is understandable that many of the Buddha's listeners would have been at this level of understanding. When the Buddha moved to illustrate the negative side of the pleasures, it is imaginable that a good part of the listeners left the assembly or even if they were there physically, they were not following what the Buddha was saying for it went beyond the worldly state of their mind. The Buddha moved to what is referred to as 'the elevating (*sam* + *ukkaṃsa* + *ika*) instruction' (in the above translation, 'special to') only when he knew that his listeners were ready to follow the higher level of instruction. In this particular story, Upāli was ready to go beyond the ordinary level of understanding. In the story of Raṭṭhapāla, he was ready to go even further and to renounce the household life.

The assumption behind this progressive way of teaching is the obvious matter that people have different levels of understanding. According to a well-known classification found in the discourses, there are four types of individuals relative to their intellectual capacity: one who understands quickly (*ugghaṭitaññū*), one who understands through elaboration (*vipacitaññū*), one who needs to be guided (*neyya*), and one for whom the word is the maximum (*padaparama*), i.e. their understanding cannot penetrate beyond the words (A.II.135). An equally important but somewhat less known analysis relevant to the intellectual capacity of persons is the following: one whose discernment (*paṭībhāna*) is incisive but not free-flowing, one whose discernment is free-flowing but not incisive, one whose discernments is both incisive and free-flowing, and one whose discernment is neither incisive nor free-flowing (A.II.135). The last of these four categories is implied to be one who is not intellectually equipped to benefit from the Dhamma in any manner.

In addition to intellectual capacity, there is another very important distinction among people: the level of their psychological inclination towards inner development.

> Just as in a pond of blue or red or white lotuses, some lotuses that are born and grow in the water thrive immersed in the water without rising out of it, and some other lotuses that are born and grow in the water rest on the water's surface, and some other lotuses that are born and grow in the water rise out of the water and stand clear, unwetted by it; so too, surveying the world with the eye of a Buddha, I saw *beings with little dust in their eyes and with much dust in their eyes, with keen faculties and with dull faculties, with good qualities and with bad qualities, easy to teach and hard to teach, and some who dwelt seeing fear in blame and in the other world.* (M.I.169, emphasis added)

The phenomenon referred to here is of utmost importance in the Buddhist path, the ultimate goal of which is the total cessation of all worldly desires and attachments, and the suffering these bring: even if a person is equipped with intellectual capacity s/he will not be persuaded to follow the path unless s/he has that inclination.

The progressive method of instruction of the Buddha, however, is not a mere matter of logicality of his method of instruction necessitated by the differences in the intellectual capacity and inner inclination of the listener. It has a direct relevance to the gradually deepening character of the path to be practised: 'Just as the great ocean slants, slopes, and inclines gradually, not dropping off abruptly, so too, in this Dhamma and discipline penetration to final knowledge occurs by gradual training, gradual activity, and gradual practice, not abruptly' (A.IV.200–201). This gradually deepening character of the Dhamma, along with intellectual and spiritual differences of people, should show that the ideal position attributed to the Dhamma is too narrow to capture the reality of the intellectual and emotional diversity of its followers.

This may be further illustrated with reference to two key concepts in the Buddhist ethical discourse, namely skilful and unskilful (*kusala* and *akusala*) states of mind and actions, and 'meritorious', or morally good, and evil acts (*puñña* and *pāpa*). The *akusala* ones are characterised by attachment (*lobha*), aversion (*dosa*) and delusion (*moha*), and the *kusala* ones are those characterised by the opposites of these: non-attachment (*alobha*), non-aversion (*adosa*) and non-delusion (*amoha*). The terms '*kusala*' and '*akusala*' carry deeper psychological import than their usual English renderings 'skilful' and 'unskilful' (or 'wholesome' and 'unwholesome') would convey. According to the Buddhist analysis of mind, the unenlightened person's behaviour is coloured by attachment, aversion and delusion, which are called the roots of unskilfulness. These roots will often be active even when they are engaged in performing what is considered morally good or meritorious acts.

There is a significant difference between the nature of skilful and unskilful and meritorious and evil deeds. Relevant here is the Buddhist distinction between *puthujjanas*, 'worldlings' or 'ordinary folk', and spiritually 'noble' people, who have some degree of enlightenment – Stream-enterers, Once-returners, Non-returners and *Arahants* – who have destroyed some or all (for *Arahants*) of the spiritual fetters that bind a person to *saṃsāra*. Worldlings always have the roots of unskilfulness in their mind. Hence, whatever they do is motivated by these roots to some extent. When they do meritorious deeds they do so only by temporarily subduing unskilful phenomena. But their mind is not totally free of such phenomena even when they do meritorious acts in the hope of gaining heavenly pleasures. This explains the reason why Raṭṭhapāla, mentioned above, did not concede to the suggestion made by his parents, who were shocked at his decision to renounce household life, that instead of renouncing the household life he should stay home, enjoy pleasures and perform meritorious deeds. Meritorious deeds are within the scope of *saṃsāra*; they make one's samsaric journey pleasurable which, nevertheless, is to keep one within *saṃsāra* and to prolong it. It should be clear that this is not acceptable to a person who had made up his mind to move beyond the samsaric existence.

Evil deeds (*pāpa*) are socially harmful ways of behaviour also motivated by the roots of unskilfulness. The ordinary person's behaviour, insofar as it is not socially harmful, is not evil even though it is motivated to some degree by the roots of unskilfulness. In other words, all behaviour motivated by unskilful roots is not evil (*pāpa*) even though all evil behaviour is motivated by unskilful roots. The conclusion is that an ordinary person has not yet started to escape the roots of unskilfulness, and hence the samsaric existence is marked by the persistence of these roots. When Buddhist practice is viewed from these two classifications, namely *puñña* and *pāpa* and *kusala* and *akusala*, it becomes clear that Buddhism has two dimensions, samsaric and nirvanic, which, broadly speaking, the lay person and the monastic are respectively supposed to follow – though in practice, from the time of the Buddha, there have been lay people who are noble ones (M.I.490–493) and monastics who are worldlings.

Buddhism and war

From the nirvanic (*kusala*) point of view, war is out of the question. The only war that is possible is the one with Māra or the Evil One, the personification of evil according to the Buddhist tradition, namely defilements of the mind such as the greed, hatred and delusion (*lobha, dosa, moha*) referred to above. Talking about war, let alone engaging in it, was prohibited for monks and nuns, and the question of humanising war naturally cannot arise. As mentioned in the *vinaya*,[5] a monk who advised an executioner to do his work swiftly so that the victim's pain would be minimal was found guilty of supporting killing, which resulted in his excommunication from the Sangha (Vin.III.86). According to this *vinaya* judgment a monk or nun concurring with killing-permitting aspects of IHL, even on humanitarian grounds, could face serious *vinaya* consequences. Whether or how this could affect a modern-day Buddhist monk or a nun, who is striving to combine both samsaric and nirvanic dimensions within their own practice, remains to be considered.

Taking the samsaric dimension of Buddhist ethics into consideration, we know that what is said above is not the only Buddhist position. It is well known that the Buddha did not impose *vinaya* rules for the laity. In Buddhism the laity was always under secular rule. When army-deserters wished to join the Sangha (without proper release), the Buddha's ruling was not to accept them (Vin.I.74). This suggests that, although the Buddha did not like war, he respected the state rules, though these are not concerned as such with ethics and the working of karma. Lay life includes sexual relations, money to be earned, families to be raised, competitive examinations to pass etc., which do or can involve *akusala* actions and states of mind. State law regulates such actions to minimise aspects harmful to others, but do the *akusala* aspects mean that lay people, as scholars like Max Weber held, are not really a part of Buddhism?

Evidence seems to suggest otherwise. If we take seriously the *Vinaya-piṭaka* story of Yasa and his friends who joined the Buddhist monastic Sangha at the very beginning of the Buddha's mission, and whose parents (and possibly other family members) became lay followers of the Buddha at the same time, the laity appeared in Buddhism almost simultaneously with the monastic community (Vin.I.15–18). Subsequently, the male and female lay followers (*upāsaka* and *upāsikā*) came to comprise two constituents of the four-fold Buddhist society, the other two being the *bhikkhu* and *bhikkhunī*.

The path of the laity is different from that of monastics. This difference is not in kind but in degree. In what follows the difference has been described with reference to a peacock, which is colourful but slow, and a swan, which is simple but fast:

> Even as the crested (peacock), blue-eyed, (the bird) that soars in the sky never will reach the speed of the swan, even so the householder cannot emulate (to match) the monk, the sage (leading a life) of seclusion contemplating in the forest. (Sn.221)

The two groups follow the same path at different speeds. The lay person's is the samsaric life with *puñña* and *akusala* combined with occasional moments of *kusala*, which is what is feasible for a large majority of lay people.[6]

Within this category of lay people were rulers and soldiers, the former who made the decisions to wage war and the latter who fought them, among both of whom were followers of the Buddha. It is quite clear from the texts that the Buddha did not approve of war. On the other hand, that war was a part of worldly affairs cannot have been unknown to the Buddha, who knew about the workings of *lobha, dosa* and *moha* better than anyone else. For his part, the Buddha endeavoured to prevent people from going to war[7] and stop and dissuade those who had already gone to war.[8] But he did not ask kings to disband their armies.[9]

In the *Jātaka* literature,[10] a good source for the samsaric aspect of Buddhist ethics, where the Bodhisatta (Pali, Sanskrit Bodhisattva), the future Buddha, is the main character, there are many stories in which he played an important political role as a ruler or adviser to a ruler. In these stories, the emphasis is to avoid war. But the Bodhisatta kings would usually maintain their armies, accepting in this manner the necessity of power.[11]

In the discourses in which the Buddha comes up with what may be called his political philosophy, the universal ruler (*rājā cakkavatti*) possesses an army and brings all other kings under his righteous reign with the help of this power which, of course, he does not have to use violently (*Cakkavatti-sīhanada Sutta*, D.III.58–79). But if any of the kings, through whose territory the universal ruler marches his army, oppose this exercise, it is hard to imagine what the final result would be. In these discourses, interestingly, we do not find any mention of good behaviour in war, perhaps for the simple reason that the universal ruler did not have to engage in war. However, we have some relevant information in the discourses (e.g. S.I.221–222) referring to the wars Sakka, the king of gods, fought with *Asuras*, his enemies.[12] In the later Buddhist literature of the Indian Mahāyāna we also find some specific instructions on good behaviour in war, discussed by K. N. Jayatilleke (2009, 472).

War is an instance of using force or violence. It appears that Buddhism accepts using force in certain circumstances. As the *Abhayarājakumāra Sutta* (M. *sutta* 58) points out, the Buddha sometimes had to use unpleasant words, provided that they were true and spiritually useful (M.I.395). The simile mentioned in the discourse, that the king would use force, even at the risk of inflicting pain, to remove a bone stuck in his child's throat, suggests that force used with good intention is permissible, at least when used on the person it benefits. A relevant example from the *vinaya*, which deals with the organisational aspect of the Sangha and has to do with the monastic system of law in contrast to *sīla* (morality) which is personal and soteriological, is the presence of punishments for the violators of rules which are basically psychological – not speaking to an offender, for example. Another instance occurring in the section on punishments (*Kamma-khandhaka*) in the *vinaya* (Vin.II.12), suggestive of use of force, is that the Buddha asked Sāriputta and Moggallāna, his two chief disciples, to impose the punishment of banishment (*pabbājanīya-kamma*) on two ill-behaved monks called Assaji and Punabbasu, and, taking note of the possibility of rough and rowdy behaviour by them, asked his two chief disciples to be accompanied by a large group of monks.

The intriguing *Rajja Sutta* (S.I.116–117), however, seems to leave the question of use of force open. This *sutta* refers to the Buddha who was thinking whether or not it is possible to rule righteously without killing and causing to kill and without conquering and causing to conquer. At that moment Māra appears and tries to persuade the Buddha to rule, saying: 'Venerable sir, if the Blessed One wishes, he need only resolve that the Himalayas, the king of mountains, should become gold, and it would turn to gold'. The Buddha dismisses Māra saying:

> If there were a mountain made of gold – made entirely of solid gold,
>
> Not double this would suffice for one – Having known this, fare evenly.

This statement does not answer the initial question but hints at a broader principle of governance, equality. The concept of *'sama'* (equal) along with *'dhamma'* (righteousness) is often referred to in the *Jātaka* stories in describing the rule of good kings. Nevertheless, the good rulers we come across in the *Jātaka* stories who ruled following these broad principles did not exclude the possibility of war altogether, though they often tried to avoid it. Clearly the two concepts are context dependent and require more precise formulation depending on particular situations. Without providing a definitive answer to the questions he himself raised, the fact that the Buddha left the matter open is not without significance.[13] Therefore, the *Rajja Sutta* may be taken as indicating both the Buddha's uneasiness about the manner of governance of the rulers of his time, and his awareness of the unavoidability of war given the nature of the ordinary worldly (*puthujjana*) mind of the rulers and their subjects. What the Buddha once said to the king of Kosala who had been defeated by the king of Magadha – namely, 'The victor breeds enmity; the vanquished sleeps unhappy. The peaceful [Arahant[14]], leaving behind both victory and defeat, sleeps happily' (*Dhammapada* 201) – alludes to the ideal transcending both victory and defeat which the Buddha knew to be beyond the reach of the King of Kosala. The *Rajja Sutta* seems to indicate that the Buddha knew that the practicalities of actual rule were not so simple.

If the Buddha knew that war was an aspect of samsaric existence, the question is, why did he not develop a set of rules to make war more humane? One way to answer this question would be to show how the Buddha advised rulers on righteous ways of behaviour such as the well-known 'ten royal virtues'[15] (*dasa rāja-dhamma*, e.g. Jat.I.260 and 399) and 'noble duties of a universal monarch' (*ariya cakkavatti vatta, Cakkavatti-sīhanāda-sutta*, D. III.61). If adhered to, these would make war unnecessary, and if war had to be waged, the king would behave in a just and humane manner. The Buddha seems to have been satisfied with outlining the foundational principles of righteous behaviour for the rulers rather than producing a set of rules on how to behave in a war, an act that could have diluted the Buddha's goal of making war unnecessary.

Discussing the Buddhist contribution to international law, Jayatilleke (2009, 472–475) refers to the *Śānti Parvan* ('Book of Peace') in Hindu literature, in the great epic on war, the *Mahābhārata*, which contains a developed set of rules to regularising behaviour in war. Jayatilleke shows how these aspects of Hindu statecraft had been shaped under the influence of Buddhist thought which laid emphasis on such virtues for rulers as humaneness, non-violence and righteousness.

Historical practice

The historical experience of Buddhism in the lands where it spread shows that Buddhist rulers (in general) have often adhered to the basic non-aggressive stand on relations with other countries or other political entities. The outstanding example is the mid-third century BCE Indian emperor Asoka, whom subsequent Buddhist rulers throughout history have regarded as the ideal king. Asoka gave up war after waging a successful but bloody campaign in Kaliṅga, modern Orissa (Kaliṅga Rock Edict, Nikam and McKeon 1959, 27–30). But in Asoka we do not have evidence of good practices in war for the simple reason that he did not wage war after he became a follower of Buddha's teachings.

In Sri Lanka we have the much-discussed war that Duṭṭhagāmaṇi (101–77 BCE) felt obliged to wage against a South Indian Tamil occupier of Sri Lanka in order to protect the country and its culture, religion and economy.[16] There are two clear instances in which Duṭṭhagāmaṇi's Buddhist influence comes to light. One is his decision to fight Eḷāra, the king of the opposing side, one-on-one so that the damage to life could be minimised. The other is that after winning the war Duṭṭhagāmaṇi became regretful rather than elated (*Mahāvaṃsa* XXV, v.103), which means that Duṭṭhagāmaṇi knew that what he had done was violent and unpleasant. He had nevertheless chosen to go to war because there were so many things at stake. It is obvious that he was faced with a moral dilemma, and he chose war with a hardened conscience. The fact that Duṭṭhagāmaṇi did not have anything against Eḷāra as a person but was only concerned about the damage caused to the country and religion by his rule (*Mahāvamsa* XXIII, vv.9–10) is shown by his post-mortem treatment of the enemy as worthy of respect.

The *Mahāvaṃsa* account says that a group of Arahants consoled the regret-stricken ruler by saying that he had killed only one and half human beings (*Mahāvaṃsa* XXV, vv.103–112) – an idea that has come under universal and unconditional censure from scholars who have discussed this matter.[17] In this case, the claimed Arahants seem to have had two choices: one was to tell the king point-blank that he will be born in the hell due to this violent act (whether in his next life, or later), thus causing great frustration in him; the other was to console the mind of a ruler who had done for the sake of others what he himself actually considered morally questionable. The 'Arahants' are portrayed as choosing to do the second. The reasoning given, no doubt, is outrageous. Nevertheless, the statement, unprecedented in the whole history of the country, needs to be understood in its proper context within this semi-historical chronicle. We must not forget that even the Buddha waited until the questioner asked the question three times to respond that a soldier who is killed in the war will be born in a woeful existence (*Yodhājiva Sutta*, S.IV.308–09).[18] Both the Buddha and the claimed Arahants in Duṭṭhagāmaṇi's case may be understood as practising *Upāya-kauśalya*[19] ('skill-in-means') to determine the proper response to these specific difficult situations.[20]

After Duṭṭhagāmaṇi, subsequent rulers of Sri Lanka are also recorded as having gone to war with invaders. In this they are regarded not as aggressors but as defenders of that which, as rulers, they were obliged to defend. During the medieval period there were a few instances of Sinhala rulers invading parts of Southern India (Sena II 853–887; Mahā Parākramabāhu 1153–1186; Nissanka-Malla 1187–1196; and Parākramabāhu VI 1412–1467). All these events, according to the *Mahāvaṃsa*, could be seen as responses of these kings to acts of foreign aggression or wrongdoing. This, however, does not mean that the kings of Sri Lanka did not have their own share of in-fighting and struggles for power among themselves.

Conclusion

From the nirvanic point of view, the eradication or total removal of suffering is the goal of Buddhism. When the Buddha explained to his son Rāhula that one should not do any act if it causes pain to oneself, another or both, he did not specify the degrees of pain (*Ambalaṭṭhika-Rāhulovāda-sutta*, M. *sutta* 61, M. I.414–20). In contrast, the IHL goal of minimising suffering is rooted in the assumption that causing some suffering is justifiable and acceptable under certain conditions. As far as Buddhism is concerned, this can be accepted only from the perspective of samsaric Buddhism, which allows the use of force and inflicting pain within limits and provides space for its followers to lead pleasurable but ethical lives. In nirvanic Buddhism minimising suffering may be accepted, though without justifying the use of physical injury, only as a general principle deriving from its goal of total eradication of suffering.

Returning to the subject of the interface between IHL and Buddhism, IHL consists of a set of rules agreed to by states, relevant to the conduct of war. We know that Buddhism has not developed a similar set of rules, only the rudiments of them. The issue is, in the absence of such a well-developed system of Buddhist rules, whether or not Buddhists should accept those of IHL. The position developed in this article is that, within the samsaric dimension of Buddhism, there is no difficulty in concurring with IHL rules in principle.

At this point, it is possible to raise an objection against accepting as good something on which the Buddha has not said anything directly or something that is not found in the Buddhist tradition. There are some guidelines in the teaching of the Buddha itself to be followed in similar situations. Key among such guidelines is the criterion called the 'great indicator' (*mahā apadesa*) according to which any statement that does not contradict the doctrine

(*Dhamma*) and discipline (*vinaya*) may be accepted as the teaching of the Buddha.[21] It is clear that the principle behind this criterion is coherence: what coheres with what the Buddha taught may also be taken as his teaching. Another such guideline is: 'whatever is well spoken is all the word of the Blessed One' (*sabbaṁ subhāsitaṁ tassa bhagavato vacanaṁ*, A.IV.164). The concept of well-spokenness could be understood as that which pertains to the eradication of suffering. These criteria allow a broad scope for accommodating what is good and acceptable, regardless of its source.

On the basis of these criteria, IHL may be accepted because it is conducive to the minimisation of human and other forms of suffering. Furthermore, perhaps inspired by this same openness of thought, the Buddhist tradition, which has a history of accepting good things from other traditions, has not had any problem in accepting what is good in modernity in general, and in modern science and technology in particular. Unlike some other religious traditions, Buddhism does not have a history of waging war against science and (appropriate) technology. This means that Buddhism does not have a difficulty in concurring with what is good whether it is ancient or modern.

In sum, accepting or rejecting IHL depends on the Buddhist attitude to war, or, in other words, on whether or not Buddhism accepts the possibility of war. The Buddhist attitude to war is an extension of the Buddhist attitude to using force as a means of solving problems. From our discussion above we saw that there is a distinction between nirvanic and samsaric forms of Buddhism, and that according to the latter, both war and the use of force were accommodated within Buddhism subject to restrictions. Once this is accepted, it goes without saying that when war is waged as the last resort the parties involved should be guided by some basic principles and procedures leading to minimisation of suffering.

Notes

1. For more on the difference between *jus in bello* (IHL) and *jus ad bellum* see: https://www.icrc.org/en/document/what-are-jus-ad-bellum-and-jus-bello-0. Also: https://www.icrc.org/en/war-and-law/ihl-other-legal-regmies/jus-in-bello-jus-ad-bellum.
2. See Rahula (1978, 84) for a similar position.
3. The wheel of existence in which beings are subject to repeated birth and death.
4. Indeed, the *Mahāvacchagotta Sutta*, at M.I.490–493, refers to fewer monks and nuns (far more than 1000) who had attained full enlightenment than male and female lay disciples who had attained a lesser level of enlightenment (far more than 2000). S.V.406 also says that that are more monastics that have attained a lower level of enlightenment than those who have attained a higher level.
5. *Vinaya* refers to the system of law applied to monks and nuns and administered internally by the Sangha, the monastic community, itself. It is contained in the collection called *Vinaya-piṭaka* (Basket of Discipline) forming one of the three 'baskets' of the Theravāda canon.

6. This, however, does not mean that the higher states in the path leading to nirvana are totally beyond the reach of lay people. Discourses do refer to some lay men and women who attained such states. For one instance refer to the *Mahāvacchagotta-sutta*, M. *sutta* 73 (M.I.490–493).
7. E.g. when Sunīdha and Vassakāra, Ajatasattu's ministers, informed the Buddha that the latter was getting ready to wage war against Vajjis, the Buddha tried to convince them that it was not a wise decision (*Mahāparinibbāna Sutta*).
8. The source of this criterion is the *Mahāparinibbāna-sutta*, D. *sutta* 16, D.II.72–76.
9. E.g. the imminent war between Sakyas and Koliyas on the waters of Rohini River (Jat.V.412–414).
10. A part of the Buddhist canonical literature containing the stories related to the past births of the Buddha.
11. See Premasiri in this volume.
12. See Premasiri in this volume.
13. See Premasiri in this volume.
14. That is, one who has realised the highest state of purity in Buddhist soteriology.
15. See Premasiri in this volume.
16. See Premasiri in this volume.
17. E.g. Harvey (2000, 257).
18. See Harvey in this volume.
19. The Buddhist ethical principle that takes into consideration context and practicality in making moral judgements.
20. For a different perspective on this story, see Harvey in this volume.
21. The source of this criterion is the *Mahāparinibbāna-sutta*, D. *sutta* 16, D.II.124–125.

Abbreviations

A. *Aṅguttara-nikaya* vol.I (1961, 2nd ed.), vol. II (1888, repr. 1976), edited by R. Morris. Vols. III–V (1897, 1899, 1900, repr. 1958), edited by E. Hardy. London: Pali Text Society, as translated by Bhikkhu Bodhi, *The Numerical Discourses of the Buddha*. Boston: Wisdom Publications, 2012.

D. *Digha-nikaya* vols. I–III, (1890, 1893, 1911, repr. 1976), edited by J. E. Carpenter. London: Pali Text Society, as translated by M. Walshe, *The Long Discourses of the Buddha*, Massachusetts: Wisdom Publications, 1995.

D-a. *Dīgha Nikāya Aṭṭhakathā*, vols. I–III, 2nd ed. (1968, 1971), Pali Text Society: commentary on the *Dīgha Nikāya*, untranslated, edited by T. W. R. Davids and J. E. Carpenter (I and II) and W. Stede (III).

Jat. *The Jātaka, Together with Its Commentary*, Ed. by V. Fausboll, 6 vols. London, Luzac and Co. (vol.1), & Tibner and Co. (vols 2–6), 1877–1896. The Pali, and English translations all of them are available at: https://jatakastories.div.ed.ac.uk. The translations are those done by various hands under E. B. Cowell, *The Jātaka or Stories of the Buddha's Former Births*, 6 vols., London: Pali Text Society, 1895–1907. Newer translations are the following. N. Appleton and S. Shaw, *The Ten Great Birth Stories of the Buddha: The Mahānipāta of the Jātakavaṇṇanā*, Chiang Mai: Silkworm, 2 volumes, 2015; this translates the final 10 and longest *Jātakas*: nos. 538–547. S. Shaw, *The Jātakas: Birth Stories of the Bodhisatta*, New Delhi: Penguin, 2006, translates 26 of the *Jātakas*: nos. 1, 9, 20, 37, 48, 55, 75, 94, 95, 99, 106, 108, 121,128, 248, 273, 313, 316, 385, 402, 407, 476, 506, 538, 539, and 540.

M. *Majjhima-nikaya* I–III (1888, 1898, 1899, repr. 1979), edited by V. Trenckener. London: Pali Text Society, as translated by Ñāṇamoli Bhikkhu and Bhikkhu Bodhi. *The Middle Length Discourses of the Buddha*. Boston: Wisdom Publications, 2001.

S. *Saṃyutta-nikaya* vols. I–V (1884–1898, repr. 1973–1976), edited by M. L. Feer. London: Pali Text Society, as translated by Bhikkhu Bodhi. *The Connected Discourses of the Buddha*. Boston: Wisdom Publications, 2000.

Sn. *Suttanipāta*, translated by N. A. Jayawickrama, *Suttanipāta: Text and Translation*. Colombo: Postgraduate Institute of Pali and Buddhist Studies, 2001.

Vin. *Vinaya-pitakam* vols. I–V, edited by H. Oldenberg. London: Pali Text Society, 1879–1883, repr. 1969. Translated by I. B. Horner as *The Book of the Discipline*, 5 vols., London: Pali Text Society, 1938–1966.

References to Sn. are by verse number; those to the other texts above are by the volume and page number of the Pali text, the page numbers being shown in their translations within square brackets. In the case of Vin., vols. I and II of the Pali are vols. IV and V in the translations.

Disclosure statement

This article has been supported by the International Committee of the Red Cross (ICRC).

References

Harvey, P. 2000. *An Introduction to Buddhist Ethics: Foundations, Values and Issues*. Cambridge: Cambridge University Press.

Jayatilleke, K. N. 2009. "The Principles of International Law in Buddhist Doctrine." In *Facets of Buddhist Thought: Collected Essays*, 371–482. Kandy: Buddhist Publication Society.

Nikam, N. A., and R. McKeon. 1959. *The Edicts of Asoka*. Chicago and London: University of Chicago Press.

Rahula, W. 1978. *What the Buddha Taught*. London: Gordon Fraser.

ICRC

THE PARADOX OF THE BUDDHIST SOLDIER

Daniel Ratheiser and Sunil Kariyakarawana

ABSTRACT

At first glance, a military life and practising Buddhism may seem like two pursuits at odds. Buddhism sets the moral bar very high and nowhere in its teachings can one find any evidence in support of violence, whether in word, thought or deed. One could therefore argue that Buddhism and the military are two strange bedfellows, and some may find it difficult to conceive of serving in the military whilst adhering to the ethos, values and standards of Buddhism. This article challenges this popular myth and resolves this apparent paradox between Buddhism and the military. By drawing on canonical Buddhist teachings as well as voices from the Sangha and Buddhist military practitioners, we demystify the 'Buddhist soldier' and clear common misconceptions regarding: the fundamental teachings of *ahiṃsā*, karma and skilful (*kusala*) action; Buddhist teachings being equated to pacifism; the duty of soldiers and the State to protect; soldiering as a 'right livelihood'; and the karmic implications of military professions. Using international humanitarian law, the body of law regulating the conduct of war, as a natural reference point, we explore what guidance Buddhist teachings provide to soldiers and how they potentially can contribute towards reducing suffering in war, including through application in military training. Buddhism endorses the concept of maintaining disciplined, virtuous and skilled military forces to protect what is good. At all times one needs to aim at not causing suffering to others, but never at the expense of preventing even worse suffering.

Introduction

At first glance, a military life and practising Buddhism[1] may seem like two pursuits at odds. Buddhism sets the moral bar very high and nowhere in its teachings does one find any evidence in support of violence, whether in word, thought or deed. On the contrary, the entire Buddhist teachings and practices are geared towards the principle of *ahiṃsā* (non-harming), for the benefit of oneself and others.

In the line of duty, soldiers may be forced to take tough actions, including those that result in death. Although professional militaries are increasingly

DOI: 10.4324/9781003439820-7

sensitive, disciplined and regulated by laws, instances of vicious military action have sometimes cast a bad light on the armed forces. Many therefore see the military as a 'no-go area' for practising Buddhists, and some even go so far as saying that military careers are a 'wrong livelihood'. Given that all Buddhist nations have militaries, how does one square these differences or reconcile this paradox?

War, religious belief and the meaning of death are connected at a very fundamental level. Warriors, faced with the imminence of death, sought purpose in their religious traditions. Buddhism itself evolved in this environment and became intimately tied to the topic of war. Buddhism recognises that in this worldly existence (*saṃsāra*) situations when war becomes unavoidable can arise,[2] which makes understanding the conduct of war in its context highly relevant.

Warfare has been subject to certain principles and customs since time immemorial. International humanitarian law (IHL), the law of armed conflict, is built on this legacy of religious and philosophical traditions. IHL focuses on conduct during war (*jus in bello*) irrespective of the question of whether wars are justifiable (*jus ad bellum*). Its objective is to reduce suffering during armed conflict by balancing military necessity with humanitarian concerns (Melzer 2019, 17–56). IHL provides us with a natural reference point and a particularly fruitful interpretive lens for seeking to understand Buddhism in the context of warfare. As all soldiers are legally required to act in accordance with IHL, it is relevant for Buddhist combatants to look at it from the perspective of their own traditions, identifying convergences as well as distinct traits.

By drawing on canonical Buddhist teachings as well as voices from the Sangha and Buddhist military practitioners, we try to demystify the enigma of the 'Buddhist soldier' and explore how Buddhist teachings potentially can contribute to reducing suffering in war, including through application in military training. Reflections from current and former members of the armed forces with their experience of the realities of warfare provide useful insights for bridging the gap between scriptural guidance and military practice.

This article argues that the deceptive incompatibility between Buddhism and the military mainly stems from a misunderstanding of the Buddhist concepts of *ahiṃsā*, karma and skilful (*kusala*) action, and from failing to recognise the soldier's duty to protect. Whilst Buddhism has no place for aggression or any other behaviour intended to cause harm, it does not rule out the use of military force for wholesome purposes. The canonical texts endorse the concept of maintaining disciplined, virtuous and skilled military forces to protect what is good. At all times one needs to aim at not causing suffering to others, but never at the expense of preventing even worse suffering.

Ahiṃsā

Although there is much diversity within Buddhism and Buddhist practices, all traditions are in agreement in their pursuit of moral, ethical conduct, *sīla* (Sanskrit: *śīla*). It is one of the three components constituting the Noble Eightfold Path, which provides a code of conduct committing to self-restraint with the principal motivation being to avoid harm. From a Buddhist perspective, ethics are causative, with karma (literally 'action') leaving imprints on the individual mind that by consequence influence the future – intention[3] constitutes the underlying force. Buddhist ethics are mainly governed by examining whether a certain action is likely to be harmful to oneself or others, with the morality of one's actions being appraised by evaluating one's intention. Because it is bad states of mind that result in harmful conduct, there is much emphasis on the cultivation of virtues.

The teaching on karma explains that one's future is shaped through one's intentional acts. Action (whether by body, speech or thought) is constituted by two components, the actual behaviour and the intention underlying that behaviour. Psychological impulses behind actions plant 'karmic seeds' and set in motion a chain of causes culminating in 'karmic fruits'.[4] To illustrate, deliberately harming a living being would plant seeds that will naturally mature into unpleasant results in the future, while accidentally causing harm does not generate a negative karmic effect in and of itself.[5] Seeing karma fatalistically, however, would be an incorrect understanding of the concept. The present experience of pain and pleasure is the consequence of actions taken both in the past and in the present, among other factors such as organic ones in the body (Sn.36.21). This creates the possibility to act with right intent by one's free will and to end suffering before the karmic seeds of past actions come to fruition.

> *Cetanāhaṃ, bhikkhave, kammaṃ vadāmi. Cetayitvā kammaṃ karoti: kāyena, vācāya, manasā.* – 'Intention, oh monks, I call karma. Intending, one does karma by way of body, speech, and mind.' (An.6.63)

The Buddha suggested that 'intention is karma', identifying mental intent, what one has in mind to make happen, as the principal factor of karmic accumulation and human suffering. *Cetanā*[6] (intention) is the mental factor that urges the mind in a particular direction, towards a specific goal. *Cetanā* obtains its ethical distinctiveness through mental factors known as *mūla*s (roots): 'Monks, there are these three roots of what is unskilful. Which three? Greed is a root of what is unskillful, hatred is a root of what is unskillful, delusion is a root of what is unskillful' (*Mūla Sutta*, An.3.69).

As one's actions result in consequences, one must show 'skilfulness'. A mind that is skilful avoids actions that are likely to cause suffering. The Buddhist terms used in the ethical evaluation of human conduct are *kusala* (skilful, wholesome) and *akusala* (unskilful, unwholesome). Actions which are *akusala* are seen as being rooted in the *akusala mūlas*, the unskilful roots (also known as the Three Poisons), i.e. greed (*lobha*), hatred (*dosa*) and delusion (*moha*), thus resulting in unpleasant karmic results. Those which are *kusala* are seen as being rooted in their opposites, i.e. generosity/non-greed (*alobha*), loving-kindness/non-hatred (*adosa*) and wisdom/non-delusion (*amoha*), thus bringing about positive karmic results.

Analogous to breaches in law resulting in legal consequences, intentionally causing unnecessary suffering has bad karmic consequences, although these are seen as natural results, not punishments. Yet Buddhism takes an even more comprehensive outlook, the most unmistakable difference being that already all thought and speech bear karmic consequences. It thus aims at the stage where all atrocities ultimately take their origin and where suffering caused to others, whether by rhetoric or bodily action, can still be prevented.

Buddhism follows a non-dogmatic approach, empowering each individual, having carefully weighed the roots and karmic consequences of possible actions, to do what is right depending on each situation. There are no commandments, but precepts, principles intended to guide action, providing the means to avoid harm to oneself and others, but also leaving room for transgression under exceptional circumstances. The *pañcaśīla* (Pali: *pañcasīla*), five precepts, are commitments to abstain from killing living beings, stealing, sexual misconduct, lying and intoxication.

Underlying all of the five precepts is *ahiṃsā*, a foundational step on the Dharma path and a practical necessity to liberate oneself from the Three Poisons. While in English language '*ahiṃsā*' is often misleadingly translated as 'non-violence' (and '*hiṃsā*' as 'violence'), its actual meaning is refraining from intentional harm to any living being whether in thought, speech or physical action (Jenkins 2011). The term 'non-harming' captures better the intimate relationship to all living things, where any harmful conduct also results in self-harm. Harbouring harmful intentions fosters the very cognitive states that Buddhism tries to overcome, thereby also directly causing harm to oneself.

A cardinal problem arises when conflating the English word 'violence' with the Buddhist concepts of *hiṃsā/ahiṃsā*, which are fundamentally different from the English-language concepts of violence and the absence thereof.[7] According to the Oxford dictionary (Lexico 2021), 'violence' is defined as 'behaviour involving physical force intended to hurt, damage, or kill someone or something'.[8]

In colloquial use 'violence' is designated very loosely and subjectively, conveying a general sense of moral condemnation of what the observer deems to be unacceptable use of physical force, including towards objects (another foundational difference to *hiṃsā/ahiṃsā*, which instead extends to other living beings, also covering verbal and psychological harm). Some might call a vigorous defence resulting in brutal injury violence in this sense – this depends on the eye of the beholder. When seeing the final result of injury caused, one cannot classify it as *hiṃsā* without understanding the underlying intent, which could have been entirely compassionate. Sometimes strong physical action resulting in injury might be the comparatively less harmful choice.

The difference between violence and *hiṃsā* is more than a nuance and decisively affects the understanding of Buddhist classifications of conflict situations.[9] Many have searched for and ostensibly found justifications for violence in the Buddhist scriptures, but it is important to understand that those are never justifications in the *hiṃsā–ahiṃsā* context or justifications of any conduct where the underlying intention is to cause harm. Trying to justify violence in Buddhist terms is an inherently futile endeavour.

Buddhist teachings are pragmatic at their very core and recognise the complexity of decision-making under difficult circumstances, such as when confronted with situations where one could be compelled to apply physical force. Virtually anybody honestly asking themselves under what circumstances they would use strong physical force that potentially could cause injury to others, even if that was not the intent, could envision a specific set of circumstances where that might occur – for example, when protecting themselves or their loved ones.

Not killing any living being is a precept that one always should follow and yet no one can ever completely adhere to, as every human being causes the destruction of tiny animals during their lifetime. In the Dharmic traditions one finds a realisation that duties can entail causing injury. Even when working the land already many small animals are harmed, but this is not the intention of farmers and occurs in line of their duty.[10] In Buddhism working in agriculture or other duties is not intrinsically considered to stand in contradiction of *ahiṃsā*.[11]

Buddhism considers *ahiṃsā* not as a rule, but as a principle. Rules and principles both are decision-guiding considerations. A principle can be understood as a fundamental belief influencing actions. Principles leave room for interpretation, providing a guiding beacon towards the right direction, internally motivating to act in a way that seems good and right. Stringent rules, while easy to understand, implement and enforce, lack flexibility to cope with unusual situations. For principles instead it is a continuous endeavour to adhere to them, while being fully aware that exceptions can be made, thus giving flexibility to exercise individual judgement. This allows for more nuanced, context-dependent action better reflecting complex ethical situations, such as those prevalent in war.

Buddhism, war and the State

Buddhism is frequently equated to pacifism, 'the belief that war and violence are unjustifiable and that all disputes should be settled by peaceful means'

(Oxford Reference 2021). Pacificism arguably covers a wide spectrum from absolute pacifism (the belief that no reason whatsoever can justify the taking of human life, even for military defence) to conditional and selective pacificism (which accepts that there are certain circumstances where military action could be considered to be the lesser evil). The Buddhist teachings found in the canonical texts certainly do not equate to absolute pacifism, which would not even allow for a country to defend itself by military means if necessary.

The understanding of 'true Buddhism' to be unconditionally pacifist is a modern, Western-inspired interpretation[12] that is challenged not only by its history, but also by scripture. This being said, out of this cultural encounter new directions in Buddhist thought and practice emerged, some aligning themselves more closely with various forms of pacifism. When taken as a general guiding principle, pacifism is not in conflict with Buddhist teachings. Buddhism condones seeking non-harmful solutions to situations of conflict at all times, even expanding the narrow focus on human life to the protection of other forms of life.

In conflict situations, the close proximity of the State and the Sangha sometimes creates the perception that Buddhism is implicitly supporting violence. It is easy for observers who conflate Buddhism with absolute pacifism to interpret voices from the Sangha in support of the military as hypocrisy and a reflection of their human failings. They see malign intent and corruption, for example, arguing that the Sangha is trying to ingratiate itself with the State to receive further patronage.[13]

Trying to reconcile the history of Buddhist participation in wars with an idealised Buddhism standing in opposition to any form of military action, some allege sheer realpolitik to explain why the Buddha in his many discourses to political leaders never counsels to abandon war. Actions taken by Buddhists that they may personally disapprove of, such as calls to defend the nation by military means, are denounced as inauthentic and/or corrupt expressions of Buddhism,[14] thereby venerating their own idealised notions while denigrating Buddhist communities. While the Sangha, like any other group of human beings, is not without human failings, one needs to be mindful when ascribing unwholesome intentions by mere judgement of external acts.

Strong physical force itself is neutral. It is the underlying intention that gives it its ethical quality. One may ask, if *people* are allowed to defend themselves, why should it be called violence when a *society* defends itself? Bhikkhu Bodhi brings this into historical perspective:

> I don't think in any way one could justify, on Buddha's principles, even by stretching them to a great extent, the idea of a just offensive war or war of aggression. There is an arguable case [which] can be made and has been made, and actually has been practiced throughout Buddhist history, that engaging in

> warfare defensively is justifiable and virtually all the Buddhist countries of South, Southeast Asia have engaged in those kinds of wars. (Bhikkhu Bodhi in Wright 2020)

In Buddhist historiography wars characteristically are explained as necessary reactions to others' improper conduct and by emphasising the compassionate intent on the side of righteous rulers. Wars of conquest would indeed be problematic in light of the precept against taking what is not freely given. The wider debate about what constitutes a defensive war is nevertheless more complex. One might imagine scenarios where initiating an attack becomes necessary for better defence and for preventing more suffering to arise. Nonetheless, in Buddhism (as in the other Dharmic traditions) warfare is considered to be a perilous course of action and it is very difficult to predict its consequences (Wu 2019).

Regardless of one's position on the various examples of Buddhist participation in historical wars, religion is only one among many factors in a conflict, often strongly overlapping with ethnic identity. When observers talk about 'Buddhist warfare', more often than not, it is because one of the groups in a conflict identifies themselves as being Buddhist. Even in societies where virtuous beliefs are widely held, one finds a similar range of human failings so evident throughout history. All the major religions contain scriptural interdictions on violence, yet all have followers who commit bad acts claiming religious justifications. Buddhist thinkers time and again have acknowledged that there is a profound difference between merely assenting to a belief and actually acting in accordance with that belief. Being Buddhist does not imply that one's acts are Buddhist or representative of Buddhism. In order to live according to Buddhist principles, one must perennially cultivate oneself through disciplined practice.

As the history of humankind continuously manifests itself in people's greed, hatred and delusion, i.e. the Three Poisons, the occurrence of war, a state of prolonged armed conflict, is an inseparable part of *saṃsāra*, our mundane world, where violence begets violence and one war ends for others to follow. *Saṃsāra* will always be filled with suffering (*duḥkha/dukkha*) – that is the first Noble Truth.

Warfare was also common in the Buddha's time, and war is a recurrent motif throughout the discourses. Kosuta (1997, para. 11) notes that 'if all the military sutta and passages were collected together in one text, they could form a separate volume of the Canon, as together they number over five hundred pages in length'. The sheer number of allegories related to warfare in the Pali Canon, where the military is generally referred to in favourable terms, is indeed striking. The language of combat and war is used myriad times for transmitting important spiritual messages.

One finds many accounts of human warfare, but wars are also fought at other levels, such as in the *Saṃyutta Nikāya* accounts of the *deva-asura* war[15] and the battle against the tempter-deity Māra (literally 'causing death', 'killing'), the personification of death and all forces antagonistic to attaining enlightenment. We also find Lokapāla, Dharma-protecting guardians that appear as generals, each endowed with their own special armour and weapons.

Śāriputra (Pali: Sāriputta), considered the first of the Buddha's two chief disciples, famed for his wisdom and teaching ability, earned the title *dhamma-senāpati* ('General of the Dharma'), just as a king has his army general. The image of the heroic warrior is a recurrent theme when illustrating commendable character traits. The numerous positive similes comparing certain qualities of monks to those of soldiers convey a message that the military was a respected institution in early Buddhism.

In fact, Buddhist teachings evolved and were mastered, disseminated and patronised by many people who in their formative stage were great warriors. The Buddha himself was born as the son of a ruler (and so came to be seen as belonging to the warrior class), was probably trained in the military skills, and in his previous existences as Bodhisattva is said to have held important military roles that did not hinder his path towards nirvana. He thus spoke from personal experience when using the language of warriors and conquest in order to provide Dharma guidance, but also when describing the horrors of war. In the *Mahādukkhakkhandha Sutta* (*The Greater Discourse on the Mass of Suffering*) the Buddha vividly narrates the conditions of war and points to the underlying reason for them to emerge:

> for the sake of sensual pleasures they don their sword and shield, fasten their bow and arrows, and charge wetly plastered bastions, with arrows and spears flying and swords flashing. There they are struck with arrows and spears, splashed with dung, crushed with spiked blocks, and their heads are chopped off, resulting in death and deadly pain. (Mn.13; PTS I.86–87)

The 'Buddhist social contract' is explained in much detail in the *Dīgha Nikāya*. In this concept of society, the responsibilities of citizens and their ruler are neatly intertwined: the ruler is bound to protect his subjects and maintain order in society, which in turn gives the ruler the legitimacy to rule. In the *Aggañña* ('Knowledge of the Highest') *Sutta*, the Buddha explains the emergence of the warrior class (*kṣatriya/khattiya*; 'lord of the fields') as a conscious choice by the people to select the most able among them to act as a protector. 'They originated among these very same beings, like ourselves, no different, and in accordance with Dhamma, not otherwise' (Dn.27; PTS Pali III.93).

The State has a duty to protect its citizens and maintains a monopoly on the legitimate administration of physical harm,[16] except in the case of immediate self-defence. In a Buddhist equivalent to secularism, the State and the Sangha mutually support each other, but have their very specific respective responsibilities, with the Sangha giving its blessings to the State, which in turn offers protection to the Sangha. Concurrently the Sangha is offering moral guidance to society, thereby contributing to the State being held accountable by its citizens.

The *cakkavatti* (Sanskrit: *cakravartin*), who rules according to Dharma wherever his wheels carry him, is presented as an ideal leader, a secular counterpart to the Buddha, whose central role is to maintain order. Two of the *cakkavatti*'s seven *ratana* ('jewels', 'gems') are the two mounts of soldiers and quintessential battle stations of warfare in ancient India: the horse and the elephant.[17] One of the five qualities a king needs to 'abide where he himself has conquered' is 'his strength in the four divisions of his army, loyal and alert to commands' (An.5.134).

In prior births the Buddha himself numerous times was a *cakkavatti*, 'conquering the four ends of the earth, bringing stability to the country, possessing the seven gems' and having 'more than a thousand sons, valiant, vigorous, crushers of enemy-hosts' (An.7.62). For a king's eldest son to become a worthy successor he needs to be fully trained 'in matters of skill that belong to anointed warrior rajahs: elephant, horse, chariot, bow and sword skill' (An.5.135). Yet even a *cakkavatti*'s rule remains fragile and the exhibition of military potential remains warranted (Dn.17, 26; PTS Pali II.172–173, III.63–67). The historical *cakkavatti* exemplar, Ashoka, also did not disband his forces or stop applying them to keep his realm safe. In his edicts he warns the forest tribes of his military potential, retains physical punishment and asks his heirs when seeking further military conquest to employ 'forbearance and light punishment' (Eka.13).

The extreme of a State not having defensive forces to protect its citizens is never presented as a viable option in the scriptures.[18] On the contrary, the failure to fulfil one's duty to protect the citizens would have negative karmic repercussions for rulers. If there are no armed forces, people would live in fear of serious internal strife and invasion. Insecurity contributes to an environment where actions take root in fear, which directly ties to suffering and accruing negative karma, thus impeding one's progress on the path. A reflection of this is found, for example, in the concept of *abhayadāna* ('Gift of Fearlessness'), where the gift is considered to be an assurance of protection to those who require it.[19]

IHL and Buddhist law

IHL comprises a set of rules and underlying principles aimed at reducing suffering in times of armed conflict. Direct sources of IHL include treaties (particularly the Geneva Conventions and their Protocols), general principles of law and customary international law, the latter being a fount to all others. Customary law indeed is a rich reservoir of the religious traditions and moral principles of the world.

The development of customary IHL depends upon State practice (*usus*) undertaken out of a sense of legal obligation (*opinio juris*) – understandings of which are influenced by different traditions, religious norms and principles. By engaging in comprehensive study of the vast body of learning on how different cultures understand armed conflict, including from Buddhist traditions and communities around the world, this repository of traditions and principles is increasingly being applied to gradually universalise IHL and to overcome perceptions of it being a Western-imposed system, thereby bolstering awareness and adherence.

Legal systems function well in an environment where people fear consequences, but in armed conflict that frequently is not the case. However, IHL also functions as a moral system, the term 'humanitarian' revealing this nature. To some extent, the reluctance of States to legislate and restrict conduct in armed conflict stems from the extraordinary nature of war and the existential threat that it poses. Given the extreme environment of war and the bendiness of some of the law's provisions, in order for IHL to function effectively (i.e. to actually reduce the suffering caused by armed conflict), it is of utmost importance to further strengthen its underlying ethical dimensions. By seeking common ground and engaging with the world's cultural and religious traditions, such as Buddhism, the law's ethical foundations can be solidified so that combatants make choices that lead to better humanitarian outcomes – even absent any potential legal consequences compelling them to do so.

Of particular reference value here is the *Vinaya* ('Discipline'), the body of rules governing the lives of monks and nuns. Both 'Buddhist law', such as in the *Vinaya*, and IHL are manmade constructs that can be adapted and improved upon depending on circumstances. The Buddha started this process, and different *Vinaya* traditions have continued it to varying extents. Upon Mahākaccāna's[20] request, the Buddha laid down special rules for the convenience of the monks of Avantidakkhināpatha (Central India) and other border countries (Vin.I.197–198) – for instance, allowing monks to wear clothing suitable to the different cultural and climatic conditions. While the *Vinaya* aims at monastics, it also provides a guide towards values held beyond the monastic context. Laypeople are not expected to follow the monastic rules, but their underlying principles are highly relevant to them. Laypeople and monastics follow the same path towards the one final goal, only at different speeds.[21]

Buddhism nowhere teaches that one is not allowed to protect oneself from physical harm. Even Buddhist monks are allowed to carry a stick to fend off attacks, but not with unwholesome intent.[22] *Vinaya* rule *Pācittiya* 74

(Thanissaro Bhikkhu 1995) says that if a monk engages in a violent act on another monk out of anger, it is a *pācittiya* offence (a minor violation requiring atonement). If this act occurred towards any other living being, it is considered a *dukkaṭa* (wrong doing), the lightest grade of offence for having engaged in an unskilful action that requires confession to another monk.

However, a monk who 'trapped in a difficult situation, gives a blow "desiring freedom"' (Thanissaro Bhikkhu 1995, on *Pācittiya* 74) does not engage in any offence. This blow is understood to include hitting out with one's own body (fist, elbow, kicking, etc.), with something attached to the body (stick, knife, etc.) or with something that can be 'thrown' (rock, shooting an arrow, etc.). If one harms another out of self-defence, it is a non-offence, even if anger arises in one's mind. If one's attacker dies, it is not considered to be a breach of the first precept if there was no intention to kill. As these rules are applicable to monastics, at the very minimum laymen are allowed to protect themselves, too, as long as they do not act unskilfully (*akusala*).

Monastic regulations treat intentionally bringing about the death of a human being, whether by killing the person, arranging for a person to be killed, inciting the person to die, or describing the advantages of death, as one of the four *pārājika* ('defeat') offences, which result in immediate expulsion from the Sangha for life; killing other sentient beings is a lesser offence. A monk's action leading to the demise of a human being only constitutes a *pārājika* offence if the monk intended his action to result in death. In all cases intention is a necessity for constituting the offence. This corresponds with IHL and the modern criminal legal system, where intent (*mens rea*), is one of two elements that must be proven in order to convict (the other being the actual act, *actus reus*). The taking of life is not considered murder when, for example, the accused acted out of self-defence, therefore negating the required intent because the killing was not done out of the desire to take the victim's life.

Although motive and intent are often treated as distinct concepts in law, no logical separation can be discerned between intentions and more ultimate intentions, i.e. motivations.[23] In legal practice there always has been an overlap, and also the legal sciences increasingly question this strict dichotomy, which emerged as a rhetorical construct in nineteenth-century criminal law in an effort to introduce scientific rather than moral norms, moving away from subjective desiderative standards towards standards of objective reasonableness (Binder 2002). The moral worth of underlying motives is difficult to codify as it has to be assessed case by case, thus undermining the predictability of laws and risking to punish the accused for their supposed character rather than their acts.

As in IHL and criminal law, the *Vinaya* does not deem the wider background motives to be central to judging culpability. What outside observers ascribe to motive is subject to conjecture as it demands a thorough understanding of and insight into others' mental processes. Even the culprits themselves might very well not know, given the difficulty of successfully monitoring one's mental factors all the time. By focusing on that part of the culpability that can be shown by standards of reasonableness, i.e. the actual prohibited conduct plus the willingness to engage in it, regardless of presumed wider motivations, arbitrary punishment can be minimised. Man-made laws judged by fallible humans have to take utmost care in their assessment of culpability. This is very different from karmic law, which unfailingly provides justice for everybody, resonating well in a world where the perpetrators of crimes often face no legal consequences, including for violations of IHL.

The Sangha and the military have their own individual duties in society. From the perspective of the Sangha, the State is accepted as an institution, including its military powers. It is a symbiotic relationship where the secular and spiritual wheels of Dharma mutually benefit from each other's protection: monks benefit from the physical protection of the military, while the military benefits from the spiritual protection offered by the Sangha. Crucially, the Sangha also provides psychological support to combatants who are inescapably concerned about the karmic consequences of their actions. Naturally the two spheres frequently interact and at times even intersect, when soldiers turn monks and vice versa.

The *Vinaya* plays a central role in regulating monk–army relations. According to the *Bhikkhunī Pāṭimokkha* (rules 129–131) and *Pācittiya* (48–50), monks and nuns alike are allowed to see an army on active duty if they have a suitable reason. They may even stay with an army for two or three nights, but not see them in combat, roll calls or parades, or otherwise they engage in a *dukkaṭa*. When the border provinces of Magadha were in turmoil, king Seniya Bimbisāra solicited the Buddha to stop soldiers from escaping their duty by joining the Sangha. The Buddha duly decreed that the ordination of anybody currently serving in the army or other royal services (for instance, tax collectors) results in a *dukkaṭa* (*Mahāvagga* 40, Vin.I.74). By preventing soldiers from becoming monks, the Buddha intrinsically recognised their duty as well as the king's duty to protect the realm.

Wu (2019) explores the *Vinaya* accounts of Ajātaśatru's war with the Vṛjis. There, Buddhist jurists recount cases of war and conflict-related sexual violence, which shows that those were of real-life concern to them. In several *Vinaya* traditions nuns were prohibited to visit places affected by armed conflict due to prior instances of sexual abuse endured by nuns when wandering into battle zones. We also learn from these accounts about the complex and ever-changing nature of wars, which makes it extremely hard to predict their outcome. Notwithstanding, all *Vinaya*s agree that monks are allowed to make predictions on the outcome of a war.

Means of protection

For a State to be able to protect its citizens it must take preparations and offer means of protection, such as in the form of arms and fortifications. In one of the most popular Buddhist works, the *Milinda Pañha* (*Questions of Milinda*), one finds a reflection of this need to maintain an army to ward off ever-present danger:[24]

> 'Have rival kings ever risen up to oppose you, O king?'
> 'Yes they have.'
> 'Was it only then that you made preparations for battle?'
> 'Not at all. All that had been done beforehand in order to ward off future danger.' (Mp. PTS I.81)

Various scriptural foundations for military action to protect against harm are presented by Sangharaja Vajirañāṇa, the Supreme Patriarch of the Kingdom of Siam and his generation's leading intellectual, in his 'The Buddhist Attitude Towards National Defense and Administration', published in 1916. There he also illustrates the need to proactively prepare:

> The defence against external foes is one of the policies of governance, and is one that cannot be neglected. War generally occurs suddenly, and victory cannot be won solely by having a large number of men, arms, and munitions; it must also depend upon Presence of Mind (Sati), Knowledge (Paññā), Bravery, Experience, Readiness in Commands, and good fighting positions, and so forth, in order to make victory certain. Therefore, war must be prepared for, even in time of peace, otherwise one would not be in time and one would be in a disadvantageous position towards one's foe. (Vajiranana 1916, 19)

Moreover, in the *Nagarūpama Sutta* (Simile of the Frontier Fortress, An.7.67) the Buddha lists seven defences that make a frontier fortress unassailable: a deep and unshakeable foundation, an encircling moat wide and deep, an encircling road wide and high, ramparts thick, high and covered by plaster, a wise and competent gatekeeper, a great armoury of weapons (both missiles, shot as in arrows or hurled as in spears, and handheld, such as swords) and many different types of troops. Listed next to cavalry, chariots and the elephant corps, we learn here about the complex composition of foot soldiers, which included archers, standard-bearers, battle marshals organising the battle arrays, the supply corps, experienced noble princes, frontline commandos, veteran heroes and shield-bearing soldiers.

Frontier forts occupied a central position in warfare. They acted as a crucial deterrence encouraging peaceful existence, provided shelter to the armed forces and arrested the onslaught of invaders. Capture of these strategic strongholds was necessary for decisive victory and this could be achieved by elephants breaking open their gates. One such assault is recorded in the *Saṃgāmāvacara Jātaka*, where the Buddha in one of his prior Bodhisattva rebirths was the mahout of the king's elephant. When it turned in fear during the attack on Benares, the Bodhisattva successfully restored the elephant's confidence and encouraged it:

> O Elephant, a hero you, whose home is in the battlefield:
> There stands the gate before you now: why do you turn and yield?
> Make haste! break through the iron bar, and beat the pillars down!
> Crash through the gates, made fast for war, and enter in the town! (Jat.182)

In ancient India elephants were a unique combination of a weapon (often characterised as early versions of battle tanks), the foundation of an army division, and a vital means of protection, yet also much-cherished fellow living beings renowned for their intelligence and majesty. The use of elephants in war was a military innovation that emerged in the centuries preceding the Buddha and that entirely changed the equilibrium in battles.[25] Elephants quickly became the dominant force in Indian warfare and continued so until well after the advent of firearms (Trautmann 2015, 108–119).

In early Vedic (c. 1500–1000 BCE) symbolism the elephant was only seen on the margins, but this rapidly changed in congruence with their taming for use in warfare (Trautmann 2015, 95–102). The army (*bala*) itself came to be conceived as a four-legged (*caturaṅga*) animal, the *caturaṅga-bala*, a fourfold army of foot soldiers, charioteers, cavalry and the elephant corps. The most powerful individual weapon in battle was the bow. Elephants provided an elevated platform for archers[26] and offered the king as well as other military commanders a better vantage point from which to steer their forces. War elephants were also used for trampling and intimidation, breaching of battle formations, inspiring awe and causing fear among enemy troops as well as their horses and, as we have seen in the *Nagarūpama Sutta*, for battering down enemy fortifications.[27]

Throughout the Pali Canon elephants are much revered and mentioned more often than any other animal. Among many other characteristics, we learn in detail about their behaviour and different classifications, how they are tracked in the jungle and captured for training, how they are tamed and trained for combat by endurance exercises as well as exposure to mock attacks with spears, and even their weak spots in battle (Dhammika 2015). The Buddha and monks are often compared with elephants, as for example in the *Sotar Sutta*, where the qualities of a worthy monk are matched to the qualities of a king's war elephant:

> Endowed with five qualities, a king's elephant is worthy of a king, is a king's asset, counts as a very limb of his king. Which five? There is the case where a king's elephant is a listener, a destroyer, a protector, an endurer, and a goer.
>
> And how is a king's elephant a listener? There is the case where, whenever the tamer of tameable elephants gives him a task, then – regardless of whether he has or hasn't done it before – he pays attention, applies his whole mind, and lends ear.

> ... a destroyer? There is the case where a king's elephant, having gone into battle, destroys an elephant together with its rider, destroys a horse together with its rider, destroys a chariot together with its driver, destroys a foot soldier.
>
> ... a protector? There is the case where a king's elephant, having gone into battle, protects his forequarters, protects his hindquarters, protects his forefeet, protects his hindfeet, protects his head, protects his ears, protects his tusks, protects his trunk, protects his tail, protects his rider.
>
> ... an endurer? There is the case where a king's elephant, having gone into battle, endures blows from spears, swords, arrows, and axes; he endures the resounding din of drums, cymbals, conchs, and tom-toms.
>
> ... a goer? There is the case where – in whichever direction the tamer of tameable elephants sends him, regardless of whether he has or hasn't gone there before – a king's elephant goes there right away. (An.5.140)

Wild elephants are seen as symbols of the uncontrolled mind, the most dangerous of weapons. They are contrasted to the king's elephant whose mind is tamed and disciplined, and can be directed to destroy any obstacle. As with the human mind, the destructive force of elephants demands restraint (Dhp.326).

The association of elephants with nobility and divinity, shared across the Dharmic traditions, emerged in congruence with their domestication for use in battle. War elephants are intimately linked to kingship and the display of power, impressive emblems of military might, to be displayed in ceremonies and royal processions (not unlike the display of war assets in modern military parades). The elephant was indeed one of the seven jewels of kingship.

In several *Jātaka*s the Bodhisattva takes birth as an elephant, such as a white Chaddanta ('having six tusks') king (Jat.514). The white elephant also appears in the form of Airāvata (Pali: Erāvana), the mount of Indra,[28] king of the gods and their leader in war (Snp.379). In the canonical texts Indra is mostly referred to as Śakra (Pali: Sakka; 'mighty'), the ruler over Trāyastriṃśa (Pali: Tāvatiṃsa; 'belonging to the thirty-three gods'), a highly sought rebirth in *saṃsāra*, which one can only reach as consequence of accumulating very good karma. The precious rarity of white elephants, symbols of purity, is also present in the Buddha's birth story, where his mother Māyādevī dreams of him entering her side in the form of a white elephant.[29]

Soldiering and 'right livelihood'

Widely held assumptions that Buddhism demands absolute pacifism have made Buddhists vulnerable to unfounded criticism for neglecting legal and pragmatic concerns[30] in a global environment where armed conflict is prevalent. Due to these same assumptions, Buddhist soldiers also often find themselves the object of misunderstanding in their communities, which puts them under additional stress. In fact, there are Buddhists serving in militaries across the world and, just like other countries, Buddhist nations maintain armed forces to protect their citizens and national interests. The majority of soldiers in the militaries of Bhutan, Cambodia, Laos, Myanmar, Sri Lanka and Thailand are Buddhists, for example.

Whether soldiers can be good Buddhists is a controversial topic in some circles. In Buddhism the thought of taking somebody's life is so reprehensible that a small subsection of (often Western) Buddhists would answer that one should not serve in the armed forces. Much of where one stands in this debate depends on one's own perceptions of the ethical nature of militaries. It is easy to comprehend that for those who see the military as inherently malevolent, joining the service becomes morally unacceptable.

Being a member of the military or any other armed group is clearly not without difficult ethical conundrums for a Buddhist. While the role of a soldier involves many kinds of tasks, it can involve taking the lives of people or supporting others who do. Prima facie, one could therefore argue that Buddhism and the military are strange bedfellows, and some may find it difficult to conceive of serving in the military whilst adhering to the ethos, values and standards of Buddhism.

Nonetheless, soldiers also play a central role in helping to prevent suffering from arising – they can be a force for wholesome objectives. The military is not only meant for conducting warfare; it acts as a crucial deterrent and supports local communities in many other capacities, such as rescue operations, emergency relief and reconstruction. Serving members in the military forces generally profess their clear intention to serve society, keep their communities safe, support law and order, maintain peace and other worthy endeavours. Some, misunderstanding the purpose of militaries, might perceive soldiering to be a wrong livelihood and yet they benefit from the safety this profession provides to them. Abolishing the military would result in a lack of safety, implicitly allowing more suffering to arise.

Military careers in the light of Buddhist ethics were discussed in some detail during the first Armed Forces Buddhist Community Conference[31] in the UK. Ajahn Brahmavaṃso,[32] arguing that Buddhist philosophy should not be reduced to pacifism, explained that one needs to understand the pragmatics of a situation. When it comes to moral decision-making in one's career, what is most important is what one's intentions are, rather than what the career is itself. It is important to bear in mind that working in other professions also comes with discrete ethical conundrums that one needs to carefully navigate. According to the highly influential Thai ascetic-philosopher Buddhadāsa Bhikkhu, 'No matter what kind of activity we carry out – be it politics, economics, or, indeed, even war – if done morally will maintain the natural, harmonious balance of all things, and will be consistent with the original plan of nature' (Buddhadāsa Bhikkhu 1986, 119–120).

In the Pali Canon, the life, service or practice of soldiers is not judged more harshly than any other mundane profession. Countering notions of warfare being the unique domain of the *kṣatriya*, in the *Issatta* ('Archery') *Sutta* the Buddha talks about military recruitment being based on merit of fighting skill rather than social stratification:

> 'Great king, you have a battle to be fought, then warrior youths not trained and without experience in archery, who would be frightened and would run away from the battlefield, come. Would you recruit them, would they serve the purpose?'
>
> 'Venerable sir, I will not recruit them and they would not serve my purpose.' ...
>
> 'Then Brahmin youths, ... householder youths, ... outcaste youths, trained and experienced in archery, who would not be frightened and would not run away from the battlefield, come. Would you recruit them, would they serve the purpose?'
>
> 'Venerable sir, I will recruit them, they would serve my purpose.' ...
>
> Then the Blessed One further said, 'Any youth skilled in archery, powerful and energetic, would be employed by a king going to war – unskilled people are not employed just because of their high caste.' (Sn.3.24)

In the *Dīghajāṇu Sutta* (An.8.54), a key text for understanding Buddhist lay ethics, when listing conditions for people to reach wealth and happiness in this life, the Buddha explicitly included archery (the most emblematic of military services) and service under the king (which also included tax collectors, for example) among the suggested careers, and advocated for developing skilfulness in these professions.

Providing archers with bows and arrows consequently required the manufacture of weapons, which brings us to another relevant topic, the condemnation of the trade in weapons, included as the fifth factor in the Noble Eightfold Path that deals with 'right livelihood' (*sammā ājīva*). The *Vaṇijjā* ('trade', 'trading', 'trading as a means of livelihood') *Sutta* states 'a lay follower should not engage in five types of trading activities. Which five? Trading of weapons, human beings, meat, intoxicants and poison' (An.5.177).[33] It is not a condemnation of weapons or their manufacture, but arguably rather of the distribution of tools used for taking life.[34] Prohibiting the development and manufacturing of weapons would have stood in direct conflict with a ruler's duty to ensure the safety of the people and to maintain protective forces.[35]

The manufacture of weapons, such as swords, lances, knives, arrowheads and spearheads, to provide soldiers with the tools and implements of warfare, was mainly conducted by blacksmiths (*kammāra*). The *kammāra* were tightly organised into their own guild and their guild chiefs were closely coordinating their affairs with the royal court. The Buddha himself is said to have been a *kammāra* in one of his previous rebirths as a Bodhisattva (*Sūci Jātaka*,

Jat.387), where he pursues the daughter of another blacksmith who is characterised as 'dear to the king' (*rājavallabha*). In the *Setaketu Jātaka* (Jat.377) the Bodhisattva, in the form of the king's priest, arms laymen with shields and weapons and appoints them to the king's service.

From the *Dhammapada* Commentary (Dhp-a.II.24–28) we learn that a hunter's wife is not held karmically responsible for preparing his weapons as she is only fulfiling her husband's request. This is part of the commentary on 'Just as the hand that has no wound is not affected by poison, so also, there are no evil outcomes for those who do no evil' (Dhp.124), showing that disregarding external appearances, one needs to understand the underlying duties and state of mind for being able to gauge intentions.

The question of 'right livelihood' is also of direct relevance to the many soldiers who are involved in the development and manufacturing of weapons worldwide. In one of his Dharma discussions Master Chin Kung (Jing Kong 淨空), an eminent master of the Pure Land school, directly addresses this intersection:

> This is a question from a layman in China. He says, there is a layman who sincerely studies Buddhism. However, he is a soldier and engaged in combat plans and weapons manufacturing every day. He is puzzled by this issue, may Master mercifully expound.
>
> There is no fault to be engaged in this vocation. Why? Your vocation, your job is to protect the nation, protect life and property of people. This is called the 'Gift of Fearlessness'. There is no fault. In this world, every nation must have soldiers for defence. Singapore, though it is a small country, has its own military force. . . .
>
> To explain from a different perspective, we can never wage war and invade others without a reason. This is right. So for a defensive war, a war of resistance . . . , Buddha and Bodhisattvas all agree that this is not wrong. Then the taking of life takes place under special circumstances. This means lifting the precepts [kai jie 开戒], not breaking the precepts [po jie 破戒]. You as a soldier, having taken Bodhisattva Precept or Five Precepts, if you are protecting your nation, you confront the enemy, do you kill or not kill them? At this moment do you think 'Oh, I have taken the precept of not taking life, if I kill them I will break my precept'? Alright. When the enemy breaks through, then in our city, our country, how many people will die because of your failed responsibility to protect? Then you will have committed a most serious sin. So you must do your duty even though sacrificing yourself. Your job is to defend against the enemy. The teachings of the Buddha are reasonable and logical. Your vocation is to protect nation and territory. This is the duty you have to fulfil. Without doubt, you are not sinful at all. (Chin 2017)

Accordingly, under close watch of the government Buddhists can be soldiers or be involved with weapon manufacturing. If it is their duty, they will not be regarded as karmically liable as long as they are skilful, meaning their intentions are not rooted in the Three Poisons. This, however, is by no means a blanket endorsement of weapons. From both a Buddhist and an IHL perspective, the unnecessary, indiscriminate and prolonged suffering caused by some forms of arms, such as biological, chemical and nuclear weapons, is immensely problematic.[36]

IHL's principle of humanity forbids the infliction of all suffering unnecessary for achieving one's side's legitimate purpose of a conflict and it requires that those who have fallen into enemy hands are to be treated humanely at all times (Melzer 2019). Moreover, the famed 'Martens Clause', which appears in numerous IHL treaties, states:

> In cases not covered by this Protocol or by other international agreements, civilians and combatants remain under the protection and authority of the principles of international law derived from established custom, from the principles of humanity and from the dictates of public conscience.[37]

Therefore, even during situations of armed conflict which are not covered by more specific laws, the principles of humanity and the dictates of public conscience should continue to guide belligerents' behaviour and provide a minimum level of protection for both civilians and combatants against the ravages of war.

Buddhist principles apply evenly at all times regardless of whether there is war or not, and certainly also contradict views that 'in war everything that is not legally forbidden is permitted'. Instead, everything is geared towards reducing suffering by practising *ahiṃsā*.[38] While both IHL and Buddhism acknowledge the realities of war and share their concerns about the suffering caused by weapons, Buddhism takes aim at the pinnacle of disarmament, which is the disarmament of the mind.

Karmic implications of soldiering

For Buddhist military practitioners the most common and important discussions are those related to ethical issues soldiers face before, during and after combat, particularly pertaining the karmic consequences of military service and the morality of taking life.[39] A unique perspective here is provided by Buddhist military chaplains, who work at the very intersection of Buddhism and the military, and fulfil important roles in imparting military ethics. Formal and informal Buddhist military chaplaincies exist in several Asian countries, including India, Indonesia, Myanmar and Thailand. In recent years Western militaries also started to enrol Buddhist chaplains. An interesting example from the field is provided to us here by Captain Thomas Dyer, the first Buddhist chaplain in the US Army, deployed to Iraq in 2009:

> During a battle in Iraq, an American Buddhist soldier fired at an armed insurgent crouching on the balcony of a house. The shots killed not only the insurgent, but went through to the house, killing the insurgent's pregnant wife and six-year-old son. The soldier went to Thomas Dyer for help. Dyer recalls, 'The soldier

recounted a sutra from the Saṃyutta Nikāya. In short, the sutra says that if a warrior kills someone while exerting himself in battle, he will be reborn in hell. As a Buddhist chaplain, how could I help this Buddhist soldier? What could I say?' Dyer told the soldier 'although bad things happen in combat, this world cannot sustain itself without protecting forces. We talked about the good military has done ... then I affirmed him as a soldier, reminding him that his service is valuable and needed and that he ... did the right action at the right time. As a Buddhist soldier, if his motives are good, his karma is good.' (Bosco 2014, 837)

Often referenced (and also misrepresented as in the quote above), the *Gāmaṇi-saṃyutta* contains accounts of the Buddha's sermons to various *Gāmaṇi* (village headmen, community leaders) regarding the karmic implications of the professions that their communities engage in. In three similar discourses there, the *Yodhājīva Sutta* (Sn.42.3), the *Hatthāroha Sutta* (Sn.42.4), and the *Assāroha Sutta* (Sn.42.5), the Buddha talks to the headmen of the *yodhājīva* (literally 'one making a living through fighting', thus referring to professionalised warriors), elephant mahouts and cavalrymen. As the *yodhājīva* community is contrasted to mahouts and cavalrymen, who bound by their profession were staying in settlements close to their animals (Singh 1989), *yodhājīva* appears to be a broad term potentially encompassing the foot soldiers in the king's army.[40]

If he, as a [*yodhājīva*], strives and exerts himself in battle; if his mind is already inferior, depraved, and misdirected [with the thought] 'Let these sentient beings be killed, bound, annihilated, perished, or never exist'; and then if others kill him and finish [him] off [while he is] striving and exerting himself [in battle], then, after death with the break-up of the body he is reborn in the hell named Sarājita.' (Sugiki 2020, 8, n. 28)

Some understand this to imply that all soldiers who die in battle end up in battle-hell (Sarājita),[41] basing this on their assumption that the intention of soldiers in battle necessarily is to kill and annihilate. Rather, what all three discourses state is that it is those soldiers who die in a misdirected mind having base thoughts intending to kill and annihilate, that do – it is evil intention that determines the unfavourable rebirth.

The three Suttas are preceded by the *Tālapuṭa Sutta* (Sn.42.2), where in analogy when talking to the headman of a community of performers, Tālapuṭa, rather than making a blanket statement that all people in his community will take rebirth in the laughter hell, the Buddha says it is those performers who are intoxicated with greed, hatred and delusion, who are heedless and who make others heedless, who will do so. Once again, it is the state of mind and intentions that are central – Tālapuṭa, even though having been their leader and thus karmically implicated in their performances, became an *arhat* (Thag.19.1).

In the *Mahā Kammavibhanga Sutta*[42] (*The Great Exposition of Kamma*), the Buddha expounds that somebody who kills a living being does not necessarily in their next life take rebirth in a hell realm and can even take rebirth in a heaven realm instead. This is explained by the complexity of the human mind and accumulating many different kinds of karma in lifetimes. Also, one's last state of mind at the time of death (*maraṇa-citta*) can have great impact on one's rebirth.

These discourses show that professions do not define us; rather, we can define how we go about our work. Buddhist combatants need to reflect carefully on what their mental state is when fighting in war and be aware that if their intention is to kill and destroy, then this invariably involves bad states of mind that lead to adverse karmic effects.

Buddhist scriptures also talk about the obligation of the State towards safeguarding and respecting its troops. In the *Cakkavatti-sīhanāda Sutta* kings are advised to 'establish guard, ward and protection according to Dhamma for your own household, your troops in the Army, . . . ' (Dn.26; PTS Pali III.61). In the *Saṃvara Jātaka* the king is praised for paying all divisions of the armed forces their appropriate wages[43] and the *Sāma Jātaka* lists among the ten duties for kings to be able to reach heavens their duty towards their own soldiers.[44]

A recognition of the duty towards one's own troops is also found in IHL. War crimes occur when unnecessary suffering is inflicted. Following law and logic, it can be argued that this includes crimes committed against one's own forces, as belonging to the same side should not be a legitimate reason to deny victims protection under IHL.[45] While IHL only comments on crimes committed against one's own forces in certain circumstances, related bodies of law such as military law and human rights law also reflect this duty to ensure the welfare of one's soldiers.

According to common interpretations of Buddhism's moral code, the laws of a country need to be respected. If the law requires one to be conscripted to the army without any possibility to object and one is fundamentally opposed to joining any war, one can try to influence the security landscape or the legal environment – one can also take the vows and join the Sangha. During a conference on the topic of 'Reducing Suffering During Armed Conflict: The Interface Between Buddhism and IHL'[46] held in Sri Lanka in 2019, a former army general highlighted the need to pay more attention to the decision-making politicians:

> People fail to make a distinction between the hand that strikes and the head that takes the decision. It is the duty of soldiers to fight. Everybody is always talking about the soldier. You have to think about the policymakers. . . . It is the failures of some that ultimately necessitate the bravery of others. The soldiers' intention is to save people. (ICRC 2019)

Soldiers are duty-bound to serve the State. They need to make choices about how to manage their karma according to their duties and circumstances in order to minimise suffering as far as possible. As under IHL, this duty does not entail blindly following orders, though. From a Buddhist perspective, when one person orders another person to act, both the orderer and the ordered are responsible for resulting actions.[47] The orderer is not free of responsibility solely because of not having done the final act, and the ordered is not free of responsibility because they were 'only obeying orders'. While the orderer has the greater responsibility, the ordered has a responsibility to not obey immoral orders and to speak up.[48] This well aligns with IHL's emphasis on the individual soldier's responsibility to disobey illegal orders – orders to kill civilians, for example (Henckaerts and Doswald-Beck 2005, 563, Rule 154). This also extends to commanders being held responsible if they are aware of war crimes being committed by their subordinates and do not attempt to prevent them, or, after the fact, do not punish the persons responsible (Henckaerts and Doswald-Beck 2005, 558, Rule 153).

The *Rājaparikathā-ratnamālā (The Precious Garland of Advice for the King)* attributed to Nāgārjuna (second/third century CE), considered among the most important Buddhist philosophers, offers advice on what constitutes good government, including: 'Appoint these as leaders of the armed forces who are magnanimous, free of attachment, brave, gentle, steadfast, ever-heedful and follow the Dharma' (Rpr.3.24).

Relevant in this context are the cases of the Generals Ajita ('Invincible') and Sīha ('Lion') of the Licchavi clan, both followers of the Buddha. As the commanders behind lethal conflict that frequently occurred in their time in service[49] they hold high karmic responsibility, yet still had a chance to reach heaven[50] and even achieve full awakening. General Ajita immediately after his death was reborn in the company of the 'thirty-three gods' (Dn.24; PTS Pali III.14–15). From the *Aṅguttara Nikāya* we learn that the Buddha, instead of advising General Sīha to leave the army, asked him to properly discharge his duties. Sīha achieved becoming a *sotāpanna* (An.8.12), which literally means 'one who entered (*āpanna*) the stream (*sota*)', using the metaphor of the Noble Eightfold Path being a stream leading to the vast ocean of nirvana (Sn.55.5). For *sotāpanna* enlightenment becomes inevitable within at most seven rebirths and, if diligent, they may fully awaken within their present life.

The influential *Abhidharmakośa-bhāṣya* (*Commentary on the Treasury of Abhidharma*), an auto-commentary to the *Abhidharmakośa-kārikā* (*Verses on the Treasury of Abhidharma*), authored by the Gandhāran monk Vasubandhu around the fifth century CE, does not karmically condemn the military profession either. When one joins any group that is united in its intention to kill, whether it is a group of hunters, intent on killing an animal, or a fighting force whose intention is to annihilate human life, even if only one amongst them actually kills, all of them are equally karmically responsible, as they were united in their intention to kill. Even when forced to join such a group, one is karmically responsible unless one rejects the group's murderous intention by vowing not to take life, even in protection of one's own.[51] It is again intention that is the defining element. The interpretation that anybody joining a military force will be held equally karmically responsible for any death that occurs in the military's line of duty hinges on the misconception of militaries being killing machines united by an intention to kill. When professional soldiers are on assignment, their intention will generally be more wholesome.

The following is a thoughtful set of reflections by a Buddhist Lt. Colonel in the British Army:

> I think that there is a serious military side which we simply cannot ignore. It is a difficult one. What we cannot have in the military is a situation where our soldiers/officers hesitate on the battlefield. ... I am not suggesting that we blindly follow orders if those orders are illegal, but then all soldiers are taught this in any case. If an order is illegal then it is a different thing. So, in my opinion, this is why I personally frequently contemplate my position:
>
> Do I trust that my Government are correctly motivated in their considerations over the use of their Armed Forces? Does our Army still function in as humanitarian manner as possible? Do I think that we are still acting as a force for good in what we are doing? If I can truthfully answer 'yes' to all these then I am content that I can remain in this profession, but it is a personal decision. It is my karma. If I have doubts over any of these questions then I would have to leave.
>
> But one thing is for sure: if I have remained in the Army and the time comes for me to carry out or give an order that involved taking life, then I must do so, but in full mindfulness about that decision, and with full cognisance as to the karmic consequences. But I must not hesitate. The decision about my profession must be made before I am in that situation. On the battlefield is not the time to make such considerations.
>
> But at the same time, my religious beliefs will make me conscious of others suffering. I will do all I can to reduce suffering. I will show kindness and compassion whenever I can. I will always try to be a force for good. (cited in Kariyakarawana and Gilbert 2011, 7)

Conduct in war

Buddhist teachings provide rich source material relevant to conduct in war. Nonetheless, already from a pragmatic standpoint it would not have made sense for the Buddha to give advice concerning when and how to conduct war. What conceivably can be permitted in a particular set of circumstances cannot be generalised and if the Buddha had laid out clear rules under what preconditions one can go to war, this could have incited people to engage in warfare. Giving specific guidance on how to conduct war would have distracted from the ultimate objective to avoid war altogether. What he advocated for instead was a different kind of 'war', that against the evil roots in oneself.

The teachings focus on wider ethical principles, but not without offering guidance also directly applicable to restrain the conduct of hostilities, for instance when condemning siege warfare[52] and prohibiting attacks against the weaponless. From the *Vasala Sutta* we learn that the Buddha said 'Whosoever destroys or lays siege to villages and towns, ... let one know him as an outcast' (Snp.118). The *Dhammapada* emphasises that 'All tremble at the rod, all are fearful of death. Drawing the parallel to yourself, neither kill nor get others to kill' (Dhp.129), which is a version of the Golden Rule, an ethic of reciprocity to treat others as one wants to be treated, which naturally flows from *ahiṃsā*, as nobody would want others to act in ill-intent towards them. It also lists severe karmic results for 'those who do harm with weapons to those who are unarmed and harmless' (Dhp.137–140).

As a commander in conflict, the aim should not be to cause harm, but to quickly end the hostilities, and if this can be achieved with minimum suffering caused, it is beneficial for all parties. This is reflected in the *Milinda Pañha*:

> Just, Nâgasena, as the strong man who, when he enters into a terrible battle, is able the most quickly to get hold of his enemies' heads under his armpit, and dragging them along to bring them prisoners to his lord, that is the champion who is regarded, in the world, as the ablest hero – just as that surgeon who is able the most quickly to extract the dart, and allay the disease, is considered the most clever. (Mp. PTS 293)

Skilfulness in battle means to quickly get over the disease without causing superfluous harm.[53]

In the worst-case scenario of being burdened with the duty to take others' lives under someone else's command, the soldier's intention cannot merely be determined by seeing an act and its outcome. An observation of two people engaging in a fight with weapons cannot gauge their underlying intentions. In one of the major Mahāyāna sutras, the *Mahāyāna Mahāparinirvāṇa Sūtra*, the Buddha elaborates:

> Furthermore, good man, it is like two people fighting with a sword or lance. Suppose one using a blade to defend himself wounds the other, causing him to bleed and death results. But if he had no intention to kill, the karmic consequences will be light, not heavy. For one who comes to the Buddha with no intention of killing, even if that person were to cause the Buddha to bleed, the karmic effect would also be light, not heavy. (Mm.9.6)

The renowned Sri Lankan Buddhist monk and scholar Venerable K. Sri Dhammananda relates this to the wider military:

> Buddhists should not be the aggressors even in protecting their religion or anything else. They must try their best to avoid any kind of violent act. Sometimes they may be forced to go to war by others who do not respect the concept of the brotherhood of humans as taught by the Buddha. They may be called upon to defend their country from external aggression, and as long as they have not renounced the worldly life, they are duty-bound to join in the struggle for peace and freedom. Under these circumstances, they cannot be blamed for becoming soldiers or being involved in defence. ...
>
> It is natural and every living being struggles and attacks others for self-protection but the karmic effect of the aggression depends on their mental attitude. During the struggle to protect himself, if a man happens to kill his opponent although he had no intention to kill, then he does not create bad karma resulting from that death. On the other hand, if he kills another person under any circumstances with the intention to kill, then he is not free from the karmic reaction; he has to face the consequences. (Dhammananda 2002, 383–390)

The ethics of the use of lethal force is highly complex. In the Mahāyāna tradition one finds the concept of *upāya-kauśalya* ('skilful in means') being applied to situations involving the intentional use of lethal force. *Upāya-kauśalya* expresses the notion of using expedient methods that fit different people and situations in order to minimise suffering and ideally prevent bad karma.

One of the most elaborate discourses related to warfare is found in the (early Mahāyāna) *Ārya-Satyakaparivarta* (*Noble Discourse of the Truth-teller*), which teaches that, for kings, compassion requires them to implement appropriate measures to protect their people. As Jenkins (2010) and Sugiki (2020) lay out, the text includes discourses on policies to avoid war and on how to confront opposing forces without resorting to killing. However, if all attempts to prevent armed confrontation fail, then the king should engage in warfare with three thoughts in his mind: that he protects his people, defeats the enemy and captures the enemy forces alive.

> Even if the king, [who] is skillful in means and [who] has a thorough knowledge of warfare, kills or wounds the [warriors of the] foreign army, by that, for the king, there is little fault, there is little vice, and receiving the [karmic] consequence [of it] also becomes uncertain. Why is this? [It is] because in this way he has performed that task with compassion and never abandoning in mind. As he has performed that task by completely abandoning himself and [his] wealth for the sake of thorough protection of the people and [for the sake of his] son, wife, and clan, immeasurable merit will also grow. (Sugiki 2020, 14)

Thus, kings do not acquire the same karmic repercussions as a killer, when they engage in war out of compassion towards their subjects and after all other avenues have been exhausted. The *Ārya-Satyakaparivarta* limits permissible forms of warfare and sets strict conditions for taking life in battle. It also talks about the need for humane treatment of prisoners of war as well as protection of infrastructure and the natural environment. And even at times of war there are opportunities to accumulate merit. However, there is no indication that warfare itself brings merit here, but rather the compassionate intention to limit harm in the course of war, both to one's own people and to one's opponents.

Another well-known example for the taking of life as 'skilful in means' is found in the *Upāya-kauśalya Sūtra*,[54] where in the absence of any other karmically less adverse options, the captain of a ship (the Buddha's past rebirth as a Bodhisattva) decides to kill a robber to prevent him from accruing the negative karmic effects of killing a group of merchants. If the captain had warned the traders, they instead would have killed the robber and accrued the negative karma. The captain willingly took on the karmic implications of taking human life, possibly resulting in many rebirths in hell, in order to prevent others from incurring even worse karma, thereby saving both the robber and the merchants – and, through self-sacrifice and compassionate intention, ultimately himself.

This willingness to take on bad karma to prevent others from doing so is also demonstrated by the first Buddhist Chaplain in the US Air Force, Brett Campbell:

> I won't deny support to anybody, even if that person's actions are causing suffering. … I support the Air Force mission by helping Airmen stay spiritually resilient. If that means that I am bringing negative karma my way, so be it, I will gladly accept that karmic debt for the opportunity to help these Airmen stay spiritually and psychologically healthy. (cited in Thieme 2017)

Buddhist teachings illustrate difficult moral choices, where one has to weigh the serious karmic consequences of non-action, against actions in violation of the five precepts. Candrakīrti, a famous seventh-century scholar of the Madhyamaka school, cites the example of a hunter's two sons arguing at the edge of a precipice. When one of the two grabs the other, intent to thrust both of them over the cliff, the father is left with the only option to shoot one son with an arrow to be able to save at least one of the two (Jenkins 2011, 314). In this example non-action would lead to comparatively more harm than taking action resulting in injury, a case where proportionality and the sum total of harm are at the centre, showing once more that one can intentionally cause physical injury to prevent even greater harm to arise without engaging in *hiṃsā*. Another comparison that is frequently made is life-saving, but conceivably lethal, surgery.

Because *ahiṃsā* is based on intention, it leaves space for the skilful use of strong physical force. Crucially, acting in accordance with *ahiṃsā* can sometimes require using strong force, while restraint from applying force can sometimes be harmful. One does not find a licence to kill here; quite the contrary, taking any life with any hint of unwholesome intent is inherently bad. It requires utmost skilfulness to use potentially lethal force without generating harmful mental attitudes. Being aware of potentially bad karmic consequences whenever transgressing the precepts is important, particularly the cardinal one not to take life. This awareness is a means by itself, causing one to be heedful and act cautiously. Self-sacrifice, willingly taking on bad karma for protecting others, is a wholesome mitigating factor. Yet the karmic implications of using lethal force are difficult to predict, so it is only ever warranted after all other alternatives are exhausted.

Similarly, during armed conflict IHL strikes a balance between military necessity and humanitarian exigencies. Its principle of military necessity permits 'only that degree and kind of force required to achieve the legitimate purpose of a conflict, i.e. the complete or partial submission of the enemy at the earliest possible moment with the minimum expenditure of life and resources' (ICRC 2014, 6). From this balance directly flows the prohibition of superfluous injury and unnecessary suffering.

IHL's principle of distinction requires that the parties to an armed conflict distinguish at all times between civilian and military targets and that attacks may only be directed at military objectives. Furthermore, IHL requires that all feasible precautions must be taken to avoid civilian casualties and damage to civilian objects (ICRC 2014, 48). Causing deliberate or indiscriminate harm to civilians and the natural environment would certainly be in violation of *ahiṃsā* as well.

IHL's principle of proportionality, a corollary to the principle of distinction, dictates that incidental harm caused by military action must not be excessive in relation to the concrete military advantage anticipated (ICRC 2014, 47). The proportionality principle is about weighing competing considerations and taking a difficult choice based on a moral judgement, where the law does not provide clear and direct guidance. Under the extraordinary conditions in war the legitimacy of killing is often taken for granted, which makes it of utmost importance to have a moral compass. Buddhism has much to say about taking difficult moral decisions, and through its rich principles it provides many guiding beacons to combatants.

The *Makasa* ('Mosquito') *Jātaka* offers good examples for the need to use force wisely and proportionally. There the Bodhisattva comes across a village of wounded men and on enquiry learns that bugged by mosquitos, the villagers had decided to go to war with them using bows and arrows, only to end up shooting each other. He then recounts a similar story where a carpenter's son, in order to help his father drive away a mosquito, employs an axe with the intention to hit it, but splits his father's head instead. 'Better than such a friend is an enemy with sense, whom fear of men's vengeance will deter from killing a man' (Jat.44). Both are examples of senselessly using weapons disproportional to the intended outcome. Disregarding intentions, the treacherous nature of strong physical force also requires restraint by wisdom and skill.

Buddhism and military training

Training lies at the heart of both Buddhism and IHL. Both consider continuous training to be a necessity for practical implementation. From a Buddhist perspective, an accumulation of karmic imprints ends up forming behaviours and reactions. Continuous training strengthens one's own capacity to work in even the most chaotic situations, which refers to chaotic external environments as well as the chaos in one's own head. Monastic training itself can be seen as an example of taking forceful action for a wholesome purpose: '*Chinda sotaṃ parakkamma, kāme panuda* – Exert yourself and cut off the stream of craving, drive away sense desires' (Dhp.383).

In a message of gratitude for having been invited to the 2009 Armed Forces Buddhist Community Conference in the UK, His Holiness the Dalai Lama outlines parallels between soldiers and monks:

> I have always admired those who are prepared to act in the defence of others for their courage and determination. In fact, it may surprise you to know that I think that monks and soldiers, sailors and airmen have more in common than at first meets the eye. Strict discipline is important to us all, we all wear a uniform and we rely on the companionship and support of our comrades.
>
> Although the public may think that physical strength is what is most important, I believe that what makes a good soldier, sailor or airman, just as what makes a good monk, is inner strength. And inner strength depends on having a firm positive motivation. The difference lies in whether ultimately you want to ensure others' wellbeing or whether you wantonly wish to do them harm.
>
> Naturally, there are some times when we need to take what on the surface appears to be harsh or tough action, but if our motivation is good our action is actually non-violent in nature. On the other hand if we use sweet words and gestures to deceive, exploit and take advantage of others, our conduct may appear agreeable, while we are actually engaged in quite unacceptable violence. (Dalai Lama 2010)

Monks, like soldiers, need continuous training and strict discipline. Both emphasise patiently enduring difficult situations and not giving way to surges of emotion. A simile in the *Milinda Pañha* illustrates:

> How do they show the manifold restraints of the holy life? Just, O king, as a coward, when he has gone to a battle and is surrounded by the forces of the enemy on all sides, will turn back and take flight for fear of his life; so too, whoever are unrestrained, shameless, impatient and fickle, when they renounce the world they are unable to carry out the manifold precepts and revert to the lower state. (Mp. PTS 251)

Monks need self-discipline[55] for overcoming greed, hatred and delusion, and cultivating their opposites. In the *Dhammapada* one finds this simile: 'As an elephant in the battlefield withstands the arrows shot from a bow, even so will I endure abuse; truly, most people are undisciplined' (Dhp.320). In the military, discipline is often regarded to be the most important attribute. Considered to be foundational, it improves self-control, helps conquer fear and promotes integrity, which all ultimately enhance the protection of those not directly participating in the hostilities.

Military training regimes find many resources in Buddhism, such as in its diverse range of meditation techniques. Capt. Somya Malasri, Buddhist chaplain in the US Army, elucidates: 'I think the Soldiers have stress in their minds, so I can help them with meditation. I can teach them how to meditate and how to get rid of stress, anger or anxiety' (cited in Bosco 2014, 834). Research indeed shows that meditative training is highly effective in lowering aggression levels and reducing the number of disciplinary violations in the military.[56]

In Buddhism meditation is an instrument for achieving positive change. Different Buddhist schools of teaching focus on different meditation techniques. For example, some of the earliest texts focus on *ānāpānasati* (mindfulness of breathing), which is still a core meditation practice in Theravāda, Tiāntāi and Chán (Zen/Seon/Thiền) traditions. Different forms of meditation techniques aim at developing different characteristics, such as *sati* (mindfulness), *samādhi* (concentration), *samatha* (calming the mind) and *vipassanā* (gaining insight). Importantly, all forms are preceded by and combined with practices such as moral restraint and right effort, which aid in developing wholesome states of mind.[57]

Mindfulness constitutes an essential part of Buddhist practice. It is the first factor of the Seven Factors of Awakening, and 'right mindfulness' is the seventh element of the Noble Eightfold Path. Broadly speaking, mindfulness practice involves the process of developing the skill of bringing one's attention to whatever is happening in the present moment. In Buddhism there is a direct connection between the practice of mindfulness and the cultivation of morality. Conscious attention is essential for combatting the natural tendency to act mindlessly, thus enabling one to take compassionate action instead.

Certainly, mental insight into oneself and the world are essential for soldiers who must minimise the infliction of harm and prevent IHL violations, while attaining their military objectives in high-stress combat situations. Mindfulness practice also builds up mental resilience in combatants, offering a preventive strategy against mental health problems. Just as physical exercise produces changes in the physique, mental exercises allow the mind to become 'fitter' and better cope with complex challenges.

Kaji Sherpa, a former Gurkha officer with the British Armed Forces, cites his participation in the delicate United Nations peacekeeping mission in East Timor in 1999, where his training in Buddhist mindfulness allowed him a better understanding and calmer mind in face of a very volatile situation on the ground. He explains, 'In Tibetan Buddhism during times of conflict it is not losing our country what we fear most. What we fear even more is losing our compassion' (ICRC 2019). This need for compassion is also attested by a Buddhist US Air Force Cadet:

> we realize that war is certainly a thing that we don't want to have to do, but sometimes it is absolutely necessary, and it requires compassion for your country, your family, the people that you are protecting. I think Buddhism definitely has a place there ... (Bosco 2014, 843)

When Venerable Thich Nhat Hanh was asked whether there are 'times when it is right to use violence in order to protect yourself, or your family, or nation', he explained: 'If you see someone who is trying to shoot, to destroy, you have to do your best in order to prevent him or her to do so. You must. But you must do it out of your compassion, of your willingness to protect, and not out of anger. That is the key.' The interviewer, following up: 'Some see a conflict between what is necessary for a police officer to do, which is violent sometimes – to enforce the law, on the one hand – and your teachings on the other'. In reply: 'Well, you carry a gun, but it's perfectly possible to carry a gun with a lot of compassion inside. You carry a gun to say, "You should not do that. If you do that, you may get into trouble." But that is a message that can go together with compassion' (PBS 2003).

From a Buddhist perspective, compassion is something that can be cultivated and one finds various practices aimed at developing one's virtues. For example, there are the *brahmavihāras*, four Buddhist virtues and the meditation practices that cultivate them: loving-kindness, compassion, empathetic joy and equanimity. When preaching to soldiers, monks often emphasise teachings of compassion to help them minimise the negative karma resulting from their military service. As negative states of mind are harmful to oneself, compassion offers combatants a strong form of protection from the surge of bad emotions amidst the horrors of war. And even in the course of war, compassionate intentions present soldiers the opportunity to generate merit.

Finding increasing application in the military as well, traditional forms of martial arts[58] are another area where there is a confluence between Buddhism and fighting. There is a notable tendency to either amplify and embellish the connection between Buddhism and martial arts, or, conversely, to see their many congruences as merely incidental or anecdotal, when indeed it is a natural relationship that connects them at the most fundamental level. Warriors who practised martial arts took an acute interest in the relevance of their religion and how to apply it to their work. They required a sense of purpose, a moral code and, prepared to die in battle in service of their lord, a way to face death. Inevitably, the realms of Buddhism, martial arts and combat became intimately intertwined.

Martial arts essentially are the art of learning to control and restrain strong physical force. Through continuous training one develops the ability to use sophisticated techniques to avoid harm, using only the amount of physical force needed to refuse the aggression that one is being offered. Research studies[59] consistently show that, like meditation, martial arts help practitioners to better gain a sense of control over both the situational environment and themselves, leading to fewer negative emotional responses and an overall reduction in violent behaviour.

There is also a further dimension to this confluence of Buddhism and martial arts. When meditating, simultaneously maintaining an ideal physical posture, controlling one's thoughts and breath for extended periods of time, not being distracted by bodily discomfort, requires both physical and mental fortitude.[60] Martial arts training establishes a solid foundation for meditation practice and furthers practice discipline. Both Buddhism's Eightfold Path and traditional martial arts are conduct- and discipline-oriented. Daily practice and perennial repetition aim to retrain the mind. Battling the enemy within, soaking the intense training into one's bones, also leads to a direct experiential realisation of the interconnectedness of all life and in that fosters compassion for others.

A natural response to attack is fear, with aggression often following in its wake, clouding one's ability to effectively respond. When one's thoughts attach to fear, one oftentimes responds with unnecessary force, inflicting greater harm to the attacker than is ethically or legally justifiable. By overcoming attachment and by developing confidence in the ability to defend oneself, one learns to better control one's fear and other mental dispositions. A stable, calm mind present in the moment, overcoming all distractions, is of paramount importance in the heat of battle. Being able not to act upon negative impulses gives one the possibility to act with wholesome intent.

Martial arts practices, when combined with their traditional emphasis on character-building principles such as discipline, humility and respect, can indeed also benefit the military. IHL's principle of honour demands a degree of fairness and mutual respect between adversaries as fellow warriors, members of a common profession that fights not out of personal enmity but out of a sense of duty. Honour has been vital to the development of IHL, drawing from the warrior codes of many cultures and time periods (US Department of Defense 2016, 65–66). Beyond the confines of the law, the realm of ethics and religion taps into people's identities and underlying motivations in a way that IHL often cannot. There is an important place for religious traditions, such as Buddhism, to further the ethical values that underpin IHL.

By highlighting as well as strengthening the underlying ethics, combatants can connect with IHL in a more meaningful way than only considering them as abstract legal demands externally imposed on them. This is also in line with the findings of the ICRC study 'Roots of Restraint in War'.[61] Ethical values play a strong complementary role to the law, discouraging unwanted behaviour not only because it is 'against the rules' but also because it is 'against who we are'.

During the earlier mentioned conference on the 'Interface Between Buddhism and IHL' (ICRC 2019), serving and retired military personnel recounted how they applied IHL principles and Buddhist teachings in their profession. Buddhist ethics and military values were not perceived as being in conflict by them, but rather seen as being complementary. Buddhism emphasises training and the cultivation of virtues, from which wholesome acts then take shape. Arguably, Buddhist soldiers have karmic incentives to become trained in both IHL and in the ethical teachings of their religion. In a profession entrusted with taking decisions over life and death, it is immensely important to maintain forces that are disciplined, virtuous and skilled – skilful both in the arts of their vocation and in the wholesomeness of their intentions.

Conclusion

Buddhism never wavers in upholding its high ethical principles, such as *ahiṃsā*, but it recognises the need to continuously adapt to the conditions of the real world. Contrary to what is often assumed from the outside, in canonical scriptures the concept of *ahiṃsā* was never understood to stand in contradiction to maintaining armed forces and protecting what is good – if necessary, by military means. The use of lethal force for wholesome purposes was at no time completely ruled out. War is assumed to be unavoidable, arising out of human failings in our imperfection-marred *saṃsāra*. A disciplined, virtuous and skilled army is seen as necessary for protection, their very existence often being the reason that conflict is avoided and without which the people would live in fear, resulting in more suffering to arise.

What stands out in the highly pragmatic perspective of Buddhism, where the ethical quality of conduct is determined by its contribution towards reducing suffering, is the supreme importance of intention, which lies at the very root of karma. Because it focuses on volition, *ahiṃsā* leaves room for military action based on wholesome objectives. To minimise suffering, one must restrain evil. In the rare instances where it cannot be avoided, this can even result in armed conflict. Because the use of military force (like the outcome of wars) is so unpredictable, however, it must only be applied absent other less harmful options and in a protective posture.

This is no Buddhist justification for violence, but to the contrary: while violence implies intention to cause harm, Buddhism demands that force is restrained by purely wholesome intentions aimed at minimising overall harm, an utmost high ethical requirement. This restraint is even extended to thought and speech, the precursors before aggressive physical actions can ensue. Due to the cyclical nature of karma where violence begets violence and where one's misconduct in war would create conditions for future conflict to arise, this ultimately appeals to everyone's self-interest.

There is no fundamental contradiction between adhering to *ahiṃsā* and working in the military. As in other professions, what is most important is how one goes about one's work and what intentions one has. In the teachings one finds a recognition of the extraordinary circumstances prevalent in war and of the State's as well as the soldier's duty to protect. As a soldier in combat, one may have to transgress the cardinal precept not to take life, potentially impeding one's progress on the path. It takes much heedfulness to ensure that one's intentions are in no way tainted by greed, hatred or delusion.

Buddhist soldiers not only need to guard themselves against harmful thought, word and deed, they also need to practise the antidotes, i.e. generosity, loving-kindness and wisdom, and thus take meritorious actions. Just like monks, they need to be well trained. Discipline, self-control, patience, endurance, mental insight, skilfulness – all these factors contribute to reducing suffering in armed conflict situations. Imperatively, this applies to all levels of the military and extends to political decision makers.

Buddhism indeed provides us an invaluable resource for contemplating warfare in the present age. Its scripture supplies a fount of stratagems on how to avoid war, but military deployment remains as a last resort. By resorting to narrative, Buddhist ethical teachings are capable of maintaining tensions and ambiguities, challenging the listeners to immerse themselves in various scenarios and experience the complex choices one must confront.

Although Buddhism is already widely applied in the contexts of conflict prevention and resolution, it also offers many teachings relevant to conduct in war. It offers profound inspiration to the 'law of armed conflict', IHL, for advancing its humanitarian aspirations. Its teachings engage with many IHL-relevant topics and show many commonalities in spirit. Both Buddhism and IHL accept the reality of conflict and try to find a path aimed at reducing suffering.

Whilst there is arguably wide common ground, their differences also prove to be insightful. Buddhist principles apply at all times evenly and it is another type of 'war' that takes centre stage here, the war against the evil roots in oneself, directed at the disarmament of the mind. From a Buddhist viewpoint the legal rules need to be complemented by strong ethical restraint. While the intention behind an act is of relevance in IHL, unwholesome mental states, such as vengeance, do not play a direct role in its compliance. For

IHL to work effectively in this environment, it needs continuous cultivation of its underlying ethics.

Those who ignore the reality of conflicts, denounce the military and deny Buddhists their legitimate right to protect themselves disengage themselves from the important dialogue on how Buddhist teachings can contribute to reducing suffering in armed conflict. Ostracising or spiritually condemning soldiers is also not conducive to developing virtuous as well as skilled soldiers, thus negatively impacting conduct. As we have shown, a 'Buddhist soldier' is a paradox, not a contradiction, difficult to understand because on their surface Buddhism and the military appear to reflect conflicting characteristics – yet this paradox reveals to us a hidden truth.

Notes

1. Buddhism encompasses a variety of traditions, beliefs and spiritual practices. This diversity is partly reflected by the different use of scriptures as well as the divergent interpretations of Buddhist traditions according to different lineages or persuasions. While this article focuses on common principles and canonical texts, it also appreciates this complex cultural, historical and philosophical diversity.
2. See Asanga Tilakaratne in this volume.
3. 'Intention' widely overlaps with the concept of 'motivation'. Both terms refer to mental forces behind goal-directed behaviour and are often used interchangeably. This differs from their very narrow legal definitions, which creates a false dichotomy (as is shown in the section on 'IHL and Buddhist law'). Motivation, however, is a broader concept that is applied in relation to wider background and underlying reasons. Greed and hatred, for example, are often cited as motivations, but would not be used when referring to intentions.
4. See Peter Harvey in this volume.
5. Although there can be cases of culpable carelessness.
6. Cetanā (Sanskrit, Pali) is commonly translated as 'intention', 'motivation', 'volition', 'purpose', 'directionality of mind' or 'that which drives one to act', which all are interrelated concepts. The translation used throughout this article is 'intention', which is a suitable term reflecting that the cognitive and purposive aspects of the mind are intertwined and closely interact.
7. For more detailed discussions on this subject, see the work of Prof. Stephen Jenkins – for example, Jenkins (2011).
8. This definition is also consistent with other major dictionaries, such as Merriam-Webster: 'the use of physical force so as to injure, abuse, damage, or destroy' (Merriam-Webster 2021).
9. In a valiant effort to stay in the English language HH the Dalai Lama delineates the Buddhist use of the English word 'violence': 'Violence–Nonviolence demarcation [is] much related to motivation. Any action, even some wrathful action, verbal as well as physical action, motivated by compassion, sense of concern of others' well-being, essentially that is non-violence. ... So, physical level, violence, but that sort of violence is permissible' (Dalai Lama 2009).
10. See, for example, the *Manu-smṛti*: 'People think that agriculture is something wholesome. Yet it is an occupation condemned by good people; the plough

with an iron tip lacerates the ground as well as creatures living in it' (Olivelle 2004, 212).

11. In Jainism one finds a more critical perspective on agriculture.
12. See, for example, Frydenlund (2017).
13. See, for example, Gethin (2007, 73–74).
14. For example, Schmithausen (1999, 53) describes this as an almost schizophrenic 'compartmentalisation of values', where Buddhists say one thing and do another.
15. See P. D. Premasiri in this volume.
16. For example: 'Those who administer torture and maiming are called kings' (Vin. III.46–47).
17. See, for example: Dn.17, 26; An.7.62; and Sn.55.1.
18. We find much evidence, though, that the use of one's armed forces is not always the best way to defend the country against invaders and that when one can lead by virtue and prevent bloodshed one should always do so – such as in the *Seyya Jātaka* (Jat.282) and *Mahāsīlava Jātaka* (Jat.51).
19. See Christina Kilby in this volume.
20. Mahākaccāna (Sanskrit: Mahākātyāyana) is one of the Buddha's ten principal disciples.
21. See Asanga Tilakaratne in this volume.
22. Even the much-quoted *Kakacūpama Sutta (The Simile of the Saw)* does not preclude monks from skilful self-defence: 'Monks, even if bandits were to carve you up savagely, limb by limb, with a two-handled saw, he among you who let his heart get angered even at that would not be doing my bidding. Even then you should train yourselves: "Our minds will be unaffected and we will say no evil words. We will remain sympathetic, with a mind of goodwill, and with no inner hate. We will keep pervading these people with an awareness imbued with goodwill and, beginning with them, we will keep pervading the all-encompassing world with an awareness imbued with goodwill – abundant, enlarged, immeasurable, free from hostility, free from ill will." That's how you should train yourselves' (Mn.21; PTS Pali I.129).
23. '[M]otive is ulterior intention – the intention with which an intentional act is done. Intention, when distinguished from motive, relates to the means, motive to the end; yet the end may be the means to another end, and the word "intention" is appropriate to such medial end. Much of what men do involves a chain of intention' (Williams 1961, 48).
24. The *Milinda Pañha*, according to the Burmese Pali Canon the eighteenth book of the *Khuddaka Nikāya*, provides many examples for the use of military imagery when conveying important spiritual messages.
25. Kautilya in his *Arthaśāstra*, ancient India's seminal treatise on statecraft, economics and military affairs, repeatedly affirms the supreme military importance of elephants. For instance, 'A king's victory is principally dependent on elephants. For elephants, with their huge-sized bodies and being capable of life-destroying acts, can annihilate an enemy's soldiers, battle formations, forts, and camps' (As.2.2.13–14).
26. For example, in the Ajanta frescoes (Cave 17) one can see three archers on top of the elephants.
27. The elephant's power to clear anything in its path is also reflected in the Hindu traditions where one finds the elephant-headed Ganeśa as the remover of obstacles (Vighneśvara).

28. In early Vedic times, Indra is described as riding a chariot, but in the later Vedic period he acquires Airāvata as his *vahana* ('that which carries, that which pulls'). Notably, the decline of the chariot in warfare, rapidly being replaced by the elephant corps as the elite unit of the armed forces, and also the increased prestige of riding one's mount (as a king on his elephant), is mirrored in Dharmic symbolism by deities acquiring their individual *vahana* (Trautmann 2015, 100).
29. To the present day, Southeast Asian Theravāda States still maintain the tradition to identify white elephants, either albino or particularly fair-skinned, as symbols of power and good fortune for the State.
30. Such as safeguarding the integrity of one's country's territory and population.
31. In 2007, the First Armed Forces Buddhist Conference was organised in the UK at Amport House, the Tri-service Armed Forces Chaplaincy Centre.
32. A well-known UK-born monk trained in the Thai Forest Tradition and the abbot of Bodhinyana Monastery in Australia.
33. Incidentally, these five are also covered in two Jain canonical texts, where Mahāvīra lays out 15 types of prohibited trading commodities (Jaini 1979, 172).
34. According to the *Milinda Pañha* weapons are not allowed to be gifted either: 'There are ten sorts of gifts, Nâgasena, in the world that are commonly disapproved of as gifts. And what are the ten? Strong drink, Nâgasena, and festivals in high places, and women, and buffaloes, and suggestive painting, and weapons, and poison, and chains, and fowls, and swine, and false weights and measures' (Mp. PTS 278–279).
35. The nineteenth and twentieth centuries brought the emergence of entirely new forms of highly destructive weapons. In a series of texts analysed by Venturi (2014), the 13th Dalai Lama uses a range of Buddhist tenets to express his conviction that the development of modern weapons and military forces are essential in the protection of the State.
36. See, for example, Soka Gakkai's longstanding work promoting nuclear disarmament (more on this in Daiki Kinoshita's article in this volume). The International Red Cross and Red Crescent Movement started its call for a ban on nuclear weapons in 1945.
37. This is the formulation of the Martens Clause used in Article 1(2) of Additional Protocol I to the Geneva Conventions of 1949.
38. One might hope that minimising harm would also be the central objective in arms development.
39. See, for example, Bosco (2014) and Kent (2008).
40. In four discourses from the *Aṅguttara Nikāya*, which are each called *Yodhājīva Sutta* (An.3.133, 4.181, 5.75, 5.76), the Buddha lays out desirable traits found in soldiers that also monks should emulate: 'Bhikkus(Monks), possessing four factors, a warrior is worthy of a king, an accessory of a king, and reckoned a factor of kingship. What four? Here, a soldier is skilled in places, a long-distance shooter, a sharp-shooter, and one who splits a great body. Possessing these four factors, a soldier is worthy of a king, an accessory of a king, and reckoned a factor of kingship' (An.5.75). He compares the victorious monk to a victorious soldier, 'who can handle the cloud of dust, the top of the enemy's banner, the tumult, and hand-to-hand combat' (An.5.75) and 'who taking his sword and shield, strapping on his bow and quiver – goes down into the thick of battle' (An.5.76).
41. Cf. Peter Harvey in this volume.

42. 'Now there is the person who has killed living beings here ... has had wrong view. And on the dissolution of the body, after death, he reappears in a happy destination, in the heavenly world. But (perhaps) the good kamma producing his happiness was done by him earlier, or the good kamma producing his happiness was done by him later, or right view was undertaken and completed by him at the time of his death' (Mn.136; PTS.III.214).
43. 'Elephant troops and chariotmen, guard royal, infantry – I took no toll of daily dole, but paid them all their fee' (Jat.462).
44. 'Then the Great Being said, "O king, if you wish to reach the world of the gods (angels) and enjoy divine happiness there, you must practise these ten duties:... fulfill your duty, warrior king, ... to your soldiers with their different arms"' (Jat.540).
45. For examples of how certain provisions could apply equally to one's own troops as to the enemy, see Nicholson (2015) and Vishakha Wijenayake in this volume.
46. From 4 to 6 September 2019, approximately 120 participants from around the world gathered in Dambulla, Sri Lanka, for a conference on 'Reducing Suffering During Armed Conflict: The Interface Between Buddhism and International Humanitarian Law (IHL)'. The conference was organised by the ICRC in collaboration with a number of universities and organisations, including Buddhist scholars, monks, legal experts and military personnel from the Theravāda, Mahāyāna and Vajrayāna traditions.
47. A recognition of this is reflected by the fact that both Buddhist leaders and soldiers who have been involved in wars often attempt to counteract negative karmic effects by engaging in compensatory acts of merit, such as alms giving or the building of pagodas.
48. See Vin.III.53 and 75, and Harvey (1999, 280).
49. See, for example, the account of General Sīha crushing Ajātaśatru's forces in Wu (2019).
50. Also in the rigorous *ahiṃsā* tradition of the Jains one finds examples of warriors who had taken enemy lives in battle and attained heaven afterwards, in one case partly due to the 'resolve not to be the first to strike but to fight only in self-defence' (Wu 2015, 106).
51. See *Abhidharmakośa-bhāṣya* IV.72c–d: La Vallée Poussin (1923–1931 and Zhang (2009).
52. For an exploration of siege warfare as found in the *Jātaka*s see Nishara Mendis in this volume.
53. The comparison to surgeons is also made in the modern military term 'surgical strike', which denotes military attacks intended to damage legitimate military targets with no or minimal collateral damage.
54. See, for example, Tatz (1994, 73–76).
55. This is also reflected by the name of the monastic regulations, the *Vinaya* ('Discipline').
56. For more on research regarding the use of meditation in military training see Charya Samarakoon in this volume.
57. For more on the role of Buddhist ethics in meditation and on the use of Koan practice in military environments see Noel Trew in this volume.
58. 'Martial arts' is a broad term covering a variety of codified traditions that originated as methods of combat and incorporate certain mental or spiritual qualities. For more on the historical congruences between Buddhism and martial arts see Bartles-Smith et al. (2021).

59. See, for example, Harwood, Lavidor and Rassovsky (2017).
60. See, for example, Mann (2012).
61. 'An exclusive focus on the law is not as effective at influencing behaviour as a combination of the law and the values underpinning it' (Terry and McQuinn 2018, 9).

Acknowledgements

We would like to record our sincere thanks to Prof. Peter Gilbert, Mr Keith Munnings, Prof. Upul Ranjith Hewawitanagamage, Prof. Peter Harvey, Prof. Stephen Jenkins, Prof. Matthew Kosuta, Prof. Stefania Travagnin, Prof. Kate Crosby, Prof. Asanga Tilakaratne, Prof. Christina Kilby, Dr Noel J. M. Trew and Mr Andrew Bartles-Smith for their comments and suggestions in the making of the paper. The framework for this article was developed by Dr Sunil Kariyakarawana. Any shortcomings and all views presented here are of the authors alone.

Disclosure statement

This article has been supported by the International Committee of the Red Cross (ICRC).

Abbreviations

An *Aṅguttara Nikāya. The Book of the Gradual Sayings, Anguttara Nikaya or More Numbered Suttas*, 5 vols. Tr. F. L. Woodward and E. M. Hare, Oxford: Pali Text

Society, [1932–1936] 2001. Also: *The Numerical Discourses of the Buddha*. Bhikkhu Bodhi, Boston: Wisdom, 2012. An.5.140: *Sotar Sutta: The Listener*. Translated from the Pali by Ṭhānissaro Bhikkhu, 1998. https://www.accesstoinsight.org/tipitaka/an/an05/an05.140.than.html

As *Arthaśāstra. The Kauṭilīya Arthaśāstra*. 3 parts. R. P. Kangle, Bombay: University of Bombay, 1965–1972.

Dhp *Dhammapada. The Dhammapada: A Translation*. Tr. Thanissaro Bhikkhu, 1997. Also: *The Dhammapada: The Buddha's Path of Wisdom*. Translated from the Pali by Acharya Buddharakkhita with an introduction by Bhikkhu Bodhi, 1996. https://www.accesstoinsight.org/tipitaka/kn/dhp/index.html

Dhp-a *Dhammapada-aṭṭhakathā. Buddhist Legends*. 3 vols. Tr. E. W. Burlingame, Harvard Oriental Series, Cambridge: Harvard University Press, 1921.

Dn *Dīgha Nikāya. Long Discourses of the Buddha*. Tr. M. Walshe, 2nd revised edition, Boston: Wisdom, 1996.

Eka Edicts of King Ashoka. *The Edicts of King Asoka*. An English rendering by Ven. S. Dhammika. https://www.accesstoinsight.org/lib/authors/dhammika/wheel386.html

Jat *Jātaka. The Jātaka or Stories of the Buddha's Former Births*. 6 vols. Translated by various hands under E. B. Cowell, London: Pali Text Society, 1895–1907.

Mn *Majjhima Nikāya. The Middle Discourses*. Tr. Bhikkhu Sujato, SuttaCentral, 2018: https://suttacentral.net/mn. Also: *The Middle Length Discourses of the Buddha: A Translation of the Majjhima Nikaya*. Ñāṇamoli Bhikkhu and Bhikkhu Bodhi, Somerville: Wisdom, 1995.

Mm *Mahāyāna Mahāparinirvāṇa Sūtra. The Mahayana Mahaparinirvana Sutra*. Translated into English by K. Yamamoto, Taisho Tripitaka Vol. 12: 374, 1973. Also: Yamamoto, K., and T. Page. 2007. *The Mahayana Mahaparinirvana Sutra*. Tr. K. Yamamoto. Edited and revised by T. Page. http://lirs.ru/do/Mahaparinirvana_Sutra,Yamamoto,Page,2007.pdf

Mp *Milinda Pañha. The Debate of King Milinda*. Edited by Bhikkhu Pesala, published by Motilal Banarsidass in 1991, revised 1998, Inward Path: Penang, 2001. Online PDF edition updated in August 2021. http://www.aimwell.org/milinda.html. Also: tr. I. B. Horner, *Milinda's Questions*, 2 vols, London, Pali Text Society, 1969. Also: tr. T. W. Rhys Davids, The Questions of King Milinda, 2 vols. Sacred Books of the East, 1890 and 1894. https://www.sacred-texts.com/bud/milinda.htm

PTS Pali Text Society.

Thag *Theragāthā* (eighth book of the *Khuddaka Nikāya*). *The Verses of the Arahant Talaputa Thera*. Translated from the Pali with some reflections by Bhikkhu Khantipalo, Kandy, BPS, 1996.

Rpr *Rājaparikathā-ratnamālā. Nagarjuna: Ratnavali*. G. Tucci, *Journal of the Royal Asiatic Society of Great Britain and Ireland*, 1934, pp. 307–325; 1936, pp. 237–252, 423–435.

Sn *Saṃyutta Nikāya. The Connected Discourses of the Buddha: A Translation of the Saṃyutta Nikāya*. Bhikkhu Bodhi, Boston: Wisdom, 2000.

Snp *Sutta Nipāta* (sutta collection in the *Khuddaka Nikāya*). *Sutta-Nipata (Sacred Books of the East)*. V. Fausböll, Oxford: Clarendon, 1881. Tr. K. R. Norman, *The Group of Discourses*, London, PTS, 1984. Also: tr. K. R. Norman, *The Group of Discourses* Vol.II, London, PTS, 1992, revised translation with introduction and notes.

Vin *Vinaya Piṭaka. The Book of the Discipline*. 6 vols. Tr. I. B. Horner, London: Pali Text Society, 1938–1966. Reference by volume and page number of Pali Text Society edition of the Pali text.

The authors take full responsibility for their use of translations based on the resources listed above. To find additional source material and translations for comparison, also see: *Wikipitaka – The Completing Tipitaka* (https://tipitaka.fandom.com/).

References

Bartles-Smith, A., K. Crosby, P. Harvey, P. D. Premasiri, A. Tilakaratne, D. Ratheiser, M. Deegalle, N. M. Trew, S. Travagnin, and E. Harris. 2021. "Reducing Suffering During Conflict: The Interface Between Buddhism and International Humanitarian Law." *Contemporary Buddhism* 21 (1–2): 369–435.

Binder, G. 2002. "The Rhetoric of Motive and Intent." *Buffalo Criminal Law Review* 6 (1): 1–96. doi:10.1525/nclr.2002.6.1.1.

Bosco, R. 2014. "Battlefield Dharma: American Buddhists in American Wars." *Journal of Buddhist Ethics* 21: 827–849.

Buddhadāsa Bhikkhu. 1986. "A Socialism Capable of Benefiting the World." In *Dhammic Socialism*, edited by D. Swearer, 19–44. Bangkok: Thai Inter-Religious Commission for Development.

Chin, K. (淨空). 2017. "Are Soldiers Sinful to Kill Enemy? Buddhist Master Chin-Kung (淨空法師) Speaks Dharma." https://www.youtube.com/watch?v=0zheNeoksGw

Dalai Lama. 2009. "Educating the Heart." Cambridge: Harvard Graduate School of Education and Harvard Divinity School. Memorial Church. April 30. https://www.youtube.com/watch?v=7Ycq5KUYlpw

Dalai Lama. 2010. "The Dalai Lama's Message to the Armed Forces." *Buddhist Military Sangha: An Online Resource for Buddhists Associated with the United States Armed Forces*, June 21. http://buddhistmilitarysangha.blogspot.com/2010/06/dalai-lamas-message-to-armed-forces.html

Dhammananda, K. S. 2002. *What Buddhists Believe*. Expanded 4th ed. Kuala Lumpur: Buddhist Missionary Society Malaysia.

Dhammika, S. 2015. *Nature and the Environment in Early Buddhism*. Singapore: Buddha Dhamma Mandala Society.

Frydenlund, I. 2017. "'Buddhism Has Made Asia Mild': The Modernist Construction of Buddhism as Pacifism." In *Buddhist Modernities: Re-Inventing Tradition in the Globalizing Modern World*, edited by H. Havnevik, U. Hüsken, M. Teeuwen, V. Tikhonov, and K. Wellens, 204–221. Abingdon: Routledge.

Gethin, R. 2007. "Buddhist Monks, Buddhist Kings, Buddhist Violence: On the Early Buddhist Attitudes to Violence." In *Religion and Violence in South Asia: Theory and Practice*, edited by J. R. Hinnells and R. King, 62–82. London: Routledge.

Harvey, P. 1999. "Vinaya Principles for Assigning Degrees of Culpability." *Journal of Buddhist Ethics* 6: 271–291. https://blogs.dickinson.edu/buddhistethics/2010/04/07/vinaya-principles-for-assigning-degrees-of-culpability/

Harwood, A., M. Lavidor, and Y. Rassovsky. 2017. "Reducing Aggression with Martial Arts: A Meta-Analysis of Child and Youth Studies." *Aggression and Violent Behavior* 34: 96–101. doi:10.1016/j.avb.2017.03.001.

ICRC. 2005. *Customary International Humanitarian Law. Volume I: Rules*, edited by Henckaerts, J. and L. Doswald-Beck. Cambridge: Cambridge University Press.

ICRC. 2014. *International Humanitarian Law: Answers to Your Questions*. Geneva: ICRC. https://www.icrc.org/en/publication/0703-international-humanitarian-law-answers-your-questions

ICRC. 2019. *Reducing Suffering During Armed Conflict: The Interface Between Buddhism and International Humanitarian Law (IHL)*. Conference in Dambulla, Sri Lanka. September 4-6.

Jaini, P. 1979. *The Jaina Path of Purification*. Berkeley: University of California Press.

Jenkins, S. 2010. "Making Merit Through Warfare and Torture According to the Ārya-Bodhisattva-gocara-upāyaviṣaya-vikurvaṇa-nirdeśa Sūtra." In *Buddhist Warfare*, edited by M. Jerryson and M. Juergensmeyer, 59–75. New York: Oxford University Press.

Jenkins, S. 2011. "On the Auspiciousness of Compassionate Violence." *The Journal of the International Association of Buddhist Studies* 33: 299–331.

Kariyakarawana, S., and P. Gilbert. 2011. "Military Careers and Buddhist Ethics." *The International Journal of Leadership in Public Services* 7 (2): 99–108.

Kent, D. 2008. "Shelter for You, Nirvana for Our Sons: Buddhist Belief and Practice in the Sri Lankan Army." PhD Thesis. Department of Religious Studies, University of Virginia. https://thecarthaginiansolution.files.wordpress.com/2011/08/buddhist-belief-practise-in-sl-army.pdf

Kosuta, M. 1997. "The Buddha and the Four-Limbed Army: The Military in the Pali Canon." *Religiologiques,* Rituels Sauvages 16 (automne 1997): 105–112.

La Vallée Poussin, L. de, ed. 1923–1931. *L'Abhidharmakosa de Vasubandhu*. 6 volumes. Paris: Paul Geuthner.

Lexico. 2021. "Violence." *Lexico Powered by Oxford*. https://www.lexico.com/definition/Violence

Mann, J. 2012. *When Buddhists Attack: The Curious Relationship Between Zen and the Martial Arts*. Rutland: Tuttle.

Melzer, N. 2019. *International Humanitarian Law: A Comprehensive Introduction*. Geneva: ICRC. https://www.icrc.org/en/publication/4231-international-humanitarian-law-comprehensive-introduction

Merriam-Webster. 2021. "Violence." *Merriam-Webster Dictionary*. https://www.merriam-webster.com/dictionary/violence

Nicholson, J. 2015. "Can War Crimes Be Committed by Military Personnel Against Members of Non-Opposing Forces?" *International Crimes Database*. http://www.internationalcrimesdatabase.org/upload/documents/20151209T150352-Nicholoson%20ICD%20Format.pdf

Olivelle, P. 2004. *Manu's Code of Law: A Critical Edition and Translation of the Manava-Dharmaśastra (South Asia Research)*. New York: Oxford University Press.

Oxford Reference. 2021. *Pacifism*. New York: Oxford University Press. https://www.oxfordreference.com/

PBS. 2003. *Religion & Ethics NewsWeekly: Thich Nhat Hanh*. https://www.pbs.org/wnet/religionandethics/2003/09/19/september-19-2003-thich-nhat-hanh/

Schmithausen, L. 1999. "Aspects of the Buddhist Attitude Towards War." In *Violence Denied: Violence, Non-Violence and the Rationalization of Violence in South Asian Cultural History*, edited by J. Houben and K. van Kooij, 45–67. Boston: Brill.

Singh, S. 1989. *Ancient Indian Warfare: With Special Reference to the Vedic Period*. Delhi: Motilal Banarsidass.

Sugiki, T. 2020. "Compassion, Self-Sacrifice, and Karma in Warfare: Buddhist Discourse on Warfare as an Ethical and Soteriological Instruction for Warriors." *Religions* 11 (2): 66–88. https://www.mdpi.com/2077-1444/11/2/66

Tatz, M., trans. 1994. *The Skill in Means (Upāyakauśalya) Sūtra*. Delhi: Motilal Banarsidass.

Terry, F., and B. McQuinn. 2018. *The Roots of Restraint in War*. Geneva: International Committee of the Red Cross.

Thanissaro Bhikkhu. 1995. *The Buddhist Monastic Code: The Patimokkha Training Rules*. Valley Center: Metta Forest Monastery. https://www.nku.edu/kenneyr/Buddhism/lib/modern/bmc/index.html

Thieme, B. 2017. "First Buddhist Chaplain in the U.S. Air Force: Brett Campbell." *Naropa Magazine*. Fall. http://magazine.naropa.edu/2017-fall/features/first-buddhist-chaplain-air-force-brett-campbell.php

Trautmann, T. 2015. *Elephants and Kings: An Environmental History*. Chicago: University of Chicago Press.

US Department of Defense. 2016. *Law of War Manual*. Washington, DC: US Government. https://dod.defense.gov/Portals/1/Documents/pubs/DoD%20Law%20of%20War%20Manual%20-%20June%202015%20Updated%20Dec%202016.pdf

Vajiranana (Prince Wachirayanawarorot, Son of Mongkut, King of Siam, Supreme Patriarch). 1916. *The Buddhist Attitude Towards National Defence and Administration: A Special Allocution by His Holiness Prince Vajiranana*. Bangkok.

Venturi, F. 2014. "The Thirteenth Dalai Lama on Warfare, Weapons, and the Right to Self-Defense." In *Trails of the Tibetan Tradition: Papers for Elliot Sperling*, edited by R. Vitali, 483–509. Dharamshala: Amnye Machen Institute.

Williams, G. 1961. *Criminal Law: The General Part*. 2nd ed. London: Stevens & Sons.

Wright, R. 2020. "Buddhism and War | Robert Wright & Bhikkhu Bodhi [The Wright Show]." *YouTube*. https://www.youtube.com/watch?v=fl3mADy46xQ

Wu, J. 2015. "Comparing Buddhist and Jaina Attitudes Towards Warfare: Some Notes on Stories of King Ajātaśatru's/Kūṇika's War Against the Vṛjis and Related Material." *Annual Report of the International Research Institute for Advanced Buddhology at Soka University (ARIRIAB)* 18: 95–112.

Wu, J. 2019. "War as a Backdrop for Legislation: Stories of Ajātaśatru's Warfare in Indian Buddhist Monastic Law Codes." *Indo-Iranian Journal* 62 (4): 293–339.

Zhang, X., ed. 2009. *阿毗达磨俱舍论梵汉对勘 Abhidharmakośabhāṣya, Sanskrit Text and Chinese Translations by Paramārtha and Xuanzang*. Beijing: Research Institute of Sanskrit Manuscripts & Buddhist Literature, Peking University.

ICRC

BUDDHIST EMPIRICAL REALISM AND THE CONDUCT OF ARMED CONFLICT

Elizabeth J. Harris

ABSTRACT

This article argues, through examples drawn mainly from the *Sutta Piṭaka*, that the Pali texts are characterised by an empirical realism that avoids neither the grim realities of conflict nor the underlying forces that drive it. *Suttas* such as the *Cakkavatti-sīhanāda Sutta* and the *Mahā-dukkha-kkhanda Sutta* are obvious examples of this realism. So also is the *Aṅgulimāla Sutta*, which deals with the phenomenon of a serial killer. Other texts examine causation, the *Mahā-nidāna Sutta*, for instance, which applies Buddhist causation theories to conflict and other forms of disruption in society. All focus on the almost intractable nature of conflict, when greed, hatred and delusion are embodied within human cultures and communities, producing diverse constructions of reality, fed by *papañca*, proliferating thought. I will argue that the empirical realism shown by texts such as the above can throw light on some of the bitter contexts of armed conflict that Buddhists are caught up in within the contemporary world, as combatants, humanitarian workers or members of civilian communities. They point to the difficulties that can arise, for instance, when humanitarian workers seek to enter zones of armed conflict to protect civilians and to encourage compliance with international humanitarian law (IHL) as set out in customary law and treaties such as the Geneva Conventions and its Additional Protocols. The strength of the diverse constructions of reality present can mean that IHL, and also the demands of compassion, are subordinated to other concerns. This article therefore argues that Buddhism offers not only tools for effective compliance with IHL within situations of armed conflict, but also an analytical model for understanding why some contexts of armed conflict are resistant to the principles embodied in this law. It also suggests a primary initial role for external authorities in guarding against IHL abuses, before armed services personnel can cultivate mindful inner discipline in line with Buddhist ideals.

Introduction

When I began to read the Pali texts well over 30 years ago, I was amazed at how realistic and down-to-earth the discourses attributed to the Buddha were. I was living in Sri Lanka at the time, doing postgraduate work in

DOI: 10.4324/9781003439820-8

Buddhist studies, and was very concerned about the growing level of violence in both the north and the south of the country. The north was under the control of the Indian Peacekeeping Force (IPKF), who were fighting the Liberation Tigers of Tamil Eelam (LTTE), and the south was experiencing the terrorism of the Janatha Vimukti Peramuna (JVP, People's Liberation Front), a militant Sinhala youth movement. As part of my master of arts in Buddhist studies, therefore, I wrote a dissertation on *Violence and Disruption in Society: A Study of the Early Buddhist Texts*, which was later published by the Buddhist Publication Society in Kandy (Harris 1994). This article draws on that early study but expands it considerably. The premises that undergird it are threefold:

(1) That the conditioning contexts for the Buddha's teaching on the gaining of serenity and insight were the political and social realities of India at the Buddha's time, including the potential for war and conflict, and that these realities are represented in the Pali Canon with considerable empirical realism, namely with an emphasis on observation and experience rather than theory.[1]
(2) That Buddhism developed a radical and hard-hitting analysis not only of the causes of conflict but also of the dynamics at work within conflict.
(3) That the empirical realism present in Early Buddhism has relevance for the study of the relationship between Buddhism and international humanitarian law (IHL) in that it can throw light on the bitter, seemingly intractable, contexts of armed conflict within which Buddhists (and others) are involved in the contemporary world as combatants, humanitarian workers or members of civilian communities. It can, for instance, illuminate the resistance that can arise when humanitarian workers seek to enter zones of conflict to protect and provide assistance to civilians and to encourage compliance with IHL as set out in customary law and treaties such as the Geneva Conventions and its Additional Protocols.

To develop these premises, therefore, I divide this article into four sections. First, I will give some indicative examples of what I have termed the 'empirical realism' found in the Pali texts on the topics of violence, war and conflict. Second, I will examine the doctrinal framework within which this realism is placed. Third, I will draw on a wider selection of texts to examine whether a Buddhist model can be developed for understanding why, within some contexts of armed conflict, humanitarian workers have experienced resistance, even from Buddhist stakeholders in the conflict, and why restraint in war can be lacking. Fourth, I reflect on what indicative texts in the Pali Canon say about the regulation of armed conflict, including the encouraging of restraint in war and the managing of retaliation. Although my study is therefore predominantly textual, with an emphasis on the Pali Canon, my focus is the application of this data to contemporary situations of war and conflict.

The empirical realism in the Pali texts

One of the most graphic texts in the Pali Canon on the topic of conflict, war and torture is the *Mahā-dukkha-kkhanda Sutta* (The Greater Discourse on the Mass of Suffering) within the *Majjhima Nikāya* (M.I.83–90). The narrative trigger for the discourse is a question concerning the gratification and the dangers of sensual pleasures. In his answer, the Buddha examines the fear experienced by those attached to sensual pleasures for the security of their possessions, and the quarrels that arise between different groups of people for similar reasons – kings with kings, friends with friends. He then moves to this:

> Again, with sensual pleasures as the cause ... men take swords and shields and buckle on bows and quiver, and they charge into battle massed in double array with arrows and spears flying and swords flashing; and there they are wounded by arrows and spears, and their heads are cut off by swords, whereby they incur death or deadly suffering ... (M.I.86)

Charges on the 'bastions' of a town are then described, with armies being 'splashed with boiling liquids and crushed under heavy weights', and then burglary, together with the tortures meted out by kings on thieves who are caught. The tortures are reminiscent of those used today by rogue governments and include the 'fiery wreath', 'meat hooks' and being 'splashed with boiling oil' or 'impaled alive on stakes' (M.I.87). I would argue that there is a graphic realism in this discourse that still speaks today, although contemporary methods of warfare are very different.

The *Mahā-nidāna Sutta* (The Great Discourse on Origination) in the *Dīgha Nikāya* (D.II.55–71) uses similar language to the *Mahā-dukkha-kkhanda Sutta*. The discourse offers a detailed account of *paṭicca-samuppāda* (Dependent Origination), offering examples of the conditioning factors that nurture the arising of craving (*taṇhā*), and its destructive results, including this:

> And so, Ānanda [the Buddha's closest monastic companion], feeling conditions craving, craving conditions seeking, seeking conditions acquisition, acquisition conditions decision-making, decision-making conditions lustful desire, lustful desire conditions attachment, attachment conditions appropriation, appropriation conditions avarice, avarice conditions guarding of possessions, and because of the guarding of possessions there arise the taking up of the stick and sword, quarrels, disputes, arguments, strife, abuse, lying and other evil unskilled states. (D.II.58–59)[2]

Within the context of war, 'possessions' can also include land, identity, status and power. The most hard-hitting discourse for me, however, in terms of its realism is the *Cakkavatti-sīhanāda Sutta* (The Lion's Roar on the Turning of the Wheel). It contains a mythical story told by the Buddha to illustrate what can happen within a society when a 'wheel-turning' monarch, namely one who governs righteously according to dhammic principles, fails to honour one of his responsibilities, as 'he did not give property to the needy' (D.III.64). The immediate result of this monarch failing to give 'property' to the needy is that poverty increases. One of those affected by poverty then commits theft. The monarch, discovering that this person was forced to steal because of poverty, gives him property but does not then tackle the wider issue of deprivation within the population. Inevitably, the rumour then spreads that the king is giving property to those who steal. So stealing becomes rife. The king then makes a U-turn and decapitates one of the offenders. People copy this and begin to commit murder in order to gain what they need to live. As the violence increases, the lifespan of the community decreases and morality in general degenerates. In effect, the discourse describes a once-orderly society falling into violent anarchy, until it comes to the point when there is what the discourse terms a 'sword-period' of seven days, when people mistake each other for wild beasts and kill indiscriminately. At this point, some within the community realise that there could be an alternative to violence and retreat into the forest, again for seven days. When they return, they choose a morally positive path and help to end the killing.

In this discourse, humanitarian concerns hardly feature in the slide to anarchy. The monarch is shown to make a bungling attempt at a humanitarian approach but fails. It is only at the end, when some society members choose a different path, that humanitarian values return. Although this discourse is placed within a mythical framework, I would argue that it holds a fundamental and timeless insight, namely that conflict, war and societal collapse is often driven by failures of the state to enable all to live in food and property security. There is a realism in the myth that deeply moved me when I first read it. I could see parallels to it in the contemporary world, for instance in the genocides and the bitter internal wars that marked the twentieth century.

In the *Cakkavatti-sīhanāda Sutta*, the cause of violence is state-induced poverty and deprivation. In the *Aṅgulimāla Sutta* (On Aṅgulimāla; M.II.97–105), violence springs from an individual, a serial killer who terrorises 'villages, towns and districts' in the kingdom of Kosala. He is described as 'bloody-handed, given to blows and violence, merciless to living beings' and as wearing the fingers of those he has killed around his neck (M.II.98–99). Although the later Pali commentary provides a background story to explain his conduct, we are not told in the *sutta* how he became such a violent person. Had he himself suffered abuse or violence as a child? Had his mind become unbalanced by the experience of war? We do not know. We are told that people normally went in large groups along the roads he frequented but that even this did not give them security. The Buddha then goes out to encounter him, against the advice of the villagers, and uses supernormal powers to stop Aṅgulimāla catching up with him. Aṅgulimāla demands that he stop, but the Buddha replies that he *has* stopped – stopped violence towards others – and that it is Aṅgulimāla who should now, likewise, *stop*. Aṅgulimāla, being very impressed that the Buddha has come, without fear, to teach him, becomes his disciple, resolves to stop his killing, and develops into an exemplary Buddhist monk, a *bhikkhu*.

Matching the *Aṅgulimāla Sutta* in the violence that is evoked to illustrate the Buddha's teachings is an image within the *Kakacūpama Sutta* (The Simile of the Saw; M.I.122–129). Its aim is to stress the kind of mind *bhikkhu*s should develop through meditative practice, and this is its last simile:

> Bhikkhus, even if bandits were to sever you savagely limb by limb with a two-handled saw, he who gave rise to a mind of hate towards them would not be carrying out my teaching. Herein, bhikkhus, you should train thus: 'Our minds will remain unaffected, and we shall utter no evil words; we shall abide compassionate for their welfare, with a mind of loving kindness, without inner hate'. (M.I.129)

A textual narrative about a *bhikkhu* named Puṇṇa can be taken as an example of this attitude of mind. Puṇṇa's intention is to go to Sunāparanta, an area considered to be part of contemporary Myanmar (S.IV.60–63). The people there were known to be 'wild and rough'. The Buddha, therefore, asks him what he will do if he is attacked, presenting Puṇṇa with a progression of ever worsening attacks and ending with: 'But Puṇṇa, if the people of Sunāparanta do take your life with a sharp knife, what will you think about that?' Even faced with this possibility, Puṇṇa refuses to speak of retaliation, only of thanks, in this case that death, which some people seek, would have come to him without him having to go far to find it. According to the *sutta*, Puṇṇa then goes to Sunāparanta and creates 500 lay male followers and 500 lay female followers and he himself attains liberation (*nibbāna*). He dies there; we are not told whether this was through violence.

For the purposes of this article, it is again the empirical realism behind these discourses that I would highlight. Our contemporary world is familiar with these genres of violence and terrorism, these pathologies of violence. They are no longer carried out with swords and arrows but with suicide bombs, knives or poison-laced substances. They demonstrate that the Buddha's teaching was honed and communicated to lay and ordained followers alike against a political, social and economic backdrop that was shot through with violence. Neither the Buddha nor his followers distanced themselves from the reality of conflict around them. As I wrote in 1994:

> [The Buddha's] concern for the human predicament made him acutely aware of the potential for violence within the economic and political forces around him. The political milieu of rival republics and monarchies in northern India forms a backdrop to his teaching, whether the rivalries between the kingdoms of Kosala and Magadha or the struggles of the republics to maintain their traditions and their independence in the face of the rising monarchies. (Harris 1994, 6–7, drawing on Thapar 1966, chapter 3)

The doctrinal framework within which this realism is placed: a world enmeshed in craving

I have demonstrated in the first section that, according to the Pali texts, the Buddha did not communicate religious truth as an abstract philosophy, divorced from social and political contexts. He contextually embedded it within Indian society and illustrated it through the realities of that society, using principles honoured by effective teachers throughout history. This is very relevant to the theme of Buddhism and IHL. One task for those who follow the Buddha's teaching is to create new metaphors, new illustrations, which have the potential to speak to us now in the most violent of situations, including modern warfare, where IHL obliges belligerents to limit their methods and means of warfare and to protect civilians and combatants who are out of action (*hors de combat*).

These new metaphors and illustrations, however, must be consistent with Buddhism's overall assessment of human society, which is that it is enmeshed in egotistical craving, *taṇhā*. A passage from the *Aṅguttara Nikāya* captures this perfectly:

> Bhikkhus, I will teach you about craving – the ensnarer, streaming, widespread, and sticky – by which this world has been smothered and enveloped, and by which it has become a tangled skein, a knotted ball of thread, a mass of reeds and rushes, so that it does not pass beyond the plane of misery, the bad destination, the lower world, *saṃsāra*. (A.II.211–212)

The currents of craving that this discourse then examines, 36 of them, are all connected with the sense of 'I am', the ego: *what* 'I am' or am not, aspirations for 'I' in the present and in the future, and putative external causes of all this. The *Attadaṇḍa Sutta* in the *Sutta-nipāta* offers another important illustration of this assessment of human society. The narrator sees people 'floundering, like fish in little water', 'opposed to one another', running 'in all directions' and is afraid, until he sees 'a barb . . ..nestling in the heart', the barb of craving and delusion, which causes societal disruption (Sn.935–939).

When these two discourses are taken together, they embrace both the individual and the community. The 'barb' of craving pierces the individual but it is also present collectively within the 'world'. Both individuals and communities can possess an 'ego', from which comes a determination to create a particular future for 'I' or 'us', a future that is 'eternal', no matter what suffering is caused to others.

According to the Pali Canon, one antidote to attachment to the 'I', whether individual or collective, is meditation on old age, death and the decomposition of the body after death. It is this that can help individuals and communities see things as they are, namely as impermanent and subject to decay and death. Significant for the topic of this volume is that the description of these meditations evokes sights that are seen in conflict and its aftermath, particularly when mass graves, proof of the brutality of armed conflict, are discovered. This is one of the 'charnel ground contemplations' from the *Kāyagatā-sati Sutta* (M.III.88–98), aimed at developing awareness of the body's impermanence:

> Again, bhikkhus, as though he were to see a corpse thrown aside in a charnel ground, one, two, three days dead, bloated, livid, and oozing matter, a bhikkhu compares this same body with it thus: 'This body too is of the same nature, it will be like that, it is not exempt from that fate'. As he abides thus diligent .... That too is how a bhikkhu develops mindfulness of the body.

More images are then added – of 'a corpse ... being devoured by crows, hawks, vultures, dogs, jackals, or various kinds of worms' and of a skeleton 'smeared with blood, held together with sinews ... a skeleton without flesh and blood, held together with sinews ... disconnected bones scattered in all directions ... '. (M.III.91–92). This perhaps represents the ultimate in empirical realism, in the context of Buddhism's doctrinal framework. Contemporary cremation practices hide these realities nowadays, but war and conflict resurrect them, and this 'resurrection' can be in the form of graphic, uncensored images of the aftermath of suicide bombings, including on social media. For the Buddhist who has meditated on these realities, compassion for all caught in the cycle of birth and death, including enemies, should result. The empirical realism in the texts, in general, should encourage people to see things as they are, namely as frequently shot through with the consequences of unchecked greed, hatred and delusion.

Constructions of reality and dis-ease of the mind

In this third section of my article, I examine whether a Buddhist model can be developed for understanding why, within some contexts of armed conflict, humanitarian workers have experienced resistance, even from Buddhist stakeholders in the conflict, and why restraint in war is often lacking. Buddhism emphasises loving kindness, *mettā*, and compassion, *karunā*, and promotes an ethic of empathy, namely that we should stand in the shoes of others, including those with whom we are in discord. These should lead, among

Buddhists, to immediate sympathy with the aims and principles of IHL. However, this has not always been the case. This part of my article argues that such a model can be developed through the Pali texts themselves.

The key to this model is the teaching given in the texts about the capacity for the unenlightened mind not to see things as they really are but to construct 'realities' based on premises conditioned by what Buddhism calls the *āsava* – corruptions, taints, cankers or intoxicating inclinations – and the defilements (*kilesa*), and the difficulty for such a mind to eradicate these corruptions and defilements. There are four *āsavas*: sense desire (*kāmāsava*); the desire for existence, usually interpreted as eternal existence for the self (*bhavāsava*); wrong views (*diṭṭhāsava*); and ignorance (*avijjāsava*). There are 10 *kilesa*: greed (*lobha*); hate (*dosa*); delusion (*moha*); conceit (*māna*); fixed and speculative views (*diṭṭhi*); doubt (*vicikicchā*); mental laziness (*thīna*); restlessness (*uddhacca*); shamelessness (*ahirika*); and lack of concern for consequences (*anottappa*). The first three of the latter are separately listed in the Pali texts as poisons or unwholesome roots (*mūla*). I have already touched on the dangers of the first *āsava*, as expressed by the *Mahā-dukkha-kkhanda Sutta*. Other discourses could also be cited, for instance the *Potaliya Sutta* (To Potaliya; M.I.359–368), when attachment to sensual pleasures and clinging to material possessions are to be undermined by comparing them to meatless bone, a blazing grass torch held against the wind and a charcoal pit full of blazing coals (M.I.364–365). The *Sabbāsava Sutta* (M.I.6–12) also gives an excellent account of the *āsavas*. Clinging to the idea of an eternal self and speculating about that self, for instance, is described in this way:

> The speculative view, bhikkhus, is called the thicket of views, the wilderness of views, the contortion of views, the vacillation of views, the fetter of views. Fettered by the fetter of views, the untaught ordinary person is not freed from birth, ageing, and death, from sorrow, lamentation, pain, grief, and despair; he is not freed from suffering, I say. (M.I.8)

The corruptions and defilements are presented in texts such as these as leading to suffering for oneself and, by extension, to suffering in society. But it could be asked: 'If the dangers of these are so clear in Buddhist teaching, why can there be resistance, even among Buddhists, to the implementation of compassionate principles in warfare?' The answer given in the texts concerns their sheer tenacity. The Buddha is reported as saying:

> Bhikkhus, there are these two kinds of illnesses. Which two? Bodily illness and mental illness. People are found who can claim to enjoy bodily health for one, two, three, four, and five years; for ten, twenty, thirty, forty, and fifty years; and even for a hundred years and more. But apart from those whose taints [*āsavas*] have been destroyed, it is hard to find people in the world who can claim to enjoy mental health even for a moment. (A.II.142–143)

To completely eradicate the *āsavas*, therefore, is not easy. An illustration of their tenacity is presented in the *Cūḷa-dukkha-kkhanda Sutta* (The Shorter Discourse on the Mass of Suffering; M.I.91–95), when a lay person comes to the Buddha and asks why greed, hatred and confusion or delusion (*moha*) persist in his mind, although he knows the dangers associated with them. The Buddha tells him that attachments connected with the householder life are the reason for his inability to practise what he knows will lead to the lessening of suffering. The implicit message is that he should become a monk, a *bhikkhu*, and give himself to meditative practice, if he really wants to progress along the Buddhist path. However, there are numerous discourses that imply even the monastic communities were not always models of harmony or intensive meditative practice, at the Buddha's time or subsequently, when the Pali texts were being compiled. For instance, in the *Kosambiya Sutta* (The Kosambians; M.I.320–325), a group of monastics who have 'taken to quarrelling and brawling and are deep in disputes, stabbing each other with verbal daggers' is described (M.I.321). In the *Anaṅgaṇa Sutta* (Without Blemishes; M. I.24–32), jealousy and competition within the monastic community, when *bhikkhus* hide their faults and unwholesome thoughts, and seek honours from lay people, lead to this simile:

> Suppose a metal bowl were brought from a shop or a smithy clean and bright; and the owners put the carcass of a snake or a dog or a human being in it and, covering it with another bowl, went back to the market; then people seeing it said: 'What is that you are carrying about like a treasure?' Then, raising the lid and uncovering it, they looked in, and as soon as they saw they were inspired with such loathing, repugnance, and disgust that even those who were hungry would not want to eat, not to speak of those who were full. (M.I.30)

The moral of the illustration is that the Buddhist monk who may appear to have abandoned the *āsavas* may really still have them within, like the poison of a dead snake or dog.[3] In the *Dvedhā-vitakka Sutta* (On Two Kinds of Thought; M.I.114–118), the Buddha gives advice to his monastic followers on what to do if unwholesome thoughts connected with the corruptions and the defilements persist even during meditative practice. After outlining a number of strategies for the restraint of unwholesome thoughts, the Buddha, as a last resort, advises, 'with his teeth clenched and his tongue pressed against the roof of his mouth, he [the bhikkhu] should beat down, constrain, and crush mind with mind' (M.I.120). The implication of the discourse is that this would not be an unusual point to reach. Thoughts connected with the corruptions and the defilements are strong and are not easily eradicated. And if this was so for the monastic community, how much more so for lay people! Bewilderment, *mohanasmiṃ pagāḷho*, according to the Pali Canon, is something that most humans often feel. Moreover, since most humans usually associate only with those like-minded to themselves, those attached to sensual pleasures and the accumulation of possessions will make friends only with those who have similar attachments. Their attitude to themselves and to life, and their 'constructed realities', will never, therefore, be challenged or questioned.[4]

In the context of conflict and war, the fact that our 'realities', under the influence of the *āsavas* and *kilesas*, are constructed and do not represent things as they really are is crucial to the discussion of IHL. John Paul Lederach (2001), a Mennonite peace activist, wrote after the attack on the Twin Towers on 9/11:

> Always remember that realities are constructed. Conflict is, among other things, the process of building and sustaining very different perceptions and interpretations of reality. This means that we have at the same time multiple realities defined as such by those in conflict.[5]

This could have been taken out of a Buddhist peace manual. It admirably applies the theory I have outlined. Lederach went on to explain that communities can hold constructed realities that, in their eyes, might seem perfectly logical but which to those outside that community might appear bizarre, false or dangerous. Caroline Brazier, a Western *Buddhist* and trained psychologist, describes our constructed realities through the vocabulary of addiction and presents it as an imprisonment:

> [B]ut it should be clear from what we have seen so far [Brazier's explanation of Buddhist philosophy] that what we are looking at in *Buddhist* psychology is a psychology of addiction. But to what are we addicted? For most of us, it is an addiction to self. The self we create is the source of security and comfort to which we turn when life gets difficult; and this habitual pattern of refuge is just as persistent and just as falsely based as any substance addiction. (Brazier 2003, 33)

The *Madhupiṇḍika Sutta* (M.I.108–114; the Honeyball Discourse) mentions a Pali term that is relevant here: *papañca*.[6] Most often translated as proliferation, although I. B. Horner translated it as 'obsessions', *papañca* is the proliferation of thoughts, feelings and judgements in the unenlightened mind. The Honeyball Discourse declares that *papañca* is the cause of such things as taking up weapons, quarrelling, contending, disputing and slander, and that the defeat of *papañca* is the way to end such actions. So it declares:

> Bhikkhus [monks], as to the source through which perceptions and notions tinged by mental proliferation [*papañca*] beset a man [person]; if nothing is found there to delight in, welcome and hold to, this is the end of the underlying tendency to lust, of the underlying tendency to aversion, of the underlying tendency to views, of the underlying tendency to doubt, of the underlying tendency to conceit, of the underlying tendency to desire for being, of the underlying tendency to ignorance; this is the end of resorting to rods and weapons, of quarrels, brawls, disputes, recrimination, malice, and false speech . . . (M.I.109–110)

An early analysis of *papañca* was made by Bhikkhu Ñāṇānanda in 1971 (*Concept and Reality*). He described *papañca* as the spreading out of concepts that occurs in the last stages of our mental cognition processes, when our thoughts and feelings run riot. He then added a most interesting point based on the grammatical structure of the Pali. When this 'spreading out' happens, he pointed out, we become the victims of our own mental and linguistic constructions. So, drawing from the *Madhupiṇḍika Sutta*, he wrote:

> Like the legendary resurrected tiger which devoured the magician who restored it to life out of its skeletal bones, the concepts and linguistic conventions overwhelm the worldling who evolved them. At the final and crucial stage of sense-perception, the concepts are, as it were, invested with an objective character. (Ñāṇananda 1971, 29; quoted in Harris 1994, 29)

His evidence is the *sutta*'s description of what arises in the mind when the senses engage with sense objects, for instance in connection with visual consciousness:

> Dependent on the eye and forms [visible objects], eye-consciousness arises. The meeting of the three is contact. With contact as condition, there is feeling. What one feels, that one perceives. What one perceives, that one thinks about. What one thinks about, that one mentally proliferates [*papañca*]. With what one has mentally proliferated as the source, perceptions and notions tinged by mental proliferations beset a man with respect to past, future, and present forms cognizable to the eye. (M.I.111–112)

The Pali word (*samudācaranti*) translated as 'beset' in the above extract implies a reversal of the usual process of thought, according to Ñāṇānanda. The thoughts take on a life of their own and 'beset' the thinker; that is, they make the thinker the victim. The thinker can no longer control or restrain thought.

Ñāṇananda emphasised that *papañca* happens in the unenlightened mind and that it works through craving (*taṅhā*), conceit (*māna* – the tendency to measure yourself up against others) and views that flow from egocentric consciousness. He also emphasised that language reinforces this, by creating a dualism between subject and object in the individual or collective mind: 'I like this', 'I want to be rid of this', 'We like this'. In 2015, a further study of *papañca* was published by an organisational psychologist, Maya Shobrook. Shobrook, *Helpless to Selfless*). It took Ñāṇananda's thought further, by comparing *papañca* to 'automatic thoughts' in Cognitive Therapy, and offered a developed analysis of the dangers of thinking through the concepts of 'I' and 'mine'. As Ñāṇananda, she argued that we become 'helpless' under the influence of *papañca* and cannot hope to make a clear assessment of the problems that beset us, unless we interrogate our use and abuse of the concept of 'Self' (Shobrook, *Helpless to Selfless*).

In 1994, using Ñāṇananda, I imagined what a sequence of thoughts influenced by *papañca* could look like if it were to foster conflict or violence. I adapt it here:

> I feel aversion to this group (or community or religion). I am right to feel aversion. This group is morally corrupt (or inferior or violent). Therefore, it is worthy of my aversion. Even more, this group threatens my identity and not only my identity but also that of my whole community. Therefore, to protect my community, this group must be eradicated. I cannot survive unless this happens. So it is my duty to work for the eradication of this group (or another object) for my sake and the sake of others.

In this sequence, 'I feel aversion' (*dosa*) comes first. *Dosa* is the second *kilesa*. It is a mental state that is contingent on experience, on conditioning, on personal likes and dislikes. The conditioned nature of this state, however, is lost sight of in the sequence of thoughts that follows, which universalises the state so that it becomes a conviction that is seen both as empirically verifiable and as an imperative for action (Harris 2017). This conviction and imperative to action are then clung to with a 'This alone is truth' mentality, an attitude that is criticised in many discourses in the Pali Canon, because, in the unenlightened mind, such statements are usually rooted in ignorance.[7] In the context of violent conflict, other factions may have constructed a completely different argument, equally held as 'This alone is truth'. Such limited, fixed views (*diṭṭhi*) narrow people's focus and stop them seeing differing perspectives on the shared world of the human situation.

In my imagined example, 'aversion' or *dosa* could be replaced by fear, jealousy, anger[8] or a feeling of being threatened. In 2017, when examining the dangers of *papañca* with reference to Ñāṇananda's thought, I wrote, 'If we use the image of the resurrected tiger seriously, this kind of proliferation can kill us in some way – can destroy us and our communities' (Harris 2017). It can also destroy and endanger proper compliance with IHL.

'Constructed realities' as a threat to compliance with IHL

In war and conflict, I would suggest, whole communities can be affected by the proliferation of thoughts that are based on premises rooted in the *āsavas* and *kilesas*. This proliferation can result in attachment to land and religious sites, to convictions of communal or racial moral superiority, to memories of past greatness and the wish to restore this greatness, or to anger conditioned by perceived slights and betrayals. The Buddha's teaching would condemn all such attachments as the fruit of craving, as forms of clinging to individual or communal 'selves'.

When attachments rooted in one of the corruptions or the defilements become, through the dynamics of *papañca*, supposedly empirically verifiable truths for a whole community, a constructed reality arises, which can become all but impermeable to other arguments or 'realities', often now spread and reinforced by algorithm-driven 'bubbles' in social media. Such constructed 'realities' can be present within radicalised religious groups, state forces, ethnic majorities and minorities, and a variety of other communities. They can be present within the four categories of armed group organisations studied by the International Committee of the Red Cross (ICRC): integrated state armed forces, centralised non-state armed groups, decentralised non-state armed groups; community-embedded armed groups (ICRC 2018). When they are present in contexts of war, considerations connected with IHL, such as the protection and humane treatment of civilians and captured combatants on the other side, can be forgotten because of the strength of these constructed realities, which can deny humanity to the perceived enemy and make violence a virtue to gain the desired end. A 2004 ICRC study points out that 'It is perfectly possible for people to know that an act is illegal but to consider it to be legitimate', for instance when 'the enemy is demonised and considered as vermin' (ICRC 2004, 9–10). Buddhism might attribute this to *papañca* and the 'constructed realities' it nurtures. The very conduct of hostilities, therefore, can be conditioned by the dynamics of *papañca*, resulting in cycles of violations of IHL and resistance or opposition to the presence of those who seek to ensure compliance with the law.

I have not named particular conflicts in this article. However, I have had personal experience of conflicts in Bosnia, Ireland, Israel/Palestine, Pakistan and Sri Lanka, and have supervised research students working on conflict in various parts of Africa. In all these contexts, I have witnessed the devastation that constructed realities can create. Of course, these 'realities' usually have some grounding in fact, for instance in experiences of violence and terrorism from a perceived enemy. A Buddhist lens, however, can reveal points where *papañca* has prevented communities from seeing things as they really are and empathising with religious and ethnic others. Recognising how people construct their 'realities', their world, can help people lessen the degree to which they are captured by these, and help them to engage with the lived experience of others.

The existence of 'constructed realities' on all sides of armed conflict can also hinder the work of humanitarian organisations when they seek to provide practical support to victims of armed conflict. The ICRC report *The Roots of Restraint in War* speaks of the importance of trust between humanitarian organisations and armed forces and armed groups.[9] State armed forces and non-state armed groups need to have trust that humanitarian organisations such as the ICRC will live up to their ethic of neutrality and not act through partisan motives. The existence of 'constructed realities' among belligerents, however, can influence the judgements that lead to trust. Humanitarian organisations have been barred from some conflict zones because their actions have been perceived to be partisan by one of the parties to the conflict, even though empirical evidence might prove otherwise. 'Constructed realities' can also trigger armed conflict in the first place and then influence how hostilities are conducted and whether violations of IHL occur.

The regulation of armed conflict

Other articles[10] in this volume examine forms of Buddhist mental culture that aim to help combatants control and/or purify their minds in conflict situations so that self-regulation occurs. They appeal to what can be called 'internal authority' whereby combatants accept the benefit of mental culture, see its truth and attempt to act accordingly so that excessive use of force is mitigated. Combatants and indeed humanitarian workers should be trained in these forms of self-regulation so that they become autonomous moral agents, guided by cultural or religious values.[11] I will not, however, concentrate on Buddhist mental culture here. For, in the heat of battle, self-regulation is rarely enough on its own. Therefore, I investigate in this section a strand within the Pali texts that refers to external authority, namely to leadership by those imbued with authority, in religious, state and military fields.

A foundational text within this strand is the *Aggañña Sutta* (Knowledge of Beginnings, D.III.80–98), which, within another myth, describes the development of craving, possessiveness, theft, false speech and interpersonal violence within a newly formed society without an executive or judicial procedures. The arising of these 'evils' eventually prompts some members of the society to recognise that a force of authority is needed – a being 'who would show anger where anger was due, censure those who deserved it, and banish those who deserved banishment!' They go to the person whom they believe is best qualified for this, with both personal charisma and capability, and a social contract ensues, within which this chosen authority figure is provided with livelihood by the people in return for enforcing order (D.III.92).

It is significant that the showing of 'anger' (*kodha*) in the face of evil, by a person imbued with authority to punish, is justified in this discourse. Banishment of evil-doers to protect the health of the wider community is also endorsed. Although the expression of anger is unwholesome (*akusala*) within Buddhist ethics,[12] this strand within the Pali texts sees it as a necessary part of the proper exercise of power in societies that are riven with conflict. A controversial further example of this is when Pasenadi, ruler of Kosala, is shown in conflict with Ajātasattu, ruler of Magadha. Ajātasattu is the aggressor at first and Pasenadi defends his kingdom, only to be defeated. At this point, the Buddha, when he hears what has happened, is recorded as saying:

> Bhikkhus, King Ajātasattu of Magadha has evil friends, evil companions, evil comrades. King Pasenadi of Kosala has good friends, good companions, good comrades. Yet for this day, bhikkhus, King Pasenadi, having been defeated, will sleep badly tonight. (S.I.82; see Harris 1994, 18–19)

Although Pasenadi has used defensive force, there is no condemnation at this point of his decision to do so, implying that such force, however regrettable, is part of exercising the authority of kingship or the state. In the next battle, however, it is Pasenadi who is the victor. He allows Ajātasattu his life but, in a retaliatory overreaction, confiscates all his troops and elephants. When news of this reaches the Buddha, his response is different. The verse he is recorded as uttering judges both sides through appeal to the principle of karma in war: 'The killer begets a killer, one who conquers, a conqueror. The abuser begets abuse, the reviler, one who reviles' (S.I.85). Both Pasenadi and Ajātasattu, in this second battle, fall short of proper conduct between states.

According to this strand of the Pali texts, therefore, the exercise of authority at the level of kingship or the state might involve the use of defensive force. I would argue that this is also part of Buddhism's 'empirical realism' in a craving-filled world, although the theoretical ideal within Buddhism is always that violence only breeds violence. Yet such force is always subject to the principle of karma, under which it stands condemned. As the Pasenadi/Ajātasattu example suggests, however, if war is entered into, humanitarian standards are expected, which invites the question: how should conflict and war be regulated once it has broken out, according to this textual strand, particularly retaliatory violence, which frequently is prey to excessive force?

Self-regulation within individual combatants is one option. Yet, as I have suggested above, fear of death and mental constructions of the 'enemy' may prove stronger in the heat of battle than any mental training undertaken. External authority, therefore, has to enter. The Pali texts of Theravāda Buddhism speak of four specifically religious external sources of authority (here, for the authenticity of a teaching), the *mahāpadesa*: the Buddha, an Order of monks that contains an elder monk, a group of learned elder monks and a sole elder monk.[13] But what would be the recognised external sources in war and conflict? I suggest that these would be the state and military commanders (*senānāyakas*), who, ideally, should see themselves as subject to dhammic principles.

I would suggest there are three Buddhist principles or teachings that could be used by such sources of external authority for the regulation of conflict and excessive retaliation. The first principle is that of karma,[14] which can be used to instil in combatants that there can be no impunity for violations of IHL or the excessive use of force, at both legal and religious levels. In other words, combatants must be convinced that those who are guilty of violations will be held accountable before the law as well as under the principle of karma. In doing this, appeal can be made to a second teaching of the Buddha, namely that moral shame (*hiri*) and fear of blame and other consequences (*ottappa*) are the forces that enable human society to function. The Buddha is recorded as saying this:

> Bhikkhus, these two bright qualities protect the world. What two? Moral shame and moral dread. If these two bright qualities did not protect the world, there would not be seen here [any restraint regarding] one's mother, aunts or wives of one's teachers and [other] respected people. The world would become promiscuous, like goats and sheep, chickens and pigs, dogs and jackals (A.I.52).

Again, the empirical realism of Buddhism can be seen. Transferred to the fields of war and conflict, this is directly relevant to rape and sexual abuse, but also, by extension, to any violation of IHL. External authority, through creating a military culture where violations of IHL are not tolerated, can utilise as a regulatory strategy the inherent capacity of all humans to fear shame, blame and punishment, because 'army values' have been broken.[15]

The third principle within the Pali canon is simply its stress on discipline and gradual training. Discipline in spiritual practice is a *sine qua non* for progress in the Buddhist path towards liberation. In the textual strand that I am highlighting, however, it is also a *sine qua non* of governance and the exercise of authority. In the Pali texts, the metaphor of a trained and disciplined animal in war is often used to illustrate the necessity for a trained mind.[16] For instance, the need for a ruler to employ trained, brave and experienced people for his army is used by the Buddha as an illustration of the value of giving gifts to those who have trained their minds, namely the monastic community (A.I.99). The texts see a direct correlation between disciplined spiritual lives and discipline at every level in society, led by those in authority, and expressed both in war and in peace.

This has implications for the training of combatants in war. The ICRC stresses, in *The Roots of Restraint in War*, 'Empirical studies have shown that training increases restraint in the battlefield' (ICRC 2018, 28). Training is not the focus of this article and is covered by other contributors. However, the Pali Canon promotes gradual training as the most efficacious. An illustration that I used in 1994 is worth citing again. The *Dantabhūmi Sutta* in the *Majjhima Nikāya* shows a confused novice monk coming to the Buddha and lamenting that a prince had not responded to his teaching of the Dhamma. The Buddha takes the novice by the hand, as it were, and kindly points out that a prince, steeped in his possessions and his love of the sensual, would not be able to absorb the kind of teaching that the Buddha was giving to his monastic pupils. Significantly, he uses an illustration from warfare. Just as a king's elephant has to be trained gradually to go into battle and withstand the noise and weapons of war, so it is with human beings. They have to be trained gradually in the teaching of the Buddha. So, it would have been far better if the novice had started at a different place (M.III.128–137; Harris 1994, 35–38).

Applying this to the training of combatants, starting with meditation training and the complete eradication of anger, hatred or fear may not be wise or even possible if results are expected. Starting with the rule of law, including IHL, and the very real possibility of sanctions and punishment for those who violate this could be more efficacious. This point was made strongly by the ICRC in their early publication, *The Roots of Behaviour in War*, which stressed not only that 'any failure to obey an order must be sanctioned' but also that it was essential to reach those who had influence over combatants so that orders were in compliance with IHL.[17] Yet gradual training can also be used in the development of values such as the capacity to feel empathy. For Buddhists, the following verse from the *Dhammapada* is often used to support absolute non-violence – 'All beings tremble at the rod; Life is dear to all. Seeing their likeness to yourself, You should neither kill nor cause to kill' (v. 130). Even though combatants can rarely avoid killing, the principle of empathy present in this verse can nevertheless be utilised in training, particularly in the context of IHL, offering a 'value-based motivation' that can be 'as powerful a motivator of combatant behaviour as the threat of punishment' (ICRC 2018, 32) Training in mindfulness can then come later.

Concluding thoughts

In the first part of this article, I sought to demonstrate that the Buddha taught against the backdrop of the political and social realities of his time, with their potential for violence and conflict, and used these realities in metaphors, similes and illustrations. In the second part, I demonstrated that the use of these metaphors and illustrations supported the Buddha's teaching that the world is enmeshed in craving and that the only escape from the consequences of this is to work towards the eradication of selfish craving and the gaining of insight, namely the ability to see things as they really are. In the third part of the article, I set myself the challenge of creating a Buddhist analytical model for understanding why, within some contexts of armed conflict, even when there are Buddhist combatants, IHL has been violated in the conduct of hostilities and humanitarian workers have experienced resistance to their work. I argued that the Pali texts themselves can provide such a model through its teaching about the sheer tenacity of the corruptions (*āsavas*) and the defilements (*kilesa*) within the mind. I focussed particularly on what happens in the mind when thoughts, based on premises rooted in the corruptions or defilements, result in *papañca*, a proliferation of thoughts that victimise the thinker and result in constructed 'realities' that lead individuals and communities away from seeing things as they really are. Most people, including Buddhists, remain susceptible to what this article terms 'constructed realities'. It is in war and conflict, I would suggest, that these constructed realities become most dangerous. They are one of the most pernicious obstacles to ensuring compliance with IHL. In the last section of the article I reflected on whether the Pali textual tradition endorses the initiation of defensive violence and whether principles and teachings from the tradition can be utilised to better regulate the conduct of hostilities and excessive retaliation to prevent violations of IHL, even in the presence of constructed realities. I pointed to sources of internal and external authority and argued that external authority that is subject to dhammic principles has a role in enforcing the rule of law in conflict, through the proper exercise of sanctions and punishment, and the utilisation of the human fear of blame and shame. Although this article recognises that Buddhism ideally condemns all forms of violence and war, it nevertheless argues that it also offers realistic and pragmatic tools for the understanding of conflict and its regulation so that excessive force is not used, and an 'enemy' population is not harmed by obstructing the work of humanitarian workers.

Notes

1. Empirical work and empirical judgements are based on direct observation and experience rather than theory. I use the phrase 'empirical realism' in this article to denote the ability of the Pali texts to represent violence and conflict, through the empirical, namely through what can be observed through the senses, resulting in a graphic and sometimes disturbing realism.
2. See also S.II.118, which describes the consequences of ignorance, one of the causes of craving, in terms of a swelling or surging: 'Bhikkhus, the ocean surging causes the rivers to surge; the rivers surging cause the streams to surge; the streams surging causes the lakes to surge; the lakes surging cause the pools to surge. So too, ignorance surging causes volitional formations to surge; volitional formations surging causes consciousness to surge; consciousness surging causes name-and-form to surge; name-and-form surging causes the six sense bases to surge [etc.]. . .'.
3. Many more discourses could be mentioned that describe dissension and quarrelling within the monastic Sangha, e.g. the *Sāmagāma Sutta* (At Sāmagāma; M.II.243–251) and the *Upakkilesa Sutta* (On Imperfections or Corruptions; M.III.153–162).
4. For instance, see *Sunakkhatta Sutta* (To Sunakkhatta) M.II.252–261.
5. Lederach (2001).
6. I have written on *papañca* before and draw from these sources: see Harris (1994, 27–30) and Harris (2017).
7. See for example the *Aggivacchagotta Sutta* (To Vacchagotta on Fire; M.I.483–489) and the *Dīghanaka Sutta* (To Dīghanaka: M.I.497–501) for a critique of the view that 'This alone is truth'.
8. One text illustrates anger with reference to snakes, a figure that is a familiar one in this article. A person who is quick to anger, for instance, but whose anger does not last long is like a snake that is possessed of poison but is not fiercely

poisonous, and a person who is neither quick to anger nor has anger that lasts long is like a snake that is neither fierce nor venomous (A.II.110–111). Anger is thus also seen as a negative quality that poisons any situation or body politic.

9. ICRC (2018, 67).
10. For example, see the Harvey and Trew articles in this volume.
11. The importance both of moral values rooted in culture or religion and law/authority is stressed in ICRC (2018, e.g. 35 and 65).
12. See for example the *Kodha Vagga* (Chapter on Anger) in the *Dhammpada* (vv. 221–234).
13. See for instance the *Mahāparinibbāna Sutta*, D.II.123–24.
14. See e.g. the Harvey article in this volume.
15. See ICRC (2018, 9 and 32).
16. See for instance *Dhammapada* v. 321: 'Folk take the tamed one into battle; The king mounts the tamed one. The tamed one, who endures abusive speech, is the best among human beings' (Dhp. 321).
17. ICRC (2004, 16).

Disclosure statement

This article has been supported by the International Committee of the Red Cross (ICRC).

Abbreviations

A. *Aṅguttara-nikāya*; as translated by Bhikkhu Bodhi, *The Numerical Discourses of the Buddha: A Translation of the Aṅguttara Nikāya*, Bristol: Pali Text Society, 2012.

D. *Dīgha-nikāya*; as translated by M. Walshe, *The Long Discourses of the Buddha*, Boston: Wisdom, 1995.

Dhp. *Dhammapada*; as translated by V. J. Roebuck, *The Dhammapada*, London: Penguin, 2010.

M. *Majjhima-nikaya*; as translated by Ñāṇamoli Bhikkhu and Bodhi Bhikkhu, *The Middle Length Discourses of the Buddha*. Boston: Wisdom, 1995.

S. *Saṃyutta-nikāya*; as translated by Bhikkhu Bodhi, *The Connected Discourses of the Buddha: A Translation of the Saṃyutta Nikāya*. Boston: Wisdom, 2000.

Sn. *Suttanipāta*, translated by K. R. Norman, *The Group of Discourses (Sutta Nipāta)*, 2nd ed. Oxford: Pali Text Society, 2001.

Translations in this article are those of the above. Reference to A., D., M. and S. are to volume and page number of the Pali Text Society editions of the Pali text, as indicated in the translations (Pali page numbers are shown in square brackets within the translation). For Dhp. and Sn. reference is to verse number.

References

Brazier, C. 2003. *Buddhist Psychology: Liberate Your Mind: Embrace Life*. London: Robinson.

Harris, E. 1994. *Violence and Disruption in Society: A Study of the Early Buddhist Texts*. Kandy: Buddhist Publication Society.

Harris, E. 2017. "Understanding Conflicts over Land: Insights from the Buddhist Tradition". Paper given at "Israel-Palestine and theology of Land", a conference held in Windsor. December. https://ctbi.org.uk/Israel-palestine-and-theology-of-land/

ICRC. 2004. *The Roots of Behaviour in War*. Geneva: ICRC.

ICRC. 2018. *The Roots of Restraint in War*. Geneva: ICRC.

Lederach, J. P. 2001. 'The Challenge of Terror: A Travelling Essay'. https://www.mediate.com/articles/terror911.cfm

Ñāṇananda, B. 1971. *Concept and Reality in Early Buddhist Thought*. Kandy: Buddhist Publication Society.

Shobrook, M. 2015. *From Helpless to Selfless: "Mine" and "I" in Papanca and Cognitive Therapy*. Saarbrücken: Lambert Academic Publishing.

Thapar, R. 1966. *A History of India*. London: Pelican Books.

ICRC

FUNDAMENTAL INTELLIGENCE, A BUDDHIST JUSTIFICATION FOR THE UNIVERSAL PRINCIPLES UNDERLYING IHL

Diane Denis

ABSTRACT

All of us agree that a civilian population is inevitably and profoundly affected by a war, regardless of where this population stands in the scheme of things. A civilian population is hostage to the forces at work, not only physically, economically and socially, but also intimately, emotionally, psychologically and spiritually. In fact, everyone involved in a conflict has to deal with the chaos in his or her own mind and in his or her own environment. The formulation of international humanitarian law (IHL) was influenced by a socially oriented intellectual culture that has often failed to address the inner workings of the individual consciousness. Buddhism's contribution here may be just that: its insistence on the process of cognition as the ground for both the creation of and the liberation from suffering. More specifically, this paper focuses on the *Dharmadharmatāvibhāga* (DDV), an ancient North Indian Buddhist text. The premise is that many such ancient texts have something important to contribute to our contemporary world, by offering some insight into 'universal principles' in the workings of the mind and in human interactions. The question then is: how can these ideas contribute to the development of individual willingness to care and embody ethical conduct even during armed conflicts?

The *Dharmadharmatāvibhāga* and the notion of 'support'[1]

The title of this text, the *Dharmadharmatāvibhāga* (DDV),[2] can be translated as *The Distinction between Phenomena*[3] *and their Nature*. It is a fourth-century North Indian Buddhist text resulting from a series of debates (in *abhidharma* circles), as well as from intensive contemplative practices (meditation). The original target audience was definitely practice-oriented (*Yogācāra*[4]). Within the Tibetan canon, the DDV is classified as a philosophical text.[5] Amongst the commentaries (*śāstra*) on the words of the Buddha (*buddhavacana*), it is associated with the development of wisdom[6] inseparable from

DOI: 10.4324/9781003439820-9

compassion.[7] The Tibetan tradition attributes its composition to Maitreya and its writing to Asaṅga. As the title indicates, its intention is to distinguish between the dualistic appearance of things (i.e. subject–object/me–other/us–them) and their essentially non-dual nature. Within its semantic structure is the notion of reliance, support or basis.[8] In brief, the foundation of human existence is said to be fundamental intelligence, though its expression is often obscured by confusion during conflicts.[9]

IHL and the DDV's justifications for it

In a pragmatic way, it is said that IHL[10] regulates general and even some specific aspects of the conduct of individuals during hostilities on the basis of certain core principles, including the following as described by the International Committee of the Red Cross (ICRC, 2014):

> [. . .] IHL also regulates the general conduct of hostilities on the basis of three core principles: distinction, proportionality, and precaution. The principle of **distinction** requires that the parties to an armed conflict distinguish at all times between civilians and civilian objects on the one hand, and combatants and military objectives on the other, and that attacks may only be directed against combatants and military objectives. The purpose of this is to protect individual civilians, civilian property, and the civilian population as a whole. Under this principle, indiscriminate attacks are prohibited. The principle of **proportionality**, a corollary to the principle of distinction, dictates that incidental loss of civilian life and property or injury to civilians must not be excessive in relation to the concrete and direct military advantage anticipated. In order to implement the restrictions and prohibitions on targeting, the principle of **precaution** requires all parties to an armed conflict to take specific precautions such as, when conducting an attack, to verify that targets are military objectives or to give the civilian population an effective warning before the attack. It can also entail restrictions on the timing and location of an attack. In addition, Articles 35(3) and 55 of [Additional Protocols] AP I prohibit methods and means of warfare that cause widespread, long-term and severe damage to the natural environment. The rules on the conduct of hostilities also grant specific protection to certain objects, including cultural property and places of worship (the 1954 Hague Convention for the Protection of Cultural Property in the Event of Armed Conflict; AP I, Article 53; AP II, Article 16), objects indispensable to the survival of the civilian population (AP I, Article 54; AP II, Article 14), and 'works and installations containing dangerous forces' (AP I, Article 56; AP II, Article 15). Such works and installations, as well as cultural property and civil defence personnel and facilities, can be identified by specific symbols [. . .] (2014, 3–4)

These all involve a process of discrimination that comprises development of knowledge, ethics and dignified conduct. However, exemplary conduct informed by Buddhist principles would possibly require an even greater sense of individual responsibility, for which inner training is necessary.

While restrictions on armed conflict are found in many ancient cultures and in the development of military philosophies, at its inception IHL was influenced by the intellectual culture of its time, which sought to embrace common or universal values rather than necessarily address the inner workings and peculiarities of the individual consciousness.[11] In fact, Jean Pictet, a Swiss jurist responsible for the elaboration of the Geneva Convention after the Second World War, says:[12]

> The modern world has placed its hopes in internationalism and therein no doubt its future lies. Now, in an international environment, [hu]man's rights can only be based on what is universal, on ideas capable of bringing together men [and women] of all races . . .

Pictet highlights the need for consensus amongst cultures in regard to IHL, and goes on to say that:

> The plurality of cultures and the need to take an interest in them and study them in depth is recognized. This leads to an awareness that humanitarian principles are common to all human communities wherever they may be. When different customs, ethics and philosophies are gathered for comparison, and when they are melted down, their particularities eliminated and only what is general extracted, one is left with a pure substance which is the heritage of all [hu]mankind. (1988, 3–4)

As with many areas of law, individual motive and intention are relevant to IHL and to judging infringements of it. However, over the years, the notion of 'universality' implicit to IHL has sometimes been criticised and seen as a product of 'Western' political, cultural, social and even religious history. Whether accurate or not about the origin of IHL, the argument against the idea of 'universality' is that although this notion creates possibilities for common-sense agreement, it also triggers culturally specific disagreement. In other words, on the one hand, we have complementary bodies of law such as IHL and the human rights law, which are seeking a universal ground and which should apply to every human being, and on the other, we have the idea that no 'moral' or 'ethical' principles can be made to apply to all cultures.[13] Facing this dichotomy, one may argue in accordance with Pictet that some aspects of these two bodies of international law can trigger cultural differences, but that surely the right for civilians not to be indiscriminately killed or maimed in war can be respected by everyone. Or again, that soldiers should not intentionally target non-combatants! Most Buddhist thinkers would agree with these arguments, including the author of the DDV. It should be noted here that IHL and human rights law are separate yet complementary bodies of law. IHL's philosophical roots are ancient, and its aims are modest – to preserve some humanity amidst the inhumanity of war. Human rights law is rooted in 'Western' culture, and demands more of political leaders. Therefore, it is sometimes possible to get agreement on IHL matters, even when a state is sceptical about the notion of human rights. Perhaps the fact that IHL and human rights law have different philosophical roots might make it easier for IHL to engage with different cultural traditions than human rights law.[14]

From the DDV's perspective, it would be helpful here to look not only at the content of the law, or at the ways it can be fruitful, but also at the inner 'workings of perception' implicit to any living organisms and to all interaction. In this context, words and concepts are clearly the instruments of any process of perception. When active, an individual's 'process' of perception operates by identifying specificities and differences in a sequence of action. According to early philosophical descriptions, first there is a perception (*saṃjñā*) which is the act of identifying the specific traits of an object – whether this object is seen, heard, tasted, smelt, touched or thought of. This perception leads to the fabrication of a barely noticeable concept (*parikalpa*) which allows an act of discrimination (*vikalpa*) which in turns separates this perception from what is different from it; then, based on that discrimination, an elaboration (*prapañca*) takes place . . ..[15] These inner workings of individual minds are part of what make up cultures and societies. All societies have a propensity to elaborate codes of behaviour, and this is a basic principle at work everywhere. The main enactors of ideas are individual processes of perception. Any debate and culturally specific agreement or disagreement come about because ideas and concepts are born out of a process of distinctions and discriminations. Rules based on cultures and religious beliefs are often bound to bring disagreements between individuals. So, in many ways, we could say that IHL is trying to create a 'common culture' around armed conflict where everyone can find some kind of agreement.

Yet I suggest here that the 'pure substance' sought by Pictet can probably not be found in ideas alone because of the very nature of ideas and of the 'process of perception'. Could this 'pure substance' then be found in acknowledging the process of cognition common to all beings? In many ways, the acknowledgement of the dualistic workings of consciousness, and to some extent of the non-duality of subject and object and of fundamental intelligence inherent to all living creatures, provides a Buddhist justification for the universal protections under IHL. It also provides a justification for attending to basic human needs as well as fulfiling the 'humanitarian' aspiration of IHL.

When Pictet claims that *although* [. . . people] *are different, human nature is the same the world over* (1988, 3–4), the DDV agrees with him but goes even further. Human nature is not only the same the world over, all beings, and the environment, are of the same nature; nothing is completely separate; all and everything is interrelated. At the very heart of all of this, from the DDV's point of view, is non-duality (the interdependence of the subject perceiving and the object perceived) and fundamental intelligence. Our task as socially concerned individuals is to create the conditions for it to express itself whenever possible, and there are many ways to go about this. Seeking common values is one of them.

Recently, 15 scholars of economics, law and the natural sciences published an article online called 'From the Anthropocene to Mutual Thriving',[16] inviting thinkers to shift from the dichotomies of a subject versus object view of the world to an 'Ecozoic'[17] understanding of mutually enhancing subject–subject relationships. With these discussions, they envision a shift from an 'ontology' of separation to one of interconnectedness; from an axiology of material development to a plurality of values for world and meaning making. In his book *The Social Face of Buddhism*, Jones (2003) makes a similar call by bringing the notion of non-duality as the hallmark of interdependence and as the very nature of the process of cognition, thus rethinking the relationship of the individual and society, subject and object, and beings and their environment. His main thesis is that inner liberation is the ultimate precondition for a collective and sustainable outer liberation.[18] This implies that, in an effort to reduce suffering, we must invest in the inner development of individual character.

In the same way, one of the reasons that I suggest that the DDV can be of help in a discussion on armed conflict, and to support the work of the Red Cross and Red Crescent with regard to promoting IHL, is that this text is specifically intended to inform the act of being in the world, of engaging in relationships and of experiencing the experiencer himself or herself (i.e. reflexive awareness). In other words, it includes individual experience in its analysis and emphasises the importance of this individual experience during a conflict. This text is intended to bring profound and unwavering support for individuals in their inevitable struggle to navigate the rugged geography of experience, whether peaceful or chaotic. And, as with many Buddhist philosophical texts, it necessarily starts with mapping the geography of experience by offering a structural framework to help assess the situation and offer guidance.

The threefold framework for assessment and guidance

In its intention to inform individuals about the process of perception, in the first part of stanza 12, the DDV presents the general state of affairs: 'Whenever beings move around somewhere, there are supports upon which rests the unending cycle of suffering. In this vicious circle, there is what the experience of "beings" relies on; and there is the environment that serves as support[19] . . .' (12).

The notion of 'support' – also found under the Sanskrit terms *āśraya* (basis), *sthāna* (stance, place or foundation), *pratiṣṭhā* (to rely on)[20] and so on – permeates several traditions of Buddhist thought, almost to an obsessive degree. It is often used in an instrumental sense (i.e. what beings gain benefit from) and at other times used in a more fundamental sense (i.e. what causes beings to experience a particular state). Perhaps this obsession is not only a Buddhist thing, but a fundamental human concern for security, and for its continuous quest to find meaning. Nevertheless, in a Buddhist context, the notion of support inevitably relates to the notions of 'interdependence' and 'causality'.

From the perspective of relative reality, any experience is considered neither without causes nor without conditions. Moreover, in the interaction of causes and conditions, no one is a passive receptor. Perception implies the action of grasping (Sk. *graha*). The working of perception here can be compared to a 'process'; it is impersonal, yet it is an activity with a consequence. This activity and its consequences can be described as the result of a constant interaction, or as a fine and subtle conversation between countless events. It is dynamic, situational, momentary and continuously in movement. The chain of causes and conditions is thought of as so complex that it is inconceivable, beyond the reach of intellectual understanding. From this perspective, the simple fact of 'being', 'seeing', 'thinking' ... occurs through a natural tendency to grasp (*graha*), to construct (*kalpanā, parikalpa, vikalpa*) and to elaborate (*prapañca*). Everything, including a conception of the world, has a consequence on the following sequence of thoughts, emotions, actions, etc. Like a circle engendering its next round, *ad infinitum* ...

Far from being fatalistic and abstract, the idea of 'support' in this Buddhist description of the process of perception reminds all who want to hear it that people have access to a practical and immediate handle on some things: awareness. In other words, the invitation here is to move from a repetitive habit of ignoring the inner workings of the mind (irresponsibility) to a momentary dynamic of awareness and individual 'responsibility'. And this is so from the very first texts attributed to the Buddha, i.e. the *Dharmacakrapravartana-sūtra* and the *Anātmalakṣaṇa-sūtra*, to later Mahāyāna texts such as the *Aṣṭasāhasrikā Prajñāpāramitā-sūtra*, to 'treatises' like the DDV that take on the specific task of addressing the issue of 'what one relies on'. This idea of 'support', in my view, is key in examining the interface between Buddhism[21] and IHL – it focuses attention on a possible 'universal principle' at work in any human encounter as well as on a justification for its implementation.

Thus, from a Buddhist perspective, if one does not acknowledge the workings of the mind in an armed conflict, one cannot offer an appropriate response to the situation at hand. Blind, habitual conditioned responses are bound to create suffering for oneself or/and others. Why? Partly because they are not in accord with the specificity of a situation. The opposite is also true.

According to these ancient texts, when one can appreciate the actual complex and fabricated state of affairs, ethical conduct can be an accurate response and a key in reducing suffering.

Along these same lines, in his short but fascinating book called *Ethical Know-How, Action, Wisdom, and Cognition*, the biologist, philosopher and neuroscientist Francisco[22] Varela (1999) calls for training in ethical spontaneity after revisiting the notion of ethical conduct:

> As a first approximation, let me say that a wise (or virtuous) person is one who knows what is good and spontaneously does it. It is the immediacy of perception and action which we want to examine critically. This approach stands in stark contrast to the usual way of investigating ethical behavior, which begins by analysing the intentional content of an act and ends by evaluating the rationality of particular moral judgements. (1999, 4)

With his findings, Varela focuses on the proper units of knowledge, and defines them as a concrete, lived experience based on immediate perception. Varela associates these embodied experiences in action with innate wisdom. Here he does not deny the importance of deliberation and analysis, but he insists on the necessity to consider both modes of cognition (analytical and immediate) in the discussions on ethics:

> In other words, cognitive science is waking up to the simple fact that just *being there*, immediate coping, is far from simple or reflexive. Immediate coping is, in fact, the real 'hard work' since it took the longest evolutionary time to develop. The ability to make intentional, rational analyses during breakdowns appeared only recently and very rapidly in evolutionary terms. (1999, 18)

For Varela, there is no doubt that many Buddhist teachings, although completely different from scientific research in their approach and outlook, are in accord with his neuroscience findings. More importantly for him, these teachings can act as one of the possible guides for training in refining natural, inherent abilities, a type of training in spontaneity. This may be a possible avenue for further research for IHL scholars.

In brief, this first part of the stanza says that when considering a situation, there are at least two interactive phenomena to take into account. These two interactive phenomena are also a way to expose dualistic thinking:

(1) individual beings with their 'process of perception' (subject),
(2) and the form that the environment takes for individuals (object).

Borrowed from earlier Indian schools of thought, this is a classic Indian presentation: there is the container – acting as the support (i.e. environment or womb); and the contained – acting as what is supported (i.e. beings, seeds or potential).[23] We could also think of it as a division between mind and matter, i.e. the mind of an individual and their physical environment, but the DDV insists on the overall importance of the mind. Suffering occurs within the experience of individuals in this dynamic. In other words, from the DDV's point of view, there is no experience of the world without an active process of perception. There is no experience of suffering without the process of cognition. This suggests that when one's goal is to reduce suffering, one must consider the process of cognition as the 'building block' upon which everything else rests. From this perspective, a division between the inner and the outer (duality) is more apparent than real; the process of cognition is *the* determinant factor in all situations. That is probably why, in the last part of stanza 12, the DDV further divides the process of cognition into two aspects: 'What the experience of "beings" relies on can be divided into what is shared by them (i.e. what is relationally produced), and what is not shared by them (i.e. what is intimate and personal)'[24] (12).

When combining the first part and the last part of stanza 12, we end up with a threefold framework for assessing situations in general, and more specifically here for IHL:

(1) what seems shared by beings (object);
(2) what is interdependently shared (relations);
(3) and what is not shared, or intimate to each individual (subject).[25]

The first element of this framework refers to the environmental and external circumstances. The term 'seems' puts emphasis on the fact that where suffering is concerned, the mind is foremost. The experience of external circumstances depends on the mind. The second refers to the relational aspect of a situation. The DDV indicates here that all relational activities are caused and determined in reciprocity.[26] We could say that they are non-dual in that they are interdependent – not separate. All relations get hooked to each other in repetitive patterns until the process of perception is clearly brought to awareness. The third element refers to sensory consciousnesses (visual, auditory, olfactory, gustative, tactile) to which we add the mental consciousness interacting with thoughts and with the dynamic of conditioning. The third element of this threefold framework focuses on the way one experiences the world and relationships (i.e. on the 'process of perception'). In other words, to repeat, it is *the* determinant factor. Mind is foremost, even in times of conflict. So, what does this mean for IHL? How does this internal process apply to a civilian population and to soldiers during armed conflict?

Amongst the many qualities to be developed on the Buddhist path in the context of armed conflict, forbearance (*kṣānti*) – a form of non-violent communication or training – plays a particularly important role. The meaning of the equivalent Pāli term *khanti* is described by Sasaki[27] as a 'willingness' to calmly engage all things and/or views along with their implications, without detriment to oneself or others. In the description of this term, the consequences of one's views and actions are at the heart of the matter. Any view has its consequences, and the view of non-duality is thought here to yield the best results. In practical terms, when a seeming separation between self and other is held to be real, the consequence is suffering, unease; when it is seen as misleading, one tends to better embrace the importance of the practice of forbearance (Sk. *kṣānti* or the calm commitment to being with what is) and benevolence (Sk. *maitrī*) for those on one's 'own' side, as well as for those on the 'other' side. The key lies in understanding the workings of the mind in the sense of what yields the best result.

In the DDV's framework, the dynamic of conditioning leads to the conclusion that the appearance of duality (i.e. a complete separation between subject and object) does not actually exist in the way it appears. How is that? It is said that by the time an object of perception is brought to awareness, a process of perception (i.e. grasping, constructing and elaborating) has already occurred. What is actually seen (e.g. an enemy) has been mentally organised to appear in such a way. So what is seen is not the 'object' itself, but an interpretation of the 'object'.[28] All perceptions are fabricated; all appearances are *interpretation-only*.[29] Perceptions are coloured by individual predispositions; dressed up and conditioned by previous experiences.

The appearance of duality, although unprompted and involuntary, is misleading because what is perceived is the product of one's own process of perception. No division between subject and object is ever possible. Duality appears to individuals just as a mirage, an illusion, or a magical display. This is why, on the quest to reduce suffering, the unquestioned belief and reliance on dualistic perception is identified as the subtlest form of aggression/ignorance, and as the basis of all conflicts and suffering. With this analysis and these examples, we end up understanding that, as individuals, we are all bound to work with dualistic perceptions, but that we can learn to not be fooled by the 'process'. Just like when seeing a rabbit coming out of a magician's hat, one can understand that a process is behind the illusion.

In his search for a Buddhist social theory influenced by the Zen tradition, Jones (2003) examines the consequences of such possibility: 'when self (subject) gives up its struggle to sustain its sense of separation from all that is other (object) it opens to an at-oneness' (2003, 14).[30] In other words, a Dharmic view is not only assessed and appreciated according to its coherence and 'truthfulness', but also according to its implications and repercussions on individual and collective realities. A sense of separated-ness from others, from the world and from nature is not only a misinterpretation, it also leads inevitably to tension, conflict and suffering. Accordingly, the Australian philosopher Chadha (2018) says that the view of interdependence associated here with non-duality (the absence of existence of an independent self/subject) is not only a logical conclusion to analysis, it is *the* preferred ethical stance: 'The Abhidharma Buddhist revisionary metaphysics aims to provide an intellectually and morally preferred picture of the world that lacks a self' (2018, 1). Although Chadha here writes specifically about the Abhidharma view, her statement about the self applies to most schools of Buddhist thought. For example, non-duality in the DDV indicates that there is no perception of an object without a subject perceiving it, and vice versa; they are interdependent.

More importantly, though, Chadha implies that ethics is not separate from the development of wisdom (e.g. recollection of the view of interdependence). The *Dīgha Nikāya* I.124 says that ethics and wisdom are like two hands washing each other. In non-dualistic terms, ethics is understood as the actual embodiment of wisdom. From an ideal way of being in the world, it progressively becomes a natural lived embodied experience in action. Ethical conduct is the willingness and commitment to be there with what appears. With this willingness, one becomes responsible for one's own perceptions and projections, neither rejecting them and losing track of relative reality, nor fixating on them (i.e. crystallising them into fixed realities) and being fooled by appearances. In the best scenarios, this presentation can bring light to one's responsibility in participating in the creation of the best conditions in any situation by recollecting a view of the situation that is conducive to virtue – in other words, manifesting an exemplary ethical conduct, particularly important in difficult, conflicted situations.

Assessment and guidance

As shown above, this threefold framework is an interesting device for individuals assessing their own situation. From this perspective, this description is concerned with the development of individual characters, yet it can also, and simultaneously, serve organisations. When assessing the situation of a civilian population, organisations could use this same framework and consider:

(1) the external circumstances of the civilian population and their physical situation,
(2) the relationship of the civilian population to the conflict itself, to humanitarian aid and to the armed forces or soldiers,
(3) and, finally, the individual experience that may vary widely from one person to another (including spiritual and future concerns).

Although such an assessment is aimed at simply understanding the state of affairs, it can also be motivated by the desire to facilitate the creation of the best conditions for the well-being of each and every being and group. Buddhist communities have sometimes used this framework to offer governing, legal and humanitarian guidance. It can be observed, for example, to operate centuries before the composition of the DDV during the time of the Buddhist king Aśoka, around 272–236 BCE in Central India. As attested by Pillar Edict number 4, there are concerns (1) for the social environment, (2) for the relational reality of individuals and (3) for personal situation and individual experience, including a concern for the workings of consciousness and its consequence in future times.[31] Hultzsch's (1925) translation reads as follows:

> For the following is to be desired, that there should be both uniformity in judicial proceedings and impartiality in punishments (1).
>
> And my order [reaches] even so far [that] a respite of three days is granted by me to persons lying in prison on whom punishment has been passed, [and] who have been condemned to death.[32]
>
> [In this way] either [their] relatives will persuade those [Lajūkas] to [grant] their life (2), or, if there is none who persuades [them], they will bestow gifts or will undergo fasts in order to [attain happiness] in the other [world] (3).
>
> For my desire is this, that, even when the time [of respite] has expired, they should attain [happiness] in the other [world] (3).
>
> And various moral practices, self-control, [and] the distribution of gifts are [thus] promoted among the people (2).[33] [numbers added for emphasis]

Norman (1975) analysed the language of the above edict and does not see it as making any reference to the death penalty:

> And even up to now (this has been) my practice. To those persons who have been imprisoned, have completed their punishments, have received their beatings, an allowance has been given by me for three days. And their relatives will make (them) think of a refuge to save their lives. Being made to think indeed of death as the end (of life), they will either make a gift connected with the next world, or perform a fast.
>
> For my desire is that even in the limited time (remaining to them), they may thus attain the next world. (1975, 21)

Despite possible problems of translation, what can be observed here is that the threefold framework is used in an effort to organise human interaction in cross-cultural contexts. In terms of the development of individual characters, the qualities of generosity and inner discipline, which are integral to Buddhist training, are encouraged. The statement on the treatment of prisoners is concerned with apparent down-to-earth realities, perhaps best expressed as *uniformity in judicial procedure*. Ethics and clear rules are presented as key in organising the coherent workings of a society and in creating conducive conditions for the well-being of individuals. Moreover, the role of friends and family is empowered through the possibility of intervening. This is an example of legal, ethical and spiritual preoccupations working together to foster care and dignity. Yet the DDV goes further than this in its pursuit of offering guidance in embodied, ethical wisdom.

Fundamental intelligence as ground for ethics

Even if we usually think of ethics/morals in terms of 'dos' and 'don'ts' – good behaviour versus bad behaviour, and consequently in times of conflict what is good (our tradition/culture) versus what is bad (what threatens it) – a Buddhist perspective prevents simplistic dualistic interpretation and responses. Of course, Buddhist communities make a distinction between what is wholesome (*kuśala*) and unwholesome (*akuśala*), yet, as Damien Keown points out, Buddhist ethics (*śīla*) is not normative but concerned with causes and effects of action (1996, 338). It looks to the causative roots of actions – attraction, aversion, ignorance; it looks to their opposites when adopting the path, and it also looks at the results of these actions, with an emphasis:

- on the future result (not simply the present situation);
- on the formation of individual character (i.e. path/journey);
- on liberation or enlightenment.

In the same way, in the DDV, ethics are necessarily linked to wisdom (inseparable from compassion). The principle said to operate in Buddhist ethics is that actions – of body, speech and mind – leave imprints (predispositions associated with volition) on each individual mind stream (intimate individual experience). As a result, these imprints influence the future course of events and therefore the dynamic of relationships and societies. Even if thoughts about future results of an action may be one component in deciding whether to do something or not, from a Buddhist perspective the dynamic of conditioning occurs whether one believes or not in past and future lives. In other words, it is apersonal, acultural; it does not relate to likes or dislikes, or simply to the conscious will of an individual.[34] During an armed conflict, the ethical conduct operating – for a combatant, a prisoner or a civilian – necessarily involves an encounter with intimately stored inner imprints. The external conflict as experienced by an individual is inevitably an inner journey. And it may, if apprehended consciously, become an incursion into the strengthening of one's own capacity to work within heightened and chaotic situations.

Thus, how might this influence conduct in line with, or against, the principles of IHL? As it is with the edict of Aśoka and with the threefold framework offered by the DDV, an external law is essential (*uniformity in judicial procedure*), but it is only one of the ingredients to success; a personal and a collective concern for the development of individual characters and for the relational realities are also important. The emphasis here is put on the individual capacity to discriminate.[35] There is a distinction between a process of discrimination leading to 'dogma' (strong habitual tendencies based on a simplistic opposition of good vs. bad) and a process of discrimination leading to 'nonpartisan logic'[36] with an ability to consider the complexity of a situation at hand. From this perspective, views, values, rules and trainings are not there to simply impose a particular behaviour, but to inform the inherent process of discrimination, the innate capacity for liberation.

So, from this point of view, when concerned with the development of individual character, a view, a rule or a law acts as a framework to develop critical thinking,[37] to develop a capacity to apply basic philosophical principles and to develop ethical expertise. In the DDV, and as it is found in several other Buddhist philosophical texts, ethical expertise is first developed through remembering again and again that everything that appears is 'interpretation-only'. Another way to train in this type of ethical expertise would be to remember the impermanence, the interdependence and/or the composite-ness of all that appears. The advantage with the training in 'interpretation-only' lies in the implied responsibility for one's own perception of reality – the reality appears in such and such a way because 'one's own' particular process of perception makes it appear so. The notion of responsability here is not retroactive by nature, it does not entail blame nor does it imply culpabilty for wrongdoings or failures; on the contrary, it is proactive in the development of wisdom with strong ethical implications. One changes the very framework of habitual tendencies. It is by taking the process of cognition into account that one turns the mind onto itself and liberates it from its tendencies. Yet simply changing a habit or a view for another is not the aim of such texts; its aim is much more radical than this.

In a later stanza,[38] one is further invited to consider everything that appears from the perspective of *dharmatā*. The term *dharmatā* is usually translated as the nature of phenomena, the nature of all that appears – in other words, the nature of external things like mountains and guns; the nature of relational realities like friends and enemies; and the nature of internal ones like fear and relief. It would thus include the experience of kindness as much as of cruelty, of love as much as of hatred, and compliance with, or violation of, laws like IHL and so on – whatever appears, its very nature is suchness (Sk. *tathatā*): the as-it-is-ness of things as they are. Suchness is neither good nor bad, it is just so without divisions: '. . . the nature of all that appears is suchness without a separation between an object grasped and a subject grasping or [between] what is designated and the designation'[39] (6).

The term suchness can be understood as non-duality, egolessness or selflessness,[40] or emptiness. What it means in concrete terms is that no matter how things appear, reality cannot be reduced to a division between subject and object, to a dualistic interpretation; it cannot be reduced to ideas, to words or to what these words refer to; and it cannot be reduced to a strict separation between friends and enemies.

The first steps dealing with the dynamic of conditioning put an emphasis on the 'intention' or the 'motivation'. Traditionally, for Buddhists, this may mean taking refuge in the Buddha/Dharma/Sangha: in a wakeful state of mind throughout the day. It is a way to remind oneself of one's most profound aspiration to be free of confusion and suffering; the idea of refuge here is also associated with the wish to be wholesome or useful (Sk. *kuśala*). It is worth noting here that people like John Makransky (2017) are actually developing this idea of refuge outside of the specificity of Buddhist communities as a way to develop sustainable compassion.[41] Traditionally, this motivation is also further nourished by the development of many qualities, amongst which we mentioned the idea of tolerance (*kṣānti*). Now with suchness, the quality that is being developed is equal-mindedness (*samatā*) towards beings and towards circumstances, whatever they may be. In this context, the development of wisdom supports the development of ethical conduct. It is further supported by an initial commitment to be mindful and aware. This 'equal-mindedness' (an attitude that sees an equality (*samatā*) between beings, and between circumstances) favours the full expression of one's potential. So, in spite of the fact that things appear separate, appearances are but a product of a process of perception; and any interpretation has its limits. According to the DDV, this is so in part due to our reliance on words and ideas. Knowing the limitation of our interpretation is already a sign of clear thinking. One acts according to one's interpretation while clearly understanding its limits. The notion of suchness in this context becomes a doorway to non-conceptual, natural, inherent, ethical know-how, also called fundamental intelligence. It creates the necessary space for a breath of fresh air during times of conflict.

Fundamental intelligence as a universal principle

In its quest to identify a reliable ground, the DDV equates suchness (i.e. things as they are) with non-dual, non-conceptual fundamental intelligence.[42] In other texts and contexts, this is also called wisdom (*jñāna* or *prajñā*) or Buddha-nature (*tathāgatagarbha* or *gotra*), and is seen as basic goodness, emptiness (*śūnyatā*[43]) and also luminosity (*prabhāsvara*[44]), perfection of wisdom (*prajñāpāramitā*) and so on. In stanza 33,[45] it is identified as the ground from which the full potential of beings is actualised (i.e. free from all suffering and endowed with exceptional qualities). And in stanza 50.2, this ground is described in the following way:

> Fundamental non-conceptual intelligence is without reference, without any dualistic distinction.
>
> It involves no object grasped nor any grasping subject, since it has the particularity of using no referents.[46] (50.2)

At this point, one comes to consider that non-dual fundamental intelligence is simply present; it is unconditioned, all-encompassing, the nature of all beings. From the DDV's perspective, fundamental intelligence is accessible at all times. It may not be noticed, yet this unconditioned realm of suchness is never beyond reach. Non-duality is the ground from which duality manifests, just as one can say that the infinite embraces finiteness.

So, if one is to rely on something conducive to reduce suffering, one needs to rely on this sound and sensible groundless ground. Fundamental intelligence is sound because it can be logically coherent (interestingly resonating with Varela's research); it is sensible because it is conducive to ethical conduct; and it is groundless because it does not rely on apparent duality. Rather, this groundless ground is a direct natural experience, and according to the first chapter of one of the foundational texts of Mahāyāna, the *Aṣtasāhasrikā Prajñāpāramitā-sūtra*, it is the expression of skilful means in itself (i.e. compassion[47]). This innate wisdom can be associated here with basic, good common sense and considered, from the Mahāyāna point of view, a universal principle at work in all living organisms. In practical terms, this means that with appreciation and confidence in one's own capacity to respond adequately to situations, one is already better equipped to face the chaos in one's environment and in one's own mind. And with the sense that everyone around is endowed with this same basic nature, dignified conduct becomes evident. So how can this notion further serve to inform IHL's aim of reducing suffering?

More on the development of individual characters

Many questions remain, but based on the idea of universal access to fundamental intelligence, some of the Buddhist methods, as Varela indicates, can be a guide for individuals; they can offer practical ideas and trainings that go beyond what sceptics may think of as a 'barren' or as a 'naïve' foundational justification for IHL. Throughout this article, I have hinted at some possible ways to train,[48] the main one being the development of non-dual awareness based on an understanding that all that appears to the mind is the result of a process of interpretation.

Sceptics *could* already argue that if one takes the point of view that 'everything is interpretation-only', one ends up with unbridled relativism, 'alternative facts', and no common ground to agree on within a society. Against this argument, it is best to point out that the expression 'interpretation-only' is another way to speak of interdependence, the only difference from earlier schools being a stronger emphasis on the process of perception/interpretation/projection. It is a way to say that there are limits to any interpretations. It is also used as part of mindfulness training.

Central to all Buddhist schools and practices, recollection/mindfulness (*smṛti* or *anusmṛti*[49]) may be defined as an act of remembering; of preventing ideas from 'floating away'; of counteracting forgetfulness, carelessness and distraction. It is linked to an informed way of watching and it is relevant to all three trainings: ethics, meditation and wisdom. In the DDV, recollecting a view like 'interpretation-only' is training in being mindful – that is, cultivating one's growing understanding of the way mental and physical appearances come to be and come to disappear based on informed experience.

To give other examples of such practices, in the *Satipaṭṭhāna Sutta* (MN 10) which is often associated with early schools, the emphasis is placed on watching arising and ceasing:

> In this way, she lives watching mind within as mind, or she lives watching mind without as mind, or she lives watching mind within and without as mind. She lives watching the way things arise in the case of mind; or she lives watching the way things pass in the case of mind; or she lives watching the way things arise and pass in the case of mind. Furthermore, her mindfulness that there is mind is established so that there is knowledge and recollection in full degree; she lives independently, not holding on to anything in the world. This is how a practitioner lives watching mind as mind.[50]

This observation of the arising and passing away of states of mind, without attachment or rejection, is essential on the path. Mind events are seen, observed and taught as ephemeral processes, and the meditator is asked here to watch the dynamic of arising and ceasing. I see a common mindfulness-thread between early schools and later schools. In many sections of the *Prajñāpāramitā-sūtra* literature most often associated with later schools, one can find such mindfulness instructions. In the case of the *Aṣṭa*, the emphasis is put on the 'not holding on to anything'. The act of recollecting is informed here to counteract the tendency to make experienced events into 'something':

> Subhuti then said to Sakra: Now, Kausika, listen and attend well. I will teach you how a Bodhisattva should stand in perfect wisdom .... Armed with the great armor, the Bodhisattva should so develop that [s]he does not take h[er] stand on the ideas that 'form, etc., is permanent, [or] impermanent'; that 'form is ease or ill'; that 'form is the self, or not the self', that 'form is lovely or repulsive', that 'form is empty', or apprehended as something.[51]

Regardless of philosophical debates between schools, living mindfully in both cases is about not holding on to anything. And this way of living is said to lead to seeing the way things are, to Nirvāṇa. An example of the result of other such 'informed watching' is also found in a later colourful description offered by the Indian tantric scholar Ratnākaraśānti (1000 CE), known as Śāntipa, associated with the Mahāsiddha tradition: 'Then, one's own mind, in which the whole world appears, is seen to be like the stainless sky on an autumn day at noon: contentless, unending bare manifestation'.[52]

The aim of most of these recollection/mindfulness practices is to learn to let go of the production of projections and generic ideas about reality, and to actually taste the specificity and particularity of one's own experience as it is. It is to draw insight from what is there, rather than from extrapolations, habits and interpretations. Stanza 37 of the DDV gives more specific steps to help anchor this understanding into experience:

> An access into fundamental non-conceptual intelligence is established through correct practice in four steps:
> (1) the practice with a point of view: 'interpretation-only',
> (2) the practice without an object,
> (3) the practice without a subject,
> (4) and the practice with neither subject nor object as referent.[53] (37)

Although this stanza may seem cryptic, these four steps are extraordinarily efficient. Their efficiency depends on a strong commitment to hold a particular point of view (i.e. one conducive to insight). First, the individual trains by adopting the view that everything that appears is 'interpretation-only' (1). The simple fact of remembering again and again the view 'interpretation-only' is itself conducive to gaining insight into the nature of things. It is thought that these types of practices create an inner space necessary for fundamental intelligence to express itself and to become the leading force in daily activity as well as in difficult situations. And with this first step, one already gets a sense that the external world and circumstances do not exist exactly as they appear; appearances do not exist independently from the process of perception. Relying on or resting within this insight is the second step (2). When the seeming solidity of external objects falls away, the subject who tends to look outwards automatically becomes the object of attention. And as it is with the object, the subject is also 'interpretation-only'. The sense of an individual self being separate from others is as much a fabrication; it is as much an interpretation as everything else. Relying on this insight is the third step (3). Finally, this realisation opens the space of non-dual awareness (4).

Coming to terms with the reality of the absence of inherent existence here does not lead to carelessness and aloofness. On the contrary, when one is profoundly aware of the workings of the process of cognition, one gains inner space, a release of extraneous tension. In this space, inherent wisdom can express itself and become the ground for exemplary conduct. What is observed by Buddhist communities is that this awareness brings a deep sense of caring. It manifests as full awareness in action; it yields a sense of connectedness with people and the world. The natural act of 'caring' comes from the understanding that one is never completely separate from the situation at hand; it comes from the clarity of one's sharp, critical assessment of the situation.[54]

As with most Buddhist approaches, Varela insists on repetitive exposure as the natural learning process of all organisms. Central to the leading theories on the notion and dynamic of 'expertise' is the idea that one becomes an expert through brute repetition. Just like a beginner musician plays the scales over and over again on their instrument, expertise occurs through a high level of automation yielding spontaneous naturalness. With repetition, in this process, one integrates and embodies the view that leads to ethical behaviour; reactions become more natural and more adapted to the situation at hand. Varela indicates that in traditional communities, the ethical expert, the Wise One, is usually clearly identified and can act as a role model. In modern societies, it has become difficult to identify ethical role models. This is problematic (1999, 24). It may be time to change this state of affairs. For Makransky, a professor of Buddhism and comparative theology at Boston College and a meditation teacher, the sense of connectedness is *the* key. He insists on the fact that there is no real solution to violence without an impartial sense of connectedness and wisdom.[55]

Conclusion

To summarise briefly, the first key to reducing suffering in times of conflict, from the DDV's point of view, comes from a proper assessment of a situation. Organised in a threefold framework (external, relational and internal circumstances), this text's framework relies on an understanding of the workings of the process of cognition and its result: dualistic thinking. From this perspective, an interface between IHL and Buddhism is best served when one considers the misleading role that appearances, based on the belief in a complete separation between self and other, play in our ability to see clearly. Based on this consideration, the next key involves non-duality and fundamental intelligence as the most basic principles at work in any living situation. If one embraces this state of affairs, then views, values and rules are seen not to impose a particular behaviour, but to inform the inherent process of discrimination, and to invite the natural expression of fundamental intelligence. If the notions of non-duality and fundamental intelligence are useful for developing individual characters, they also provide a Buddhist justification for the universal principles underlying IHL. The emphasis here is on individuals' commitment to manifesting care and dignity within their respective communities (including allies and enemies) even when navigating the rugged geography of the experience of chaos and suffering.

While, in this paper, I have focussed on an outlook and mental attitude that is supportive of non-aggressive caring, and thus respect for human dignity in the context of IHL, I have also emphasised the importance of repeated *training in building beneficial character traits*, which would be valuable for those who go on to be active in armed conflict against those conventionally designated as 'enemies', as well as for those who are caught up or have to work in armed conflict situations.

Notes

1. This paper has greatly benefitted from Kate Crosby, Andrew Bartles-Smith and Peter Harvey's bright and insightful comments and from Charby Slemin's close reading. My sincere gratitude goes to all of them.
2. The full Sanskrit original of this text has not been found; only fragments remain. There are several Tibetan editions of the entire text of both prose (DDV) and versified versions (DDVK-*kārikā*); there are very recent Chinese translations based on Tibetan editions. In this paper, I offer an original translation of some stanzas of a *Derge* Tibetan versified version (DDVK) often used in the Kagyu lineage of Tibetan Buddhism. In its original form, the DDV is quite technical and so I have chosen to adapt the language for our purpose. Faithful translations of the stanzas are offered in the notes.
3. The term 'phenomena' here is a translation of the Sanskrit term *dharma*. For more information on this term, see, amongst others, the works of Geiger and Geiger ([1920] 1973), Stcherbatsky (1923), Carter (1976, 1978), Cox (2004), Gethin (2004) and, more recently, Denis (2017).
4. Although the *Dharmadharmatāvibhāga* is most often associated with the Yogācāra school, I find that it is best to see it as belonging to the general Mahāyāna literature closely linked to the *Prajñāpāramitā* literature, and more specifically to chapters one and two of the *Aṣṭasāhasrikā Prajñāpāramitā-sūtra*: the 8000 lines. The connection is made through the notion of reliance (see my forthcoming article on the structure of the DDV); hence the main question of this article: 'What can one rely on during times of conflict?'.
5. Philosophy in this Buddhist context is seen as an operative device, meaning that a conception of the world has an inevitable consequence for individual experience.
6. Sk. *prajñā*; Tib. *shes rab*. In its usage, this term has two aspects: initially it is conceptual (based on scriptures and reasoning); when perfected, it is non-conceptual and non-dual.
7. Sk. *karuṇā*; Tib. *snying rje*. The Sanskrit term relates to the root *kṛ* (to do); the Tibetan term refers to an excellence of the heart.
8. Sk. *āśraya, sthāna*; Tib. *gnas, rten*. In this intellectual tradition, as Nance (2007, 149–150) notes, in traditions of Indian and Tibetan Buddhist scholasticism one is often instructed to check one's understanding against 'scripture and reasoning' (respectively, Skt. *āgama, yukti*; Tib. *lung, rigs pa*) in order to determine

whether one has comprehended a particular point. Typically, this injunction is invoked in the course of advocating a particular interpretation of Buddhist doctrinal claims . . .. In Sanskrit texts, the terms are typically found juxtaposed as a *dvandva* compound, voiced in the dual. *Āgama* and *yukti* are thus to be distinguished from one another and are portrayed as constituting two separable interpretive tools and/or warrants. Noting this distinction, recent scholars have sometimes formulated it in terms of the distinction between 'dogma', on the one hand, and 'nonpartisan logic', on the other.

9. Sk. *nirvikalpa-jñāna*; Tib. *rnam par mi rtog pa ye shes*. Although the term 'intelligence' is often considered an active changing process, here it is used to translate *nirvikalpajñāna*, meaning 'inherent non-conceptual non-dual wisdom'.
10. Considering that IHL evolved from general concerns for humans in relation to the military requirements during armed conflict, it may be important to remind ourselves of the basic rules implied under such a law. These can be summed up in four precepts according to David (2002, 921–922): do not attack non-combatants; attack combatants only by legal means; treat persons in your power humanely; and protect the victims. David's book is cited in Sassòli et al. (2020, I.921–922).
11. In Buddhist context in general, one speaks of five sensory consciousnesses, plus one mental consciousness. In texts like the DDV, one adds to these six capacities to be aware, the all-base consciousness seen as responsible for the dynamic of conditioning, plus what is called *kleśa*-mind or afflictive-mind: a way Buddhist thinkers have found to identify the dynamic of the sense of 'I', 'me', 'mine' – henceforth, 'we', 'us', 'our'.
12. Note here that I have changed obvious sexist language in the quotation.
13. For more debates on universality, see: https://www.globalpolicy.org/home/163-general/29441.html. In a nutshell, the socially oriented critics of the notion of 'universality' have argued that the principles embedded in the Universal Declaration of Human Rights (1948) are the product of Western political history. The origins of this declaration are rooted in political landmarks in Western history, such as the Magna Carta of the United Kingdom (1215), the French Revolution (1789) and the American Bill of Rights (1791). From this perspective, relativists argue that universalism, in its historical attempt to extend a Western ideal to the rest of the world, is a form of cultural imperialism. The problem is particularly obvious when looking at the establishment of post-conflict ad hoc tribunals for Rwanda and the Former Yugoslavia in the 1990s and the International Criminal Court in 2002. As they do not involve 'traditional' or local approaches to justice, doing so could be more efficient in post-conflict reconciliation, therein also considering future implications.
14. For a discussion on the philosophical roots of IHL and those of the human rights law: https://international-review.icrc.org/sites/default/files/S0020860400071539a.pdf.
15. See, amongst many others, Williams (1980) and Dreyfus (1997).
16. In this discourse there is a shift from an epistemology of domination to a more egalitarian, relational conception of knowledge production also relevant to IHL. See Roncancio et al. (2019).
17. This term was popularised by Thomas Berry (1914–2009), a cultural historian and scholar of the world's religions, especially Asian traditions. Later he studied earth history and evolution and developed ecological concerns.

18. In his book, Jones writes: 'the sense of coercion is never far below the surface in most social sectors, in the workplace and school, on the streets, in politics, in government and the law, and in constant reminders in the new media' (2003, 143). An armed conflict is an extension of these realities. As Jones says, a law is authoritatively efficient through compliance because those who comply assume it to be reasonable, or because of habits and conditioning, or unfortunately, at other times when people have a sense of powerlessness. However, as Jones says, a law stays superficial unless embraced with understanding (2003, 151).
19. This part of stanza 12 reads literally as follows: 'as soon as there are [beings] who move around somewhere, the supports upon which rests the unending [cycle of suffering] are present. [In this wheel], there are [supports] that pertain to "beings" and those that pertain to the "container"'. Tib. *gang zhig gang du 'khor ba na / de ni kun tu gnas pas ste / sems can khams dang snod kyi khams / . . . .*
20. Tib. *gnas, gzhi, sten.*
21. The term 'Buddh-ism' is a neologism, a new word created by the studies of religions. This area of studies emerged as a formal discipline during the nineteenth century. Its methods and approaches are borrowed from different disciplines. Its main task is to look at the history, origins and functions of religion. For some scholars, the notion of universality has been central to this quest; many others end up finding more differences than similarities.
22. Francisco Varela is one of the founders of the Mind and Life Institute engaged in a dialogue between science and Buddhism.
23. Individual beings (Sk. *sattva-loka*; Tib. *sems can gyi 'jig rten*) and the environment or 'vessel' (Sk. *bhājana-loka*; Tib. *snod kyi 'jig rten*).
24. This part of stanza 12 reads more literally as follows: 'What pertains to "beings" [can be divided into] what is shared by them [i.e. what is interdependently or relationally produced], and what is not shared by them [i.e. what is intimate or personal]'. Tib. . . . *sems can khams ni thun mong dang / yang na thun mong ma yin pa'o /.*
25. In several commentaries, both Indian and Tibetan, this threefold framework is associated amongst other things with body, speech and mind; or with the five *skandhas*: form (body); sensation, perception, formation (speech); consciousnesses (mind). 1. The body here can refer to beings' bodies, the environment, external circumstances, sense faculties and/or all the external objects. This idea of the world is often illustrated by the six realms of rebirth and to the specificity of the suffering that is experienced in each one. 2. Speech can refer to all types of relational activity (internal and external – including the interaction of sensations, perceptions and formations). 3. Mind refers to the capacity to experience, the capacity to perceive, the capacity to accumulate information and impressions. In its analysis, the DDV concludes that in the end, the individual process of cognition (3) is the determinant factor in the way relationships evolve and in how external circumstances are experienced.
26. Stanza 13 reads like this: 'more precisely, what is relationally relevant is 1- the birth experience [i.e. inter-being of mother, father and baby]; 2- conventions [necessary to communication and cultures]; 3–4- help or coercion; 5–6- benefit or oppression; 7–8- and [the development of] qualities or faults, are all caused and determined in reciprocity'. Tib. *de yang skye dang tha snyad dang / rjes su gzung dang tshar gcod dan / phan pa dang ni gnod pa dang / yon tan skyon ni phan tshun du / bdag po nyid kyis phan tshun rgyu / yin pa'i phir na thun mong pa'o /.*

27. See Sasaki (1986, particularly 64 and 133–140).
28. The similarity of experiences is said to stem from the similarity of individual predispositions. Saying that there are similar predispositions at play does not mean that people agree on the content of experience; it means that there are similarities in the way the process of cognition occurs. If there were no similarities, the commonality or the conflict would not appear; it could not even take place.
29. Sk. *vijñaptimātra*; Tib. *rnam par rig tsam*.
30. Different from a Tibetan Buddhist approach, Jones' work is influenced by the Zen tradition for which the notion of Self and the notion of one-ness is not a problem. Other Buddhist traditions would probably never explain this experience in this same way.
31. The Dharmic approach illustrated by this edict is perhaps the earliest example of the threefold framework applied in a social context.
32. Tieken (2002) says that what is clearly meant here is a three-day stay of the execution. In this edict, the king is concerned with the 'gift of life'.
33. Although I have used the translation of the edict done by E. Hultzsch and published in *Inscriptions of Asoka* (1925, 119), there has been a lot of discussion about the meaning of these lines; see, amongst others, Norman (1975) and Herman Tieken (2002). For more information on the discovery of King Aśoka's story, see also the work of Charles Allen (2014).
34. The role of volition here is fascinating. On the one hand there is the notion of motivation and intention at work in the dynamic of *karma* and the development on the path. Yet volition is not the only factor to have a consequence on the way things appear and evolve. The Buddhist analysis of volition is not simplistic.
35. Sk. *vibhāga*; Tib. *rnam par 'byed pa*.
36. As Nance (2007) says, it may be useful to situate the analysis (Sk. *yukti*; Tib. *rigs pa*) within the broader categories. In Vasubandhu's *Abhidharmakośabhāṣya* and elsewhere, analysis is portrayed as contributing to the development of what Buddhist thinkers call 'discriminating insight caused by reflection'. This form of insight is the second step of a three-step model of wisdom acquired though listening, reflecting and meditating. According to Vasubandhu, the wisdom acquired through reflection also falls under 'what is born from investigation by means of reasoning' (*yuktinidhyānajā*). These three forms of discriminating insight are said to arise successively in meditative concentration (*samādhi*). So, we end up here with the idea that the three trainings in the development of wisdom are intricately connected or inseparable. This applies to life in general, as well as to the development of profound insight (*vipaśyanā*) during meditation.
37. Sk. *yukti*; Tib. *rigs pa*. More recently, Jay L. Garfeild (2021) published a book on the intimate relationship between philosophy/wisdom and ethics from a Buddhist perspective titled *Buddhist Ethics: a Philosophical Exploration*.
38. Stanza 35 offers a list of ideas that need to be abandoned on the path; there are four steps. These steps are also found in the *Avikalpadeśadhāraṇī*. The first step consists of abandoning what is contra-productive by using remedies (e.g. addictive behaviours are abandoned by looking at the negative qualities of their objects); then one is invited to abandon these remedies by embracing suchness (e.g. in the nature of phenomena notions of good and bad are superfluous); after which one abandon suchness (e.g. when suchness is made

into a thing it becomes an obstacle); and finally, one abandons all notions of realisation – all hopes and fears (e.g. in the end the idea that there is something to be realised becomes a subtle obstacle to be abandoned).

39. Closer to the Tibetan version, one reads: 'the nature of phenomena is suchness without a separation between an object grasped and a subject grasping or [between] what is designated and the designation'. Tib. *gzhan yang chos nyid mtshan nyid ni / gzung ba dang ni 'dzin pa dang / brjod par bya dang rjod par byed / khad med de bzhin nyid yin no /.*
40. In his *Identités Meurtrières*, an essay translated into English under the title *In the Name of Identity, Violence and the Need to Belong*, Amin Maalouf (2000), a writer of Lebanese origin living in France whose philosophical background is not Buddhism, also sees in the separation between self and other the root of a grave confusion.
41. See also e.g. Foundation for Active Compassion – Transformational Practices for a Better World, https://foundationforactivecompassion.org/.
42. Sk. *nirvikalpajñāna*; Tib. *rnam par mi rtog pa ye shes.*
43. The term 'emptiness' is used in several ways in the Mahāyāna. In the *Prajñāpāramitā* literature it sometimes refers to the middle way, meaning 'neither existent nor not existent'; in response to the Abhidharma literature, it sometimes means empty of intrinsic existence (*svabhāva*); in some Tathāgatagarbha texts, it refers to the absence of defilements in the Buddha-nature; in the DDV, if it was used, it would refer to the absence of duality, to suchness (*tathatā*) and to fundamental non-conceptual intelligence/wisdom (*nirvikalpajñāna*).
44. References to the luminosity of the mind are found in early texts, but start being clearly formulated in texts such as the *Prajñāpāramitā-sūtra*, the *Laṅkāvatāra-sūtra* and so on.
45. The translation of stanza 33 reads as follows: 'An access to a profound change of what one relies on occurs through considering the ground or basis, that is, through considering the fundamental non-conceptual intelligence in six ways: [the way to] orient the mind; the attributes to be abandoned; the correct practice; the characteristics of this intelligence; its benefits; and a thorough understanding [of its particularities]'. The Sanskrit fragment reads as follows: *āśrayo ... praveśaḥ ... ṣaḍākāranirvikalpajñānapraveśāt ṣaḍākārapraveśaḥ punarālambanato nimittaparivarjanataḥ samyakprayogato lakṣaṇato 'nuśaṃsataḥ parijñānataś ca* (Saṅkṛtyāyana 1938, 163, note 1). The Tibetan translation reads like this: *gnas sam rten la 'jug pa ni /rnam par mi rtog ye shes la / 'jug pa rnam pa drug gis te / dmigs dang mtshan ma spangs pa dang / yang dag pa yi sbyor ba dang / mtshan nyid dang ni phan yon dang / yongs su shes la 'jug pas so.*
46. Tib. . . . *de gnyis khyad par mi dmigs pa/ de ni rnam par mi rtogs pa'i/ ye shes yul med dmigs med pa/ mtshan ma thams cad mi dmigs pas/ rab phye ba ni yin phyir ro /.*
47. On the interchangeability of *prajñā-pāramitā* and *upāya-kauśalya* – 'perfection of wisdom' and 'skill in means' – see amongst others de Breet (1992).
48. In all Buddhist trainings, three principles are necessary for the process of an exemplary conduct to develop: listening, reflecting and meditating. The training starts with the reception of ideas (i.e. listening) and goes to analysis and examination according to one's own experience (i.e. reflection). Finally, the idea gets integrated through habituation. Meditation here is understood as a process of habituation and cultivation (i.e. repetitive exposure). For more information on this subject, see also note 36.

49. Tib. *dran pa*.
50. This is an adaptation of Rupert Gethin's translation (2008, 147) of this '*Establishing Mindfulness*' *Sutta* (2013).
51. This is an adaptation of Edward Conze's translation (1973, 97). Following Willis' (2002) reading of the word *bodhisattva*, I have used the feminine interchangeably with the masculine – see note 114, p. 63: 'Bodhisattva literally means "one whose whole being (*sattva*)" is intent on ultimate enlightenment (*bodhi*). Strictly speaking, then, there is no limitation associated with the term as to the sex of such a one'.
52. See Tomlinson (2018), 12.
53. Stanza 37 reads more literally as follows: 'An access [into fundamental non-conceptual intelligence is established] through correct practice in four steps: the practice [of a specific way] to rest one's attention [on phenomena], the practice without [an object-grasped] on which to rest one's attention, the practice without an attention on which to rest one's attention, [that is, without a grasping-subject], and the practice of the attention without attention, [that is, without subject and object]'. Tib. *yang dag pa yi sbyor ba la / 'jug pa yang ni rnam bzhi ste / dmigs pa yi ni sbyor ba dang / mi dmigs pa yi sbyor ba dang / dmigs pa mi dmigs sbyor ba dang / mi dmigs dmigs pa'i sbyor ba'o*. The reconstitution: *atha samyakprayoge'pi pravṛttis tu caturvidhā / ālambanaprayogaś ca nirālambaprayogitā // lambālambaprayogaś ca tathā nirlambayojanam /* (Phuntsok 1990, 62).
54. There are examples of ethical military training of sorts amongst Buddhist traditions that sees itself as a non-aggressive protective force, one of which developed in the US and in Europe in the 1980s; I think here of the Kasung training associated with the Dharma Protectors of the Tibetan tradition and I quote from their website: 'As part of their practice the Dorje Kasung wear uniforms to communicate, delight in the disciplines of egolessness [non-duality] and simplicity, service to others by being present and available to help, commitment to the continuous path of waking up, and manifesting care and dignity. The military forms used by the Dorje Kasung were chosen as a reminder that we need to transmute aggression if we are to create enlightened society, and because these forms resemble the traditional monastic Buddhist discipline'. See Dorje Kasung – Montréal Shambhala Meditation Centre: https://montreal.shambhala.org/kasung/?lang=en. The emphasis is put on training the mind – it is not clear whether the use of modern military weapons would be involved in this type of training or not.
55. See online: http://www.johnmakransky.org/summary.html. Makransky is currently developing a training of sorts based on Active Compassion.

Disclosure statement

This article has been supported by the International Committee of the Red Cross (ICRC).

References

Allen, C. 2014. *King Aśoka: The Search for India's Lost Emperor*. London: Abacus.

Aṅgulimāla Sutta. 2013. M 86. Translated from Pāli by Thanissaro Bhikkhu. https://www.dhammatalks.org/suttas/MN/MN86.html

Carter, J. R. and J. Ross. 1976. "Traditional Definitions of the Term 'Dhamma'." *Philosophy East and West* 26 (3): 329–337. doi:10.2307/1397863.

Carter, J. R. 1978. *Dhamma. Western Academic and Sinhalese Buddhist Interpretations. A Study of a Religious Concept*. Tokyo: Hokuseido Press.

Chadha, M. 2018. "No-Self and the Phenomenology of Ownership." *Australasian Journal of Philosophy* 96 (1): 14–27. doi:10.1080/00048402.2017.1307236.

Conze, E. 1973. *The Perfection of Wisdom in Eight Thousand Lines & Its Verse Summary*. Bolinas: Four Seasons Foundation.

Cox, C. 2004. "From Category to Ontology: The Changing Role of Dharma in *Sarvāstivāda* Abhidharma." *Journal of Indian Philosophy* 32 (5–6): 543–597. doi:10.1007/s10781-004-8635-4.

David, É. 2002. *Principes de droit des conflits armés*. Bruxelles: Bruylant.

de Breet, J. A. 1992. "The Concept of 'Upāyakauśalya' in the *Aṣṭasāhasrikā Prajñāpāramitā Sūtra*." *Vienna Journal of South Asian Studies* 36: 203–216.

Denis, D. 2017. "La traduction du terme '*dharma*' (tib. *chos*) dans le contexte du *Dharmadharmatāvibhāga*, texte bouddhique de l'Inde du IVe siècle." *Laval Théologique et Philosophique* 73 (1): 3–29. doi:10.7202/1041631ar.

Doswald-Beck, L., and S. Vité. 1993. "International Humanitarian Law and Human Rights Law." *International Review of the Red Cross* 293. https://international-review.icrc.org/sites/default/files/S0020860400071539a.pdf

Dreyfus, G. 1997. *Recognizing Reality*. New York: State University of New York Press.

Garfeild, J. L. 2021. *Buddhist Ethics: A Philosophical Exploration*. Oxford: Oxford University Press.

Geiger, W., and M. Geiger. [1920] 1973. "Pāli Dhamma vornehmlich in der kanonischen Literatur." *Kleine Schriften zur Indologie und Buddhismuskunde* 6: 101–228.

Gethin, R. 2004. "He Who Sees Dhamma Sees Dhammas: Dhamma in Early Buddhism." *Journal of Indian Philosophy* 32 (5–6): 513–542. doi:10.1007/s10781-004-8633-6.

Gethin, R. 2008. "Establishing Mindfulness (*Majjhima Nikāya* 10)." In *Sayings of the Buddha: New Translations by Rupert Gethin from the Pali Nikāyas*, 141–151. Oxford: Oxford University Press.

Hultzsch, E. 1925. "Inscriptions of Asoka, New Edition." In *Corpus Inscriptionum Indicarum*, Vol. I. Oxford: Clarendon Press. https://archive.org/details/InscriptionsOfAsoka.NewEditionByE.Hultzsch/page/n291

International Committee of the Red Cross. 2014. *What is IHL?* https://www.icrc.org/en/download/file/4541/what-is-ihl-factsheet.pdf

Jones, K. 2003. *The New Social Face of Buddhism: An Alternative Sociopolitical Perspective*. Boston: Wisdom Publications.

Keown, D. 1996. "Karma, Character, and Consequentialism." *Journal of Religious Ethics* 24: 329–350.

Maalouf, A. 2000. *In the Name of Identity, Violence and the Need to Belong*. Translated by Barbara Bray. New York: Arcade Publishing.

Makransky, J. 2017. *Awakening Through Love: Unveiling Your Deepest Goodness*. Somerville: Wisdom Publication.

Nance, R. 2007. "What Do We Rely on When We Rely on Reasoning?" *Journal of Indian Philosophy* 35 (2): 149–167. doi:10.1007/s10781-007-9013-9.

Norman, K. R. 1975. "Aśoka and Capital Punishment." *Journal of the Royal Asiatic Society* 107 (1): 16–24.

Pictet, J. 1988. "Humanitarian Ideas Shared by Different Schools of Thought and Cultural Traditions." In *International Dimensions of Humanitarian Law*, 3–5. Paris: Unesco.

Phuntsok, T. 1990. *Dharmadharmatāvibhāgakārikā* (with Commentary by Vasubandhu – Tibetan Version, Sanskrit Restoration and Hindi Translation). Sarnath: Central Institute of Higher Tibetan Studies.

Roncancio, I. V., L. Temper, J. Sterlin, N. Smolyar, S. Sellers, M. Moore, R. Melgar-Melgar, et al. 2019. "From the Anthropocene to Mutual Thriving: An Agenda for Higher Education in the Ecozoic." *Sustainability (MDPI)* 11 (12): 1–19. https://www.mdpi.com/2071-1050/11/12

Sāṅkṛtyāyana, R. 1938. "Search for Manuscript in Tibet." *The Journal of the Bihar Research Society* 24 (4): 137–163.

Sasaki, G. H. 1986. *Linguistic Approach to Buddhist Thought*. Delhi: Motilal Banarsidass.

Sassòli, M., A. Bouvier, and A. Quintin, eds. 2020. *How Does Law Protect in War? Cases, Documents and Teaching Materials on Contemporary Practice in International Humanitarian Law*. 3rd ed. Vol. I, Outline of International Humanitarian Law. Brussels: ICRC.

Shambala Kasung Training. Centre de méditation Shambhala de Montréal. https://montreal.shambhala.org/kasung/?lang=en

Stcherbatsky, T. 1923. *The Central Conception of Buddhism and the Meaning of the Word "Dharma"*. Delhi: Motilal Banarsidass.

Tieken, H. 2002. "The Dissemination of Aśoka's Rock and Pillar Edicts." *Wiener Zeitschrift Für Die Kunde Südasiens/Vienna Journal of South Asian Studies* 46: 5–42.

Tomlinson, D. K. 2018. "The Tantric Context of Ratnākaraśānti's Philosophy of Mind." *Journal of Indian Philosophy* 46 (2): 355–372. doi:10.1007/s10781-018-9351-9.

Varela, F. J. 1999. *Ethical Know-How, Action, Wisdom, and Cognition*. Stanford: Stanford University Press.

Williams, P. 1980. "Some Aspects of Language and Construction in the Madhyamaka." *Journal of Indian Philosophy* 8 (1): 1–45. doi:10.1007/BF02539785.

Willis, J. 2002. *On Knowing Reality*. Delhi: Motilal Banarsidass.

Part II

The Military and the Conduct of War

ICRC

THE BUDDHIST SOLDIER: A MADHYAMAKA INQUIRY

Dharmacārin Siṃhanāda

ABSTRACT

Dialogue between international humanitarian law (IHL) and Buddhism draws attention to the challenging question of the nature and identity of the Buddhist soldier. Here, the Buddhist soldier is considered not as a simple binary contradiction but as a complex dynamic paradox that can be unfolded, explored and understood through the use of Buddhist philosophy. The dialectical logic of Madhyamaka is harnessed through dialectical process analysis (DPA), a method that shows complex dynamic relationships in relatively accessible and legible spatial form, as maps. DPA maps are used to analyse the complex, dynamic nature of military duty, the soldier as responsible individual, and the soldier in socio-political context. Connections between the Mahāyāna Buddhist ideal of the bodhisattva and the Jungian Warrior Hero archetype are explored. A model is proposed for the ethical conduct of military operations in accordance with IHL, which includes the failure of ethics and law in the case of military atrocity. Ethics are discussed in both Buddhist and more general terms as 'natural ethics', for the critical test is not some parochial religious orthodoxy, but practical compliance with IHL in the field of conflict. Difficulties that the practice of ethical soldiering faces are noted. These will not be overcome without significant change, so implications are noted for management education, cultural change and organisational development in military training.

Introduction and overview

In recent years, a global resurgence of traditional religion has led the International Committee of the Red Cross (ICRC) to examine the alignment of international humanitarian law (IHL) with world religions. In Buddhism, it finds a particularly promising partner. Both are concerned with the maintenance of human dignity and the minimisation of suffering in a world marked by violent conflict. Whilst Buddhism has both humanistic and transcendental dimensions, its humanistic dimension aligns closely with the strategic mission of the ICRC, and Buddhist ethics fit well with the standards of IHL.

DOI: 10.4324/9781003439820-11

Dialogue between Buddhism and IHL focuses attention upon the concept of the Buddhist soldier, for the entire enterprise depends upon the Buddhist soldier being a robust and coherent idea. This is a problem because whilst on the one hand Buddhist soldiers clearly exist, on the other the Buddhist soldier appears to be a contradiction. Here is a thorny issue. Are we to conclude that the Buddhist soldier – whether ethnic or convert – takes an inherently false position? If not, how then is Buddhist non-violence to be reconciled with the soldier's professional engagement with violence? Rather than look to examples of how Buddhist principles might apply within the military context – which, apparent contradiction notwithstanding, is one potentially constructive approach to the reduction of suffering – this article seeks to disentangle, open and unfold the question of the Buddhist soldier itself. It takes a Buddhist approach to a Buddhist issue, pursuing an inquiry rooted in Madhyamaka to seek an understanding of the Buddhist soldier.

Madhyamaka is the earliest school of Buddhist philosophy to develop within Mahāyāna Buddhism. Founded by around the second century CE, it places great emphasis on epistemology, and methods for challenging received and fixed views.[1] The inquiry in this article makes selective and original use of core ideas from within the Madhyamaka tradition. It hinges upon a key feature of Madhyamaka logic: its capacity to disentangle, resolve and transcend paradox by revealing the interconnection of apparent opposites.[2] This interconnection is explored using a method for mapping complex dialectics that I have developed from Barry Johnson's (1996) polarity management, a method he advanced for modelling and managing complex dilemmas within organisations. I developed dialectical process analysis (DPA) to harness Madhyamaka as a way of opening and unfolding apparent contradictions to understand them better. DPA provides a form of mapping which, for our purposes here, tackles the problem of the nature of the Buddhist soldier. It does so by demonstrating that the Buddhist soldier is not a binary contradiction, but rather a complex relational paradox whose dialectics merit and require exploration. I shall illustrate how DPA works below. In applying it to our present conundrum, the soldier in general and the Buddhist soldier in particular are viewed from three angles: as an ideal, as an individual and in social context. The ideal soldier as archetypal Warrior Hero is compared with the ideal Buddhist as bodhisattva, one whose being and action are characterised by the qualities perfected, the 'perfections' (*pāramitā*), on the Bodhisattva Path. The duty of the soldier as responsible individual is mapped in terms of dialectical interplay between *Active* and *Receptive* poles. Duty in social context is mapped as dialectical interplay between poles of *Support* and *Challenge*. These poles will be explained below. These dialectical dynamics are presented in the form of maps, which provide a visual aid to improve the legibility of complex processes.

My intention is that the tone of this inquiry should be transparent, curious and exploratory: it aims to ask good questions, to see what emerges from them and where they lead. In keeping with Buddhist tradition, it strives to ensure that abstract ideas are anchored in concrete practical illustration.

The ideal soldier

The ICRC and the Buddhist tradition have in common a commitment to the definition and pursuit of high ideals. Are these ideals mutually consistent? How does the ideal soldier compare to the ideal Buddhist?

The ideal soldier can be modelled in terms of the Warrior Hero archetype as originally defined by Carl Jung (1991, [1933] 2001) and subsequently developed by Jungians including Joseph Campbell ([1949] 2012), and Moore and Gillette (1990). In Jung's analysis, archetypes are deep transpersonal dynamics that may find expression at the personal level, within the thought and action of the individual. From the emergence of the Mahāyāna onwards, the ideal Buddhist is defined as the bodhisattva, the archetypal hero of the Buddhist life, whose way involves the cultivation of the *pāramitā*s of the Bodhisattva Path.[3] Are these ideals compatible?

Indeed they are, for it is clear that, from the earliest origins of the tradition, Buddhism and soldiering are comrades-in-arms. The Buddha came to be seen as an ex-warrior prince, and was given to the use of military metaphor to emphasise key points in his teaching. Perhaps the best-known example of this narrative habit is the celebrated Parable of the Arrow,[4] in which the human predicament is presented as that of a soldier wounded on the field of battle, in mortal danger and in urgent need of skilled assistance. Military symbolism remains prominent and purposeful throughout subsequent Buddhist history. Prominent examples within Tibetan iconography include the flaming diamond sword of Mañjuśrī[5] and the *vajra* thunderbolt, which Padmasambhava[6] and Vajrapāṇi[7] wield and with which Vajrasattva[8] plays.

Table 1 juxtaposes the qualities of the Jungian Warrior Hero archetype (Moore and Gillette 1990) against the *pāramitā*s of the Bodhisattva Path, to reveal some close and suggestive correspondence. This correspondence indicates that the Warrior Hero archetype and the Bodhisattva draw upon a common underlying human potential.

Table 1. Eight qualities of the Warrior Hero in relation to the six parāmitās.

Warrior Hero quality		Parāmitā	
Destroyer	Capable of abandoning that which limits or blocks potential. Breaks unhelpful boundaries, taboos and group norms.	***Dāna pāramitā*** Perfection of generosity *Leads to* ↓	Able to offer appropriate and unconditional gifts (sustenance, time, attention, money and – most importantly – The Dharma) with the intention to alleviate suffering and spiritual ignorance. Includes *abhaya*, the gift of fearlessness, and *tyāga*, as the supreme generosity of self-sacrifice.
Self-controlled	Engages fully in training to develop vision, skill and integration of knowledge. Takes responsibility for own actions.	***Śila pāramitā*** Perfection of ethics *Leads to* ↓	Activity that arises out of deepening awareness and faith in conditionality and the wisdom of *śūnyatā*. Skilful and appropriate activity encouraged by the Wise for the benefit of all.
Tactician	Evaluates what is happening. Able to develop strategies to achieve aims.		
Unconquerable	Has the mental strength to bear trials and adversity. Able to bear the unbearable and the unknown.	***Kṣānti pāramitā*** Perfection of patience (patient endurance) *Leads to* ↓	Ability to tolerate and not abandon the truth/reality, including suffering (*duḥkha*). Ability to stay in relation to difficulty and difference.
Aggressive	Has energy that rouses, energises, motivates. Always appropriate to the situation.	***Vīrya pāramitā*** Perfection of energy in pursuit of the good *Leads to* ↓	Directed and appropriate use of energy. Harnessed and used skilfully for the benefit of the many.
Self-aware	Knows own capacities and limitations. Motivated by awareness of the proximity of death and fragility of life.		
Alert	Uses clarity and discernment through thinking, observing and wakefulness.	***Samādhi pāramitā*** Perfection of meditative absorption *Leads to* ↓	Skill in focus, concentration, mindfulness. Ability to direct thought and generate clarity and conditions for reflection.
Loyal to the transpersonal	Choices and activity arise out of bond with vision and goal. Life as service to the transpersonal.	***Prajñā pāramitā*** Perfection of wisdom ↑ *Leads 'back' to* ***Dāna***	Seeing things as they really are. Vision of the conventionally true yet fundamentally illusory nature of self and other. Knowing interconnectedness. Embodied knowing of universal conditionality.

The dark side

These standards of being and conduct represent a sublime and demanding ideal. They represent a route to perfection only if all aspects are integrated and connected in dynamic equilibrium, understood with due insight, within a robust ethical context. However, the ideal casts a shadow. It is sobering to reflect that the Buddhist analysis of the *pṛthagjana* (worldly) state indicates that we are likely not starting from a promising place. The Warrior archetype is rather easy to grasp wrongly. Its Destroyer and Aggressive aspects, especially, can be stripped of their ethical context and used to rationalise and glorify violence, not unusually through an ideology of 'holy war'.[9] The Jungian analysis proposes that, awareness notwithstanding, transpersonal archetypal energies are always at work, and will surely find expression through the individual psyche. Failure to engage with Warrior Hero energy in a conscious, healthy and integrated way results in a repression that drives energy into manifestation in 'shadow' forms. Shadow manifestation is essentially unbalanced, a disequilibrium. It occurs primarily because energy has become detached or alienated from the tempering and balancing influence of the other archetypes, particularly King and Lover (Moore and Gillette 1990), which are equally bases of a healthy and relational life. Energy that is repressed will seep out, semiconsciously, subconsciously and/or unconsciously shaping attitudes and behaviour.

Table 2. Shadow aspects of the Warrior Hero (derived from Moore and Gillette 1990).

Masochistic manifestation	Sadistic manifestation
Workaholic, stemming from isolation and sense of deep anxiety, absence or lack. Unable to delegate or work collectively/co-operatively. Has difficulty in simply being.	Perceived humiliation feeding imagined grievance. Avenging spirit that wants to punish the source of rage or fear.
Inability to generate self-care for mental and physical well-being.	Relishes carnage and cruelty.
Crushingly low self-esteem. Self-loathing. Inability to acknowledge value of personal qualities and simple presence.	Hatred of the weak and the vulnerable.
Insecure inner personality structure relies on outer activity and external affirmation to bolster chronic inner sense of lack and intrinsic worth. Rooted in deprivation of unconditional love: must perform in order to assert existence and worth. *'I work therefore I am'.*	Polarisation and antagonism towards what is described as the feminine due to fear of intimacy and the relational life.
Self-punishing behaviour due to falling short of deluded fantasies of perfection or inflated capability. *'Those obsessed with success have already failed'.*	Disruptive and confrontational when uncertain, and threatened around personal power and authority.

Table 2 summarises the most visible forms of the shadow aspect of the Warrior Hero archetype, in its masochistic (inflicted on self) and sadistic (inflicted on other) forms. Here is a portrait of the psychopathology of military atrocity; fundamental disequilibrium in profoundly negative form. Madhyamaka dialectic can be used to predict and model both the loss of equilibrium and its recovery. Whilst the healthy expression of archetypal energy initially transforms into its opposite when blocked, this dynamic is part of a larger process that subsequently leads to the eventual recovery of equilibrium. Staying in balance involves lurches, wobbles and recovery. Jung called this *enantiodromia*, the tendency of a complex system to lose balance, restore balance and maintain its dynamic equilibrium through the assertion of counterposed forces.[10]

Is the Buddhist soldier a problem?

The argument up to this point has demonstrated multiple connections between Buddhism and the military in terms of history, symbolism and the construction of ideal type. There is clear evidence of a relationship. However, that relationship has so far been shown to be no more than one of positive correlation, a description of parallels. It remains to move beyond description into analysis, to further investigate those parallels and to explore what might lie within them. The Buddhist soldier is not a flat contradiction, yet it remains problematic. So what sort of problem is it?

Answering this question starts with recognising that problems differ in nature. A key distinction is that between the binary and the complex problem. Binary problems are essentially simple in form, genuinely 'black and white'. They can be solved, closed and brought to rest because their exclusive either/or logical structure leads to win–lose outcomes and closure. With a genuine binary, every win brings with it a loss: there is no Middle Way between dead and alive. Complex problems are of a higher order. They involve 'shades of grey'. You know you have run into one of these when 'there is something to be said for both sides', but yet the sides prove difficult to reconcile. Complex problems cannot be finally solved, closed and brought to rest. Their inclusive, both/and logical structure offers the opportunity to achieve win–win outcomes, but also the risk of a disastrous lose–lose. Because they are by nature open, dynamic and relational, resolving them involves managing paradoxically opposed yet connected poles by keeping them in balance. Staying on your bike means following The Middle Way: leaning to both right and left, sometimes lurching, wobbling and recovering, to maintain the dynamic equilibrium of balance. Polarise exclusively in favour of right or left, and you fall off your bike.

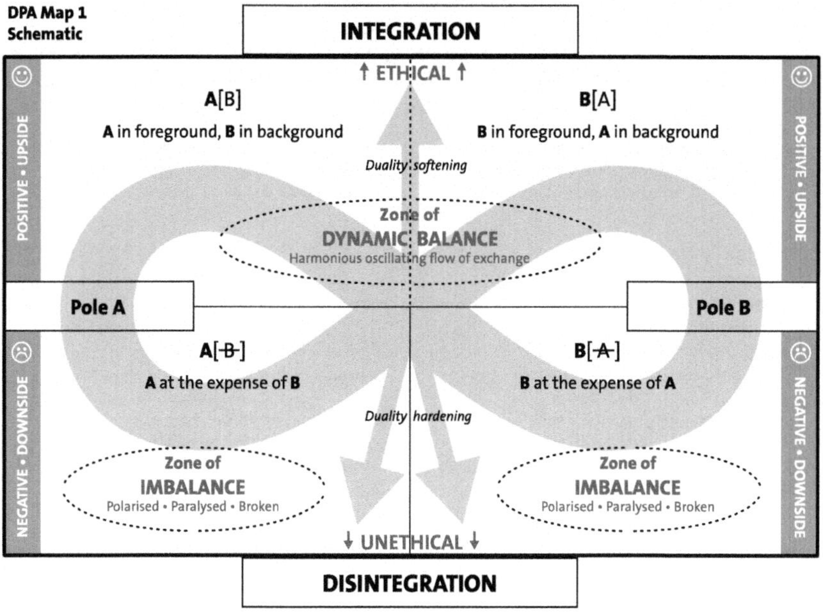

Figure 1. DPA Map 1: Schematic.

If the Buddhist soldier is not a binary contradiction, is it a complex paradox? To bring the method of Madhyamaka to bear upon this question is to investigate the possibility that 'Buddhist' versus 'soldier' is not an irreconcilable opposition, but a dialectical polarity. That is, each term is a pole that is *both* opposed *and* connected to the other. If evidence of both opposition and connection can be found in the relationship between the poles, then that relationship is dialectical and the problem is a complex paradox.

DPA[11] is a method for investigating complex paradox though mapping. How does a dialectical polarity map work? Figure 1 is a general dialectical polarity map in schematic form. This is a complex diagram because it represents complex processes. The first main point to grasp is that all the positive conditions lie in the upper quadrants. They remain positive because in the healthy, skilful (*kuśala*) state of the system, there is a continuous oscillating flow of harmonious dynamic balance between them. The lower quadrants contain all the negative conditions. These are negative because they arise out of polarised imbalance. To bring this down to earth, consider Figure 2, which translates abstract into concrete terms through an analysis of the dialectical nature of duty. The schematic will make increased sense as its specific concrete forms are considered in Figures 2–4. Duty is a useful example, because it is self-evidently not a simple binary but complex, relational and interactive by nature. Its logic is both/and: the soldier operating under IHL is simultaneously both an individual responsible under law and an actor within a social context.

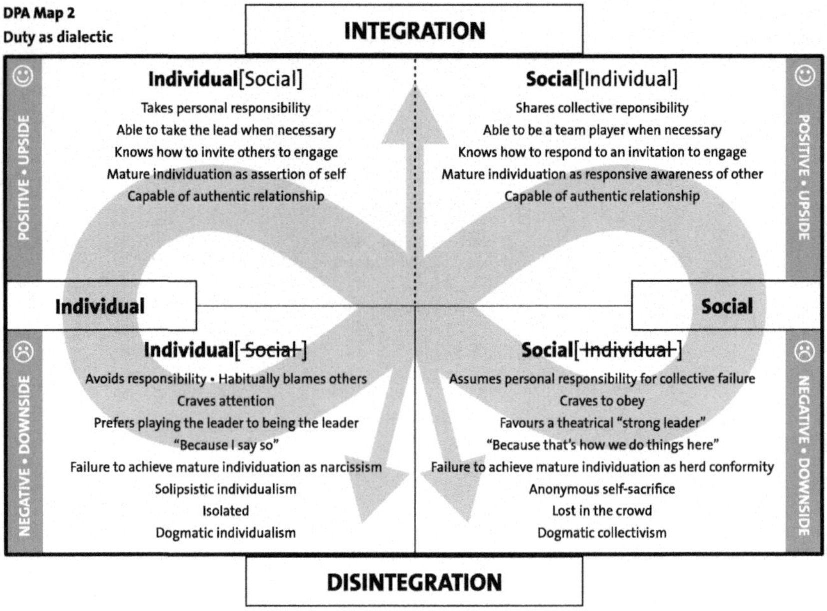

Figure 2. DPA Map 2: Duty as dialectic.

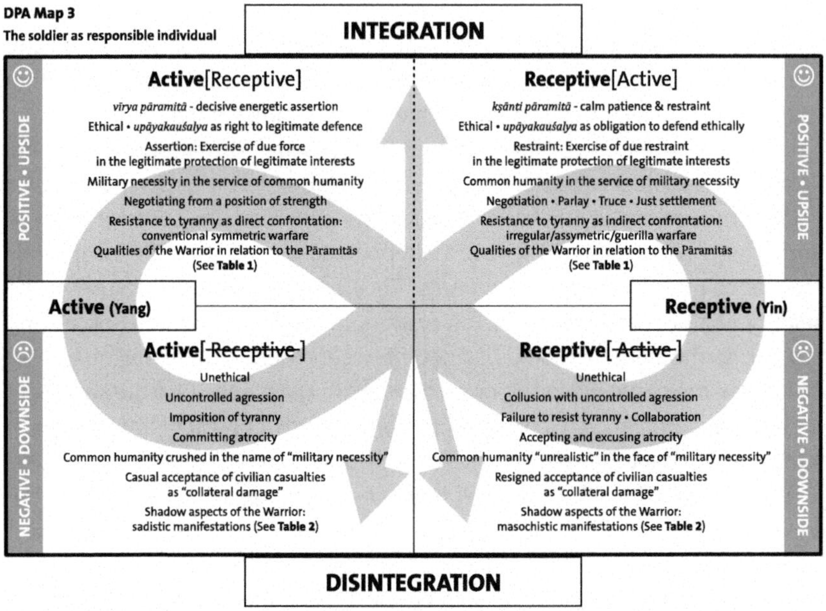

Figure 3. DPA Map 3: The soldier as responsible individual.

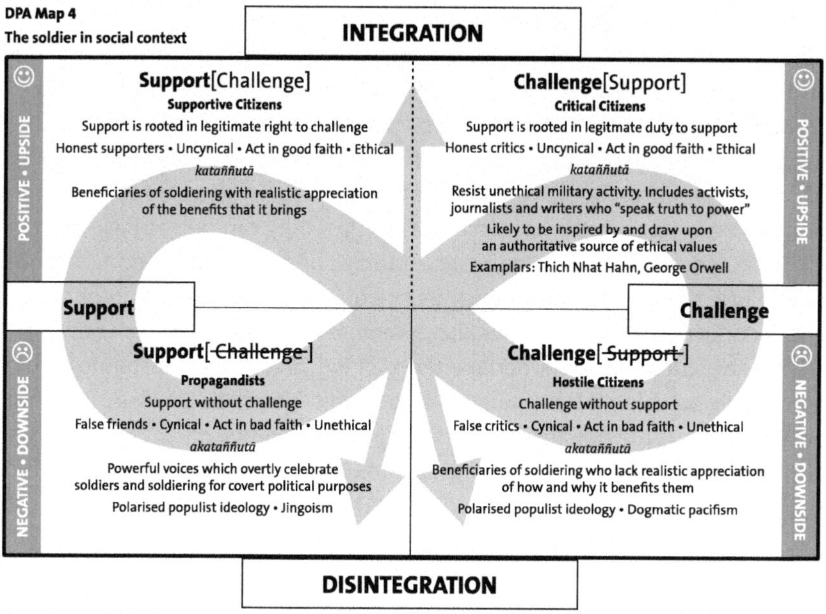

Figure 4. DPA Map 4: The soldier in social context.

Figure 2 explores the dialectics of the soldier's duty as a dynamic balance between *Individual* and *Social* poles. Each of these poles in turn is further unfolded and analysed: Figure 3 unfolds the soldier as responsible individual, and Figure 4 unfolds the soldier in social context.

The soldier as responsible individual

Figure 3 identifies the exemplary Buddhist soldier as an individual whose activity, like that of any ideal Buddhist, is entirely skilful (*kuśala*): a practitioner of skill in means (*upāya-kauśalya*), integrating and balancing Active and Receptive modes. The practice of *upāya-kauśalya* involves bringing the most imaginative and appropriate creative response to any situation. Whilst cognisant and respectful of relevant external schemata – such as the principles of IHL – it never involves mere rigid adherence to external codes. *Upāya-kauśalya* is never unthinking obedience, nor is it ever wilful disobedience. It perfectly integrates effectiveness and efficiency, consistently doing the right things and doing them well. Maximising effectiveness and efficiency bring consistency, for example, with the principles expounded by the influential ancient (sixth century BCE) Chinese military strategist Sun Tzu: 'Win all without fighting' and 'Avoid strength, attack weakness' (McNeilly 2003, vii).

Taking a dialectical stance within a system of ethics tends to resolve otherwise thorny problems around contested questions of chivalry, honour and Warrior Code. Whilst Rain Liivoja (2012) demonstrates the persistence of certain chivalric concepts within contemporary IHL, jurist and soldier VanLandigham (2015) attacks and dismisses the concept of chivalry in favour of an IHL based on a 'shared sense of humanity'. To the extent that both positions rely upon common ethical principles, they can be reconciled.

Particularly in the Mahāyāna, *upāya-kauśalya* underpins the Buddhist stance on the use of force. Buddhist ethics are unequivocally non-violent in principle. The First Ethical Precept – *pāṇātipātā veramaṇī sikkhāpadaṃ samādiyāmi* – affirms the intention to 'undertake the training principle of abstention from harming living beings'. However, this is not a rigid, dogmatic pacifism. Buddhist ethical precepts are not absolute binary commandments, nor indeed are they any kind of commandment. They are pragmatic training principles to be applied in good faith within the demanding complexity of everyday life,[12] and military situations are apt to be complex and demanding. *Upāya-kauśalya* is the skilful management of these demands in a quest for the best outcomes available. Accordingly, *faute de mieux*, minimally violent action may possibly involve the pursuit of peace through the conscious and skilful exercise of force. The stance is realistic: a complex and nuanced dynamic response to a complex and nuanced dynamic reality. Rights and obligations are dialectically balanced: the right to act is always connected to the duty of restraint. Proceeding from the skilful reading of conditions, *upāya-kauśalya* may manifest as an exercise of the legitimate right to defence or as legitimate obligation to defend ethically. Legitimate protection of legitimate interests may involve the exercise of due force, or due restraint, which to be legitimate must also meet or exceed the standards set by IHL. Resistance to tyranny may involve the direct symmetrical confrontation of conventional warfare, or the indirect asymmetrical confrontation of guerrilla resistance. The Buddhist soldier knows how and when to negotiate from a position of strength, how and when to negotiate, to call truce and parlay to attain just settlement. This strength as dynamic fluidity is succinct in Churchill's rhetoric: 'In war: resolution. In defeat: defiance. In victory: magnanimity. In peace: good will'. When considering the Buddhist soldier in relation to IHL, especially on the question of individual responsibility under the law, it should be noted that Buddhist ethics place great emphasis upon individual responsibility, for it is a principal purpose of the Buddhist life to become a genuinely responsible person. This is not a mere politicised and polarised individualism which evades, whenever convenient, the reality of social context, but a dialectical vision of true individuality as a simultaneously personal and social actualisation of human potential.

The dialectical interplay of the individual and social aspects of the soldier is evident in ethicist Shannon French's (2017) analysis of Warrior Code. French's analysis is implicitly dialectical, modelling the ethics of soldiering as an effort to resolve the tension between the abhorrence of murder and the violence of armed conflict. French notes that the exercise of ethical restraint during armed conflict tends to catalyse and expedite peaceful resolution. Whilst it is axiomatic that compliance with IHL serves to protect the innocent, French sees further than this, to the insight that the soldier faces distinctive moral peril and risk of psychological trauma: 'The most compelling reason for warriors to accept restraint may be the internal moral damage they risk if they fail to do so, and the serious psychological damage they may suffer' (67). French cites Shay's (1994) work on post-traumatic stress disorder among Vietnam veterans, which highlights the heavy impacts of moral, as well as physical, violence.

The power of dialectical analysis in this area can be illustrated by examining one of Rain Liivoja's arguments around chivalry. Liivoja (2012) seeks 'to call into question the popular idea that the entire law of armed conflict reflects a delicate balance between the fundamentally conflicting notions of military necessity and humanity'. Against Dinstein's (2004, 16) claim that the law of armed conflict 'in its entirety is predicated on a subtle equilibrium between two diametrically opposite impulses: military necessity and humanitarian considerations', Liivoja argues that these forces are not necessarily opposed, as it is well known that the exercise of humanitarian restraint may serve the strategic purpose of winning 'hearts and minds' among a civilian population. But Liivoja stops there. Having scored a hit on the 'diametric opposition' in Dinstein's argument, he misses the 'subtle equilibrium'. He does not interrogate the logic further.

But what might be revealed if the logic is interrogated further? As stated above, dialectical analysis proposes: *if evidence of both opposition and connection can be found in the relationship between the poles, then that relationship is dialectical and the problem is a complex paradox*. Military necessity sometimes threatens common humanity; sometimes it co-operates with common humanity. The key point is that *both* outcomes can arise. Once this is understood, Dinstein's 'subtle equilibrium' looks very much like a dialectical process.

The soldier in social context

Figure 4 models legitimate soldiering as the free interplay of *Support* and *Challenge*. 'Legitimate soldiering' is here defined as military activity conducted in accordance with IHL. All soldiering involves individuals acting within a social context. Here, legitimate soldiering is understood in terms of the maintenance of authentic ethical relations with the citizenry whom the soldier serves and protects. Ethical authenticity requires that there exists a dialectical balance between rights and duties. Where this is so, citizens are ready, willing and able – on the basis of informed judgement and according to circumstance – to exercise, collectively or individually, the duty to support or the right to challenge the actions of their armed forces. It is also necessary that competent independent external bodies (e.g. International Criminal Court, ICRC) are similarly free to exercise judgement in support or challenge, on behalf of all persons affected by military activity. Such action may be that of the armed forces of affected citizens' own state, or of another, such as multinational or occupying forces. The key test of the validity of all support or challenge is adherence to the requirements of IHL. The effective operation of IHL depends upon this freedom and opportunity to engage.

The Supportive Citizen acts ethically and in good faith, a beneficiary of soldiering with a realistic appreciation of the benefits that it brings. In Buddhist terms, they are *kataññutā*: mindful and appreciative of what has been done for and to them. Their support is authentic and robust because it is rooted in a right to challenge when necessary. This right is not exercised lightly and when it is, the Supportive Citizen becomes a Critical Citizen, one whose challenge proceeds from concomitant duty to support, expressed through loyalty to, and appeal to, legitimate standards such as the standards of IHL. Critical Citizens provide an essential balancing counterweight to those wielding dangerous weapons and draconian powers of enforcement. They include activists, journalists and writers, often inspired by an authoritative source of ethics (possibly Buddhist), who critically analyse military activity. Giants among them include Thich Nhat Hanh and George Orwell.

Dialectical balance may be broken in two ways. Polarisation as Support without Challenge is the work of Propagandists, the stuff of populist rhetoric, the voice of those who cheer from a safe distance whilst others do the fighting. On the other side, polarisation as Challenge without Support manifests as the Hostile Citizen, a beneficiary of soldiering who fails to appreciate how it benefits them. The Hostile Citizen acts unethically and in bad faith. In Buddhist terms, this is *akataññutā*: failure to be mindful and appreciative of what has been done for and to one. The Hostile Citizen breaks the balance of rights and duties, exercising the right to challenge whilst neglecting the duty to support. Distinguishing between the Critical Citizen and the Hostile Citizen may prove difficult, but the hallmark of the Hostile Citizen is polarised thinking: rigid adherence to an ideology which denies legitimacy to the soldier under all circumstances. Dogmatic pacifism may be found here.

The balanced healthy state of the system is a dynamic within which the military and the society that it serves and protects are in adult dialogue. Soldiers do their duty in dialogue with their citizenry, aware that the legitimacy of that duty depends upon the maintenance of due regard to its social context and impact. Citizens remain in dialogue with their soldiery, aware of the benefits conferred, supporting whilst feeling free to question and challenge when necessary. This is the consensual basis of military activity in a functioning democracy. The system is unbalanced and unhealthy to the extent that polarisation breaks adult dialogue and the mutual trust upon which it depends into a regressed adversarial exchange of slogans. Soldiers are all too aware that it falls to them to step in when civilian politics fail. For all their rhetoric of 'patriotism', politicians who exploit the processes of democratic governance to profit from populist polarisation threaten their military, their citizenry and the very basis of democracy.

Conclusions

The overall aim of this inquiry is to contribute to dialogue with Buddhism in the service of IHL, for the benefit of all, by subjecting the concept of the Buddhist soldier to rigorous investigation. This is hardly the last word on the Buddhist soldier, but it does offer some indication of the results that can be obtained when an enigmatic problem is examined from a Buddhist perspective. Buddhist thinking has a way of opening up the seemingly closed. Here, that attempt to open up and unfold the enigmatic has made original use of Buddhist Madhyamaka philosophy to penetrate some way beyond the commonplace view that the Buddhist soldier is a mere contradiction. It has demonstrated, through the use of dialectical analysis, that the forbidding initial appearance of the Buddhist soldier construct can be opened and unfolded to reveal a phenomenon of complexity, richness and significance.

Close parallels between Buddhism and the military in terms of key aspects of Buddhist doctrine and iconography have been pointed out. Buddhism and the military have been shown to hold mutually consistent, even synonymous, visions of the archetypal ideal. Unfolding through dialectical analysis has explored the nature of duty as dynamic balance between Individual and Social poles. Each of these poles has been further unfolded to explore the dialectics of the soldier as an ethically responsible individual acting within a context of social responsibility. The positive consequences of achieving balance and the negative consequences of falling into imbalance have been indicated.

For the ICRC project on Buddhism and IHL, this modelling is surely significant. The soldier operating in dialectical balance between energy (*vīrya*) and patience (*kṣānti*), authentically actualising the Warrior Hero archetype in a social context of legitimate support open to legitimate challenge, offers ideal prospects for the observance of IHL. By the same token, the prospects for IHL are bleak where these balances are not understood, valued, cultivated and maintained.

Does this mean that the Buddhist soldier is the ideal soldier? Consistency between the ideals of Buddhism and the military at the archetypal level leans towards this conclusion. Whilst there is scant originality in seeing the ideal Buddhist as a Warrior Hero, to see the ideal Warrior Hero as a Buddhist is more original, and has significant implications for the ICRC Buddhism and IHL project. But to privilege the Buddhist soldier over the soldier of other faiths (or none) is clearly a gross and dangerous error. That error can be avoided by distinguishing between a Buddhist and one who embodies values shared with Buddhists, with due regard to the transcendental and humanistic dimensions of Buddhism. This inquiry opened by distinguishing between these dimensions and proposing that dialogue between Buddhism and IHL focus on the humanistic dimension, leaving it free to focus on questions of ethical conduct in the world. This hardly dilutes the Buddhism, as ethical conduct is essential to Buddhist identity: it is axiomatic within the tradition that one is only truly a Buddhist to the extent that one acts like a Buddhist. Similarly, one can act in congruence with Buddhist ethical principles without identifying as a Buddhist. Ethical conduct is what matters. The nature of Buddhist ethics is helpful here. Buddhist ethics are held to be natural, in accordance with the true nature of reality. This is why, on a DPA map, the positive upper regions converge and point towards an integration which is ethical, whist the negative lower regions split into a disintegration which is unethical. It may be concluded, therefore, that the ideal soldier is one who acts in accordance with Buddhist principles, consciously and deliberately or not, whatever faith (or none) they may profess, for acting in accordance with Buddhist principles means acting in consistency with IHL.

This suggests that the Buddhism and IHL project might consider setting itself two related long-term objectives. A minimum objective could be the *Compliant Soldier*: a soldier whose action complies with IHL as a professional requirement. A maximum objective could be the *Ethical Soldier*: a soldier whose action complies with IHL not only as a professional requirement, but as a minimum standard of ethical conduct. Those ethics derive from an authoritative source, which may or not be Buddhist: compatibility with IHL is the test.

The Ethical Soldier may not face promising circumstances. As things currently stand, it is surely the case that, whilst life for the Critical Citizen may turn rough, the situation of the Ethical Soldier may well be riskier still. The most basic element in the politics of soldiering is the hierarchy of command. It would be naïve to assume that politics and ethics sit easily together in that hierarchy. The history of the 'superior orders' defence (Dinstein 2012), from the execution of Peter von Hagenbach (1474) through the Nuremberg Trials (1945), the massacres at Kafr Qassim (1956) and My Lai (1968), to the Iraq War (2003), is one of logical inconsistency and political expediency.[13] Even though obeying illegal orders is itself an IHL violation, the soldier who faces a conflict between acting legally or ethically on the one hand and obedience to command on the other is likely to be in serious difficulty. The Ethical Soldier will not develop, let alone thrive, in such an environment.

The Ethical Soldier's action is rooted in a full understanding of their identity, duty and potential. The impact of that understanding depends upon it being robustly established and active across several distinct but related spheres: in the mind of the individual soldier, at all levels of the armed forces within which they serve, in the wider cultural context within which they operate, within civic and governmental bodies, and among independent external bodies, such as the ICRC. In response to a mindset that rejects dialectical thinking, it can be pointed out that prime examples of competent dialectical thought and action in complex, demanding and fast-changing conditions include the Prussian Field Marshall Helmuth von Moltke's insistence upon agile flexibility in response to the dynamic flow of emergent circumstance on the field of battle: 'No plan of action survives first contact with the enemy' (Hughes 1993, 92). Similar understanding is evident among such celebrated military strategists as Sun Tzu, Napoleon Bonaparte ('I have never had a plan of operations')[14] and Carl von Clausewitz ([1832] 1989).

An agenda for action

Developing the Ethical Soldier means cultivating potential. This analysis will be of little real use unless it leads to action and change. Here is an agenda for original, imaginative and creative action on organisational development and management learning among military leaders and political decision-makers, as well as within engaged civilian organisations such as the ICRC. Key competences requiring further development include capacity around the identification, analysis and resolution of complex problems, including the modelling of key dialectics through DPA analysis, and the development of knowledge, skill and attitude in working with the archetypal dimension of mind. Nothing less will give the Ethical Soldier and the rule of IHL a fighting chance.

Notes

1. The founder of Madhyamaka is Nāgārjuna, supported by Āryadeva, conventionally dated 150–250 CE. Nāgārjuna's importance within the Buddhist tradition is such that he is sometimes known as a 'Second Buddha'. However, Nāgārjuna insists that his work is entirely consistent with the original Buddhist tradition, which it seeks to reinstate. This is a core theme of the Mahāyāna. Nāgārjuna's *Mūlamadhyamakakārikā*, the foundational text of Madhyamaka, cites the Buddha's Discourse with Kaccayāna from the Pali Canon (*Kaccayānagotta Sutta, Saṃyutta Nikāya* 12.15; for a translation see Thanissaro Bhikkhu 1997). Nāgārjuna's consistency with other original Pali sources, such as the *Aṭṭhakavagga* and *Pārāyanavagga* of the *Sutta-Nipāta*, is emphasised by e.g.

Kalupahana (1994). For authoritative contemporary commentary on Nāgārjuna and *Mūlamadhyamakakārikā*, see e.g. Garfield (1995), and Siderits and Katsura (2013).

2. Capacity to explore the interconnection between apparent opposites is not unique to Madhyamaka, for it is common to any philosophical method based on dialectical logic. What is unique to Madhyamaka is that its dialectics are rooted in insight into the empty nature of phenomena (*Śūnyatā*), which is why it is preferred here.
3. Buddhist tradition enumerates the *pāramitās* in various ways. In the Pali Canon, the *Buddhavaṃsa* (*Khuddaka Nikāya* 14) lists 10 perfections. In the Mahāyāna tradition, *the Prajñāpāramitā Sūtras* list six, whilst amongst them the *Saddharmapuṇḍarīka* (White Lotus) *Sūtra* adds a seventh: *upāya aramita*, Perfection of (Skilful) Means. The Theravādin commentator Dhammapāla (identity and dates uncertain, but pre-twelfth century CE) equates the sets of 10 and six. The lists of Buddhist doctrine are no more (and no less) than analytic schemata, mnemonic devices that evolved during the early oral tradition of Buddhism. Content matters more than number. For a contemporary discussion, see e.g. Wright (2009).
4. Cula-Malunkyovada Sutta, Majjhima Nikaya 63. For a translation see Thanissaro Bhikkhu (1998).
5. Examples of the iconography of Mañjuśrī: https://www.google.co.uk/search?source=univ&tbm=isch&q=manjushri+images&sa=X&ved=2ahUKEwjZkJv8vLLtAhVDC-wKHVGaCK0QjJkEegQIAxAB&biw=2560&bih=1329.
6. Examples of the iconography of Padmasambhava: https://www.google.co.uk/search?source=univ&tbm=isch&q=padmasambhava+images&sa=X&ved=2ahUKEwjG-oS4qd3tAhXHVsAKHSNIAbUQjJkEegQIBRAB&biw=2560&bih=1329&dpr=2.
7. Examples of the iconography of Vajrapāṇi: https://www.google.co.uk/search?source=univ&tbm=isch&q=vajrapani+images&sa=X&ved=2ahUKEwiY7YGzvrLtAhXKvKQKHRLqAQkQjJkEegQIAxAB&biw=2560&bih=1329.
8. Examples of the iconography of Vajrasattva: https://www.google.co.uk/search?q=vajrasattva+images&tbm=isch&ved=2ahUKEwjyirq0vrLtAhWJiqQKHfKEDRAQ2-cCegQIABAA&oq=vajrasattva+images&gs_lcp=CgNpbWcQAzICCAA6BAgAEEM6BggAEAcQHlCV3QRY5ewEYljwBGgAcAB4AIABdIgB1wWSAQQxMC4xmAEAoAEBqgELZ3dzLXdpei1pbWfAAQE&sclient=img&ei=lDTJX_LwHlmVkgXyibaAAQ&bih=1329&biw=2560.
9. The ideology of 'holy war' is all too familiar within the major world religions. Buddhism is sometimes considered to be an exception, but for an analysis of the perversion of Buddhist doctrine in the service of Japanese militarism, see Victoria (2006).
10. Jung (1990, para. 709) defines *enantiodromia* as 'the emergence of the unconscious opposite in the course of time. This characteristic phenomenon practically always occurs when an extreme, one-sided tendency dominates conscious life; in time an equally powerful counterposition is built up which first inhibits the conscious performance and subsequently breaks through the conscious control'. As Jung (2014) notes, this thinking is found in the Western tradition as far back as Heraclitus. It is evident in Plato's *Phaedo* and the dialectics of Socrates, as well as being fundamental within the Buddhist and Taoist traditions.

11. See note 2.
12. See e.g. Sangharakshita (1986).
13. For details of these events, and a history of the Superior Orders defence, see https://en.wikipedia.org/wiki/Superior_orders.
14. Quoted by von Moltke (Hughes 1993, 92).

Disclosure statement

This article has been supported by the International Committee of the Red Cross (ICRC).

ORCID

Dharmacārin Siṃhanāda http://orcid.org/0000-0003-0258-5121

References

Campbell, J. [1949] 2012. *The Hero with a Thousand Faces. Collected Works of Joseph Campbell*. 3rd ed. Novato: New World Library.
Dinstein, Y. 2004. *The Conduct of Hostilities under the Law of Armed Conflict*. Cambridge: Cambridge University Press.
Dinstein, Y. 2012. *The Defence of Obedience to Superior Orders in International Law*. Oxford: Oxford University Press.
French, S. E. 2017. "The Code of the Warrior: Ideals of Warrior Cultures Throughout History." *Journal of Character & Leadership Integration* 4 (1): 64–71.
Garfield, J. 1995. *The Fundamental Wisdom of the Middle Way: Nāgārjuna's Mūlamadhyamakakārikā*. New York: Oxford University Press.
Hughes, D. J., ed. 1993. *Moltke on the Art of War: Selected Writings*. New York: Presidio Press.
Johnson, B. 1996. *Polarity Management: Identifying & Managing Unsolvable Problems*. 2nd ed. Amhurst: HRD Press.
Jung, C. G. 1990. *Psychological Types*. London: Routledge.
Jung, C. G. 1991. *The Archetypes and the Collective Unconscious. Collected Works of C.G. Jung*. London: Routledge.
Jung, C. G. [1933] 2001. *Modern Man in Search of a Soul*. London: Routledge.

Jung, C. G. 2014. *Two Essays on Analytical Psychology*. London: Routledge.
Kalupahana, D. J. 1994. *A History of Buddhist Philosophy*. Delhi: Motilal Banarsidass.
Liivoja, R. 2012. "Chivalry without a Horse: Military Honour and the Modern Law of Armed Conflict." In *The Law of Armed Conflict: Historical and Contemporary Perspectives*, edited by R. Liivoja and A. Saumets, 75–100. Tartu: Tartu University Press.
McNeilly, M. 2003. *Sun Tzu and the Art of Modern Warfare*. New York: Oxford University Press.
Moore, R., and D. Gillette. 1990. *King, Warrior, Magician, Lover: Rediscovering the Archetypes of the Mature Masculine*. New York: HarperOne.
Sangharakshita. 1986. *Sangharakshita, Alternative Traditions*. Glasgow: Windhorse.
Shay, J. 1994. *Achilles in Vietnam: Combat Trauma and the Undoing of Character*. New York: Simon & Schuster.
Siderits, M., and S. Katsura. 2013. *Nāgārjuna's Middle Way: Mūlamadhyamakakārikā*. Boston: Wisdom.
Thanissaro Bhikkhu, trans. 1997. "Kaccayānagotta Sutta: On Right View. Saṃyutta Nikāya 12.15." *Access to Insight*. https://www.accesstoinsight.org/tipitaka/sn/sn12/sn12.015.than.html
Thanissaro Bhikkhu, trans. 1998. "Cūḷa-Māluṅkyovāda Sutta: The Shorter Instructions to Māluṅkyā. Majjhima Nikāya 63." *Access to Insight*. https://www.accesstoinsight.org/tipitaka/mn/mn.063.than.html
VanLandigham, R. 2015. "The Law of War Is Not about 'Chivalry'." *Just Security*. https://www.justsecurity.org/24773/laws-war-chivalry/
Victoria, B. D. 2006. *Zen at War*. 2nd ed. Lanham: Rowman & Littlefield.
von Clausewitz, C. [1832] 1989. *On War (Vom Kriege)*. Edited by M. Howard and P. Paret. Princeton: Princeton University Press.
Wright, D. S. 2009. *The Six Perfections: Buddhism and the Cultivation of Character*. New York: Oxford University Press.

ICRC

LIMITING THE RISK TO COMBATANT LIVES: CONFLUENCES BETWEEN INTERNATIONAL HUMANITARIAN LAW AND BUDDHISM

Vishakha Wijenayake

ABSTRACT

This article places international humanitarian law (IHL) side by side with Buddhist narratives as seen through the *Jātakas*, to investigate how they view the expectation placed on soldiers to risk their lives in battle. To this end, I delve into the notion of reciprocity of risk in battle from an IHL perspective, which I argue is crucial to infusing warfare with restraint. Similarly, Buddhism acknowledges the importance of reciprocity as an ethical principle that leads to non-violence. I demonstrate how IHL tries to ensure that the risk combatants undertake in combat is limited through its rule of surrender. I compare this argument with the *Seyyaṃsa* or *Seyya Jātaka* (no. 282), which illustrates the need to cease violence in cases of surrender. The way militaries treat their own combatants is crucial to the meaningful practice of surrender and thereby the limits and restraints of warfare. Buddhism too encourages rulers to value the lives of their soldiers and not to put their lives at unnecessary risk. I conclude that to maximise the combatant's choice to limit the risk he takes in battle, IHL should pay more attention to the orders that militaries and armed groups issue to their combatants. Buddhism, for its part, can facilitate the constructive use of military orders because it projects positive images of rulers who are reluctant to order their soldiers to take unnecessary risks in war.

Introduction

War is a way of framing political violence around which various narratives are constructed (Kahn 2013, 202). One such narrative is that pertaining to death. Death in wartime is not viewed with the same lens as it is viewed in peacetime. This is even more applicable to how combatants' deaths are seen in comparison to civilian deaths. While in peacetime it is illegal to kill another, in war it is legal to kill an enemy combatant (Additional Protocol I, Article 42). There is an acceptance that those who join the military have a high probability of dying. Likewise, morality in times of war and as applied within the

DOI: 10.4324/9781003439820-12

military is different to that of civilian society (Durkheim 1951, 198; McMahan 2009, 36).[1] Militaries and armed groups seem to 'lay down their own precepts and presume to establish their own hierarchies of norms' (Cover 1983, 33). However, the boundaries of even sectarian communities such as the military can be porous. The principles that establish the worldview of a community, including the military, tend to mirror the cultural constructs of the community within which it resides (Cover 1983, 33). A combatant does not exclusively reflect his attitudes *qua* military man but is also influenced by social, economic, political or religious affiliations (Huntington 1957, 60). Therefore, societal and religious norms and expectations continue to play a role in defining the value of a soldier's life, actions and eventual death.

Buddhism does not encourage violence and is pacifist in terms of its outlook towards war.[2] However, this is not to say that Buddhist narratives are entirely silent on this issue. For example, the circumstances that resulted in the Buddha narrating the *Vaḍḍhakisūkara Jātaka* (no. 283) involved a monk by the name of Dhanuggaha Tissa who is described as a clever military strategist. During the time when the Buddha narrated this *Jātaka*, the King of Kosala had sent spies to hang around the monasteries to overhear military strategies communicated by monk Dhauggaha Tissa to monk Upatissa, for example:

> In warfare there are three strategies such as Paduma Bruha, Cakra Bruha and Sataka Bruha. In the Sataka Bruha, positioning the army on either side, fighting for some time and retreating suddenly, then rushing into the middle of the enemy camp like the army of Mara, is one strategy of capture. If one fights using this strategy beside that mountain, one could defeat the enemy easily. (Jat. II.404) (Obeyesekere 2016, 251)

The spies duly informed their king of this strategy. The king in turn carried out wartime preparations accordingly and captured King Ajātasattu (Obeyesekere 2016, 252).[3] While this story is clear on the fact that the monk did not engage in giving direct advice to the king on how to fight war, it is an apt example to show that Buddhist lore contains narratives that speak of war and view it from the perspective of a non-participating observer. In this article, I choose to focus primarily on such narratives as seen through the *Jātakas*. The *Jātakas*, or stories of the past lives of the Buddha during which he was mastering the qualities that would enable him to become a Buddha, form an integral part of Buddhist lore. Even if *Jātakas* may not be strictly Buddhist in origin and may have been taken from the wider Indian context, one cannot dismiss these stories given that they have been a popular part of Buddhism for over 2000 years (Appleton 2010, 10). Likewise, they are the stories with which Buddhist communities grow up, and they shape their cultural sensibilities (Schober 1997, 1). Appleton (2010, 2) states that especially in Theravāda Buddhist countries, *Jātakas* are infused into people's daily lives through 'illustrations in temples, their presence in sermons, children's story books, plays, television programmes, theatre, dance and poetry'. These tales influence not only the cultural sensibilities of Buddhist societies but also their ethical principles. Therefore, the pursuit of identifying messages that the *Jātakas* project about war, and the image of the soldier that they paint, is an important one, given that they have the capacity to influence how militaries make decisions about how their combatants engage in battle.

This article places international humanitarian law (IHL) side by side with Buddhist narratives as seen through the *Jātakas*, to investigate how they view the expectation placed on soldiers to risk their lives in battle. To this end, firstly, I delve into the notion of reciprocity of risk in battle from an IHL perspective, which I argue is crucial to infusing warfare with restraint. It must be noted, however, that the notion of reciprocity of risk is not one that finds expression in the black letter of IHL. My argument, through an exploration of warfare as an interactional practice, is that reciprocity of risk in warfare acts as an undercurrent to IHL's objective of increasing restraint in warfare. Similarly, Buddhism acknowledges the importance of reciprocity as an ethical principle which leads to non-violence. Secondly, I demonstrate how IHL tries to ensure that the risk combatants undertake in combat is limited through its rule of surrender. I compare this argument with the *Seyyaṃsa* or *Seyya Jātaka* (no. 282), which illustrates the need to cease violence in cases of surrender. Thirdly, I establish that the manner in which militaries treat their own combatants is crucial to the meaningful practice of surrender and thereby the limits and restraints of warfare. I argue that Buddhism too encourages rulers to value the lives of their soldiers and not to put their lives at unnecessary risk. I conclude that in order to maximise the combatant's choice to limit the risk he takes in battle, IHL should pay more attention to the orders that militaries and armed groups issue to their combatants. Buddhism, for its part, can facilitate this by projecting positive images of rulers who are reluctant to order their soldiers to take unnecessary risks in war.

Reciprocity and restraint in war

War, since pre-historic times, has been a reciprocal enterprise (Keely 2012, 11). René Provost (2012) argues that the notion of reciprocity undergirds IHL. The chivalric codes of mediaeval Europe supported reciprocal trust between knights, including with those on the opposing side. These codes have been assimilated into modern wartime practices (Pilloud et al. 1987, 434). However, with the universal ratification of the Geneva Conventions of 1949, all states now have an obligation to respect IHL regardless of whether it is being respected by the opposing parties to a conflict (International Committee of the Red Cross 2016, 119; Provost 2012, 19; Dörmann and Serralvo 2014; Mégret 2013).[4] Common Article 1 to the Geneva Conventions provides that '[t]he High Contracting Parties undertake to respect and ensure respect for the present Convention *in all circumstances*' [emphasis added], emphasising the automatic application of the Conventions.[5] Therefore, it may be argued that reciprocity is now less important in order for IHL rules to apply to warring parties. In spite of this shift, I argue that reciprocity remains relevant to how combatants risk their lives in combat. The 'reciprocity of risk in combat' speaks to the mutual danger and vulnerability experienced between adversaries (Kahn 2013, 218). This 'bond of mutual risk' brings human interaction into war, where ordinary social relations otherwise experience a breakdown (Mégret 2013, 1310). Accordingly, when combatants confront each other on the battlefield they engage in a reciprocal interaction (Provost 2012, 36). Reciprocity of risk, therefore, marks an 'internal morality of combat' (Kahn 2013, 201) and can be seen as reinforcing IHL given that it acts as a pragmatic *raison d'être* for restraint in warfare (Evangelidi 2018, 100).

The mutually reinforcing relationship between reciprocity and restraint can also be seen in Buddhist ethics (Scheible 2009, 212). The *Dhammapada* contains verses considered to be delivered by the Buddha preserved in the form of an anthology in the Pali language in Sri Lanka and Southeast Asia. Parallel versions of this text are found in many languages from throughout the Buddhist world, and it is the most translated Buddhist text into non-Asian languages because of its succinct and accessible presentation of Buddhist teachings. The Pali version (Carter and Palihawadana 1987, 202–203) states thus:

> All are frightened of the rod.
> Of death all are afraid.
> Having made oneself the example,
> One should neither slay nor cause to slay.
>
> All are frightened of the rod.
> For all, life is dear.
> Having made oneself example,
> One should neither slay nor cause to slay.

Charles Hallisey states that using the terms 'Having made oneself the example' to mean 'As I am, so are other beings', and that to prevent oneself from harming another indicates 'an awareness of an underlying 'kinship, or sameness in a defining experience, that can be used as a guide for actions' (Hallisey 2009, 136). Norman (1997, 20) offers an alternative translation to the third line, rendering 'Having made oneself the example' as 'Comparing (others) with oneself'. This makes even more clear the point about how one can better relate to the experience of others by looking inward. Moreover, the fifth-century Pali treatise the *Visuddhimagga* contains a meditation that mirrors the verses from the *Dhammapada*:

> On traversing all directions with the mind
> One finds no one anywhere dearer than oneself.
> Likewise everyone holds himself most dear,
> Hence one who loves himself should not harm another.

(Ireland 1997, 62)

Both the *Visuddhimagga* and the *Dhammapada* present an ethical argument that appeals to the ability to empathise with others, putting oneself in their place. According to Kristin Scheible (2009, 122), this requires determining how one wants or would want to be treated, and then projecting the quality of one's own self-interest onto others.

Similarly, in war, the notion of reciprocity 'reflects the fact that most agents will agree to be bound by a norm on the basis that they thereby obtain a benefit' (Provost 2012, 18). Likewise, IHL provides combatants with a combatant's privilege, a right to legally kill other combatants on the grounds that these combatants would have an equal right to target them.[6] While IHL itself does not expressly expand on this idea in the following manner, as just war scholar Michael Walzer puts it: 'You can't kill unless you are prepared to die' (Walzer 2004, 101). This speaks to an ethos that undergirds the interactional nature of warfare. Likewise, Bryan Peeler argues that reciprocal behaviour by parties to a conflict, when repeated over time, can create a possibility for mutual restraint in warfare (Peeler 2019, 23). Without such a norm, there is a risk of losing restraint imposed through law in times of conflict, leading to warfare that is excessive (Greenspan 1959, 319). The understanding that to cause harm to an adversary, a combatant has to assume a similar risk of harm to himself, prevents unbridled violence from taking place (Robinson 1999, 682). In other words, my argument is that while a reciprocity of risk in combat is not a rule that is expressly featured in IHL, it is in fact a rationale underlying how restraint in war is maintained. The corollary of this equation is that where the adversary does not pose a threat, the legitimacy of targeting one's opponent founded on reciprocal threat would also fail. The manner in which this practice of reciprocity leads to restraint is best demonstrated in how surrender operates on the battlefield.

Limiting the risk to life of combatants through surrender

Obligations are reciprocal if they depend on 'the existence of connected obligations on others' (Provost 2002, 121). Surrender, therefore, is a practice that depends on a shared understanding of how one party will be treated by the other in the case of a combatant ceasing to fight. Surrendering communicates a limit to the risk that a combatant is willing to take in battle: If you will not surrender or be taken prisoner, and torture or kill those who surrender to you, your enemies will not allow you to be taken or to surrender' (Keely 2012, 10).

A look at Buddhist *Jātaka* tales further demonstrates this need to grant mercy to those who refuse to fight in battle through acts of surrender. In the *Seyyaṃsa Jātaka* (no. 282), the Bodhisattva, being born as the King of Benares, overcomes his enemy by meditating on compassion. When a foreign army invades his kingdom, the soldiers in his city go to the king to inform him about the arrival of the King of Kosala, thereby requesting to fight him. The King of Benares commands them not to fight, and then gives the order for the palace gates to be opened. The King of Kosala, confident, captures and imprisons the King and Queen. While in prison, the King of Benares, who is in this case the Bodhisattva, meditates on compassion, the power of which causes the King of Kosala to feel his body burn unbearably. This is due to the fact that he captured the kingdom of a king who practises meditation based on compassion. The King of Kosala releases both the King of Benares and the other prisoners. The Bodhisattva, surrounded by his ministers, tells them that by the power of the thoughts of compassion and loving kindness he was able to save his life as well as theirs (Obeyesekere 2016, 249–250).

Through the acts of the Bodhisattva King of Benares, Buddhist lore accepts surrender as a legitimate option to take in war. The *Seyyamsa Jātaka* demonstrates the need for violence in war to be reciprocal, and therefore when one party refuses to engage in combat, violence must cease. Not only does the *Jātaka* approve of the practice of surrender, it demands that such practice be respected by the victor. Likewise, the obligation to not harm the surrendering party is prompted by the King of Kosala feeling burning sensations in his body. This is an indication that if a party to a conflict were not to grant mercy to those who surrender, it would bear adverse repercussions. While the *Jātaka* presents the repercussions as an immediate adverse physical reaction, at a more universally practical level, an adverse repercussion might, for example, result in the party not being shown respect in the future. Therefore, the refusal to grant mercy to those who surrender would make the foundations of reciprocal restraint crumble. Another facet of the story speaks of how the Bodhisattva King was conscious of the need to limit harm to his own soldiers. The king states that by avoiding going into battle and by meditating on compassion, he was able to save the lives of his officials, including those of his soldiers. This is a recognition that the Bodhisattva valued the lives of his own troops and realised that surrendering would limit the risk they would have to take if they were to engage in battle. This demonstrates that the notion of limited warfare is contingent not only on how a party treats its opponents but also on how a military decides to treat the lives of its own troops.

In its development, IHL created obligations on the party receiving a surrender to accept it. Article 41 of Additional Protocol I to the Geneva Conventions speaks of safeguarding an enemy who has been rendered *hors de combat*. The obligation on the adverse party is to cease fire immediately upon being communicated a clear intention of surrender. Accordingly, surrender as per Additional Protocol I to the Geneva Conventions is unconditional. It is prohibited to refuse an offer of surrender and 'no argument of military necessity may be invoked' to do so (Pilloud et al. 1987, 488). In IHL, a belligerent can no longer choose whether or not to accept a surrender by a warring party based on how its own combatants' offers of surrender were received by the adversary. In other words, belligerents are obliged to accept surrender whether this practice is reciprocated by the adversary or not. Even while IHL attempts to make the practice of surrender less reciprocal, however, reciprocity still continues to play a role in how surrender takes place in battle. Hersch Lauterpacht (1953) claims that 'it is impossible to visualise the conduct of hostilities in which one side would be bound by rules of warfare without benefiting from them and the other side would benefit from rules of warfare without being bound by them'. In this case he views benefits and obligations as deriving from the conduct of the adversary. The next section of the article notes that, in the case of surrender, a party to the conflict may deny the acceptance of surrender due to combatants of such party themselves being prevented from being able to surrender through the internal rules of their own military. That is, for meaningful reciprocity and restraint to be practised in war, it is important to look into how and to what extent militaries demand their own soldiers to risk their lives in combat.

Importance of how a military treats its own troops to limited risk in warfare

Historically, armed groups have often determined the degree of risk their own combatants are expected to take in battle, by making it difficult for combatants to practise surrender. For example, 'in Aztec combat in which soldiers fought in units and sought to maintain cohesion, it was difficult for an individual to separate himself physically in order to surrender to the enemy' (Hassig 2012, 116–117). Any Roman who surrendered chose disgrace for himself and his family (de Libero 2012, 33). Accordingly, a soldier was expected to sacrifice his life rather than surrender (Kortüm 2012, 43). Today's legislation governing military discipline does not contain stringent prohibitions against surrender. However, remnants of historical practice that frowns upon surrender remain. This is seen in the fact that current laws in some countries try to ensure that surrender is only used as a last resort. Command and leadership play a significant role in establishing whether soldiers can engage in surrender or not. Therefore, internal military rules on when one is able to give up fighting are directly applicable to commanders.[7] Surrender is only permitted if exercised in situations where successful defence is not possible. Such laws indicate to commanders that a decision to surrender can only be exercised as a last resort and cannot be made lightly, even when one's forces are at great risk.

Furthermore, certain provisions in national legislation make it an offence to engage in acts that could be indicative of surrender. For example, the Army Act 1949 of Sri Lanka (as amended) makes it an offence for any military person to send a flag of truce to the enemy. The law does not expressly refer to the intent of the combatant who uses a white flag or the circumstances in which the flag is used. Law in Ireland penalises combatants who treacherously or without due authority send a flag of truce to the enemy.[8] This provision, however, envisages a situation where a white flag can be used to surrender when this is done as per due authority. During international armed conflicts, the main right those who are surrendering can claim is to be treated as prisoners of war (Pilloud et al. 1987, 488).[9] Certain legislation limits the capacity of a military's own soldiers to stop fighting through rules that prohibit being captured by the enemy.[10] With the effect of such provisions, individual soldiers are barred from taking measures warranted under IHL for them to exercise a legal surrender. Therefore, while IHL may dictate that once an intention to surrender is expressed the adversary is obligated to respect it, the aforementioned provisions penalise a combatant for making an offer of surrender in the first place.

Such prohibitions against surrendering or being taken prisoner shatter the equation of reciprocity as it relates to the practice of surrender, which is based on a risk of death which is limited. To a combatant who has been ordered to fight to the death or who has no or limited option of surrender, what incentives are there to empathise with someone who would want to give up fighting in order to preserve his or her own life? The restraint embedded in the idea of reciprocal risk in combat rests on both parties understanding that, at the point a combatant ceases to be a threat, there will no longer be a risk of being targeted by him or her. However, where there is certainty of death, a combatant cannot envisage a point at which the other side ceases to be a threat. Accordingly, the manner in which the internal structures and ethos of militaries and armed groups minimise or magnify the risk to their own troops must be of concern to IHL.

The notion of reciprocity of risk must be assessed in the context of how different cultures decide to draw the limits to risk in battle. According to Walzer (2006, 23) restraints that are observed in war are determined by each society. Each cultural context tends to determine 'who can fight, what tactics are acceptable, when battle has to be broken off, and what prerogatives go with victory into the idea of war itself'. Walzer (2006, 24–25) argues that while war tends to be limited, how it is limited and the extent of its limits are specific to each time and place. It is pertinent, therefore, to examine how the cultural context created through Buddhist narratives approaches the issue of how a military should treat is own troops.

Buddhism speaks strongly of the manner in which one's own troops are to be treated. For example, a '*cakkavartin*' or universal monarch[11] is meant to keep his armed forces in good health and condition. The Buddhist approach to such treatment would not be limited to a mere utilitarian need to ensure the good health of one's forces but would also demonstrate compassion and give dignity to all. The Buddha, according to the *Jātaka*s, urged warrior nobles to see value in the lives of their soldiers, by encouraging them to recognise how much was lost if they were sacrificed. For example, in the *Culla Kāliṅga*

Jātaka (no. 301) minister Nandisena takes a thousand of the king's personal guards up a cliff. He then asks them whether they are prepared to risk their lives by jumping off the cliff in order to save their king's life. To this the warriors unhesitatingly answer yes (Obeyesekere 2016, 305). The minister, however, states 'What use is there in falling off this cliff? Go ahead and fight without retreating and help our king' (Obeyesekere 2016, 306). While the story discourages retreating from battle, it also indicates that Buddhism does not approve of the kind of extreme altruism that requires disregard for the value of one's own life.[12] This *Jātaka* mirrors IHL principles where the duty of utmost exertion cannot be interpreted as extending to an obligation to recklessly fight to death. In modern legislation, the term 'utmost exertion' speaks to the degree of risk a soldier is supposed to take prior to being legitimately capable of giving up fighting. The National Defence Act of Canada at section 74 makes it an offence for any military person, when ordered to carry out an operation of war, to fail to use his utmost exertion to carry out the orders. These legal provisions should be interpreted in a manner consistent with IHL. To this end, the utmost exertion clause must be read in light of, and so as not to contravene, the rule on surrender and foundational notions of restraint in IHL.

In the *Supatta Jātaka* (no. 292), the virtue of a king as well as the virtue of the solider is measured by the willingness of the soldier to sacrifice his life in the name of the king (Obeyesekere 2016, 280–281). In this story, the Bodhisattva was born as a crow known by the name Supatta, the king of 80,000 other crows. The Bodhisattva's chief queen developed a pregnancy craving for royal human food. His general, Sumukha, planned to fly down and topple the lids when the cook in the royal kitchen came out carrying the food for the human king. Four of the other crows would then swoop down and scoop out some rice. He knew he would get caught. But he asked the other crows not to tell the King and Queen that he was caught (Obeyesekere 2016, 280). It is important to note that the general, Sumukha, did not want his king to find out that he was sacrificing his life in order to get his queen royal food. He states that if they were to find out, they would refuse to eat the food. This shows that the king did not take pleasure in soldiers sacrificing their lives for him and would not give an order to that effect.

Similarly, I argue that IHL should be updated to the effect that military leaders are prevented from leading their own forces to needlessly give up their lives. Such a development would not be wholly alien to the existing provisions and developing trends in IHL. Common Article 1 to the Geneva Conventions enshrines the duty to ensure respect for IHL, which applies first and foremost to the High Contracting Parties themselves, including their armed forces and other persons and groups acting on their behalf (International Committee of the Red Cross 2016, 118). Moreover, in the case of *The Prosecutor v. Bosco Ntaganda* (2014), the International Criminal Court's Pre-Trial Chamber addressed allegations that Ntaganda committed the war crimes of rape and sexual slavery – involving children forcibly recruited into his armed group, the Union des Patriotes Congolais/Forces Patriotiques pour la Libération du Congo (UPC/FPLC). The court determined that these war crimes would extend to the acts of armed groups in relation to their own troops.[13] While in this case, such protection applied in the context of child soldiers, the ICRC Updated Commentary to Common Article 3 to the Geneva Conventions (International Committee of the Red Cross 2016, 547–549) argues that 'all parties to the conflict should, as a minimum, grant humane treatment to their own armed forces based on Common Article 3'. Furthermore, Article 40 of Additional Protocol I to the Geneva Conventions prohibits taking or threatening the adversary to take no survivors. Making this a separate article from Article 41 (which requires belligerents to accept surrenders) was one way of underlining the fundamental importance of the idea that 'combatants who went on defending themselves to the limit of their strength and finally surrendered and laid down their arms, should not be exterminated' (Pilloud et al. 1987, 476). Article 40 speaks to those who are in the power of the enemy, anyone who is rendered *hors de combat*, or is surrendering. When reading the rule prohibiting no quarter in conjunction with the principle of surrender, I propose that for these provisions to be meaningful in practice, it must be implicit in IHL that the risks that combatants undertake in warfare are limited not only through the acts of the adversary but also through the internal military culture to which they belong.

Conclusion

While the image of warfare painted by IHL accepts a risk to combatants as an occupational hazard of engaging in hostilities, it does not expect a combatant to necessarily die in battle simply as a precondition of war. However, in the military context, sometimes norms of obedience are so strong that they can create a presumption of obedience to authority even when the actions ordered would otherwise be perceived as immoral or illegal (Osiel 2001, 55).[14] Historical experiences of mass atrocities have enlightened international law to the fact that there needs to be a balance between the need to maintain discipline on the field and deterring soldiers from engaging in war crimes (Ziv 2014, 20; Posner and Sykes 2007, 129). Today, the duty to disobey a manifestly unlawful order is a rule of customary international law that is intrinsic to combatants respecting the principles of IHL, regardless of their superior orders. Likewise, customary law as set out in ICRC Customary IHL study's Rule 154 tends to suggest that acts which, if committed, would amount to war crimes would necessarily have to be disobeyed. This rule still leaves it unclear whether due obedience pertaining to anything but the most egregious offences such as war crimes would be a violation of the duty to disobey manifestly unlawful orders

(Osiel 2001). Therefore, combatants have to decide which orders are manifestly unlawful, in which case they would have a duty to disobey such orders under general international law. If an order is 'lawful', on the other hand, they have a duty to obey such an order under domestic legislation governing military discipline. While it is debatable whether an order that requires a combatant to fight to the death or expose themselves to extreme risk is manifestly unlawful, as argued in this article, such an order can render the principle of surrender in IHL redundant. However, some scholars argue that, given that combatants are liable to be killed in any case, while 'any rule that limits the intensity and duration of combat or the suffering of soldiers is to be welcomed', the violation of such a norm would not result in universal disapprobation (Walzer 2006, 42). Therefore, it would seem that an order to fight to the death is not one that is so manifestly unlawful that a combatant has a duty to disobey it. This highlights a need for IHL to take steps to ensure clarity through express rules on how armed forces treat their own combatants, in particular with regard to the use of orders to fight to the death or laws prohibiting surrender.

However, where IHL rules may not provide clarity, other cultural influences, such as religious narratives, can come into play and discourage combatants from engaging in practices that challenge restraint in warfare. This appeal to something other than merely the 'law' to preserve humanity in war can be seen in the adoption of the Martens Clause. The Martens Clause has formed a part of the laws of armed conflict since its first appearance in the preamble to the 1899 Hague Convention (II) with respect to the laws and customs of war on land, and appeals to 'public conscience' as a safety net where principles of international law provide no cover. The notion of public conscience is not a monolith, and a combatant's choice to act is influenced by how good or bad is understood by the public to which he or she is most related. This is particularly the case where the law's requirements are not obvious (such as where the illegality of a superior's order is not fully manifest). Therefore, religious narratives can help combatants 'exercise practical judgment in the circumstances where bright-line rules do not provide clear guidance' (Walzer 2006, 37).

As this article has highlighted, Buddhism responds to such existential and ethical questions that may preoccupy the soldier. It emphasises that there is a duty of care on the part of those in command to conduct hostilities in a manner that preserves the lives of their own troops where at all possible. Accordingly, in the *Jātaka* stories, the justness and virtue of a king is measured by his reluctance to sacrifice the lives of his soldiers. The article has argued that recent developments in IHL point in the direction of generating a norm that binds parties to a conflict to look into treating their own forces with humanity and dignity. However, given that the choice exercised by individual combatants is limited, normative frameworks in war need to be strengthened so that militaries cannot prevent combatants from exercising their choice to surrender, thereby leading such combatants to unduly risk their lives. Buddhism lends cultural credibility to the efforts of the international lawyer who cares for the humanity of the combatant. This confluence between Buddhism and IHL is particularly important as narratives that influence those who engage in war can hardly be compartmentalised into separate boxes. They intermingle and create webs of meaning. IHL and Buddhism are two such narratives based on which soldiers and the forces to which they belong can generate their own meaning regarding how soldiers are to be treated in war. Therefore, a commingling of IHL and Buddhism would result in better treatment by the armed forces of their own soldiers.

Notes

1. McMahan (2009, 36) acknowledges the argument that 'war is fundamentally different morally, from other forms of conflict and all other types of activity'.
2. The first of the Five Precepts of Buddhism is to abstain from killing and there are no exceptions to this principle for times of war. However, this idea is debated by Buddhist and international humanitarian law scholars. More elaborate discussions on this debate can be found in other articles of this volume.
3. In referring to this work in the remainder of this article, proper names have been changed to the Pali version.
4. This shift away from the principle of reciprocity in IHL can be seen in rules regulating reprisals in attack. 'Customary IHL – Rule 145. Reprisals'. https://ihl-databases.icrc.org/customary-ihl/eng/docs/v1_rul_rule145.
5. International Committee of the Red Cross (ICRC), *Geneva Convention for the Amelioration of the Condition of the Wounded and Sick in Armed Forces in the Field (First Geneva Convention)*, 12 August 1949, 75 UNTS 31 at Art 1; International Committee of the Red Cross (ICRC), *Geneva Convention for the Amelioration of the Condition of Wounded, Sick and Shipwrecked Members of Armed Forces at Sea* (*Second Geneva Convention*), 12 August 1949, 75 UNTS 85 at Art 1; International Committee of the Red Cross (ICRC), *Geneva Convention for the Amelioration of the Condition of Wounded, Sick and Shipwrecked Members of Armed Forces at Sea* (*Second Geneva Convention*), 12 August 1949, 75 UNTS 85 at Art 1; International Committee of the Red Cross (ICRC), *Geneva Convention Relative to the Protection of Civilian Persons in Time of War* (*Fourth Geneva Convention*), 12 August 1949, 75 UNTS 287 at Art. 1.
6. Combatant privilege does not expressly apply in the context of non-international armed conflicts. Scholars debate the impact of this asymmetry in the recognition of combatants on the reciprocal foundations of IHL.
7. Surrender is only permitted if exercised in situations where successful defence is not possible. Such laws indicate to commanders that a decision to surrender can only be exercised as a last resort and cannot be made lightly, even when one's forces are at great risk: National Defence Act, 1985 of Canada last amended in 2019, at 73; Defence Act No. 18 of 1954 of Ireland, at 124(b); The Gambia Armed Forces Act, 1985 of Gambia, at 37(c); Military Penal Code, No. 13 of 1940 of Iraq, at 55; Armed Forces Act, 1968 of Kenya, at 15(d).
8. Defence Act of Ireland, note 9 at 125 (b) and (c). Also see The Army Act, 1950 of India at 34(f).

9. During non-international armed conflicts, detainees are not entitled to prisoner of war status, but according to Common Article 3 to the 1949 Geneva Conventions, they must be treated humanely.
10. Armed Forces Act, 1970 of Malta at 41(1); Armed Forces Act of Malaysia, note 16 at 43(1); Armed Forces Act, 1972 of Singapore; Defence Force Act of Botswana, note 22 at 31(1); Armed Forces Act, 1968 of Kenya at 21(1).
11. A universal monarch is considered an ideal universal king, who reigns ethically and compassionately over the entire world.
12. See also the 'story of the present' from the *Kuṇāla Jātaka* (no. 536, Jat V.412–414), where the Buddha confronted the Sākiyans and Koliyas who were about to attack each other over rights to the water of a shared river at a time of drought. He did so by asking them whether they should sacrifice something of great value – the lives of the warrior-nobles – for something of lesser value – water.
13. ICC, Ntaganda Decision on the Confirmation of Charges, 2014: 76–82, https://www.icc-cpi.int/CourtRecords/CR2014_04750.PDF
14. *US v. von Leeb*, 11 Nuremberg Military Tribunals 511 (1948) (the High Command Trial): 'within certain limitations, [a soldier] has the right to assume that the orders of his superiors ... are in conformity to international law'.

Acknowledgements

For their helpful input on earlier drafts, I thank Professor René Provost, Dr Noel Trew, Dr Elizabeth Harris, Professor Kate Crosby and Andrew Bartles-Smith.

Disclosure statement

This article has been supported by the International Committee of the Red Cross (ICRC).

References

Appleton, N. 2010. *Jātaka Stories in Theravāda Buddhism: Narrating the Bodhisatta Path*. Farnham: Ashgate.

Carter, J. R., and M. Palihawadana. 1987. *The Dhammapada*. New York: Oxford University Press.

Cover, R. 1983. "Nomos and Narrative." *Harvard Law Review* 97 (1): 4–68.

de Libero, L. 2012. "Surrender in Ancient Rome." In *How Fighting Ends: A History of Surrender*, edited by H. Afflerbach and H. Strachan, 8–14. Oxford: Oxford University Press.

Dörmann, K., and J. Serralvo. 2014. "Common Article 1 to the Geneva Conventions and the Obligation to Prevent International Humanitarian Law Violations." *International Review of the Red Cross* 96 (895/896): 707–736. doi:10.1017/S181638311400037X.

Durkheim, E. 1951. *Suicide: A Study in Sociology*. 2nd ed. London: Routledge.

Evangelidi, E. 2018. "Restraint in Bello: Some Thoughts on Reciprocity and Humanity." In *International Humanitarian Law and Justice: Historical and Sociological Perspectives*, edited by M. Deland, M. Klamberg, and P. Wrange, 100–113. Oxfordshire: Routledge.

Greenspan, M. 1959. *The Modern Law of Land Warfare*. Berkeley: University of California Press.

Hallisey, C. 2009. "The Golden Rule in Buddhism [II]." In *The Golden Rule: The Ethics of Reciprocity in World Religions*, edited by J. Neusner and B. D. Chilton, 129–145. London: Bloomsbury.

Hassig, R. 2012. "How Fighting Ended in the Aztec Empire and Its Surrender to the Europeans." In *How Fighting Ends: A History of Surrender*, edited by H. Afflerbach and H. Strachan, 113–123. Oxford: Oxford University Press.

Huntington, S. P. 1957. *The Soldier and the State: The Theory and Politics of Civil–Military Relations*. Cambridge: Harvard University Press.

International Committee of the Red Cross. 2016. *Commentary on the First Geneva Convention: Convention (I) for the Amelioration of the Condition of the Wounded and Sick in Armed Forces in the Field*. Cambridge: Cambridge University Press.

Ireland, J., trans. 1997. *The Udāna: Inspired Utterances of the Buddha*. Kandy: Buddhist Publication Society.

Kahn, P. W. 2013. "Imagining Warfare." *European Journal of International Law* 24 (1): 199–226. doi:10.1093/ejil/chs086.

Keely, L. H. 2012. "Surrender and Prisoners in Prehistoric and Tribal Societies." In *How Fighting Ends: A History of Surrender*, edited by H. Afflerbach and H. Strachan, 7–13. Oxford: Oxford University Press.

Kortüm, H. 2012. "Surrender in Medieval Times." In *How Fighting Ends: A History of Surrender*, edited by H. Afflerbach and H. Strachan, 41–54. Oxford: Oxford University Press.

Lauterpacht, H. 1953. "The Limits of the Operation of the Law of War." *British Year Book of International Law* 30: 206–243.

McMahan, J. 2009. *Killing in War*. Oxford: Clarendon.

Mégret, F. 2013. "The Humanitarian Problem with Drones." *Utah Law Review* 5: 1283–1319.

Norman, K. R. 1997. *The Word of the Doctrine Dhammapada*. London: Pali Text Society.

Obeyesekere, R. 2016. *The Revered Book of Five Hundred and Fifty Jataka Stories: Volume II. Translated from the 14th Century Sinhala Version*. Colombo: Gunasena.

Osiel, M. J. 2001. *Obeying Orders: Atrocity, Military Discipline and the Law of War.* Somerset: Routledge.

Peeler, P. 2019. *The Persistence of Reciprocity in International Humanitarian Law.* Cambridge: Cambridge University Press.

Pilloud, C., Y. Sandoz, C. Swinarski, and B. Zimmermann. 1987. *Commentary on the Additional Protocols of 8 June 1977 to the Geneva Conventions of 12 August 1949.* Geneva: International Committee of the Red Cross.

Posner, E., and A. Sykes. 2007. "An Economic Analysis of State and Individual Responsibility under International Law." *American Law and Economics Review* 9 (1): 72–134. doi:10.1093/aler/ahm001.

Provost, R. 2002. *International Human Rights and Humanitarian Law.* Cambridge: Cambridge University Press.

Provost, R. 2012. "Asymmetrical Reciprocity and Compliance with the Laws of War." In *Modern Warfare: Armed Groups, Private Militaries, Humanitarian Organizations, and the Law*, edited by B. Perrin, 17–42. Vancouver: UBC Press.

Robinson, P. 1999. "'Ready to Kill but Not to Die': NATO Strategy in Kosovo." *International Journal: Canada's Journal of Global Policy Analysis* 54 (4): 671–682.

Scheible, K. 2009. "The Formulation and Significance of the Golden Rule in Buddhism [I]." In *The Golden Rule: The Ethics of Reciprocity in World Religions*, edited by J. Neusner and B. D. Chilton, 116–128. London: Bloomsbury.

Schober, J. 1997. *Sacred Biography in the Buddhist Traditions of South and Southeast Asia.* Honolulu: University of Hawaii Press.

Walzer, M. 2004. *Arguing About War.* New Haven: Yale University Press.

Walzer, M. 2006. *Just and Unjust Wars: A Moral Argument with Historical Illustrations.* 4th ed. New York: Basic Books.

Ziv, B. 2014. "The Superior Orders Defense: A Principal-Agent Analysis." *Georgia Journal of International and Comparative Law* 41: 1–74.

ICRC

'NOT KNOWING IS MOST INTIMATE': KOAN PRACTICE AND THE FOG OF WAR

Noel Maurer Trew

ABSTRACT

The branch of international humanitarian law (IHL) pertaining to targeting is notoriously challenging for decision makers to apply in practice. The rules of distinction, precautions and proportionality in attack form the bedrock of targeting law, but compliance with these rules requires combatants to correctly understand what is happening in the battlespace. Those who decide upon, plan or execute an attack may not always have access to the right kind or amount of information needed to correctly set up an attack. Furthermore, they may not even know what information they need. Given the ambiguity posed by inadequate intelligence or information overload, how can combatants train themselves to successfully cut through the fog of war? In Japanese Zen (Chinese: *Chan*) Buddhism, adherents typically practice meditation methods featuring elements of open monitoring and focused attention. One style of focused attention, known as kōan practice, is often used by those in the Rinzai and (to a lesser extent) Sōtō schools of Zen. Kōans are short stories that Zen teachers use to communicate those Buddhist insights that cannot be expressed through direct communication, such as the experience of 'nonduality'. Although kōans are often described as riddles or puzzles, they are not intended to be solved logically. Rather, the practitioner focuses their attention upon the kōan and observes what happens when linguistic and logical means of 'solving' it fall away. By training the mind to recognise its attachments to particular concepts or habitual ways of problem-solving, those who take up this practice in its proper context may find themselves better prepared to make decisions based on ambiguous information, and to spot errors in their perception or thinking when considering such matters of grave importance.

Attention! Master Jizo asked Hogen, 'Where have you come from?' 'I pilgrimage aimlessly', replied Hogen. 'What is the matter of your pilgrimage?' asked Jizo. 'I don't know', replied Hogen. 'Not knowing is the most intimate', remarked Jizo. At that, Hogen experienced great enlightenment. [*The Book of Equanimity*, Case 20] (Wick 2005, 63)

DOI: 10.4324/9781003439820-13

Introduction

International humanitarian law (IHL),[1] or the law of armed conflict, requires combatants to make reasonable decisions about who or what may be targeted and who or what must be protected in war. In practice, the good-faith application of this body of law can be difficult even in the best of times. It is even more challenging to apply in targeting situations that seem ambiguous, either because of a lack of information about the battlespace or because of information overload.

It has become commonplace for introductory IHL texts to invoke the universality of the law's principles by stressing that many religions and cultures have independently concluded there should be limits to the use of force, even in war.[2] For example, Zen not only prohibits an 'anything goes' approach to *jus in bello* (if practiced properly), but Zen kōan practice may be particularly useful in helping practitioners navigate the balance between military necessity and humanity required by targeting law.[3] For centuries, Zen practitioners have used kōan introspection, a meditative practice in which adherents focus on an unsolvable problem, to break past logical, discursive thought and achieve an intuitive understanding of enlightenment. This practice also helps one break habitual patterns of thought and hold contradictory viewpoints without becoming emotionally or intellectually invested in one perspective or another.

Even if kōan introspection helps combatants make better decisions in situations of stress or ambiguity, it is important to note that there are limitations to this practice. First, it is not generally a technique that can be learned in a short period of time and applied immediately. Second, progress through the kōan curriculum[4] requires a steady dialogue between teacher and student. Finally, kōan practice by itself, without a good grounding in Buddhist precepts, could result in a person making decisions that run counter to IHL. This is because the practice does not have an independent ethical orientation.

While there is good evidence that kōan introspection can help commanders, military planners and front-line combatants to question their habitual ways of thinking and to resolve ambiguity more easily, I would not necessarily prescribe kōan work (or any other meditative technique) as an instrumentalist way to achieve compliance with IHL in a secular context. Rather, it may prove to be an effective way for those who have already taken up the practice to uphold their commitments under targeting law, when used *alongside the Buddhist precepts.*

A brief summary of the *jus in bello* rules on targeting in modern IHL

Distinction

In the International Committee of the Red Cross (ICRC)'s estimation, the crowning achievement of the Diplomatic Conference of 1977 was the adoption of certain protections for the civilian population in the Additional Protocols (APs) (Pilloud 1987, 583). Traditionally, the Geneva Conventions protected the *victims* of hostilities and the Hague Conventions had regulated the *conduct* of hostilities (Boothby 2012, 5), but the ICRC was concerned that Hague law had not been sufficiently updated to reflect lessons learned after the Second World War, particularly with respect to aerial bombardment – which did not yet exist when these laws were written. The ICRC therefore saw the development of the APs as 'bringing together the two strands' of IHL into one legal framework: the protection of victims on the one hand and the conduct of hostilities on the other (Boothby 2012, 5). In particular, Additional Protocol I (API) clarified the principle of distinction and the rules of proportionality and precautions in attack. These are codified in Part IV, Section I of API, beginning with the Basic Rule:

> Article 48. In order to ensure respect for and protection of the civilian population and civilian objects, the Parties to the conflict shall at all times distinguish between the civilian population and combatants and between civilian objects and military objectives and accordingly shall direct their operations only against military objectives.

The Basic Rule is the cornerstone of modern IHL and has been recognised as having achieved customary status for both international armed conflict[5] and non-international armed conflict (NIAC).[6]

In theory, the application of this principle would not be difficult in situations where there is a clear difference between the civilian population and military objectives. However, the framers of API recognised that when military objectives are located near civilians and civilian objects, commanders might be tempted to subject the civilian population to an unacceptable level of risk while engaging legitimate military targets. To address these concerns, Article 51 prohibits not only direct attacks against the civilian population but also those operations that amount to indiscriminate attacks. Article 57 then requires attackers to take positive steps to mitigate the effects of their operations on the civilian population.

Proportionality in attack

A key test of whether an attack could be considered indiscriminate is the proportionality rule: given what a commander knows about a target and the likely effects of using a particular weapon (or weapons), will the collateral damage associated with the attack be excessive in relation to the military advantage gained from striking the target? The modern conception of this rule is widely accepted[7] to have been set forth in Article 51 of API:

> Article 51(4). Indiscriminate attacks are prohibited ... (5) Among others, the following types of attacks are to be considered as indiscriminate ... (b) an attack which may be expected to cause incidental loss of civilian life, injury to civilians, damage to civilian objects, or a combination thereof, which would be excessive in relation to the concrete and direct military advantage anticipated.

It is important to note that the values a commander or military planner must compare – expected civilian loss and anticipated military advantage – are incommensurable and cannot be calculated numerically.

Precautions in attack

Whereas API Article 51(5)(b) sets forth the negative requirement for combatants to refrain from launching disproportionate attacks, Article 57 establishes concrete, positive measures to which combatants must adhere to ensure their attacks are proportionate:

> Article 57(2)(a). [T]hose who plan or decide upon an attack shall: i) do everything feasible to verify that the objectives to be attacked are neither civilians nor civilian objects and are not subject to special protection but are military objectives ...; ii) take all feasible precautions in the choice of means and methods of attack with a view to avoiding, and in any event to minimizing, incidental loss of civilian life, injury to civilians and damage to civilian objects; iii) refrain from deciding to launch any attack which may be expected to cause incidental loss of civilian life, injury to civilians, damage to civilian objects, or a combination thereof, which would be excessive in relation to the concrete and direct military advantage anticipated.

The attack precautions enumerated in API Article 57 include actions that need to be taken before commanders or planners perform the proportionality assessment, such as verifying the target's military nature; but they also include actions to be taken after the assessment in order to further minimise the likelihood of collateral damage, such as issuing warnings to the civilian population.[8]

Before a commander or military planner can accurately perform a proportionality calculation for an attack, they must have enough information about the situation to answer the following questions:

(1) Is the target a legitimate military objective?[9]
(2) What is the military advantage that might be gained from attacking the target?[10]
(3) What is the concentration of civilians or civilian objects nearby?[11]
(4) What means are available to engage the target?[12] and
(5) What are the likely effects of employing those means?[13]

The answers to the first, second and fourth questions may be immediately available to the commander or a military planner, but the answers to the third and fifth will likely require additional investigation. If, after employing all feasible measures to ascertain the nature of the proposed target, there is still doubt as to its character, Articles 50(1) and 52(3) state that it should be presumed to be civilian. As a final sense-check, if it becomes apparent during a mission that a strike would cause excessive collateral damage, Article 57(b) requires that the attack be suspended or cancelled.

The reasonable military commander test

While the International Criminal Tribunal of the former Yugoslavia (ICTY) is best known for its decisions on the conduct of civil and military figures from the Balkans, the Office of the Prosecutor was also called upon to examine the legality of the North Atlantic Treaty Organization (NATO)'s use of airpower during the wars. In a report to the Office of the Prosecutor (OTP) in 2000, the Committee Established to Review the NATO Bombing Campaign developed a 'reasonable military commander' standard to gauge whether those involved with the air campaign had complied with their obligation not to launch strikes that were expected to cause excessive collateral damage. The committee reasoned that:

> It is unlikely that a human rights lawyer and an experienced combat commander would assign the same relative values to military advantage and to injury to noncombatants. Further, it is unlikely that military commanders with different doctrinal backgrounds and differing degrees of combat experience or national military histories would always agree in close cases. It is suggested that the determination of relative values must be that of the 'reasonable military commander'. Although there will be room for argument in close cases, there will be many cases where reasonable military commanders will agree that the injury to noncombatants or the damage to civilian objects was clearly disproportionate to the military advantage gained. (International Criminal Tribunal for the Former Yugoslavia 2000, para. 50)

With this standard in mind, the committee analysed both the bombing mission as a whole and specific strikes that human rights organisations like Amnesty International and Human Rights Watch had suggested were in contravention of international law. While in some cases the civilian casualties were considered to be high, the committee reasoned there was insufficient evidence to ascertain the reasonableness of the strikes or to open a formal war crimes investigation.

The reasonable military commander standard has since been cited approvingly by other judicial and non-judicial bodies as the appropriate way to ascertain a commander's adherence to the rules of both precautions and proportionality in attack.[14] Moreover, the US Law of War Manual does not seem to view 'feasible precautions' as being different in meaning from 'reasonable precautions' (US Department of Defense 2016, 191–197).[15] Although imperfect, this reasonableness standard represents the best benchmark for determining whether a commander, planner or front-line combatant acted lawfully with regards to the rules governing proportionality and precautions in attack.

Meditative practices within the Buddhist tradition are designed to help a practitioner to cultivate the virtue of equanimity (Sanskrit: *upekṣā*; Pali: *upekkhā*). In translating this Buddhist concept for a medical/scientific audience, Desbordes et al. (2015, 357) defined equanimity as

> an even-minded mental state or dispositional tendency toward all experiences or objects, regardless of their affective valence (pleasant, unpleasant or neutral) or source. ... Equanimity also involves a level of impartiality (i.e. being not partial or biased), such that one can experience unpleasant thoughts or emotions without repressing, denying, judging, or having aversion for them.

Although the term may conjure an image of cold aloofness, the Buddhist understanding of equanimity does not denote indifference. Rather, it describes an imperturbable mental state where a person's experiences are fully felt, yet not dwelled upon. Desbordes and her colleagues describe three ways researchers can measure the experience of equanimity: self-report questionnaires, physiological markers (such as the strength of a person's startle reflex) and neural markers (such as patterns of activation in the amygdala, which is responsible for emotional arousal). Using such measures as indicators of an equanimous mental state, their survey of prior research showed that certain types of meditation – both religious and secular – have been shown to promote practitioners' ability to hold an equanimous mental state.

It is important to be clear that the concept of a reasonable military commander does not imply a person who necessarily makes rational or clear-headed decisions. Moreover, the reasonable military commander test is forward-looking and it must not take into account situational factors that could only be known in hindsight. In practice, judges and other judicial actors have applied this test in a manner that gives military commanders a broad margin of appreciation for decisions that appear to have been made in good faith – even if they are incorrect

(Trew 2017, 124–126). Although certainly not required by the law, a person who trains themselves to maintain equanimity in the face of adversity and to overcome their habitual ways of thinking may be better situated to make a reasonable assessment of any given situation – and to make more reasonable decisions based upon that assessment. This could help to improve compliance with the law and prevent the sorts of errors in judgement that lead to IHL violations.

The reality of targeting in modern warfare

The three categories of targeting

The law of targeting begins with the absolute prohibition against targeting civilians and civilian objects (or other protected persons or objects, such as medical units), i.e. distinction. The rules of proportionality and precautions specify how to operationalise distinction in cases where there is a risk that civilians or civilian objects may be near a military objective. To put these rules into practice, decision makers (i.e. commanders and military planners) must make finely balanced assessments about what is really going on in the battlespace and about what they believe the likely effects of their attacks will be. Many armed forces divide the various targeting processes into roughly three categories: deliberate targeting, dynamic targeting and combat engagement.

In deliberate targeting, commanders and military planners have relatively more time to collect and analyse intelligence about the battlespace and to explore the possible effects of a proposed attack on civilians or civilian objects. The deliberate targeting cycle is highly process-driven and includes input from multiple actors, as one former US Air Force officer recounted:

> With targeting, it's so algorithmic, there's not a lot of philosophical moments of deep thinking – It's checklists, and procedures. There're multiple people running through them and there're criteria that are either met or not met . . .. A lot of what we were doing had a lawyer or legal review included in the strike decks [target lists] and the packages. So, in that sense, you have to ask, 'what went into the creation of those checklists and those criteria and where are they coming from?' I can't speak to that. I think that most people on the ground in a combat zone are past that point …. They are solely implementing [procedures].[16]

Despite these safeguards, in deliberate targeting decision makers are not omniscient or infallible. Even when the decision to execute a particular target is data-driven and dispassionate, biases can still creep in at the level on which the targeting criteria, procedures or rules of engagement (RoE) are drafted. Also, those implementing such procedures still have some margin of discretion for deciding whether the targeting criteria are met. Nevertheless, it is telling that relatively little collateral damage is caused during deliberate targeting missions compared to dynamic targeting or combat engagements (Human Rights Watch 2008, 29–33).

Dynamic targeting involves engaging targets of opportunity. As such, time pressures may not allow commanders, support staff or front-line troops to collect or analyse as much information as they would during deliberate targeting scenarios. However, they must still reasonably assess the situation as they find it, using the information to which they do have access.

By necessity, combat engagements (e.g. when troops are directly engaged in a firefight with the enemy) are even more ad hoc in nature and are not subject to the same processes as either deliberative or dynamic targeting (NATO 2016, 1:2–1:3).[17] In combat engagements, the unit under fire, with the aid of a few support elements, must collect information about the operating environment and engage targets based on their best understanding of the situation prevailing at the time.

Commanders, military planners and front-line troops will be given tactics, techniques and procedures (TTPs) and RoE that take into consideration the *jus in bello* principle of distinction, and the rules of proportionality and precautions in attack appropriate for each category of targeting. Even so, in all three cases the proverbial 'fog of war'[18] can introduce ambiguity into targeting analyses, creating opportunities for individuals to bring their own biases into the process, particularly when stressed or pressed for time.

The fog of war

The fog of war arises because in war it is difficult for an individual or even a group of individuals to have access to the right information about the battlespace at the right time. In addition, misinformation intentionally generated by the enemy can further complicate combatants' efforts to correctly perceive a given situation. In earlier wars it may have been difficult for decision makers to obtain enough information about the battlespace (e.g. access to the right maps, photographs or human intelligence about a target). Although still a potential difficulty in contemporary armed conflicts, now there is the additional problem that commanders and their staff may have access to more information than can be reasonably analysed in a timely manner.

In one highly publicised US attack in 2011, a drone operator seemed to be preoccupied with reports of a possible threat posed by nearby enemy forces and failed to notice reports that a group of vehicles and people in the area were likely civilians and not enemy troops. When pressed to decide whether to target the vehicles the operator cleared a helicopter to fire upon them, believing them to be a Taliban convoy. The cause of the violation, which left 23 Afghan civilians dead, was attributed to information overload:

> 'Information overload – an accurate description', said one senior military officer, who was briefed on the inquiry [of the airstrike] and spoke on the condition of anonymity because the case might yet result in a court martial. The deaths would have been prevented, he said, '*if we had just slowed things down and thought deliberately*'. (Shanker and Richtel 2011) [my emphasis]

Information overload poses such great challenges for combatants involved with targeting in modern warfare that some military researchers have proposed outfitting troops with multi-sensory interfaces to spread incoming information across a user's different sensory channels (Elliott and Redden 2012). Others have suggested using artificial intelligence to analyse imagery and only alert the human operator when something is out of the ordinary (e.g. as described in Johnson and Wald 2017). Some have even proposed building computers that can respond dynamically to combatants' brain activity, automatically adjusting the amount of information presented based on how mentally taxed the computer believes the human operator to be (Lance and McDowell 2012).

Whether caused by misinformation, lack of information or information overload, the fog of war can foster a sense of ambiguity and uncertainty that makes it difficult for combatants to fully understand the military advantage of a potential target or to be able to reliably predict the effects of a proposed attack on civilians or civilian objects. In such an environment – and particularly when under stress (Yu 2016) – it becomes likely that combatants will fall back on heuristics and cognitive biases to make decisions, given their perceptions of the available information at the time. In cognitive psychology, a heuristic refers to the mind's predisposition to automatic ways of thinking based more on bias and intuition than on effortful reasoning (Kahneman, Slovic and Tversky 1982). Similarly, the concept of vāsanā in Yogācāra Buddhist psychology denotes the habitual tendency or disposition for a person to think or act in an automatic manner based on what has been imprinted in their 'storehouse-consciousness' (Keown 2004, 212).

Building upon earlier work on heuristics and IHL by Tomer Broude and Ashley Deeks, a US Navy legal adviser, Luke Whittemore (2016), analysed several ways that heuristics may affect the quality of targeting decisions. For example, the availability heuristic describes the tendency for an individual to act upon information that is easy to access in memory rather than information that is difficult to recall. When affected by this heuristic, a commander or planner may be more likely to consider reports of low collateral damage from recent or more emotionally salient attacks to indicate a low risk of collateral damage for the next strike – even if the overall historical trend of civilian casualties has been steadily increasing. Similarly, the *confirmation bias* describes how a person will tend to seek out and accept information that confirms their understanding of a situation, while discounting evidence that undermines it. Military planners affected by this heuristic may try to look for information which confirms their theory about the intentions of, say, the behaviour of a group of people depicted in drone footage of an urban battlespace. Information that suggests that the group is directly participating in hostilities may be given greater weight than conflicting evidence that suggests the group is civilian (such as in the 2011 example discussed above).

The ICRC study on the *Roots of Restraint in War* (Terry and McQuinn 2018, 29) claims that immediate pre-deployment briefings present a key opportunity for military leaders to reinforce norms of restraint before troops have to put the somewhat abstract principles of IHL into concrete practice. Similarly, Whittemore's scholarship stresses the effect that commanders' own pre-mission briefings have on their adherence to IHL. Based in part on his personal experience advising commanders on targeting decisions, he suggested that they might be affected by two heuristics in particular: *framing* and the *endowment effect*. Framing describes the tendency for a person to consider different options to be more or less attractive based solely on the *way* in which information about the options is presented. For instance, a commander may be more willing to authorise an airstrike if the person briefing the attack emphasises the value of the anticipated military advantage. Conversely, they may be less likely to authorise it if the briefer emphasises the severity of the expected collateral damage. In either case, the objective facts of the scenario did not change and in both cases the commander is exposed to the same values for the anticipated military advantage and the expected collateral damage – the only change is the way the briefer emphasised the relative gains or losses of the attack.

Additionally, the endowment effect may cause a commander to deviate from making rational decisions. This effect describes the tendency for people to value an object (or idea) more if they own it. For example, if a pre-mission briefing is prepared in such a way as to give the commander a sense of ownership over the successful completion of the mission, they may find it difficult to call off the strike when it becomes apparent, mid-mission, that the expected collateral damage could be excessive. Whittemore rightly stressed that heuristic thinking is not necessarily wrong in all cases – indeed, these quick decision-making 'shortcuts' may even enhance civilian protection in some situations. Nevertheless, he suggested that subtle changes in the structure of a commander's pre-mission briefing may encourage military planners and decision makers to hew closer to the 'reasonable military commander' standard.

In addition to such practical measures for managing heuristic thinking, meditation and mindfulness practices also hold some promise for helping to improve the quality of targeting decisions – especially those made under stress.

Cutting through the fog: kōan introspection

The benefits of meditation for combatants

Given the uncertainty posed by both inadequate intelligence and information overload, and the concomitant tendency for military planners and front-line combatants in uncertain circumstances to fall back on heuristics-based reasoning and biases, what can be done to help cut through the fog of war? In addition to the technological and organisational approaches proposed earlier, meditation may offer a way for combatants to develop better awareness and make better decisions. Studies from the fields of psychology and neuroscience have shown that Buddhist meditative practices can have profound effects on the mind and – in the case of experienced individuals – even create structural changes in the brain (Austin 1999).

According to Braboszcz, Hahusseau, and Delorme (2010), mind wandering is generally associated with a reduced ability to process external stimuli, while meditative practices tend to clarify perceptions of external events. While these claims likely would not surprise experienced meditators, what may be of interest is the way certain practices encourage particular developments in cognition or brain structure. For example, those who practise 'open-monitoring' styles of meditation (such as vipassanā or zazen) tend to resist habituating to their environment. Instead, they seem better able to continuously perceive the world as if for the first time, and are therefore better at shifting their attention and spotting changes in their surroundings more easily, even when not meditating. By comparison, those who practise 'focused attention' styles of meditation (such as kōan introspection) may not perceive changes in the environment as readily, but they appear able to hold conflicting stimuli in mind more easily than those who practise open monitoring. Moreover, experienced meditators who practise focused attention show decreased metabolic activity in areas of the brain associated with sustained attention compared with beginners, suggesting they possess a more automatic and efficient use of attentional resources.

The promise shown by meditation in helping with information overload has not been lost on military researchers. For instance, the US military has trialled a meditation regime called 'mindfulness-based mind fitness training' or MMFT (Stanley et al. 2011). Although a secular practice and not explicitly connected with Buddhism, both the technique and its results would be familiar to Buddhists who practise an open-monitoring style of meditation:

> 'The whole question we're asking is whether we can rewire the functioning of the attention system through mindfulness', said one of the researchers, Elizabeth A. Stanley, an assistant professor of security studies at Georgetown University.

> Recently she received financing to bring the training to a Marine base, and preliminary results from a related pilot study she did with Amishi Jha, a neuroscientist at the University of Miami, found that it helped Marines to focus. (Shanker and Richtel 2011)

Although some of the rhetoric around the use of mindfulness training in the military has focused on how it promises to make troops more effective or resilient,[19] those who conduct research on the matter have also highlighted how mindfulness training could help troops to avoid the sort of automatic thinking that leads to targeting errors. As neuroscientist Amishi Jha claims:

> Being in a high-stress situation degrades the capacity to be discerning. Under high stress, we just don't see what's going on. We go on autopilot. We react based on stereotypes. So the training helps soldiers base their decisions on what is actually in front of them instead of on assumptions. Being more discerning is what it means to be a better soldier. (Jha in Senauke and Gates 2014)

Research in this area has kept apace, and a recent study by Zanesco et al. (2019) has shown that a specially crafted form of open-awareness meditation improved special operations troops' performance in a sustained attention task in the laboratory. This suggests that the benefits of both open-awareness and focused attention styles of meditation could be blended to help military members better perceive changes in their surroundings, and successfully focus their attention in a way that improves decision-making in armed conflict.

Some Western Buddhists, such as Michael Stone (2014) and Robert Purser (2014), have expressed concern about attempts to introduce secular meditation and mindfulness techniques like MMFT to the military in order to – as Stone puts it – 'optimize organized violence'. One of the core criticisms both Stone and Purser present is that mindfulness and meditation should not be divorced from the religious teachings which gave rise to them – teachings that include strong ethical prohibitions against intentional killing. Purser suggests that even if it were possible to use meditation and mindfulness to help military decision makers to avoid collateral damage, Buddhism's strong ethical injunction against killing of any sort would preclude the use of its teachings in association with *any* military action:

> MMFT proponents view it as a form of 'harm reduction', as the training improves working memory capacity that can prevent soldiers from overreacting and overgeneralizing, coupled with higher levels of emotional regulation that can even improve their ethical decision-making. With greater mindfulness, soldiers can purportedly be more 'discriminating' of their targets, thus 'reducing harm'. … Perhaps in the circumscribed world of 'military ethics', sparing the lives of civilians while taking better aim at the designated enemy is considered exemplary practice. But it is orthogonal to Buddhist practice where ethical decision-making is based on intentions of nonharming, noninjuriousness, and

> universal metta and compassion for all sentient beings. It is also far removed from the Hippocratic oath of medical practice of *primum non nocere*, to first do no harm – the very context from which MBSR[20] was rooted. (Purser 2014)

Whilst this argument is consistent with a widely held interpretation of Buddhist ethics, it unfortunately offers little instruction for how a Buddhist combatant should navigate difficult situations in armed conflict skilfully – other than to try to find another occupation.

Indeed, it would be a stretch to say that Buddhist ethics condones the use of violence. However, there is a story in the *Skill-with-Means* (*Upāya-kauśalya*) *Sūtra*[21] (Tatz 1994, 73–76), a first-century BCE Mahāyāna text, which evokes the sort of tension between necessity and humanity that underpins IHL in general and targeting law in particular. In the Sutra, the 'Story of the Compassionate Ship's Captain' recounts a previous life of Shakyamuni Buddha when he was the captain, named 'Great Compassionate', of a merchant ship. On one voyage, the captain discovered a robber among the passengers who was planning to kill all 500 of those onboard, so that he could steal the ship's cargo. After exhausting all other options, the captain concluded that the karmic consequences of letting the robber kill 500 people would be dire and that it would be better to kill the robber – skilfully and with compassion – than it would be to let him carry out his plan or to have the other passengers kill the robber with malice. In so doing, the captain saved 500 lives and the robber was spared the aeons in hell that would have awaited him had he been allowed to commit the murders. In the end, Great Compassionate acted with such skill in this instance that he himself was spared most of the karmic consequences of having killed the robber.

In this classic story, the compassionate captain is confronted with a situation where all of his possible responses have negative karmic consequences – either for himself or for others. In weighing the value of each course of action, he ultimately chooses the one that causes the least amount of suffering overall. This is not exactly the sort of balancing act envisaged by the principle of proportionality in IHL, since in the Buddhist view, it is not inherently good, righteous or legitimate to take the life of the robber. Rather, the robber is at the same time considered to be a legitimate target *and* collateral damage. Moreover, it is important to note that the captain *did not expect to escape the consequences of murdering the robber* merely because he intended to protect the lives of 500 others – that is, he was willing to take on the negative karma associated with his action even if that karma did not, except minimally, later materialise in fact. In some situations, all actions (or inactions) may carry wrong or unfortunate consequences, but a person will still require some discernment to determine the course of action that might be necessary to reduce suffering overall.

It is important not to overextend the significance of the Story of the Compassionate Ship's Captain or to read it out of context from the rest of the Sūtra's discourse on skilful means. Nevertheless, the story could act as an ethical touchstone for Mahāyāna Buddhists who find themselves in the position of having to make difficult targeting decisions during armed conflict.

As much as some Buddhists may be concerned that armed forces' use of secular mindfulness training programmes may omit core religious and ethical teachings, some ethicists express the inverse objection: that it is impossible to divorce mindfulness from its religious roots. In this view, secular mindfulness training could pose a challenge to the liberal neutrality of a state's institutions. For example, Andreas Schmidt (2016, 451) posits: 'One set of worries concerns the question as to whether MBIs [mindfulness-based interventions] constitute an illegitimate promotion of a particular worldview or way of life'. Despite this worry, Schmidt reckons that in most instances, the use of purely *secular* mindfulness training by government institutions would be generally compatible with liberal neutrality. For her part, Amishi Jha claimed:

> I have had an easier time speaking at the Pentagon and talking to generals than I have convincing some Buddhists that what we're doing is okay. The angriest, flaming responses I've had to my research have come from Buddhists more so than the military. This really surprised me. (Jha in Senauke and Gates 2014)

This would suggest that the main ethical concerns about the use of secular mindfulness training by state institutions seem to come from the Buddhist community, rather than from the state, the military or other secular institutions.

To be clear, in this paper, my aim is not to prescribe the use of scientifically evaluated secular mindfulness practices to non-Buddhists in order to enhance compliance with IHL. I also am not discouraging its use for this purpose. Rather, my point is that – *regardless of the ethics of its use by the armed forces* – the evidence gathered to date on secular mindfulness training in the military strongly suggests that Buddhist meditative practices could indeed help combatants *who are already Buddhist* to better uphold their obligations under IHL, should they find themselves in an armed conflict.

The role of Kōan introspection in Zen

In Zen Buddhism, adherents typically practise meditation styles featuring elements of both open monitoring and focused attention. One style of focused attention meditation unique to Zen is known as kōan introspection (also known as kōan study or practice). Kōan introspection is specifically used by those in the Rinzai (Chinese: *Linji*), and – to a lesser extent – Sōtō schools of Zen, and is especially popular in the Harada-Yasutani lineage, which heavily influenced the development of Zen as practised in the West. Kōan introspection developed in China as Mahāyāna Buddhist masters adapted their teaching methods to accommodate the cultural and linguistic milieu in which they found themselves, as my teacher, Roshi Sarah Bender, explains

> Those [Pali] scriptures were not coming out of a tradition in which the Chinese were rooted and there were translation issues at first .... In each leap – from India to China and from China to Japan and Southeast Asia, the kōans specifically mention translation issues sometimes. One of the reasons the kōan curriculum evolved as it did was because you couldn't rely on the scriptural knowledge of the people you were talking to, and their language was challenging. I think that big batch of kōan teachers from 700CE to 900CE were going directly to people's own experience as expedient means.[22]

The Japanese word *'kōan'* comes from the Chinese word *'gong'an'* meaning 'public case' – as in a court case. In much the same way that prior legal cases set precedents, kōans are a record of 'precedents' set by earlier Zen masters.

Each kōan features a short story that Zen teachers use to guide students to learn certain ineffable Buddhist insights which can lead the student to experience kenshō. Peter Harvey defines kenshō as

> a blissful realisation where a person's inner nature, the originally pure, is directly known in a sudden re-ordering of his or her perception of the world. All appears vividly; each thing retaining its individuality, yet empty of separateness, so being unified with all else, including the meditator. There is just an indescribable thusness, beyond the duality of subject and object, a thusness which is dynamic and immanent in the world. (Harvey 2013, 369)

One well-known kōan in Western popular culture is: 'What is the sound of one hand clapping?' Although kōans are often described as riddles or puzzles, they are not intended to be solved logically. Rather, the student is meant to focus their attention upon the kōan and observe what happens when the mind abandons linguistic and logical means of 'solving' it. As Roshi Gerry Wick explains: 'In order to penetrate a kōan, the student must drop away attachments to images, beliefs, and projections'. (2005, 5). While students should be thinking about the kōan – both during meditation and during daily life – insight will not come from analysing it logically.

The complete record of around 1700 classic kōans spans several centuries and covers a range of topics. Many – at least on the surface – seem to be about everyday matters, such as making tea or washing one's bowl. Others may seem more pertinent to armed conflict. One kōan, for example, implores the practitioner to 'stop the fighting across the river'. Often, these stories involve a dialogue between a Zen master and a monk. Such is the case with the first kōan many students encounter, 'Joshu's Mu':

> Attention! A monk asked Master Joshu, 'Does a dog have Buddha Nature?' Joshu replied, 'Yes'. And then the monk said, 'Since it has, how did it get into that bag of skin?' Joshu said, 'Because knowingly, he purposefully offends'. On

> another occasion a monk asked Joshu, 'Does a dog have Buddha Nature?' Joshu said, 'No!' [in Japanese: '*Mu!*'] Then the monk said, 'All beings have Buddha Nature.[23] Why doesn't the dog have it?' Joshu said, 'It is because of his having karmic consciousness'. [*The Book of Equanimity*, Case 18] (Wick 2005, 57)

Despite the apparent paradox, Joshu told each monk what he needed to hear. While working with this kōan, often teachers will ask the student to concentrate on the *huatou* or 'head' of the kōan, a short phrase which summarises the whole case. In this instance, what is the meaning of Joshu's 'Yes'? What is the meaning of his 'Mu'?

Roshi Bender states,

> There are categories of kōans. Some of them are going to focus more on just the fundamental nature of 'what is this?', 'what am I?', 'what's the deal here?'. That's what [Roshi] Bernie Glassman says is the fundamental kōan – they're all just 'what's the deal here?'[24]

But the content of a kōan's story is not necessarily as important as how the student works with it. A skilful teacher will select the kōan that will help their student to most effectively grapple with the mental or conceptual stumbling block to which they seem most attached at that point in their practice.

Roshi James Ford explains that, at least initially, the practice is meant to elicit 'Great Doubt' from the practitioner: 'Turning doubt on ourselves, questioning each thought that arises, we strive to manifest that bumper-sticker truth: "Don't believe everything you think". However, the invitation here is even more radical: "Don't believe anything you think"' (2018, 92). Roshi Bender remarks that kōan practice is

> training in holding paradox and not falling on one side or another, learning how to take a position without being married to a position .... One of the fundamental kōan lines that undergirds the whole practice is: 'abiding nowhere, the heart-mind comes forth'.[25]

The ability of those who practise kōan introspection to hold paradoxes in this way has been recognised recently by researchers in the field of clinical psychology, such as Lars Didriksen (2018), who believes that it could potentially have some therapeutic utility. Many psychosocial difficulties are accompanied by unhelpful self-talk, categorising and/or artificially framing a given situation as a dilemma. While seasoned practitioners would caution against viewing Zen or kōan practice itself as a form of psychotherapy, some elements of the practice may indeed disrupt unhelpful modes of thinking; and under the right conditions, kōan introspection may provide therapists with another tool with which to engage their clients.

Although the point of kōan practice is sometimes presented as helping a student to embrace paradox as a path to kenshō, this is not the whole practice. Rather, the student must also be able to integrate that experience and any insights gleaned along the way during meditation into their everyday life. Roshi Ford states, 'The full value of the kōan is to be found in how it is lived into. I can't emphasise this point too strenuously. It is critical if we want to understand the kōan way' (2018, 117). But can this practice of holding paradox without falling on one side or the other help prepare combatants to make better decisions (particularly targeting decisions) in the face of the fog of war?

Kōan introspection in time of armed conflict

Bushidō (which could be translated literally as 'military-knight-ways') was a warrior code that developed during Japan's feudal period. In his seminal treatise, *Bushido: The Soul of Japan*, Inazo Nitobe (1908) considered Buddhism – and Zen in particular – to be one of its primary sources. Additionally, Seisen Fueoka claimed in his introductory text, *A Zen Primer*, that:

> Zen was introduced into Japan at the beginning of the Kamakura period [1185–1333], at a time when Bushido had risen to power. The simple and direct teachings of Zen coincided with the straightforward and resolute spirit of samurai discipline. In particular, the Zen teaching on life and death was strikingly clear and thorough. Because samurai stood on the edge between life and death, this teaching was very appropriate for their training. They very quickly came to revere and have faith in it. (Seisen in Victoria 2006, 99–100)

Given Zen's history and its purported interaction with Bushidō, it is not surprising that it could have a different approach towards war and killing compared with other strands of Buddhism.

However, more recent scholarship on Bushidō by Oleg Benesch (2014) calls into question the strength of the relationship between Zen and Bushidō in Japanese history. Rather than representing an accurate account of the interaction between Zen and Bushidō, Benesch claims that much of what was written on the topic during the late nineteenth and early twentieth centuries was either exaggerated or invented out of whole cloth. The actual evidence linking Zen to Bushidō is tenuous, but from the mid-1800s until the end of the Second World War, Japanese Buddhist leaders – and especially those in the Zen schools – were keen to demonstrate their patriotism by promoting the supposed influence of Zen on Bushidō (and vice versa) during the Kamakura period (Benesch 2014, 135–140). Nevertheless, even if the influence of Zen on Japanese martial culture is somewhat apocryphal, the 'effectiveness' of Zen training as a tool to help soldiers overcome fear of death and to enhance their operational prowess in *modern* warfare is well documented, most notably by Brian Victoria (2006) in his critical examination of the support that the Zen schools provided to the Japanese war effort during the Second World War.

In spite of its ability to become co-opted for unwholesome aims, *when taken up correctly*, Zen practice – including kōan introspection – could also prepare a person to uphold the rules of war. As Roshi Bender put it: 'They're really about how to be a human being. Do you want somebody in war to have practised the art of being a human being? Yes!'[26] Koan practice forces Zen students to consider paradoxes in order to confront the limits of 'either/or' ways of reasoning, and it invites the student to see what happens when they embrace 'both/and' ways of understanding a problem (Didriksen 2018, 403–404). This ability to consider 'both/and' ways of thinking seems to give the student space to better hold ambiguity, even when not meditating. While by no means foolproof, Zen practitioners who are presented with ambiguous situations in combat may be able to act with greater discernment in armed conflict compared with those who have not taken up such training.

To help me explore the potential ways kōan practice might help members of the armed forces who are already Zen practitioners to embrace ambiguity and overcome bias or heuristic thinking in times of armed conflict – specifically with the aim of enhancing respect for IHL – I sought the views of a focus group of three former US Air Force officers who have been deployed and who practised Zen meditation before they left. The following is intended to share the experiences of combatants who have undertaken a kōan introspection as a way to show how the theory discussed above has played out as lived experience. It is not intended to represent a scientific account.

All three participants agreed that practising zazen and taking up kōan work *before* their deployments was helpful. Two former officers explained:

> As for kōan work ... sitting with an absurd question and trying to find truth within it – that's war, right? Having gone through the process of sitting with something that doesn't make sense and trying to sift through it and not find an academic, self-aggrandising answer to the question – maybe, in theory, that could help somebody sit in the 'kōan' of war too.[27]

> When you get into a conflict zone, you get a lot of ideas. Depending on how much conflict you're dealing with, those ideas dissipate very quickly .... It gets a hell of a lot less intellectual and academic as you go – well, welcome to kōan work.[28]

Sitting with an impossible question – time and time again – becomes a way to train the mind to handle ambiguity or absurdity, like having a personal wargaming exercise available wherever one happens to be. However, one member of the focus group cautioned against viewing Zen as a tool that can fully prepare one mentally for the realities of serving in a combat zone:

> On a very practical, individual level, what's nice about Zen practice is that it tends to be more embedded into routine than in some other spiritual practices, so it's akin to working out – how physically, spiritually and mentally fit are you to walk into extreme stress? However, just as being the fittest person in the world doesn't prepare you for combat or war; being a lama or a roshi doesn't inherently prepare you for war either.[29]

The parallel with physical fitness described above is apt. Kōan introspection is not the sort of practice that a person can learn in a one-day training session; it is a practice that takes a lifetime to master. The more one practises, the more 'fit' one becomes.

The views of the group on whether kōan introspection was helpful to take up while deployed were more mixed. The general view was that, unless one had already started a regular kōan practice before going to war, it would probably be best not to take it up during a deployment.[22] As one former officer put it:

> Going into a conflict zone, you need to be confident in your capability and you need to know you can do certain things, so training is paramount. To remove biases, you need to have 'beginner's mind'. Kōan work is about beginner's mind. There's an inherent conflict between confidence … and beginner's mind. The ideal warrior can probably mix the two – you know, a samurai. However, when you try to do that and you don't have previous experience with it, I don't think that's a good idea.[30]

If one already has a regular kōan practice, it does seem that it could be immensely helpful to further develop one's ability to handle ambiguity; but one should be very careful about which kōan one takes into the combat zone. As one former officer's experience reveals:

> In terms of kōan work, the series that you happen to be working on may be important. I was actively working one over there ['Stop the fighting across the river!'] and it was – weird. On the other hand – not necessarily to the benefit of anyone I was working with or fighting against – I don't think I will ever have a clearer experience of any kōan than I will of that one in particular because of what it was and where I was. … I had some very interesting ideas about it before I went: 'Aha! How nice! I'm stopping the fighting across the river. I'm going to clean up after the fighting across the river'. … I can certainly see a parallel between certain initial kōans, at least in our tradition, and this notion of dropping all of that crap in your head – letting it fall away – as you're in harm's way and just getting on with doing what you need to do: 'what is the most important thing; who is the most important person; what is the best action in any given moment?' … What had happened was when I came home, I was just angry and I was angry all the time. … I remember that I finally broke down and it really wasn't in response to kōan work, but I called Roshi and I said, 'you've got to help me – I just can't stop being angry' and it had been months since we talked. He asked me, 'which kōan are you working on?' and I remember when I told him, there was just this pregnant pause on the other end of the phone. Before he even opened his mouth, I had realised what had gone on. He said, 'First off, you've passed it. Secondly, you need to put it down. You need to

> let it go'. . . . That (at least for me) was not the one to be taking to Iraq, because it made the transition back home a hell of a lot more difficult. It was probably just my naivety with kōan work. I got to the point where the kōan was doing me, rather than I was doing it.[31]

The role of the teacher in guiding a student through the kōan curriculum cannot be stressed enough. Because of the distance (especially if there is a time zone change) or long work hours, a deployed Zen student may be tempted to continue practising despite being unable to regularly consult their teacher. But because the strength of the practice depends upon regular dialogue with one's teacher in order to keep from developing unhelpful mental states, this is not advisable. The kōan curriculum was originally developed in a monastic tradition in which teachers lived alongside their students and saw them often in one-to-one sessions. Any meditative practice, including kōan introspection, involves opening oneself fully to an experience and armed conflict may not be the best place for a student to do so, particularly without an adequate support structure to help them process that experience. As another former officer remarked:

> Just from a psychological standpoint, you need to compartmentalise in that moment and if you're sitting and letting these things come up and you don't have a container to manage whatever is coming up, I think it would be detrimental, actually. Unless you have a really good sensei [teacher] or a really good roshi, or a really good combat stress clinic, I think that at that point, compartmentalisation *is* your protection – that's what your mind should be doing. But, before and after – that's where [kōan practice] could be helpful. In the moment – I think it could be proper dangerous, actually.[32]

So while kōan introspection can provide some much-needed perspective in difficult or ambiguous situations, the main value of the practice seems to be in helping to *prepare* a person for deployment, rather than necessarily being of benefit in a combat zone. If a student wishes to continue kōan work while deployed, it would seem prudent for them to agree a kōan with their teacher ahead of time which is likely to work for them in that environment, and for the student to regularly consult their teacher throughout the deployment and immediately afterwards.

The precepts as a moral anchor

Without an ethical mooring, it is possible to co-opt the 'spiritual technologies' that Zen has developed, including kōan introspection, and use them to merely inoculate troops against fear of death or to make them better at killing. Such was the case with Imperial-state Zen, in which Zen institutions in Japan adapted themselves and their teachings to support the emperor and the war effort during the Second World War. Rather than using the practice to encourage soldiers to uphold Buddhist ethics, in many cases Zen teachers and masters promoted fealty to the state as the highest 'virtue' to which a soldier could aspire (Victoria 2006, 95–129).

In Zen, many teachings refer to two aspects of reality: the 'absolute' (Japanese: *Ri*) and the 'relative' (Japanese: *Ji*). These are related to the concepts of 'emptiness' and 'form', respectively. In her commentary on Master Sekito Kisen's *The Identity of Relative and Absolute* (Japanese: *Sandokai*), Sōtō Priest Domyo Burk helps to explain the relationship between the absolute and the relative:

> [I]t can often feel like the absolute and relative dimensions of our lives are very separate. When we perceive the absolute – unity, non-separation, everything complete just-as-it-is – the relative seems to recede, and when the relative intrudes – individuality, separation, action, worldly success, conflict, suffering – the absolute aspect seems to disappear. In reality, though, everything exists in both the absolute and relative sense simultaneously, and the two aspects don't interfere with or impede each other at all. One or the other aspect may be more salient in our experience at any given moment, but we should know neither ceases to function when the other is front and center. (Burk 2018)

During Zen training, it is sometimes possible for a student to become 'stuck' in the absolute perspective and reject or no longer view the world in relative terms. In the fourth verse of the *Sandokai*, Sekito warns against this, saying, 'Grasping at things [i.e. seeing reality only from the relative perspective] is surely delusion; according with sameness [i.e. seeing reality only from the absolute perspective] is still not enlightenment' (Sekito in Burk 2018).

Since kōan introspection can sometimes allow a person to experience (or get stuck in) the absolute aspect of reality in a way that transcends ethical teachings, it is particularly important for a combatant who studies Zen to have a good ethical baseline before and while taking up the practice. As one of my focus group participants warned, it is very important to keep the precepts close when undertaking kōan introspection:

> When thinking about kōan work in particular, I think it's like any other aspect of practice in Zen. If … you're attempting to inoculate yourself into some false sense of non-dualism: 'well, I can't really hurt anyone because there's nobody to hurt', you're doing it 'wrong'. One of the things that Roshi would say at length is that one of the most dangerous times for any practitioner is when they have had a really good, hard, deep opening or *kenshō*, because of that sense of 'it's all okay' … If you're a samurai or you're a soldier, I can certainly see a certain degree of stoicism being helpful to get through the day … [I]f you are not getting stuck in the absolute … then it affords you a great clarity of vision. It prepares you as an individual to deal with who and what is most important in any given moment with as little of your nonsense getting in the way as possible. So, I don't necessarily see Zen practice or kōan work having a direct impact on the law of armed conflict, writ large, but as somebody who is going in, trying to accomplish a mission and to do it without causing any more harm than you

> have to, . . . if you're doing it right, I think Zen can be *immensely* helpful for that. I think that the risk for Zen in particular is, . . . there is also an *immense* risk for getting it wrong.[33]

For instance, Zen Master Takuan Soho (1573–1645), who was himself a swordsman, once wrote in his instructions to a samurai:

> The uplifted sword has no will of its own, it is all of emptiness. It is a flash of lightning. The man who is about to be struck down is also of emptiness, as is the one who wields the sword . . .. Do not get your mind stopped with the sword you raise; forget about what you are doing, and strike the enemy. Do not keep your mind on the person before you. They are all of emptiness, but beware of your mind being caught in emptiness. (Takuan in Aitken 1984, 5)

Despite Master Takuan's warning against getting caught in emptiness, this passage could be seen as an example of Zen 'getting it wrong'. As Roshi Robert Aitken explains, Master Takuan is correct that from a perspective seated in emptiness, or the absolute, there is nothing to be called death (and therefore no killing). Nevertheless, he rebukes Takuan, suggesting that practitioners should not take up the perspective of the absolute exclusively since the consequences of killing from the perspective of the everyday world of form are very real:

> If there is no sword, no swing of the sword, no decapitation, then what about all the blood? What about the wails of the widow and children? The absolute position, when isolated, omits human details completely. Doctrines, including Buddhism, are meant to be used. Beware of them taking a life of their own, for then they use us. Nirvana, the purity and clarity of the void, is the same name we give to the total peace one experiences in deepest realization. But that is the same sea that we experience rising and falling in samsara, the relative world of coming and going. We cannot abstract depth from surface, nor surface from depth. Killing, even in an exalted state of mind, cannot be separated from suffering. (Aitken 1984, 17–18)

Rather than producing the perfect, fearless soldier who can overcome not only information overload, but also aversion to killing, Roshi Bender explains that it is extremely important for a combatant who practises kōan introspection to be thoroughly inculcated into the precepts:

> You want the person to be so deeply *stained* by the precepts – and by the practice of facing impossible questions – that they are able to come forth from a place of deep integrity at an instant. I think kōan practice does do that.[34]

Likewise, I would argue that it is vitally important for any Buddhist meditative practice, including kōan introspection, to be taken up in conjunction with Buddhist precept study. The First Precept becomes especially important for guiding the conduct of combatants who take up such practices during armed conflict. As Roshi Aitken explains:

> The First Precept plainly means 'Don't kill', but it also expresses social concern: 'Let us encourage life', and it relates to the mind: 'There is no thought of killing'. There are three elements that the Zen teacher uses in conveying the precepts: the literal, the compassionate, and the essential . . .' (Aitken 1984, 16)

The literal, the compassionate and the essential elements of a precept are often mutually reinforcing. For example, by not killing, one helps to encourage life and to cultivate a mind where there is no thought of killing.

However, what is one to do if the compassionate element (e.g. to encourage life, including one's own life) conflicts with the literal element (e.g. the prohibition on killing)? In applying this understanding of the First Precept to dilemmas in the real world, a practitioner may consider it necessary to take a life in order to sustain or protect the lives of others. Nevertheless, even if one considers it necessary to take a life, at no point should one – including a soldier in times of armed conflict – ever 'take a life for granted' (Roshi George Burch in Emery 2007). Whilst many Buddhists may seek to avoid military service altogether, many have joined and will continue to join the profession of arms – either by volunteering or through conscription. In such cases, a Buddhist combatant must learn how to continuously return to their vow of supporting life and abstaining from killing – in the knowledge that it will be an impossible vow to keep, especially in times of armed conflict. There can be no rationalising or reconciling this contradiction. In a way, the practice of keeping the First Precept in armed conflict can itself become a kōan.

Conclusions

The available evidence on the benefits of meditative practices, including kōan introspection, suggests that it could help combatants recognise their cognitive biases and better deal with situations of ambiguity in a way that enables more reasonable decision-making related to targeting. Nevertheless, this article represents only a surface-level foray into the matter, and more research could provide better empirical data to determine whether this particular practice does indeed have a robust effect.

Even if, in principle, kōan introspection could reliably enhance combatants' abilities to make decisions in line with IHL, it may be prudent not to promote kōan introspection as a stand-alone compliance measure – even for Buddhists. It is not a practice that can be taught in a short training session and practised for a few hours shortly before deployment, and it would not be wise to take up kōan introspection for the first time in a conflict zone. Moreover, a student's progress through the kōan curriculum depends to a great degree on the student having regular dialogue with their teacher, which is difficult to maintain during a deployment. Finally, kōan introspection should not be divorced from its ethical and spiritual roots. Without a solid ethical grounding, if a practitioner has a kenshō – an experiential understanding of the absolute aspect of reality – they might be unable to integrate the experience into a particular ethical orientation that would be compatible with adherence to IHL.

Nevertheless, for those military Zen practitioners who develop their kōan practice before going to war, it could give them helpful insights into their understanding of the battlespace, and it could help them to hold multiple perspectives in mind at the same time before deciding upon a course of action. Such an ability should help them to make more reasonable targeting decisions, even when faced with the fog of war.

Acknowledgements

I thank everyone who has had to put up with me waxing on about Buddhism and IHL; however, there are several folks without whose help I would not have been able to fit the pieces of this paper together. I am very grateful to my teacher, Sarah Bender, Roshi, for allowing me to seek her thoughts on kōan introspection generally and on its specific applications to the military profession. I also thank my fellow Zen practitioners and former US Air Force officers, Andrew Galbraith, Stuart Lloyd and Erinn Woodside, for entertaining my questions as a part of a focus group on meditation, kōan introspection and military deployment. Many thanks as well to Professors Kate Crosby and Peter Harvey, and Doctors Elizabeth Harris, Christina A. Kilby and Stefania Travagnin for kindly reviewing my drafts from a Buddhist studies perspective and providing valuable feedback on how to improve it. Finally, Lauren Trew, thank you for our dharma chats, your editing prowess and your patience and lovingkindness while I was writing this article.

Notes

1. The views set forth herein are expressed in my personal capacity and do not necessarily reflect those of my institutional affiliation. The British Red Cross is a religiously neutral humanitarian organisation that welcomes supporters, volunteers and beneficiaries of all religions or none.
2. See e.g. Solis (2010, 3–6).
3. In this article, I use the term 'targeting law' in the same manner as William Boothby to describe the subset of principles or rules in the IHL branch governing the conduct of hostilities as they relate to targeting.
4. Formal kōan study dates to the tenth century in China (Wick 2005, 1). There are roughly 1700 classic kōans – of which 500–600 continue to be used today (Schumaker and Woerner 1986, 182). Some of these kōans have been compiled into anthologies, such as the *Blue Cliff Record* (compiled in the twelfth century), the *Gateless Gate* (thirteenth century), the *Book of Equanimity* (thirteenth century), the *Transmission of Light* (fourteenth century) and *Entangling Vines* (c. seventeenth century). Of those Chan/Zen lineages which include formal kōan study, different lineages have developed different sequences, or 'curricula', for taking up particular kōans or kōan series, and some Zen groups may use more recently developed kōans in addition to the classic anthologies.

5. One would be hard pressed to find a principle in IHL more widely accepted than the Basic Rule. Evidence for its acceptance by states can be found in numerous military manuals and in Rule 7 of the ICRC's Customary International Humanitarian Law (CIHL) Study (Henckaerts and Doswald-Beck 2005, 25–29). The experts who drafted Rule 10 for the HPCR Manual on Air and Missile Warfare likewise regard the Basic Rule to be a fundamental tenet of the law of armed conflict (Harvard Program on Humanitarian Policy and Conflict Research 2010, 83–86).
6. The version of distinction articulated in APII (for NIACs) is not as strong as that stated in the Basic Rule. However, the ICRC CIHL Study puts forth a convincing case for the applicability of the Basic Rule in non-international armed conflict. The authors cite military manuals, the adoption of the rule into amended protocols II and III to the Certain Conventional Weapons Treaty (which is applicable in NIAC) and domestic legislation as evidence of states' acceptance of the rule during NIAC (Henckaerts and Doswald-Beck 2005, 25–28). The HPCR Manual on Air and Missile Warfare (2010, 83) confirms this view.
7. See e.g. Cannizzaro (2014, 335); Kolb and Hyde (2008, 136); Solis (2010, 273); Boothby (2012, 170); Henckaerts and Doswald-Beck (2005, 46).
8. I.e. API Article 57(2)(c).
9. API Articles 48 & 57(2)(a)(i). The HPCR Group of Experts clarify: 'To facilitate verification that a target is a lawful target and does not benefit from specific protection, command echelons must utilize all technical assets (such as intelligence, reconnaissance and surveillance systems) at their disposal, to the extent that these assets are reasonably available, and utilizing them is militarily sound in the context of the overall air campaign' (Harvard Program on Humanitarian Policy and Conflict Research 2010, 126).
10. Again, this is implied by Article 57(2)(a)(iii).
11. This is implied by Article 57(2)(a)(iii).
12. This is implied by Article 57(2)(a)(ii).
13. Article 57(2)(a)(ii). The HPCR Group of Experts clarify: 'For instance, an attacker ought to choose a weapon with greater precision or lesser explosive force if doing so would minimize the likelihood of collateral damage, assuming the selection is militarily feasible .... Similarly, angle of attack is one of the factors that determine where a bomb may land if it falls short of, or beyond, the target. Thus, to spare a building located, e.g. to the west of a target, it may be advisable to attack from the north or the south' (Harvard Program on Humanitarian Policy and Conflict Research 2010, 127).
14. See e.g. *Public Committee against Torture in Israel v. Government of Israel* (2006, 512–513) and German Federal Prosecutor (2010, 69); see also, for a reference to an 'unreasonable' decision to authorise a strike, US Department of Defense (2015, 54); and see, for non-attack related military decisions, *Beit Sourik Village Council v. the Government of Israel* (2004, 27).
15. This understanding of the word 'feasible' would have been controversial at the time of the negotiation of the APs, as the Rapporteur of the Diplomatic Conference Working Group explained: 'Certain words [in draft Article 50 (which later became Article 57 AP I] created problems, particularly the choice between "feasible" and "reasonable" .... The Rapporteur understands "feasible", which was the term chosen by the Working Group, to mean that which is practicable, or practically possible. "Reasonable" struck many representatives as too subjective a term'.
16. Focus Group with Zen Practitioners from the US Air Force, interview by Noel Trew (06 July 2019).

17. For ease in this instance, I reference NATO targeting doctrine since it covers the processes of a number of (western) countries; however, it is important to keep in mind that other states may operationalise their IHL targeting law obligations in a different manner.
18. Though he never used the phrase 'fog of war', the origin of this metaphor is widely attributed to the nineteenth-century Prussian strategist, Carl von Clausewitz: 'War is the realm of uncertainty; three quarters of the factors on which action in war is based are wrapped in a fog of greater or lesser uncertainty. A sensitive and discriminating judgement is called for; a skilled intelligence to scent out the truth' (1976, 101).
19. See e.g. Carter and Mortlock (2019) and Stanley and Jha (2009).
20. MBSR stands for 'mindfulness-based stress reduction'. It is a secular meditation technique which is used in a clinical setting.
21. For a more in-depth commentary on the story of Captain Great Compassionate and how *Upāya-kauśalya* can be seen in some circumstances as overriding the precepts in Mahāyāna ethics, see Harvey (2000, 134–138).
22. Bender, Sarah. 2019. Interview by Noel Trew. July 07.
23. It is a central tenet of East Asian Mahāyāna Buddhism that 'Buddha nature pervades the whole universe, existing right here now'.
24. Bender, Sarah. 2019. Interview by Noel Trew. July 07.
25. Bender, Sarah. 2019. Interview by Noel Trew. July 07.
26. Bender, Sarah. 2019. Interview by Noel Trew. July 07.
27. Focus Group with Zen Practitioners from the US Air Force, interview by Noel Trew (06 July 2019).
28. Focus Group with Zen Practitioners from the US Air Force, interview by Noel Trew (06 July 2019).
29. Focus Group with Zen Practitioners from the US Air Force, interview by Noel Trew (06 July 2019).
30. Focus Group with Zen Practitioners from the US Air Force, interview by Noel Trew (06 July 2019).
31. Focus Group with Zen Practitioners from the US Air Force, interview by Noel Trew (06 July 2019).
32. Focus Group with Zen Practitioners from the US Air Force, interview by Noel Trew (06 July 2019).
33. Focus Group with Zen Practitioners from the US Air Force, interview by Noel Trew (06 July 2019).
34. Bender, Sarah. 2019. Interview by Noel Trew. July 07.

Disclosure statement

This article was supported by the International Committee of the Red Cross (ICRC).

ORCID

Noel Maurer Trew http://orcid.org/0000-0002-2261-8341

References

Aitken, R. 1984. *The Mind of Clover: Essays in Zen Buddhist Ethics*. New York: North Point Press.

Austin, J. 1999. *Zen and the Brain: Toward an Understanding of Meditation and Consciousness*. Cambridge: MIT Press.

Beit Sourik Village Council v. the Government of Israel. 2004. *HCJ 2056/04*. Israeli High Court of Justice.

Benesch, O. 2014. *Inventing the Way of the Samurai*. Oxford: Oxford University Press.

Boothby, W. 2012. *The Law of Targeting*. Oxford: Oxford University Press.

Braboszcz, C., S. Hahusseau, and A. Delorme. 2010. "Meditation and Neuroscience: From Basic Research to Clinical Practice." In *Handbook of Integrative Clinical Psychology: Perspectives, Practices and Research*, edited by R. Carlstedt, 1910–1929. New York: Springer.

Burk, D. *"Sekito Kisen's Sandokai: The Identity of Relative and Absolute – Part 1."* 27 September 2018. https://zenstudiespodcast.com/sandokai-1/

Cannizzaro, E. 2014. "Proportionality in the Law of Armed Conflict." In *The Oxford Handbook of International Law in Armed Conflict*, edited by P. Gaeta and A. Clapham. Oxford: Oxford University Press.

Carter, A., and J. Tobias Mortlock. 2019. *Mindfulness in the Military: Improving Mental Fitness in the UK Armed Forces Using Next Generation Team Mindfulness Training*. Brighton: Institute of Employment Studies.

Desbordes, G., T. Gard, E. A. Hoge, B. K. Hölzel, C. Kerr, S. W. Lazar, A. Olendzk and D. R. Vago. 2015. "Moving beyond Mindfulness: Defining Equanimity as an Outcome Measure in Meditation and Contemplative Research." *Mindfulness* 6: 356–372. doi: 10.1007/s12671-013-0269-8.

Didriksen, L. 2018. "A Paradox of Koan Study and Why Psychology Should Take Note." *Human Arenas* 1 (4): 396–408. doi:10.1007/s42087-018-0036-4.

Elliott, L., and E. Redden. 2012. "Reducing Workload: A Multisensory Approach." In *Designing Soldier Systems: Current Issues in Human Factors*, edited by P. Savage-Knepshield, J. Martin, J. Lockett and L. Allender, 69–96. New York: Ashgate.

Emery, E. "A Place to Find Peace." *The Denver Post*. 29 October 2007. https://www.denverpost.com/2007/10/29/a-place-to-find-peace/

Ford, J. 2018. *Introduction to Zen Koans: Learning the Language of Dragons*. Somerville: Wisdom.

German Federal Prosecutor. 2010. *Investigation against Col Klein and Sgt W. on Suspicion of a Criminal Offense under the International Crimes Code and Other Offenses*.

Harvey, P. 2000. *An Introduction to Buddhist Ethics: Foundations, Values and Issues*. Cambridge: Cambridge University Press.

Harvey, P. 2013. *An Introduction to Buddhism: Teachings History and Practices*. 2nd ed. Cambridge: Cambridge University Press.

Harvard Program on Humanitarian Policy and Conflict Research. 2010. *Commentary on the HPCR Manual on International Law Applicable to Air and Missle Warfare*. Cambridge.

Henckaerts, J.-M., and L. Doswald-Beck. 2005. *Customary International Humanitarian Law - Rules*. Vol. 1. Cambridge: Cambridge University Press.

Human Rights Watch. 2008. *Troops in Contact: Airstrikes and Civilian Deaths in Afghanistan*.

International Criminal Tribunal for the Former Yugoslavia. 2000. "Final Report to the Prosecutor by the Committee Esatblished to Review the NATO Bombing Campaign against the Federal Republic of Yugoslavia." The Hague.

Johnson, T., and C. Wald. "The Military Should Teach AI to Watch Drone Footage." *Wired*. 26 November 2017. https://www.wired.com/story/the-military-should-teach-ai-to-watch-drone-footage/

Kahneman, D., S. P. Slovic, and A. Tversky. 1982. *Judgement under Uncertainty: Heuristics and Biases*. Cambridge: Cambridge University Press.

Keown, D. 2004. *A Dictionary of Buddhism*. Oxford: Oxford University Press.

Kolb, R., and R. Hyde. 2008. *An Introduction to the International Law of Armed Conflicts*. Portland: Hart.

Lance, B. J., and K. McDowell. 2012. "Future Soldier-System Design Concepts: Brain-Computer Interaction Technologies." In *Designing Soldier Systems: Current Issues in Human Factors*, edited by P. Savage-Knepshield, J. Martin, J. Lockett and L. Allender, 249–274. New York: Ashgate.

NATO. 2016. *Allied Joint Doctrine for Joint Targeting*. No. AJP-3.9. Nato Standardization Office.

Nitobe, I. 1908. *Bushido: The Soul of Japan*. 13th ed.

Pilloud, C. 1987. *Commentary on the Additional Protocols of 8 June 1977 to the Geneva Conventions of 12 August 1949*. Edited by C. Swinarski, Y. Sandoz and B. Zimmerman. Leiden: Martinus Nijhoff.

Public Committee against Torture in Israel v. Government of Israel. 2006. *Government of Israel*. HCJ 769/02. Israeli High Court of Justice.

Purser, R. 2014. "The Militarization of Mindfulness." *Inquiring Mind* 30 (2). https://www.inquiringmind.com/article/3002_17_purser-the-militarization-of-mindfulness/

Schmidt, A. 2016. "The Ethics and Politics of Mindfulness-based Interventions." *J Med Ethics* 42 (7): 450–454. doi:10.1136/medethics-2015-102942.

Schumaker, S., and G. Woerner. 1986. *The Rider Encyclopedia of Eastern Philosophy and Religion: Buddhism, Hinduism, Taoism, Zen*. London and Melbourne: Rider Books.

Senauke, A., and B. Gates. 2014. "Interview with Neuroscientist Amishi Jha: Mental Armor." *Inquiring Mind* 30 (2). https://www.inquiringmind.com/article/3002_18_w_jah-interview-with-neuroscientist-amishi-jha-mental-armor/

Shanker, T., and M. Richtel. "In New Military, Data Overload Can Be Deadly." *The New York Times*, 16 January 2011.

Solis, G. 2010. *The Law of Armed Conflict: International Humanitarian Law in War*. New York: Cambridge University Press.

Stanley, E., and A. Jha. 2009. "Mind Fitness: Improving Operational Effectiveness and Building Warrior Resilience." *Joint Forces Quarterly* 55: 145–151.

Stanley, E., J. Schaldach, A. Kiyonaga, and A. Jha. 2011. "Mindfulness-Based Mind Fitness Training: A Case Study of a High-Stress Predeployment Military Cohort." *Cognitive and Behavioral Practice* 18 (4): 566–576. doi:10.1016/j.cbpra.2010.08.002.

Stone, M. 2014. "Abusing the Buddha: How the U.S. Army and Google Co-opt Mindfulness." *Salon*, March 18. https://www.salon.com/2014/03/17/abusing_the_buddha_how_the_u_s_army_and_google_co_opt_mindfulness/

Tatz, M., trans. 1994. *The Skill in Means (Upayakausalya) Sutra*. Delhi: Motilal Banarsidass.

Terry, F., and B. McQuinn. 2018. *Roots of Restraint in War*. Geneva: ICRC.

Trew, N. 2017. *Dead Letter Law Arising from Strategic Choices: The Difficulty of Achieving Accountability for the Jus in Bello Rules on Proportionality and Precautions in Attack*. Exeter: University of Exeter. https://ore.exeter.ac.uk/repository/handle/10871/33168

US Department of Government Defense. 2016. *Law of War Manual (2016 Update)*. Washington, D.C.

US Department of Defense. "Investigation Report of the Airstrike on the Médecins sans Frontières/Doctors Without Borders Trauma Center in Kunduz, Afghanistan." 3 October 2015.

Victoria, B. D. 2006. *Zen at War*. Lanham: Rowman & Littlefield.

Von Clausewitz, C. 1976. *On War*. Translated by M. Howard and P. Paret. Princeton: Princeton University Press.

Whittemore, L. 2016. "Proportionality Decision Making in Targeting: Heuristics, Cognitive Biases and the Law." *Harvard National Security Journal* 3: 577–636.

Wick, G. S., trans. 2005. *The Book of Equanimity*. Sommerville: Wisdom.

Yu, R. 2016. "Stress Potentiates Decision Biases: A Stress Induced Deliberation-to-Intuition Model." *Neurobiology of Stress* 3: 83–95.

Zanesco, A., E. Denkova, S. Rogers, W. MacNulty and A. Jha. 2019. "Mindfulness Training as Cognitive Training in High-Demand Cohorts: An Initial Study in Elite Military Servicememebers." *Progress in Brain Research* 244: 323–354.

ICRC

SIEGE WARFARE AND THE PROHIBITION OF INTENTIONAL STARVATION OF CIVILIANS: THE CONVERGENCE OF IHL AND BUDDHIST ETHICS

Nishara Mendis

ABSTRACT

Sieges and threatening the besieged population with starvation are methods of warfare as old as civilisation. While sieges are not explicitly prohibited under international humanitarian law (IHL), the starvation of civilians as a method of warfare has been prohibited since the Geneva Conventions of 1949 and the Additional Protocols of 1977. This article discusses whether Buddhist ethics can contribute towards and enhance the existing IHL guidance on the subject. Buddhist texts and philosophy clearly declare that one must avoid actions that cause suffering to oneself or others, and that this principle of 'no-harm' (*ahimsā*) is applicable even during a war. The *Jātaka* stories of the past births of the Buddha and other figures illustrate wrong action and its karmic consequences. The article analyses two *Jātaka* stories: the *Ummagga Jātaka* (no. 546) which describes a potential siege and the tactics used by the *Bodhisattva* (Buddha-to-be) Mahosadha to avoid it, and the *Asātarūpa Jātaka* (no. 100) which provides a moral judgement on the actual use of siege warfare in the former births of Suppavāsā and her son, the *arhat* (enlightened saint) Sīvali. The narratives are useful for discussion and teaching of IHL, particularly in Buddhist societies, as they not only emphasise responsibility for ones' own actions but also provide psychological hope for spiritual progress based on the concept of intention.

The convergence between IHL and Buddhism

It is generally recognised that Buddhism as a whole is directed towards the minimising of suffering of oneself and others and the extension of compassion to all beings, including 'enemies' in a time of war. The concept of *ahiṃsā* or doing no harm or injury and the first precept of not taking life cannot be reconciled with violence and killing in war. The *Dhammapada* also states in many verses the admonition not to commit violence against others and not to encourage violence. For example:

The ultimate objective isn't putting a villain in jail but making the infliction of starvation so morally toxic that it is unthinkable. (Alex de Waal 2019)

DOI: 10.4324/9781003439820-14

Dhammapada verse 129: All tremble at force, of death are all afraid. Likening others to oneself, kill not nor cause to kill.

Dhammapada verse 405: Him I call a *brahmana* [a holy man], who has laid aside the use of force towards all beings, the perturbed as well as the unperturbed (*arhats*),[1] and who does not kill or cause others to kill.[2]

Although verse 405 specifically addresses the behaviour of monks and nuns rather than laypeople,[3] the verses of the *Dhammapada*, where they can be applied generally, can also be taken as admonitions to laity. Furthermore, they could be applicable for any situation: whether there is peace or war, it does not change the principle of non-harm. Buddhism does not specify that emergencies or war may be used as situations where exceptions or waivers to the prohibitions on violence and killing can be applied.

Some may argue that this universal guidance to avoid harm means that Buddhism has no relevance for wartime, but only applies during peace.[4] It can also be argued that it is *initiating* of warfare that is prohibited according to Buddhism, thus aligning with the prohibition of the 'crime of aggression'[5] and the current United Nations Charter framework for the regulation of the use of force. However, there is also no absolute prohibition of self-defence in Buddhism, and it could be argued that the Buddhist restrictions on self-defence by a nation are similar to the framework of the international law on self-defence or current *jus ad bellum* rules, as well as the international law on the peaceful settlement of disputes.

Regarding decision-making in a situation of ongoing war, the *jus in bello* (laws in war) or international humanitarian law (hereinafter IHL) rules come into play. It can be assumed that Buddhism, while being against the imposition of suffering and taking of life, recognises that when a conflict is underway there arises a need to minimise suffering, for example by avoiding collateral civilian deaths. Buddhism would therefore have something to say about the ethics of and *karmic* consequences of killing or causing harm – as a soldier or a commander of armed forces and also for civilian decision makers and advisors.

It is where the debate becomes technical and legalistic that the convergence between Buddhist ethics and IHL can become important for focusing on the core values of underlying both and the choice of action. This study considers how Buddhism could contribute, by focusing on a specific issue in IHL – siege during armed conflict. Buddhist writings, specifically those *Jātaka* stories that are relevant to situations of siege during armed conflict, are explored in order to discover to what extent they offer support to the existing core concepts of IHL and how Buddhist ethics could contribute towards the balancing of humanitarian values and military necessity in a difficult situation.

Introducing siege warfare, blockade and starvation in historical context

Today, the terms 'siege' and 'starvation' are likely to raise images of ancient and medieval warfare, with citizens behind stone city walls facing a prolonged campaign by invading armies. However, these methods are not entirely absent from modern warfare, as we can hear of similar issues on news reports of current conflicts. The recent and continuing humanitarian tragedies in the non-international and internationalised conflicts occurring in Yemen, Syria and South Sudan show that there is a need to revisit and strengthen the implementation of relevant IHL. There is thus a need to discuss the legality of siege and blockade in light of the principles and obligations in modern IHL, which have been developed in relation to the prohibition of starvation as a method of warfare.

According to commentary by experts on behalf of the International Committee of the Red Cross (ICRC), 'siege' is defined as: 'encircling an enemy location, cutting off those inside from any communication in order to bring about their surrender'. [6]

A term connected to siege is 'blockade', which is defined as consisting of 'disrupting the maritime trade of a country or one of its coastal provinces'.[7] The tactic of blockade by its very nature usually fails to apply the crucial IHL principle of distinction, i.e. between legitimate and illegitimate targets. To do so, those using the tactic would need to differentiate between military and civilian supplies, whereas a blockade will usually often affect food and medicine as well as the military objectives of preventing access to fuel and military supplies. While a blockade is not *per se* illegal, it is still subject to limits in terms of what a state is allowed to accomplish. According to the *San Remo Manual*, a blockade where the sole objective is the intentional starvation of civilians is prohibited.[8] Furthermore, the principle of proportionality must be applied to the commencement and the continuation of a blockade. In the context of the laws of war both on land and at sea, it could therefore be argued that siege and blockade can be conducted within the framework of IHL, if there is continued access to food, water and medicine for the civilian population and there is therefore a balancing of military necessity with humanity.

With regard to the term 'starvation', it has been stated by IHL experts that: 'The term "starvation" means the action of subjecting people to famine, i.e., extreme and general scarcity of food'.[9] They further explain: '*To use it as a method of warfare would be to provoke it deliberately*, causing the population to suffer hunger, particularly by depriving it of its sources of food or of supplies' [emphasis added].[10]

Starvation has been used as a political tactic of suppression, in occupied or colonised territories, and does not necessarily have to be connected to a situation of siege in wartime (de Waal 2017). The '*An Gorta Mor*' (Irish for 'great hunger') in 1840s Ireland (see Kelly 2012; Coogan 2013), the '*Holodomor*' – Ukrainian for 'murder by starvation', as Stalin's starvation of Ukraine during 1932–1934 is now called (see Wolny 2017; Graziosi, Hajda, and Hryn 2013) and the Bengal famine of 1943 (see Mukerjee 2018) can be identified as such 'political famines'. They were the direct result of political decision-making to deprive populations of existing food supplies in order to divert agricultural lands and available food to imperial or occupying powers. This article, however, will focus not on these types of famines, but on the use of starvation tactics associated with siege warfare or blockade.

Siege and starvation tactics were tragically part of the suffering of civilians in beleaguered cities during World War II. The Nazi's *Hungerplan* was a planned tactic of starvation against civilians and prisoners of war that was to be implemented in occupied territories, particularly the Soviet Union (Gerhard 2015). At this time, the starving of a population by besieging a city was not clearly prohibited under the laws of war. In the High Command Case, *The United States of America v. Wilhelm von Leeb, et al.*, a US post-war military commission stated that laying siege and 'cutting off every source of sustenance' was not unlawful under the laws of war at the time and therefore they acquitted German Field Marshall Wilhelm von Leeb for his role in the siege of Leningrad during September 1941–January 1944, where starvation killed at least half a million Russian civilians.[11] The judgement explicitly stated that:

> The propriety of attempting to reduce it [the population of Leningrad] by starvation is not questioned ... We might wish the law were otherwise, but we must administer it as we find it. Consequently, we hold no criminality attaches on this charge.[12]

The scale of the starvation at Leningrad has been highlighted by Michael Walzer, stating that '[m]ore civilians died in the siege of Leningrad than the modernist infernos of Hamburg, Dresden, Tokyo, Hiroshima and Nagasaki taken together' (Walzer 2015, 160). Thus, starvation is as much a part of the horrors of modern warfare as firebombing and the use of nuclear weapons. Even the victorious allies of World War II used starvation tactics against enemy civilians. The US blockade of Japan in 1945 was code-named 'Operation Starvation'. It was carried out by an aerial mining campaign dropping mines into harbours to prevent imports of food and fuel (Mason 2002). The extent of the suffering and starvation of Japanese civilians due to this blockade is not clear, as there are conflicting statistics, and Japan in any event surrendered before many months had passed.

The use of siege and starvation as tactics of war seem to be increasing again, observing the massive ongoing humanitarian crisis in the war in Yemen, the starvation used in South Sudan, the use of siege methods against cities in Syria and, recently, in the conflict with 'Islamic State' forces in Iraq (Todman 2017; de Waal 2009; Ferguson 2018). While aid agencies struggle with the practical aspects of providing adequate aid to civilians in such dire situations, academics and policymakers grapple with the legality of these methods at an intellectual level. For example, Susan Power has considered whether the starvation of civilians during siege warfare can be prosecuted as a war crime, focusing on the situation in Syria. She concludes that the deliberate denial of food and other conditions of life with the intent to cause death will amount to wilful killing under grave breaches of IHL (Power 2016; see also Mikos-Skuza 2018). De Waal goes further and describes intentional starvation as a method of war as 'new atrocity famines' which should be compared to the crime of genocide (de Waal 2018).

The situation in Yemen has also been dire, with aid agencies reporting large numbers of Yemenis suffering from starvation and related disease – apparently more than the number killed in battle or air raids. In 2014, the United Nations (UN) Security Council approved and extended an arms embargo relating to certain parties to the conflict within Yemen, particularly affecting the Red Sea port of al-Hoedaida.[13] It is stated that this embargo should not negatively impact humanitarian assistance and food supplies. Parties to the conflict agreed to redeploy their forces from Hodeidah, as agreed in the December 2018 Stockholm Agreement, in order for vital humanitarian food aid to reach Yemeni civilians.[14] The United Nations Mission to Support the Hodeidah Agreement (UNMHA) has been working on this issue since then, with the Security Council adopting Resolution 2534 on 14 July 2020, extending the mandate of the UNMHA until 15 July 2021. The involvement of Saudi Arabia (with support from the United States and the United Kingdom) and allegedly Iran, in the Yemeni conflict, has unfortunately overshadowed the needs of the civilians facing humanitarian crisis and starvation in the country, and allegedly muted the United Nations Security Council response to the problem. Yemen is being supported with food aid from the World Food Programme (WFP), which apparently feeds more than 10 million people per month, but the distribution of this aid is a fragile mechanism.[15] In October and November 2020, the UN Security Council and the UN Secretary General again made a statement on the dangers of famine in Yemen.[16]

In the context of the Syrian conflict, the United Nations Security Council in 2014, 'recalling that starvation of civilians as a method of combat is prohibited by international humanitarian law', called for an immediate lifting of all 'siege of populated areas' and demanded 'that all parties allow the delivery of humanitarian assistance ... and enable the rapid, safe and unhindered evacuation of all civilians who wish to leave'.[17] Again in 2015, the UN Security Council recalled with concern the legal obligation of parties under IHL with regard to 'the use of starvation of civilians as a method of combat, including by the besiegement of populated areas . . . '.[18] In 2018, an important resolution on conflict-related food insecurity was adopted unanimously by the 15-member Security Council.[19] This Resolution 2417 (2018) emphasised the relationship between armed conflict and conflict-induced food insecurity and the threat of famine and 'strongly condemned' the use of starvation of civilians as a method of warfare and the unlawful denial of humanitarian access as violations of IHL.[20] The same resolution stated, in paragraph 10, that the Security Council 'strongly urged' states to investigate and take action against those responsible for the use of starvation as a method of warfare 'with a view to reinforcing preventive measures' and 'ensuring accountability'.

The Food and Agriculture Organization of the United Nations (FAO) has also commented in support of Resolution 2417, adding that the number of people affected by hunger has been rising in recent years, although there had been a decrease in the previous decade. It identified armed conflict as the 'main driver of this reversal'.[21] FAO and WFP informed the UN Security Council in a recent joint report that food insecurity is currently a major issue for 16 countries – namely, Afghanistan, Burundi, the Central African Republic, the Democratic Republic of the Congo, Guinea-Bissau, Haiti, Iraq, Lebanon regarding Syrian refugees, Liberia, Mali, Somalia, South Sudan, Sudan, Syrian Arab Republic, Ukraine and Yemen – plus the transboundary Lake Chad Basin area.[22] As can be seen from this list, the majority are affected by ongoing armed conflict. Currently, there are no South Asian or Eastern Asian countries on this list; however, Afghanistan, a South-Central Asian Muslim country with a rich Buddhist heritage, is included.

The IHL prohibition on the starvation of civilians

The starvation of civilians gradually came to be recognised as an act against the laws and customs of war only during the last 100 years. The Lieber Code, one of the earliest of modern IHL documents, did not prohibit starvation as a method of warfare. In fact, Article 18 of the 1863 Lieber Code even states that:

> When a commander of a besieged place expels the non-combatants, in order to lessen the number of those who consume his stock of provisions, it is lawful, though an extreme measure, to drive them back, so as to hasten on the surrender.

This implies that strategies that could cause starvation of non-combatants were considered unfortunate but not illegal.[23] It should be noted however, that the principle of proportionality should apply to arguments for either mitigation or prohibition of such strategies. Modern IHL in fact goes further than just the application of proportionality, to explicitly identify a prohibition of starvation of civilians in treaty and customary law.

The first document that can be cited in support of the principle of prohibiting starvation as a method of warfare is dated after the First World War, when the 1919 Report of the Commission on Responsibility listed 'deliberate starvation of civilians' as a violation of the laws and customs of war and furthermore recommended that it be considered a criminal offence that should be prosecuted by courts.[24] Yet it is only in the post-World War II context that starvation of civilians became explicitly prohibited in IHL under the Additional Protocols, which built upon some of the provisions already in Geneva Convention IV of 1949.[25] The Geneva Convention IV on the treatment of civilians did not in itself specifically prohibit sieges, but only specified measures that can mitigate its effects. Article 54(1) of Additional Protocol I explicitly prohibits starvation as a method of warfare and Article 14 of Additional Protocol II includes the wording of Article 54(2), that '[S]tarvation of civilians as a method of warfare is prohibited'. Article 14 of Additional Protocol II states further (similar to the wording of Article 54(2) of Protocol I) that:

> It is therefore prohibited to attack, destroy, remove or render useless, for that purpose, objects indispensable to the survival of the civilian population, such as foodstuffs, agricultural areas for the production of foodstuffs, crops, livestock, drinking water installations and supplies and irrigation works.

The ICRC Commentary of 1987 specifically mentions that this article is a simplified version of Article 54 of Additional Protocol I.[26] It also explains that the objective of this provision 'is to prohibit the deliberate provocation of such a situation [of starvation] and to preserve the means of subsistence of the civilian population'.[27] The commentary also clarifies that the prohibition on using starvation against civilians is a non-derogable rule[28] (since no mention was made of imperative military necessity) meaning that there can be no exceptions to the rule.[29] Intentionally starving a civilian population would always be prohibited. However, the use of both siege and blockade as methods of warfare could remain legitimate if they are directed exclusively against combatants.[30] The incidental effect of starvation of civilians, where the intention of the siege or blockade is directed towards combatants, is something that could occur and yet not be considered a violation of IHL. Concerning humanitarian assistance to civilians, the ICRC Commentary adds that 'the possibility of refusing a relief action or relief consignments is not a matter of discretion; such refusals should thus remain exceptional'.[31]

According to the ICRC study on customary international law, Customary Rule 53 states that the use of starvation of the civilian population as a method of warfare is prohibited in customary international law as applicable for both international armed conflict and non-international armed conflict.[32] Thus, starvation tactics against combatants are not covered by this and are therefore not prohibited under customary international law, in either form of conflict.

In terms of individual and command responsibility for using starvation tactics, it is notable that the *original* Article 8(2)(b)(xxv) of the Statute of the International Criminal Court (ICC) of 1998, provided that 'intentionally using starvation of civilians as a method of warfare' is a war crime only in international armed conflicts and not in non-international armed conflicts.[33] This was changed by an Amendment in 2019, which recognised that starvation is a war crime for non-international armed conflict as well.[34] Currently there are only five ratifications for this agreement (Andorra, Croatia, Netherlands, New Zealand and Norway) but it is possible that there will be other states following suit soon, as this appears to be a relatively uncontroversial amendment. There has as yet been no prosecution in the ICC on this particular type of violation. However, there is the example of *Prosecutor v Perisic and Others*, a judgement of the District Court of Zadar, Croatia under the Croatian Penal Code, which cites Article 14 of Additional Protocol II.[35]

In terms of academic responses, there are critiques of a strict IHL standard from the perspective of military strategy. Yoram Dinstein has critiqued the Additional Protocols' prohibitions as making it unfeasible to carry siege out lawfully despite it being a valuable military tactic (Dinstein 1991, 150–151). Sean Watts agrees with Dinstein insofar as current IHL 'greatly constrains siege operations as classically conceived and executed' (Watts 2014, 20). But Watts is less critical of the IHL framework than Dinstein, and notes that there appears to be an encouragement of evacuation of civilians during a siege (under Additional Protocol I in particular) in order to be more humane – which is a framework that allows for a balancing of military necessity and humanity. In a 2019 Chatham House briefing, Emanuela-Chiara Gillard comments that the achievement of the military objectives of the siege can be delayed if IHL is complied with, and also concludes that parties to a conflict should strive to conclude agreements to evacuate civilians and the wounded and sick (Gillard 2019). Gillard suggests that the interpretation of the standard in Article 54 of Additional Protocol I prohibits only the deliberate starvation of civilians, with the principle of proportionality applicable in situations where starvation of civilians is not the purpose of the siege but is foreseeable and incidentally occurring. An academic blog post by Gloria Gaggioli also questions whether the IHL principle of proportionality should be applied for the restriction of sieges causing incidental starvation, rather than a complete prohibition of all sieges (Gaggioli 2019). Beth Van Schaack, former Deputy to the US Ambassador-at-Large for War Crimes Issues in the US State Department, acknowledges the difficulty for a commander to carry out a siege that is both successful and lawful, but supports the approach that treats deliberate starvation of civilians as a war crime (Van Schaack 2016). Thus, there appears to be some academic debate raised as to whether there should be a total prohibition of siege warfare, since in practice a siege could violate the IHL prohibition on starvation of civilians more often than not, or whether sieges could still be carried out legitimately with humanitarian assistance provided to the besieged.

The current IHL standard does not need to be the only measure by which to approach siege and starvation. Ruwanthika Gunaratne, former IHL expert to the United Nations Security Council Panels of Experts concerning Yemen (2016 to 2018) and Sudan (2014 to 2016), argues that there should be a separate designation criterion concerning actions that *contribute to* the starvation of the civilian population but do not reach the IHL threshold; and notes that the UN sanctions regime has examples of instances where 'obstructions to the delivery and distribution of humanitarian assistance' have been viewed as standalone criteria independently of the IHL criterion of intentional starvation as a method of warfare (Gunaratne 2018, 2019). The position of ICRC experts as expressed in the Commentary on Article 14 of Protocol II notes that legality is not the only measure of response to the situation of starvation:

> It should be noted that even if starvation were not subject to an official legal prohibition, it is nowadays no longer an acceptable phenomenon, irrespective of how it arises (natural disaster or induced by man). Increasingly public opinion and public conscience have forced governments to face their responsibilities and prompted the international community to organize relief actions, which are never sufficient in view of the scale of the problem worldwide.[36]

The above highlights the role of conscience in responding to the phenomenon of starvation, whether caused intentionally as a method of warfare or due to other reasons. The ICRC experts' position also recalls the language of the Martens Clause, that where there are gaps in the law, people ought to still be protected by the principle of humanity and by public conscience.[37] It is to this gap of action and response to suffering, that religion, particularly Buddhism, can make an important contribution.

Buddhist *Jātaka* stories involving siege and starvation of civilians

Buddhist tradition and philosophy recognise the complexity of life and actions taken by people in difficult circumstances. Since there are consequences to one's actions, one must show 'skilfulness' in making decisions and taking action. Here the Buddhist concepts of *kusala* (skilful or wholesome) and *akusala* (unskilful or unwholesome) come into play.[38] The core of

Buddhism is indeed this, as stated in verse 183 of the *Dhammapada*: 'Not to do evil, to cultivate "merit" (*kusalassa upasampadā*), to purify one's mind – this is the Teaching of the Buddhas'.[39]

Something that is unskilful is grounded in negative motivations based on greed, hatred or delusion – three root unskilful mental states, according to Buddhism. Skilful actions are those based on the opposite of these vices. In deciding whether or not to engage in siege warfare, *kusala* or skilful/wholesome decision-making, avoiding negative *karma*, can be useful to discuss.

Buddhist *Jātaka* stories describe the effects of past lives and *karma* (action), elucidating the consequences of both *kusala* and *akusala* action, and are thus well suited to consideration of ethical issues. The *Jātaka* stories identify and develop Buddhist ethics through application to practical situations. These situations are described as incidents from the past lives of the Buddha, and at times include past lives of other historical figures. It could be said that the stories have a 'case study approach' to teaching the application of Buddhist ethics. Set in the past, they mostly refer to people and animals in broader situations, and therefore often offer us a Buddhist view of life beyond the specific context of Buddhist monastic ethics. Moreover, as Peter Harvey has noted: 'The idea of the cycle of rebirth also provides a perspective on life which is supportive of sympathy and respect for other beings. Within the round of rebirths, all beings are part of the same cycle of lives' (Harvey 2000, 29).

The *Jātaka* stories are framed in terms of different times and spaces. The 'present' in the stories is the monastic settlement (usually in Jetavana or at Sāvatthī) where the Buddha responds to some event or problem in the present by reflecting on a similar event in the past. The 'past' or former birth stories refer to a past king, city and kingdom, most often referring to the King Brahmadatta of Bārānasī or Kāsī (Roy 1996). It can be argued that this framing of the stories, which crosses into both monastic and secular spaces, and the distancing in terms of time allows for the laity of any time period to apply the ethical principles raised in the story narrative to any suitably appropriate secular political, historical or legal context.

It is relevant to note at this point the observations by Oskar von Hinüber, commenting on the creation of monastic rules in the Theravāda Buddhist tradition, that

> ... rules are derived from experience and based on the practical need to avoid certain forms of behavior in future. This means at the same time that the cause for a rule is always due to the wrong behavior of a certain person. (von Hinüber 1995, 22)

This practical aspect is similar to IHL, which was created in response to unconscionable behaviour with a view towards preventing its repetition in the future. The importance of Buddhist *Jātaka* stories, which are used in teaching rules, ethics and behaviour to both Buddhist clergy and laity, is that there is often a description of situations in which rules, ethics or expected behaviour were not followed, and the consequences that ensued. These consequences occur according to disciplinary procedures under monastic law, the application of the (secular) 'law of the land' or the operation of '*karmic* law'.

The *Jātaka* stories often highlight the *karmic* consequences more than the possibility of punishment under monastic procedures or the 'law of the land'. However, there is no exclusion of the possibility of the 'law of the land' making an attempt to implement the standards of morality depicted in the stories. This adaptation to the given environment, consideration of existing frameworks and responsiveness to new events and behaviours means that we find a correspondence between Buddhism and IHL in terms of process, where IHL seeks to respond to new means and methods of warfare. In this space between the existing law and moral law of *karma*, Buddhism and IHL, with their similar processes, may be able to come together to strengthen the convergences in law and practice. Let me now turn to specific *Jātaka*s as examples. In *Jātaka*, the Buddha-to-be or *Bodhisattva* is often the hero or main protagonist displaying a particular virtue that he must perfect on his route to Buddhahood (although in some stories he is a minor character observing the action, or even a bad character whose behaviour is transformed in the story).

The *Ummagga Jātaka* (no. 546)

There is a well-known, detailed description of a siege in the *Ummagga Jātaka* (also known as the *Mahosadha Jātaka*), a story whose hero exemplifies the virtue of wisdom. It describes the siege of the city of Mithilā by King Chulani Brahmadatta of Pañcāla and 101 allied princes. The hero of the story is the *Bodhisattva* Mahosadha, the Chief Advisor to the King Vedeha of Mithilā. The *Jātaka* describes Mithilā as being besieged on all sides by a massive army, 'as it were by stars on all sides'.[40]

In this disheartening situation, Mahosadha responds by telling the people of the city to 'drink deep, sing and dance and make merry, shout and cheer and snap their fingers'.[41] The besieging armies cannot enter the city and are given the impression by the apparent merriment within that there is more than sufficient food. Mahosadha uses common sense to store rice paddy and firewood in preparation for siege and clever stratagems through spies and misinformation to convince those who have besieged his city that the food and firewood stores are so large that they cannot easily succeed in starving the population, thereby compelling them to abandon their plan. Even the plan to cut off water supplies to the city is undermined when Mahosadha uses misinformation to suggest that there are very deep ponds and wells within the city.

Finally, the advisor to King Chulani Brahmadatta, the Brahmin Kevatta, suggests a *Dhamma-Yuddha* ('Battle of the Dhamma', 'Battle of Righteousness') by the two advisors or sages Mahosadha and Kevatta, instead of a battle by armies to overcome Mithila. As is to be expected, the *Bodhisattva* (Buddha-to-be), i.e. Mahosadha, succeeds over the Brahmin and the country is defended by wisdom instead of warfare. As pointed out by A. T. Ariyaratne, the *Ummagga Jātaka* portrays how '*Pandith Mahaushada* conducted the war on behalf of *King Vedeha* against *King Chulani* and won the war without any bloodshed' (Ariyaratne 2003, 11). This method has also been referred to generally as a victory through *Dhamma* without any actual violent war.

The fear of hardship caused by prolonged siege is the context for this part of the *Jātaka* story, but siege warfare itself is not criticised specifically. It is the cleverness of Mahosadha in avoiding the siege that is highlighted. Why is siege warfare not criticised in the *Ummagga Jātaka*? To begin with, the reader or listener enters into the story from the point of view of the defender of the city and the besieged population, not of the attacker in the context of a siege. It does not become necessary to comment on the legality or morality of *using* siege and starvation methods, if the story is from the view of defending a location and its population.

Siege and starvation tactics were historically used in ancient India and not prohibited by Hindu ethics of war. Kaushik Roy points out, 'vedic and epic India did not generate any discussion of the military ethics of siege warfare' (Roy 2012, 38). Roy explains this conclusion by arguing that restraint in warfare develops only where there is adequate motivation for limiting the lethality of siege warfare by establishing elaborate rules and regulations, and that 'Aryans', as he identifies the purveyors of the Sanskritic culture of Hinduism, were originally pastoralist and so not motivated to develop such restrictions in warfare against urbanised enemy populations. The *Arthaśāstra*, the third-century BCE treatise on governance by Kauṭilya, which gives us a strong indication of acceptable warfare strategies, elaborates the 'Strategic Means to Capture a Fortress' in Chapter IV ('The Operation of a Siege and Storming a Fort'), Book XIII. Intrigue, spies, winning over the enemy's people, siege and assault are listed as the five means to capture a fort. Siege operations would begin when the enemy king was in a weakened state and low on supplies. It is mentioned in particular by Kauṭilya that 'Reduction (of the enemy) must precede a siege … When a people resist the attempt of the conqueror, then he may destroy their stores, crops, and granaries, and trade'.[42] It is further elaborated in Book XIII that destruction of agricultural produce and standing crops will result in the country being denuded of its people, a clear support for the general use of starvation as a method of warfare.

These methods are similar to the advice given by the Brahmin Kevatta to King Chulani Brahmadatta in the *Ummagga Jātaka*. Kevatta is a character who is described as unrighteous and also the object of derision and ridicule, and identified as a previous birth of Devadatta, the cousin of the Buddha who represents rivalry and jealousy of the Buddha's power. These tactics described in the *Arthaśāstra* are, moreover, all *offensive* tactics advocating the use of starvation, and the complete opposite of Mahosadha's *defensive* tactics of using spies and misinformation to mislead the besieging armies and defend the people. The *Ummagga Jātaka* places the *Bodhisattva* as a defender in a military context and thereby evokes the sympathies of the Buddhist reader or listener with the people of Mithila, subtly criticising the use of siege warfare.

We can also see siege warfare in early Buddhist art. There is a highly detailed relief on the Sanchi *stūpa*, the building of which goes back to the emperor Ashoka in the third century BCE. It shows the Mallas defending their city of Kuśīnagara against besieging armies, an event that took place during the fifth century BCE. It is relevant that this siege took place in the context of a dispute between Buddhist kingdoms over the relics of the Buddha, who according to legend had attained his *mahā-parinibbāna* (final *nibbāna* at death) at Kuśīnagara, with the Mallas hosting his funeral, as described in the *Mahāparinibbāna Sutta*. The modern site of Kuśīnagara is an important pilgrimage site for Buddhists around 2500 years later, reclaimed as a Buddhist site in the modern period. The war over the relics of the Buddha depicted in the Sanchi relief occurred when seven other claimants to the relics were ready to wage war with Kuśīnagara, but it is recorded that the Brahmin Droṇa successfully argued for a non-violent and peaceful sharing of the relics equally among the kingdoms, reflecting the kind of advice the Buddha himself would have offered (Singh 2017, 260–261).

There is no specific prohibition of siege or starvation as a method of warfare with regard to *jus in bello* to be ascertained from this story depicted in the Sanchi *stūpa*, as it seems that the war is averted by application of Buddhist principles of peaceful settlement of disputes at the early stage of the conflict. The use of this story depicted at Sanchi is usually seen as being in support of Ashoka's position for a peaceful handover of the dispersed relics for common worship during his own era.[43] It could also have reminded the kingdoms of the previous war for the relics, and the suffering that would be the consequence of siege warfare. Thus, it is necessary to see whether there is a more direct *Jātaka* or other Buddhist story that supports the prohibition of siege and/or starvation in a *jus in bello* context.

The *Asātarūpa Jātaka* (no. 100)[44]

We can find a more telling discussion of the ethics of conducting siege warfare in the *Asātarūpa Jātaka*. This offers a better source for considering a Buddhist approach to the principles and rules of IHL and international criminal law than did the *Ummagga Jātaka*. The *Asātarūpa Jātaka* offers an explanation of the birth of the monk Sīvali, an important and highly respected disciple of the Buddha, and in so doing provides a rare Buddhist story on methods of war and *karmic* consequences for decisions by military leaders and their advisors.

The story begins during the time of the Buddha, with the impending delivery of a son by Suppavāsā, who was a daughter to the King of Koliya. Her pregnancy is described as being of seven years' duration with a labour of seven days, during which she is said to have sent her husband to the Buddha to tell of her agony and ask for his blessing. A healthy child is born, who speaks seven days after his birth to the elder Sāriputta, describing his seven-year suffering in his mother's womb. In later life Sīvali became an *arhat*, an enlightened saint, and was considered most wise and fortunate, but his difficult breach birth ('stuck crossways in the womb'[45]) was a matter for discussion by his fellow monks. The Buddha, told of this discussion by other monks, decides to relate the past life story of Sīvali and Suppavāsā.

In this past life story, the Buddha is the deceased king of the city of Bārānasī, who was killed during an invasion by the King of Kosol, Suppavāsā is the queen of Bārānasī and Sīvali is her son, the young prince in exile. The young prince returns and camps with his army, sending a message demanding surrender or battle, to which the King of Kosol replies that he is ready to fight. The mother of the prince advises a siege of the city instead of open battle. Her argument is that surrounding the city and waiting until supplies of food, water and firewood are gone, and people are starving, would result in capturing the city without a battle. The prince follows his mother's advice and after suffering a seven-day siege, the people of Bārānasī decide to behead the conquering King of Kosol and open the gates of the city, and the prince regains his kingdom. It is for the advice and carrying out of the siege, respectively, causing suffering for the people of the city, that Suppavāsā and Sīvali suffer in their future lifetime.

There are many fascinating elements to this *Jātaka* story. Is it significant that the suffering people are not 'the enemy' but the prince's own people, or is that irrelevant? It certainly raises the issue of non-international armed conflict where the impact of starvation is on citizens of one's own country, and is therefore closer to the situations in Yemen, Syria and South Sudan. There is of course an international aspect to the conflict between Bārānasī and Kosol, and there is clearly internationalisation of the conflicts in Yemen and Syria.

The choices before the prince of Bārānasī are (1) to risk the lives of himself and his soldiers in battle or (2) to follow the advice of his mother to put pressure on the people of the city. From a military commander's point of view, if the military objective is to gain control of a city, town or area of territory, the military strategy would include how to achieve the objective with minimal casualties to one's soldiers. As Sean Watts notes:

> It is not surprising, then, that throughout history commanders have declined to advance into urban areas, resorting instead to encirclement and siege to reduce enemy resistance or provoke surrender. Even for numerically and technically superior forces, sieges may be tactically and strategically compelled. *Siege operations are often necessary to avoid the high attacking-force casualty rates associated with urban combat* …. (Watts 2014, emphasis added)

IHL is usually described as an attempt to balance military necessity with humanity. Military necessity would support siege warfare as a strategy or tactic that may avoid battle and save lives of soldiers, but the conceptualisation of 'humanity' in IHL does not encompass a decision of military commanders to save lives of soldiers over causing civilian suffering and death. Modern humanitarian law appears to prioritise the protection of the lives of civilians over the lives of soldiers in such a situation, which would be a dilemma for the decision makers.

Kum Kum Roy, examining concepts of justice in the *Jātaka*s, reminds us that they are more than mere folktales, but often present complex problematic issues in terms of conflicting interests (Roy 1996, 27). This is clear in the choice faced by the young prince; in avoiding outright bloodshed that could result in casualties of not only his soldiers but also his own citizens within the besieged city, he chooses instead to apply starvation tactics during a siege, that would affect only the civilians. One may question whether the prince made the better choice or not, but in terms of Buddhist ethics, perhaps the answer is that there is no right choice as such in war – only different methods and different *karmic* consequences to match.

The *Asātarūpa Jātaka* concerns a relatively short seven-day siege. Could this story be used and applied in the context of very complex, long-term conflict situations? We are familiar with international and non-international armed conflicts that continue for many years – often referred to as 'protracted conflicts'. Since it is ultimately the suffering of the people who are trapped that is highlighted in both the *Jātaka* story and in IHL generally, it could be argued that the length of the siege (or blockade, or even of sanctions) does not matter in terms of evaluating the decision-making of the attacking forces' commanders and their advisors in terms of IHL.

The story plays a role in developing empathy with the trapped people, who are, significantly, the prince's own subjects. They are not an 'enemy' but only a people caught between two alternative rulers. It is interesting that the people are forced into action themselves, to execute the King of Kosol who is in control of the city and open the doors to their own prince. They too are caught in a difficult situation where they have to choose between two evils – their own suffering or to kill another human being. In terms of Buddhist ethics, there is no justification for killing. The *Jātaka* is silent regarding any moral judgement on the people and there is an implied justification, but not necessarily a Buddhist justification, of necessity being suggested. The *Jātaka* does not address the *karmic* consequences for their choice, since the story focuses only on the past lives of Sīvali and Suppavāsā and their sufferings in their current life.

The responsibility of commanders and advisors

The text of the *Asātarūpa Jātaka* is particularly interesting to analyse, since there is significant moral blame of both the prince, who is later reborn as Sīvali, and of the queen, who is later reborn as Suppavāsā. The difficult and unrealistically long pregnancy and the agony of labour pains that Suppavāsā is subjected to seem to be given slightly more significance in the amount of text describing her suffering,[46] as compared to the single short sentence where the infant Sīvali describes his suffering in the womb. Yet it is Sīvali's uterine 'confinement' that closely matches the restriction of movement of the besieged people. The text clearly communicates both the pain of pregnancy and childbirth and the claustrophobia of a foetus struggling to be born, and thereby also the fear and suffering of besieged people. What can be more evocative than these particular images of a helpless mother and foetus? In the story, the monks who know of Sīvali's difficult birth question 'How great must have been the pains of mother and child! Of what deeds were their pains the fruit?' (Chalmers 1895).

It is also notable that both the *Asātarūpa Jātaka* and the *Ummagga Jātaka* feature advisors to kings and princes. In the *Ummagga Jātaka* past life story, the King Chūlani Brahmadatta is advised by the wise queen mother Talathā Devī as well as the Brahmin Kevatta. There is even a passage in the *Ummagga Jātaka* which praises Talathā Devī for her wisdom in judicial matters. Both these *Jātaka* stories make it clear that while good advice is a worthy and valuable service, there is *karmic* responsibility for wrongdoing as an advisor when it leads to a ruler or military commander violating norms of ethics or morality. Although civilian advisors are usually not perceived by the general public as being potential violators of modern IHL (compared to military officers and soldiers), the *Asātarūpa Jātaka* story highlights the role of those who are 'behind the scenes' in military decision-making. Likewise, IHL in fact covers not only military personnel but also civilian personnel, and the gender of the accused does not have any significance with regard to the criminal charges that can ensue due to violations of IHL.

While the story of the siege in the *Asātarūpa Jātaka* is almost unrealistically short, being described as only seven days in duration, the *karmic* consequences are unrealistically long, with Sīvali trapped in the womb for seven days' labour and the pregnancy of Suppavāsā being of seven years' duration. It could be explored whether this pattern of 'sevens' suggests a gradation in terms of *karmic* responsibility. The prince, who may have carried out the actions with perhaps little thought other than following advice, suffers in a later birth, but suffers less pain and for a shorter time period than the queen, who has implicitly thought through the use of the method and advises the course of action.[47]

According to the ICC Statute of 1998, Article 25(3)a–c, individual criminal responsibility can arise if an individual commits a crime individually or jointly; 'orders, solicits or induces the commission of such a crime'; 'aids, abets or otherwise assists in its commission or its attempted commission, including providing the means for its commission'; or 'in any other way contributes to the commission or attempted commission of such a crime by a group of persons acting with a common purpose'. As can be seen, this refers to not only the person who commands the carrying out of a crime against international law, but also those involved in the decision-making, and this can include civilian advisors.

Although an example not of IHL violations (war crimes), but of crimes against humanity,[48] the arrest warrant issued in 2012 for Simone Gbagbo as an indirect co-perpetrator on charges of four counts of crimes against humanity, allegedly committed during post-election violence in Côte d'Ivoire in 2010–2011, is an interesting case in point.[49] Mrs Gbagbo was the wife of Laurent Gbagbo, formerly President of Côte d'Ivoire, and the ICC prosecutor stated that there was sufficient evidence of a plan that led to the commission of the alleged crimes that was prepared by Mr Gbagbo *and his inner circle, including Mrs Gbagbo*. Thus, close associates, advisors and even family members who give advice leading to the planning and carrying out of offences against international law can be held criminally responsible in the ICC. Domestic courts can also choose to follow this standard in their criminal law. Simone Gbagbo was never handed over to the ICC, but in 2015 she was sentenced to 20 years in jail for crimes against humanity in the domestic courts of the Côte d'Ivoire. She was later pardoned under a general amnesty in 2018 after serving three years of a 20-year sentence in her own country. A similar situation could occur if there was a real-life incident comparable to the

Asātarūpa Jātaka, of planning the starvation of civilians during wartime, where civilian advisors to military commanders could be held liable for war crimes in either international or domestic courts.

It should be noted that soldiers and commanders can be both morally and legally obliged to *protect* people's access to food. A useful example is Section 23(1) the *Army Act No. 17 of 1949* of Sri Lanka. According to this legal provision, if the President of Sri Lanka finds any action or threats to deprive the people of Sri Lanka or a substantial portion of them of 'the essentials of life by interfering with the supply and distribution of food, water, fuel . . . ' he may order all or any members of the armed forces to 'perform such duties of *a non-military nature* as he may consider necessary for the maintenance of supplies and services essential to the life of the community' (emphasis added). This provision applies to both peacetime and wartime situations.

It would be an interesting follow-up to the analysis presented in this article if a quantitative study or series of key interviews was carried out on whether actual military decision-making in a predominantly Buddhist country such as Sri Lanka is influenced by religious-cultural attitudes concerning provision of food and water to civilians. Anecdotal evidence from conversations the author has had with various Sri Lankan military officers suggests that the Buddhist ethics of providing food and water to all actually did play a positive role, especially during and after May 2009 in the aftermath of the 30-year civil war in Sri Lanka, when the military had to provide food, water and shelter to displaced populations. Contrary views, such as those of Gordon Weiss and A. R. Sriskanda Rajah, claim that the Sri Lankan government *deliberately* under-estimated the numbers of the non-combatant civilian populations who had moved from their homes elsewhere and accompanied the withdrawal of Liberation Tigers of Tamil Eelam (LTTE) cadres[50] to the jungles of the Vanni region during the last stages of the war (Sriskanda Rajah 2017, 123, 128; Weiss 2011). They allege that this was done in order to reduce the amount of humanitarian aid delivered and use starvation as a tactic against the combined civilian and combatant populations surrounded by Sri Lankan armed forces.[51]

During the 30-year Sri Lankan conflict, free public services, including healthcare and education, had been provided by the Sri Lankan government to all parts of the country, including the Northern and Eastern Provinces where many areas were at various times controlled by the LTTE. However, the strategy and logistics of supplying food and medicines to civilian human shields in a jungle area where the concluding battles of an armed conflict were playing out was clearly an immense challenge at many levels. Commanders and advisers in this situation were facing a comparable dilemma to the one faced by the Prince of Bārānasī and his mother (Sīvali and Suppavāsā in their past lives), in order to win back their kingdom and their subjects while simultaneously considering the lives of both their soldiers and civilians.

It would be interesting to present the *Asātarūpa Jātaka* to military officers or civilians learning IHL, and to discuss the difficult tactical and strategic choices involved in balancing military necessity with humanity in a situation where civilians and combatants are restricted to an area without access to food and clean water, such as during the last stages of the war in Sri Lanka. Discussion of the *karmic* consequences of actions during war may be distressing to Buddhist officers if they feel that they will suffer from bad karmic results in this life or in their next rebirth regardless of their intention, so it is important to stress that *intention* to cause harm is part of the karmic equation, and is therefore relevant in Buddhism (as it is in criminal law). It may also be useful from a psychological point of view to recall how the story of Sīvali is described in relation to verse 414 of the *Dhammapada* (*Sīvalitthera Vatthu* in *Brāhmaṇavagga*). It is mentioned there that he became an *arhat* 'as soon as his head was shaved' and was foremost among all the monks in terms of receiving offerings of food and shelter. The Buddha states in verse 414, referring to Sīvali:

> Him I call a *brāhmaṇa*, who, having traversed this dangerous swamp (of passion), this difficult road (of moral defilements), the ocean of life (*saṃsāra*) and the darkness of ignorance (*moha*), and having crossed the fourfold Flood, has reached the other shore (*nibbana*); who practices Tranquility and Insight Meditation, who is free from craving and from doubt, who clings to nothing and remains in perfect peace.[52]

Sīvali had to face the *karmic* consequences during his early life in the womb for the choices that had been made in a former life, but his life was otherwise considered fortunate and blessed as he had, through a journey of many lifetimes, overcome and finally attained the status of *arhat*. In this manner, the psychological impact of the story of Sīvali as a whole could be seen as (and used for) setting a very strict standard of conduct (in terms of IHL) while also offering hope for Buddhists who want eventually to liberate themselves from *saṃsāra* and attain *nibbāna*.

Conclusions

The *Ummagga Jātaka* (no. 546) describes a potential siege and the tactics used by the *Bodhisattva* Mahosadha to avoid it, but the *Asātarūpa Jātaka* (no. 100) has a clearer moral judgement on the actual use of siege warfare and the accompanying starvation of civilians as an *akusala* action based on unwholesome mental states, with negative repercussions in the form of karmic consequences. In this *Jātaka*, Suppavāsā faces the karmic consequences for the advice she gave to her son Sīvali in a former birth to wage siege warfare, just as Sīvali faces the karmic consequences of acting upon it. The *arhat* Sīvali in his former birth was a usurped prince attempting to regain his city from a conqueror, and the besieged population were his own people. The story shows that people are individually responsible for the suffering they inflict and will themselves suffer the consequences for this, which has parallels in some respects with the principle of individual responsibility in modern international criminal law for violations of IHL. It can be presented that the *Asātarūpa Jātaka* strongly supports the total prohibition of siege warfare that results in starvation, and that it upholds individual and command responsibility for war crimes, including to the extent that civilian advisors who suggest or endorse such a strategy must face the consequences for doing so.

The ethical and moral responsibility for causing suffering to civilians through the use of siege warfare can be highlighted through sharing of religious stories like the *Asātarūpa Jātaka*. As Kum Kum Roy states, 'the Jatakas were meant to be disseminated – they were not regarded as the exclusive preserve of specialists' (Roy 1996, 23). Roy adds that the stories came from 'a pool of popular lore', and were alternatively used in both Buddhist teaching and secular oral traditions, 'and could thus flow into and out of a variety of narrative contexts' (Roy 1996, 37).

Can the Buddhist ethics expressed in these narratives be presented and taught alongside humanitarian law training for both civilians and the military to strengthen good practice and prevent IHL violations? For countries with a Buddhist cultural background, there is a strong argument for making reference to Buddhist religious texts and literature, as well as cultural practices, in the dissemination of IHL. It is possible that making these links could strengthen the application of IHL rules and principles, especially considering here the very real concern of soldiers, commanders and military advisors who are practising Buddhists regarding the *karmic* consequences of their actions. Buddhism does not provide a waiver for actions that cause harm to other living beings during war. But Buddhist ethics can support decision-making that mitigates suffering during war as far as possible, and stops the cycle of violence from continuing. The avoidance of actions that cause starvation during armed conflict, and the provision of humanitarian assistance to civilians, are examples of such ethical decisions.

Using the *Asātarūpa Jātaka* in the context of discussions on IHL raises a number of interesting questions. Firstly, can there be a role for Buddhist ethics to support the further development of the law of war concerning siege and blockade – specifically, the total prohibition of strategies and methods of war that result (even incidentally) in mass starvation, lack of access to water, medicine and sanitation for the civilian population?

Secondly, should Buddhist ethics be used to generate scholarly support for individual criminal liability for decision makers, whether military or civilian, who adopt such methods in international or non-international armed conflicts? It should also be noted that, even if individual criminal liability is not established and criminal punishment is thereby avoided, Buddhists understand that the *karmic* consequences of one's actions cannot be escaped. In this way, discussion of personal responsibility for Buddhists could have a deterrent effect and prevent future violations. In this manner, dialogue on IHL and Buddhist ethics can provoke constructive conversation in Asia and beyond, and Buddhist ethics may even provide the stimulus for reassessing the law concerning siege as a method of warfare under IHL.

As noted by Carolyn Evans in her assessment of references to religion by judges of the International Court of Justice (especially Judge Weeramantry of Sri Lanka, who has used Sri Lankan Buddhist values and principles in his judgements), it is possible to 'use religion in a way that bolsters the standing of norms developed within the international legal system' (Evans 2005, 18). However, as Evans also correctly comments, it is not suitable to use references to religion where it clashes with norms of international law, since religion is not recognised as a source of international law as such. Evans also warns that using religion can be a double-edged sword where there may be other passages in religious texts that encourage the violation of modern international law.[53] However, it can be argued that being a double-edged sword in this sense is not the case for Buddhist texts, and it is particularly not the case with regard to siege warfare and starvation of civilians, as depicted by the *Asātarūpa Jātaka*. The Buddhist ethics of 'not doing harm' combined with this specific story of consequences for wrongdoing are useful for dissemination and discussion of IHL, as well as the further development of the law in this area.

Notes

1. An *arhat* is the term given for one who gains enlightenment through the teaching of a Buddha, whereas a Buddha rediscovers the truth for themselves and then teaches it to help others.
2. Translation by the Buddha Dharma Education Association Inc., available online at https://www.buddhanet.net/.
3. Verse 129 is included in the *Daṇḍavagga*, with the commentary referring to an incident in the Jetavana monastery, when the Buddha reprimanded a group of *bhikkhus* (monks) who had beaten up another group of *bhikkhus*. He then laid down the disciplinary rule forbidding *bhikkhus* to beat others. Verse 405 is included in the *Brāhmaṇavagga*, and concerns the story of a *bhikkhu* (monk) from Jetavana who was beaten severely by a layperson due to a misunderstanding, but who did not retaliate or show anger. The Buddha confirms that this *bhikkhu* has shown the qualities of an *arhat*.
4. See further discussion on this point in the article in this volume authored by Prof. Asanga Tilakaratne.

5. See further, for the development of this concept, Article 10 of The Covenant of the League of Nations of 1919 and the Kellogg–Briand Pact of 1928, where aggressive war as an instrument of national policy was deplored. Individual criminal liability under international law for the crime of aggression was first included in the Charter of the International Military Tribunal at Nuremberg in its Article 6(a) and repeated in Article 5(a) of the Charter for the International Military Tribunal at Tokyo. The amended Article 8 *bis* (1) defines the crime of aggression for the Statute of the International Criminal Court (operational from 2018).
6. International Committee of the Red Cross (Pilloud et al. 1987), *Commentary on the Additional Protocols of 8 June 1977 to the Geneva Conventions of 12 August 1949*, Article 14 of Additional Protocol II: Protection of Objects Indispensable to the Survival of the Civilian Population, para. 4797.
7. International Committee of the Red Cross (Pilloud et al. 1987), *Commentary on the Additional Protocols of 8 June 1977 to the Geneva Conventions of 12 August 1949*, Article 14 of Additional Protocol II: Protection of Objects Indispensable to the Survival of the Civilian Population, para. 4797. For naval blockade see further the *San Remo Manual on International Law Applicable to Armed Conflicts at Sea*, 12 June 1994, Art 102. For aerial blockage see the *Manual on International Law Relating to Air and Missile Warfare*, 15 May 2009, Art 157a.
8. See *San Remo Manual on International Law Applicable to Armed Conflicts at Sea*, 12 June 1994, Art 102:

   'The declaration or establishment of a blockade is prohibited if: (a) it has the sole purpose of starving the civilian population or denying it other objects essential for its survival; or (b) the damage to the civilian population is, or may be expected to be, excessive in relation to the concrete and direct military advantage anticipated from the blockade'.
9. International Committee of the Red Cross (Pilloud et al. 1987), *Commentary on the Additional Protocols of 8 June 1977 to the Geneva Conventions of 12 August 1949*, Article 14 of Protocol II: Protection of Objects Indispensable to the Survival of the Civilian Population, para. 4791.
10. International Committee of the Red Cross (Pilloud et al. 1987), *Commentary on the Additional Protocols of 8 June 1977 to the Geneva Conventions of 12 August 1949*, Article 54 of Protocol I: Protection of Objects Indispensable to the Survival of the Civilian Population, para. 2089.
11. See the High Command Case, *The United States of America v. Wilhelm von Leeb* 12 LRTWC 1 at 59 (1948). Also available in United Nations War Crimes Commission, *Law Reports of Trials of War Criminals, Volume XII: The German High Command Trial, Case No 72: von Leeb*, 1949, available online, https://www.loc.gov/rr/frd/Military_Law/pdf/Law-Reports_Vol-12.pdf.
12. See the High Command Case, *The United States of America v. Wilhelm von Leeb* 12 LRTWC 1 at 59 (1948). Also available in United Nations War Crimes Commission, *Law Reports of Trials of War Criminals, Volume XII: The German High Command Trial, Case No 72: von Leeb*, 1949, available online, https://www.loc.gov/rr/frd/Military_Law/pdf/Law-Reports_Vol-12.pdf.
13. Security Council Resolution 2140, 26 February 2014, supporting the implementation of the National Dialogue outcomes, reaffirming the need for the full and timely implementation of the political transition, and establishing a sanctions regime under Chapter VII of the United Nations Charter, S/RES/2140 (2014). See also Security Council Resolution 2511, 25 February 2020, renewing the sanctions against Yemen imposed by Security Council Resolution 2140 (2014) until

26 February 2021 and extension of the mandate of the Panel of Experts until 28 March 2021, S/RES/2511 (2020); and Security Council Resolution 2534, 14 July 2020, extending until 15 July 2021 the mandate of the United Nations Mission to support the Hodeidah Agreement (UNMHA), S/RES/2534 (2020).

14. United Nations Security Council Press Release, 'Parties to Conflict in Yemen Have Accepted Plan for Redeployment of Forces from Hodeidah Port, Special Envoy Tells Security Council', SC/13780, 8512TH Meeting, 15 April 2019, https://www.un.org/press/en/2019/sc13780.doc.htm.
15. See 'Yemen's Houthis and WFP Dispute Aid Control as Millions Starve', 4 June 2019, https://www.reuters.com/article/us-yemen-security-wfp/yemens-houthis-and-wfp-dispute-aid-control-as-millions-starve-idUSKCN1T51YO.
16. UN, 'Security Council Press Statement on Yemen', 17 October 2020, https://osesgy.unmissions.org/security-council-press-statement-yemen-1; UN, 'Statement by The Secretary-General – On Yemen', 20 November 2020, https://osesgy.unmissions.org/statement-secretary-general-%E2%80%93-yemen.
17. Security Council Resolution 2139 (2014), adopted by the Security Council at its 7116th meeting, on 22 February 2014, S/RES/2139 (2014).
18. Security Council Resolution 2258 (2015), adopted by the Security Council at its 7595th meeting, on 22 December 2015, S/RES/2258 (2015).
19. Security Council Resolution 2417 (2018), adopted by the Security Council at its 8267th meeting, on 24 May 2018, S/RES/2417 (2018).
20. Ibid, Security Council Resolution 2417 (2018), paras. 5 and 6.
21. FAO/WFP (2018), FAO Hails UN Security Council Resolution on Hunger and Conflict, 24 May 2018, Rome, http://www.fao.org/news/story/en/item/1135838/icode/.
22. FAO/WFP (2018), 'Monitoring Food Security in Countries with Conflict Situations: A Joint FAO/WFP Update for the United Nations Security Council', January 2018, Issue No. 3, http://www.fao.org/3/I8386EN/i8386en.pdf.
23. Note that these phrases from The Lieber Code were also referred to in the High Command Case, *The United States of America v. Wilhelm von Leeb* 12 LRTWC 1 at 59 (1948); see notes 11 and 12 above.
24. Paris Peace Conference (1919–1920), *Commission on the Responsibility of the Authors of the War and on Enforcement of Penalties: Violation of the Laws and Customs of War*, https://archive.org/stream/violationoflawsc00pariuoft/violationoflawsc00pariuoft_djvu.txt.
25. Note also the general 'humane treatment' standard included in Common Article 3 and Article 27 of Geneva Convention IV, which can be used in argumentation that denial of food or other humanitarian assistance would be a violation of the humane treatment standard.
26. International Committee of the Red Cross (Pilloud et al. 1987), *Commentary on the Additional Protocols of 8 June 1977 to the Geneva Conventions of 12 August 1949*, Article 14 of Additional Protocol II: Protection of Objects Indispensable to the Survival of the Civilian Population, para. 4792.
27. International Committee of the Red Cross (Pilloud et al. 1987), *Commentary on the Additional Protocols of 8 June 1977 to the Geneva Conventions of 12 August 1949*, Article 14 of Additional Protocol II: Protection of Objects Indispensable to the Survival of the Civilian Population, para. 4791.

28. In the context of a state's legal obligations, this is a term that refers to a rule or right that cannot be limited or suspended under any circumstance, or where no exception to the application of the rule can be applied.
29. International Committee of the Red Cross (Pilloud et al. 1987), *Commentary on the Additional Protocols of 8 June 1977 to the Geneva Conventions of 12 August 1949*, Article 14 of Additional Protocol II: Protection of Objects Indispensable to the Survival of the Civilian Population, para. 4795.
30. International Committee of the Red Cross (Pilloud et al. 1987), *Commentary on the Additional Protocols of 8 June 1977 to the Geneva Conventions of 12 August 1949*, para. 4795.
31. International Committee of the Red Cross (Pilloud et al. 1987), *Commentary on the Additional Protocols of 8 June 1977 to the Geneva Conventions of 12 August 1949*, para. 2808.
32. See https://ihl-databases.icrc.org/customary-ihl/eng/docs/v1_cha_chapter17_rule53#Fn_5496F01F_00014.
33. Article 8(2)(b)(xxv) of the Statute of the International Criminal Court (ICC): 'Intentionally using starvation of civilians as a method of warfare by depriving them of objects indispensable to their survival, including wilfully impeding relief supplies as provided for under the Geneva Convention'.
34. Amendment to Article 8 of the Rome Statute of the International Criminal Court, Intentionally Using Starvation of Civilians, 6 December 2019, C.N.394.2020. TREATIES-XVIII.10.g., https://treaties.un.org/doc/Publication/CN/2020/CN.394.2020-Eng.pdf.
35. *The Prosecutor v Perisic and others*, District Court in Zadar, Croatia (Hrvatska), case number K. 74/96, 24 April 1997, available at http://www.internationalcrimesdatabase.org/Case/1053. The Court in *Perisic and others* convicted 19 officers of the Yugoslav People's Army (JNA) *in absentia* for the siege of the city of Zadar, 'which caused the death of at least 30 civilians and the destruction of significant parts of the city – including facilities and objects of large economic and cultural significance – without any military necessity to do so'.

    See further ICRC Customary International Law Database, 'Customary Rule 53. The Use of Starvation of the Civilian Population as a Method of Warfare Is Prohibited', https://ihl-databases.icrc.org/customary-ihl/eng/docs/v1_cha_chapter17_rule53#Fn_5496F01F_00014.
36. International Committee of the Red Cross (Pilloud et al. 1987), *Commentary on the Additional Protocols of 8 June 1977 to the Geneva Conventions of 12 August 1949*, Article 14 of Additional Protocol II: Protection of Objects Indispensable to the Survival of the Civilian Population, para. 4799.
37. The 'Martens Clause' refers to the language expressed originally in the preamble to the 1899 Hague Convention (II) with respect to the laws and customs of war on land, and which has been used in later IHL documents and convention provisions:

    'Until a more complete code of the laws of war is issued, the High Contracting Parties think it right to declare that in cases not included in the Regulations adopted by them, populations and belligerents remain under the protection and empire of the principles of international law, as they result from the usages established between civilized nations, from the laws of humanity and the requirements of the public conscience'.

It is named after Fyodor Fyodorovich Martens (1845–1909), the Russian delegate at the Hague Peace Conferences 1899, whose declaration was used to draft the above paragraph.

38. See further Bhikkhu Thich Nhat-Tu, 'Kusala and Akusala as Criteria of Buddhist Ethics', http://www.buddhivihara.org/kusala-and-akusala-as-criteria-of-buddhist-ethics/. See also Premasiri (1976), discussing the concepts of *punna* and *kusala*; and Harvey (2010).
39. This is the first of the three verses that make up the *Ānandatthera-paha Vatthu* (which is included in the *Buddha-vagga*), where the Buddha responds to the question of Ānanda *Thera*, who asked what the fundamental instructions are, and whether they are the same instructions given by all Buddhas.

    Peter Harvey's comment on this article is useful to include here, as he pointed out that 'Merit is the usual (though still problematic) translation of *puñña*, the power of an action to bring pleasant karmic results. *Kusala* is about the wholesome and wise nature of the action itself, and it motivating roots'.
40. E. B. Cowell and W. H. D. Rouse, 1907, translation, The *Jātaka*, Vol. VI, first published by Cambridge University Press in 1895, http://www.sacred-texts.com/bud/j6/j6012.htm.
41. E. B. Cowell and W. H. D. Rouse, 1907, translation, *The Jātaka*, Vol. VI, first published by Cambridge University Press in 1895, http://www.sacred-texts.com/bud/j6/j6012.htm.
42. Kautilya, *The Arthashastra*, 'Strategic Means to Capture a Fortress' in Chapter IV ('The Operation of a Siege and Storming a Fort'), Book XIII.
43. See, further, the interesting analysis by Strong (1989) that refers to narratives in the *Aśokāvadāna* and *Mahāvamsa* that link the spiritual and political dimensions of the distribution of the Buddha's relics.
44. Also referred to in some texts as the *Aghātarūpa Jātaka* (see the Sinhala translation available through the University of Sri Jayawardenapura, Sri Lanka, available at https://www.sjp.ac.lk/buddhism/download-buddhist-555-jathaka-katha-free-pdf/), and referred to in some collections as *Jātaka* Story No. 99 (see Obeyesekera 2014). However, these may be errors, as the majority of texts and collections appear to refer to the spellings and numbering I choose to refer to in this article.
45. Obeyesekera (2014, 393).
46. A similar admonition to a woman giving wrong advice to a male is the story of Eve in the Bible, where the Judeo-Christian God punishes Eve for advising Adam to eat the fruit of the tree of knowledge, stating 'I will greatly multiply thy sorrow and thy conception; in sorrow thou shalt bring forth children' (Genesis 3:16 – King James Version).

    The karmic result of the wrong advice given by a woman is suffering in labour and childbirth (and also being subject to a husband), but Adam's punishment is that he must toil ('labour') in order to live. This is similar to Suppavāsā being *karmically* punished in the form of difficult labour for the wrong advice given to her son in a previous birth.

    See further, for reference to unrealistically long pregnancies in Buddhist stories, Tatelman (1996). In his thesis, Tatelman discusses a Nepali Buddhist narrative that appears to have been added to the original story of *Yashodharā* (the wife of the Buddha), which chronicles *Yashodharā*'s 'six-year pregnancy' and other tribulations.

47. Note that there is some commentary on the consequences of actions. In the Dhammapada Commentary (Buddhaghosa) it is stated as follows:

    'A certain countryman buys a comb of honey for a thousand pieces of money and presents it to the Buddha [Vipassi]. In a later existence as King of Benares, he lays siege to a certain city for seven years and seven months. His mother, learning that he has blockaded the four principal gates of the city and left the lesser gates open, sends word to him to close the lesser gates and blockade the city completely. The king does so. On the seventh day the residents of the besieged city kill their king, and hand over the kingdom to the invader. Because Sivali in his previous existence as a king besieged this city, he was reborn in hell, and because he closed the lesser gates, he remained in the womb of his mother for seven days and seven months and seven years; because in his previous existence as a countryman he gave the comb of honey to the Buddha, he reached the pinnacle of gain and honor' (103–104).

    'Sivali remained in the womb of his mother for seven days and seven months and seven years for no other reason than that in a previous existence he once blockaded a city and reduced the inhabitants to starvation' (33).

    Burlingame, E. W., 1921, *Buddhist Legends; Translated from the Dhammapada Commentary*, Harvard University Press. http://www.columbia.edu/cu/lweb/digital/collections/cul/texts/ldpd_6072311_001/ldpd_6072311_001.pdf.
48. It should also be noted that starvation of a population during 'peacetime' can be considered a crime against humanity, since the ICC Statute provisions defining crimes against humanity are open-ended, and a widespread or systematic attack directed against any civilian population falls under its definition and covers, respectively:

    Article 7(1)(b): 'Extermination' – (defined in 7(2)(b) as 'the intentional infliction of conditions of life, *inter alia* the deprivation of access to food and medicine, calculated to bring about the destruction of part of a population'.

    Article 7(1)(k): 'Other inhumane acts of a similar character intentionally causing great suffering, or serious injury to body or to mental or physical health'.
49. *The Prosecutor v. Simone Gbagbo*, ICC-02/11-01/12, https://www.icc-cpi.int/cdi/simone-gbagbo.
50. The Liberation Tigers of Tamil Eelam was a separatist armed group which has also been categorised as a terrorist organisation, particularly in light of its use of suicide attacks, targeting of civilians, ethnic cleansing, assassinations of political opponents and critics, and use of child soldiers. Allegations of war crimes have been made against both sides during the war, with a comparably small number of domestic criminal investigations and convictions carried out in response to the allegations.
51. Weiss was the UN spokesman in Sri Lanka during the final months of the war.
52. Translated by Daw Mya Tin, 1986, *The Dhammapada: Verses and Stories*, Burma Tipitaka Association Rangoon, Burma, https://www.tipitaka.net/tipitaka/dhp/verseload.php?verse=414.
53. Evans (2005, 20) citing M. Khadduri, 1955, *War and Peace in the Law of Islam*, that 'jihadists are permitted to besiege enemy cities' and contaminate water sources.

Acknowledgements

The author greatly appreciates the valuable comments and edits on this article made by Peter Harvey, Kate Crosby, Noel Trew and Andrew Bartles-Smith.

Disclosure statement

This article has been supported by the International Committee of the Red Cross (ICRC).

Case law

The United States of America v. Wilhelm von Leeb High Command Case. 12 LRTWC 1 at 59 (1948).

The Prosecutor v. Simone Gbagbo, ICC-02/11-01/12. https://www.icc-cpi.int/cdi/simone-gbagbo

The Prosecutor v Perisic and others, District Court in Zadar, Croatia (Hrvatska), case number K. 74/96, 24 April 1997. http://www.internationalcrimesdatabase.org/Case/1053

References

Ariyaratne, A. T. 2003. "Buddhism and International Humanitarian Law." *Sri Lanka Journal of International Law* 15: 11–16.

Chalmers, R., trans. 1895. *The Jātaka*. Vol. I. Cambridge: Cambridge University Press. https://www.sacred-texts.com/bud/j1/j1103.htm

Coogan, T. P. 2013. *The Famine Plot: England's Role in Ireland's Greatest Tragedy*. New York: St. Martin's.

Cowell, E. B., and W. H. D. Rouse, trans. 1907. *The Jātaka*. Vol. VI. Cambridge: Cambridge University Press. https://www.sacred-texts.com/bud/j6/j6012.htm

de Waal, A. 2017. "Counter-Humanitarianism and the Return of Famine as a Weapon of War." *London Review of Books* 39 (12): 9–12. A more complete version is available online: https://sites.tufts.edu/reinventingpeace/files/2017/06/Operation-Starvation-extended-20170616.pdf

de Waal, A. 2018. *Mass Starvation: The History and Future of Famine*. Cambridge: Polity.

de Waal, A. 2019. "Mass Starvation Is a Crime - It's Time We Treated It that Way." *Boston Review*, January 14. http://bostonreview.net/global-justice/alex-de-waal-mass-starvation-crime%E2%80%94its-time-we-treated-it-way (this is an adapted version of the Seventh Annual Overseas Development Institute lecture, given in London on 6 December 2018)

Dinstein, Y. 1991. "Siege Warfare and the Starvation of Civilians." In *Humanitarian Law of Armed Conflict: Challenges Ahead: Essays in Honour of Frits Kalshoven*, edited by A. J. M. Delissen and G. J. Tanja, 145–152. Leiden: Martinus Nijhoff.

Evans, C. 2005. "The Double-Edged Sword: Religious Influences on International Humanitarian Law." *Melbourne Journal of International Law* 6 (1): 1–32.

Ferguson, J. 2018. "Is Intentional Starvation the Future of War?" *The New Yorker*, July 11. https://www.newyorker.com/news/news-desk/is-yemen-intentional-starvation-the-future-of-war

Gaggioli, G. 2019. "Joint Blog Series on International Law and Armed Conflict: Are Sieges Prohibited under Contemporary IHL?" *EJIL:Talk!*, January 30. https://www.ejiltalk.org/joint-blog-series-on-international-law-and-armed-conflict-are-sieges-prohibited-under-contemporary-ihl/

Gerhard, G. 2015. *Nazi Hunger Politics: A History of Food in the Third Reich*. Lanham: Rowman and Littlefield.

Gillard, E.-C. 2019. "Sieges, the Law and Protecting Civilians." *Chatham House Briefing* 27 (June). https://www.chathamhouse.org/2019/06/sieges-law-and-protecting-civilians-0/iii-rules-international-humanitarian-law-particularly

Graziosi, A., L. A. Hajda, and H. Hryn, eds. 2013. *After the Holodomor: The Enduring Impact of the Great Famine on Ukraine*. Cambridge: Harvard University Press for the Ukrainian Research Institute.

Gunaratne, R. 2018. "Advocating for a Separate Designation Criterion on Starvation." *Just Security*, June 6. https://www.justsecurity.org/57480/advocating-separate-designation-criterion-starvation/

Gunaratne, R. 2019. "Humanitarian Assistance and Security Council Sanctions: Different Approaches to International Humanitarian Law." *EJIL:Talk!*, April 11. https://www.ejiltalk.org/humanitarian-assistance-a nd-security-council-sanctions-different-approaches-to-international-humanitarian-law/

Harvey, P. 2000. *An Introduction to Buddhist Ethics: Foundations, Values and Issues*. Cambridge: Cambridge University Press.

Harvey, P. 2010. "An Analysis of Factors Related to the *Kusala/akusala* Quality of Actions in the Pāli Tradition." *Journal of the International Association of Buddhist Studies* 33 (1–2): 175–209.

Kelly, J. 2012. *The Graves are Walking: The History of the Great Irish Famine*. New York: Picador.

Mason, G. A. 2002. *Operation Starvation*. Report no. AU/AWC/2002-02. Maxwell Air Force Base: Air University, Air War College. https://apps.dtic.mil/dtic/tr/fulltext/u2/a420650.pdf

Mikos-Skuza, E. 2018. "Siege Warfare in the 21 St Century from the Perspective of International Humanitarian Law." *Wroclaw Review of Law, Administration and Economics* 8 (2): 319–330. doi:10.1515/wrlae-2018-0050.

Mukerjee, M. 2018. *Churchill's Secret War: The British Empire and the Ravaging of India during World War II*. New Delhi: Penguin Random House India.

Obeyesekera, R., ed. 2014. *The Revered Book of Five Hundred and Fifty Jātaka Stories, Volume I*. Colombo: Gunasena.

Pilloud, C., Y. Sandoz, C. Swinarski, and B. Zimmermann. 1987. *Commentary on the Additional Protocols of 8 June 1977 to the Geneva Conventions of 12 August 1949*. Geneva: International Committee of the Red Cross.

Power, S. R. 2016. "Starvation by Siege: Applying the Law of Armed Conflict in Syria." *Amsterdam Law Forum* 8 (2): 1–22. doi:10.37974/ALF.282.

Premasiri, P. D. 1976. "Interpretation of Two Principle Ethical Terms in Early Buddhism." *Sri Lanka Journal of the Humanities* 2 (1): 63–74.

Roy, K. 1996. "*Justice in the Jātakas*." *Social Scientist* 24 (4/6): 23–40. doi:10.2307/3517789.

Roy, K. 2012. *Hinduism and the Ethics of Warfare in South Asia: From Antiquity to the Present*. Cambridge: Cambridge University Press.

Singh, U. 2017. *Political Violence in Ancient India*. Cambridge: Harvard University Press.

Sriskanda Rajah, A. R. 2017. *Government and Politics in Sri Lanka: Biopolitics and Security*. Routledge Studies in South Asian Politics. Vol. 11. London and New York: Taylor & Francis.

Strong, J. S. 1989. *The Legend of King Aśoka: A Study and Translation of the Aśokāvadāna*. New Delhi: Motilal Banarsidass.

Tatelman, J. 1996. *The Trials of Yashodharā: A Critical Edition, Annotated Translation and Study of Bhadrakalpāvadāna II–V, Part I: Text*. Thesis submitted for the degree of Doctor of Philosophy, Wolfson College, University of Oxford. https://www.academia.edu/20955477/The_trials_of_Yasodhara_a_critical_edition_annotated_translation_and_study_of_Bhadrakalpavadana_II_V

Todman, W. 2017. "The Resurgence of Siege Warfare." *Georgetown University, Center for Contemporary Arab Studies' Newsmagazine, Fall/Winter*. https://issuu.com/georgetownsfs/docs/ccasnewsfw2017_final_issue

Van Schaack, B. 2016. "Siege Warfare and the Starvation of Civilians as a Weapon of War and War Crime." *Just Security*. https://www.justsecurity.org/29157/siege-warfare-starvation-civilians-war-crime/

von Hinüber, O. 1995. "Buddhist Law according to the Theravada-Vinaya: A Survey of Theory and Practice." *Journal of the International Association of Buddhist Studies* 18 (1): 7–45.

Walzer, M. 2015. *Just and Unjust Wars: A Moral Argument with Historical Illustrations*. Fifth ed. New York: Basic Books.

Watts, S. 2014. *Under Siege: International Humanitarian Law and Security Council Practice concerning Urban Siege Operation*. Harvard Law School Brookings Project on Law and Security: Counterterrorism and Humanitarian Engagement Project. http://blogs.harvard.edu/cheproject/files/2013/10/CHE-Project-IHL-and-SC-Practice-concerning-Urban-Siege-Operations.pdf

Weiss, G. 2011. *The Cage: The Fight for Sri Lanka and the Last Days of the Tamil Tigers*. Sydney: Pan Macmillan Australia.

Wolny, P. 2017. *Holodomor: The Ukrainian Famine-Genocide Bearing Witness: Genocide and Ethnic Cleansing*. New York: Rosen Young Adult.

Part III

Minimising Harm and Practical Values

ICRC

'FREEDOM FROM HATRED': THE ROLE OF *KHANTI* IN COMPLEMENTING THE WORK OF INTERNATIONAL HUMANITARIAN LAW (IHL)

Alex Wakefield

ABSTRACT

This article explores the Buddhist quality of *khanti*. *Khanti/kṣānti* translates as patience, forbearance or tolerance, and includes the notions of non-retaliation and forgiveness. Understood in Buddhist texts as the opposite of anger and hatred, *khanti* may support measures of international humanitarian law (IHL) which prevent unlawful reprisals and other atrocities motivated by revenge in the context of war. As with IHL, Buddhism emphasises common humanity through the recognition of universal suffering. By drawing on Buddhist narratives and treatises, which apply the analysis of non-self (anattā) to anger itself as a basis for khanti, this article demonstrates that khanti is regarded as particularly appropriate for dealing with conflict. *Khanti* addresses the immediate psychological responses of victims of violence during conflict, thus offering immediate relief of suffering and preventing its further escalation. This article suggests that the *brahmavihārās*, particularly loving-kindness (*mettā*), may practically develop the quality of *khanti*. Just as mindfulness meditations have been used in the secular and global contexts, so too *mettā* practice as the development of *khanti* could be utilised alongside military training and the work of the International Committee of the Red Cross to enhance compliance with IHL.

Introduction

Buddhism is often acknowledged as possessing a strongly pacifistic position, yet it also does not seek to deny that war is a lived experience for many. Conflict remains an inevitable fact of life; precious time and resources may be wasted in ongoing arguments for its abolition, whereas efforts to minimise its consequences may prove more productive. This is the position taken by international humanitarian law (IHL), which aims to reduce the effects of war – to limit the adverse 'humanitarian consequences of armed conflicts' (Melzer 2016, 17). Thus, the laws of IHL find common ground with several Buddhist teachings, considering how suffering can be mitigated, and especially suffering that is a result of military action.

DOI: 10.4324/9781003439820-16

One such teaching is that of *khanti* (Pali) or *ksānti* (Sanskrit). This is the Buddhist concept of patience, forbearance and tolerance: the capacity to let go of interpersonal resentment and to cultivate a quality of acceptance and forgiveness. As one of the *pāramitā*s or perfections (see Bodhi 1978), which are associated with virtuous conduct, Buddhism has long considered *khanti* a core aspect of its path of moral practice. Particular to Buddhism is the understanding that the self is 'interpenetratively co-dependent with others'. James Whitehill describes this as allowing the *pāramitā*s to 'flow necessarily into the community on many levels, materially, verbally, and mentally, in a subtle, looping reciprocity' (Whitehill 2000, 26). Thus, the practices work both on the level of the individual and for greater humanity. Pertinent links may be uncovered between the Buddhist concept of *khanti* and the humanitarian basis of IHL. By exploring the distinctive quality of this Buddhist virtue, one may discern new methods with which both Buddhism and IHL may deal with adversity in times of war.

This paper will explore the theoretical links between the Buddhist concept of *khanti* and the principles of IHL, and propose certain applications for its support of the latter. Beginning with an exploration of the context behind IHL, and how *khanti* has been understood in the Buddhist textual tradition, it will explore the role the virtue has taken in Buddhist thought, primarily as a response to the unwholesome/unskilful quality of anger. Finally, it will suggest a practical application for the cultivation of *khanti* through the four meditative techniques, the *brahmavihārā*s (and particularly that of loving-kindness, *mettā*) as a means of harnessing the benefits of patience for potential use within the work of IHL.

Khanti and the ethical framework of IHL

The virtue of *khanti* consists of an enduring patience, forbearance and forgiveness. In Buddhism, it acts as one of the six or ten *pāramitā*s, perfections, which characterise a virtuous person, cited by James Whitehill as informing moral efforts not only for oneself but also for the wider community (Whitehill 2000, 26). *Khanti* as a *pāramitā* attests to its core position at the heart of Buddhist ethical practice.

The *Dhammasaṅgaṇī* (section 1341), the first book of the Abhidhamma Piṭaka section of the Theravāda scriptural canon, defines this *pāramitā* as 'That patience which is long-suffering, compliance, absence of rudeness and abruptness, complacency [in the sense of contentment, *attamanatā*] of heart'. Caroline A. F. Rhys Davids notes here that the final three stand in direct opposition to synonyms of *dosa* (Pali), covering anger, hatred and aversion (Rhys Davids 1974, 324). *Dosa* is one of the three roots of unwholesome actions, which are so defined precisely because of the suffering (Pali *dukkha*) that they bring either to oneself or to others (Harvey 2000, 48). In contrast, *khanti* as non-hatred/non-anger contributes to wholesome actions that are free from these results, moving the practitioner instead towards a state free from such suffering (Harvey 2000, 48).

A fundamental acknowledgement of the human condition is an attitude found across Buddhist ethical teaching, based on our shared journey through the cycle of rebirths. The Buddha considers this point himself:

> It is not easy, bhikkhus, to find a being who in this long course has not previously been your mother ... your father ... your brother ... your sister ... your son ... your daughter. For what reason? Because, bhikkhus, this *saṃsāra* is without discoverable beginning .... (SN 15.14–19)

A similar understanding of mankind's common humanity allows IHL to establish and maintain its ethical framework. The minimisation of suffering becomes possible through adherence to certain principles of IHL – the balance of humanity and military necessity, distinction, proportionality, precaution, humane treatment and the prohibition of unnecessary suffering (ICRC 2014). They govern decisions on who may or may not be targeted, the humane treatment of prisoners of war, and how to impartially administer aid to the wounded based on need alone. Acts of retribution against protected persons, and those that do not fulfil a strict military purpose, are forbidden, and a culture of reciprocity is encouraged regarding the observance of IHL rules.

Non-retaliation, or non-vengeance, is fundamentally about a response to anger. When certain principles of IHL are not adhered to in conflict (for instance, by using weapons that have been banned because they cause superfluous injury), retribution may be an option chosen by wronged parties who are angered by unnecessary suffering. This response is often not limited to military personnel; the father who has lost his son may seek revenge on the serviceman who killed him or those he associates with the perpetrator. IHL is in some respects an antidote to this cycle of retribution – while it does not deal explicitly with conflict resolution, it is understood that the prevalence of atrocities or violations of IHL may provoke further ones in return, thereby exacerbating and prolonging a conflict (Muñoz-Rojas and Frésard 2004, 8). This parallels the structure within which Buddhism perceives anger to be functioning; it is easy for hatred to warrant hatred in return. Sallie B. King notes:

> Due to the law of karma, violence produces further violence. Violent acts sow karmic seeds that bear fruit in retaliatory violence from the one who suffered the original blow. One may win today, only to suffer the revenge of the defeated later .... (King 2013, 633)

This understanding is best summarised with the verse from the *Dhammapada* that 'never here [in this world] do hatreds cease by hatred. By freedom from hatred they cease: This is a perennial truth' (Dhp.5). With the knowledge that revenge is potentially a continuous tragedy, that has anger or hatred as its cause, practical approaches may be established to temper its effects. While not necessarily commenting on the psychology that gives rise to cycles of violations, some of the rules of IHL reduce the risk that the parties to a conflict might commit tit-for-tat atrocities, particularly those aimed at the civilian population. For example, IHL prohibits military actions whose primary purpose is to induce terror in the population at large (Melzer 2016, 85) and attacks against civilians by way of reprisal (Melzer 2016, 86).

A closer exploration of the Buddhist understanding of anger, and *khanti* as its response, will be offered below, but it is enough at this stage to identify how the virtue closely aligns with IHL. If anger is allowed to persist, unlawful retributive actions may be carried out, prompting further unlawful retributive acts in return. To deal with vengeful responses requires cultivating patience, tolerance and fortitude. One also needs to develop a far-reaching perspective as one considers how anger will manifest further in the future as well as in the immediate present. This is the role that Buddhism envisages *khanti* as fulfilling.

A few words must be said here about the particular circumstances of establishing such patience in warfare. As suffering experienced in conflict becomes far more extreme than that in daily life, so too the nature of *khanti* must change to meet these heightened demands. One must ask to what extent it is appropriate to encourage parties in conflict (civilian or otherwise) to cultivate a forgiving attitude even as conflict continues, or whether it is a viable process when the dangers of a lack of safety or security still exist. It is therefore important to note that the fostering of the virtue should act independently from considerations of justice; 'forgiveness' as an aspect of *khanti* has little to say about the pardoning of crimes committed during wartime. Achieving justice, while often perceived as a retributive measure, must be seen as distinctly concerned with preventing similar crimes from happening again. Nor should the tolerance and patience of *khanti* be equated with reconciliation during war. Ṭhānissaro Bhikkhu considers that reconciliation is instead 'a return to amicability … requiring the re-establishment of trust' (Ṭhānissaro Bhikkhu 2011). The practice of *khanti* will often, and must, take place in circumstances where such reconciliation is not possible. Reconciliation should therefore not be a prerequisite for *khanti* to work, nor should it even be its primary concern. Moreover, reconciliation falls outside the remit of IHL, since it concerns the after-effects of armed conflict.

Equally, the practical application of *khanti* during war should also be made distinct from a concept of amnesty. Amnesties are legislative decisions where criminal prosecutions and their subsequent penalties are effectively cancelled

(ICRC 2017). There are various reasons why this would be an appropriate course of action to take, not least in achieving a swift resolution to hostilities (ICRC 2017). Once again, however, wartime amnesties should not function as 'proof' that forgiveness or patience has been reached, regardless of the motives behind their use. How *khanti* is understood in Buddhism is less to do with the pardoning or acceptance of crime and far more to do with limiting the potential dangers of the consequences of that crime for any or all involved.

Clearly the virtue of *khanti* overlaps in many respects with the humanitarian concerns of IHL. This can now be elaborated from a Buddhist perspective, as we consider how the virtue has traditionally functioned in Buddhist teaching and in practice.

The role of *khanti* in Buddhist thought

As with all Buddhist teachings, *khanti* is envisioned as a means to achieve an end to *dukkha*. More specifically, however, the most clearly elucidated role of *khanti* is as a response to the unwholesome qualities of anger and hate. A recurring idea in Buddhist literature is the danger in allowing the latter to fester. The Pali *Nikāyas* often emphasise the particularly damaging results that anger may bring and the necessity in eliminating it, as here in the *Saṃyutta Nikāya*:

> Having slain anger, one sleeps soundly;
> Having slain anger, one does not sorrow;
> The killing of anger . . .
> With its poisoned root and honeyed tip;
> This is the killing the noble ones praise . . . (SN.11.21)

By positing the two as directly opposed, this not only emphasises the damage that anger (*kodha*) may cause, but in turn highlights the value of *khanti*, as a patient non-anger, in subduing it. It is worth considering here the wider moral framework within which *kodha* and *dosa* are understood in Buddhism.

Wholesome and unwholesome *(kusala/akusala)* behaviours

Dosa (*dveṣa* in Sanskrit), i.e. hatred or aversion, acts as one of the three unwholesome roots alongside delusion, *moha*; and greed, *lobha* (e.g. AN 3.69). They are considered to be the roots of all other defilements (*kilesa* in Pali; *kleśa* in Sanskrit) and thus an essential problem to be surmounted on the Buddhist path towards awakening. These roots form the bases of 'all the unskilful mental states which characterise the un-Awakened mind and bind the unenlightened person in the cycle of existence, and it is from the defilements that the Buddhist seeks liberation' (Crosby and Skilton 1998, xxxvii). An action that is considered 'unwholesome' arises from one or more of the three roots, and leads to suffering for oneself and/or others, whether immediately or later in one's karmic future (Harvey 2000, 48). This implies certain consequences for the practitioner within their Buddhist ethical framework. Christopher Gowans highlights that what is 'fundamental to determining whether actions are good or bad' is essentially the psychology of the agent, and particularly the intention behind said actions (Gowans 2013, 435). Establishing the distinction between wholesome and unwholesome at the level of the mental stages resulting in action, rather than at the level of the individual as a whole, means there cannot be any concept of a person as 'truly evil' in Buddhism; no person can ever be seen as inherently or irredeemably evil, but rather as acting because of one or more of the unwholesome roots. Indeed, a number of figures in the *Nikāya*s are described as committing crimes only to be later transformed through discovery of the Buddha and his teachings. The most famous of these is the serial killer Aṅgulimāla, who not only changes from a hardened criminal to a member of the Sangha, but is shown to progress all the way to enlightenment, becoming no longer subject to *saṃsāra*; this is possible through a radical improvement of mind and behaviour inspired by the Buddha (MN.86). It is not the man as such who is being judged here, but rather the consequences of his thoughts and actions, which are dictated by his defilements. Ultimately, this is where Buddhism will see the beginnings of such wrongdoing: unwholesome actions that are influenced by the three core roots of greed, hatred and delusion. The benefits of *khanti* are therefore made possible as one realises the roots may be weakened and then destroyed, thus opening the practitioner to the potential for sincere change in their actions.

Martin Southwold suggests that the difference between cultures with a concept of evil in the strongest sense, and those without, falls to the issue of forgiveness (Southwold 2003, 430). Establishing a difference between 'the evil person' and 'the unwholesome act' opens up a pragmatic structure for the virtue of *khanti* to work. Such patience is made possible by appealing to the cause of unwholesome behaviour as not an essential part of the one who commits it. Aṅgulimāla goes from among the worst of society to one of the very best, and it comes through the choice to change, to change actions from what is *akusala* to what is *kusala*. This attitude aligns the practice with IHL as it shares a well-conceived message of universality – the benefits of *khanti* are, and must be, available to all.

Khanti in response to anger

Khanti is often expounded, in both canonical and commentarial literature, as antithetical to anger or resentment. This role of *khanti* is therefore seen as a supremely advantageous quality:

Patience, endurance, is the highest asceticism. (Dhp.184)

Of goals that culminate in one's own good
None is found better than patience. (SN.11.4)

Contrasted with *dosa*, *khanti* is thereby described as a virtue ingrained in the path of practice. Yet one may argue here that exalting patience as an abstract and virtuous quality does little to support a practical value in complementing the work of IHL. Warfare would surely test the patience, forbearance and forgiveness of its parties to the extreme. However, the value of *khanti* in such violent situations has, in fact, been explored throughout the literature.

In the *Khantivādī Jātaka* (no. 313), the tale of the 'one professing forbearance', the Buddha in a previous life (the Bodhisatta) is described as a sage who encounters the rage of the king of Kāsi (Horner 1957, 43–49). When the king falls asleep in the park where the sage is staying, the royal harem takes the opportunity to approach the sage and ask him to give a talk on *Dhamma*, to which they listen with rapt attention. On waking, the king is angered that the Bodhisatta has stolen his entertainers away from him, and asks him what the doctrine he has been teaching is: 'I teach the doctrine of forbearance [*khanti*]' which is ' . . . not being angry with others who are abusive, violent and slanderous' (Shaw 2006, 110). Exemplifying anger in contrast, the enraged king proceeds to order his executioner to progressively injure the Bodhisatta: scourging him with thorns, cutting off his hands and feet, and mutilating his face. After each injury, the king spitefully asks again the doctrine that the Bodhisatta teaches, to which the reply is always the doctrine of *khanti*, which is not skin-deep, but 'established deep in the recesses of my heart' (Shaw 2006, 111).

In this *Jātaka*, the connotations of *khanti* as both patience and endurance are drawn out in the face of incredible pain and suffering, albeit with a specific purpose. Andrew Skilton notes: 'The lengthy mutilation scene is . . . utilised skilfully to allow the Bodhisatta to assert that his teaching is deep seated, not superficial or insincere – not located in his hands and feet or ears and nose, but in his heart' (Skilton 2002, 121).

The violent imagery is necessary here to emphasise *khanti* as deeply embedded and, importantly, far-sighted; it is understood that true patience endures, and is not easily destroyed in those who have eliminated anger successfully. The Bodhisatta does not give in to anger with the king, the text considering that hatred and anger are what motivated the king to act wrongly in the first place. The real challenge is therefore not towards the abuser, but towards the anger that prompted their action.

The author Śāntideva expresses this same point in his *Bodhicaryāvatāra*, by considering the capacity of *khanti* (here, *kṣānti*) for tolerance in enduring suffering, and particularly suffering as a result of the actions of others

(Edelglass 2009, 390). Here it is examined by use of an analysis in which the person on the receiving end separates the abuser, or their action, from the anger that compels them: 'If, disregarding the principle cause, such as a stick or other weapon, I become angry with the person who impels it, he too is impelled by hatred. It is better that I hate that hatred' (Bca.VI.41).

Accordingly, animosity should not be directed towards the person; they are acting merely as vehicles for their defilements. Śāntideva draws attention to the root cause of the hatred within both the abuser and the abused, identifying the common enemy that they share even while in conflict with one another. Furthermore, the author touches here on his understanding of causality. It remains short-sighted to consider the act of aggression (here, being hit with a stick) as independent of other conditions that prompt the abuser. Śāntideva expresses this point clearly:

> A person does not get angry at will, having decided 'I shall get angry', nor does anger well up after deciding 'I shall well up'.
>
> Whatever transgressions and evil deeds of various kinds there are, all arise through the power of conditioning factors, while there is nothing that arises independently. (Bca.VI.24–25)

The understanding of causal conditioning therefore becomes how one can separate a person's anger from the person themselves. Consequently, the patience and forgiving qualities of *khanti* become easier to cultivate. It will be seen below how these are necessary for a successful incorporation of the virtue within IHL.

Returning to the *Khantivādī Jātaka*, we also see highlighted the power of forbearance as resilience, as the purity of mind of the Bodhisatta is contrasted with that of the king. This expression of resilience in the face of *dukkha* is attested to elsewhere in the canonical literature; in the *Kakacūpama Sutta*, the Buddha states, 'Bhikkhus, even if bandits were to sever you savagely limb by limb with a two-handled saw, he who gave rise to a mind of hate towards them would not be carrying out my teaching'. (MN.I.129). Here powerful imagery is used to reinforce the practice of *khanti* as enduring and unshakeable. It is valuable to note here, in relation to its applicability to IHL, the firm Buddhist belief that this state of mind is possible even in such severe occurrences, attesting to the long-lasting value that the virtue may bring for the practitioner. Once again, it should be noted that this is separate from legal justice for such crimes. Rather, *khanti* acts as a psychological method for alleviating suffering and preventing the creation of further suffering. The suffering that may be caused by allowing the prevalence of anger and hatred is greater than that which may be physically overwhelming in the present moment. In this manner, *khanti* is understood as a powerful practice that maintains the strength of the mind and holds back *dukkha* even in the most painful of circumstances.

Non-self (*anattā*)

The concept of non-self (*anattā* in Pali; *anātman* in Sanskrit) – that it is inappropriate to take anything as a permanent, essential self or its possession – also provides context for understanding how Buddhism can use *khanti* for practical purposes. Non-self suggests that, beyond a 'conventional validity', there is nothing that can constitute a permanent, unchanging self or personhood (Bodhi and Ñāṇamoli 1995, 28). What may be conventionally described as a person is, in fact, a composite of aggregates – bundles of mental and physical processes – that together create the picture of a 'self'; yet the aggregates provide no inherent justification for the impression of a self that exists either within or independently of them.

Becoming too far trapped by notions of an essential 'self' is related to an even deeper vague sense of 'I am': self-centredness, an ego that serves to separate oneself from others, or to see others on varying levels of importance. The Buddha instead explicitly says that happiness is consistently achieved only after the aggregates constituting the conventional self are properly regarded as being 'not yours' (MN.I.140–141). The doctrine of non-self eliminates an 'us and them' mentality, and instead proposes a means to examine the universality apparent across humankind. Important groundwork is provided here for a Buddhist notion of forgiveness, as the place that it comes from – a refusal to see fundamental differences between oneself and others – can be the method for how it is achieved.

In the *Bodhicaryāvatāra*, the issue of non-self is used to support Śāntideva's discussion of the perfection of *khanti/kṣānti* in a similar manner. We have seen the author separate the person from their anger, but he goes even further by analysing away what we mistakenly think is the essence of the person whom we consider to be the root cause of our anger. Śāntideva explains: 'I feel no anger towards bile and the like, even though they cause intense suffering. Why am I angry with the sentient? They too have their reasons for anger' (Bca.VI.22).

This mirrors an attitude found in the fifth-century Pali treatise the *Visuddhimagga* of Buddhaghosa, where he suggests approaching anger through 'resolution into elements', asking the practitioner to try and locate the object of anger in another person: 'When you are angry with him, what is it you are angry with? Is it head hairs you are angry with? Or body hairs? … For when he tries the resolution into elements, his anger finds no foothold …' (Vism.IX.38).

With this understanding, one realises the hard-to-grasp nature of anger, as one tries and fails to find the precise object of hatred in another. The reasoning, based on the Buddhist teaching of lack of a self-essence, allows one to consider the emptiness of the object of one's anger and thereby of anger itself. Śāntideva elaborates on this point by bringing forbearance back to the defilements, as the reasons for unwholesome actions, and so suggesting the virtue of *khanti/kṣānti* as the way to sympathise with their agent, rather than to become angry with them in return. Crosby and Skilton (1998, 46) summarise this in the following manner:

> 'If the actions of people and objects are determined by a network of other conditions, how can any individual person or object be held to blame for the consequence, and, in that light, how can anger be justified?'

By separating the question of person from the suffering they bring, *khanti/kṣānti* becomes a far more realistic proposal. In fact, the *Bodhicaryāvatāra* offers a more direct example where this may be beneficial in the context of war:

> 'The person who realises that hatred is an enemy, since it creates such sufferings as these, and who persistently strikes it down, is happy in this world and the next' (Bca.VI.6).

By this reasoning, one is reminded of soldiers who are encouraged to see the opposing side as 'the enemy', yet the verse here suggests that in order to placate arising hatred, one instead should recognise hatred itself as the true enemy. The manner to achieve this is the patient, enduring and forgiving nature of *khanti*; all of these come into play in establishing how the cultivation of the virtue may reduce the suffering of those caught in conflict, and begin to encourage the spirit of non-retaliation.

Incorporating *khanti* within IHL

IHL provides a legal framework for the prevention and punishment of IHL violations, especially war crimes (ICRC 2002). Nevertheless, there will remain instances when legal justice, even if achieved, will remain unsatisfactory. Justice in legal terms rarely supersedes the pain and suffering caused by actions in conflict. Psychologically, it can only go so far to mend broken families and the trauma that has been prevalent, especially when considering that warfare may be ongoing in many of these instances.

Khanti alleviates psychological suffering in the present moment, with a view to avoiding its manifestation in the future. As we have seen through its inherent opposition to the manifestation of anger, and its probing analysis of the agent/object of that anger, *khanti* can complement IHL, discouraging unlawful retaliatory violence by emphasising the interdependence or common humanity of parties to armed conflict. Once again, the Pali *Nikāyas* often themselves place this quality of patience in a wartime context. Returning to the *Saṃyutta Nikāya*, we hear of Sakka, lord of the *devas*, who has won his battle against the *asuras*, and captured their leader, Vepacitti (SN.11.4). The prisoner, despite being at the mercy of the victors, angrily slanders them, which Sakka patiently endures without response. When pressed, he offers this reason for his practice of *khanti*:

> One who repays an angry man with anger
> Thereby makes things worse for himself.
> Not repaying an angry man with anger,
> One wins a battle hard to win.
>
> He practises for the welfare of both,
> His own and the other's,
> When, knowing that his foe is angry,
> He mindfully maintains his peace. (SN.11.4)

By this logic, *khanti* is understood to possess far-reaching benefits to all parties in conflict. This also draws out the quality of *khanti* as forgiveness; here, we may understand forgiveness to be a conscious letting go of one's negative emotions towards another person. Even if one is the victim of wrongdoing, one may still avoid a clouded mind. This aspect of *khanti* removes the harbouring of pain and humiliation, and the elimination of anger removes the temptation, or possibility, to seek a corrupted form of justice through acts of revenge, whether in a military or a civilian context. *Khanti* may support the upholding of IHL through practical methods (see below) by which this quality of forgiveness is encouraged, even in the face of violations by the opposing party in conflict. The breaking of humanitarian law by one side does not release the other side from their own obligations (Melzer 2016, 17). Equally, as noted by Śāntideva, *khanti* provides a means by which anger is separated from the individual, lessening the impetus for retaliatory actions targeting perceived victimisers.

Vengeance is understood to be a natural outcome of allowing *dosa* and *kodha* to take hold, when forgiveness is not encouraged. Warnings against its consequences are attested throughout canonical literature. In the *Vinaya's Mahāvagga*, one finds the story of Prince Dīghāvu, who witnesses the death of his parents at the hands of rival king Brahmadatta (Mv 10.2.3–20, Ṭhānissaro Bhikkhu 2013). Despite initially setting out to avenge this crime, the moral of the tale is captured by the king's final words to his son, to remember that 'vengeance is not settled through vengeance. Vengeance is settled through non-vengeance'. The tale of Prince Dīghāvu exemplifies how revenge can be avoided by tempering the anger that causes it. Recollecting his father's praise for patience, the young prince is encouraged to eliminate his anger and avoid his desire for revenge, and is therefore spared from committing an act with terrible karmic consequences. In this manner, the story makes clear the iterative and cumulative nature of acts of anger, as only through shedding this anger can the series be stopped. A willingness to put an end to the cycle of violence is of benefit to all involved. This can only be achieved through a practice of *khanti*, maintaining patience, forbearance and ultimately forgiveness.

The virtue clearly has benefits within such violent contexts. How patience may be encouraged under such conditions is another matter. Here, one may look to meditation on the qualities known as the *brahmavihārā*s to provide a practical means for the cultivation of *khanti*.

The *brahmavihārās*

The *brahmavihārā*s comprise loving-kindness (*mettā*), compassion (*karunā*), sympathetic joy (*muditā*) and equanimity (*upekkhā*). The term '*brahmavihārā*' literally means 'divine abiding' or 'behaving or living like a brahmā deity', which underlines the heavenly states of mind that they are associated with. In the *Visuddhimagga*, Buddhaghosa begins his chapter on the *brahmavihārā*s with a collection of sayings from the *Nikāya*s extolling the benefits of patience in response to the dangers of hatred (*dosa*) (Vism.IX.2ff). Consequently, while the individual practices may be seen as antidotes to specific unwholesome states of mind, the implication here is that they feed into a greater framework of *khanti*, which is again being described in direct opposition to *dosa*.

The foundational practice is that of *mettā*. The connotations of 'loving-kindness' in English do not reach the weight of the Pali word, which includes friendliness, deep goodwill and caring concern. *Mettā* is a powerful practice that can substantially alter a person's state of mind towards themselves and towards others. It will ultimately be the primary vehicle to cultivate *khanti*, as *mettā* forms a relationship with others that is not based on anger. Edelglass points out that as meditation, *mettā* is used particularly to alleviate the defilement of anger (Edelglass 2009, 391), thereby becoming a meditative tool for the development of patience.

Karunā will serve to strengthen the basis provided by loving-kindness. In fact, this *brahmavihārā* may be seen as an even more radical proposition, as Buddhaghosa describes how compassion should be aroused for a person who has committed wrongdoing even if they remain happy, or free from repercussions: 'he deserves the meditator's compassion; and so he does too in any case, even with no such ruin, thus "In reality he is unhappy", because he is not exempt from the suffering of the round [of becoming]' (Vism.IX.81).

These words underline that despite no immediate repercussions, the wrongdoer may in fact face suffering in the future (almost certainly, according to the Buddhist perspective, due to the karma of his wrongdoing). From this perspective, *karunā* also exemplifies an investment in our shared humanity; everyone in the world will face suffering, and they deserve compassion in response. As Buddhaghosa notes, like everyone else the wrongdoer is not exempt from *dukkha*, as he continues to live with rebirth as a fundamental truth. In such a manner, compassion for all living beings is natural when one considers that the great majority of them are not freed from the rounds of rebirth.

Sympathetic joy (*muditā*) is closely tied with compassion, as compassionate sympathy gives way to happiness at the thriving of others. When one can take pleasure in the achievements and happiness of others, envy or resentment (leading to anger) are kept in check. Śāntideva suggests that the latter are traits that deceive and disturb the practitioner from 'the feeling of sympathetic joy', which must not be derailed 'even at the arrival of something extremely unwelcome' (Bca.VI.9). Allowing *muditā* to persist, even in the face of what is unwholesome, keeps a positive mind towards others regardless of their wrongdoing towards you. One should note that, as with all the *brahmavihārā*s, a distinctive sense of strength is implied for the practitioner, a resilience that can be maintained through these meditative practices.

Upekkhā will elaborate and consolidate the value of *mettā* with particular reference to this universality. Nyanaponika Thera clarifies:

> Equanimity rooted in insight is the guiding and restraining power for the other three sublime states. It points out to them the direction they have to take, and sees to it that this direction is followed . . . it endows it [loving-kindness] with the great virtue of patience. (Nyanaponika Thera 1998, 23)

Upekkhā is, in fact, a logical conclusion when considering that anger does not originate with the wrongdoer, who is more a vehicle for the action rather than its prime cause. Equanimity considers all of us players in a complex causality, the heart of Buddhist metaphysics. As such, there is no use in attaching one's ideas of anger to another person, as humanity is bound together in this web of causality. More than just a comment on humanity's interpersonal relations, it provides striking insight into the common causal conditioning behind unwholesome states such as anger. We return here to the interrelationships commented upon by the *Bodhicaryāvatāra*. Śāntideva considers: 'Everything is dependent upon something else. Even that thing upon which each is dependent is not independent. Since, like a magical display, phenomena do not initiate activity, at what does one get angry . . . ?' (Bca.IV.31). As such, the virtue of *khanti* may be directly linked with the *brahmavihārā*s, as they – beginning with loving-kindness – become meditative practices to encourage the fulfilment of patience in response to anger.

Mettā in IHL

The effective dissemination of IHL rests on educational programmes that inform people the world over as to its rules and purpose. This sound knowledge of IHL remains a 'condition of respect [for IHL]' (ICRC 2003). These programmes often work to incorporate the study of the law into the training of the armed forces, who ultimately will have the main responsibility for adhering to it. Yet public authorities among states must also work to make knowledge of humanitarian law well understood by the civilian population, including the specific laws of IHL. Familiarising both civilian and military populations with IHL contributes to a broad understanding and respect for the law. In situations where combatants are inevitably recruited as ordinary citizens, this has direct consequences on increasing awareness of IHL among active participants in the conflict. A practice of forgiveness and non-retaliation as expressed through *khanti* and facilitated by *mettā* may be integrated into such programmes, opening its benefits to secular and non-secular persons of all spiritual traditions. During conflict, it becomes even more imperative to step up the understanding of IHL, and the methods it may take to reduce *dukkha* become even more pertinent. As such, proposing the reasons for a doctrine of forbearance as practised through loving-kindness meditation, demonstrating how and why it works, can serve to aid IHL in reducing the potential for misery in war.

As custodians of IHL, the International Committee of the Red Cross (ICRC) works to promote knowledge and implementation of IHL alongside providing aid to the victims of conflict (ICRC 2009, 6). Four approaches are taken in its work, namely the protection approach (to protect both the dignity and lives of those suffering under armed conflict), the assistance approach (assisting victims through addressing the consequences of armed conflict), the cooperation approach (coordinating relief efforts during armed conflict) and the prevention approach (the attempt to prevent suffering through the promotion of IHL and other humanitarian principles) (ICRC 2009, 14–16). A prevention approach works to 'foster an environment that is conducive to respect for the lives and dignity of those who may be adversely affected by armed conflict' (ICRC 2009, 16). This will involve communication and promotion of IHL by influencing parties who may have a direct impact on the fate of those living under conflict. To incorporate here a practice of loving-kindness through meditation and the kind of unpacking of causality involved in the development of *khanti* may encourage a similar respect for the values of tolerance and forgiveness. Often it is the emotional weight of victimisation that inspires claimed justifications for further violations of humanitarian law (Muñoz-Rojas and Frésard 2004, 8–10). *Mettā* addresses the vengeful impulse, guiding the practitioner to see unchecked anger for what it is, reemphasising the message of IHL that there are no justifications for retributive acts that violate international law. By reducing suffering in the present through *mettā* and *khanti*, the future manifestation of suffering is avoided. This may easily form part of a multi-disciplinary approach in promoting a culture of forgiveness across various situations of conflict.

War is both traumatic and devastating, yet Buddhism does not question that the cultivation of forbearance is possible even in the most egregious of circumstances. As in the *Kakacūpama Sutta*, *khanti* is understood as unshakeable and having far-reaching benefits. It is not to be pushed aside in war; rather, the canonical literature uses war as among the most pertinent examples of when the value of patience is necessary. Its consequences for the present moment, achieved through meditation, carry across time in eliminating lasting anger and breaking the cycle of continuing conflict. The integration of *mettā* with the instructional programmes of IHL therefore offers a potential application for both present crises and long-term planning. Appleby (2012, 354) observes: 'Peacebuilding, which encompasses conflict prevention, conflict resolution, and post-violence social reconstruction, operates according to a long-term horizon. Religions, accustomed to thinking and enacting missions in larger blocs of time, bring distinctive and essential resources to this sustained activity'.

Here we see the potential for Buddhist teachings and practices to influence and aid the work of IHL practitioners, not only in an ongoing conflict but past the point of its ending. These ideas are not just abstractions, but highly practical methods created for the alleviation of suffering. Buddhism recognises that changing the present will change the future. To incorporate a practice of *khanti* into the application of IHL, through *mettā*, may radically decrease the prevalence of suffering during conflict.

Conclusion

It is true to say that Buddhism, as a religion and ethical system, does not see any virtue in violence. However, the popular perception of Buddhism as therefore immutably opposed to warfare often shuts down any productive conversation regarding its value during such circumstances. Yet conversations about this possibility are necessary if we are to establish that Buddhist ethics can, and will, help complement humanitarian systems in wartime.

Buddhist teaching reveals a mutual compatibility with the aims and principles of IHL in lessening the impact of suffering during wartime. The virtue of *khanti* has often been emphasised by canonical and commentarial literature as advantageous precisely in the face of extreme adversity, and reveals Buddhist authors grappling with the realities of conflict. The establishing of *khanti*, a *patient, forgiving forbearance*, is explicitly contrasted with the unwholesome qualities of anger. To deal with the consequences of anger, the virtue is supported by the Buddhist non-acceptance of an essential self, an unpacking of causality, as well as the greater ethical framework of establishing what actions are wholesome or otherwise. *Khanti* therefore may complement the work of IHL in encouraging an environment of non-retaliation, where unlawful retributive acts are tempered by addressing the underlying anger.

Considering the Buddhist proposal of *mettā* as an antidote to hatred and anger, this paper has proposed that the capacity for *khanti* may be developed through loving-kindness meditation, supported by the other *brahmavihārās*. To date, the practice of mindfulness has been found advantageous in secular contexts such as schools and universities across the world; in recent years, its benefits have been extended to military and humanitarian institutions to lessen the impact of conflict. *Mettā*, however, is still underdeveloped as a potential tool in these environments. What some have called 'kindfulness' (Brahm 2016) is a good complement to mindfulness. Its cultivation of patience in subduing anger is just one advantage it may have for wartime. Further research in this area may prove useful in establishing its practical value to the work of IHL.

Abbreviations

AN *Aṅguttara Nikāya*, Bodhi (2012) translation, cited by *nipāta* and *sutta*.

Bca *Bodhicaryāvatāra*, Crosby and Skilton (1998) translation, cited by chapter and verse number.

Dhp *Dhammapada*, Roebuck (2010) translation, cited by verse number.

MN *Majjhima Nikāya*, Bodhi and Ñāṇamoli (1995) translation, cited by *sutta* number or volume and page number of Pali Text Society Pali edition.

SN *Saṃyutta Nikāya*, Bodhi (2000) translation, cited by *saṃyutta* and *sutta* number.

Vism *Visuddhimagga*, Ñāṇamoli (1991) translation, cited by chapter and section number.

Disclosure statement

This article has been supported by the International Committee of the Red Cross (ICRC).

ORCID

Alex Wakefield http://orcid.org/0000-0002-8052-4554

References

Appleby, R. S. 2012. "Religion, Violence and the Right to Peace." In *Religion and Human Rights*, edited by J. Witte Jr. and C. M. Green, 346–359. New York: Oxford University Press.

Bodhi, B., trans. 2000. *The Connected Discourses of the Buddha: A Translation of the Saṃyutta Nikāya*. Boston: Wisdom.

Bodhi, B., trans. 2012. *The Numerical Discourses of the Buddha: A Translation of the Aṅguttara Nikāya*. Boston: Wisdom.

Bodhi, B. 1978. "A Treatise on the Pāramīs." Translated from the *Cariyāpiṭaka* Commentary. In *The Discourse on the All-embracing New of Views: The Brahmajāla Sutta and Its Commentaries*, edited by B. Bodhi, 254–330. Kandy: Buddhist Publication Society.

Bodhi, B., and B. Ñāṇamoli, trans. 1995. *The Middle Length Discourses of the Buddha: A Translation of the Majjhima Nikāya*. Boston: Wisdom.

Brahm, A. 2016. *Kindfulness*. Boston: Wisdom.

Crosby, K., and A. Skilton, trans. 1998. *Śāntideva: The Bodhicaryāvatāra*. Oxford and New York: Oxford University Press.

Edelglass, W. 2009. "The Bodhisattva Path: Śāntideva's *Bodhicaryāvatāra*." In *Buddhist Philosophy: Essential Readings*, edited by W. Edelglass and J. A. Garfield, 388–399. Oxford and New York: Oxford University Press.

Gowans, C. W. 2013. "Ethical Thought in Indian Buddhism." In *A Companion to Buddhist Philosophy*, edited by S. M. Emmanuel, 429–451. Oxford: Wiley-Blackwell.

Harvey, P. 2000. *An Introduction to Buddhist Ethics: Foundations, Values and Issues*. Cambridge: Cambridge University Press.

Horner, I. B. 1957. *Ten Jātaka Stories, Each Illustrating One of the Ten Pāramitā with Pali Text*. London: Luzac.

ICRC. 2002. *Implementing International Humanitarian Law: From Law to Action*. ICRC. https://www.icrc.org/en/document/implementing-international-humanitarian-law-law-action

ICRC. 2003. *The Obligation to Disseminate International Humanitarian Law*. ICRC. https://www.icrc.org/en/document/obligation-disseminate-international-humanitarian-law-factsheet

ICRC. 2009. *The ICRC: Its Mission and Work*. Geneva: ICRC.

ICRC. 2014. *What is international humanitarian law?* ICRC. https://www.icrc.org/en/document/what-international-humanitarian-law

ICRC. 2017. *Amnesties and International Humanitarian Law: Purpose and Scope*. ICRC. https://www.icrc.org/en/document/amnesties-and-ihl-purpose-and-scope

King, S. B. 2013. "War and Peace in Buddhist Philosophy." In *A Companion to Buddhist Philosophy*, edited by S. M. Emmanuel, 631–650. Oxford: Wiley-Blackwell.

Melzer, N. 2016. *International Humanitarian Law: A Comprehensive Introduction*. Geneva: ICRC.

Muñoz-Rojas, D., and J. Frésard. 2004. *The Roots of Behaviour in War: Understanding and Preventing IHL Violations*. Geneva: ICRC.

Ñāṇamoli, B., trans. 1991. *The Path of Purification (Visuddhimagga)*. Kandy: Buddhist Publication Society.

Nyanaponika Thera. 1998. *The Four Sublime States: Contemplations on Love, Compassion, Sympathetic Joy, and Equanimity*. Kandy: Buddhist Publication Society. https://www.accesstoinsight.org/lib/authors/nyanaponika/wheel006.html

Rhys Davids, C. A. F., trans. 1974 (2012 reprint). *A Buddhist Manual of Psychological Ethics*. 3rd ed. Bristol: Pali Text Society.

Roebuck, V., trans. 2010. *The Dhammapada*. London: Penguin Books.

Shaw, S., trans. 2006. *The Jātakas: Birth Stories of the Bodhisatta*. New Delhi and New York: Penguin Books.

Skilton, A. 2002. "An Early Mahāyāna Transformation of the Story of *Kṣāntivādin* - 'The Teacher of Forbearance'." *Buddhist Studies Review* 19 (2): 115–136.

Southwold, M. 2003. "Buddhism and Evil." In *Philosophy of Religion: An Anthology*, edited by C. Taliaferro and P. Griffiths, 424–431. Hoboken: Blackwell.

Ṭhānissaro Bhikkhu. 2011. "Reconciliation, Right & Wrong." *Access to Insight (BCBS Edition)*. https://www.accesstoinsight.org/lib/authors/thanissaro/reconciliation.html

Ṭhānissaro Bhikkhu, trans. 2013. "Dighavu-kumara Vatthu: The Story of Prince Dighavu." Mv 10.2.3-20. *Access to Insight (BCBS Edition)*. https://www.accesstoinsight.org/tipitaka/vin/mv/mv.10.02.03-20.than.html

Whitehill, J. 2000. "Buddhism and the Virtues." In *Contemporary Buddhist Ethics*, edited by D. Keown, 17–36. Richmond: Curzon Press.

ICRC

RESTRAINT IN WARFARE AND APPAMĀDA: THE CONCEPT OF COLLATERAL DAMAGE IN INTERNATIONAL HUMANITARIAN LAW IN LIGHT OF THE BUDDHA'S LAST WORDS

Bhagya Samarakoon

ABSTRACT

In international humanitarian law (IHL), collateral damage to civilians caught in warfare is restrained through the rule of proportionality. The first part of this chapter explains how this increasingly controversial area is dependent on the perceptions, values and good faith of the military commander in the specific instance. In determining which Buddhist teachings can guide the mind in this grey area, the quality of *appamāda*, 'heedfulness', is significant. The Buddha refers to it several times in his sermons (*suttas*) and, most importantly, included it in his final words before his demise. The second part explores what the Buddha meant by *appamāda* and argues that the concept has a moral dimension useful in decision-making for Buddhists engaged in warfare. The third part discusses Emperor Ashoka to whom the monk Nigrodha preached the *Appamāda Vagga*. The change in Emperor Ashoka's manner of ruling and conquering as manifested in his many edict inscriptions proves that Buddhist values can be practically applied by the laity, not just monastics. The fourth analyses how *appamāda* could guide the minds of Buddhists engaged in warfare, and proposes that this could be done through sermons (to transform intention) and meditation (to aid such transformation).

Introduction

International humanitarian law (IHL) has made great strides in regulating the conduct of hostilities. However, implementation of IHL is not wholly successful without genuine commitment to its ideals. This necessitates establishing that IHL is not a foreign body of law but that its core principles of humanity and reducing suffering are also found in local religions. With this broad aim in view, this chapter seeks to build a dialogue between IHL and Buddhism by examining how the Buddha's teachings can ensure greater compliance with

DOI: 10.4324/9781003439820-17

IHL among Buddhist communities. This article is presented in four parts. The first discusses collateral damage, its controversial nature and the issue of subjectivity from an IHL perspective. The second deals with the concept of *appamāda*, 'heedfulness', and how it can guide decision-making in instances of potential collateral damage to civilians. The third part discusses the positive impact of Buddhism in times of war in relation to the conversion of Emperor Ashoka to whom the monk or novice Nigrodha famously preached the *Appamāda-vagga*, and the fourth explores how in modern times, Buddhist monks could play a role in influencing Buddhists engaged in warfare through sermons and discussions. This analysis is based on the teachings and practices of Theravāda Buddhism as it is practised in Sri Lanka.

The broad aim of this article is to identify how a particular Buddhist concept or teaching can be interpreted in warfare to reduce suffering. Despite certain limitations in this study, one necessarily finds that the two disciplines can meet on some plane, because both have the aim of addressing human suffering, albeit from different perspectives.

Collateral damage

The concept

In this section, I shall first explain collateral damage, which is an increasingly controversial concept in IHL. The International Committee of the Red Cross (ICRC) glossary of terms used in IHL defines 'collateral damage' as

> the incidental damage, loss or injury that is caused to civilians and civilian objects in the course of an attack against a legitimate military target despite the taking of all necessary precautions to prevent or to minimise such damage, loss or injury. (ICRC 2009, 5)

The rule of proportionality in *jus in bello* restrains collateral damage. It is a principle of IHL that requires that the expected civilian deaths, injuries to civilians and damage to civilian objects incidental to an attack on a military objective must not be excessive compared to the military advantage anticipated from that attack (ICRC 2009, 11). At the diplomatic conference leading to the adoption of Additional Protocol I (AP I) to the Geneva Conventions, several states expressed concern that the principle of proportionality contained a danger for the protection of the civilian population because it meant that incidental loss of civilian life could be justified in some instances, but conceded that there was no workable alternative solution (ICRC 2005, 46–47).

AP I codifies the rule of proportionality. It provides that one should refrain from launching any attack that may be expected to cause incidental loss to civilian life, injury to civilians, damage to civilian objects or a combination thereof which would be excessive in relation to the concrete and direct military advantage anticipated (Article 51(5) b). Relatedly, Article 57 of AP

I elaborates on the manner in which all feasible precautions should be taken to avoid and, in any event, minimise incidental loss to civilians (ICRC 1977). With regard to non-international armed conflicts, there is no express reference to the principle of proportionality in Additional Protocol II to the Geneva Conventions (AP II). However, it has been argued that it is inherent in the principle of humanity explicitly mentioned in its provisions (ICRC 2005, 48). Apart from this, recent treaty law (e.g. Amended Protocol II to the Convention on Conventional Weapons) and military manuals (e.g. of Canada, Croatia, Germany, South Africa) also reiterate the applicability of the principle to non-international armed conflicts (ICRC 2005, 48).

Further, Rule 14 of the ICRC Customary IHL Study affirms that the provisions of AP I Article 51(5) b reflect the state of customary IHL, applicable in both international and non-international armed conflicts (ICRC 2005, 46). This is important because customary IHL is binding on all parties to a conflict, independent of treaty law. The customary nature of the rule has also been mentioned in some jurisprudence of various international tribunals. For instance, the *Military Junta* case judgement by the National Appeals Court of Argentina and the *Martić* case of the International Criminal Tribunal for Yugoslavia (ICTY) can be considered. In the latter case, Martić was charged with wanton destruction of villages and attacks on civilians among other charges. The Trial Chamber in this instance emphasised that disproportionate attacks could not be justified in relation to such concepts as distinction and collateral damage (ICTY 2007, 29, 35).

In the 'Advisory Opinion of the International Court of Justice (ICJ 1996a) on the Legality of the Threat or Use of Nuclear Weapons', the opinion of the Court considers the concept of proportionality in determining the legality of the use or threat of use of nuclear weapons. The dissenting opinion of Judge Weeramantry (the Sri Lankan-born jurist Christopher Gregory Weeramantry, 1926–2017, who has also written about Buddhism and IHL) is based on the proposition that the use or threat of use of nuclear weapons is illegal in any circumstances whatsoever (ICJ 1996b, 433). This opinion maintained that the principles of humanitarian law governed this situation and that from the very beginning, humanitarian law took into account a realistic perception of the brutalities of war, and the need to restrain them in accordance with the dictates of humanity. The opinion of Judge Weeramantry concludes with a reference to the appeal in the Russell–Einstein Manifesto to 'remember your humanity and forget the rest', without which the risk arises of universal death (ICJ 1996b, 554).

Nevertheless, whether the principle of proportionality is customary international law is debated by some scholars, and therefore its effect on states that have not ratified AP I is uncertain.

Controversies and new standards

The concept of collateral damage has been described as perhaps the most puzzling and subjective concept in IHL (Sloane 2015, 301–302). This article looks to Buddhist teachings, which can be made relevant to this area due to three main factors. First, while IHL offers guidelines in the practical application of the rule of proportionality, some inadequacy remains. Secondly, unforeseen developments in modern warfare add complexities. Thirdly, there is an inherent issue which is that claiming innocent lives are collateral damage is ethically unacceptable.

If the first factor is considered, it is clear that experts have attempted to reduce the subjectivity embedded in the concept mainly through the introduction of the 'reasonable military commander' standard. This standard first seems to appear in the 'Final Report to the Prosecutor by the Committee Established to Review the NATO Bombing Campaign Against the Federal Republic of Yugoslavia' (ICTY 2000, 15). In black and white cases, it would be very easy to decide whether the incidental loss is acceptable or not, but most instances are not black and white. When we add into the equation the fact that the speculation of incommensurables has to be done *ex ante* (before the event, based on forecasts rather than actual results) and under pressure, assessment of acceptable loss is not easy (Sloane 2015, 312). Further, as the Final Report mentioned above states, 'commanders with different doctrinal backgrounds and differing degrees of combat experience or national military histories would not always agree in close cases' (Fenrick 2009, 279). The implication is that the standard of reasonableness introduced to reduce subjectivity is itself subject to some subjectivity.

Even experts cannot agree on an exact definition for collateral damage or what amounts to collateral damage in a given situation. At the International Experts Meeting 2016 on the Principle of Proportionality, in Quebec, it was agreed that there are definitional problems with regard to when damage is concrete and direct and in what circumstances damage could be said to be excessive. There are also difficulties in defining and identifying instances of reverberating effects and dynamic targeting, as opposed to pre-planned deliberate targeting (ICRC 2016, 224). Reverberating effects are consequences that are not directly and immediately caused by an attack but which are nevertheless a result of the attack. Dynamic targeting occurs when a target was not anticipated, such as when targets are passed to aircraft already airborne as hostile forces are identified, thereby limiting the opportunity for comprehensive target analysis. In contrast, pre-planned deliberate targeting, as the term conveys, occurs when a target is anticipated beforehand and information on it is comprehensively analysed within a longer time frame (Schmitt 2009, 337; Roorda 2015, 158).

Secondly, the changing face of modern warfare increases the possibility of civilian losses. Perhaps the main factor contributing to this is that warfare is shifting from 'traditional battlefields' to densely populated urban areas. One need only look at the recent conflict in Syria to fully grasp the gravity of this fact. Another reason is the prevalence of non-international armed conflicts (NIACs) and other internal armed conflicts (rather than international armed conflicts) with the result that in most instances, the non-state belligerent parties resort to such tactics as guerrilla fighting and the use of human shields, all of which make the civilian population caught in the midst of the battle more vulnerable (ICRC 2017).

Thirdly, at issue is whether death, injury and other losses to civilians are justifiable even as collateral damage. In IHL too, civilians and civilian objectives have been granted considerable protection, most notably in the principle of distinction, which states that civilians and civilian objectives may never be directly targeted in attack (ICRC 2005, 3). While there are widely differing opinions on this, the short answer would be that while it is not morally acceptable or justified, in practical terms it is acceptable.

Determining the practical application of the rule of proportionality is difficult as it offers no binary answer. The example of a soldier who decided to fire a weapon that could malfunction and so detonate before reaching the target 5% of the time, and might therefore kill numerous civilians, is illustrative of this situation. Here there is a low risk of a high amount of collateral damage. The reverse situation could also obtain, where there is a high risk of a low amount of collateral damage (Sloane 2015, 314).

Notwithstanding the controversial aspect of the concept of collateral damage, this article does not attempt to address any of these controversies. Instead, it will examine the subjectivity embedded in the concept. It cannot be denied that there is an element of subjectivity in decision-making in the practical application of the rule of proportionality, and in many instances proportionality could be a value judgement. The Commentary to AP I, referring to this, states:

> it seemed necessary to leave a *fairly broad margin of appreciation* to those who will have to apply the rules. Thus, their effectiveness will depend to a large extent on the *good faith of the belligerents* and on their *wish to conform to the requirements of humanity*. (ICRC 1987, 589, emphasis added)

While this leeway is necessary, it could in reality transform itself into a grey area for decision-making, which in turn means that collateral damage (justifiable in IHL) could easily become 'wanton destruction', which is never acceptable. The concept of collateral damage itself is controversial, but what is more problematic is that the subjectivity inherent in the concept makes way for increasing 'wanton destruction' in the guise of collateral damage (Bica

2007). Wanton destruction can be defined as violence that is not justified by the principle of military necessity in IHL. However, there have been instances where belligerents attempt to justify such violence by trying to pass it off as collateral damage (Bica 2007). In an area rife with such controversy there is a need to explore which Buddhist teachings might guide combatants in their decision-making.

Appamāda – heedfulness

The concept of appamāda

An exploration of the concept of *appamāda* demonstrates that it was an integral idea in early Buddhism. It has been variously rendered as heedfulness, conscientiousness, care, non-complacency and sometimes mindfulness (Glossology s.v. *appamāda*), and Bhikkhu Bodhi renders it 'diligence' in his *Saṃyutta Nikāya* (SN) translation (Bodhi 2000, 77, 179). These different terms highlight the fact that it is hard to find an exact equivalent of the term in English. Something is lost in translation. Buddhologist Ernst Steinkellner renders the concept into German as '*wachsame Sorge*', 'watchful/vigilant care' (cited in Batchelor 2005, 8). When broken into the constituent parts, it is '*a* + *(p)pa* + *māda*'. The prefix '*a*' is a negative signifying the absence of the quality described (when the negative 'a' is added before the '(p)pamāda', it signifies that the quality of 'pamāda' is absent). The root word is '*mad*' which means intoxication. Some related words are '*matta*' (maddened, intoxicated) and '*majja*' (intoxication). '*Pa*' is a prefix signifying that the action is carried to extremes (Jayarava 2009). Thus *pamajja* would be not only 'drunkenness' but 'blind drunkenness' to an extent that it is delinquent and is a source of danger to others. *Appamāda*, then, is the opposite of this and is further elaborated as the vivid, clear watchfulness one might have when confronted with a poisonous snake or a hungry tiger (Jayarava 2009). This metaphor is significant as it shows the standard of heedfulness one needs to exercise at all times and especially before making decisions that could impact on oneself and others. Metaphorically, the 'dangerous beast' is the passions, prejudice, hatred, lack of clarity and rashness that can cloud one's mind.

Why appamāda?

But why is *appamāda* being considered in the context of this article? Why not any other Buddhist teaching? The quality of *appamāda* is clearly a skill vital in our daily actions, as the Pali Canon refers to it repeatedly. For instance, the *Appamāda Sutta* (SN 3.17, Thanissaro Bhikkhu 2013) recounts the tale of how King Pasenadi asked the Buddha whether there was any one quality which could bring benefit in both this life and the lives to come. The Buddha replies by saying that this one quality is *appamāda*, which, just as the footprint of the elephant can encompass the footprint of all other animals, contains and is supreme among all qualities (Batchelor 2005, 9).

The *Dhammapada* (v. 21), in the chapter called *Appamāda-vagga*, says that heedfulness is the path to deathlessness:

> By sustained effort, discipline and self-control, the wise man makes for himself an island, which no flood overflows [An island on a higher level cannot be flooded by the floods of sense desire – (*kāma*), false beliefs (*diṭṭhi*), craving for existence (*bhava*) and ignorance (*avijjā*)]. (*Dhammapada* v. 25, translation by Narada Thera 1954, 27)

Monk Nigrodha preached the *Appamāda-vagga* to Emperor Ashoka and the concept seems to have made a deep impression on him, as will be discussed later. Further, the *Saṃyutta Nikāya* contains an *Appamāda-vagga* (SN.45.139–148) as well as many scattered *suttas* on *appamāda* (SN.1.36; 3.17–18; 12.22; 20.1–2; 35.97; 35.134; 46.31; 48.56; 55.40).

While the *Mahā-parinibbāna Sutta* does not elaborate on this quality, despite being the longest *sutta* in the canon, and covering the final three months of the Buddha's life, it further heightens the significance the Buddha gave to the concept in recording his last words as follows:

> Handa dāni bhikkhave āmantayāmi vo:
>
> Vayadhammā sankhārā appamādena sampādetha
>
> Behold now, bhikkhus [monks], I exhort you:
>
> All compounded things are subject to vanish. Strive with earnestness!
>
> (*Mahāparinibbānna Sutta* v. 324, DN 16, 6.8 (DN.II.156), translation by Sister Vajira and F. Story 1998)

As Batchelor comments, the Buddha, as an experienced teacher of almost 45 years, was aware of the impending end of his life, and would have looked for a unifying concept embracing all that he had preached to be part of his last words (Batchelor 2005, 9). *Appamāda* is, then, a rich and significant concept that Ven. Nārada justly sums up as the ethical essence of Buddhism (Narada Thera 1954, 24).

Appamāda is also associated with the quality of restraint and therefore is possibly the most relevant quality one could cultivate for awareness of one's actions and their consequences:

> If one dwells with restraint (*saṃvara*) over the eye faculty, the mind is not soiled among forms cognizable by the eye. If the mind is not soiled, gladness is born. When one is gladdened, rapture is born. When the mind is uplifted by rapture, the body becomes tranquil. One tranquil in body experiences happiness. The mind of one who is happy becomes concentrated. When the mind is concentrated, phenomena become manifest [*dhammānaṃ pātubhāvā*], one is reckoned as 'one who dwells diligently'. (Jayarava 2009)

As maintained throughout this article, the issue with the concept of collateral damage is that it leaves a margin of discretion for those applying the rule of proportionality. Thus, restraint over the sense organs and mind in decision-making is necessary and *appamāda* as a quality could guide individuals for their own betterment in terms of merit (good karma) and benefit both themselves and others through reduced suffering.

Since the control of the mind is central in decision-making, analysis of the thought process in Buddhist metaphysics is relevant. As shown in Table 1, there are altogether 52 mental factors (*cetasika*) which can, in different combinations, go into the making of a given consciousness (*citta*). Out of these, seven are called 'universals' or 'essentials' because all of them are present in all states of consciousness. Then there are six more that are called 'particulars' because they are not invariably present in consciousness. They can be part of a wholesome or unwholesome consciousness, and their presence intensifies its strength. Next there are 14 unwholesome mental factors, and these associate with the 13 factors mentioned above (the universals and particulars) in various combinations to give rise to an unwholesome consciousness, as shown in Figure 1 (Baptist 2008, 2–5).

Then, there are 19 beautiful or wholesome mental factors and six additional beautiful or wholesome factors. All the 19 factors have to be present to give rise to any beautiful or wholesome consciousness. As we can see in Figure 2, when these 25 wholesome mental factors (with the 19 wholesome factors necessarily present) combine in different ways with the 13 factors ('universals' and 'particulars') mentioned before, they can give rise to a wholesome consciousness (Baptist 2008, 2–5).

It is important to observe that this analysis indicates a beautiful consciousness requires more mental factors to go into its making than the number of mental factors needed to form an unwholesome consciousness. A necessary implication of this would be that doing what is good or wholesome is harder and requires more effort, whereas it is easier for an unwholesome consciousness to arise.

Appamāda can be translated and understood as 'mindfulness' and as a mental quality that is related to *manasikāra, ekaggatā, viriya*, etc., but it does not appear in the list of *cetasikas* (52 mental factors), given in Table 1. Rather than a separate state of mind, *appamāda* might be best seen as a quality with which one might try to imbue *sati* (Lomas 2015). *Appamāda* is thus, a quality that must be carefully cultivated to control one's mind through

Table 1. The 52 mental factors (*cetasika*) listed in Theravāda *Abhidhamma*.

The seven essentials or universals (*sabba-citta -sādhārana*)	1. Contact (*phassa*)
	2. Feeling (*vedanā*)
	3. Perception (*saññā*)
	4. Volition (*cetanā*)
	5. One-pointedness (*ekaggatā*)
	6. Psychic life (*jīvitindritya*)
	7. Attention or mental advertence (*manasikāra*)
The six particulars (*pakiṇṇaka*)	1. Initial application (*vitakka*)
	2. Sustained application (*vicāra*)
	3. Deciding (*adhimokkha*)
	4. Effort (*viriya*)
	5. Interest, joy (*pīti*)
	6. Desire-to-do or intention (*chanda*)
The 14 unwholesome mental factors (*akusala cetasika*)	1. Dullness or delusion (*moha*)
	2. Lack of moral self-respect (*ahirika*)
	3. Lack of concern for consequences of actions (*anottappa*)
	4. Restlessness (*uddhacca*)
	5. Greed (*lobha*)
	6. Wrong view (*diṭṭhi*)
	7. Conceit (*māna*)
	8. Hate (*dosa*)
	9. Envy (*issā*)
	10. Sloth (*thīna*)
	11. Torpor (*middha*)
	12. Selfishness (*macchariya*)
	13. Sceptical doubt (*vicikicchā*)
	14. Worry (*kukkucca*)
The 19 essential beautiful (wholesome) mental factors (*sobhana cetasika*)	1. Faith (*saddhā*)
	2. Mindfulness (*sati*)
	3. Self-respect/sense of moral integrity (*hiri*)
	4. Concern for consequences of actions (*ottappa*)
	5. Non-greed (*alobha*)
	6. Non-hate, amity (*adosa*)
	7. Equipoise (*tatra-majjhattatā*)
	The six pairs:
	8. and 9. Composure/tranquillity (*passaddhi*) of mental properties and of mind
	10. and 11. Buoyancy (*lahutā*) of mental properties and of mind
	12. and 13. Pliancy (*mudutā*) of mental properties and of mind
	14. and 15. Fitness to work (*kammaññatā*) of mental properties and of mind
	16. and 17. Proficiency (*pāguññatā*) of mental properties and of mind
	18. and 19. Rectitude/straightforwardness (*ujjukatā*) of mental properties and of mind

(*Continued*)

Table 1. (Continued).

The six additional beautiful mental factors	The three abstinences: 1. Right speech (*sammā-vācā*) 2. Right action (*sammā-kammanta*) 3. Right livelihood (*sammā-ājīva*) The two illimitables (*appamañña*): 4. Compassion (*karuṇā*) and 5. Appreciative joy (*muditā*) 6. Wisdom (*paññā*)

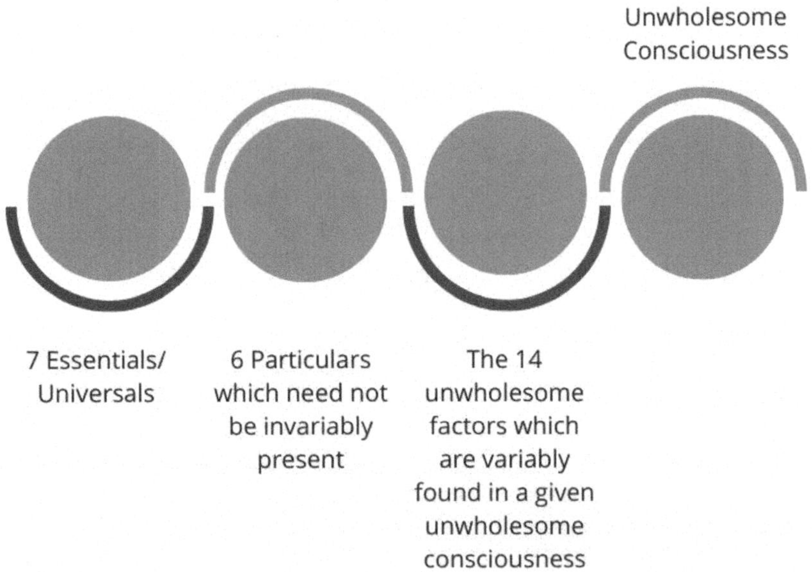

Figure 1. The combination of mental factors in an unwholesome consciousness.

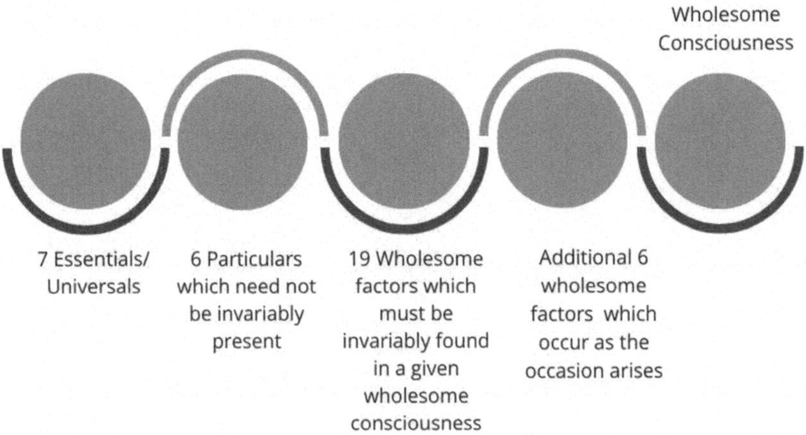

Figure 2. The combination of mental factors in a wholesome consciousness.

heedfulness of *cetasikas*. It has been said that the prime importance of *appamāda* is that it introduces an ethical dimension to mindfulness practice. One is not just aware of what is happening (i.e. *sati*); one explicitly connects it to Buddhist teachings on ethics and morality (Lomas 2015). Hence, the quality of *appamāda* (heedfulness) would be vital in energetically guarding one's consciousness against the arising of an unwholesome consciousness.

Emperor Ashoka – a character study

Conversion to Buddhism (transforming intention)

None would deny that Ashoka (mid-third-century BCE) was one of those Buddhist rulers who left his mark on the religion that had influenced so many aspects of his political vision. His own inscription records that he sent missionaries – termed messengers of Dharma – to outlying regions and countries, while the Sri Lankan chronicles relate how he sent his own son Mahinda Thera to the island as one such missionary (Guruge 1993, 157–160).

Some scholars believe that there was a subtle political design in these attempts to propagate Buddhism – or at least Dharma in a broader sense – in neighbouring regions. This seems to be especially pertinent in Sri Lanka, to which country he also – again, according the island's chronicles – sent the Mauryan regalia inviting his friend Tissa, the king of Sri Lanka, to perform a second coronation according to the Mauryan tradition and embrace Buddhism as he himself had done (Guruge 1993, 407). If the significance of the powerful Mauryan emperor instructing the ruler of the neighbouring island in this manner is examined critically, one would have to agree that the above view, namely that there was political design in Ashoka's attempts to spread Dharma, is not so far off the mark. However, the approach taken by Ashoka also indicates the influence Buddhism had on his character and worldview. Where earlier he would have set off with armies to conquer regions, here he is sending missionaries. Instead of following his previous policy of conquest through violence and intimidation, he had in the course of a few years shifted to a policy of conquest by Dharma (*dhamma-vijaya*) (Guruge 1993, 490–491). One could argue that Ashoka had come to a position from which he could influence neighbouring rulers with such non-violent methods because of the terrible wars he had launched earlier and the fierce reputation he had built upon them. This article does not present the view that wars should be prevented altogether, but that violence and suffering should be minimised during armed conflicts that are to some extent inevitable. This makes Ashoka an important figure in our consideration of Buddhism and IHL.

In assessing the impact Buddhist teachings could have on Buddhists engaged in warfare, one could look to the conversion of Emperor Ashoka and the influence it had on his world view. According to the *Mahāvaṃsa* (v. 189), Ashoka was earlier called *Candāśoka* 'Ashoka the Wicked' because of his evil deeds (Guruge 1993, 74). Other sources explain that this epithet was conferred on him for fratricide, the killing of 99 half-brothers in his wars of succession (Guruge 1993, 78–81). Ananda Guruge mentions that there is a difference between the portrayal of Ashoka in the Northern Buddhist sources (the *Divyāvadāna* and Chinese and Tibetan Buddhist sources) and that provided in the Pali sources of Sri Lanka. The former portrays Ashoka as ruthless and vicious, recounting his many evil deeds, perhaps in order to accentuate the saving grace of Buddhism. However, as many scholars including Guruge argue, these accounts are so incredible (with numerous supernatural embellishments) as to be improbable (Guruge 1993, 81–87). In contrast, the Pali sources depict Ashoka as having committed low deeds but also as an individual with a consciousness about right and wrong. For instance, the Sri Lankan chronicle, the *Dīpavaṃsa* describes the years after his ascension to the throne as a time when Ashoka actively searched for truth in religion. In his search for Dharma he invited many religious persons to the palace and questioned them. According to the *Samantapāsādikā*, this was also a search for persons with *antosāra* (inner essence) (Guruge 1993, 99). It was at this time that Ashoka came upon the monk Nigrodha, and there are two versions describing the manner in which Ashoka was converted by him. The first explains that Ashoka took refuge in the *Buddha, Dhamma* and the *Saṅgha* on the same day following a sermon on *Appamāda-vagga*, the Chapter on Heedfulness:

> Hearing the king's spirited words, Nigrodha who was well-versed in the comprehension of the nine-fold doctrine pondered over the precious Tripiṭaka. He saw the excellent discourse on Heedfulness: 'Heedfulness is the path to immortality. Heedlessness is the way to death.
>
> The heedful never die and the heedless are like the dead'. (*Dipavamsa* VI.52–53, cited in Guruge 1993, 101)

The second version, in contrast, portrays Nigrodha as a young novice whom the king saw through a palace window and, pleased by his calm demeanour, invited to the palace for a meal.

> At the end of the meal, the king asked, 'Do you know any advice given to you by your teacher?'
>
> 'I know, Great king, from one sermon'. (*Samantapāsādikā*, cited in Guruge 1993, 104)

It then describes how he expounded the *Appamāda-vagga* of the *Dhammapada* and how Ashoka, pleased with Nigrodha's manner and conduct, was introduced to other senior monks who could discourse on

Buddhism at length with the king. The *Mahāvamsa* (vv. 71–72) too does not describe the king's conversion as taking place on the same day (Guruge 1993, 102).

Dr Guruge states that in considering these sometimes contradictory accounts, what is closer to the truth and more probable is that, first, Ashoka was not wholly evil as some sources portray him to be, and, secondly, he was not miraculously converted in one day upon hearing one sermon by a young novice. In this regard, Guruge writes 'the text that a *sāmanera* of tender years is most likely to know is the *Dhammapada*. Nigrodha's statement that the verse he recited was all that he knew from one discourse is quite understandable' (Guruge 1993, 105–108).

This fact is quite important for the furtherance of the idea presented in this article because it shows the effect that Buddhism has had on ordinary individuals, much like the average individual one would find in military forces in modern times – a person who is neither wholly evil nor saintly but something in between. Secondly and more importantly, it shows that Ashoka did not in one day convert to Buddhism but that it was a gradual process beginning from his growing consciousness about right and wrong, which aspect will now be examined as a character study for the quality of *appamāda* in the context of his edicts and inscriptions. It is best to analyse the impact of Buddhist teachings on Asoka through what he has expressed in these, rather than any other historical source, because they show who he was, or aspired to be, in his own words (it should be noted that in his inscriptions, Ashoka describes his own conversion as owing mainly to the carnage he witnessed during the Kaliṅga War).

Appamāda as manifested in Ashoka inscriptions

One cannot conclusively state that *appamāda*, the quality described in the first sermon preached by the monk Nigrodha to the emperor, made a significant change in the emperor's character. It is more likely that a combination of teachings by the Buddhist monks that the emperor began to associate with would have been instrumental in transforming his character. However, it can be argued that this particular Buddhist concept made a deep impression on Ashoka as ideas similar to heedfulness appear quite often in his inscriptions.

For instance, in his first Major Rock Edict, Ashoka recounts how he reduced the number of animals killed for food in the palace kitchens, manifesting how Ashoka heeded the consequences of his own actions and restrained the killing of living beings, even though it was killing done for the purpose of sustenance. The ninth Major Rock Edict also advocates restrained behaviour towards all living beings. His fourth Major Rock Edict reflects an idea that is embedded in the concept of heedfulness: one must be always watchful of one's intentions and where one fails to guard against bad thoughts, one must not be complacent but strive again and again. In a similar vein, the fifth Major Rock Edict states that doing good is difficult. It was discussed earlier how a wholesome consciousness takes much more effort to develop than an unwholesome consciousness. This inscription captures that idea succinctly.

Further, the first Separate Edict (at Dhauli and Jaugada) to the officers and city magistrates at Tosali/Samapa states,

> you are in charge of many thousands of living beings. You should gain the affection of men. All men are my children ... You should strive to practice impartiality. But it cannot be practiced by one possessing any one of these faults – jealousy, shortness of temper, harshness, rashness, obstinacy, idleness or slackness. You should wish to avoid such faults. The root of all this is to be even tempered and not rash in your work ... (Thapar 1961, 257)

This inscription is important as it admonishes rulers and administrative officers against unwholesome thoughts. Such strenuous guarding against unwholesome thoughts would be important for belligerents to prevent them from taking hasty decisions out of unwholesome motives such as anger, obstinacy and hatred.

Buddhist concepts in practice

How can appamāda guide decision-making?

In this section, we will examine the manner in which *appamāda* can guide decision-making during warfare, by navigating with skill and care the subjectivity present in the practical application of proportionality. The concept of proportionality could in practice very easily be abused by belligerents due to wanton disregard or because of negative states of mind such as anger, hatred, prejudice or revenge.

The standards that have evolved so far in the legal sphere to guide decision-making with regard to the application of proportionality are the requirement for good faith, the desire to conform to the requirements of humanity and the 'reasonable military commander' standard. Scholars agree that while these standards might be nebulous, they are the best acceptable standards for now (Sloane 2015, 318). In contexts where compliance with legal requirements is not satisfactory and laws are flouted, we are also interested in whether Buddhism can be a compulsive force in relation to Buddhist communities in encouraging heedfulness of one's own actions. Firstly, one could ask the question, what does good faith mean to Buddhists? As good faith in belligerents is important in deciding difficult questions of proportionality, and given the emphasis on the quality of *appamāda* in summing up Buddhist teachings, the concept of *appamāda* could be used in defining good faith for Buddhists. One could argue that it means an awareness of one's own intentions and whether such intentions are bad or good, or whether one is thinking in such a way as to give rise to a wholesome consciousness.

Secondly, how would Buddhists be compelled to conform to 'the requirements of humanity'? In this instance, the compulsion to conform to an acceptable standard of conduct would be both an internal one (arising from one's own understanding of Buddhist teachings and need to adhere to such teachings) and a social one. It is here that the role of Buddhist monks and the influence they exert over the laity is crucial. When Buddhist monks advise on the manner in which one engaged in warfare should conduct himself, this creates public opinion and carries considerable weight. Belligerents who act in contravention of the requirements of humanity at both the political and military command levels would be subject to social judgement, which could also have politically adverse effects for them.

Thirdly, it has to be considered how the reasonable military commander standard would apply to Buddhists. Reasonableness, even though it is an acceptable and often used criterion in both domestic and international legal spheres, can also be subjective. Sloane writes, 'as every first-year law student learns, the number and variety of questions begged by the legal device of the reasonable person are legion, and there is a sense in which it restates rather than answers those questions' (Sloane 2015, 318). It could be said that this standard requires a commander to act with good faith and within reason in a rational manner. In acting rationally, too, the heed paid to one's intention would guide the decision maker to think with a calm mind, unclouded by negative thoughts, and of course to be careful to ascertain the facts of the situation as far as possible in the given circumstances. In this regard, it is also important to pay attention to a new theory, the *as if* theory, which dictates that a military commander should determine the acceptable levels of collateral damage *as if* the civilians at risk were civilians of his own state/group (Sloane 2015, 323–331). In the context of conflict between two belligerents belonging to two ethnic groups, for instance in the civil war between the Sri Lankan government and the Liberation Tigers of Tamil Eelam (LTTE), the Sri Lankan army, the majority of which is Sinhalese, would have to treat Tamil civilians the same as Sinhalese civilians. In Sri Lanka, this duty applies to the government in any case, since it has a responsibility towards all citizens regardless of ethnicity.

Sloane writes that while there is value in this theory, no military has ever conducted armed conflict in this manner, or even aspires to do so (Sloane 2015, 326). Perhaps, but this theory is in consonance with the high ideals of IHL, as well as Buddhist teachings such as *mettā* (loving kindness – 'just as a mother would protect her only child with her life even so let one cultivate a boundless love towards all beings') taught in the *Karaṇīyamettā Sutta* (*Karaṇīyamettā Sutta*, translation Piyadassi Thera 1999).

This article has discussed how *appamāda*, if cultivated, could guide decision-making to reduce suffering during conflict. Indeed, the importance of *appamāda* for combatants was already recognised by the third-century CE Buddhist philosopher Nāgārjuna, who in his *Ratnāvalī*, addressed to a king, refers to heedfulness (*appamāda*, Sanskrit *apramāda*) as a requirement for commanders, using the term *nityāpramatta*, meaning ever (*nitya*) heedful (*apramatta*):

> *akṣudrāṃs tyāginaḥ śūrān snigdhān sambhoginaḥ sthirān kuru nityāpramattāṃs ca dhārmikān daṇḍa-nāyakān.*
>
> As army commander, appoint someone who is magnanimous, free of attachment, courageous, gentle, reliable, ever-conscientious and is a follower of dharma. (translation by Tamas Agocs, in Harvey 2018, chapter 4, v. 12)

However, the question remains how this quality can be cultivated, especially in soldiers whose focus admittedly needs to be more on intensive military training rather than the training of the mind on the Buddha's path. For this, one needs to understand the significant role Buddhist monks play in their interactions with military forces before, during and after warfare. Secondly, one needs to examine the value of sermons and meditation in inspiring a Buddhist way of thinking and transforming intention.

The role of Buddhist monks

Buddhist monks play an important role during warfare. While this is sometimes considered an 'anomaly' because some believe that monks should lead a secluded life and not associate with military men, others believe that monks have the potential to play an active role in advising and guiding those engaged in warfare (Kent 2008, 77, 105). Perhaps there is a duty for Buddhist monks to advise and guide those who genuinely attempt to take refuge in the *Buddha, Dhamma* and *Saṅgha* (i.e. practising Buddhists) regardless of their profession (Kent 2008, 121–122). Regardless of which position one would adopt, monks have and will continue to influence Buddhists who fight. The role of Buddhist monks in reducing unnecessary violence and promoting calmness and intentionality in a soldier's mind has great potential to reduce suffering during conflict. A combatant's mind must be calm during conflict because he has a deadly weapon in his hand that can inflict great suffering on others, and must not be used heedlessly (Kent 2008, 129–134).

Most of the conclusions drawn in this part of the article are based on practical research done in Sri Lanka by Daniel Kent in *Shelter for You, Nirvana for Our Sons: Buddhist Belief and Practice in the Sri Lankan Army*, through interviews with Buddhist monks and soldiers during the years 2004–2007 – so, two years before the end of the civil war in 2009 (Kent 2008).

The role of the Buddhist preaching tradition is often underestimated by historians of religion and Buddhologists (Deegalle 1997, 429). It is easier to comprehend the value of sermons if one looks to them '*as actions meant to produce intended effect rather than didactic pronouncements*' (Kent 2008, 93, emphasis added). However, the performative aspect of Buddhist sermons depends on three aspects: firstly, the original authority or the source of the sacred words – that is, the Buddha and the veneration accorded to him; secondly, the way in which doctrine becomes a sacred object symbolising cultural heritage; and, thirdly, the authority of the religious expert who is reciting them (Kent 2008, 79). If the first of these factors is considered, *appamāda* would have considerable appeal to all Buddhists simply because the concept is emphasised in the famous last words of the Buddha, found in the *Mahā-parinibbāna Sutta* (see above). Any Buddhist reading this *Sutta* would not fail to be moved by the demise of the great teacher, and the last address of the Buddha to the monks around him would make a deep impression. The use of narrative and stories in sermons can also increase their appeal to the laity (Kent 2008, 91–125). With regard to the authority of the religious expert, it is important to note that the appearance, demeanour and conduct of Buddhist monks preaching would play a role in commanding the respect of the laity (Kent 2008, 115). As discussed earlier, this was one of the reasons why Emperor Ashoka was so impressed with the monk Nigrodha.

Apart from these three factors, the ideal sermon has to be *kālīna* and *uccita* (timely and appropriate) (Kent 2008, 95). Amidst the uncertainty in the battlefield, the immediate need is not for nirvana but for mental stability and protection. The topic of a sermon for those entering battle therefore should look at both aspects of Buddhism, though primarily the worldly (*lokika*) rather than the transcendent (*lokuttara*). The attainment of nirvana is a long-term goal; progressing on the Buddhist path is a gradual process and, as such, making mundane topics relevant to this life is also important in sermons (Kent 2008, 80–81, 126).

Having observed the value of sermons, how exactly could one develop *appamāda* or heedfulness in a soldier through them? This is done by transforming intention, as will be discussed now.

The judgement of the International Military Tribunal at Nuremberg states that 'crimes against international law are committed by men, not by abstract entities' (United Nations 2005, 374). From a Buddhist perspective, one might expand on this to say that crimes begin in the minds of men. Similarly, in his study of the use of sermons in relation to soldiers, Daniel Kent cites the monk Maduluwawe Sobhitha Thero's explanation:

> 'according to the Buddhist position, all wars are fought within the hearts of people . . . there are no conflicts where there is no greed, hatred and ignorance. No matter how terrible the reality of a war may be, every single war has one of these unwholesome roots at its core'. (Kent 2008, 10)

It is not to be denied by anyone, even those who justify Buddhists engaging in warfare, that negative karma is created when one engages in warfare with blatantly negative emotions such as anger, hatred and revenge. Kent also cites the monk Ven. Dhammalankara as saying, 'on the battlefield there is a war between two groups and people from both sides die. However, we can't condone the killing of innocent Tamils, Muslims or Sinhala. We tell them never to do such things' (Kent 2008, 131).

Thus, we find to some extent a dichotomy between Buddhism in theory and Buddhism in practice. Theravāda Buddhism in theory preaches non-violence and loving kindness towards all. But in practice, when advising soldiers, monks are compelled to acknowledge the reality of war and preach accordingly. In the difficult task of reconciling these aspects, Buddhist monks preach about the 'ideal' in 'Buddhist *practice*', the selfless soldier fighting without mental defilement only because he needs to fight to protect himself and others from harm and not out of anger or feelings of revenge (Kent 2008, 73). What is interesting is that the IHL ideal, based on the balance between military necessity and humanity, is the same. IHL envisages a soldier fighting only to the extent that military necessity requires, and cognisant always of humanitarian considerations. Perhaps this is where the two concepts can meet in practice.

In practice, then, Buddhist monks, when preaching to soldiers, do not concern themselves with whether war is justified or not. The focus, rather, is on the individual karma of one's actions (Kent 2008, 134). The majority of Buddhist monks and soldiers believe that some negative karma is necessarily created when engaged in battle and therefore monks, for the greater part, make an effort through their preaching and sermons to reduce unnecessary violence and the resultant bad karma. This is done by transforming intention, so that one does not kill with a mind clouded by unwholesome emotions or thoughts (Kent 2008, 59). This is in consonance with the quality of *appamāda* which cautions care with regard to our intentions, unwholesome intentions being the 'hungry tiger' and the 'poisonous snake' that cause self-harm by the infliction of unnecessary suffering on others which generates negative karma.

Meditation – training the mind

As a practice familiar to Buddhists from all over the world, meditation has a significant role in shaping the understanding and behaviour of persons from Buddhist communities. In addition to sermons, mindfulness meditation could be used as a means of training the mind, complementing the function of sermons in transforming intention.

Buddhism identifies three forms or levels of mindfulness which can be developed through mindfulness meditation practice. The first is *sati*, or awareness suffused with the spirit of recollection. This constitutes awareness of one's present moment or being mindful of one's own thoughts, feelings and actions. The second level of mindfulness is *appamāda* – that is, awareness suffused with a spirit of ethical care. The third level of mindfulness is *sampajañña*, or awareness suffused with a sense of spiritual development. It is the second of these, the development of *appamāda* in order to improve the standard of decision-making by combatants during armed conflict, which is of interest to us here. According to Buddhist teachings, *appamāda* (mindfulness infused with a spirit of ethical care) can be developed through mindfulness meditation practices (Lomas 2015). In order to develop the quality of *appamāda* through meditation, one must go beyond a mere awareness of what is happening and connect it to Buddhist teachings on ethics and morality. Mindfulness meditation training to develop the quality of *appamāda* must therefore go beyond simply being aware of one's thoughts, feelings and actions, to reflecting on whether one's actions are ethically sound. From such training emerge behavioural guidelines that engage mindfully in positive *karma* rooted in positive intentions (Lomas 2015).

Research has demonstrated with empirical data that mindfulness-based meditative training results in improvements in moral reasoning and ethical decision-making, mindful attention, emotion, and well-being. According to psychologists, there are four key components of moral reasoning, namely moral sensitivity, moral judgement, moral motivation and commitment, and moral character and competence. The first component, moral sensitivity, is defined as the awareness a person has regarding their actions (or inactions) and the potential effects their behaviour has on others (Shapiro, Jazaieri, and Goldin 2012, 2). Therefore, the foundation for moral reasoning lies in awareness or *appamāda*. The first step on the path to making moral judgements and moral commitment and thus developing one's moral character is awareness. Thus, meditation would help the mind think with clarity, be unclouded in urgent situations and respond with a clear awareness of one's own intentions. It could be successfully employed to guide the ethical reasoning and decision-making of combatants from Buddhist communities and give them practical training in practising the quality of *appamāda*.

Conclusion

It would be too idealistic to imagine that Buddhist teachings could prevent unnecessary suffering in warfare wholly and at all times. However, as the above discussion makes clear, it is possible that Buddhist teachings can exert a strong restraining force in instances where laws sometimes fail to exert influence.

Firstly, this is because religion is close to people's hearts and is something on which their faith, belief systems and cultures are founded. Thus, even where one thinks that something is not particularly illegal, if it is prohibited by one's religious teachings then the moral opprobrium attached to such action would deter belligerents from carrying it out. Secondly, even where one expects to escape the grasp of the law, Buddhists believe that there is no escape from the karmic results of one's intentions and actions.

In this article, I have focused on the quality of *appamāda* – heedfulness – showing its significance as a fundamental Buddhist teaching, both at the time of the Buddha and in transforming the character of Emperor Ashoka. By looking at the *Abhidhamma* analysis of the components of thought processes, I have demonstrated that wholesome thought processes in fact require more effort and more wholesome factors, meaning that it is easier to act with negative intentions and negative consequences than positive ones. This makes *appamāda* particularly important in guarding against the presence of negative intentions. Due to the fundamental nature of *appamāda* in Buddhist teachings and in safeguarding against unethical and ill-considered action, I have then argued for the importance of *appamāda* in combatants. I have proposed that *appamāda* can be developed in belligerents from Buddhist communities through sermons by Buddhist monks, identifying four factors that make sermons effective. These four factors include the high regard Buddhist communities hold for Buddhist monks and sermons conducted by them. Additionally, meditation on mindfulness could enhance *appamāda*, training the minds of soldiers and commanders to act according to the ethical values expressed in such sermons. Thus, the presence of the quality of *appamāda* in the decision-making of belligerents can to a certain extent fill the gap caused by the subjectivity and definitional problems inherent in the IHL rule of proportionality, and potentially reduce unnecessary suffering of civilians during conflict. This would reduce the problem of wanton destruction, allowing military decision makers at all levels to make better assessments of proportionality. It would also help judges assess the nature of what constitutes a reasonable commander within a Buddhist context, since *appamāda* can be understood as a quality to be expected of a reasonable commander from a Buddhist background. This would not be the first time that Buddhist principles have been used in such a context. For instance, in his dissenting opinion to the Advisory Opinion on the Legality of the Threat or Use of Nuclear Weapons, Judge Weeramantry uses religious principles to argue against the use of nuclear weapons. The opinion recognises that the pacifist tradition of Buddhism could under no circumstances lend its sanction to weapons of destruction – least of all to a weapon such as the nuclear bomb, which destroys without any consideration as to principles of proportionality and distinction.

Acknowledgements

The author gratefully acknowledges the comments and guidance given by Prof. Kate Crosby, Andrew Bartles-Smith, Dr Noel Trew and Daniel Ratheiser in the revision of this article. The author is also thankful for the insights and guidance provided by Prof. Asanga Tilakaratne on the Buddhist philosophical aspects it contains.

Disclosure statement

This article has been supported by the International Committee of the Red Cross (ICRC).

References

Baptist, E. 2008. *Abhidhamma for the Beginner*. Colombo: Buddhist Cultural Centre.

Batchelor, S. 2005. "The Buddha's Last Word: Care." *Insight Journal* Spring: 8–11. https://www.buddhistinquiry.org/article/the-buddhas-last-word-care/

Bica, C. 2007. "Collateral Damage: A Military Euphemism for Murder." *ZNET*. https://zcomm.org/znetarticle/collateral-damage-a-military-euphemism-for-murder-by-camillo-mac-bica/

Bodhi, B. 2000. *The Connected Discourses of the Buddha (A New Translation of the Samyutta Nikaya). Vol. 1*. Boston: Wisdom.

Deegalle, M. 1997. "Reconsidering Buddhist Preaching: Bana Tradition in Sri Lanka." In *Recent Researches in Buddhist Studies: Essays in Honour of Y. Karunadasa*, edited by B. K. L. Dhammajoti, A. Tilakaratne, and K. Abhayawansa, 427–453. Colombo: Y. Karunadasa Felicitation Committee.

Fenrick, W. 2009. "Applying IHL Targeting Rules to Practical Situations: Proportionality and Military Objectives." *Windsor Yearbook of Access to Justice* 27 (2): 271–283. doi:10.22329/wyaj.v27i2.4535.

Glossology. "Appamāda." https://obo.genaud.net/backmatter/glossology/glossology/appamada.htm

Guruge, A. W. 1993. *Aśoka, the Righteous: A Definitive Biography*. Colombo: Central Cultural Fund.

Harvey, P., ed. 2018. *Common Buddhist Text: Guidance and Insight from the Buddha*. Ayutthaya: Mahachulalongkornrajavidyalaya University Press. http://www.icdv.net/pdf/cbt_final_dec29%202015.pdf

ICRC. 1977. "Protocol Additional to the Geneva Conventions of 12 August 1949, and Relating to the Protection of Victims of International Armed Conflicts (Protocol I)." Accessed June 8 1977, entered into force 7 December 1978. 1125 UNTS 3. https://ihl-databases.icrc.org/ihl/INTRO/470

ICRC. 1987. *Commentary on the Additional Protocols of 8 June 1977 to the Geneva Conventions of 12 August 1949*. Edited by Y. Sandoz, C. Swinarski and B. Zimmermann. Geneva: Martinus Nijhoff.

ICRC. 2005. *Customary International Humanitarian Law. Volume I: Rules*. Edited by J. Henckaerts and L. Doswald-Beck. Cambridge: Cambridge University Press. https://www.icrc.org/en/doc/assets/files/other/customary-international-humanitarian-law-i-icrc-eng.pdf

ICRC. 2009. "Exploring Humanitarian Law: Glossary." https://www.icrc.org/en/doc/what-we-do/building-respect-ihl/education-outreach/ehl/ehl-other-language-versions/ehl-english-glossary.pdf

ICRC. 2016. "International Expert Meeting Report: The Principle of Proportionality." https://www.icrc.org/en/document/international-expert-meeting-report-principle-proportionality

ICRC. 2017. "War in Cities: What Is at Stake?" https://www.icrc.org/en/document/war-cities-what-stake-0

International Court of Justice (ICJ). 1996a. "Advisory Opinion of the International Court of Justice on the Legality of the Threat or Use of Nuclear Weapons, Advisory Opinion of 8 July 1996." https://www.icj-cij.org/public/files/case-related/95/095-19960708-ADV-01-00-EN.pdf

International Court of Justice (ICJ). 1996b. "Advisory Opinion of the International Court of Justice on the Legality of the Threat or Use of Nuclear Weapons, 8 July 1996 (Dissenting Opinion of Judge Weeramantry)." https://www.icj-cij.org/public/files/case-related/95/095-19960708-ADV-01-12-EN.pdf

International Criminal Tribunal for the Former Yugoslavia (ICTY). 2000. "Final Report to the Prosecutor by the Committee Established to Review the NATO Bombing Campaign against the Federal Republic of Yugoslavia." International Criminal Tribunal for the Former Yugoslavia/United Nations International Criminal Tribunal for the Former Yugoslavia. https://www.icty.org/en/press/final-report-prosecutor-committee-established-review-nato-bombing-campaign-against-federal

International Criminal Tribunal for the Former Yugoslavia (ICTY). 2007. "Prosecutor V. Milan Martić." International Criminal Tribunal for the Former Yugoslavia/United Nations International Criminal Tribunal for the Former Yugoslavia. https://www.icty.org/en/case/martic

Jayarava, D. 2009. "The Last Words of the Buddha." *Jayarava.org*. http://www.jayarava.org/buddhas-last-words.html

Kent, D. 2008. *Shelter for You, Nirvana for Our Sons: Buddhist Belief and Practice in the Sri Lankan Army*. PhD diss., University of Virginia. https://thecarthaginiansolution.files.wordpress.com/2011/08/buddhist-belief-practise-in-sl-army.pdf

Lomas, T. 2015. "Nourishment from the Roots: Engaging with the Buddhist Foundations of Mindfulness." In *Mindfulness in Positive Psychology: The Science of Meditation and Wellbeing*, edited by I. Ivtzan and T. Lomas, 265–279. London: Routledge.

Narada Thera. 1954. *Dhammapada with Translation, Explanatory Texts and Notes*. Reprint ed. Taiwan: Buddha Educational Foundation. https://archive.org/stream/DhammapadaWithNotes/Dhammapada%20with%20notes_djvu.txt

Piyadassi Thera, trans. 1999. "Karaṇīyamettā Sutta, Sutta-nipāta 1.8." *Access to Insight*. https://www.accesstoinsight.org/tipitaka/kn/snp/snp.1.08.piya.html

Roorda, M. 2015. "NATO's Targeting Process: Ensuring Human Control Over (and Lawful Use of) 'Autonomous' Weapons." In *Autonomous Systems: Issues for Defence Policymakers*, edited by A. Williams and P. Scharre, 152–168. Norfolk: Headquarters Supreme Allied Commander Transformation.

Schmitt, M. 2009. "Targeting and International Humanitarian Law in Afghanistan." *International Law Studies* 85: 307–339. https://digital-commons.usnwc.edu/cgi/viewcontent.cgi?article=1126&context=ils

Shapiro, S. L., H. Jazaieri, and P. Goldin. 2012. "Mindfulness-based Stress Reduction Effects on Moral Reasoning and Decision Making." *The Journal of Positive Psychology* 1: 1–12. https://www.researchgate.net/publication/233421440_Mindfulness-based_stress_reduction_effects_on_moral_reasoning_and_decision_making

Sister Vajira and F. Story 1998. "Mahāparinibbānna Sutta: Last Days of the Buddha (DN 16)." *Access to Insight (BCBS Edition)*. https://www.accesstoinsight.org/tipitaka/dn/dn.16.1-6.vaji.html

Sloane, R. 2015. "Puzzles of Proportion and the Reasonable Military Commander: Reflections on the Law, Ethics and Geopolitics of Proportionality." *Harvard National Security Journal* 6: 299–343. https://papers.ssrn.com/sol3/papers.cfm?abstract_id=2613413

Thapar, R. 1961. *Aśoka and the Decline of the Mauryas*. New York: Oxford University Press.

Thanissaro Bhikkhu, trans. 2013. "Appamāda Sutta: Heedfulness (SN 3.17)." *Access to Insight (BCBS Edition)*. https://www.accesstoinsight.org/tipitaka/sn/sn03/sn03.017.than.html

United Nations. 2005. "Principles of International Law Recognized in the Charter of the Nuremberg Tribunal and in the Judgment of the Tribunal with Commentaries (1950)." https://legal.un.org/ilc/texts/instruments/english/draft_articles/7_1_1950

ICRC

THE GIFT OF FEARLESSNESS: A BUDDHIST FRAMEWORK FOR THE PROTECTION OF VULNERABLE POPULATIONS UNDER INTERNATIONAL HUMANITARIAN LAW

Christina A. Kilby

ABSTRACT

In this article, I present *abhayadāna* ('the gift of fearlessness') as a Buddhist framework for the protection of populations who are vulnerable to violence, terror or displacement during times of conflict. *Abhayadāna* is an ancient Indian ethic that inspired the political activism of Hindu leader Mohandas Gandhi. Although seldom invoked by Buddhists today (one notable exception is Aung San Suu Kyi's appeal to *abhayadāna* in her 1990 essay 'Freedom from Fear'), *abhayadāna* is also deeply rooted in the Buddhist tradition and holds vital potential for transforming the way that Buddhist-majority societies conceive of their Buddhist identity and their responsibility to protect the vulnerable during times of conflict. In this article, I argue that *abhayadāna* offers a Buddhist principle of protection that in substantial ways complements and strengthens the principle of protection enshrined in international humanitarian law (IHL).

The gift of fearlessness in classical context

The principle of protection, which is a cornerstone of international humanitarian law (IHL), has ancient roots in the Buddhist tradition as *abhayadāna. Abhayadāna* has been understood in classical Hindu, Jain and Buddhist texts as the gift of protection for those who are without a protector and are vulnerable to violence. The fear that is relieved by the gift of fearlessness is, specifically, fear for one's life. Extending protection to refugees and extending mercy to animals destined for slaughter are common examples of *abhayadāna* that these traditions invoke.[1] While often translated into English as 'the gift of fearlessness', *abhayadāna* may also be rightly translated as 'the gift of protection', 'the gift of security', or 'the gift of assurance'.[2] This gift is symbolised by the *abhaya-mudrā*, the gesture of a raised hand with palm facing outward to

DOI: 10.4324/9781003439820-18

express benevolence and to dispel fear. The Buddha is sometimes depicted with the *abhayamudrā* in sacred art because his teachings offer a path for overcoming the fundamental insecurity of life; *dukkha*, which the Buddhist path aims to alleviate, can mean not only 'suffering' (as it is usually translated), but also 'insecure' (Crosby 2014, 17).

Because Buddhism is a tradition rich in psychological analysis, an understanding of fear as well as the suffering, delusion and hatred that it can precipitate is taken seriously in Buddhist texts. IHL shares a concern for the acute suffering that mortal fear entails. The whole of IHL could be read as an agreed standard of protection meant to relieve those who are not (or no longer) directly participating in hostilities from the fear of danger, in addition to the danger itself, that accompanies armed conflict. Rule 2 of the International Committee of the Red Cross (ICRC, 2005) Customary IHL Study prohibits 'acts or threats of violence the primary purpose of which is to spread terror among the civilian population'.[3] In this customary rule, we see IHL's role in reducing the mental as well as physical suffering of civilians during times of war. Terror and mortal fear constitute forms of psychological injury, or trauma, that can leave lasting and debilitating effects. Another recent ICRC study even suggests that considerations of the mental health toll on civilians should be factored into evaluations of proportionality in attacks (Gillard 2018, 32–33).

Buddhist insights into fear and fearlessness can extend IHL's applications to the psychological dimensions of wartime suffering. IHL aims to offer many forms of psychological assurance to the non-combatant population: primarily, the assurances that they will not be targeted in attacks and that their land, food, medical access, cultural property and other resources indispensable to their survival will be protected, as far as military necessity allows (ICRC 2005).[4] When non-combatants can better trust that humanitarian principles will be respected during a time of conflict, not only will the psychological trauma of warfare be reduced, but less disruption of agriculture and trade as well as less human displacement will occur.[5]

It is important to note, however, that in Indian tradition the gift of fearlessness is the gift not only of an emotional or psychological state, but of a socio-political one: it is the gift of the conditions of protection and security by which beings can live and flourish free from the fear of mortal danger.[6] The concrete aspect of *abhayadāna* is made obvious in Hindu digests that list the 'nine types of superior gifts' as 'food, curds, honey, protection [= fearlessness], cows, land, gold, horses, and elephants' (Hibbets 1999, 441). Because fearlessness frequently appears in lists of tangible goods, we are reminded that fearlessness has been classically understood not only as a psychological sense of security but also as a gift of the tangible conditions of safety, as tangible as a Red Cross tent or a residency permit. It may not always be possible to cultivate another's *feelings* of security, but it is entirely possible to cultivate the *conditions* for another's security. *Abhayadāna* and IHL complement each other to encompass a robust understanding of the interwoven physical and psychological dimensions of human security.

Rethinking the 'gift': humanity, karma and the restraint of power

If the gift of fearlessness is a practice of creating secure conditions for the vulnerable in order to protect their lives and to relieve their fear, it follows that *abhayadāna* speaks most directly to those who are in positions of power to create these conditions. During times of war, the ethic of *abhayadāna* is highly relevant for governmental leaders and military personnel whose decisions shape the collective experience of so many, for good or for ill. In classical Hindu treatises, such as the *Laws of Manu*, the gift of fearlessness is treated as an ethical responsibility assigned to kings because a king's position of authority gives him the power to decide who lives and who dies. These Hindu texts, as well as the Buddhist traditions that draw upon them, envision the righteous or dharmic king as one who extends protection to those who come to him for safety and one who refrains from excessive or disproportionate violence (a trait that correlates in important ways to IHL's principle of proportionality).

The classical framing of protection as a 'gift' of the righteous king should not be misunderstood to imply that the gift of fearlessness is a moral luxury that the king or state may exercise on a whim. On the contrary, the gift of fearlessness is fundamental to the humanity of those without protection. Maslow's well-known hierarchy of needs (1943) reflects the Buddhist understanding that when suffering and insecurity are severe, they prevent our pursuit of truth and self-actualisation as human beings. When in fear for our lives, we are forced to seek out the most basic conditions for our survival before we can pursue the loftier goals of material, intellectual and spiritual development that reflect the height of our human potential. The 'gift' of protection enables those who are acutely vulnerable to violence to regain their humanity: to move from fear and terror into a fuller experience of life with the freedoms and advantages that in Buddhist thought characterise a precious human birth. It is the king's duty to preserve the lives and the humanity of the vulnerable. IHL also appeals to the principle of humanity, balanced with military necessity, for its persuasive power.

The Buddhist doctrine of karma, which teaches that our circumstances are the results of causes that were in part set in motion by our own past actions, does not absolve leaders of their responsibility to offer protection to the vulnerable. Although the idea of karma might perhaps be used to explain the sufferings that others endure in a way that excuses those who inflict them, Buddhist tradition challenges this misunderstanding of karma. First, in the Pāli Canon, the Buddha specifies certain limits of karma in determining our present situations. He criticises three theories of determinism: that all experiences are due to past karma, that all experiences are due to the creation of a god, and that all experiences are due to pure chance (Harvey 2007, 57). The causes of suffering and insecurity cannot be definitively attributed to karma. Furthermore, 'karmic results of a particular action are actually seen to vary, so past karma does not inflexibly determine a fixed result, produced in a mechanical-like way' (Harvey 2007, 59). The complexity of karma is, as the Buddha advised, imponderable (Harvey 2007, 60).

Even when past karma may be understood as a cause for someone's present suffering, this does not remove the moral responsibility of those in power who provide the immediate conditions for either well-being or suffering to arise. In the Mahāyāna tradition, one Tibetan commentator challenges the explanatory power of karma when he argues,

> In any and every world system, the good and evil that befall people, both collectively and individually, is indeed the fruition of their karma that is shared or unshared; but, conventionally speaking, in any place, the waxing and waning of the Buddha's teachings, and the respective happiness or misery of beings, all follow as a consequence of the words and actions of the kings and ministers of that land. [...] Therefore, [...] merit and non-merit and happiness and misery, whatever befalls [the people], follows as a consequence of the powerful rulers of that place – and there is no place where that isn't the case. (Sumpa Khenpo 2001, 471)

A king who fails to understand his own culpability in the sufferings of his subjects does not properly understand cause and effect, for with power comes moral responsibility.

It is significant that the classical understanding of fearlessness as a 'gift' unequivocally positions it as something meant for others, not for oneself. Nowhere in my reading do Buddhist texts use *abhayadāna* as a justification for rulers to act fearlessly, meaning with impunity or without regard for the effects of their actions upon others.[7] Fearlessness is meant as a gift for the powerless. For those in power, Buddhist tradition enjoins training in compassion, wisdom and restraint.[8]

When turned upon oneself, the gift of fearlessness is framed not as a gift but as a weapon: a weapon against one's own ego and greed. Giving fearlessness is a critical duty for rulers precisely because giving 'is the best weapon against greed (*lobha*), the first of the three unwholesome motivational roots' (De Silva 1995, para. 2). Furthermore, 'the *Devatāsaṃyutta* equates giving to a battle [...]. One has to fight the evil forces of greed' (De Silva 1995, para. 3). In this extended metaphor of war, rulers must fight against their own greed using the gift of fearlessness as their weapon. By likening the practice of protection to a battle, the *Devatāsaṃyutta* makes a compelling case that a king's giving of fearlessness should be equal to (or greater than) his potential for violence. By engaging in the battle against his own greed for power, a king conquers his people's most threatening enemy: himself (Hibbets 1999). When the *Sūtra on the Upāsaka Precepts* enumerates the many dangers that beings may fear, kings are first on the list: 'If the bodhisattva sees sentient beings in fear of kings, lions, tigers, wolves, floods, fires, or robbers and saves them, this is called the giving of fearlessness' (Shih 1991, 107). We find kings at the front of a similar list in the *Cariyāpiṭaka Aṭṭhakathā*: 'The giving of fearlessness is the giving of protection to beings when they have become frightened on account of kings, thieves, fire, water, enemies, lions, tigers, other wild beasts, dragons, ogres, demons, goblins, etc'. (Dhammapāla 1978, para. 10). *Abhayadāna* protects those without a protector, but also *creates* the protector by ensuring that the ruler serves to safeguard rather than to abuse others.

Security as a sovereign responsibility

Fearlessness is not only a gift meant for times of crisis or war, but it is also 'the gift that kings give when they ensure that *their subjects live in security*' (Hibbets 1999, 441; emphasis mine). Specifically, a king should 'grant his subjects protection from fear of mutilation, imprisonment, banishment, beatings, thievery, and dishonor' (Heim 2004, 122). The logical connection between security and fearlessness is clear when we consider that if each state provided its domestic population with real security, no one would be without a protector. A king who gives fearlessness by providing for the people's security refrains from creating new vulnerable populations who must seek the gift of fearlessness elsewhere. This emphasis on the gift of security as a gift of prevention, and not only a response to crisis, corresponds well to IHL's treatment of displacement. According to the ICRC Study of Customary IHL, parties to a conflict have the responsibility to protect the displaced (Rule 131) and to refrain from displacing people in the first place, except when that population's security or imperative military objectives necessitate it (Rule 129). The gift of fearlessness provides a robust vision for what security entails: not only protection in response to a problem, but the proactive cultivation of restraint and precaution in order to protect the vulnerable from the effects of hostilities more generally.

In the *Laws of Manu* (4.232), it is written that 'a bestower of fearlessness receives [in turn] *sovereignty*' (Hibbets 1999, 442). Traditionally, a ruler's authority to govern follows from his or her capacity to grant fearlessness to a population. Fearlessness, not fear, is a prerequisite for rulership. As Hibbets explains, 'Whoever can ensure the protection of the people is entitled to rule . . .; since one of the primary functions of the king is protection of his subjects, he is, in fact, empowered by his "gift" of security' (442). The practice of protection is the *sine qua non* of a powerful and sovereign leader.[9] A compelling parallel can be found in the *Aggañña-sutta* (*Dīgha-nikāya* sutta 27, at III.92–93), which provides a narrative account of the origins of human civilisation. The text describes the first king as one elected by the people for the purpose of ensuring food security by punishing theft.

Abhayadāna could, then, be used as a framework for understanding the sovereignty of a state or for justifying intervention when a state has failed in its obligations to provide security for its population. A government unable to offer fearlessness to the vulnerable within that state's borders could be considered to have ceded its sovereignty temporarily. In contemporary instances of armed conflict, the provision of fearlessness must sometimes be demanded, and even seized when it has been denied to those in fear for their lives.

However, an appeal to political sovereignty within the classical explanations of *abhayadāna* poses a potential problem. It may provide an excuse for a leader or government to renounce sovereignty *only over a particular group of people*, rendering them stateless and forcing them to seek protection elsewhere. *Abhayadāna*, while promoting the good of protecting the vulnerable and while linking fearlessness to tangible conditions of security, does not necessarily compel a sovereign state to include perceived outsiders within the bounds of its sovereignty (although there is certainly room for such an interpretation). To fill this gap, practitioners must invoke other Buddhist doctrines and practices that can support the right to protection for minority groups and showcase successes of Buddhist pluralism.

Another challenge that arises in this linkage of *abhayadāna* to state sovereignty is the distinction in IHL between international armed conflicts (IACs) and non-international armed conflicts (NIACs). Increasingly, armed conflicts involve groups that are not states and do not assert themselves as states. An armed group that is not a state and does not claim sovereignty over any particular territory or population may not be as easily persuaded by the classical understanding of *abhayadāna* that focuses on the duties of the sovereign king or state. Yet the other moral and karmic imperatives of *abhayadāna* can still apply to those groups because in Buddhist tradition, *abhayadāna* is the purview not merely of kings, but of every person at every level in society.

***Abhayadāna* as foundational to Buddhist identity and practice**

Abhayadāna is typically discussed in Buddhist commentaries on the perfection of generosity where gifts are classified into three types: 'the giving of material things (*amisadāna*), the giving of fearlessness (*abhayadāna*), and the giving of the Dhamma (*dhammadāna*)' (Dhammapāla 1978, para. 2). Most commonly discussed in Buddhist commentaries are gifts of dharma and gifts of material things, the ultimate being the gift of one's own body sacrificed for others.[10] Giving material goods is understood as a responsibility of the lay community, and giving dharma is understood as a responsibility of the monastic community. Who gives the gift of fearlessness, then, and how does that gift function within a Buddhist society?

While Hindu sources discuss *abhayadāna* primarily in the context of kingship, they also extend the practice of *abhayadāna* to yogins who undertake the discipline of refraining from harm of living creatures, as well as to ordinary lay people who can at least protect the lives of certain animals and insects (Hibbets 1999, 442). The extension of *abhayadāna* beyond the role of kings to ascetics and lay people contextualises the gift of fearlessness within any relationship of power. The gift of fearlessness is the practice of restraining one's own violent potential, whether for rulers who hold power over the life and death of their subjects or for ordinary people who hold power only over the fates of the smallest of creatures. Following Hinduism's extension of *abhayadāna* beyond the role of the king, Buddhist texts describe *abhayadāna* as an ethical discipline for everyone, not only for the elite or powerful. One well-known Tibetan commentator, Patrul Rinpoché, glossed the gift of fearlessness as

> actually doing whatever you can to help others in difficulty. It includes, for instance, providing a refuge for those without any place of safety, giving protection to those without any protector, and being with those who have no other companion. It refers particularly to such actions as forbidding hunting and fishing wherever you have the power to do so, buying back sheep on the way to the slaughter, and saving the lives of dying fish, worms, flies and other creatures. (Patrul 1998, 238)

Patrul's brief list of actions that constitute *abhayadāna* includes giving political protection, offering social support and solidarity, protecting physical environments, and using economic power to intervene in harmful practices. Importantly, this description encompasses a range of activities that can be undertaken by people with varying levels of social and political power.

In the Pāli Canon, the practice of giving fearlessness is equated with the observance of the five precepts, the most basic and ubiquitous markers of Buddhist identity: not to take life, not to take what is not given, not to engage in sexual misconduct, not to engage in wrong speech and not to consume intoxicants. As one Theravāda commentator summarises,

> The *Aṅguttara Nikāya mentions five great gifts which have been held in high esteem by noble-minded men from ancient times. [. . .] These great givings comprise the meticulous observance of the Five Precepts. By doing so one gives fearlessness, love and benevolence to all beings. If one human being can give security and freedom from fear to others by his behavior, that is the highest form of* dāna *one can give, not only to mankind, but to all living beings. (De Silva 1995, para. 10)*

Similarly, from the Mahāyāna tradition, the *Sūtra on the Upāsaka Precepts* equates the gift of fearlessness with the code of conduct for all who call themselves Buddhists by equating *abhayadāna* with the five precepts. While *abhayadāna* corresponds most closely to the first precept (not to take life), this sutra understands each of the five precepts as the gift of a particular type of fearlessness, as specified in the next section of this paper. The sutra reads,

> Good son, among various kinds of giving, the giving of fearlessness is foremost. Therefore I say that the five great kinds of giving are the five precepts that keep sentient beings away from the five kinds of fear. These five kinds of giving are easy to practice, for not only do they free one from obstructions but they do not cost anything; furthermore, they reward those who practice them with immeasurable blessings and virtues. (Shih 1991, 151)

The sutra also reads that 'One who has taken refuge in the Three Treasures [Jewels] should protect sentient beings from fear. If he can give fearlessness, he attains the *upāsaka* precepts and even unsurpassed, perfect enlightenment' (Shih 1991, 107). In this text, the gift of fearlessness *is* the practice of Buddhism. There is no refuge, no precept, no practice and no enlightenment without *abhayadāna.*

Although not as well known or frequently discussed in Buddhist texts as material and dharmic gifts, the gift of fearlessness is presented by these scriptural sources from both Theravāda and Mahāyāna canons as the most important among the three types of gifts – even more important than dharma. Without fundamental protection and security for their physical life, beings are not free to receive either the gift of material flourishing or the gift of spiritual development. The gift of fearlessness undergirds and enables the other two gifts. For the recipient, fearlessness is the gift of life itself, and for the giver, *abhayadāna* is the basis of the path to perfect liberation.

Abhayadāna holds a highly privileged place within the Buddhist tradition. This Buddhist principle of protection may be especially relevant to the capacities of those with political power, but it is so fundamental to Buddhist practice and identity that it is meant for all Buddhists in all times and circumstances. This means that no Buddhist soldier, Buddhist government official or Buddhist civilian can abandon the practice of protecting the vulnerable, even in times of conflict and difficulty, without forfeiting their practice of Buddhism.

Applications of *Abhayadāna* to IHL

The mutual concerns of IHL and the Buddhist tradition are many. The foundation of IHL is the protection of non-combatants during times of war, and the principle of protection runs deep in the Buddhist ethic of *abhayadāna* as inherited from India. Both IHL and the *abhayadāna* tradition emphasise the responsibilities that accompany the capacity for violence, whether through IHL's language of duty or the Buddhist tradition's language of gift giving. In both cases, the power to exercise violence, whether at high echelons or low, comes with a commensurate responsibility to protect the vulnerable by enacting restraint. Both IHL and *abhayadāna* appeal to their own notions of humanity in order to moderate the use of violence.

Because IHL and the *abhayadāna* tradition share an overarching framework for protection, there are numerous correspondences between them in the specific practices that comprise this framework. In particular, the Buddhist tradition offers a taxonomy of vulnerability that could prove useful for the interpretation and application of IHL. The *Sūtra on the Upāsaka Precepts* makes the case that each of the five precepts corresponds to a particular type of fear or vulnerability, and many of IHL's customary rules, as described by the ICRC Study, map onto these categories of vulnerability.

- The first precept (not to take life) is the gift of protection to those vulnerable to mortal violence, mapping readily onto Rule 89 prohibiting 'violence to life', Rule 53 prohibiting 'starvation as a method of warfare' and Rule 97 prohibiting the use of 'human shields'.[11]
- The second precept (not to take what is not given) is the gift of protection to those vulnerable to the violence of theft and exploitation; this precept maps onto Rule 51 specifying that in occupied territory, 'private property must be respected and may not be confiscated; except where destruction or seizure of such property is required by imperative military necessity'. This precept also maps onto Rule 52 prohibiting 'pillage', Rule 94 prohibiting 'slavery and slave trade' and Rule 95 prohibiting 'forced labor'.
- The third precept (not to engage in sexual misconduct) is protection from violent exploitation of the vulnerabilities that human sexualities and family relationships pose; this precept maps onto Rule 93 prohibiting 'rape and other forms of sexual violence', Rule 119 on 'accommodation for women deprived of their liberty', and Rule 134 on respecting 'the specific protection, health and assistance needs of women'. The particular vulnerabilities of children and their dependence upon their families can also be addressed by this precept, mapping onto Rule 105 on 'respect for family life', Rule 120 stating that 'children who are deprived of their liberty must be held in quarters separate from those of adults, except where families are accommodated as family units', Rule 131 specifying that 'in case of displacement, [...] members of the same family are not separated', and Rule 135 on the 'special respect and protection' of children more generally.
- The fourth precept (not to engage in wrong speech) is the gift of protection for those vulnerable to the violent consequences of false or destructive speech. This precept has particularly strong implications for IHL because treaties, agreements and propaganda are central to the conduct of war. This precept maps onto Rule 2 prohibiting 'threats of

violence the primary purpose of which is to spread terror among the civilian population' and Rule 46 prohibiting 'orders or threats that no quarter will be given'. This precept also maps onto the prohibition in Rule 64 against 'conclusion of an agreement to suspend combat with the intention of attacking by surprise the adversary relying on it', and onto Rule 65 prohibiting 'perfidy', as well as several rules requiring the appropriate use of emblems such as the flag of truce or Red Cross and Red Crescent emblems (ICRC 2005, Rules 58–63).
- The fifth precept (not to consume intoxicants that cloud the mind) requires more interpretive creativity to map onto the ICRC study's customary IHL rules. In Buddhist tradition, the fifth precept is designed to mitigate against the harm caused by the loss of one's mental clarity and moral agency. In the context of customary IHL, there are many rules and practices that emphasise discrimination and clarity of knowledge. Rule 1 on 'the principle of distinction between civilians and combatants', Rule 7 on 'the principle of distinction between civilian objects and military objectives', and Rule 11 prohibiting 'indiscriminate attacks' all require the executive clarity to make – and rigorously verify, assess and enforce – the critical distinctions between civilian and military targets that form the foundation of IHL. Rules restricting the use of landmines (Rules 81–83) as well as other 'weapons that are by nature indiscriminate' (Rule 71) can also relate to the fifth precept because loss of the ability to clearly discriminate between military and civilian targets causes immense harm to non-combatants. Without a rigorous standard of clarity in assessment, those involved in armed conflict severely limit their own capacities to implement the other aspects of IHL.

The five basic precepts of Buddhist practice helpfully frame the customary rules of IHL in terms of five primary types of fear and vulnerability to violence, emphasising the inextricability of physical and psychological forms of suffering. Buddhist sources also extend the concerns of IHL beyond the human world to the non-human world. For IHL, the vulnerable groups among the non-combatant population identified as needing special protection include: journalists; displaced persons; women and children; the elderly, disabled and infirm; wounded, sick, shipwrecked, and captured combatants; medical and religious personnel; and humanitarian workers (ICRC 2005, chapters I, II and V). All of these are groups who, in times of war, are not in the fight but nevertheless may be in legitimate fear for their lives. While the classical texts of the *abhayadāna* tradition do not name each of these groups, they do include a strong concern for people without protection, for non-human animals (which are not specifically protected under IHL) and for the natural environment (which is protected in some measure under IHL as seen in Rules 43–45).

Conclusion

The gift of fearlessness provides a Buddhist framework for addressing standards for security, sovereignty, governance and ethics in the context of armed conflict. One great merit of the gift of fearlessness is that, like IHL, its successful implementation depends upon kings or states as well as upon the monastic sangha and lay people. While states or non-state armed groups hold more power, and thus more responsibility for human well-being, *abhayadāna* as an expression of the five precepts extends to every member of the Buddhist community, high and low, ordained and lay. *Abhayadāna* holds rich possibilities for a contemporary Buddhist vision of human security that includes protection for the vulnerable as well as the prevention of suffering through responsible governance and ethical action, enacted by every member of society, even during the worst of times.

Notes

1. For an application of *abhayadāna* to the political ethics of refugee resettlement, see Kilby (2019).
2. My thanks to an anonymous reviewer for suggesting these alternate translations.
3. It should be noted that the prohibition on spreading terror applies only to terrorising the civilian population. Under IHL, it is lawful to use tactics that intimidate or demoralise enemy troops who are still in the fight. Also, the prohibition only covers acts or threats of violence whose *primary purpose* is to spread terror. Attacks directed against military objectives may be terrifying for nearby civilians, but they are not considered unlawful because such terror is incidental to the attack's legitimate primary purpose (i.e. destroying the military objective).
4. These provisions are primarily addressed in the ICRC Customary IHL Study (2005), Rules 11, 23, 24, 28, 35, 38, 40, 44, 53 and 54.
5. The role of fear in human displacement is well reflected in the 1951 Refugee Convention, which defines refugees as those who flee their countries of nationality or residence because of 'well-founded fear' of persecution (*United Nations Convention Relating to the Status of Refugees*, 1951; Chapter One, Article 1.A.2). Note that international refugee law is a separate body of law from IHL.
6. I have previously explored this topic in Kilby (2019).
7. The gift of fearlessness is distinct from the four fearlessnesses of a Buddha, which pertain to transcendent realisations. However, in the *Cariyāpiṭaka Aṭṭhakathā*, the gift of fearlessness and the four fearlessnesses of a Buddha coincide in the power and virtue of a bodhisattva, who is both 'fearless and a giver of fearlessness' (Dhammapāla 1978, printed version, 260).
8. See S.M.M.P. Bhagya Samarakoon's contribution on *Appamāda* in this volume.
9. See Deng et al. (2010) for a contemporary argument that state sovereignty should depend upon the responsibility to protect the domestic population.
10. See Reiko Ohnuma's discussion of the relationship between these two types of gifts (1998, 323–359).

11. In the context of war, this rule does not apply to those directly participating in hostilities.

Disclosure statement

This article has been supported by the International Committee of the Red Cross (ICRC).

References

Crosby, K. 2014. *Theravada Buddhism: Continuity, Diversity, Identity*. Oxford: Blackwell-Wiley.

De Silva, L. 1995. "Giving in the Pali Canon." In *Dana, the Practice of Giving, Selected Essays*, edited by B. Bodhi. Published by Access to Insight. https://www.accesstoinsight.org/lib/authors/various/wheel367.html

Deng, F. M., S. Kimaro, G. Lyons, D. Rothchild, and I. W. Zartman. 2010. *Sovereignty as Responsibility: Conflict Management in Africa*. Washington, DC: Brookings Institution Press.

Dhammapāla, Ā. 1978 [n.d.]. *Cariyāpiṭaka Aṭṭhakathā. Translated by Bhikkhu Bodhi in the Discourse on the All-Embracing Net of Views: The Brahmajāla Sutta and Its Commentaries*, pp. 254–330. Kandy: Buddhist Publication Society. Extracts (pp. 289-96 and 322-23) in *Dana: The Practice of Giving selected essays* edited by Bhikkhu Bodhi. https://www.accesstoinsight.org/lib/authors/various/wheel367.html#perfect

Gillard, E. 2018. "Proportionality in the Conduct of Hostilities: The Incidental Harm Side of the Assessment." Research paper published by *Chatham House: The Royal Institute of International Affairs*. https://www.chathamhouse.org/sites/default/files/publications/research/2018-12-10-proportionality-conduct-hostilities-incidental-harm-gillard-final.pdf#page=33

Harvey, P. 2007. "'Freedom of the Will' in the Light of Theravāda Buddhist Teachings." *Journal of Buddhist Ethics* 14: 35–98.

Heim, M. 2004. *Theories of the Gift in South Asia: Hindu, Buddhist, and Jain Reflections on Dāna*. New York: Routledge.

Hibbets, M. 1999. "Saving Them from Yourself: An Inquiry into the South Asian Gift of Fearlessness." *Journal of Religious Ethics* 27 (3): 435–462.

ICRC. 2005. "IHL Database: Customary IHL." https://ihl-databases.icrc.org/customary-ihl/eng/docs/v1_rul

Kilby, C. 2019. "The Global Refugee Crisis and the Gift of Fearlessness." *Journal of Buddhist Ethics* 26: 307–327.

Maslow, A. H. 1943. "A Theory of Human Motivation." *Psychological Review* 50 (4): 370–396.

Ohnuma, R. 1998. "The Gift of the Body and the Gift of Dharma." *History of Religions* 37 (4): 323–359.

Patrul Rinpoché (dpal sprul O rgyan 'jigs med chos kyi dbang po). 1998 [19th c. original]. *Words of My Perfect Teacher*. Translated by the Padmakara Translation Group. Boston: Shambala.

Shih, H. (translator). 1991. *Upāsakaśīlasūtra (The Sutra on Upāsaka Precepts)*. Berkeley: Bukkhyo Dendo Kyokai.

Sumpa Khenpo (sum pa mkhan po ye shes dpal 'byor). 2001 [18th c. original]. "*paN+Di Ta Sum Pa Ye Shes Dpal 'Byor Mchog Gi Spyod Tshul Brjod Pa Sgra 'Dzin Bcud Len (Expressing the Conduct of the Supreme Pandita Sumpa Yeshé Penjor: Alchemy for the Ear)*." Buddhist Digital Resource Center work ID W25006, 15–776. Beijing: Tibetan Civilization Publishing House of China (krung go'i bod kyi shes rig dpe skrun khang).

United Nations. 1951 Convention Relating to the Status of Refugees. Chapter One, Article 1.A.2.

ICRC

ADDRESSING THE CAUSES OF CONFLICT-RELATED SEXUAL VIOLENCE WITH THE BUDDHIST DOCTRINE OF LACK OF A PERMANENT SELF AND MEDITATION TRAINING

Charya Samarakoon

ABSTRACT

Conflict-related sexual violence (CRSV) against both male and female combatants, as well as civilians, remains a reality of war despite global efforts to address it. International humanitarian law (IHL) unequivocally condemns sexual violence in armed conflict, and there are specific measures addressing this issue in IHL. However, Buddhist teachings and practices to address sexual violence in armed conflict have not been extensively researched, despite the prevalence of sexual violence in situations of armed conflict involving Buddhist communities. This article examines Buddhist teachings and practices relevant to addressing this challenge, identifying where these align with IHL, as well as proposing how Buddhist teachings may reduce the likelihood of CRSV. It is proposed that insight into the Buddhist teaching on lack of a permanent, essential self, as expounded in the *Anattalakkhaṇa Sutta*, coupled with meditation, is a practical means of dispelling the toxic conceptions of gender that exacerbate sexual violence in armed conflict and of fostering compassionate behaviour towards others. As brought to light by recent neurological research, Buddhist meditation practices lessen the 'self'-focused outlook common to humans and increase the capacity for compassion, active empathy and resilience to peer pressure. Training in Buddhist meditation, supported by explanation of relevant Buddhist teachings, may therefore significantly reduce the cultural and individual attitudes that currently exacerbate the risks of CRSV.

Introduction

The purpose of this study on the interface between Buddhism and international humanitarian law (IHL) is not to legitimise IHL values by showing consistency with a religious group's values, such as by selectively quoting from important Buddhist texts. However, we should note that adopting principles of law that embody IHL values, whether this be in treaty, customary law or even jurisprudence, is just the first step in the inculcation of these values (Mack and Pejic 2020). Hence, this article seeks to bridge the gap

DOI: 10.4324/9781003439820-19

between law and its implementation, which is necessary to ensure that these formulations do not remain mere words on paper. Bridging this gap is an exercise in social transformation, and such transformation can only take place within a living cultural context (Fernando 1997). This position is supported by the findings of the International Committee of the Red Cross (ICRC) study *Roots of Restraint in War*, which concludes that

> an exclusive focus on the law is not as effective at influencing behaviour as a combination of the law and the values underpinning it. Linking the law to local norms and values gives it greater traction. The role of law is vital in setting standards, but encouraging individuals to internalize the values it represents through socialization is a more durable way of promoting restraint. (ICRC 2018, 9)

Conflict-related sexual violence (CRSV) has been historically present and remains an extreme source of suffering during armed conflict. In such conflict, the objectives of power and dominance often manifest themselves in the form of sexual violence, to which both men and women are vulnerable. Regardless of the actual gender of the perpetrator or victim, the characteristic of masculinity is attributed to the perpetrator and femininity to the victim. The fixed binaries of gender are not adequate to understand and address the realities of CRSV. The intention of the rape may be to 'lower' the social status of the male survivor by reducing him to a 'feminised male'. Castration and violence against male organs in conflict can be done to remove the procreative ability, and therefore the 'virility' or 'manliness', of the victim (Sivakumaran 2007, 253).

Until recently CRSV has for the most part gone unrecorded and therefore unpunished. From the Lieber Code of 1863 to the Additional Protocols of 1977 of the Geneva Conventions, legislative instruments on IHL have been concerned about CRSV (Lyth 2001, 4). Additionally, the ICRC has identified several rules of Customary International Humanitarian Law that also address the issue of CRSV. For instance, Rules 93 and 94 of Customary International Humanitarian Law prohibit rape and other forms of sexual violence as well as sexual slavery. Additionally, Rule 156 recognises sexual violence as a war crime, while Rule 134 states that the specific protection, health and assistance needs of women affected by armed conflict must be respected (ICRC 2005). The statutes of the International Criminal Tribunal for former-Yugoslavia (ICTY) 1993 and the International Criminal Tribunal for Rwanda (ICTR) 1994 as well as the jurisprudence of these ad hoc tribunals have been groundbreaking in confronting the humanitarian challenge posed by CRSV (ICRC 2005, 326–327). They have given recognition to the varied forms of CRSV and established a precedent of accountability.

On the whole, there is increasing recognition of the need for prevention and accountability. However, many measures of IHL seem not to have achieved their maximum potential with regard to protection from sexual violence in armed conflict as well as ensuring accountability. This particular trend has been called 'a triumph of form over substance' by international legal scholars, signifying the need to remove obstacles in the way of practical implementation (Gardam and Jarvis 2001, 29). Moreover, the dismissive attitude towards CRSV where instances of grave and widespread CRSV are discounted and denied by tribunals and other domestic bodies charged with investigating abuses (as we shall see in the cases of Cambodia and Sri Lanka, both countries with Buddhist communities) is a major hindrance to the implementation of the IHL rules against sexual violence in armed conflict.

Another major obstacle is the stigma associated with CRSV, making survivors of CRSV reluctant to come forward and give evidence against perpetrators. Moreover, due to the stigmatisation associated with sexual violence as well as the attendant difficulties in obtaining evidence, judicial and other bodies charged with investigating conflict-related crimes show a reluctance to acknowledge the reality of sexual violence during conflict.

In such a setting, the stigmatisation of sexual violence (Benshoof 2014), rather than its survivors, and the willingness to hold perpetrators accountable can only be achieved through integrating the rules of IHL into the moral fabric of society (Eisenbruch 2018b). A means of doing this is to draw parallels between IHL values and the inherent value systems in that society. This article is an attempt to do just that, aimed at identifying Buddhist teachings and practices relevant to the IHL measures in place to address CRSV and to determine where IHL aligns with Buddhist doctrines and traditions. It further proposes how Buddhist teachings can be used to deconstruct fixed gender binaries and enhance understanding of the importance of reducing suffering for others as well as for oneself. It further suggests that meditation practices can be used to enhance the comprehension of such doctrines, and to develop prosociality, active compassion and resilience, while maintaining the effective military functioning of the combatant. The combination of training in relevant teachings and meditation techniques within Buddhist contexts is a way of harnessing culturally embedded values to reduce the likelihood of CRSV.

This research is centred on customary as well as convention-based IHL rules on CRSV, and includes a brief historical review of the development of the present law. It also refers to the statutes as well as the jurisprudence of the International Criminal Court (ICC) and various ad hoc tribunals on armed conflict, to present IHL measures to address CRSV.

It must be noted here that combatants are by no means the only perpetrators of CRSV and there are many instances where non-combatants also perpetrate and/or condone CRSV. However, there are a variety of factors leading to CRSV ranging from the intention to terrorise or humiliate civilians of the opposing group, to control resources and territory, to gain information, or to effect ethnic cleansing or genocide. Combatants may also take advantage of their position of power and lack of accountability to perpetrate sexual violence. This article will focus on Buddhist principles and practices to address CRSV as perpetrated by combatants during armed conflict.

The gradual recognition of CRSV in IHL

In the period since the end of the Second World War there have been over 250 armed conflicts (Pettersson and Wallensteen 2015). Violent conflict in protracted low-intensity wars by design intrudes into the home and family, intensifying the levels of sexual violence in armed conflict (Manchanda 2001).

Sexual violence is not explicitly recognised as constituting 'grave breaches' of IHL, nor under common Article 3 of the Geneva Conventions, which sets out minimum protections to be followed during armed conflict. For rape to be considered a grave breach it has to be interpreted as coming within the crimes of 'wilful killing, torture or inhumane treatment' or 'wilfully causing great suffering or serious injury to body and health'. However, early on in the conflict in former Yugoslavia, the ICRC declared that the grave breach of the 1949 Geneva Conventions constituted by 'wilfully causing great suffering or serious injury to body and health' obviously does cover not only rape but also any other attack on a woman's dignity (Gardam and Jarvis 2001, 29). Article 27 of the Convention Relative to the Protection of Civilian Persons in the Time of War (GC IV), Articles 75(2) and 76 of the Additional Protocol I to the Geneva Conventions (AP I) and Article 4(2)(e) of the Additional Protocol II to the Geneva Conventions (AP II) address the issue of sexual violence in armed conflict. Rules 93 and 94 of the ICRC's Customary International Humanitarian Law Study recognise some forms of sexual violence as war crimes (ICRC 2005). As a matter of international criminal law, the Statutes of the ICTY 1993 and of the ICTR 1994 explicitly recognised rape as a crime against humanity (Lyth 2001).

The focus placed on sexual violence by these international bodies contributed to the end of the invisibility of sexual violence, and led to important new developments in the interpretation of relevant IHL norms. Although the precedential value of these ad hoc tribunals is limited both by their origin as Security Council measures and by their geographical scope, the normative effect of these initiatives is much more widespread (Lyth 2001).

Historically in IHL, women have been subsumed under the general category of civilians, and little account had been taken of the distinctive experience of women in armed conflict. Early legal and judicial procedures such as the Lieber Code, the Hague Conventions and the International Military Tribunal at Nuremberg and the Far East make limited reference to addressing CRSV (Lyth 2001). In 1998, the ICRC initiated a study to examine how women are affected by armed conflict around the world. The findings of this study served as guidelines for all parties involved in combating CRSV (Suk and Skjelsbæk 2010; Gardam and Jarvis 2001). However, more recent research has identified that multiple forms of sexual violence exist in the context of armed conflicts, and that women are not the only victims of CRSV (Dolan 2014; Wood 2014). Men as well as persons belonging to sexual minorities are also often victims of CRSV, and there are additional barriers to identifying these survivors based on a lack of recognition of the realities of sexual violence in conflict situations. The position presented in this article, namely cultivating understanding and compassion through meditative training, is sufficiently broad to encompass all these forms of sexual violence perpetrated against different groups of people during armed conflict.

CRSV in Cambodia, Sri Lanka and Myanmar and the need for the cultural integration of IHL values

Although law has a powerful role in constructing the way we see the world and has significantly improved the position of survivors of CRSV, the reluctance to acknowledge, and thus to address, the underlying factors of stigmatisation and social rejection that account for so many of the difficulties that survivors of sexual violence in armed conflict experience is a barrier to the implementation of IHL's legal protections. This stigmatisation has resulted in survivors of CRSV often being hesitant to break the silence and give evidence and/or prosecutors being reluctant to prosecute CRSV due to a lack of evidence, leading them to question the efficacy of conventional and customary IHL as well as international judicial proceedings to prevent and prosecute CRSV (Ministry for Foreign Affairs Sweden 2007; Goodley 2019).

The experiences of several domestic transitional justice tribunals and processes mirror this dismissive attitude towards CRSV. Until as recently as 2011, the sexual violence perpetrated by Khmer Rouge troops in Cambodia was not acknowledged or redressed (Carmichael 2019; Eisenbruch 2018b). The Extraordinary Chambers in the Courts of Cambodia (ECCC) established to carry out the transitional justice processes has consistently resisted taking up sexual crimes for full deliberation (Carmichael 2019; Extraordinary Chambers in the Courts of Cambodia 2012). In Sri Lanka, despite consistent and serious allegations of CRSV during the civil war (Office of the High Commissioner for Human Rights 2015; Fonseka 2015), the transitional justice mechanisms have failed to address them. The Lessons Learnt and Reconciliation Commission Report did not sufficiently explore allegations of sexual violence (de Mel 2013) and despite public commitments by the Government of Sri Lanka, other transitional justice processes that followed it have also failed, due to reluctance on the part of survivors of CRSV to come forward owing to the stigma attached to being a victim of sexual crimes, the lack of political will to investigate and prosecute sexual violence crimes in particular (International Crimes Evidence Project 2014; Fonseka and Woodworth 2016), and the continuing intimidation of victims and witnesses (Fonseka and Schulz 2018). Most recently, the United Nations reported a pattern of widespread CRSV against Rohingya women and girls in Myanmar from 2016 to 2017, and little has been done to ensure accountability and non-recurrence (Office of the Special Representative of the Secretary-General on Sexual Violence in Conflict 2021). All of the above are instances where sexual violence has been perpetrated in and by Buddhist communities involved in armed conflict.

In this context, it is appropriate for Buddhists to reflect on the story of the enlightened nun Uppalavaṇṇā, who was much praised by the Buddha, as one of his two chief female disciples. When she was raped, the Buddha said she had not broken the key monastic rule against sexual intercourse, as she was not willing (*Vinaya* III.35, cf. *Dhammapada* commentary II.47–52). No blame or stigma was attached to her.

Despite the presence of many IHL measures including treaty provisions, customary law as well as related international criminal law jurisprudence, CRSV is not effectively addressed in international or domestic tribunals. At the same time, although there are over half a billion Buddhists around the world, and many Buddhist societies have been torn apart by violent conflicts in the recent decades, there has so far been no systematic and focused study of the interface between Buddhism and IHL. Moreover, as the foregoing instances make clear, CRSV has been perpetrated by and in Buddhist communities, and at times even been condoned by Buddhist communities both lay and monastic (Lei 2019; Eisenbruch 2018a). In this context, we may ask how Buddhist principles could be used to prevent CRSV: why, from a Buddhist perspective, should one refrain from perpetrating sexual violence? When addressing this question, we shall keep in mind that both men and women are victims of CRSV.

The teachings on non-self in relation to gender and epistemological change

To answer this question, we now turn to look at Buddhist teachings from the Pali Canon. Aspects of Buddhism that particularly align with the position of IHL with regard to CRSV are compassion and understanding. According to Buddhist teachings, human actions are to be guided by two fundamental principles: compassion (*karuṇā*) and wisdom/understanding (*paññā/prajñā*). Indeed, it is said that the life of the Bodhisattva (the prospective Buddha) is guided by them. As regards the aspect of understanding, an important teaching is the doctrine of *anatta*, 'no-self', the notion that we have no fixed, enduring entity at the core of us, as expounded in the *Anattalakkhaṇa Sutta* (SN 22.59).[1] An insightful understanding of the doctrine of *anattā* helps in the deconstruction of the harmful gendered constructs of power and vulnerability that lead to CRSV. This position is reinforced by an analysis of Buddhist texts such as *Therīgāthā* and *Bhikkhunī Saṃyutta*[2] embodying Buddhist teachings on how the doctrine of *anattā* relates to gender.

The *Anattalakkhaṇa Sutta*, or 'Discourse on the Characteristic of Non-Self', is traditionally recorded as the second discourse of the Buddha. Being non-self – not a permanent self or anything that belongs to such a supposed thing – is one of the three characteristics of existence, the other two being impermanence (*anicca*) and unsatisfactoriness (*dukkha*). These three are interrelated and one cannot be isolated from the other two. That everything is non-self (*anattā*) means that there is no permanent, unchanging entity in anything animate or inanimate. The *Anattalakkhaṇa Sutta* analyses the make-up of all sentient beings as consisting of five *khandha*s or 'aggregates': material form, feeling, perception, volitional states (or mental formations) and consciousness. All five are identified as being impermanent and unsatisfactory and therefore unable to form an abiding self-essence in a sentient being.

Although the doctrine of *anattā* plays a culturally significant role in many Buddhist societies, many Buddhists lack a deep understanding of it. This is partly due to its complexity as well as the unwillingness to let go of conditioned constructs which many see as anchoring them in the world. These may be constructs of socio-economic class, ethnicity, religion or, importantly, gender. It has long been maintained in Buddhist teachings that Buddhist meditation training enhances the power and inner stability of the mind, which then facilitates insights into the subtle teachings on *anattā* (Harvey 1997; Kaszniak 2010; Goodman 2013, 561).

At the root of most of the sexual violence perpetrated during armed conflict are gendered socio-cultural constructs of power and vulnerability (Sivakumaran 2007). Concepts of power and invulnerability are often central to the construct of masculinity, while concepts of vulnerability and subordination frequently inform the feminine construct. Sexual violence is perpetrated on men to destroy the construct of power associated with masculinity. The penetration of the constructed impenetrable male body subverts gender norms leading to a perceived loss of the victim's masculine identity or to the victim being not a 'proper' or 'real' man and ascribing to the male victim the passive gendered identity of a woman. Testimony from survivors confirms the existence of this feminisation process (International Crimes Database 2016).

Corresponding to this essentialisation of – and attacks on – male identity, women are seen as subordinate to and possessions of the men of their own community, and sexual violence is perpetrated on them to demonstrate victory over the men of the other group who have failed to protect their women. Additionally, patriarchal notions linking female sexual 'purity' with honour is used to legitimise sexual violence perpetrated against women of the 'other' group to humiliate and control them (United Nations 2009). Moreover, constructs of subordination and passivity associated with femininity may lead to the sexualisation of women, resulting in CRSV perpetrated by combatants of their own side as well as the opposition. For instance, the Rwandan practice of *intsinzi* obliges many young girls and women to offer themselves to the military to congratulate them on their victory. During the civil war in 1994, women who refused to conform to this were accused of collaboration with the deposed regime and threatened with death (Dijkema 2001).

These toxic constructs are harmful to both men and women. Their deconstruction may be guided by the Buddhist doctrine of *anattā* and the Buddhist practice of meditation. These destructive conceptions of gender – bound up with the perpetrator's image of his 'self', projecting an image of 'I' as powerful – would be dispelled with the realisation of the illusory nature of this apparently powerful 'self'. Indeed, sexual violence may be supported by what is actually a fragile self-concept, in an attempt to compensate for this and pander to an illusion of strength. Sexual violence against both men and women of the 'other' group is caused by the attachment to an illusory sense of self, in part obtained by defining oneself and one's immediate community in opposition to another group, country, race or gender (Bergsmo and Buis 2019). Meditation reveals how this 'self' is constructed to show that any representation of self as a fixed, essential nature, whether it be based on gender, race, religion or nationality, is merely a deceptive belief (Engler 2003, 95). It is in fact a corollary of the doctrine of *anattā* that the individual has no fixed inner essence and that gendered perceptions of self are merely an imaginary attribute (Dharmasiri 1997, 152). The Buddhist teachings of *anattā*, particularly when combined with the support of feminist analysis, provides a powerful tool for the dispelling of harmful gendered constructs. For both Buddhism and feminism, conventional patterns of thinking and perceiving are a source of suffering (Gross 1993, 153), but can be changed for the better.

Moreover, analysis of Buddhist texts attributed to women, such as the *Therīgāthā* and *Bhikkhunī Saṃyutta*,[3] which provide Buddhist examples of how the doctrine of *anattā* relates to gender, clearly shows that such gendered constructs are in complete opposition to core Buddhist teachings and traditions. An example is the response of Bhikkhunī Somā to the question posed by Māra recorded in both the *Therīgāthā* and *Bhikkhunī Saṃyutta*. Māra is the representative of temptation and death within the round of rebirths, best known for his attempts to prevent the Buddha from attaining enlightenment. In the following passage, he hopes to keep the nun Somā within his clutches by undermining her confidence in her ability to reach awakening:

> Māra –
> That state so hard to achieve
> Which is to be attained by the seers,
> Can't be attained by a woman
> With her two-fingered wisdom.
> Bhikkhunī Somā –
> What does womanhood matter at all
> When the mind is concentrated well,
> When knowledge flows on steadily
> As one sees correctly into Dhamma.
> One to whom it might occur,
> 'I'm a woman' or 'I'm a man'
> Or 'I'm anything at all' –
> Is fit for Māra to address.[4]
> (Bodhi 1997)

The view that terms such as 'man' and 'woman' should be treated as local, conventional forms of speech (*janapada-nirutti*) is considered in the *Visuddhimagga* (commentary on XVII.24) (Ñāṇamoli Thera 2011, 538–539), a Theravāda Buddhist manual of doctrine and meditation by Buddhaghosa (c. fifth century) in Sri Lanka. The *Potthapāda Sutta* (DN.I.185–186, 195–201), which analyses how what people take as 'self' is sometimes perception and sometimes certain acquired meditative states, warns against being misled by or becoming attached to 'the world's designations, the world's expressions, the world's ways of speaking, the world's descriptions', because only someone entertaining such thoughts would be prey to craving, conceit, and desire (Dharmasiri 1997, 151).[5]

This effort to move beyond the gender binary[6] is gaining ground in the field of humanitarian action. Recent approaches towards preventing and addressing CRSV highlight the importance of moving away from gender equality to gender inclusivity. Acknowledging the multiple forms of sexual violence experienced differently by persons belonging to all gender identities as well as recognising the harms caused by non-sexual forms of gender-based violence is crucial in this effort (Dolan 2014).

To say that the Buddhist teachings discussed above make Buddhism an entirely egalitarian and inclusive religion where gender is concerned would be simplistic. There are many teachings and traditions within Buddhism which reinforce traditional and harmful gendered constructs. However, the doctrine of *anattā*, which is a core principle of Buddhism independent of time and place, can be used to revalorise these teachings and traditions to bring them into line with the fundamental values and vision of Buddhism (Gross 1993, 3; Wachs 2003, 271; Collett 2006, 60).

Meditations and affective change

The difficulty is that *anattā* is a considerably complex and subtle philosophical doctrine that does not lend itself to easy comprehension, but Buddhist meditation training enhances insights into it. Meditation is a major tool for self-transformation in Buddhism, such that individuals may realise and embody its principles. Buddhist teachings emphasise that meditative training increases compassionate responses to suffering and reduces aggression (Harvey 1997, 354; Kaszniak 2010). To explore the relevance of this, this article will draw on findings of recent research in neuroscience, further buttressing and demonstrating this position with empirical evidence (Condon et al. 2013). I will also draw on military research into meditation in order to ascertain practical measures to encourage meditative training among combatants.

There are different kinds of Buddhist meditation (Harvey 1997). *Vipassanā* or 'insight' meditation emphasises mindful awareness of the changing processes of body and mind, seeing them as conditioned patterns of events, rather than in terms of 'I', 'me' or 'mine'. This is the kind of practice that particularly develops insight into non-self by increasing the understanding of the constructed nature of one's self-image.[7] Nevertheless, this form of meditation needs to be handled carefully, so that in viewing persons as bundles of conditioned, impersonal processes, it does not undermine care and concern for others, or oneself. Hence, it is best complemented by other meditations. It is important that not only others but also oneself (and one's community) are seen as lacking a permanent self; otherwise, *anattā* may be misunderstood to imply that others and their concerns are less substantial than oneself and one's concerns, and even that others and their suffering are unimportant, or indeed do not really exist. In Japan, a Mahāyāna form of this argument has in fact been used in some Buddhist dialogues on warfare to justify violence (Jerryson and

Juergensmeyer 2010, 20). Care needs to be taken, therefore, to ensure the outcome of teachings and meditations on *anattā* is to reduce suffering regardless of in whom it arises.

Cultivated appropriately, meditative insight into *anattā* allows an expansion of consciousness in terms of greater awareness and wider sympathies to act from a less I-centred consciousness (Harvey 1997). In dissolving the constructed barriers between self and other, skilful recognition of the non-self characteristic aids the development of compassion for others that is more than empathy.

The kind of meditation called *samatha* develops deep calm, stillness and inner strength by cultivating strong mindfulness and concentration focused on an object such as the breathing process or on the good qualities of the Buddha, Dhamma and Saṅgha. Chanting can also have a meditative quality, developing calm and inner strength. Indeed, *samatha* helps a person to be calmer, more self-confident and resilient, and less likely to be controlled by harmful mind-states such as anger. This, in effect, helps a person to build a more harmonious and caring 'self', though one still recognised as lacking a fixed self-essence.

The cultivation of loving-kindness (*mettā*) and compassion (*karuṇā*)[8] are particular kinds of *samatha* meditation that develop a calm focus on these qualities, spreading them out to all kinds of people and other beings. Meditation on kindness and compassion also helps practitioners to contemplate the sufferings that we all share and equally wish to be free of, and so helps to widen a person's circle of concern (Rubin 2003, 399; Mendis 1978, 9; Harvey 1997).

A related key aspect of Buddhism is its ethical principle that one should not inflict on another being what one would not want done to oneself, as we all seek to avoid suffering (Harvey 2000, 33–34). Further to this, the principle of karma means that if one intentionally inflicts suffering on others, this plants a seed that will bring future suffering to oneself (Harvey 2000, 14–16). Both of these aspects are very relevant to negating any impulse to sexually abuse anyone.

The effectiveness of traditional Buddhist meditations is supported by empirical research in neuroscience and psychology. Several studies in these fields have demonstrated that certain forms of meditation enhance prosociality and reduce aggression. Meditation does this through disengaging the meditator from a self-focused outlook to a 'selfless' outlook and corresponding emotional responses (Klimecki 2012).

The response to suffering that certain forms of meditation cultivate goes beyond sympathy to active compassion. It is not just the ability to enter into and share another's suffering but the need to ask what one might do to alleviate the suffering of the other (Rubin 2003, 409; Singer and Bolz 2013, 466). Several studies find that greater physiological emotional response to others' suffering can lead to empathic distress, which is an aversive and self-oriented emotional response to the suffering of others, leading to withdrawal behaviour to protect oneself from negative emotions (Klimecki 2012, 9). Studies in neuroscience using functional magnetic resonance imaging (fMRI) demonstrate differences in response to the suffering of others between meditators and non-meditators. In non-meditators it activated the empathy-for-pain network, which they reported to be a highly aversive experience potentially reducing helping behaviours. In meditators, the suffering of others elicited the activation of compassion-related networks, and they reported more positive emotions and a willingness to engage in pro-social behaviours to alleviate the suffering of others (Singer and Bolz 2013, 530–536; Kaszniak 2010). The researchers also found that even a few days' training in meditation increased altruistic behaviours towards strangers, and compassionate response was not something that could be felt only by expert meditators (Singer and Bolz 2013, 530–536).

In addition to reducing aggression, meditation increases compassionate responses to suffering, even in the face of social pressure to avoid doing so (Condon et al. 2013, 21–27). This is a particularly significant finding in light of the group pressure that combatants may face to conform to group norms by perpetrating and/or condoning CRSV. The *Roots of Restraint* study conducted by the ICRC to understand the sources influencing soldiers and fighters to respect the principles and norms of IHL identified that socialisation (the process by which people adopt the norms and rules of a given community) is a key factor influencing combatants (ICRC 2018).

These findings demonstrate that meditation, especially those forms that cultivate loving-kindness and compassion, is a practical and effective means of negating self-centred attachment and widening a person's sympathies, in tune with the Buddhist teaching on the lack of a permanent, essential self and on our deep relationship to other beings. Seeing the non-selfness of aspects of the body–mind that we take as a fixed 'self', and developing kindness and compassion, thus work together to increase a compassionate response to suffering, which can thus result in actions to prevent and reduce suffering during armed conflict. This is directly relevant to the objectives of the IHL measures to prevent and address CRSV, as they are aimed at preventing unjustifiable and extreme suffering during armed conflict.

Military research on meditative training of combatants

Meditation has historically been a part of some warrior cultures, particularly that of the Samurai. It was believed that meditation would improve concentration and focus, in part by blocking off irrelevant thoughts.

Certain forms of meditation are currently used as part of the training of combatants in several armed forces in the world. The United States Department of Defense uses it effectively to reduce the stress experienced by combatants in conflict situations and train them to act wisely in such situations, preventing them from burning out, or acting out (the release of out-of-control aggressive or sexual impulses in order to gain relief from tension or anxiety) during prolonged stress exposure (Johnson et al. 2014; Barnes et al. 2016). It is also used widely among American veterans suffering from post-traumatic stress disorder. Several studies demonstrate that meditative training promotes self- and other-compassion among war veterans with post-traumatic stress disorder (Kearney et al. 2014). A study conducted among combatants from all ranks of the Indian army established that certain forms of meditation are effective in long-term reduction of stress. The combatants for this study were drawn from insurgency-prone and difficult areas (Assam/Jammu and Kashmir) with frequent cases of soldiers running amok. The study recommended incorporating meditative training into the combatants' morning exercise routine to manage physiological and psychological effects of stress (Cheema and Grewal 2013, 27). The implementation of a transcendental meditation (concentrating on a mantra) programme in the Brazilian military police forces showed greater relaxation among the military personnel, greater respect for the country and organisations, a reduction in disciplinary sanctions and improvement in the relationships of the officers with other community members (Roset and Schuler 1990).

Research has found that even relatively brief periods of meditation training can substantially reduce aggression without any concomitant change in executive control (the ability to carry out goal-directed behaviour using complex mental processes and cognitive abilities) (DeSteno et al. 2018). Thus, the use of meditative training as part of military training would in no way affect the ability of combatants to perform tasks requiring intense cognitive and physical capacity nor would they be required to engage in meditation for long periods of time. However, meditative training needs to be engaged in regularly to ensure that these effects are maintained consistently.

The initiation of meditative training among combatants may prove to be a challenge. At first glance, meditation would not seem a natural part of a martial culture. Also, the nature of meditation requires focused, intentional dedication. Merely making participation mandatory would not serve the purpose (Johnson et al. 2014). Combatants would have to be convinced, based on the proven benefits of meditation in terms of concentrated performance and by drawing parallels with elite military cultures that have used meditation, such as the Samurai.

The cultural familiarity of meditation in Buddhist communities (Maquet 1975, 555) is both a strength and a weakness when incorporating meditative training into the military training of Buddhist combatants. The cultural familiarity and the respect for meditation as a religious practice would make Buddhist combatants more open to the idea of engaging in meditation. However, meditation is often perceived by some lay Buddhists as merely a component of Buddhist ritual rather than a practice to engage in with the highest alertness and dedication. This should be taken into consideration when implementing meditation programmes among military personnel in Buddhist communities. Moreover, as discussed above, meditations on no-self need to be handled carefully, so as to be engaged with in a balanced way and not lead to undermining respect for others.[9]

Conclusion

The article has reported that, although developments in the interpretation of IHL since the early 1990s have led to the greater recognition of CRSV as a violation, there are still significant problems with prevention, recognition and accountability. I have examined how harmful, essentialised conceptions of gender often lie behind the use of CRSV. These conceptions also inform shame, absence of reporting and poor conviction rates. We have further noted that group culture and pressure may exacerbate its occurrence.

I have turned to two Buddhist resources to propose how to address these issues. The first is the doctrine of *anattā*, non-self, or the absence of a fixed individual identity, to undermine harmful gender essentialisation. The second is training in meaningful meditative development among combatants as well as non-combatants to create awareness and compassion, as well as to make people more resistant to negative peer pressure. Cognitive and psychological studies have confirmed greater prosociality and stronger integrity among meditators, even after relative short meditation sessions. The effectiveness of even short, easy-to-manage meditation sessions means that meditative training could form an important and heretofore overlooked aspect of military training and significantly contribute to reducing suffering during conflict. As meditation has always been valued and practised in Buddhist communities (Maquet 1975), it would be an effective starting point through which Buddhist communities can be brought closer to a genuine understanding of the significance of more complex and less familiar Buddhist doctrines and traditions, and their IHL-related implications.

Both Theravāda and Mahāyāna Buddhism place meditative training at the centre of Buddhist practice, and in many contemporary Buddhist contexts it is a practice widely engaged with by everyone, whether lay or monastic (Goodman 2013, 555), at least in simple forms, such as chanting. Nonetheless, the uptake of meditation among Buddhist communities is not uniform, with many leaving it to dedicated practitioners or to a small part of ritual practices on specific, one-off occasions. This article suggests that meditation, supported with explanations of related doctrine, could be successfully employed as a means to reduce suffering during conflict by influencing the behaviour of combatants through epistemological and affective change, which would ultimately contribute to the practical implementation of IHL measures to address CRSV. However, more attention needs to be paid to what *kind(s)* of 'meditation' are effective in combatting CRSV, and what kinds of 'meditation' have been studied in particular instances of empirical research. This article proposes specifically that the practice of *mettā* meditation cultivates calm, kindness and compassion, and the mindfulness emphasised especially in Vipassanā meditation leads to an understanding of the constructed nature of identity, including gender identity. The development of the two would result in significant changes in the understanding as well as the emotions of those practising them. The capacity of meditation to bring about such epistemological and affective change in individuals is demonstrated by drawing on Buddhist doctrine and practice and empirical evidence from recent research in neuroscience.

Notes

1. *Anattalakkhana Sutta, Saṃyutta Nikāya* 22.59 of the *Sutta Pitaka* of the Pali Canon. See Ñāṇamoli Thera (2010) for translation.
2. See Thanissaro Bhikkhu (2005) for translation of the *Therīgāthā* and https://www.accesstoinsight.org/tipitaka/sn/index.html#sn5 for translation of the *Bhikkhunī Saṃyutta*.
3. See *Somā Sutta* of *Bhikkhunī-saṃyutta* SN 5.2 (Bodhi 1997), *Therīgāthā* (Thanissaro Bhikkhu 2005) and Harvey 2000, 357–361 for detailed discussion.
4. *Somā Sutta* of *Bhikkhunī-saṃyutta* SN 5.2 (Bodhi 1997); see also *Therīgāthā* vv.60–62 (Thanissaro Bhikkhu 2005).
5. DN.I.202, as discussed in Dharmasiri (1997).
6. It should be noted that Buddhism has traditionally accepted four sexes: male, female, both and neither (Harvey 2000, 411–417).
7. Personal correspondence with Asanga Tilakaratne, 28 November 2019.
8. See Buddharakkhita (1989), Ñāṇamoli Thera (1994), Nyanaponika Thera (1994) and Sujiva (1991) for modern discussion on loving-kindness and compassion. The *Visuddhimagga*, in Chapter IX (Ñāṇamoli Thera 2011, 288–319), classifies meditation on loving-kindness and compassion as a *samatha* practice.
9. See also Noel Trew in this volume for the use and potential benefits of meditation in the military so long as it is coupled with training in Buddhist ethical precepts.

Acknowledgements

I gratefully acknowledge the comments and assistance given by Prof. Kate Crosby, Prof. Peter Harvey and Dr Noel Trew in the revision of this article. I am also thankful for the insights and guidance provided by Prof. Asanga Tilakaratne on the Buddhist philosophical aspects of this article and by Bhavani Fonseka and Zuleyka Piniella Mencia on the IHL aspects of this article.

Disclosure statement

This article has been supported by the International Committee of the Red Cross (ICRC).

ORCID

Charya Samarakoon http://orcid.org/0000-0003-3078-1082

References

Barnes, V. A., A. Monto, J. J. Williams, and J. L. Rigg. 2016. "Impact of Transcendental Meditation on Psychotropic Medication Use among Active Duty Military Service Members with Anxiety and PTSD." *Military Medicine* 181 (1): 56–63. doi:10.7205/MILMED-D-14-00333.

Benshoof, J. 2014. "The Other Red Line: The Use of Rape as an Unlawful Tactic of Warfare." *Global Policy* 5 (2): 146–158. doi:10.1111/1758-5899.12140.

Bergsmo, M., and E. J. Buis, eds. 2019. *Philosophical Foundations of International Criminal Law: Foundational Concepts*. Brussels: Torkel Opsahl Academic Epublisher.

Bodhi, B., trans. 1997. "Soma Sutta: Soma (SN 5.2)." *Access to Insight (BCBS Edition)*. 13 June 2010. http://www.accesstoinsight.org/tipitaka/sn/sn05/sn05.002.bodh.html

Buddharakkhita, A. 1989. *Mettā: The Philosophy and Practice of Universal Love. Access to Insight (BCBS Edition)*. 30 November 2013. http://www.accesstoinsight.org//lib/authors/buddharakkhita/wheel365.html

Carmichael, R. 2019. "Cambodia, War Crimes and Sexual Violence." *International Bar Association*. 1 October 2014. https://www.robertcarmichael.net/Robert_Carmichael/Articles/Entries/2014/10/1_Cambodia%2C_war_crimes_and_sexual_violence.html

Cheema, C. S. S., and C. D. S. Grewal. 2013. "Meditation for Stress Reduction in Indian Army – An Experimental Study." *IOSR Journal of Business and Management* 10 (2): 27–37. doi:10.9790/487X-1022737.

Collett, A. 2006. "Buddhism and Gender: Reframing and Refocusing the Debate". *Journal of Feminist Studies in Religion* 22 (2): 56–84. doi:10.2979/FSR.2006.22.2.55.

Condon, P., G. Desbordes, W. Miller, and D. Desteno. 2013. "Meditation Increases Compassionate Response to Suffering." *Psychological Science* 24 (10): 2125–2127. doi:10.1177/0956797613485603.

de Mel, N. 2013. *The Promise of the LLRC: Women's Testimony and Justice in Post-War Sri Lanka*. Colombo: International Centre for Ethnic Studies. http://www.ices.lk/wp-content/uploads/2013/11/the-Promise-of-the-LLRC.pdf

DeSteno, D., D. Lim, F. Duong, and P. Condon. 2018. "Meditation Inhibits Aggressive Responses to Provocations." *Mindfulness* 9 (4): 1117–1122. doi:10.1007/s12671-017-0847-2.

Dharmasiri, G. 1997. "Buddhism as the Greatest Ally of Feminism." In *Recent Researches in Buddhist Studies: Essays in Honour of Y. Karunadasa*, edited by K. L. Dhammajoti, A. Tilakaratne, and K. Abhayawansa, 138–172. Colombo: Y. Karunadasa Felicitation Committee.

Dijkema, C. 2001. "Why Study Gender and Conflict Together?" *Irénées: A Website of Resources for Peace*. http://www.irenees.net/bdf_fiche-analyse-801_en.html

Dolan, C. 2014. "Letting Go of the Gender Binary: Charting New Pathways for Humanitarian Interventions on Gender-based Violence." *International Review of the Red Cross* 96 (894): 485–501. doi:10.1017/S1816383115000120.

Eisenbruch, M. 2018a. "The Cultural Epigenesis of Gender-Based Violence in Cambodia: Local and Buddhist Perspectives." *Culture, Medicine and Psychiatry* 42: 315–349. doi:10.1007/s11013-017-9563-6.

Eisenbruch, M. 2018b. "Violence against Women in Cambodia: Towards a Culturally Responsive Theory of Change." *Culture, Medicine and Psychiatry* 42: 350–370. doi:10.1007/s11013-017-9564-5.

Engler, J. 2003. "Being Somebody and Being Nobody: A Re-examination of the Understanding of Self in Psychoanalysis and Buddhism." In *Psychoanalysis and Buddhism: An Unfolding Dialogue*, edited by J. D. Safran, 35–100. New York: Simon & Schuster.

Extraordinary Chambers in the Courts of Cambodia. 2012. "Press Release by the Trial Chamber regarding Sexual Violence Crimes." *Extraordinary Chambers in the Courts of Cambodia*. 5 June 2012. https://www.eccc.gov.kh/en/articles/press-release-trial-chamber-regarding-sexual-violence-crimes

Fernando, B. 1997. "Harmonizing Asia's Cultural Values and Human Rights: The Validity of the Approach – Sri Lankan Experience." *FOCUS*, September 1997. https://www.hurights.or.jp/archives/focus/section2/1997/09/harmonizing-asias-cultural-values-and-human-rights-the-validity-of-the-approach—sri-lankan-experience.html

Fonseka, B. 2015. *Transitional Justice in Sri Lanka and Ways Forward*. Colombo: Centre for Policy Alternatives. https://www.cpalanka.org/transitional-justice-in-sri-lanka-and-ways-forward/

Fonseka, B., and E. Schulz. 2018. "Gender and Transformative Justice in Sri Lanka." *LSE Women, Peace and Security Working Paper Series*. http://www.lse.ac.uk/women-peace-security/assets/documents/2018/WPS18Fonseka.pdf

Fonseka, B., and A. Woodworth. 2016. *Accountability and Reparations for Victims of Conflict Related Sexual Violence in Sri Lanka*. Colombo: Centre for Policy Alternatives. https://www.cpalanka.org/wp-content/uploads/2016/07/CSV-paper-June-2016.pdf

Gardam, J. G., and M. J. Jarvis. 2001. *Women, Armed Conflict and International Law*. The Hague: Kluwer Law International.

Goodley, H. 2019. "Ignoring Male Victims of Sexual Violence in Conflict is Short-sighted and Wrong." *Chatham House*. Last modified 10 January 2019. https://www.chathamhouse.org/expert/comment/ignoring-male-victims-sexual-violence-conflict-short-sighted-and-wrong

Goodman, C. 2013. "Buddhist Meditation Theory and Practice." In *A Companion to Buddhist Philosophy*, edited by S. M. Emmanuel, 555–571. Hoboken: John Wiley & Sons.

Gross, R. M. 1993. *Buddhism after Patriarchy: A Feminist History, Analysis, and Reconstruction of Buddhism*. Delhi: Sri Satguru.

Harvey, P. 1997. "Psychological Aspects of Theravāda Buddhist Meditation Training: Cultivating and I-less Self." In *Recent Researches in Buddhist Studies: Essays in Honour of Y. Karunadasa*, edited by K. L. Dhammajoti, A. Tilakaratne, and K. Abhayawansa, amended version, 341–365. Colombo: Y. Karunadasa Felicitation Committee. https://sunderland.academia.edu/PeterHarvey

Harvey, P. 2000. *An Introduction to Buddhist Ethics: Foundations, Values and Issues*. Cambridge: Cambridge University Press.

ICRC. 2005. *Customary International Humanitarian Law, Volume I: Rules*. Edited by J.-M. Henckaerts and L. Doswald-Beck. Geneva: ICRC. https://www.icrc.org/en/doc/assets/files/other/customary-international-humanitarian-law-i-icrc-eng.pdf

ICRC. 2018. *The Roots of Restraint in War*. Geneva: ICRC. https://www.icrc.org/en/publication/4352-roots-restraint-war

International Crimes Database. 2016. *Gender Jurisprudence for Gender Crimes?* International Crimes Database. The Hague: T.M.C. Asser Instituut. http://www.internationalcrimesdatabase.org/upload/documents/20160701T104109-ICD%20Brief%2020%20-%20Ruiz.pdf

International Crimes Evidence Project. 2014. *Island of Impunity? Investigation into International Crimes in the Final Stages of the Sri Lankan Civil War*. Sydney: Public Interest Advocacy Centre. https://piac.asn.au/2014/02/12/island-of-impunity/

Jerryson, M., and M. Juergensmeyer. 2010. *Buddhist Warfare*. New York: Oxford University Press.

Johnson, D., N. J. Thom, E. A. Stanley, L. Haase, A. N. Simmons, P.-A. B. Shih, W. K. Thompson, et al. 2014. "Modifying Resilience Mechanisms in At-Risk Individuals: A Controlled Study of Mindfulness Training in Marines Preparing for Deployment." *American Journal of Psychiatry* 171 (8): 844–853. doi:10.1176/appi.ajp.2014.13040502.

Kaszniak, A. 2010. "Empathy and Compassion in Buddhism and Neuroscience." *Public Broadcasting Service*. 17 March 2010. https://www.pbs.org/thebuddha/blog/2010/Mar/17/empathy-and-compassion-buddhism-and-neuroscience-a/

Kearney, D. J., C. McManus, C. A. Malte, M. E. Martinez, B. Felleman, and T. L. Simpson. 2014. "Loving-Kindness Meditation and the Broaden-and-Build Theory of Positive Emotions among Veterans with Posttraumatic Stress Disorder." *Medical Care* 52 (12): 32–38. doi:10.1097/MLR.0000000000000221.

Klimecki, O. 2012. "Training the compassionate and the empathic brain." PhD diss., University of Zurich.

Lei, Z. 2019. "Buddhist Nationalism as Social Movement in Political Transition: MaBaTha Movement in Myanmar." *International Relations and Diplomacy* 7 (2): 66–75.

Lyth, A. 2001. "The Development of the Legal Protection against Sexual Violence in Armed Conflicts – Advantages and Disadvantages." *Kvinna till Kvinna Foundation*, December 2001.

Mack, M., and J. Pejic. 2020. *Increasing Respect for International Humanitarian Law in Non-international Armed Conflicts*. Geneva: ICRC. https://www.icrc.org/en/publication/0923-increasing-respect-international-humanitarian-law-non-international-armed-conflicts

Manchanda, R. 2001. "Where are the Women in South Asian Conflicts?" In *Women, War and Peace in South Asia: Beyond Victimhood to Agency*, edited by R. Manchanda, 10–38. Michigan: Sage.

Maquet, J. 1975. "Meditation in Contemporary Sri Lanka: Idea and Practice." *Journal of Transpersonal Psychology* 7 (2): 182–196.

Mendis, K. N. G. 1978. *The Second Discourse of the Buddha on the No-Self Characteristic*. Kandy: Buddhist Publication Society.

Ministry for Foreign Affairs Sweden. 2007. *International Expert Meeting: 'Gender Perspectives on International Humanitarian Law'*. Stockholm: Ministry for Foreign Affairs Sweden. https://www.icrc.org/en/doc/assets/files/other/ihl_and_gender.pdf

Ñāṇamoli Thera, trans. 1994. *The Practice of Loving-kindness (Metta). Access to Insight (BCBS Edition)*. 30 November 2013. http://accesstoinsight.org/lib/authors/nanamoli/wheel007.html

Ñāṇamoli Thera, trans. 2010. "Anatta-lakkhana Sutta: The Discourse on the Not-self Characteristic." *Access to Insight (BCBS Edition)*. 13 June 2010. https://www.accesstoinsight.org/tipitaka/sn/sn22/sn22.059.nymo.html

Ñāṇamoli Thera, trans. 2011. *The Path of Purification: Visuddhimagga*. Kandy: Buddhist Publication Society. http://www.accesstoinsight.org/lib/authors/nanamoli/PathofPurification2011.pdf

Nyanaponika Thera, 1994. "The Four Sublime States: Contemplations on Love, Compassion, Sympathetic Joy and Equanimity." *Access to Insight (BCBS Edition)*. 30 November 2013. http://accesstoinsight.org/lib/authors/nyanaponika/wheel006.html

Office of the High Commissioner for Human Rights. 2015. "*Report of the OHCHR Investigation on Sri Lanka*." Human Rights Council. https://www.ohchr.org/EN/HRBodies/HRC/RegularSessions/Session30/Documents/A-HRC-30-2_en.doc

Office of the Special Representative of the Secretary-General on Sexual Violence in Conflict. 2021. *Myanmar*. Information Based on the Report of the Secretary-General to the Security Council (S/2021/312). Issued on 30 March 2021. https://www.un.org/sexualviolenceinconflict/countries/myanmar/

Pettersson, T., and P. Wallensteen. 2015. "Armed Conflicts, 1946–2014." *Journal of Peace Research* 52 (4): 536–550. doi:10.1177/0022343315595927.

Roset, J. L., and M. Schuler. 1990. "Implementing the Transcendental Meditation Programme in the Brazilian Military Police Forces: A Case Study." In *International Meditation Society, Rio de Janeiro, Brazil, in Conjunction with Committee of Ayurvedic Medicine*, edited by M. C. Dillbeck, 4073–4076. Brasilia: Secretary of Medical Services, Ministry of Social Welfare.

Rubin, J. 2003. "A Well-Lived Life: Psychoanalytic and Buddhist Contributions." In *Psychoanalysis and Buddhism: An Unfolding Dialogue*, edited by J. D. Safran, 387–427. New York: Simon & Schuster.

Singer, T., and M. Bolz. 2013. *Compassion: Bridging Practice and Science*. Leipzig: Max Planck Society.

Sivakumaran, S. 2007. "Sexual Violence against Men in Armed Conflict." *European Journal of International Law* 18 (2): 253–276. doi:10.1093/ejil/chm013.

Sujiva, V. 1991. *Loving-kindness Meditation: Meditation on Loving Kindness and Other Sublime States*. BuddhaNet eBooks. http://www.buddhanet.net/pdf_file/allmetta.pdf

Suk, C., and I. Skjelsbæk. 2010. "Sexual Violence in Armed Conflicts." *PRIO Policy Brief*. Vol. 1. Oslo: Peace Research Institute Oslo.

Thanissaro Bhikkhu, trans. 2005. "Therigatha: Verses of the Elder Nuns." Edited by Access to Insight. *Access to Insight (BCBS Edition)*. 30 November 2013. http://www.accesstoinsight.org/tipitaka/kn/thig/index.html

United Nations. 2009. *15 Years of the United Nations Special Rapporteur on Violence Against Women (1994-2009) – A Critical Review*. https://www.ohchr.org/Documents/Issues/Women/15YearReviewofVAWMandate.pdf

Wachs, M. 2003. "Buddhism and Women." In *Pranamalekha, Essays in Honour of Ven. Dr. Madagama*, edited by V. Wimalajothi, V. M. Pemananda, V. U. Ananda, and S. Nanayakkara, 259–277. London: London Buddhist Vihara.

Wood, E. J. 2014. "Conflict-related Sexual Violence and the Policy Implications of Recent Research." *International Review of the Red Cross* 96 (894): 457–478. doi:10.1017/S1816383115000077.

ICRC

HOW BUDDHIST PRINCIPLES CAN HELP THE PRACTICAL IMPLEMENTATION OF IHL VALUES DURING WAR WITH RESPECT TO NON-COMBATANTS

Ven Kosgama Muditha, Ven Koralegama Gnanawasa
and Ven Kirindiwela Pagngnawansa

ABSTRACT

The arising of war is almost inevitable within human societies, and IHL seeks to regulate its conduct as far as possible. According to Buddhism, mental defilements are the roots of conflict, so from the viewpoint of Dhamma, awareness of them is imperative if suffering is to be effectively reduced. The aim of this study is to examine the utility of Buddhist teachings in ensuring the humane treatment, without adverse distinctions, of those caught up in war, by the development of self-control, self-discipline and responsibility. The *Vepacitti Sutta* describes the ideal mental qualities that are required to do this, and we point out the practical implications of those qualities, as explained in the *Mahācattārīsaka Sutta*. Our argument is that cultivating the mind according to the practical path that we introduce is conducive to self-control, discipline and responsibility during a war with respect to international humanitarian law (IHL), and particularly with respect to non-combatants.

The goal of Buddhist teaching is to attain enlightenment by uprooting all defilements. Buddhism never advocates war. The purpose of Buddhism is non-violence and uprooting the causes of war. There is no space for silence in Buddhism when there is going to be a war. On the other hand, although people may think that they live free from hostility, free from violence, free from rivalry, free from ill will, free from those who are hostile, in practice this is not possible for any except enlightened persons. Most people cannot escape living with problems connected with violence and ill will: they wish to, but fail 'to live without hate, harming, hostility or malignity, and without enmity' (*averā adaṇḍā asapattā abyāpajjā viharemu averino*) (D.II.276). The arising of war is almost inevitable, therefore, within human societies. According to

DOI: 10.4324/9781003439820-20

Buddhism, defilements are the cause of conflicts, so awareness of Dhamma and of the nature of defilements is essential during a war to reduce pain.

As stated in Article 3 common to the four Geneva Conventions:

> Persons taking no active part in the hostilities, including members of armed forces who have laid down their arms and those placed 'hors de combat' by sickness, wounds, detention, or any other cause, shall in all circumstances be treated humanely, without any adverse distinction founded on race, colour, religion or faith, sex, birth or wealth, or any other similar criteria.[1]

According to Buddhism, making such adverse distinctions arises as a result of defilements. For instance, while the defilement hatred (*dosa*) is a causal factor in war, it also, once war has come about, leads to the absence of humane treatment of non-combatants because it overrides normal ethics, in turn creating violations of international humanitarian law (IHL). Awareness of the defilements can provide an antidote to problematic thinking and behaviour. If someone caught up in a war pays attention to how he or she should deal with defilements, then it is easier to practise IHL on the battlefield and in its aftermath. Paying attention to underlying defilements requires concentration on self-control, discipline and responsibility, with volition being the vital factor because it provides the entire psychological impulse behind a deed. 'Volition (*cetanā*), monks, I call karma [action]; having willed, one acts through body, speech or mind' (A.III.415). Buddhism always aims for volitional purity, namely for ensuring that volitions are not defiled by greed, hatred or ignorance. How one applies the mind to anything has a key effect on the following mental states, then actions and their results:

> Mind (*mano*) is the forerunner of all mental states. Mind is their chief; mind-made are they. If one speaks or acts with a sullied mind, because of that, suffering will follow one, even as the wheel follows the foot of the draught-ox. (Dhp.1)

Hence it is clear not only that there is a similarity between the goals of Buddhism and IHL to reduce suffering, but that Buddhism is alert to the psychological defilements that might lead one to act in contravention of such law. Being thus attuned, it offers ways of developing awareness to counter contraventions. Applying Buddhist teaching in a pragmatic manner, therefore, is one of the most effective methods of minimising breaches of IHL.

This study aims to point out the utility of Buddhist teaching in ensuring the humane treatment, without adverse distinction, of those caught up in war through the development of self-control, self-discipline and responsibility, using a threefold formula of clear vision, perseverance and mindfulness which is drawn from the Noble Eightfold Path. To develop this study, we shall draw on a number of authoritative texts from the Pāli Canon. Our primary canonical sources are the *Kalahavivāda Sutta* and the *Vāseṭṭha Sutta* of the *Sutta-nipāta*; the *Vepacitti Sutta* of the *Saṃyutta Nikāya*; the *Mahā-cattārīsaka*

Sutta and the *Madhura Sutta* of the *Majjhima Nikāya*; the *Mahā-satipaṭṭhāna Sutta* of the *Dīgha Nikāya;* and the *Sotānugata Sutta* of the *Aṅguttara-nikāya*. We extract from these texts Buddhist teachings related to the kind of context in which IHL applies, and build on these to introduce a practical Buddhist method to increase respect for IHL.

As depicted in the *Kalahavivāda Sutta*, the impulse of desire for things that are considered desirable (*piya*) is the foundation of all sorts of disputes, and defilements such as greed and anger which are the roots of war (Sn.863). When these defilements appear in the mind, they cause or worsen quarrels and disputes. During such situations, concentration is imperative. While the *Kalahavivāda Sutta* teaches how awareness of one's defilements can lead one to disengage from disputes, the issue here is how one can be conscious of these defilements within a war situation, including on a battlefield.

Sakka's calm patience in the *Vepacitti Sutta*

We can turn to the *Vepacitti Sutta*, which is one of the oldest sources in Buddhism, to explain the appropriate treatment of prisoners of war. According to the *sutta*, there was a battle between the gods and the demons or antigods, called *asuras*. Vepacitti was the lord of the *asuras*. At the beginning of the war, he ordered his forces, in the event of their victory in battle, to tie up Sakka, the leader of the gods, and bring him to the city of the *asuras*. Similarly, Sakka also ordered his forces to capture and bring back Vepacitti to the divine assembly hall, if they won.

These parallel plans of both leaders might be indicative of their respect for the principle that the ultimate goal of war is to overcome one's adversary to solve one or more problems without disproportionate harm to the retinue of the opposing forces, for neither leader wished to kill the other, or take the troops of the adversary into permanent captivity.

According to the *sutta*, the gods won and the *asuras* lost the war. So, the gods did as they had been ordered and brought Vepacitti to the divine assembly hall. As Sakka was entering and leaving the hall, Vepacitti abused and insulted him with rude, harsh words. Now Vepacitti was no longer an active participant in the war and was mentally confused, behaving in an ill-tempered manner, an example of the mentality of a war victim from the Buddhist perspective. This allows us to study the behaviour of Sakka, lord of the gods, towards Vepacitti as an authoritative Buddhist example of how to treat the captured. Despite the goading, Sakka did not respond to Vepacitti or take any action against him. This shows how self-control, discipline and responsibility are advocated, exactly those virtues required in order to adhere to IHL.

At this juncture in the story, Mātalī, the divine charioteer, posed three questions or suggestions to Sakka. First, he asked whether Sakka tolerated the harsh words of Vepacitti because of fear or weakness.

Sakka replied, 'It is neither through fear nor weakness that I am patient with Vepacitti. How can a wise person like me engage in [verbal] combat with a fool (*bāla*)?' (S.I.221). He displayed patience – a vital mental quality and one that must be practised both in battle and in its aftermath. As mentioned above, the aim of battle is to solve the problems that caused the conflict, and patience is one of the most effective means to do so. An angry and vindictive response to the curses of a captive adds nothing of worth.

Mātalī's second suggestion was that if those like Vepacitti are not punished, they will continue to repeat the same offence. Sakka's reply was that the only way to put a stop to such a fool was, while recognising the anger of the other, to remain mindful and calm oneself (*sato upasammatī'ti*) (S.I.222). Accordingly, we see here that concentration on patience, mindfulness and calm must be practised. We shall return to the question of how one can practise mindfulness and calm in the midst of hostilities below.

The third of Mātalī's suggestions was that if a fool mistakes our patience for fear then he will go after us even harder, like a cow chasing someone who runs away. Sakka replies skilfully in three verses as follows:

> Let it be whether or not he thinks, 'He endures me out of fear', of goals that culminate in one's own good none is found better than patience.
>
> When a person endowed with strength patiently endures a weakling, they call that the supreme patience; the weakling must be patient always.
>
> They call that strength no strength at all – the strength that is the strength of folly – but no one can reproach a person who is strong because guarded by Dhamma. (S.I.322)

When this context is compared with IHL, specifically the Third Geneva Convention relative to the treatment of prisoners of war,[2] it can be seen that Sakka's reply depicts how one should treat a defeated enemy without any adverse distinction. When one practises sustained patience during a war, one can more easily keep self-control and discipline and take responsibility for one's actions.

The core idea of this *sutta* is depicted by two further verses as follows:

> One who repays an angry man with anger thereby makes things worse for himself. Not repaying an angry man with anger, one wins a battle hard to win.
>
> He practises for the welfare of both, his own and the other's, when, knowing that his foe is angry, he mindfully maintains his peace. (S.I.322–323)

Here, Sakka's opinion reflects broader Buddhist ethical principles that are applicable in a war situation, especially as regards treating prisoners of war humanely:

(1) The importance of mindfully maintaining one's own peace even when aware of the foe's anger – mindfulness and clarity of consciousness or situational awareness (*sati* and *sati-sampajañña*).
(2) The realisation that the ultimate patience is showing tolerance towards those who are weak – enduring patience is the highest austerity (*khantī paramaṃ tapo titikkhā*).
(3) The importance of developing calmness (*upasammati*) – hatred is appeased by non-hatred (Dhp.5).

The importance of mindfulness and awareness

Sati-sampajaññā, the pair 'mindfulness' and 'awareness', or 'situational awareness', indicates the mental state that needs to be awoken in a situation. *Khanti*, 'patience', is the pivotal quality that leads to peace. *Upasammati*, 'to free from conflicts' or 'to calm down', implies the ideal way of keeping company with others with calm, compassion and amity.

According to the *Mahā-satipaṭṭhāna Sutta*, situational awareness – that is, clear awareness of one's bodily and vocal activities and their context – should be present in all human activities (D.II.83). The *Sati-sampajañña Sutta* in the *Aṅguttara Nikāya* gives a wider perspective on the same matter:

> Suppose there is a tree deficient in branches and foliage. Then its shoots do not grow to fullness; also its bark, softwood, and heartwood do not grow to fullness. So too, when there is no mindfulness and situational awareness, for one deficient in mindfulness and clear comprehension, the sense of moral shame (*hiri*) and moral dread (*ottappa*) lack their proximate cause. When there is no sense of moral shame and moral dread, restraint of the sense faculties lacks its proximate cause. When there is no restraint of the sense faculties, for one deficient in restraint of the sense faculties, virtuous behaviour lacks its proximate cause. (A.IV.336)

This context clearly explains that *sati-sampajañña*, mindfulness and situational awareness, is fundamental, underlying many aspects of successful functioning, and that working without them generates problems and failures. Thought with *sati-sampajañña* generates right thoughts, which bring benefits. Thought without *sati-sampajañña* causes wrong ideas, which bring problems and suffering. Speaking without mindfulness may often involve dishonesty. Hence, one should be mindful and have situational awareness in relation to whatever is said or discussed. Moreover, *sati* implies concentration in the mind, and *sampajañña* aids the maintenance of concentration in a fourfold manner as depicted in the commentary to the *Majjhima Nikāya* (Ps.I.252): awareness regarding the purpose (*sātthaka-sampajaññaṃ*), the suitability (*sappāya-sampajaññaṃ*), the domain (*gocara-sampajaññaṃ*) and the undeluded situational awareness of the activity concerned (*asammoha-sampajaññaṃ*).

During a battle, situational awareness, *sampajañña*, can pragmatically be applied: in remembering the purpose of the conflict, namely that it is not to inflict gratuitous harm but to resolve a problem by overcoming the adversary; the measures taken must correspond to this understanding, and should concur with the values of IHL, without being clouded by deluded conceptions. Moreover, being the key mental quality for carrying out activities without inner conflict, *sati-sampajañña* leads those who practise it to concentrate on ultimate patience and calmness, which is required during a war for ensuring the humanitarian treatment of those caught up in it.

The relevance of the factors of the Noble Eightfold Path

Now let us examine how these qualities can be practised to maintain self-control, discipline and responsibility during war. The Noble Eightfold Path is a summary of all the key attributes that lead to success on the Buddhist path. In this case, we find a link between mindfulness and the Noble Eightfold Path (*aṭṭhaṅgika-magga*), the seventh factor of which is right mindfulness, *sammā-sati*. Its position in the Noble Eightfold Path shows that right mindfulness is closely associated with three more of the eight factors, namely right thought (*sammā saṅkappa*), right speech (*sammā vācā*) and right action (*sammā kammanta*), which are needed for both material development and liberation.

While the Noble Eightfold Path leads to emancipation, that it is also important for success in life in general is clear from the *Mahā-cattārīsaka Sutta* (M.117), which depicts two ways of practising it:

(1) That which is affected by taints, partaking of merit, ripening on the side of attachment (*sāsavā puññabhāgiyā upadhivepakkā*).
(2) That which is noble, taintless, supramundane, a factor of the path (*ariyā anāsavā lokuttarā maggaṅgā*) (M.III.71).

The *sutta* goes through the first five factors of the path, showing how the first way improves even the lives of ordinary people, i.e. 'worldlings' (*puthujjana*), whereas the second level of the path applies to noble ones or saints. Accordingly, we must pay attention to the way in which mindfulness can be practised for the betterment of this life and how it can be applied to maintaining self-control during war.

As stated in the *Mahā-cattārīsaka Sutta*, right view (*sammā diṭṭhi*) means identifying and understanding the right and wrong paths, right effort (*sammā vāyāma*) means making an effort to avoid the wrong path and pursue the right path, right mindfulness (*sammā sati*) means abandoning the wrong path and mindfully entering upon and abiding by the right path. In this way, these three constituents encompass all the other constituents (M.III.72). In other words, this is the common formula connected with the other path-factors in order to reach either the mundane goal or the supramundane goal as depicted by the *sutta*. The *Mahā-cattārīsaka Sutta* thus depicts an inseparable interrelationship between right view, right effort and right mindfulness in order to cultivate the other constituents of the path.

Now, we draw attention to how this formula can be applied with the other factors, i.e. right intention *(sammā saṅkappa)*, right speech (*sammā vācā*), right bodily action (*sammā kammanta*) and right livelihood (*sammā ājīva*), within the mindset of a combatant so as to follow IHL.

Saṅkappa (intention or thought) is a synonym for *vitakka* (thought). *Vitakka* is one of the six particulars or occasionals (*pakiṇṇaka*) that come under the mental factors (*cetasika*) in Abhidhamma and may be karmically wholesome, unwholesome or neutral. Neutral means either that the states of consciousness and mental factors are mere *kamma*-results (*vipāka*) or that they function without karmic effects and so are part of functional consciousness, *kiriya-citta*, for example the consciousness of a Buddha. There are three kinds of karmically unwholesome (*akusala*) thoughts: sensuous thoughts (*kāma vitakka*), hating thoughts (*byāpāda vitakka*) and cruel thoughts (*vihiṃsā vitakka*). Conversely, thoughts of renunciation (*nekkhamma vitakka*), thoughts devoid of hate (*avyāpāda vitakka*) and thoughts of not harming (*avihiṃsā vitakka*) are the karmically wholesome (*kusala*) thoughts (S.II.151–152; M.III.72). The former three constituents deal with 'wrong intention' while the latter three constituents deal with 'right intention', i.e. *sammā saṅkappa*, the second factor of the Noble Eightfold Path.

We shall now explore the application of these different types of intentions during war. Sensuous thought involves thinking about, and the enjoyment of, sensual pleasures such as physical beauty, sweet sounds, etc. It is associated with greed. Conversely, thoughts of renunciation or thoughts free from lust (*nekkhamma vitakka*) are linked with the eradication of greed. Accordingly, we cannot expect eradication of greed from one who is at war, because war itself is based on greed and anger. Buddhism does not countenance the unethical enjoyment of sense pleasures, because its effect could be theft, sexual violence or other malpractices. When this is transferred to the context of war, if non-combatants are to be protected against any form of indecent assault and inhuman treatment such as sexual abuse, combatants must be able to deal ethically and mindfully with sensuous thoughts. Right intention, moreover, is applicable in thinking of delivering war victims from suffering and could therefore be directed to the protection of the values of IHL.

Byāpāda means the ill will that can lead to injuring or killing others. *Vihiṃsā* means the ill will that can lead to persecuting or torturing others. These two thoughts are motivated by hatred. When one thinks or plans to kill or cause harm by any means, it is called *vihiṃsā vitakka*. On the other hand, *avihiṃsā* means the desire to avoid harming, i.e. compassion or pity, which is the opposite of ill will. The thought that leads us to non-violent action is *avihiṃsā vitakka*. During a battle, when the defeat of others with weapons is the aim, it is impossible to uproot hateful or cruel thoughts and replace them with non-hatred, loving-kindness and compassion. However, combatants can concentrate on the thoughts that minimise violence, *avihiṃsā vitakka*, as far as practicable, especially towards non-combatants. *Avihiṃsā vitakka*, in this manner, can be applied with the aforementioned formula to abstention from the unnecessary violence and inhuman treatment that characterise IHL violations. To do this, the mindset of a combatant must concentrate on IHL principles – that is, his/her right vision (*sammā diṭṭhi*) – and he/she then would strive (*sammā vāyāma*) with mindful (*sammā sati*) intention as discussed. With frequent practice he/she would then be better able to adhere to IHL.

Moving on to right speech, we draw attention to the role of verbal discipline in engaging with others from several Buddhist perspectives. As his final disciplinary act, the Buddha decreed the ostracism (*brahma-daṇda*) of the monk Channa, formerly the charioteer of prince Siddhārtha, whereby all monks were forbidden to keep him company in order to chastise him (D. II.151). Channa fainted three times when he was informed of this punishment, as depicted in the commentary, and eventually became an Arahant (Dhp-a. II.112). This incident shows the effect of speech – or meaningful silence – to modify someone's behaviour. A well-spoken statement, according to the *Vācā Sutta*, is endowed with five characteristics; it is spoken at the right time, in truth, affectionately, beneficially and with good-will (A.III.243–244; cf. M.I.395).

Right speech, as the third path factor, simply means abstaining from lying (*musāvādā*), malicious speech (*pisunāvācā*), harsh language (*pharusāvācā*) and foolish babble (*sampappalāpā*). Right intention, moreover, is the base of right verbal expressions, because this leads to right thoughts (*vitakka*) such as ungreediness, non-hatred or non-delusion.

In the case of treating non-combatants humanely, combatants should be aware of and sympathetic to their mental situation, since they are likely to be suffering from fear, grief, anger, frustration or other negative emotions (*dukkhaṃ seti parājito* – Dhp.201 = S.I.189), and might also behave like Vepacitti, for example. In practising right speech, those dealing with captured combatants should have a clear view (*sammā diṭṭhi*) regarding speech, should make an effort (*sammā vāyāma*) to speak with calm words and should mindfully (with *sammā sati*) express their words. That is how one can apply the common formula together with right speech in the aftermath of a battle, for example.

The fourth path factor, right bodily action (*sammā kammanta*), stands for three ethical behaviours: abstaining from killing, from stealing, and from adultery or unlawful sexual intercourse. Abstaining from killing is difficult or impossible during war. Nevertheless, abusing non-combatants, i.e. killing them, stealing their property, or perpetrating rape and other forms of sexual violence, is unacceptable. Concerning right bodily action, again combatants can apply the three-fold formula: clear vision (*sammā diṭṭhi*), perseverance (*sammā vāyāma*) and mindfulness (*sammā sati*).

The fifth path factor, right livelihood (*sammā ājīva*), means abstaining from unrighteous occupations such as trading in arms, drugs or poisons, human trafficking, slaughtering or fishing, or those involving deceit, treachery, soothsaying, usury and so on. While abstaining from trading in weapons cannot perhaps be expected in a war situation, it resonates with the prohibition on the use and stockpiling of weapons that cause unnecessary suffering or superfluous injury, in line with the IHL conventions prohibiting the use of chemical and biological weapons, landmines and blinding lasers, for example.[3]

Overall, volition/intention (*cetanā*) in the form of right intention (*sammā saṅkappa*) plays a pivotal role, being the coordinator of all the path factors, as it is the base of any form of action (*kamma*) as depicted above.

Treating people equally

It is appropriate now to draw attention to Buddhist reflections on eliminating any form of adverse distinction based on racism, apartheid or separation of ethnic groups, and so on. Within Buddhism, there is no room for any sort of differentiation based on caste or race, as depicted in the *Pahārada Sutta*, which illustrates this through the metaphor of rivers pouring into the sea. The great rivers that arrive at the great ocean are simply called the great ocean without their former names and designations; similarly, the social backgrounds of people are irrelevant when they ordain in the monastic community (A.IV.201). The same notion is raised in the *Madhura Sutta*, which records the Buddha saying, 'the facts being what they are, the people of all four castes are absolutely equal (*samasamā*) and I do not see any difference between them at all in these respects' (M.II.87). To honour this, practising equanimity, calm and patience is the possible solution in suppressing adverse distinctions. The *Vāseṭṭha Sutta* (Sn.594–656) discusses equanimity in two ways, using a biological (Jayatilleke 2006, 72) and a stratification argument. Although there are different species among plants and animals, man constitutes one species (Sn.607), despite minor observable differences in such features as hair, skin colour, the shape of the head, etc. Differences among humans are a matter of convention, depending on occupation and not caste (Sn.612–620).

When it comes to IHL, combatants should realise that there is no basis for dealing with non-combatants in a divisive way, based on ethnic or social hierarchies. Rather, they should be treated in accord with ethical principles such as equanimity, calm and patience, which, in this context, can be connected with right intention in the Noble Eightfold Path. Furthermore, striving (*sammā vāyāma*) to retain mindfulness (*sammā sati*) and concentration with a clear mental vision (*sammā diṭṭhi*) is the pragmatic way of applying the common formula we have suggested, brought out from the *Mahā-cattārīsaka Sutta*.

Conclusion

We have now come to the end of our discussion of our proposed Buddhist approach to the humane treatment of non-combatants based on the Noble Eightfold Path. In this regard, insufficient knowledge or understanding may be the major cause of IHL violations. Unless frequent training takes place, practical implementation is impossible. If the teaching process and the practice are perfected, war crimes will cease and this Buddhist approach holds out the possibility of reinforcing IHL training. To this end, the threefold formula of clear vision, perseverance and mindfulness that we set out at the beginning of this article to

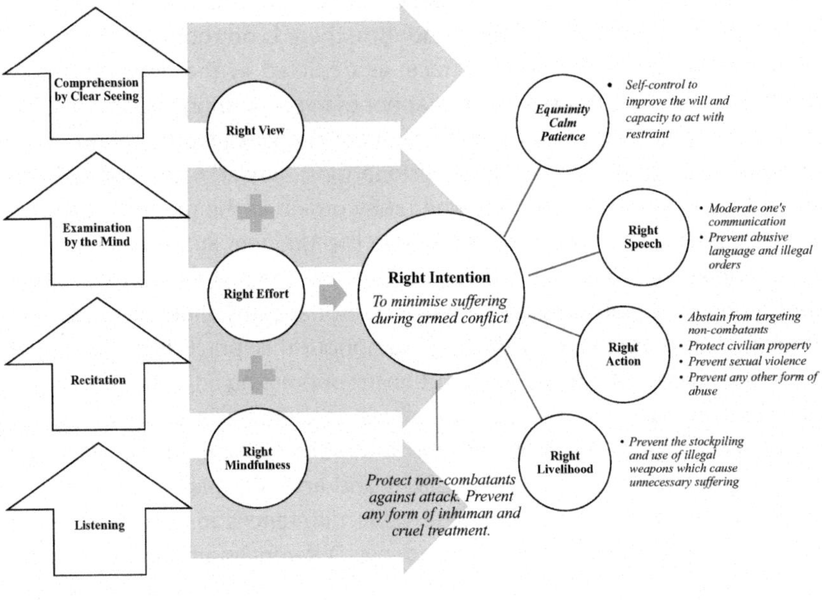

Figure 1. Practical implementation of Buddhist and international humanitarian law (IHL) values during a war.

embed IHL into the mindset of belligerents in a war situation can be enhanced by the fourfold way of practising the Dhamma, i.e. by listening, recitation, examination by the mind, and comprehension by clear seeing (*tassa te dhammā sotānugatā honti, vacasā paricitā, manasānupekkhitā, diṭṭhiyā suppaṭividdhā*) depicted in the *Sotānugata Sutta* (A.II.185). In this respect, it is particularly important for a combatant to comply with the fourfold path factors – right intention, right speech, right bodily action and right livelihood – and their IHL particularities as discussed above. For ease of implementation, recapping all of the above, Figure 1 illustrates this Buddhist approach towards the practical implementation of IHL values during a war.

To conclude, we initially discussed the problematic defilements that can both lead to war and exacerbate violations of IHL during war, drawing on both *sutta* texts and the analysis of defilements and their opposites in Abhidhamma. We also examined the mental qualities required to minimise suffering during war, before moving to the application of the Noble Eightfold Path to increase adherence to IHL in practice. Bearing these factors in mind, we suggest the application of a threefold formula – clear vision, perseverance and mindfulness – to improve self-control, discipline and responsibility during war with respect to IHL, and particularly the protection of non-combatants. All things considered, Buddhist teachings lead to the cultivation of humanitarian qualities. The cultivation of the mind (*citta*) is key, because the state of our minds determines the state of affairs in the world, not least during war (S.I.39).

Abbreviations

A. *Aṅguttara-nikāya;* as translated by Bhikkhu Bodhi, *The Numerical Discourses of the Buddha: A Translation of the Aṅguttara Nikāya*, Bristol: Pali Text Society, 2012.

D. *Dīgha-nikāya*; as translated by Maurice Walshe, *The Long Discourses of the Buddha*, Massachusetts: Wisdom, 1995.

Dhp. *Dhammapada*; our translations are based on that by Valerie J. Roebuck, *The Dhammapada*, London: Penguin, 2010.

Dhp-a. *Dhammapadaṭṭhakathā* commentary on Dhp., as translated by E. W. Burlingame, *Buddhist Legends*, 3 vols., Harvard Oriental Series, Harvard University Press, 1921; repr. London, PTS, 1995.

M. *Majjhima-nikaya*; as translated by Ñāṇamoli Bhikkhu and Bhikkhu Bodhi, *The Middle Length Discourses of the Buddha*, Boston: Wisdom, 1995.

Ps. *Papañcasūdanī;* commentary on M. (untranslated).

S. *Saṃyutta-nikāya*; as translated by Bhikkhu Bodhi, *The Connected Discourses of the Buddha: A Translation of the Saṃyutta Nikāya*, Boston: Wisdom, 2000.

Sn. *Suttanipāta*, translated by K. R. Norman, *The Group of Discourses (Sutta Nipāta)*, 2nd ed., Oxford: Pali Text Society, 2001.

Reference to A., D., M. and S. are to volume and page number of the Pali Text Society editions of the Pali text, as indicated in the translations. For Dhp. and Sn., reference is to verse number.

Notes

1. International Committee of the Red Cross, *Convention (III) relative to the Treatment of Prisoners of War*, Geneva, 12 August 1949. Conflicts Not of an International Character. https://ihl-databases.icrc.org/ihl/WebART/375-590006
2. International Committee of the Red Cross, *Convention (III) relative to the Treatment of Prisoners of War*, Geneva, 12 August 1949. Conflicts Not of an International Character. https://ihl-databases.icrc.org/ihl/WebART/375-590006
3. For more details see: https://www.icrc.org/en/war-and-law/weapons/conventional-weapons

Disclosure statement

This article has been supported by the International Committee of the Red Cross (ICRC).

Reference

Jayatilleke, N. 2006. *Dhamma Man and Law*. Dehiwala: Buddhist Cultural Center.

Part IV

Buddhist Historical and Humanitarian Dimensions

ICRC

BUDDHISM, THE ROYAL IMAGINARY AND LIMITS IN WARFARE: THE MODERATING INFLUENCE OF PRECOLONIAL MYANMAR ROYAL CAMPAIGNS ON EVERYDAY WARRIORS

Michael W. Charney

ABSTRACT

Rules on the treatment of civilians and other non-combatants in conflict are often attributed to Western origins, particularly the increasingly widening circles of empathy that grew out of the European Enlightenment and found international implementation in the twentieth century. Nevertheless, such limits were pursued or encouraged by many non-Western societies as well, particularly amongst indigenous Americans. The present article examines the case of Myanmar and the ways in which the Myanmar court set limits on violence in administration and limits on warfare. These limits were not an imposition of the West but emerged entirely within the Myanmar-Buddhist historical experience. It is argued that these provide an existing, discernible and indigenous model for limiting violence in warfare in Myanmar society. The article also explains why this model was forgotten. The removal of the king and disintegration of the standing army that came with the end of indigenous rule in 1885 did away with crucial moderating influences, while the violence of the brutal Pacification Campaign from 1885 erased from Burmese social memory the idea that there could be limits in warfare.

Introduction

Contemporary historiography on the non-Western world holds that our modern scholarly disciplines were shaped on the basis of Western systems of knowledge. In effect, Europe carved out for itself a privileged space as the only centre for the emergence of modernity. Even to the present, academic faith in European exceptionalism still exerts an overwhelming influence on a number of fields, from international relations to human rights theory. Comparatively fewer examples of non-Western modern thought are viewed as being sufficiently robust to draw into broader debates. This bias remains

DOI: 10.4324/9781003439820-22

pervasive, even over a decade after Dipesh Chakrabarty's call to provincialise Europe (Chakrabarty 2008). Nevertheless, processes comparable to the European Enlightenment occurred elsewhere as well, at roughly the same time. Myanmar, like other non-Western countries, has been shown to have undergone an indigenous process of cultural and religious reformation in the late eighteenth century that might be usefully compared to the European Enlightenment (Charney 2006). While there is no suggestion here that we should deny European peculiarities in the thought that would provide it with unique takes on such things as how to treat non-combatants in war, it is argued that there is value in looking for indigenous cognates to doctrines of limited warfare and restrictions on the application of violence against civilians and non-combatants rather than seeing these as uniquely European.

Recent research by the present author on the precolonial Myanmar provincial administration and its standing army has emphasised the importance of villagers and village ways of combat in larger campaigns that are normally understood through depictions in the chronicles that are heavily formulaic and court-scopic (Charney 2017, 2020). Beneath the veneer of ordered and obedient soldiery, however, was a chronic tension. On the one hand the court, its generals and its ministers sought to regulate the limits of warfare and administration in line with a royal imaginary predicated on beneficent rulership, Buddhist values and the establishment of universal harmony. On the other hand, local commanders and village warriors dealt with the weak administrative structures by relying on violence to achieve their assigned ends. In effect, villagers were raped, maimed, killed and sold into slavery, and administrative officials and commanders were punished, removed from office and even executed for having engaged in this activity. But over time, particularly in the last century of the Konbaung Dynasty (1751–1885), the Bamars (the dominant ethnic group) had evolved their own doctrines on the limits of violence, although this came to an end in 1885 because of the profound impact of regime change with the British colonial conquest.

The present article examines the ways in which the Myanmar court set limits on violence in administration and limits on warfare, and the impact of the removal of the king and disintegration of the standing army that came with the end of indigenous rule in 1885. These events did away with crucial moderating influences. What followed in Myanmar was a less regulated colonial approach to war and violence and a reversion in indigenous warfare to the more violent traditions of rural fighting. It is argued that there is an existing model for limiting violence in warfare that is not an imposition of the West but has emerged entirely within the Myanmar-Buddhist historical experience. Unfortunately, the violence of the Pacification Campaign from 1885 has erased this from Burmese social memory.

The lack of limits in rural warfare

No matter how large Myanmar armies grew in size, the bulk of their numbers remained assemblies of armed rural folk. The earliest practice for wartime was to call up villagers who would come in groups, armed with local weapons for war. Myanmar royal edicts claimed that the legendary King Duttabaung (said to have ruled in the fifth century BCE) had introduced assigning quotas to different towns (districts) on the basis of their population size according to whether they could produce levies in the tens, hundreds or thousands, and this same classification system was in place in the late Bagan Dynasty (eleventh to thirteenth centuries) with a new quota being recalculated in the thirteenth century. This basic system would remain in place for provincial levies during wartime to the end of the dynasty, although these levies had little to do with the standing army. Most warriors in the royal armies were thus certainly rural folk first. When they were gathered for campaigns, they came as rural folk; in the royal army, which involved no system of centralised training for levies until late in the pre-colonial period, they remained rural folk; and when they went into the field they fought as rural folk. In some cases, they were merely picked up as levies en route to the battlefield. As a result, armed rural folk brought to the enemy the kind of warfare that was waged at the local level whenever competition among rural settlements over resources led them to violence in rural Myanmar (Charney 2017).

In the late eighteenth and nineteenth centuries the political centre in Myanmar weakened on several occasions, and during these periods of weakness, or interregnums in which complete political collapse had occurred, local conflicts became accessible for scrutiny. Not all of these periods yield much data on the actual fighting, although they provide extensive evidence of inter-settlement conflict in such cases of royal decline. Perhaps we might see in these men the same kind of rural leader as Alaunghpaya (r. 1752–1760), before his rise to power, when he was merely the headman of a settlement and a rural strongman at the head of a body of his kith and kin. Nevertheless, although we find evidence of what appears to be local, rural conflict, we lack the clear descriptions by the participants themselves or direct observers that would make this a convincing argument for what was going on. Rebels in the British counterinsurgency campaign known as the Pacification Campaign (1886–1889) are generally depicted as dacoits or independent princes in the European accounts (Ghosh 2000). By contrast, in pre-1920s Myanmar accounts, the rebels are viewed either as denizens of the court or – by Bamar historians of the late colonial period and after – as nationalists. Such interpretations obscured the continuing legacy of rural warrior culture in Myanmar well into the colonial period and even after.

There were two determining factors for this kind of warfare. First, there was a low population-to-land ratio, so there was rarely a density of population anywhere sufficient to avoid relying on masses of rural levies. Second, a distant state centre challenged by weak transportation infrastructure made a centralised military institution that could train rural men in the art of war a difficult proposition. When villagers went back to their homes after war, they brought experience and booty that then entered local, rural mythologies and oral traditions unknown to court scribes. And when state rule was weak, indirect or absent on occasion, or when adverse intervention from the state through normal channels was expected, there was likely some attractiveness to inter-settlement fighting over local squabbles.

When the indigenous state collapsed and lowland rural folk became fully visible, their manner of fighting appeared very different from the descriptions of war found in the court chronicles. Importantly, the rural way of fighting was considered to be just as crude by the late Burmese court as it was in early colonial appraisals. It was noted for its violence, its lack of limits on who was and who was not a combatant, the lack of rules of war, its treatment of captives, the mutilation of the dead, and rapine. For the middle and late Konbaung court that saw order as a measure of universal harmony, rural warfare was also unacceptably disorganised. This distaste was a consequence of the gentrification of warrior elites of the earlier years of the dynasty,[1] the influence of orthodox Theravada Buddhism on these elites, and the emergence of a professional soldiery – a standing army. The interest in enforcing Theravada Buddhist orthodoxy was directed at monastic and ritual practice and included banning such obvious transgressions as the sacrifice of chickens in the Shan states under Bodawhpaya (r. 1782–1819), for example. But before that, Bamar and other precolonial kings of Myanmar also drank from skulls of defeated enemies, fornicated with the wives of their soldiery when they were away to war, encouraged their warriors to take heads and even, when necessary, condoned the eating of human flesh, although this may be a warped relation of the drinking of blood to instil a sense of comradeship. Torture, rapine, theft and other acts of violence and personal gain were condoned amongst the soldiery. Sexual violence was very common. In other words, before the early years of the Konbaung Dynasty (1752–1885), there appear to have been few limits in war, regardless of Buddhist influence in other areas of Myanmar life within the capital zone.

Limits on violence in rural administration

By the early nineteenth century, the boundaries of the Myanmar kingdom had stretched to include roughly what colonial and independent Burma would cover geographically and were held together in part by a proto-bureaucracy, a proto-national culture and a shared sense of Buddhist orthodoxy that had grown over time.[2] But an imaginary of the kingdom was also fundamental. In the royal imaginary, the king maintained peace and harmony and supported the Sangha so that monks could provide merit and continue on their path to Enlightenment. From what could be seen in the central provinces, the state space of the kingdom, peace and prosperity sustained this image. In the core of the kingdom, those areas within the direct reach of the court, the state had become so deeply rooted that the court did not have to rely on physical force to enforce laws or collect revenues. This area formed what James Scott calls the 'padi state', where it was possible to concentrate grain production and, as 'state space', terrain that was easily governable (Scott 2009, 13). The court exercised here closer administrative scrutiny. This was where the state's wealth was concentrated. It included most of the monasteries under royal patronage, the main colonies of royal bondsmen and the kingdom's richest agricultural districts.

But the reach and administrative capacity of the precolonial Burmese state even by the early nineteenth century was weak and uneven in the outlying provinces. Outside of the immediate economic, social and cultural life of the royal capital, the non-state space was dominated by highlands and wetlands that were difficult to govern. Central officials sent out to these areas found that local populations did not subscribe to the royal imaginary as easily as did those closer to the royal capital. The complex of overlapping administrative, economic and cultural structures that ensured popular submission to the court in state space were nearly wholly absent in the non-state spaces. Villages in these areas were not as tied to particular parcels of land as those in the lowland areas and are better viewed as temporary trading, fishing and agricultural colonies than as permanent settlements. If state demands became too heavy, the village moved farther out of reach unless local officials used force. As Martin Thomas has observed regarding colonial policing, 'coercive policing … was a powerful indicator of the colonial state's limited reach' (Thomas 2012, 75). Supplied only with credentials backed by a distant royal court and soldiers, Myanmar officials often relied on the force of the latter rather than on the authority that came with the former.

Such officials were thus often merciless in their imposition of demands, for soldiers for royal campaigns but in particular for revenue. As Canning described the situation in Lower Myanmar,

> the people are exposed to the unrestrained violence and exactions of [the Governor of Hanthawaddy's] Ministers and followers of every description. This system of uninvited rapine finds its excuse in the nature of the Burman Government, which allowing no salary to any of its officers and exacting on the contrary from the high in office and they again from those under them, considerable sums every year of the privation of their respective situation all

> from the Governor of a province to the lowest writer in service to plunder indiscriminately whenever power or opportunity exists. (IOR F/4/310, 29 November 1809, 64)

Evidence that violence was going too far, however, was a potential threat to the validity of the royal imaginary. This was particularly a problem during the preparations for royal military campaigns, as commanders would be charged with making use of local resources to set up supplies, build ships, form groups of levies and so on, creating a situation in which villagers would be forced to make sacrifices of revenues, crops or labour. Equally, by custom, the commander would supply his own personal needs as well, sometimes to excess, particularly if his retinue of clients and family in the royal city was substantial in size and/or given to luxury. It was on these occasions that things were most likely to go beyond local tolerance and be reported back to the court by political rivals or the villagers themselves or, worse for the court, lead to a local rebellion, which would also draw its attention. A good example was when the court became concerned after sending the royal *atwinwun* (the interior minister) to Martaban in May 1809 with 'broad powers' to go to Tavoy, build up resources for a military expedition and then lead an attack on Siam (Anonymous 1962, 149; Koenig 1990, 155). Viewed from the royal court, the *atwinwun* was a royal army commander who had been sent to Southeastern Myanmar to raise troops and build an army that would then attack the Siamese and secure the frontiers of the kingdom and hopefully deliver booty to the royal court as well. The *atwinwun* appears to have gone through the motions of acting out this role.

On the ground in his appointed province, however, the *atwinwun* prioritised the enhancement of his political strength, through the acquisition of manpower and wealth to support it. This was often carried out with much violence that was at odds with the harmony between royal rule and society that was a core element of the royal imaginary, particularly as it was mainly directed at women and children. Women shouldered much of the *corvee* labour impositions and taxation demands because it was mainly women who remained in the village after men had been conscripted for an ongoing war. The *atwinwun*'s officials punished village women with rape, and when they could not pay their taxes their children were sold into bondage. When opposed, the *atwinwun* had no qualms putting villagers to death. By this time, the early nineteenth century, this kind of official behaviour was common in outlying provinces. Central appointees sent out to run outlying areas found it expedient to engage in spectacular displays of violence to achieve their aims. This was an immediate solution to their administrative weakness as non-state space had not yet been transitioned into state space while the state remained functionally weak outside of the central, royal zone.

More importantly, the violence was not condoned by the king. In the aforementioned example from 1809, the *atwinwun* put so many people to death that it attracted the attention of the court. The king immediately intervened and gave orders releasing all of the *atwinwun*'s prisoners and initiating an investigation into why the *atwinwun* was carrying out so many executions. The *atwinwun*'s violence was not the will of the king, but in defiance of him. So long as it did not reach the royal ear, outlying officials and commanders might indeed resort to violent means to a royal end, but they risked severe punishment by the court when they violated the operating principles of the royal imaginary predicated by this time on the rule of the Dharma, the Buddhist moral law, which the king upheld.

So much was this a key part of the royal imaginary that, while these transgressions are recorded in non-central literature,[3] they are expunged from the royal record, the royal chronicles. In the royal imaginary, in the world run by the king according to Buddhist law, the king's officers and officials should not allow their charges to engage in the rape or murder of anyone. Such activities brought severe disruptions to the royal imaginary and were signs of weakness rather than strength and the sign of bad rule as opposed to good. Those who engaged in such seditious activities were punished for their immoral behaviour and even sentenced to death.

The beginning and end of indigenous ideas on limits in warfare

Prior to the Konbaung Dynasty and even well into it, the organisation of military manpower followed the same pattern for all manpower going back to the Bagan period and earlier. This approach emphasised consanguinity (through ritual blood-drinking or *thwethauk*), endogamy and occupational exclusivity (including the hereditary pre-determination of occupation) for the community as a whole. Free people were peasants who remained cultivators except when temporarily mobilised for war and came armed as they were. Similarly, war captives were planted in different parts of Myanmar in new village communities in which they were royal servicemen who spent their time, when they were not cultivating, honing their skills with a particular kind of weapon or mount, or both. Burmese sources from across the early modern period indicate that well into the late eighteenth century this approach to manpower organisation did not change. It also created a very significant obstacle to technological change across the military establishment and did not invite very much experimentation. The introduction of rudimentary Chinese firearms in the fifteenth century and better Portuguese guns in the sixteenth century thus did not bring about a revolution in Myanmar warfare or in the army (or navy) as it did in many other places.

Major change did occur in the 1760s and thereafter maintained momentum throughout the remainder of the dynasty. The Myanmar army became a standing or professional army that regularly watched for new technology, tactics, organisation and the like, experimented, and changed on a regular basis. The major stimulus for the military change in late eighteenth-century Myanmar was not technological innovation, but the spectre of imperial rivalry and conquest, presented first by Qing China and then by the British. These two imperial rivals forced the Myanmar court to reorient its military establishment towards deterring them from transgressing Myanmar's frontiers, requiring the creation of a permanent and standing military organisation around the royal capital. Understood at the time as a necessary measure to provide stability and security of the kingdom in an uncertain political and economic climate, the decision taken was to shift the army from a mass of reservist cultivators to a standing army of permanent regiments concentrated in the royal capital. This decision initially involved no change to the organisation of soldiers within units, the command structure, the way they fought or the way they were armed. The only change that occurred was that instead of being demobilised and stationed on lands in the provinces, they would be kept on a permanent war footing around the royal capital. However, this singular change created a military that could be tinkered with and made military reform per se possible.

The standing army that emerged was formed from the ranks of the *ahmudan* or royal servicemen or bondsmen. Technically they were hereditary royal slaves who specialised in certain kinds of weapons or combat and lived in special villages assigned to different *ahmudan* groups where they waited until called up for royal service. One of the many outcomes of the creation of the standing army was that the ahmudans emerged as a new landed elite in the countryside. Despite their *ahmudan* status, soldiers of the standing army asserted private ownership over state lands and used them to gain wealth through trade and other work in the private sector.

More importantly, for our purposes here, these soldiers periodically circulated between their villages and their posts in the royal capital. From the late eighteenth century, the *ahmudan*s in the standing army split their time between the royal capital and their assigned villages in the rural areas, with 10% on duty at any one time in the royal capital and the other 90% remaining in the village. The posting in the royal city and in the palace meant constant exposure to the culture of the court and its elites, central monastic institutions and symbolisms. Relieved annually by a different 10% of the *ahmudan* regiment, the circulation meant that this exposure had a regular and reinforcing influence in the rural areas. Over time central culture became the culture of these villages, and as these *ahmudan* became the new landed elite of the countryside, this culture became the 'high' culture of rural society. This included the doctrine of the Myanmar Buddhist royal imaginary that there were limits in warfare which the army and officials must respect. The *ahmudans* now garrisoned the kingdom both in the abstract as an imaginary and in practice on the ground in the core provinces of the kingdom. The limits on war were reinforced now by an army as well as by a king.

As in many other parts of the non-Western world, where strong, vibrant moral systems maintained social harmony and peaceful state relations, colonial conquest destroyed the institutions sustaining them. The British steamed up the Irrawaddy to Mandalay, shelling the three Italian-built forts on the banks of the river as they ascended, and forced Thibaw's surrender, all within three weeks in November 1885. Thibaw ordered the standing army to lay down their arms and although many did not and fled the royal capital, the standing army had effectively and permanently disintegrated. The British decided to annex Myanmar to India and to exile King Thibaw. They did not replace him with another indigenous ruler in the lowland areas (although highland *sawbwas* would remain in place). As the standing army had already fallen apart, resistance to the British took the form of a decentralised insurgency, dominated by villagers who fought using time-honoured methods of rural warfare. The royal imaginary immediately faded. The institutionally codified limits on warfare, that had emerged in the precolonial, Myanmar Buddhist tradition, first within the court and then through the rise of a standing army, were erased. The loss of the king and the loss of the standing army meant that the Buddhicising role played by both and the limitations they set on violence in war and administration were lost. This meant that Buddhist influence was relegated first to monks alone and then to lay Buddhist associations as well, outside of the institution of the military.

The idea that there were limits in war and that killing unarmed civilians was wrong was replaced by the colonial idea that the army could engage in unlimited warfare in pursuit of state security. The colonial forces of the time sanctioned weaker limits on violence based on Western experience and a Western timeline. Civilisational and racial discourse also identified Bamars as inferior to Europeans. Their welfare was thus of less concern than would be that of European opponents. The colonial army reintroduced unlimited warfare against the Bamars in the Pacification Campaign and in counterinsurgency operations later during the anti-colonial revolts. In these conflicts, villages were surrounded and burned to the ground, Bamars were decapitated and prisoners were executed. Worse, civilians were also punished if they were believed to have provided support or sustenance to the enemy or if they were suspected of not having reported such behaviour by their fellow villagers. Burning villages to the ground, including everyone's personal possessions and means of livelihood, was a routine measure that was undertaken without qualms by the army.[4]

As indigenous resistance was left to villagers who came from outside the now-defunct standing army, and who practised warfare as it had always been practised in rural areas in outlying parts of the kingdom (those areas that had not been closely administered by the central state), the limits on warfare that had indoctrinated the standing army were no longer in evidence. By all accounts, including those of Bamars, village bands that fought the British, whom the British labelled as dacoits or bandits, also burned villages, carted off valuables and women, engaged in rapine and crucified their prisoners. They also mutilated the relations of those who collaborated with the British. As Charles Crosthwaite claimed of one Bamar band's behaviour during the conflict:

> Money and food and women were demanded from the villages, and those who refused supplies were unmercifully punished, their property seized, their villages burnt, their women dishonoured, and their cattle driven off by hundreds. Those who in any way assisted the troops were the objects of special barbarities. If they could not be caught, their fathers or brothers were taken. One of his followers deposed that he was with Ya Nyun when three men who were related to a man who had assisted the British were ordered to be crucified in front of the camp. He says: 'I saw the bodies after they were crucified. They were crucified alive and then shot, their hearts cut open'. (Crosthwaite 1912, 111)

The crimes committed against civilians by both sides in this war erased any social memory of the accepted limitations on warfare and violence against non-combatants. As Mr Labouchere, Member of Parliament from Northampton, complained in the Commons in August 1886, just eight months into the campaign:

> Our conduct in that country had not been such as to be likely to win over the people. In consequence of it the country was now open to rapine on the part of Native robbers, while our soldiers were sent from village to village to punish the inhabitants by killing them and burning their villages. (House of Commons Debates 1886 August 30)

From this conflict on, British and indigenous populations would fight each other brutally.[5]

Conclusion

This article has argued that Myanmar had a code of ethics of war and administration that had emerged within the royal court and administration and then was instilled in the ranks of the standing army as it emerged from the mid-eighteenth century. Gradually, unlimited violence in war (and peace) was limited in principle and – where the court or army knew – in practice as well. This ethics was something that was enforced in theory throughout the royal imaginary. Nevertheless, in the mundane world, on the periphery of the kingdom, beyond the practical view of the court in the outer districts where Konbaung administrators, charged with extracting resources from villagers in what was effectively non-state space, violated this ethics. Spectacular violence, without limits, targeted families, men, women, children, the aged and young alike, ranging from burning villages to rape, torture and execution. When the court learned of such transgressions, it punished the perpetrators, regardless of their rank or the purpose to which this violence was put, with the deprivation of rank and wealth, imprisonment and even death. In the king's domain, there were limits on what could be done in the name of war.

This Myanmar ethics of war and administration was erased with the overthrow of the king and the standing army's collapse in 1885. Rural warfare – unlimited, local warfare, less influenced by the tenets of Buddhism and royal experience – continued to provide the template for Bamars in the village afterwards. As a result, rural conflict subsequently, partly reinforced by the unlimited colonial warfare introduced by the British, consisted of warfare without limits. These two different traditions, one indigenous and rural, and the other colonial and foreign, would influence the existing inheritance regarding how one should or should not wage war. Decolonising the way the limits in war are understood in Myanmar can be achieved by dropping the colonial example and the rural village warfare templates and looking into Buddhism and the royal traditions of war as they had evolved by the middle and late Konbaung periods.

Notes

1. For a comparable trend in early modern France, see Elias (1982). For a different view, see Carroll (2006).
2. See Lieberman (2003, 1984) and Koenig (1990).
3. From early modern Myanmar a vast variety of materials are preserved from outlying areas, in Burmese and in ethnic minority languages, that record local histories and accounts. Some of these manuscripts relate to the histories of temples, but others deal with local legend, literature, local family lineages and so on. Another important local source of information were revenue inquests, the headmens' reports to the court. Some of the latter are reproduced in translation in Trager and Koenig (1979). Many of these kinds of sources were collected in the royal library, but many more were kept in local monastic libraries and private collections, helping to explain their survival to the present.
4. This is supported by many accounts of the campaign, including, for example, statements in 'Personal Recollections of the Upper Burmah Campaign 1886–7 by Major Richard Holbeche (1850–1914)', Sutton Coldfield Local History Research Group Archive, https://sclhrg.org.uk/research/transcriptions/2182-personal-recollections-of-the-upper-burmah-campaign-1886-7-by-major-richard-holbeche-1850-1914.html.
5. See the example of highlanders fighting in 1891 that included the killing of 'all' women and children in affected villages (Watson 1967, 8).

Disclosure statement

This article has been supported by the International Committee of the Red Cross (ICRC).

ORCID

Michael W. Charney http://orcid.org/0000-0002-3910-155X

References

Anonymous. 1962. "Wung-gyi-hmu-gyi-mya Akyaung." *Journal of the Burma Research Society* 45 (2): 147–162.

Carroll, S. 2006. *Blood and Violence in Early Modern France*. Oxford: Oxford University Press.

Chakrabarty, D. 2008. *Provincializing Europe: Postcolonial Thought and Historical Difference*. Princeton: Princeton University Press.

Charney, M. 2006. *Powerful Learning. Buddhist Literati and the Throne in Burma's Last Dynasty, 1752–1885*. Ann Arbor: University of Michigan Centre for Southeast Asian Studies.

Charney, M. 2017. "Armed Rural Folk: Elements of Pre-colonial Warfare in the Artistic Representations and Written Accounts of the Pacification Campaign (1886-1889) in Burma." In *Warring Societies of Pre-colonial Southeast Asia: Local Cultures of Conflict within a Regional Context*, edited by M. Charney and K. Wellen, 155–181. Copenhagen: NIAS.

Charney, M. 2020. "Both Benevolent and Brutal: The Two Sides of Provincial Violence in Early Modern Burma." In *A Global History of Early Modern Violence*, edited by C. Erica, M. H. Erica, and P. H. Wilson, 37–51. Manchester: Manchester University Press.

Crosthwaite, C. 1912. *The Pacification of Burma*. London: Edward Arnold.

Elias, N. 1982. *The Civilizing Process Vol. 2. State Formation and Civilization*. Oxford: Blackwell.

Ghosh, P. 2000. *Brave Men of the Hills: Resistance and Rebellion in Burma, 1825-1932*. London: C. Hurst.

Holbeche, R. "Personal Recollections of the Upper Burmah Campaign 1886-7 by Major Richard Holbeche (1850-1914)." Sutton Coldfield Local History Research Group Archive. https://sclhrg.org.uk/research/transcriptions/2182-personal-recollections-of-the-upper-burmah-campaign-1886-7-by-major-richard-holbeche-1850-1914.html

"House of Commons Debates Hansard." 1886. 308: cc797–873. August, 30.

IOR [India Office Records]. *Board of Control Records 1784-1858 [F Series]*. London: British Library, Asia and Africa Collection.

Koenig, W. 1990. *The Burmese Polity, 1752-1819: Politics, Administration, and Social Organization in the Early Konbaung Period*. Ann Arbor: University of Michigan Center for South & Southeast Asian Studies.
Lieberman, V. 1984. *Burmese Administrative Cycles: Anarchy and Conquest, C. 1580-1760*. Princeton: Princeton University Press.
Lieberman, V. 2003. *Strange Parallels, Volume 1: Integration of the Mainland Southeast Asia in Global Context, C. 800–1830*. Cambridge: Cambridge University Press.
Scott, J. 2009. *The Art of Not Being Governed: An Anarchist History of Upland Southeast Asia*. New Haven: Yale University Press.
Thomas, M. 2012. *Violence and Colonial Order: Police, Workers and Protest in European Colonial Empires, 1918-1940*. Cambridge: Cambridge University Press.
Trager, F., and W. Koenig. 1979. *Burmese Sit-tans 1764-1826: Records of Rural Life and Administration. With the Assistance of Daw Yi Yi*. Tucson: University of Arizona Press.
Watson, J. 1967. *Military Operations in Burma, 1890-1892*, edited by B. R. Pearn. Ithaca: Cornell University Southeast Asia Program.

ICRC

BETWEEN COMMON HUMANITY AND PARTIALITY: THE CHOGYE BUDDHIST CHAPLAINCY MANUAL OF THE SOUTH KOREAN MILITARY AND ITS RELEVANCE TO INTERNATIONAL HUMANITARIAN LAW

Hyein Lee

ABSTRACT

The Chogye Order of Korean Buddhism (K. Chogye chong or Jogyejong 曹溪宗) compiled a booklet called *Kukkun pŏbyo chip* (*Essential Buddhist Teachings for the Armed Forces*, 國軍法要集, *EBTAF* hereafter), which is distributed in the military Buddhist temples (K. *kun sachal*; Ch. *jun sisha* 軍寺刹) of South Korea. This manual for Buddhist military personnel draws on Buddhist classical texts and teachings to provide them both with doctrinal and practical information, and guidance as well as litanies for chaplains to perform crucial rites such as funerals. At the same time the *EBTAF* contains some distinctively Korean Buddhist references and ideas, and combines them with elements of Korean nationalism. In this context, this article analyses (1) the ideal traits of Buddhist combatants suggested in the *EBTAF* and their compliance with international humanitarian law (IHL); (2) the conflicting values illustrated in the booklet between Buddhist soldiers' religious aspirations to uphold common humanity and the partiality inherent in their governmental affiliation; and (3) a passage to resolve the disparity. While the *EBTAF* aligns with IHL principles, some parts of it reflect a tension between Buddhist aspirations for peace and the military necessities of the state. Though IHL is not explicitly mentioned in the *EBTAF*, there is potential for embedding education on mutually complementary Buddhist and IHL values into Korean military chaplaincy.

Introduction[1]

The Chogye Order of Korean Buddhism[2] is a Korean Zen school with a focus on meditation practices like *Kanwha Sŏn* (Ch. *kanhua chan* 看話禪) and *Hwadu* (Ch. *huatou* 話頭). Even though its provenance can be traced much further back in history, the current form of the Chogye Order was established in 1962. As of the 2018 census, it is the largest and most influential Buddhist

DOI: 10.4324/9781003439820-23

order in South Korea, with 3185 temples, 13,327 monastics, and 12,000,000 lay followers (Ministry of Culture, Sports and Tourism 문화체육관광부 2018, 101). With its increasing interest in social engagement, it is currently one of the four religious denominations[3] that partake in the military chaplaincy service in cooperation with the Ministry of National Defence of South Korea.

The military chaplaincy institution was founded in South Korea in 1951 during the Korean War (1950–1953), inspired by the American Protestant chaplaincy service (Kang 2017, 35–54). However, during the pro-Christian Syngman Rhee's regime (1948–1960), no Buddhist monastic was officially assigned to chaplaincy service, even though Buddhism was the most prominent religion among South Koreans in the 1950s (Kang 2017). After a period of ostracisation that lasted almost two decades, the Chogye Order was finally recognised by the South Korean government in 1968 as the third religious denomination to become an official member of the military chaplaincy service (Editorial Board of Buddhist Chaplaincy 불교군종사 편찬위원회 2008, 16). In the same year, five chaplains who had completed a chaplaincy training course, as well as ten weeks of military training at the army's Infantry School, were deployed. Three of them were sent to Vietnam during the Vietnamese War (1954–1975) (Kim and Park 2020, 4).

Ever since, the Chogye Order has noticeably increased the number of military temples, with 10 monasteries in 1970, which rose to 170 by 1990, then reaching 416 in 2018. Military temples are run jointly with military camps in South Korea. They are located either within the camps or in proximity to them, for the convenience of military personnel. Subject to availability, one Buddhist military chaplain may reside in the camp or travel between temples at weekends. The activities conducted in the military temples include Dharma talks and Buddhist rituals; the latter include funerals for deceased soldiers. In 2008, the Pisung sa temple held celebrations for a South Korea–US collaborative military exercise, namely Ulchi Freedom Guardian (Editorial Board of Buddhist Chaplaincy 불교군종사 편찬위원회 2008, 395).

The need for an administrative entity for the military temples and chaplains was ardently discussed at the Chogye Order in the 1990s (Editorial Board of Buddhist Chaplaincy 불교군종사 편찬위원회 2018, 42), and in 2005, the Buddhist Military Ordinariate of the Chogye Order of Korean Buddhism (K. *Taehan pulgyo chogyejong kunjong t'ŭkpyŏl kyogu*; Ch. *dahan fojiao caoxizong junzong tebie jiaoqu*大韓佛教曹溪宗 軍宗特別教區) was established. The Ordinariate is in charge of selecting aspiring military personnel and running monasteries in conjunction with military camps. With the aid of two universities, Joong-ang Sangha University[4] and Dongguk University,[5] the Ordinariate is also responsible for educating aspiring military chaplains. In addition, it publishes the reading materials and booklets related to the Buddhist military chaplaincy service.

Contrary to a few countries where the military chaplaincy service is either completely or partially civilianised, South Korea has maintained the service under the direction of the state. The Buddhist monks and nuns[6] who are appointed are therefore military personnel, while maintaining their status as monastics at the Chogye Order. In the same fashion, the military temples are essentially military facilities, even though they are run by the Ordinariate and some of them were completed with donations from lay Buddhists with permission from the Ministry of National Defence.

The primary source for this paper is *Kukkun pŏbyo chip* (*Essential Buddhist Teachings for the Armed Forces, EBTAF*, Office of Military Ordinariate, 1997), a booklet distributed in military Buddhist temples in South Korea. The *EBTAF* is a guidebook for Buddhist military personnel who wish to abide by Buddhist teachings during their service to their country. It is compiled by the Office of Buddhist Military Ordinariate and published by the Ministry of National Defence of South Korea. The first 1000 copies were printed in 1972.[7] The *EBTAF* has already undergone several revisions in the past five decades since then. Except for the latest version from 2018, all the older booklets are over 400 pages long with extensive coverage of diverse themes. These include Buddhist rituals and core teachings, the fit mindset and disciplines for military personnel, and the correct attitudes towards one's nation. In this article, the *EBTAF* versions from 1997, 2000, 2010 and 2018 are analysed.

The tension between humanitarianism and military necessity is embedded in the booklet. As a guide for Buddhist combatants, composed by the ordained and sanctioned by the state, both common humanity and patriotism co-exist ironically yet ineluctably. This tension is similar to the ontological grounding for international humanitarian law (henceforth IHL), which is based on a balance between considerations of military necessity and of humanity, and imposes limits on the means and methods of warfare (Melzer 2019, 17, 18). A comparative analysis of the two can therefore shed light on their potential complementarity.[8]

This study answers the following questions in this regard: (1) What kind of Buddhist teachings are emphasised in the *EBTAF*?; (2) Do the Buddhist values espoused in the *EBTAF* align with IHL?; (3) How are the seemingly irreconcilable humanitarian values of Buddhism and patriotism addressed together in the *EBTAF*?; (4) How does the *EBTAF* reflect and reconcile the disparity between scriptural Buddhism and the lived reality of Buddhism?; and (5) What implications does the *EBTAF* have in terms of Buddhist military personnel's understanding of Buddhism and humanity in situations of armed conflict? By answering these questions, this study attempts to contribute to the understanding of the lived reality of Buddhists by analysing how impartiality and partiality are placed and endorsed together in the lives of Buddhist armed forces in South Korea. By so doing, it is hoped that this research will open up further engagement between the Buddhist military chaplaincy service and IHL practitioners.

Overview of the *EBTAF*

The *EBTAF* is a manual for Buddhist combatants which addresses multiple aspects of a Buddhist's life in military situations, from combat preparation to Buddhist daily practice. The content includes canonical compositions from both Mahāyāna and earlier Buddhist teachings, written in both Korean and classical Chinese. Non-canonical pieces are provided only in modern Korean; they consist of expositions and interpretations of canonical pieces or guidelines for daily life tailored to Korean Buddhist soldiers.

The *EBTAF* published in 1997 consists of 10 chapters and over 700 pages, whereas the versions from 2000 and 2010 have six chapters, with a total of 480 and 438 pages, respectively. The latest revision from 2018 has three chapters and a total of 95 pages. According to the educational director at the Ordinariate, there are three additional publications being planned in order to supplement the latest *EBTAF: Collected Buddhist Rituals in Battlefields, Buddhist Sutras for Young Soldiers* and *Manual for Rituals and Prayers.*[9] Prior to 2018, despite a number of revisions, the contents of the *EBTAF* in the past several decades remained similar except for marginal changes of structure. The list of the chapters of the four versions of the *EBTAF* is given in Table 1.

Table 1. Contents of the four versions of the *Essential Buddhist Teachings for the Armed Forces* (*EBTAF*).

1997	2000	2010	2018
I. Buddhist Ceremonies II. Guidelines for Everyday Life III. Prayers (for the Ordained) IV. Prayers (for All) V. Buddhist Etiquettes VI. Rituals VII. Buddhist Teachings VIII. Sutras for Recitations IX. Operational Discipline of Buddhist Military Temples X. Buddhist Hymns	I. Buddhist Ceremonies II. Prayers III. Buddhist Teachings IV. Sutras for Recitations V. Guidelines for Buddhist Practice VI. Buddhist Hymns	I. Buddhist Ceremonies II. Prayers III. Buddhist Teachings IV. Introduction to Buddhism	I. Buddhist Ceremonies II. Sutras for Recitations III. Basic Knowledge on Buddhism

Chapter III and Chapter IX in the version in 1997 were eliminated in the versions from 2000 and 2010. The construction and content of these two versions do not differ greatly despite changes to the title of the fourth chapter. In the 2010 version, sutras for recitations and essential Buddhist teachings are placed together under the title 'Introduction to Buddhism', with a detailed explanation.

Among the contents in Chapter I: Buddhist Ceremonies, Buddhist rituals for the deceased are noticeable. In its subchapters, topics such as ceremonies for receiving Buddhist precepts and for Buddhist observance days (Skt. *upavasatha*; Ch. *busa* 布薩) are included. In the chapter of prayers, readers can find diverse prayers which the armed forces may need during service, including prayers for patience and perseverance, prayers for courage, prayers for the soldiers who are training, prayers before carrying out operations, and prayers before dispatching warplanes.

In Chapters III and IV, Buddhist teachings as well as major sutras are introduced in both classical Chinese and Korean with explanations of the content. For instance, in the subchapters, core Mahayanist Buddhist sutras such as the *Lotus Sūtra* (Skt. *Saddharma Puṇḍarīka Sūtra*; Ch. *miaofa lianhua jing* 妙法蓮華經), the *Flower Garland Sūtra* (Skt. *Avataṃsaka Sūtra*; Ch. *dafangguang fohuayan jing* 大方廣佛華嚴經), and the *Diamond Sūtra* (Skt. *Vajracchedikā Prajñāpāramitā Sūtra*; Ch. *jingang banruo boluomi jing* 金剛般若波羅蜜經) are introduced. An apocryphal text, the *Sūtra of Filial Piety* (Ch. *fumu enzhong jing* 父母恩重經), is also included in Chapter IV. In Chapter V: Guidelines for Buddhist Practice, readers can find practical guidance related to the practice of Buddhism in daily life. Readers are informed about fundamental Buddhist courtesy and the rules of conduct including the correct way to enter a Buddhist temple, and to make offerings to the Buddha.

Chapter VI: Buddhist Hymns contains 29 Buddhist hymns and the South Korean national anthem with full scores and lyrics in sheet music. The themes of the hymns include playing Dharma drums and welcoming new Buddhist soldiers. It is notable that four of the hymns are related to death and funerals.

The ideal traits of Buddhist combatants and their compliance with IHL

In all versions of the *EBTAF*, Buddhist combatants are encouraged to remain calm and compassionate during their service. Prayers and Buddhist teachings in the *EBTAF* aim to help them develop a sound mindset and cultivate desirable personality traits through the practice of Buddhism in military camps, particularly impartiality, compassion and selflessness. Consideration for the happiness of others, sacrifice, devotion and world peace are also often discussed. For example, the meaning and implications of the Four Immeasurable Minds (Skt. *apramāṇa*; Ch. *si wuliang xin* 四無量心) are introduced and explained in full as follows:

> Buddhist teachings place a great emphasis on the relationship one has with others, to the point that Buddhist practice is ultimately perfected by doing good for others as much as for oneself. One must interact with others with the Four Immeasurable Minds, which are:
>
> (1) *Cha muryang shim* (loving-kindness; Skt. *maitrī*; Ch. *ci wuliang xin* 慈無量心): a loving and kind mind. Loving-kindness is about treating everyone with benevolence and warmth.
> (2) *Pi muryang shim* (compassion; Skt. *karuṇā*; Ch. *bei wuliang xin* 悲無量心): a compassionate mind. Compassion is about taking someone else's adversities as your own. This mind allows us to feel compassion towards suffering sentient beings.
> (3) *Hŭi muryang shim* (joy; Skt. *muditā*; Ch. *xi wuliang xin* 喜無量心): this mind assists us to be happy for others without jealousy.
> (4) *Sa muryang shim* (equanimity; Skt. *upekṣā*; Ch. *she wuliang xin* 捨無量心): with equanimity, we do not discriminate against anyone, whether he is a friend or a foe. We are not attached to or obsessed with anything, and we are fair.
>
> It is to say that Buddhism is ultimately about *chabi* (Ch: *cibei* 慈悲). *Chabi* is indeed the combination of the first and the second mind in the Four Immeasurable Minds, loving-kindness and compassion, as explained above. In other words, *chabi* denotes the mindset of treating others with gentleness and warmth as if it were one's own body (*EBTAF* 2010, 302–303).

The way in which the meaning of equanimity is construed in the *EBTAF* is note-worthy, as it argues against the distinction between a friend and a foe. The Buddhist virtues praised in the Four Immeasurable Minds are accentuated again in the way the Ten Conducts in the *Flower Garland Sūtra*[10] are fully quoted and translated in the *EBTAF*. Like the interpretation of equanimity above, the following passage on non-attachment resonates with the core attributes of IHL in its emphasis on equanimity and impartiality:

> What do we call bodhisattvas' non-attachment?[11]
>
> ...
>
> The impurity of the world does not incite hatred in bodhisattvas. This is because bodhisattvas see everything as the Buddha Dharma. That is, everything is neither pure nor impure, light nor dark, truthful nor untruthful, comfortable nor arduous, neither right nor wrong.

> ...
>
> Bodhisattvas do not think of 'self' or 'mine' even in a brief instant, do not attach to their bodies, the Dharma, thoughts, aspirations, *samādhi*, or *dhyāna*.
>
> ...
>
> Bodhisattvas conceive everything through no-self, develop *mahā-karuṇā* (great compassion) to relieve sentient beings, yet they are not defiled by their conducts. They transcend the secular realm, yet they fully live in it. This is what we call bodhisattvas' conduct of non-attachment. (*EBTAF* 2000, 314–315)

Such well-established Buddhist qualities of compassion, impartiality and equanimity are reflected in the Four Immeasurable Minds as well as the Bodhisattvas' Conduct of Non-Attachment in the *EBTAF*. These Buddhist aspirations are channelled into one of the most frequently recited prayers from the *EBTAF*. In this prayer, soldiers are encouraged to remain compassionate, loving, and impartial during service.

> Prayer Two[12]
>
> I pay homage to the divine true teacher, the Buddha, with great devotion.
>
> ...
>
> I aspire to be grateful to my mission and everyone around me.
>
> I will pray for the happiness of others rather than that of my own.
>
> I aspire to be a person who cherishes living beings and peace for the happiness of my family, my fellow comrades, and all sentient beings.
>
> I wish my prayers to lead to security of all troops and harmony among families.
>
> I aspire to be a stepping-stone to peace so that the whole world will become a Pure Land. (*EBTAF* 2018, 20–21)

The values found in the verses above correspond with IHL's core humanitarian concerns. For example, according to IHL, 'all persons who have fallen into the power of the enemy are entitled to humane treatment regardless of their status and previous function or activities without any adverse distinction founded on race, color, religion or faith' (Melzer 2019, 20).[13] IHL, therefore, requires treatment to be impartial, prioritised only according to need, in the provision of medical care and humanitarian relief.[14]

IHL also upholds human dignity during armed conflict, including that of the deceased. It imposes obligations with regard to the dead, and stipulates that parties to a conflict must take all possible measures to ensure that the remains of the deceased are respected and that they are neither mutilated nor pillaged or despoiled (Melzer 2019, 159–160).[15] The *EBTAF* pays close attention to this topic, and emphasises the importance of rituals for the dead during military service. In its preface, the significance of the rituals for the armed forces is explicitly stipulated. Consequently, there are multiple entries related to funerals in Chapter I, which provide the full procedures, with additional prayers and hymns in Chapter II and VI. The values of the Buddhist teachings in the *EBTAF* therefore guide soldiers to treat the bodies of the deceased with respect and kindness, and in compliance with IHL.

To summarise, the implications of compassion, impartiality and equanimity in the *EBTAF* for relieving suffering during military situations are twofold. Firstly, such values may relieve the participating military personnel from excessive negative emotions, and aid their mental and emotional health. Secondly, such values help them to abide by IHL.

Conflicting values in the *EBTAF*

As a booklet reflecting both military necessity and humanitarian values, the *EBTAF* has an additional dimension: nationalism. Numerous subchapters place patriotic and humanitarian terms in the same passage without conceptual distinction, articulation of their implications, or recognition of the cognitive dissonance such blending of the two may cause. As a case in point, the prayers in the booklet often show great care and compassion for others, with a nationalistic undertone.

The prayer below expresses concerns for distressed, sick and fatigued soldiers. At the same time, patriotic sentiments are observable throughout the passage, invoking a sense of belonging to the 'homeland'. An archaic character in the history of Korean Buddhism is also drawn on to add historical legitimacy to the military activities of Buddhists; Won'gwang 圓光 (555–638), an eminent monk from the mid-Silla period (514–654) is believed to have altered the five Buddhist precepts to support his king by integrating Confucian virtues with Buddhist concepts of morality (Yi 2014, 3).

He is known for a set of moral codes entitled *sesok o kye* 世俗五戒 (five worldly precepts): *sagun ich'ung* 事君以忠 (Serve the king with loyalty), *sach'in ihyo* 事親以孝 (Serve parents with filial piety), *kyou isin* 交友以信 (Befriend people with trust), *imjŏn mut'oe* 臨戰無退 (Do not retreat from battle), and *salsaeng yut'aek* 殺生有擇 (Kill with discernment).[16] His five worldly precepts are often quoted in the discourses with regard to the convergence of the state and institutional Buddhism in Korea, suggesting that the Korean Buddhist *saṃgha* has a long history of supporting the state in even a military capacity.[17]

Such a confluence of politics and Buddhism in East Asia was framed as state-protecting Buddhism (J. *gokoku bukkyō*; K. *hoguk pulgyo* 護國佛教; SPB hereafter)[18] by Japanese Buddhologists during the Meiji period (1868–1912) (Jorgensen 1997, 209–210). Buddhist intellectuals such as Eda Toshio (1898–

1957) applied *gokoku bukkyō* discourses to describe Korean Buddhism during the Japanese occupation of Korea (1910–1945) (Eda 1977, 155–169; Kamada 1987). As the concept aligned with the ideologies of the authoritarian regimes of Syngman Rhee and Park Chunghee (1948–1979), it carried increasing significance (Mohan 2006; Sorensen 2008), and by the 1970s it was adopted by Korean scholars of various disciplines (Kim 2007, 10). This concept is therefore frequently attributed to Won'gwang's alleged stance on the military involvement of the *saṃgha*. In the prayer below, the concept of SPB appears together with Won'gwang's precept.

> Prayer Before Executing Operations
>
> Dear Buddha, who guides sentient beings with compassion, please help us realize that our lives only exist because our homeland does, and peace in our homeland only exists thanks to our challenging training.
>
> . . .
>
> Let us overcome our own selves through hard work, let the teaching of Venerable Won'gwang, 'no retreat at a battlefield', live in the heart of every fellow comrade through the strength of state-protecting spirit, so that everything is accomplished by the Buddha's brilliance without obstacle.
>
> . . .
>
> Dear Buddha, who leads us to the path of limitless compassion and wisdom, please be benevolent to our troops, parents, and siblings whom we left behind and make our sacrificial lives worthy. Please heal our fellow soldiers who became sick during training, and give courage to those who are distressed and fatigued so that we can hear shouts of victory. (*EBTAF* 2000, 152)

In addition to distinctively Korean Buddhist references and ideas, various other rhetorical devices are found in the *EBTAF* that reflect conflicting values. In the prayer below, the repetition of the word 'our' rhetorically separates 'us' from 'them'. This rhetorical style is particularly perplexing, considering the exposition on the Four Immeasurable Minds in which soldiers are encouraged not to separate friends and foes, and to be loving towards both instead. At the same time, the military activity in this prayer is described as defensive, focusing on the protection of people from undesignated enemies who are not demonised.

> Prayer Before Dispatching Warplanes
>
> Dear Buddha, we, Air Force 000, the protector of the South Korean airspace, are about to execute our mission. For we have our homeland, we can fly in our airspace like birds, looking down the beautiful mountains and streams, which is the basis of our people. We bid you to lead us to victory and to grant

> us the Four Heavenly Kings' courage and strength so that we will not let the enemies rob our beautiful land which we must protect even at the cost of our lives.
>
> . . .
>
> Dear Buddha of limitless light, please answer to our earnest prayer and let us not become conceited or negligent. Let us return to our beloved homeland with our fellow comrades. (*EBTAF* 2000, 154)

However, in another entry with a reference to enemies, the contrast between the impartiality emphasised in the Four Immeasurable Minds and the sentiments in the excerpt becomes starker. The 2010 version of the *EBTAF* ends with a battlefield hymn with a reference to Māra, the demonic figure in Buddhism who represents temptation and *samsāra*. The hymn, which is placed almost at the end of the booklet in Chapter VI with the South Korean anthem, reads as follows:

> A Song for State-Protecting Buddhist Militaries
>
> Following the example of unification Buddhism of Silla, which brought the distressed nation together, hold the flag of reunification high in the sky! Let us march, let us defeat the red evil soldiers, we are invincible soldiers against Māra!
>
> Following the example of state-protecting Buddhism from Koryŏ dynasty (高麗, 918–1391) which protected the state in need, hold up the state-protecting flag! (*EBTAF* 2000, 436)

In this excerpt, the juxtaposition equates Māra with the enemy. With the ideal of reunification and the reference to the colour red, a visual symbol of communism, the lyrics seem to associate the military of North Korea with Māra. Given that a war against Māra, the mythological representation of evil, is one of the common mechanisms used in Buddhist countries when justifying state-sanctioned violence against non-Buddhist groups or socially constructed others,[19] this hymn suggests animosity towards designated 'others' which contradicts the otherwise humanitarian undertone of the *EBTAF*. Since the metaphor of Māra is often employed in a dehumanising sense, this song contradicts the principle of common humanity. Additionally, the concept of SPB reappears and frames the identity of Buddhist militaries. The way in which this hymn associates current military practices of Buddhists with historical events, and thus with the larger SPB discourses, is also notable.

In combining Buddhist, nationalistic and militaristic values, the *EBTAF* includes conflicting messages and does not provide conceptual clarification in relation to these hymns. In sum, the above pieces translated from the

EBTAF, where humanitarian concepts are placed alongside nationalistic terms, beg the question of how Buddhist combatants should understand such texts and manage the cognitive dissonance they induce.

A passage to close the gap

Elsewhere, however, the *EBTAF* acknowledges the disparity between Buddhist combatants' religious aspirations and their institutionalised loyalty to the state. In the 1997 version, the topic of the Buddhist view on warfare and taking lives during armed conflicts is discussed in detail over 10 pages. This discussion on Buddhism and warfare begins by tracing the canonical provenance of the Buddha's perspective on engagement in battles.

The *EBTAF* refers to the *Book of Gradual Sayings* (Skt. *Ekottaragama*; Ch. *zengyi ehan jing* 增一阿含經) to elaborate on the Buddha's position on war, with concrete examples in which the Buddha mediates between two antagonists and advises against violence (*EBTAF* 1997, 555–557). Quotes from the *Dharmaguptaka Vinaya* (Ch. *sifen lü* 四分律) are presented as well, to demonstrate that *bhikṣus* are prohibited from visiting military camps or staying there for more than two nights or witnessing scenes of war. With various canonical references, the *EBTAF* comments that 'Sakyamunī disapproved of war and held the value of life to the utmost priority. His perspective on war is shown in the first precept against killing. In this sense, in accordance with the thought that war equates with taking life, it seems that war itself was considered transgressive in the times of early Buddhism' (*EBTAF* 1997, 557). To summarise, the first few paragraphs of this subchapter emphasise that Buddhism is a peace-oriented religion.

The passage proceeds by contending that the Buddhist view on warfare has changed over time. It quotes the *Medicine Buddha Sutra* (Skt. *Bhaiṣajyaguru Sūtra*; Ch. *yaoshi rulai benyuan jing* 藥師如來本願經),[20] in which armed conflicts are justified in the case of defensive war and civil turmoil (*EBTAF* 1997, 559). The *Nirvana Sutra* (Skt. *Mahāyāna Mahāparinirvāṇa Sūtra*; Ch. *daban niepan jing* 大般涅槃經)[21] and the *Treatise on the Stages for Yoga Practice* (Skt. *Yogācārabhūmi-Śāstra*; Ch. *yujia shi di lun* 瑜伽師地論)[22] are also quoted in order to argue that war is condoned in the cases of protecting the Dharma or sentient beings (*EBTAF* 1997, 559–560). This subchapter concludes that 'participation in a war can be a proactive practice of compassion' (*EBTAF* 1997, 558–559). The *EBTAF* tries to resolve the tension between the humanitarian qualities embedded in Buddhism and military necessity by advocating that in certain cases, partaking in war does not contradict foundational principles in Buddhism.

Lastly, this subchapter on Buddhism and war addresses the issue of killing and warfare in the context of Korean Buddhism. The chapter stresses the aforementioned monk Won'gwang's position on precepts. Moreover, it emphasises that his contemporary Ŭijŏk 義寂 (681–?) also elaborated the issue of killing in war for soldiers in his well-received commentary on the *Brahma's Net Sutra* (Skt. *Brahmajāla Sūtra*; Ch. *fan wang jing* 梵網經) (*EBTAF* 1997, 560).[23] With the introduction of the two eminent monks from the Korean Buddhist historiography, the *EBTAF* affirms and ends with Won'gwang's five worldly precepts (*EBTAF* 1997, 562).

In the *EBTAF*, Won'gwang is described as the forefather of SPB, who set moral codes for Buddhist militaries as well as civilians (*EBTAF* 1997, 561–562). His 'kill with discernment' is cited as altering the precepts, in this case the first precept not to kill, in order to serve military purposes. Such a conventional way to read his worldly precepts is precisely how the *EBTAF* depicts them in order to close the gap between normative Buddhist ethics and the lived reality of Buddhism in practice. What is noteworthy in the *EBTAF*, however, is that it quotes the whole passage in which the precise context of the worldly precept 'kill with discernment' can be analysed.

> Won'gwang replied, 'There are ten Bodhisattva precepts in Buddhism, but since you are subjects of a king, I am afraid that you can hardly keep them.
>
> . . .
>
> It [kill with discernment] means no killing on the six purification days or in the spring and summer months. This is to choose the right time. Killing with discernment means no killing of domestic animals such as horses, cattle, fowl or dogs. No killing of organisms that are not big enough to make a morsel. This is to choose the right beings. Moreover, there should be no killing beyond what is absolutely necessary. These are the commandments for the secular world'. (Ilyon, *Memorabilia of the Three Kingdoms (三國遺事)*, v.4_342b 1–11)[24]

The context for 'kill with discernment' from the *Samguk yusa* 三國遺事 (Memorabilia of the Three Kingdoms) makes it clear that there is a logical leap in connecting this precept with any justification for the military involvement of the *saṃgha*. The original context shows that the worldly precepts were an attempt to accommodate the difficulties of maintaining the bodhisattva precepts in lay life rather than an endorsement of military action per se. While the phrase 'kill with discernment' has been widely misconstrued to justify killing due to lack of consideration for its original context, its primary connotation is that 'there should be no killing beyond what is absolutely necessary', and therefore it aligns with IHL.

Conclusion: between common humanity and partiality

Common humanity – or, in the Buddhist case, common sentience – and impartiality are emphasised in both IHL and Buddhist teachings. These are the pillars of belief wherein the two institutions overlap and can guide the armed forces in situations of armed conflict. Both can help prevent unnecessary harm and ameliorate the distress that military personnel undergo by guiding them to see that their 'enemies' are in fact no different from themselves, regardless of their different nationality and other affiliations. Such values are indeed the undertone of the *EBTAF*. However, its indiscriminate use of conceptually discrepant notions blended together requires further analysis.

The Buddhist position on warfare itself is not conclusive. This lack of clarity, complicated by the diverse cultures, political systems and historical memories of different countries, yields context-specific interpretations of the reasoning behind Buddhist involvement in military activity and its morality. Precisely because of the dearth of discussion on this issue, Buddhist military chaplains presumably receive questions from military personnel with regard to the lack of conceptual clarity between humanitarian principles and nationalism, or the Buddhist stance on state-sanctioned violence. This dearth of incisive, explicit discussion also explains the confusion and mixed accounts of common humanity and nationalism that are features of the *EBTAF*. The philosophical question here is whether one can ever be totally impartial while devoted to one's duty as a servant of a specific country, its associated values and political orientation.[25]

While this is possible for IHL because it does not seek to prohibit killing per se, for a Buddhist member of the military this is more problematic, because impartiality is taken to a higher degree in Buddhism, and requires literally treating one's enemy with the same consideration as oneself, even during armed conflict. Moreover, patriotism or national identity and the will to fight are both often invoked using othering techniques to dehumanise the opponent, in the case of the *EBTAF* by equating the enemy with Māra, the mythological representation of evil, which in Buddhism originally represents our inner weaknesses to be overcome on the spiritual journey.

Even though many of the Buddhist virtues presented in the *EBTAF* overlap with and support IHL, there is nevertheless no direct reference to IHL in the *EBTAF*. Some collaborative work between the Chogye Order, or Korean chaplaincy in general, and the International Committee of the Red Cross (ICRC) to revise the content of the *EBTAF* or the curriculum for aspiring Buddhist military chaplains could be of great benefit to the Buddhist members of the armed forces in the future.

Lastly, while there is no doubt that it is important to examine the compatibility of IHL and scriptural Buddhism, the lived reality of Buddhist combatants for whom the *EBTAF* is designed, and the specific cultural history of Buddhism that pertains to them, suggests that the context-specificity of a given region should also be taken into account when looking for areas where the two might converge. In this respect, there should be further research with empirical data to fully comprehend the realities of different Buddhisms in the plural, to whatever degree they share some core basic principles.

Notes

1. Romanisation of Korean follows the McCune–Reischauer system and the *pinyin* system is used to romanise Chinese characters. K. for Korean; Ch. for Chinese; Skt. for Sanskrit; J. for Japanese. Because all Korean words that appear in this article can be written in Chinese logographs, only rominisations are provided, followed by English translations and Chinese characters.
2. The Education Centre for the Chogye Order of Korean Buddhism published a book titled *History of the Chogye Order* (Education Centre for the Chogye Order of Korean Buddhism 대한불교조계종교육원 2001). For a concise introduction to the Order in English, see Buswell and Lopez (2014, 185). For the historical development of Buddhism in modern Korea, see Park (2014). For the contemporary monastic practices of the Chogye Order, see Buswell (1992).
3. The other three denominations are the Protestant Church, the Catholic Church and Won Buddhism. Won Buddhism was founded in 1916. There are debates on whether it should be regarded as a new religion or a form of Buddhism. It joined the chaplaincy service in 2007.
4. A higher educational institute for Buddhist monks and nuns, founded and run by the Chogye Order of Korean Buddhism.
5. A private university founded and run by the Chogye Order. Contrary to Joongang Sangha University, it is open to the unordained public as well. The Chogye Order recruits military chaplains by offering tuition fee waivers to aspiring Buddhist chaplains.
6. In 2014, the first Buddhist nun was assigned to military chaplaincy service. A recent publication by the Ordinariate, namely the *50-Year History of the Buddhist Chaplain Service*, includes interviews with four female military chaplains.
7. See the Ordinariate's official homepage: www.gunindra.com.
8. I am indebted to Noel Trew for his kind suggestions regarding IHL reading materials related to my research.
9. http://www.hyunbulnews.com/news/articleView.html?idxno=294124.
10. *Flower Garland Sutra* (Skt. *Avataṃsaka Sūtra*; Ch. *hua yan jing* 華嚴經). *Tripiṭaka Koreana* K0079; K0080; K1262. https://kabc.dongguk.edu/.
11. The Korean translation of this passage in the *EBTAF* diverges marginally from the standard one of the *Tripiṭaka Koreana* by the Institute for the Translation of Buddhist Literature at Dongguk University. No classical Chinese is provided for this passage. The *EBTAF* sometimes omits the exact bibliographical information for its canonical source. Based on the comparison of the three versions of the *Flower Garland Sutra*, the translation given above proved to be the closest to the version with 60 volumes, which was initially translated into classical Chinese by Buddhabhadra (359–429 CE).
12. Parts of the English translations of the *EBTAF* were carried out by the author without consultation regarding possible variations, due to the lack of extant research on the *EBTAF*.
13. GC I–IV, Common Art. 3(1); CIHL, Rules 87 and 88.

14. GC II, Art. 12; AP I Art. 10; ICRC study on customary IHL, Rule 55.
15. GC I, Art. 15; GC II, Art. 18; GC IV, Art. 16; AP I, Art. 34(1); CIHL, Rule 113. Recited from Melzer (2019).
16. For different interpretations of the five worldly precepts, see Yim (2014). For their ethical underpinnings, see Im (2012), Lee (1990) and Yi (2014).
17. Tikhonov notes, 'it is no accident that the chief Buddhist military temple attached to the Ministry of Defence was named in honor of the priest [Won'gwang]' (Tikhonov 2015, 15–16).
18. During the last few decades, this term and the associated ideology have met harsh criticism with a trend of Buddhist scholarship reassessing characteristics of Korean Buddhism (Kim 2013, 2014; Mohan 2006; Pak 2010; Shim 1989; Sorensen 2008). Despite diminishing acceptance among academics, however, the SPB rhetoric still prevails among and continues to shape the religious experience of South Koreans. For the doctrine and practices of SPB in East Asia, in the premodern and modern era, see Daoru (2012).
19. The rhetoric against Māra is often found in Theravada Buddhist countries. For the case of Sri Lanka, see Seneviratne (1999), Bartholomeusz (2002) and Frydenlund (2013). For Thailand, see Nilsen (2013), Tambiah (1992) and Jerryson (2010, 2011, 2013). As for Mahāyāna countries, concepts such as no-self or ethical transcendentalism – bodhisattvas transcending normative ethics – are employed as just-war ideologies. For the case of Japan, see Auerback (2013), Kleine (2006) and Victoria (2003, 2006). For China, see Yu (2005, 2010, 2013). In the case of South Korea, the discourses on state-protecting Buddhism are the most dominant in the disputes on Buddhism and war.
20. *Medicine Buddha Sutra* (Skt. *Bhaiṣajyaguru Sūtra*; Ch. *yaoshi rulai benyuan jing* 藥師如來本願經). *Tripiṭaka Koreana* K0176. https://kabc.dongguk.edu/.
21. In Fascicle III, Chapter Two: The Adamantine Body, *Nirvana Sutra* (Skt. *Mahāyāna Mahāparinirvāṇa Sūtra*; Ch. *Daban niepan jing* 大般涅槃經). *Taishō Tripiṭaka* 0374_12.0383b; 0384b. http://21dzk.l.u-tokyo.ac.jp/SAT/ddb-sat2.php.
22. In Fascicle 41, *Treatise on the Stages for Yoga Practice* (Skt. *Yogācārabhūmi-Śāstra*; Ch. *yujia shidi lun* 瑜伽師地論), *Taishō Tripiṭaka* 1579_30.0517b. http://21dzk.l.u-tokyo.ac.jp/SAT/ddb-sat2.php.
23. *Posalgyebon so* 菩薩戒本疏 (Commentary to the Code of the Bodhisattva Precepts). *Han'guk pulgyo chŏnsŏ* (The Collected Works of Korean Buddhism) H0036. https://kabc.dongguk.edu/.
24. Though my translation is indebted to Ha and Mintz (2006), any mistakes are my own.
25. Agent neutrality is a frequently debated topic in Buddhist ethics. In Theravada Buddhism, having no element of negative emotions in the moment of the act of killing is deemed impossible (Gethin 2004).

Acknowledgements

I express my gratitude to the jurors, participants and editorial board members involved in the ICRC Project on Buddhism and IHL for their invaluable comments on my first draft.

Disclosure statement

This article has been supported by the International Committee of the Red Cross (ICRC).

ORCID

Hyein Lee http://orcid.org/0000-0003-0859-2189

References

Auerback, M. 2013. "A Closer Look at Zen at War: The Battlefield Chaplaincy of Shaku Soen in the Russo-Japanese War (1904-1905)." In *Buddhism and Violence: Militarism and Buddhism in Modern Asia*, edited by V. Tikhonov and T. Brekke, 152–171. New York: Routledge.

Bartholomeusz, T. J. 2002. *In Defense of Dharma: Just-War Ideology in Buddhist Sri Lanka*. London and New York: Routledge Curzon.

Buswell, R. E. 1992. *The Zen Monastic Experience: Buddhist Practice in Contemporary Korea*. Princeton: Princeton University Press.

Buswell, R. E., and D. S. Lopez. 2014. *The Princeton Dictionary of Buddhism*. Princeton: Princeton University Press.

Daoru, W., 魏道儒, ed. 2012. *Fojiao Huguo Sixiang Yu Shijian 佛教護國思想與實踐 (State-Protecting Buddhism as a Doctrine and Practice)*. Beijing: Shehui Kexue Wenxian Chubanshe.

Eda, T., 江田俊雄. 1977. *Chōsen Bukkyōshi No Kenkyū 朝鮮佛教史の研究 (Research on the History of Chosŏn Buddhism)*. Tokyo: Kokusho kankōkai.

Editorial Board of Buddhist Chaplaincy 불교군종사 편찬위원회. 2008. *Pulgyo kunjong sa: Kunsŭng 40 nyŏn sa 불교 군종사 군승 40년사 (40-year History of the Buddhist Chaplain Service)*. Seoul: Buddhist Military Ordinariate of the Chogye Order of Korean Buddhism.

Editorial Board of Buddhist Chaplaincy 불교군종사 편찬위원회. 2018. *Pulgyo Kunjong Sa: Kunsŭng 50 Nyŏn Sa불교 군종사 군승 50년사 (50-year History of the Buddhist Chaplain Service)*. Seoul: Buddhist Military Ordinariate of the Chogye Order of Korean Buddhism.

Education Centre for the Chogye Order of Korean Buddhism 대한불교조계종교육원. 2001. *Chogyejong Sa 조계종사 (History of the Chogye Order)*. Seoul: Chogyejong Press.

Frydenlund, I. 2013. "Canonical Ambiguity and Differential Practices: Buddhism and Militarism in Contemporary Sri Lanka." In *Buddhism and Violence: Militarism and Buddhism in Modern Asia*, edited by V. Tikhonov and T. Brekke, 95–119. New York: Routledge.

Gethin, R. 2004. "Can Killing a Living Being Ever Be an Act of Compassion?" *Journal of Buddhist Ethics* 11: 162–202.

Ha, T.-H., and G. Mintz, trans. 2006. *Samguk Yusa: Legends and History of the Three Kingdoms of Ancient Korea*. Seoul: Yonsei University Press.

Im, D., 임동주. 2012. *Silla pulkyo yunli sasang yŏn'gu* 신라불교 윤리사상 연구 *(Study on Ethics of Silla Buddhism)*. PhD dissertation, Dongguk University.

Jerryson, M. 2010. "Militarizing Buddhism: Violence in Southern Thailand." In *Buddhist Warfare*, edited by M. K. Jerrison and M. Juergensmeyer, 179–209. New York: Oxford University Press.

Jerryson, M. 2011. *Buddhist Fury*. New York: Oxford University Press.

Jerryson, M. 2013. "A Path to Militant Buddhism: Thai Buddhist Monks as Representations." In *Buddhism and Violence: Militarism and Buddhism in Modern Asia*, edited by V. Tikhonov and T. Brekke, 75–94. New York: Routledge.

Jorgensen, J. 1997. "Korean Buddhist Historiography-Lessons from past to the Future." *Pulgo yŏn'gu* 14: 219–237.

Kamada, S., 鎌田茂雄. 1987. *Chōsen Bukkyōshi 朝鮮佛教史 (History of Chosŏn Buddhism)*. Tokyo: Tōkyō Daigaku Shuppankai.

Kang, I., 강인철. 2017. *Chong'gyo Wa Kundae* 종교와 군대 *(Religion and Military)*. Seoul: Hyŏnsil Munhwa.

Kim, J., 김종명. 2013. *Kugwang ŭi pulgyogwan kwa ch'igukch'aek* 국왕의 불교관과 치국책 *(Kings' Perspectives on Buddhism and Their Statecraft)*. Seoul: Han'guk Haksul Chŏngbo.

Kim, K., and C. Park. 2020. "Married Monastics and Military Life: Contradictions and Conflicted Identities within South Korea's Buddhist Chaplaincy System." *Religions* 262: 1–9.

Kim, S. 2007. "The Identity of Korean Buddhism within the Context of East Asian Buddhism." In *Korean Buddhism in East Asian Perspectives*, edited by Geumgang Center for Buddhist Studies, 23–44. Seoul: Jimoondang.

Kim, S., 김상용. 2014. "Han'guk pulgyo ŭi pop'yŏnsŏng kwa t'ŭksusŏng 한국 불교의 보편성과 특수성 (Universalities and Particularities in Korean Buddhism)." *Pulgyo Yŏn'gu* 40: 155–191.

Kleine, C. 2006. "Evil Monks with Good Intentions? Remarks on Buddhist Monastic Violence and Its Doctrinal Background." In *Buddhism and Violence*, edited by M. Zimmermann, 65–98. Lumbini: Lumbini International Research Institute.

Lee, J., 이종학. 1990. "Wŏn'gwang pŏpsa wa sesok ogye e taehan shin koch'al 원광법사와 세속오계에 대한 신고찰 (A New Study on Wŏn'gwang and his Five Worldly Precepts)." *The Journal of Silla Culture* 7: 145–168.

Melzer, N. 2019. *International Humanitarian Law: A Comprehensive Introduction*. Geneva: International Committee of the Red Cross.

Ministry of Culture, Sports and Tourism 문화체육관광부. 2018. *2018 Nyŏn han'guk ŭi chong'gyo hyŏnhwang 2018년 한국의 종교 현황 (The Current State of South Korean Religions in 2018)*. Seoul: Ministry of Culture, Sports and Tourism.

Mohan, P. N. 2006. "Beyond the Nation-Protecting Paradigm: Recent Trends in the Historical Studies of Korean Buddhism." *The Review of Korean Studies* 9 (1): 49–68.

Nilsen, M. 2013. "Military Temples and Saffron-Robed Soldiers: Legitimacy and the Securing of Buddhism in Southern Thailand." In *Buddhism and Violence: Militarism and Buddhism in Modern Asia*, edited by V. Tikhonov and T. Brekke, 37–53. New York: Routledge.

Office of Military Ordinariate. 1997. *Kukkun Pŏbyo Chip* 국군법요집 (*Essential Buddhist Teachings for the Armed Forces*). Later revised in 2000, 2010 and 2018. Seoul: Ministry of National Defense.

Pak, C., 박재현. 2010. "Chosn Chŏn'gi Pulgyogye Ŭi Inyŏm Chŏk Pyŏnhwa Kwajŏng Yŏn'gu: Ŭisŭngbyŏng ŬI Chungsim Ŭro 조선전기 불교계의 이념적 변화과정 연구: 의승병을 중심으로 (A Study on the Ideological Change Process in Choson Buddhism: Focusing on Monk Armies Raised in the Cause of Justice)." *Pulgyohak Yŏn'gu* 26: 329–358.

Park, P. 2014. "Buddhism in Modern Korea." In *The Wiley Blackwell Companion to East and Inner Asian Buddhism*, edited by M. Poceski, 466–484. Oxford: Wiley Blackwell.

Seneviratne, H. L. 1999. *The Work of Kings: The New Buddhism in Sri Lanka*. Chicago: University of Chicago Press.

Shim, J. 1989. "On the General Characteristics of Korean Buddhism – Is Korean Buddhism Syncretic?" *Seoul Journal of Korean Studies* 2: 147–157.

Sorensen, H. 2008. "Protecting the Nation': Korean Buddhism under the Rule of Park Chung Hee (1961–79)." In *Korea: The Past and the Present*, edited by S. Pares and J. Hoare, 191–204. Kent: Global Oriental.

Tambiah, S. J. 1992. *Buddhism Betrayed? Religion, Politics, and Violence in Sri Lanka*. Chicago: University of Chicago Press.

Tikhonov, V. 2015. "Militarized Masculinity with Buddhist Characteristics: Buddhist Chaplains and Their Role in the South Korean Army." *The Review of Korean Studies* 18: 7–33.

Victoria, B. D. 2003. *Zen War Stories*. London: Routledge Curzon.

Victoria, B. D. 2006. *Zen at War*. Washington: Rowman and Littlefield.

Yi, C., 이자랑. 2014. "Sesok ogye ŭi salsaeng yut'aek kye wa Won'gwang ŭi kyeyul kwan. 세속오계의 살생유택계와 원광의 계율관 (The Precept of Discriminative Killing from Principle of Five Codes for the Secular World and the Perspectives of Wŏn'gwang on Precepts)." *Han'guk sasangsa hak* 46: 1–27.

Yim, S., 임승택. 2014. "Sesok ogye ŭi paegyŏng kwa gŭn'gŏ세속오계의 배경과 근거 (A Study on the Rationale of the Five Wordly Precepts)." *Tong ashia pulgyo munhwa* 18: 93–96.

Yu, X. 2005. *Buddhism, War, and Nationalism: Chinese Monks in the Struggle against Japanese Aggression, 1931-1945*. New York: Routledge.

Yu, X. 2010. "Buddhists in China during the Korean War (1951-1953)." In *Buddhist Warfare*, edited by M. K. Jerrison and M. Juergensmeyer, 131–156. New York: Oxford University Press.

Yu, X. 2013. "Buddhism and the Justification of War with Focus on Chinese Buddhist History." In *Buddhism and Violence: Militarism and Buddhism in Modern Asia*, edited by V. Tikhonov and T. Brekke, 194–208. New York: Routledge.

ICRC

INTERNATIONAL HUMANITARIAN LAW AND NICHIREN BUDDHISM

Daiki Kinoshita

ABSTRACT

This paper explores how specific Mahāyāna ethics, namely the interpretation of the *Lotus Sūtra* by Zhiyi (536–597), Nichiren (1222–1282) and Sōka Gakkai (1930–), can relate to core principles of international humanitarian law (IHL). In particular, it also assesses and discusses how Sōka Gakkai's three key doctrines (the dignity of life, the variability of life and the interconnectedness of life) are congruent with some IHL principles. The paper then analyses how Buddhist organisations today can be advocates of IHL and specifically looks at how Sōka Gakkai agrees with – and commits to – IHL in terms of the humanitarian impact of the use of nuclear weapons.

Introduction

The teachings upheld by the Sōka Gakkai 創価学会 (Value-Creation Society), which was founded in 1930 as the Sōka Kyōiku Gakkai 創価教育学会 (Society for Value-Creating Education) and renamed the Sōka Gakkai in 1946, belong to the tradition of Buddhist humanism that originated from Shakyamuni Buddha.[1] Most notably, Sōka Gakkai is based on the doctrine proposed in the *Lotus Sūtra* (Skr: *Saddharma-puṇḍarīka-sūtra*; Ch: *Miaofa lianhua jing* 妙法蓮華經; Jp: *Myōhō-renge-kyō* [T09n0262]). The teachings of the *Lotus Sūtra* were transmitted and developed by Buddhist scholars and teachers in India, China and Japan, most notably Zhiyi 智顗 (538–597)[2] in China and Nichiren 日蓮 (1222–1282)[3] in Japan. The scholarship of Zhiyi affirmed the supremacy of the *Lotus Sūtra* with his classification of teachings and texts (*panjiao* 判教); he discerned a deeply significant distinction between the first half of the sūtra and the second half, which explores further the radically new perspective according to which all human beings are born with the potential for Buddhahood.

DOI: 10.4324/9781003439820-24

In Japan, during the Kamakura period (1192–1333), the Buddhist priest Nichiren proposed a new form of practice based on the *Lotus Sūtra*, including the recitation of its title with the formula '*Namu-myōhō-renge-kyō* 南無妙法蓮華経'[4] and its representation in the *Gohonzon* 御本尊.[5]

Following and also developing Nichiren's teaching, Sōka Gakkai was founded with the aim to become a Buddhist organisation that promotes peace, culture and education centred on respect for the dignity of life. It is now present in 192 countries and territories around the world.

This paper consists of three sections: the first part concerns Nichiren's and Sōka Gakkai's views on government, violence and war; the second section explains Sōka Gakkai's perspective on IHL; and the final part explores Sōka Gakkai's efforts to limit the use of nuclear weapons.

Nichiren and Sōka Gakkai on government, violence and war

Nichiren was born on 16 February 1222, in a small coastal hamlet in what is now Chiba Prefecture, Japan, and died from natural causes on 13 October 1282, at the age of 61. Throughout his life, Nichiren was moved by the suffering of ordinary people and sought to engage the establishment in dialogue for a more peaceful society. His best-known treatise, titled 'On Establishing the Correct Teaching for the Peace of the Land' (*Risshō Ankokuron* 立正安国論), was written in the form of a dialogue between a host and a guest, and aimed to address contemporary political leaders and provide them with a philosophy of respect for life that would lead to peace. In it, Nichiren writes: 'If you care about your personal security, you should first of all pray for order and tranquillity throughout the four quarters of the land, should you not' (Sōka Gakkai 1999, 24).

Nichiren always used persuasion and dialogue. He often called for debates with established Buddhists from different sects to discuss and clarify the original intention of Shakyamuni Buddha as taught in the sūtras. For this reason, Nichiren was perceived as being unusually outspoken; for instance, he was critical of the Japanese government of the time for cooperating with what he saw as corrupt Buddhist denominations that encouraged a sense of dependency and fatalism in the people, instead of stabilising society and saving the vulnerable. His outspokenness led to a series of persecutions from other schools and from governmental authorities.

Nichiren even experienced armed attacks, ambushes, further banishment and ultimately an attempted execution. One such example is the Komatsubara persecution in November 1264, which he describes as follows: 'Nembutsu believers[6] number in the thousands or ten thousands, and their supporters' (Sōka Gakkai 1999, 81) attacked and attempted to kill Nichiren and 10 men who were accompanying him, 'only three or four of whom were capable of offering any resistance at all' (Sōka Gakkai 1999, 81). Even in such a situation, Nichiren and his disciples were reluctant to resort to violence and thus were not armed sufficiently to fight against the assailants. Such an attitude reflects Nichiren's belief that '[t]he foremost treasure of sentient beings is none other than life itself' and that '[t]hose who take life are certain to fall into the three evil paths' (Sōka Gakkai 1999, 460), which are the realms of hell, hungry spirits and animals. Because Nichiren firmly believed in the dignity of human life and non-violence, in some extreme circumstances, such as the Komatsubara persecution, he and his disciples had no choice but to use a minimum level of force to protect themselves. In fact, he later received a sword that a disciple gave him to protect his life (Sōka Gakkai 1999, 451). However, Matsuoka 松岡 (2014, 84–85) points out that Nichiren's focus was always to avoid armed conflict and pursue dialogue and discussion rather than to arm himself and his disciples. His approach was to escape from hostile environments, thus protecting himself in a non-violent way while persisting in dialogue.

Nichiren's non-violent philosophy found application in the modern world, with the foundation of Sōka Gakkai in 1930 by Tsunesaburō Makiguchi and Jōsei Toda. With Makiguchi as its first president, the organisation began as a group of teachers focused on educational reform, but later developed into a movement dedicated to the improvement of society through a practice of individual inner transformation based on Nichiren Buddhism.

During World War II, Makiguchi and Toda resisted pressure from the militarist government of Japan to abandon their religious beliefs. The government at that time imposed the State Shintō religion – which proclaims the divinity of the emperor – to glorify its wars of aggression in Asia and suppress all forms of dissent. In 1943, Makiguchi and Toda were arrested and imprisoned as 'thought criminals'[7] for opposing a regime that contributed to warfare, and the former died in prison. After World War II, many ex-combatants, victims of war and atomic bomb survivors joined Sōka Gakkai. These people overcame the pain and suffering of their wartime experiences through Buddhist practice.

Article 5 of the Sōka Gakkai Charter states that the Sōka Gakkai will respect local cultures and customs, and the autonomy of each organisation. Each organisation will develop its activities in accordance with the laws and conditions prevailing in that country or territory and will encourage its members to contribute to society as responsible citizens (Sōka Gakkai 1995). Being a good citizen means living according to the legal system of the modern state.

Even if Sōka Gakkai members embrace the principle of revering the dignity of life, it goes without saying that those who live in countries with conscription must spend time in the army and possibly be deployed in the event of an emergency. Those who live in countries where conscientious objection is allowed may refuse as individuals to perform military service.

Sōka Gakkai's perspective on international humanitarian law

International humanitarian law (IHL hereafter), the primary instruments of which are the Geneva Conventions and their Additional Protocols, seeks to restrict the 'means and methods of warfare' and establish minimum standards to ensure the humane treatment of individuals at all stages of armed conflict (ICRC 2014).[8] IHL balances the principle of humanity with military necessity and rests on a distinction between combatants and civilians, civilian objects and military objectives, proportionality and precaution, thereby preventing superfluous and unnecessary suffering (ICRC n.d.a).

From a Buddhist point of view, every person deserves to be treated with respect based on the dignity and value of their life (respect for human dignity also being an important aspect of IHL), and one should show compassion for each individual, regardless of whether they are 'civilians' or 'combatants'. Compassion, in Nichiren's understanding, is 'like the mercy and compassion that a mother feels for her child' and 'the mercy and compassion of Nichiren and his followers' (Sōka Gakkai 2004, 43). Thus, compassion is not something far from the individual, as it is rooted in profound respect for the inherent dignity of each life – our own and that of others – and a desire to see that dignity treasured rather than any hurt or injury being suffered. Nichiren, referring to the *Nirvana Sūtra* (Skr: *Mahāyāna Mahāparinirvāṇa Sūtra*; Ch: 大般涅槃經 [T12n0374]), quotes, 'The varied sufferings that all living beings undergo – all these are the Thus Come One's [Buddha's] own sufferings' and declares that '[t]he varied sufferings that all living beings undergo – all these are Nichiren's own sufferings' (Sōka Gakkai 2004, 138). Thus, compassion means to feel the suffering of others as one's own and recognise the interconnectedness of oneself and others.

In the same way, Sōka Gakkai considers compassion to be a sense of solidarity with others – with all life – arising from a wish for mutual happiness and growth (Sōka Gakkai Study Department 2017, 159). Sōka Gakkai sees this at the heart and origin of Buddhism, and especially as articulated in the *Lotus Sūtra*, which expounds that Buddhahood, the supreme spiritual and humanistic state of life, which is characterised by boundless compassion, wisdom and courage, is inherent within every person without distinction by gender, ethnicity, social standing or intellectual ability. The *Lotus Sūtra* reads in part, 'This cluster of unsurpassed jewels has come to us unsought' (Watson 2009, 124). This passage suggests that the cluster of jewels is life itself, which contains the world of Buddhahood, and that 'the *Lotus Sūtra* enables us to most profoundly perceive and recognise the treasure of our lives' (Ikeda et al. 2000, 37). According to Sōka Gakkai, Nichiren interprets the treasure tower expounded[9] in the *Lotus Sūtra* as follows:

> In the Latter Day of the Law, no treasure tower exists other than the figures of the men and women who embrace the Lotus Sutra. It follows, therefore, that

> whether eminent or humble, high or low, those who chant Nam-myoho-renge-kyo are themselves the treasure tower, and, likewise, are themselves the Thus Come One Many Treasures. (Sōka Gakkai 1999, 299)

Principles of protection and dignity of life

IHL calls for the protection of those who do not take part in fighting, such as civilians and medical and religious personnel (ICRC n.d.b). It also protects those who have ceased to take part, such as wounded, shipwrecked and sick combatants, and prisoners of war (ICRC 1988). From a Buddhist perspective, inherent in the IHL principle of protection is respect for the dignity of life, which is central to both Buddhism and IHL.

The practice of the philosophy of respect for the dignity of life can be examined in the life of the bodhisattva. In Mahāyāna Buddhism, a bodhisattva is a sentient being who seeks enlightenment for themselves and others. A bodhisattva is literally a living being who aspires to enlightenment and carries out altruistic practices (Sōka Gakkai Study Department 2017, 319).

Respect for the dignity of life lies at the very core of the bodhisattva way of life. One example is the Never Disparaging Bodhisattva (Skr: Sadāparibhūta; Ch: Chang buqing pusa 常不輕菩薩: Jp: Jōkufyō Bosatsu) who is depicted in chapter 20 of the *Lotus Sūtra*. He was known to bow in reverence to everyone he met and praise their inherent Buddha nature. Although this practice sometimes provoked violence and abuse in return, he never disparaged anyone. He would simply retreat and repeat his practice, honouring the potential for good within his persecutors. Over time, as a result of these actions, Bodhisattva Never Disparaging's humanity came to shine, and those who had despised him became his disciples and thus entered the path of attaining Buddhahood themselves.

In times of armed conflict, Buddhist principles would suggest opting for a non-violent resolution. However, when such resolutions are not forthcoming and an impasse has been reached, they would seek for an outcome involving the least suffering and the earliest possible end to the war. Taking the example of Sōka Gakkai, this wisdom then leads to action that promotes peace through nonviolent solutions, such as engaging in dialogue and proposing ways of building peace. For instance, a major activity of Sōka Gakkai organisations around the world is awareness-raising through educational exhibitions, seminars and interactive sessions with speakers engaged in peacebuilding. One example is the Culture of Peace Distinguished Speaker Series of the Sōka Gakkai International – USA (SGI-USA hereafter), where speakers not only address an audience, but engage in active dialogue with youth representatives to help empower them to act for peace.

In addition, and again based on the ideal of the bodhisattva and the central value of the dignity of life, Sōka Gakkai members also commit to supporting ex-combatants who might suffer from physical or mental illness. For example, SGI-USA has held special conferences at its Florida Nature and Culture Center for ex-combatants to share experiences and support each other.[10] It goes without saying that Sōka Gakkai members believe it is crucial to protect and abide by rules that call for saving the vulnerable such as civilians, medical and religious personnel, as well as military personnel who have ceased to take part in conflict, the wounded, shipwrecked and sick combatants, and prisoners of war.

The variability of life

Article 35 of Additional Protocol 1 of the Geneva Conventions stipulates in part that '[i]t is prohibited to employ weapons, projectiles and material and methods of warfare of a nature to cause superfluous injury or unnecessary suffering' (ICRC n.d.c).

Nichiren Buddhism supports the ideas of Article 35 based on the principles of variability of life and dignity of life. The variability of life means that the life condition of an individual changes not only from moment to moment but over the long term. For example, a person who has a propensity for aggressive and violent behaviour can undergo an experience that transforms this tendency into a passionate belief in non-violence and the adoption of an anti-war stance.[11] The longer a person lives, the more opportunities they have to change their karma. Denying an individual their right to life – which is a basic human right – denies them the opportunity for self-reflection, inner discipline, and therefore transformation.

According to Zhiyi, this potential for transformation is explained in the Buddhist concept of the Ten Worlds (Skr: *dasa dhātavaḥ*; Ch: *shijie* 十界; Jp: *Jikkai*). The Ten Worlds are 10 states of life equally inherent within each living being at each moment. Life at each moment manifests one of the Ten Worlds. As Zhiyi states in his work *The Great Concentration and Insight* (Ch: *Mohe zhiguan* 摩訶止觀), 'life is not fixed in one or another of the Ten Worlds, but can manifest any of the ten, from hell to the state of Buddhahood' (Sōka Gakkai 2002, 416–417). In ascending order, these worlds are the worlds of: (1) hell, (2) hungry spirits, (3) animals (animality), (4) *asuras* (anger), (5) human beings, (6) heavenly beings, (7) *Śrāvakas*/voice-hearers (learning), (8) *Pratyekabuddhas*/cause-awakened ones (realisation), (9) bodhisattvas and (10) Buddhas (Sōka Gakkai Study Department 2017, 152–153).[12]

Each of these worlds possesses the potential for all 10 within it. This means that even those in the lower worlds, also known as the four evil paths (hell, hungry spirits, animals and *asuras*), possess the potential to be as compassionate and enlightened as those in the worlds of bodhisattvas and Buddhahood, because people's life states are dynamic and variable. An example of the variability of life is illustrated in Chapter 12 of the *Lotus Sūtra*, through Devadatta, a person of great evil who finally receives a prediction that he will be able to attain Buddhahood after infinite *kalpa*s of Buddhist practices.

From such a Buddhist perspective, it could be considered that by prohibiting superfluous injury and unnecessary suffering, Article 35 aims to reduce the number of deaths and ensure opportunities for all parties that live through warfare to reflect, discipline themselves, and transform themselves to attain a higher life state. Practising Buddhism enables them to change their bad karma, which comes from actions during armed conflict.

Those who trample on the dignity of life and kill humans, whether they are winners, losers, enemies or allies, all accumulate bad karma. When they die with bad karma, they suffer after death. Ikeda states in *The Wisdom of The Lotus Sutra: A Discussion*:

> While activity is the main characteristic of one's life current while alive, one's life current after death is passive. From that standpoint, we cannot independently change our state of life after we have died. For instance, while we are alive, even if our underlying tendency is that of the world of hell, through contact with other people and the influence of the environment, we may experience a variety of different worlds – heavens, humanity and so on. But in the state of death we lose touch with external stimuli, reverting to the underlying state of our own lives. (Ikeda et al. 2002, 270)

This statement suggests that it would be difficult for all those who are involved in an armed conflict to transform themselves after they die. In other words, this lifetime is the time for anyone to experience possible changes in their life states with the influences from the environment. Learning about and practising this Buddhist philosophy – the invariability of life – helps those who take part in war reflect on their conduct. They might change the methods of warfare to avoid causing superfluous injury or unnecessary suffering, thus ensuring the possibility of all parties involved to undergo positive transformation. Therefore, as the concept of the invariability of life prevails, more people will realise that the deaths of enemies should be minimised and that all parties involved in war should be allowed to live and have the opportunity to change, which reflects the ideals of IHL.

The interconnectedness of life

The *Flower Garland Sūtra* (Skr: *Avataṃsaka Sūtra*; Ch: *Huayan jing* 華嚴經; Jp: *Kegon Kyō* [T9n0278]) offers a cosmic view, showing how all the phenomena of the universe interrelate. It illustrates the concept of dependent origination (Skr: *pratītya-samutpāda*; Ch: *yuanqi* 縁起), which teaches the coexistence of all things in the universe, including human beings and nature, in interdependent relationships. The same teaching appears in other texts, including the *Lotus Sūtra*.

The oneness of life and its environment (Ch: *yizheng bu'er* 依正不二; Jp: *eshō-funi*)[13] is clarified within the theoretical framework of 'three thousand realms in a single moment of life' (Ch: *yinian sanqian* 一念三千; Jp: *ichinen sanzen*), which was formulated by Zhiyi on the basis of the teachings of the *Lotus Sūtra*. This concept provides an overarching explanation of the nature and processes of life. Zhiyi's thoughts indicate that all life is interconnected. Thus, human beings are also connected to the physical environment; in other words, a living being and its environment are a single integrated dynamic and therefore are fundamentally inseparable.

Nichiren explains this concept as follows: 'To illustrate, environment is like the shadow, and life, the body. Without the body, no shadow can exist, and without life, no environment. In the same way, life is shaped by its environment' (Sōka Gakkai 1999, 644). Life refers to the 'subjective life' (Ch: *zhengbao* 正報; Jp: *shōhō*), and its environment means the 'objective world' (Ch: *yibao* 依報; Jp: *ehō*) that surrounds it. Even though life is supported by its environment, human beings are part of nature and should preserve the environment.

Similarly, IHL also highlights the importance of protecting the environment. The 1977 Additional Protocol I of the Geneva Conventions, Article 35 stipulates in part that '[i]t is prohibited to employ methods or means of warfare which are intended, or may be expected, to cause widespread, long-term and severe damage to the natural environment'. Similarly, Article 55 stipulates that '[c]are shall be taken in warfare to protect the natural environment against widespread, long-term and severe damage' and that '[a]ttacks against the natural environment by way of reprisals are prohibited' (ICRC n.d.c).

This prohibition is paralleled in Nichiren by the concept of the oneness of life and its environment. There is no separation of the individual and their environment. To protect the environment is to protect the lives of individuals. As Nichiren writes in 'On Attaining Buddhahood in This Lifetime' (Jp: *Isshō jōbutsu shō* 一生成仏抄): '[I]f the minds of living beings are impure, their land is also impure, but if their minds are pure, so is their land. There are not two lands, pure or impure in themselves. The difference lies solely in the good or evil of our minds' (Sōka Gakkai 1999, 4). This is an illustration of the concept of the oneness of life and its environment.

IHL and Sōka Gakkai: Restrictions on nuclear weapons and tactics

As stated earlier, the Buddhist principles of the dignity of life, the variability of life and the interconnectedness of life correspond to Article 35 that prohibits means and methods of warfare that cause unnecessary suffering and destroy the environment. However, as this article does not explicitly state whether the prohibited means and methods include the usage of nuclear weapons, it has led to differing interpretations among scholars and stakeholders.

Some have argued that the use of nuclear weapons could be legal, depending on the situation. The 1868 Saint Petersburg Declaration, the first formal agreement that called for the banning of inhumane weapons in war, prohibited the use of weapons that would cause unnecessary suffering as follows:

> Considering: ... That the only legitimate object which States should endeavour to accomplish during war is to weaken the military forces of the enemy; That for this purpose it is sufficient to disable the greatest possible number of men; That this object would be exceeded by the employment of arms which uselessly aggravate the sufferings of disabled men, or render their death inevitable; That the employment of such arms would, therefore, be contrary to the laws of humanity. (ICRC n.d.d)

This declaration was groundbreaking as the authors saw the need to affirm humanitarian principles in warfare. It also formed a foundation for modern IHL. However, as the Saint Petersburg Declaration does not explicitly denounce all weapons, it does not prevent states from using nuclear weapons to 'weaken the military forces' of an enemy state.

Such interpretations of these prohibitions could conceivably encourage the proliferation of nuclear weapons and run contrary to the respect for the dignity of life and protection of the environment. Similar interpretations could be made regarding the 1996 Advisory Opinion on the Legality of the Threat or Use of Nuclear Weapons issued by the International Court of Justice. It reads,

> A threat or use of nuclear weapons should also be compatible with the requirements of the international law applicable in armed conflict, particularly those of the principles and rules of international humanitarian law, as well as with specific obligations under treaties and other undertakings which expressly deal with nuclear weapons. (ICJ 1996, 266)

The Advisory Opinion indicated that the law was not sufficiently clear on whether the use of nuclear weapons is illegal under any circumstances. For instance, Mayama (2014) points out that the use of nuclear weapons could be legal when the state in question is under existential threat or has been subject to a nuclear attack and might need to respond in kind.[14]

Another argument is that IHL bans the usage of nuclear weapons in any situation, which the Sōka Gakkai also supports based on the aforementioned Buddhist ethics (the dignity of life, the variability of life and the interconnectedness of life). Historically, the atomic bombings of Hiroshima and Nagasaki resulted in unnecessary suffering. The estimated number of combined causalities in the two cities is 199,000 (Atomic Archive n.d.), and the survivors and their offspring still suffer from aftereffects including leukaemia, trauma and social stigma. O'Connor (2014, 147) writes:

> The long-term impact of nuclear weapons also means a significantly increased risk of cancer mortality throughout the life of survivors. How the temporal aspect of the rule on unnecessary suffering does not manifest itself immediately, is to be understood, requires further analysis. That said, given the

> characteristics that would ordinarily manifest themselves from exposure to radiation, it is fair to contend that this issue must be taken into account in applying the unnecessary suffering rule.

Thus, regardless of the reason or justification behind their usage, the damage that nuclear weapons wreak would be catastrophic and absolutely detrimental to the dignity of all life on the planet. It would also affect victims in the long term. The use of nuclear weapons cannot be justified, in my opinion, as they would cause unnecessary and immeasurable suffering to both civilians and combatants.

In 2017, the United Nations General Assembly made the monumental decision to convene a diplomatic conference to negotiate the Treaty on the Prohibition of Nuclear Weapons (TPNW hereafter), which has been ratified by 66 states as of the time of writing and came into force on 21 January 2021. The preamble of the TPNW recognises the important role that organisations such as the International Red Cross and Red Crescent Movement, among other international and religious organisations and individuals, have played in contributing to the call for the total elimination of nuclear weapons, by bringing into focus the humanitarian impact of any use of nuclear weapons.

The Treaty's Article 8, paragraph 5 states that these organisations 'shall be invited to attend the meetings of States Parties and the review conferences as observers' (UN 2017). While the TPNW has not yet been adopted by a state that possess nuclear weapons, it has promoted an international conversation on whether the international community admits the use of nuclear weapons either in times of war or times of no war.

As a religious organisation that upholds the importance of the dignity of life, Sōka Gakkai also participated in the international conferences on the humanitarian impact of nuclear weapons and has consistently engaged in grassroots peace activities towards the elimination of nuclear weapons in cooperation with like-minded organisations, including other faith organisations. For some 40 years, it has engaged in creating and showing panel exhibitions calling for the abolition of nuclear weapons (Sōka Gakkai International 2018); in April 2014, Sōka Gakkai also convened an unprecedented interfaith gathering on the humanitarian impact of nuclear weapons, held at the United States Institute for Peace (USIP) in Washington, DC (Tullo 2014).

Earlier on, in 1957, the second president of Sōka Gakkai, Toda, made a declaration calling for the abolition of nuclear weapons. This was the starting point of Sōka Gakkai's activities to rid the world of nuclear weapons.

Daisaku Ikeda, who later became the third president of the organisation, has continued to spearhead the organisation's movement for the abolition of nuclear weapons and has consistently referred to the declaration in his annual peace proposals since 1983. In his 2007 peace proposal, Ikeda commented on Toda's declaration, which describes the destructive nature within any person who would use nuclear weapons as 'a devil incarnate, a fiend, a monster' (Ikeda 2007). Ikeda states:

> Those who would use nuclear weapons capable of instantaneously killing tens of millions of people exhibit the most desperate symptoms of this pathology. They have lost all sense of the dignity of life, having fallen prey to their own inner demons. (Ikeda 2007)

According to Ikeda (2007),

> Buddhism classifies the underlying destructive impulses that give rise to such behaviour as 'the three poisons'... of greed, anger and ignorance. 'The world of anger' can be thought of as the state of life of those in whom these forces have been directed outward towards others.

The following words of Nichiren well describe the world of anger:

> Since the mind of a person who is in the world of asuras [anger] desires in every moment to be superior to everyone else and cannot bear to be inferior to anyone else, he belittles and despises others and exalts himself. (Sōka Gakkai 2006, 197)

When in the world of anger, we always engage in invidious comparisons with others, always seeking to excel over them. The resulting distortions prevent us from perceiving the world accurately; we fall easily into conflict, locking horns with others at the slightest provocation. Under the sway of such anger, people can commit unimaginable acts of violence and bloodshed.

When an individual's state of mind and heart are within the three evil paths, they are unable to make reasonable judgements. When in such a state of anger, decision-making is ruled by one's ego. It is therefore not impossible that such an individual will not hesitate to kill others by using weapons as destructive as nuclear weapons.

Shakyamuni Buddha was once asked which living beings we as human beings may kill and which we must not kill. His reply was that it is enough to 'kill the will to kill'. As Ikeda (1991) comments in his lecture 'The Age of Soft Power and Inner-Motivated Philosophy' given at Harvard University:

> He [Shakyamuni Buddha] is telling us that, in seeking the kind of harmonious relationship expressed in the idea of respect for the sanctity of life, we must not limit ourselves to the phenomenal level where conflict and hostility undeniably exist – the conflict, in this case, of which living beings it is acceptable to kill and which not. We must seek it on a deeper level – a level where it is truly possible to 'kill the will to kill'. This goes beyond mere objective awareness; it refers to a state of compassion transcending distinctions between self and other; it refers to a compassionate energy that beats within the depths of all people's subjective lives; it is here that the individual and the universal life are merged.

In the 2009 proposal of steps towards the abolition of nuclear weapons, Ikeda (2009) clarified that this challenge too is one of changing the minds of human beings, stating:

> If we are to put the era of nuclear terror behind us, we must struggle against the real 'enemy'. That enemy is not nuclear weapons *per se*, nor is it the states that possess or develop them. The real enemy that we must confront is the ways of thinking that justify nuclear weapons; the readiness to annihilate others when they are seen as a threat or as a hindrance to the realization of our objectives.

In other writing, Ikeda (2007) explains:

> It is this state of mind that would countenance the use of nuclear weapons; it can equally be seen in the psychology of those who would advocate the use of such hideously cruel weapons as napalm, or, more recently, depleted uranium and cluster bombs. People in such a state of life are blinded, not only to the horrific suffering their actions wreak but also to the value of human life itself. For the sake of human dignity, we must never succumb to the numbing dehumanisation of the rampant world of anger.

In conclusion, according to Ikeda, on an individual level, the practice of Buddhism can enable individuals to master their egocentric selves, gradually lessening the influence of the 'three poisons' of greed, anger and ignorance, and bringing out the qualities that constitute Buddhahood: compassion, courage and wisdom.

Conclusion

There are commonalities between IHL and the principles stemming from Mahāyāna Buddhism; this article explained especially how the principles of the dignity, variability and interconnectedness of life, which are found in the Buddhist teachings of Zhiyi, Nichiren and Sōka Gakkai, and explained in the *Lotus Sūtra*, are paralleled in IHL. Furthermore, the principle of protection extends to the restriction of weapons, including nuclear weapons.

More specifically, the dignity of life described in the *Lotus Sūtra* seems to have a substantial overlap with the 1977 Additional Protocol I to the Geneva Conventions, Article 51, which calls for protection of civilian life, whereas the dignity, variability and interconnectedness of life, based on Zhiyi's view, relates to Article 35 of the Additional Protocol I, which focuses on the restriction of the weapons and means of warfare.

As seen with the adoption of the TPNW, dialogue among states, organisations and individuals is important, as it advocates for peaceful resolutions to contentious issues. As there is growing consensus by the international community that nuclear weapons are redundant and their very existence a threat to humanity, it is imperative that '[i]n an armed conflict, it is extremely doubtful that nuclear weapons could ever be used in accordance with the principles and rules of IHL' (ICRC 2022, 1481).

Nichiren Buddhism values the dignity of individuals' lives and holds that an individual has the potential to change and, in doing so, can effect a change in their environment. Parallel with this philosophical argument, IHL has a vital role to play to ensure that all people affected by war not only have their basic human right to life respected but also that the dignity of their life – be they ex-combatants or other vulnerable people – is protected and respected.

Notes

1. Recent scholarship on Sōka Gakkai includes Metraux (1996), Fisker-Nielsen (2012) and McLaughlin (2018).
2. For more about Zhiyi and early Tiantai interpretation of the *Lotus Sūtra* see e.g. Ziporyn (2016).
3. About Nichiren, see e.g. Satō 佐藤 (2003, 69–190).
4. Often translated as 'Glory to the Dharma of the Lotus Sutra', the formula contains a vow to embrace and manifest one's Buddha nature.
5. The *Gohonzon* ('object of devotion') is a scroll containing Chinese and Sanskrit characters aimed at aiding in the process of bringing forth the life condition of Buddhahood.
6. Followers of the practice of recitation (*nembutsu* 念仏) of Amida's name, especially in the Pure Land schools.
7. Those who violated the Peace Preservation Law in Japan during and before WWII were called 'thought criminals'.
8. The four Geneva Conventions of 1949 (GC I, II, III and IV), which have been universally ratified, constitute the core treaties of IHL. The Conventions have been supplemented by Additional Protocols I and II of 1977 (AP I and AP II) relating to the protection of victims of international and non-international armed conflict, respectively; and by Additional Protocol III of 2005 (AP III) relating to an additional distinctive emblem (the red crystal).
9. See Watson (2009, 209–220).
10. From 10 to 13 November 2017, for instance, 165 SGI-USA members joined its sixth Veterans/Active Duty Conference held at the Florida Nature and Culture Center. Details are available at https://www.worldtribune.org/2017/11/carrying-mission-kosen-rufu/.
11. The famous story of King Ashoka also suggests that Buddhism inspired him to transform his life. His story illustrates the potential for good within a life of evil acts. It is said that the Indian ruler King Ashoka (304–232 BCE) was a merciless king of the Mauryan Empire and waged many wars. He waged war against the state of Kalinga and conquered it around 261 BCE. The war led to the killing of 100,000 people and the deportation of 150,000 others. The horror of this war and of what it did left him tormented to the extent that he repented of his cruelty and vowed to never again wage war. It is said that he learnt about Buddhist teachings immediately before he started governing his realm, though he did not immediately take it to heart. Ten years after he ascended the throne, he visited the place where Shakyamuni achieved enlightenment and started his circumambulation, seeking the

Buddhist law. Over the following decades of his reign, he constructed wells, planted trees, built hospitals to cure humans and animals, encouraged cultural exchanges and erected stone pillars engraved with edicts, such as those admonishing against the taking of life. See Thapar (1997, 255).

12. For a translation of and commentary on *Mohe zhiguan* see Swanson (2017).
13. Also, non-duality of life and its environment; the principle that life and its environment, although two seemingly distinct phenomena, are essentially non-dual; they are two integral phases of a single reality. In the Japanese term *eshō-funi*, *eshō* is a compound of *shōhō*, meaning life or a living being, and *ehō*, its environment. *Funi*, meaning 'not two', indicates oneness or non-duality. It is short for *nini-funi*, which means 'two (in phenomena) but not two (in essence)'. *Hō* of *shōhō* and *ehō* means reward or effect. It indicates that 'life' constitutes a subjective self that experiences the effects of its past actions, and 'its environment' is an objective realm in which individuals' karmic rewards find expression. Each living being has its own unique environment. The effects of karma appear in oneself and in one's objective environment, because self and environment are two integral aspects of an individual. See Sōka Gakkai (2002, 477–478).
14. See also Nishimura 西村 (2004).

Disclosure statement

This article has been supported by the International Committee of the Red Cross (ICRC).

References

Atomic Archive. n.d. *The Atomic Bombings of Hiroshima and Nagasaki*. San Diego: AJ Software & Multimedia. http://www.atomicarchive.com/Docs/MED/med_chp10.shtml

Fisker-Nielsen, A. M. 2012. *Religion and Politics in Contemporary Japan: Soka Gakkai Youth and Komeito*. London: Routledge.

ICJ (International Court of Justice). 1996. *Legality of the Threat or Use of Nuclear Weapons, Advisory Opinion of 8 July 1996*. The Hague: International Court of Justice. https://www.icj-cij.org/public/files/case-related/95/095-19960708-ADV-01-00-EN.pdf

ICRC (International Committee of the Red Cross). 1988. *Protection of the Wounded, Sick and Shipwrecked*. Geneva: International Committee of the Red Cross. https://www.icrc.org/en/doc/resources/documents/misc/57jmjs.htm

ICRC (International Committee of the Red Cross). 2014. *What is International Humanitarian Law*. Geneva: International Committee of the Red Cross. https://www.icrc.org/en/doc/assets/files/other/what_is_ihl.pdf

ICRC (International Committee of the Red Cross). 2022. "The ICRC's Legal and Policy Position on Nuclear Weapons." *International Review of the Red Cross* 104 (919): 1477–1499. doi:10.1017/S1816383122000248.

ICRC (International Committee of the Red Cross). n.d.a. *Fundamental Principles of IHL*. Geneva: International Committee of the Red Cross. https://casebook.icrc.org/glossary/fundamental-principles-ihl

ICRC (International Committee of the Red Cross). n.d.b. *Protection of the Civilian Population*. Geneva: International Committee of the Red Cross. https://ihl-databases.icrc.org/ihl/WebART/470-750065

ICRC (International Committee of the Red Cross). n.d.c. *Basic Rules*. Geneva: International Committee of the Red Cross. https://ihl-databases.icrc.org/applic/ihl/ihl.nsf/Article.xsp?action=openDocument&documentId=0DF4B935977689E8C12563CD0051DAE4

ICRC (International Committee of the Red Cross). n.d.d. *Declaration Renouncing the Use, in Time of War, of Explosive Projectiles Under 400 Grammes Weight. Saint Petersburg, 29 November/11 December 1868*. Geneva: International Committee of the Red Cross. https://ihl-databases.icrc.org/applic/ihl/ihl.nsf/Article.xsp?action=openDocument&documentId=568842C2B90F4A29C12563CD0051547C

Ikeda, D. 1991. *The Age of "Soft Power" and Inner-Motivated Philosophy*. Tokyo: Sōka Gakkai. https://www.daisakuikeda.org/sub/resources/works/lect/lect-01.html

Ikeda, D. 2007. *Restoring the Human Connection: The First Step to Global Peace*. Tokyo: Sōka Gakkai. https://www.daisakuikeda.org/assets/files/pp2007.pdf

Ikeda, D. 2009. *Nuclear Abolition Proposal 2009*. Tokyo: Sōka Gakkai. https://www.daisakuikeda.org/assets/files/disarm_p2009.pdf

Ikeda, D., K. Saito, T. Endo, and H. Suda. 2000. *The Wisdom of the Lotus Sutra: A Discussion*. 2 vols. Santa Monica: World Tribune.

Ikeda, D., K. Saito, T. Endo, and H. Suda. 2002. *The Wisdom of the Lotus Sutra: A Discussion*. 4 vols. Santa Monica: World Tribune.

Matsuoka, M. 松岡幹夫. 2014. *Heiwa wo tsukuru shukyo: Nichiren buppo to Soka Gakkai 平和をつくる宗教：日蓮仏法と創価学会* [Religion to Create Peace: Nichiren Buddhism and Soka Gakkai]. Tokyo: Daisanbunmeisha.

Mayama, A. 2014. "Legality of the Use of Nuclear Weapons and the 2011 Resolution 1 of the Red Cross Movement's Council of Delegates: 'Working towards the Elimination of Nuclear Weapons'." *The Journal of Humanitarian Studies* 3: 6–18.

McLaughlin, L. 2018. *Soka Gakkai's Human Revolution: The Rise of a Mimetic Nation in Modern Japan*. Honolulu: University of Hawai'i Press.

Metraux, D. A. 1996. "The Soka Gakkai: Buddhism and the Creation of a Harmonious and Peaceful Society." In *Engaged Buddhism: Buddhist Liberation Movements in Asia*, edited by C. S. Queen and S. B. King, 365–400. Albany: SUNY Press.

Nishimura, Y. 西村弓. 2004. "Buryoku hunso ho no riko kakuho: Sogo shugi to hukkyu 武力紛争法の履行確保: 相互主義と復仇 [Ensuring Implementation of Law of Armed Conflict: Reciprocity and Reprisal]." In *Buryoku hunso no kokusai ho 武力紛争の国際法* [International Law of Armed Conflict], edited by M. Shinya 村瀬信也 and M. Akira 真山全, 685–707. Tokyo: Toshindo.

O'Connor, S. 2014. "Nuclear Weapons and the Unnecessary Suffering Rule." In *Nuclear Weapons Under International Law*, edited by G. Nystuen, S. Casey-Maslen, and A. G. Bersagel, 128–147. Cambridge: Cambridge University Press.

Satō, H. 佐藤弘夫. 2003. *Nichiren: Ware Nihon no hashira to naran 日蓮：われ日本の柱となむ* [I Will Be the Pillar of Japan]. Kyoto: Mineruva Shobō.

Sōka Gakkai. 1995. *Soka Gakkai Charter*. Tokyo: Sōka Gakkai. https://www.sokaglobal.org/resources/sgi-charter.html

Sōka Gakkai. 1999. *The Writings of Nichiren Daishonin, Volume I*. Tokyo: Sōka Gakkai.

Sōka Gakkai. 2002. *The Soka Gakkai Dictionary of Buddhism*. Tokyo: Sōka Gakkai.

Sōka Gakkai. 2004. *The Record of the Orally Transmitted Teachings*. Tokyo: Sōka Gakkai.

Sōka Gakkai. 2006. *The Writings of Nichiren Daishonin, Volume II*. Tokyo: Sōka Gakkai.

Sōka Gakkai International. 2018. *People's Decade for Nuclear Abolition II*. https://peoplesdecade2.wixsite.com/nuclear-abolition

Sōka Gakkai Study Department. 2017. *Kyōgaku yōgo shu 教学用語* [Glossary of Buddhist Terminology]. Tokyo: Seikyo Shimbun.

Swanson, P. 2017. *Clear Serenity, Quiet Insight: T'ien-T'ai Chih-I's Mo-Ho Chih-Kuan*. Honolulu: University of Hawai'i Press.

Thapar, R. 1997. *Aśoka and the Decline of the Mauryas*. Oxford: Oxford University Press.

Tullo, M. 2014. "Interfaith Leaders Jointly Call to Abolish Nuclear Arms." *Inter Press Service*, April 25. https://www.ipsnews.net/2014/04/interfaith-leaders-jointly-call-abolish-nuclear-arms/

UN (United Nations). 2017. "Treaty on the Prohibition of Nuclear Weapons." *A/CONF.229/2017/8*, July, 7. https://undocs.org/Home/Mobile?FinalSymbol=A%2FCONF.229%2F2017%2F8

Watson, B., ed. 2009. *The Lotus Sutra and Its Opening and Closing Sutras*. Tokyo: Sōka Gakkai.

Ziporyn, B. A. 2016. *Emptiness and Omnipresence: An Essential Introduction to Tiantai Buddhism*. Bloomington: Indiana University Press.

ICRC

SOCIALLY ENGAGED BUDDHISM AND PRINCIPLED HUMANITARIAN ACTION DURING ARMED CONFLICT

Ha Vinh Tho, Edith Favoreu and Noel Maurer Trew

ABSTRACT

In this paper, we will highlight the correspondences between the Socially Engaged Buddhism movement, especially as defined in the practice of the late Thich Nhat Hanh, and the core principles of humanity, impartiality, neutrality and independence originally adopted by the International Red Cross and Red Crescent Movement. These principles also underpin the neutral, impartial and independent approach to humanitarian action, used by agencies working under the auspices of the United Nations' Inter-Agency Standing Committee and Office for the Coordination of Humanitarian Affairs, along with those who have signed the Code of Conduct for the International Red Cross and Red Crescent Movement and Non-Governmental Organizations in Disaster Relief. We hope this paper is a modest but useful contribution to create better understanding and to generate dialogue among different stakeholders in the humanitarian field, particularly in the context of armed conflict.

Hatred never ceases through hatred in this world.

Through love alone, they cease. This is an eternal law.

The Dhammapada, v. 5 (Narada Thera 1978)

Introduction

Contemporary Socially Engaged Buddhism (SEB), and its founding figure, the Vietnamese Zen Master Thich Nhat Hanh (1926–2022), emphasise meeting the needs and responding to the suffering of our time (Plum Village Monastery n.d.a). From the experience of war in Vietnam, Thich Nhat Hanh's form of Buddhist activism was born of a desire to bring assistance to those suffering under the bombings and turmoil of war. This Engaged Buddhism movement has since been dedicated to the work of inner transformation for the benefit of individuals and society. It is important to keep in

DOI: 10.4324/9781003439820-25

mind that SEB does not consider itself to be a 'new movement' – rather, it regards its teachings as a restatement of early Buddhist doctrine. Indeed, Thich Nhat Hanh claims that 'Engaged Buddhism is just Buddhism' (Nhat Hanh in Malkin 2003). The movement, as understood by Thich Nhat Hanh, recognises that the Buddha-Dharma has always had the flexibility to adapt its 'skilful means' (*upāya-kauśalya*) to the historical, cultural, social and economic context of a particular place and age. In this paper, we will consider from a philosophical perspective the correspondence between the core values of SEB and humanitarian principles. In doing so, we hope to strengthen the universality of the norms that underpin each.

Contemporary SEB: Meeting the needs and suffering of our time

In the mid-twentieth century, a distinctive – yet non-centralised – movement was developed as an 'ecumenical' Buddhist endeavour to contextualise and actualise the ancient teachings of loving-kindness and compassion (respectively known as *mettā* and *karuṇā* from the four *Brahma-vihāra*s, or sublime ways of living). Intended to meet the needs and suffering of modern times, this movement was called 'Socially Engaged Buddhism' or 'Engaged Buddhism' (SEB). Although the SEB movement first appeared in a Mahāyāna context (i.e. Chan/Zen Buddhism) – and can be understood as a contemporary expression of the Bodhisattva ideal of striving to alleviate the suffering of all sentient beings – the development of Engaged Buddhism involved many teachers from nearly all Buddhist Schools.[1] Their common objective has been to translate the wisdom and compassion that is at the heart of the Buddha's teaching into 'skilful means' (*upāya-kauśalya*), in order to alleviate the suffering of all people – and of all sentient beings.

SEB was influenced by earlier efforts in the twentieth century to apply Buddhist foundational principles to address social problems in a tangible way. One notable predecessor of SEB is Dr B. R. Ambedkar's (1891–1956) neo-Buddhism movement in India, which championed social equality, particularly for those of the Dalit (a former 'untouchable') class. In addition, the Humanistic Buddhism developed by Chinese Buddhist monk Taixu 太虛 (1890–1947) served as an inspiration for the later work of the so called 'Four Heavenly Kings' of Taiwanese engaged Buddhism, namely the monks Hsing Yun 星雲 (b. 1927), Sheng Yen 聖嚴 (1931–2009) and Wei Chueh 惟覺 (1928–2016), and the nun Cheng Yen 證嚴 (b. 1937) (Sharkey 2017). Taixu's idea of *renjian fojiao (*人間佛教, i.e. 'Buddhism for this world'), was well received by Buddhist reformers in Vietnam during the 1930s and 1940s who would in turn inspire the teachings and actions of Vietnamese Zen Master Thich Nhat Hanh (DeVido 2009, 435–439; Gleig 2021). It is well known that a young Thich Nhat Hanh had the opportunity to interact very closely with the monk Yen Pei 演培 (1917–1996), another key exponent of the

Chinese movement of Humanistic Buddhism who then became active especially in Southeast Asia.[2] Nhat Hanh is widely considered to be one of SEB's founding figures and was the first to use the term 'Socially Engaged Buddhism' to describe this non-sectarian and activist strand of Buddhism (Plum Village Monastery n.d.a). In a spirit similar to that which animated Henri Dunant, the founder the of the Red Cross and Red Crescent Movement, Thich Nhat Hanh was moved to action in order to respond to the suffering caused by war:

> When bombs begin to fall on people, you cannot stay in the meditation hall all of the time. Meditation is about the awareness of what is going on – not only in your body and in your feelings, but all around you. When I was a novice in Vietnam, we young monks witnessed the suffering caused by the war and were very eager to practice Buddhism in such a way that we could bring it into society. That was not easy because the tradition did not directly offer Engaged Buddhism, so we had to do it by ourselves. That was the birth of Engaged Buddhism. (Nhat Hanh in Malkin 2003)

In 1964 during the Vietnam–American war, the country was afflicted not only by the war itself, but also by various disasters (what today might be referred to as 'complex emergencies'). All around the country people were affected by these compounding crises, unable to meet their basic needs and, in most cases, being without access to any supplies. At that time, Sister Chan Khong (b. 1938) and her teacher Thich Nhat Hanh, with a group of volunteers, founded the School of Youth and Social Service, a grassroots relief organisation. With nearly 10,000 volunteers, this politically neutral movement was based on the Buddhist principles of non-violence and compassionate action (Valente 2016). In addition, Thich Nhat Hanh created the Order of Interbeing in the early 1960s to support young monks, nuns and lay practitioners who wanted to make a positive contribution in a country torn by war (Eppsteiner 1998). Of one early intervention by the Order after a flood, Sister Chan Khong recalled:

> The flood victims that the volunteer relief workers had come to help were either on the verge of death – starving, shivering, and homeless – or else they were dead, bloated and rotting. The volunteers themselves were also in danger. They knew that at any moment they could be killed in the crossfire. (quoted in Miller 2017)

Travelling to remote impoverished areas, they started distributing rice, beans, clothing, cooking utensils and medical supplies. Besides providing this relief, they have developed a way of delivering aid with love, compassion and calm (Miller 2017).

While the movement has inspired its adherents to improve the lives of others, it is necessary to also acknowledge some of the criticisms that have been levelled at Engaged Buddhism. From a doctrinal perspective, Sallie King claims that some conservative Buddhists argue the objective of Buddhism is to cultivate an attitude of non-attachment to the problems of saṃsāra (i.e. the world of birth, death, rebirth) and SEB compels its adherents to become stuck in saṃsāra. Relatedly, in many sects of Buddhism, it is seen as a meritorious act for laypeople to give gifts to monks (i.e. dāna) – the purer the recipient of the gift, the better. There is a fear that by getting involved in (or attached to) worldly affairs, monks who are active in SEB do not allow the local laity to accrue as much merit through their dāna (King 2009, 7–8).

These criticisms seem to overlook an important dimension of Buddhist philosophy: the differentiation between two levels of reality, between relative or conventional reality (*saṁvṛti-satya*) and ultimate reality (*paramārtha-satya*). In the realm of ultimate truth, only Enlightenment can truly overcome the roots of suffering and should therefore be the focus of the practice. However, in the realm of relative truth, the aim *is* to enhance happiness for self and others and alleviate suffering for self and others through the practice of active compassion. These two aspects of the Buddhist path are related to the non-duality of Wisdom (relating to ultimate truth) and compassion (relating to relative truth).

Moreover, Thich Nhat Hanh argues that Buddhism has always been engaged in the problems of the world. He claims that while Buddhism allows for the possibility of 'solitary Buddhas', that was not the path taken by the historical Buddha – after his enlightenment, Siddhartha Gautama did not stay under the Bodhi Tree. Rather, he returned to teach both monastics and laypeople (King 2009, 9). Indeed, A. T. Ariyaratne, the founder of the Sarvodaya Shramadana Movement, claims that up until colonial times, Buddhist monks would have had a greater role in secular affairs, such as medicine, education and government. By favouring their own Western institutions, colonial governments pushed the monks out of the secular sphere. Consequently, he regards Socially Engaged Buddhist monks as simply reclaiming their traditional role in society, rather than inventing a new (modern) one (King 2009, 10).

Since the protection of lives, the preservation of the dignity of human beings, and the alleviation of suffering are all historically at the heart of SEB (and, indeed, of Buddhism more generally), these themes provide us with an entry point to explore the tradition's convergences with international humanitarian law (IHL) and the humanitarian principles.

The humanitarian principles and their relationship with IHL

The humanitarian principles have their origins in the Fundamental Principles of the International Red Cross and Red Crescent Movement (RC/RC). Although they were first proclaimed in their current form at the 20th International Conference of the Red Cross and Red Crescent in 1965, they could be considered to be a codification of the Movement's mission and ways of working since its origin a century earlier.

In 1991, the principles of humanity, impartiality and neutrality were then adopted by United Nations General Assembly (UNGA) Resolution 46/182[3] to guide the work of the newly created Inter-Agency Standing Committee (IASC), which was established to coordinate international relief actions undertaken by organisations that are active in the humanitarian sphere. In 2004, UNGA Resolution 58/114[4] added the principle of independence to this list. These principles also guide the work of the United Nations Office for the Coordination of Humanitarian Affairs (OCHA), which helps to coordinate the day-to-day operations of humanitarian actors on the ground.

The humanitarian principles have since underpinned the 'Neutral, Impartial and Independent Humanitarian Action' or 'NIIHA' approach. All agencies that work under the auspices of IASC – whether they be an RC/RC organisation, inter-governmental organisation (IGO), non-governmental organisation (NGO), or faith-based organisation (FBO), acting either individually or as part of a consortium – have agreed to be guided by these principles. This includes the Tzu Chi Foundation, an organisation that was expressly set up as an engaged Buddhist group.

The humanitarian principles have also influenced the development of the RC/RC and NGO Code of Conduct,[5] a voluntary code that guides humanitarian action outside of situations of armed conflict and which can be adopted irrespective of an organisation's affiliation with IASC. In addition, the NIIHA approach also forms part of the Core Humanitarian Standard on Quality and Accountability, another voluntary code that is widely used throughout the humanitarian sector (CHS Alliance, Groupe URD and the Sphere Project 2014, 8).

The humanitarian principles are not formally part of IHL. However, they have been recognised as being indispensable for helping humanitarian organisations to comply with their obligations under IHL, thereby maintaining the security of their personnel and their access to affected populations during armed conflict. Humanitarian actors are protected from attack in their own right during international armed conflicts[6] and they are protected during both international and non-international armed conflicts because of their medical[7] and/or civilian status.[8] However, to benefit from these protections, they must not take 'a direct part in hostilities'[9] nor (in the case of medical units) may they 'commit, outside their humanitarian function, acts harmful to the enemy'.[10] Therefore, the safety of humanitarian actors depends upon their ability to observe strict neutrality in military affairs.

IHL requires parties to a conflict to allow and facilitate humanitarian relief to civilians in need (except where restrictions are in place for reasons of imperative military necessity).[11] Although it is primarily the responsibility of the state to ensure that the basic needs of the civilian population are met, if the state is unwilling or unable to provide such assistance, then access for humanitarian actors becomes vitally important (Schwendimann 2011, 997). For their part, humanitarian actors must not 'exceed the terms of their mission',[12] and their relief must be 'impartial in character'.[13] Therefore, to maintain their access (particularly in territories controlled by the state), humanitarian actors are expected to uphold the principles of neutrality and impartiality.

In addition to the role that the principles play in helping humanitarian organisations to comply with IHL in a formal sense, adherence to these principles helps them to build trust in a more informal way, especially when working with more than one party to a conflict. For example, when working with non-state armed groups (NSAGs), humanitarian actors' independence (both real and perceived) becomes especially important and can determine whether they are able to operate in areas under the control of a particular NSAG (Geneva Call 2016).

So, it is clear that organisations working in times of armed conflict – including those associated with the SEB movement – should adhere to the humanitarian principles if they wish to benefit from the protections and access that IHL bestows upon humanitarian actors. With this in mind, it may be helpful to further explore where the tenets of SEB align with the core humanitarian principles and – equally importantly – where they might diverge or be difficult for particular SEB groups to put into practice.

Core values of SEB and humanitarianism

When studying Buddhist texts deeply, one realises that they are not only about setting boundaries to negative behaviours. They also promote the development of positive attitudes, or 'virtues' in the Aristotelian sense. Similarly, the humanitarian principles at the same time represent practical guidelines to help humanitarian actors comply with their obligations under IHL and positive values that help to build trust and guide humanitarian response to armed conflicts and other emergencies.

In the Mahāyāna tradition, this aspect of Buddhist virtue ethics underwent a profound development at Nalanda University in Northern India during the fifth to twelfth centuries CE – an era that can be considered a golden age of Indian Buddhism. The most famous text of this time is probably *The Way of the Bodhisattva* (*Bodhicaryāvatāra*) by Shantideva (c. 685–c. 763). We would like to quote a few verses from Chapter 3, considering that they make an interesting link with the mandate of most humanitarian actors, including the International Committee of the Red Cross (ICRC)

> Verse 8. For all those ailing in the world,
> Until their every sickness has been healed,
> May I myself become for them
> The doctor, nurse, the medicine itself.

> Verse 9. Raining down a flood of food and drink,
> May I dispel the ills of thirst and famine.
> And in the aeons marked by scarcity and want,
> May I myself appear as drink and sustenance.
> ...
>
> Verse 18. May I be a guard for those who are protectorless,
> A guide for those who journey on the road.
> For those who wish to cross the water,
> May I be a boat, a raft, a bridge.
> (Shantideva 2011, 48–49)

These three verses provide a sense of the deep compassion that is the guiding principle of *The Way of the Bodhisattva*. These verses of Shantideva are considered by some to be a metaphorical rather than a literal call to action. However, to Socially Engaged Buddhists this is not simply a poetic description of otherworldly virtues, but a guide on how to conduct their lives and to engage with the world.

Similarly, contemporary humanitarianism represents a way to give practical effect to lofty values. In his *Commentary to the Fundamental Principles of the International Red Cross and Red Crescent Movement*, the ICRC jurist Jean Pictet (1914–2002) defined humanitarianism in the following terms:

> Humanitarianism is a doctrine which aims at the happiness of the human species, or, if one prefers, it is the attitude of humanity towards mankind, on a basis of universality.
>
> Modern humanitarianism is an advanced and rational form of charity and justice. It is not only directed to fighting against the suffering of a given moment and of helping particular individuals, for it also has more positive aims, designed to attain the greatest possible measure of happiness for the greatest number of people. In addition, humanitarianism does not only act to cure but also to prevent suffering, to fight against evils, even over a long term of time. The Red Cross is a living example of this approach. (Pictet 1979, 13)

Of course, Pictet was writing from a Red Cross perspective. However, since the humanitarian principles have their roots in the Fundamental Principles of the Red Cross and Red Crescent Movement, his observations regarding the humanitarian spirit that underlies the principles is nevertheless helpful for our analysis.

We will limit our investigation to the four core humanitarian principles – humanity, impartiality, neutrality and independence – rather than the seven Fundamental Principles of the International Red Cross and Red Crescent Movement, as the former play a central role in humanitarian responses during armed conflicts for a wider range of organisations, including FBOs. We argue that these four principles reflect standards and practices that are aligned with SEB ethics and values. They are not merely 'imported Western norms', but rather present a way to embody Buddhist values in providing humanitarian assistance during situations of armed conflict and other emergencies.

The principle of humanity and correspondences with loving-kindness, compassion, empathetic joy and equanimity (maitrī, karuṇā, muditā and upekṣā), as well as the First Precept

It may be helpful to begin our analysis with OCHA's formulation of the principle of humanity, which describes a succinct but powerful call to action:

> Human suffering must be addressed wherever it is found. The purpose of humanitarian action is to protect life and health and ensure respect for human beings. (United Nations 2012).

The wording used to describe the same principle in the RC/RC and NGO Code of Conduct is slightly longer, but it similarly recognises that the aim of humanitarian action is to reduce human suffering:

> **The humanitarian imperative comes first**
> The right to receive humanitarian assistance, and to offer it, is a fundamental humanitarian principle which should be enjoyed by all citizens of all countries. As members of the international community, we recognise our obligation to provide humanitarian assistance wherever it is needed .... The prime motivation of our response to disaster is to alleviate human suffering amongst those least able to withstand the stress caused by disaster .... (International Federation of Red Cross and Red Crescent Societies and the ICRC 1994)

Of course, the problem of suffering is central to the teachings of Buddhism. According to tradition, the Buddha said, 'In the past, as today, I describe suffering and the cessation of suffering'.[14] Moreover, in the *Dhammacakkappavattana Sutta*, the first teaching given by the Buddha after having attained Enlightenment, the Buddha expounded the Four Noble Truths that form the common ground for all schools of Buddhism.[15] It is clear from this teaching that the fundamental goal of Buddhism is to alleviate suffering. Although this aim can be understood at a spiritual level as the aspiration towards enlightenment, it also applies to the worldly dimension of suffering, even in times of armed conflict. This is why we believe that the values and practices of SEB are fully compatible with the humanitarian principle of humanity.

One could even argue that the two first Noble Truths – (1) the truth of suffering (*duḥkha*) and (2) the truth of the origin of suffering (*samudaya*) – describe reality as it is, rather than how one might wish it to be. Similarly, IHL acknowledges that wars and conflicts are a reality of the human condition, even though one may wish it to be otherwise. The third and fourth Noble Truths – (3) the truth of the cessation of suffering (*nirodha*) and (4) the truth of the path leading to the cessation of suffering (*marga*) – show the way to transform and heal suffering in oneself, and to enable others to do the same, and are of practical relevance to humanitarian responses and principles aimed at reducing and relieving suffering.

Four sublime states of mind have been taught by the Buddha: loving-kindness (*maitrī*), compassion (*karuna*), empathetic joy (*mudita*), and equanimity (*upekṣā*). These four attitudes are said to be excellent or sublime because they are the right or ideal way of conduct towards living beings (Pali *sattesu samma patipatti*). In addition, a series of four Buddhist virtues and the meditation practices used to cultivate them, known as the 'Four Immeasurables' (*brahmavihāras*), provide answers relevant to all situations arising from social contact. They are the great removers of tension, peace-makers in social conflict, and great healers of wounds suffered in the struggle of existence. They help to level social barriers, build harmonious communities, awaken slumbering magnanimity, revive joy and hope, and promote human brotherhood against the forces of egotism. They can be seen as a key Buddhist formulation of the principle of humanity.

In addition, the first Buddhist lay precept is 'I vow to abstain from taking life'. We recognise our relationship to all life and realise that harming any living creature harms oneself. According to Sulak Sivaraksa (b. 1933), the Buddha said of the First Precept: 'Identifying ourselves with others, we can never slay or cause to slay' (Sivaraksa 1992). Here is a modern reformulation of the First Precept as used in the field of Engaged Buddhism:

> Reverence for Life – Aware of the suffering caused by the destruction of life, I am committed to cultivating the insights of interbeing and compassion, and learning ways to protect the lives of people, animals, plants, and minerals. I am determined not to kill, not to let others kill, and not to support any act of killing in the world, in my thinking, or in my way of life. Seeing that harmful actions arise from anger, fear, greed, and intolerance, which in turn come from dualistic and discriminative thinking, I will cultivate openness, non-discrimination, and non-attachment to views in order to transform violence, fanaticism, and dogmatism in myself and in the world. (Plum Village Monastery n.d.b)

Whilst most Buddhists would understand the focus of the First Precept to be on abstaining from taking life, the concept of 'reverence for life' in SEB sets forth a positive duty to cultivate compassion and to protect the lives of others – an idea which is similar to the motivation expressed in the principle of humanity. The main difference between the two is that the Western cultural background that gave rise to the principle of humanity emphasises humankind as a unique species, while Buddhist teachings speak of protecting 'all sentient beings', which would include non-human life forms such as animals. The classic formulation of this principle is expressed in the *Metta Sutta*:

> May everyone be happy and safe, and may all hearts be filled with joy. May all beings live in security and in peace – beings who are frail or strong, tall or short, big or small, invisible or visible, near or faraway, already born, or yet to be born. May all of them dwell in perfect tranquillity. (Nhat Hanh 2017)

The principle of impartiality and correspondences with the Edicts of Ashoka and equanimity (upekṣā)

Whilst the principle of humanity establishes the motivation behind humanitarian action, the other humanitarian principles set out how humanitarian action should be conducted. As such, the principle of impartiality describes the way in which assistance should be rendered to others. This principle has its roots in the requirement under IHL for states to treat the wounded of both sides 'without any adverse distinction founded on sex, race, nationality, religion, political opinions, or any other similar criteria'.[16] As above, we shall begin our analysis with the OCHA wording of the principle: 'Humanitarian action must be carried out on the basis of need alone, giving priority to the most urgent cases of distress and making no distinctions on the basis of nationality, race, gender, religious belief, class or political opinions' (United Nations 2012).

The only bases that may be used to help humanitarians decide who to assist and the order in which they will be seen are need and urgency of distress. The RC/RC and NGO Code of Conduct expands upon this principle:

> Aid is given regardless of the race, creed or nationality of the recipients and without adverse distinction of any kind. Aid priorities are calculated on the basis of need alone . . .. Human suffering must be alleviated whenever it is found; life is as precious in one part of a country as another. Thus, our provision of aid will reflect the degree of suffering it seeks to alleviate . . .. (International Federation of Red Cross and Red Crescent Societies and the ICRC 1994)

This version of the principle of impartiality restates the humanitarian imperative that requires human suffering to be met with a response. Interestingly, it also makes the claim that 'life is as precious in one part of a country as another'. This value judgement helps to explain why it is so important for humanitarian assistance to be rendered with regard to need alone and not on the basis of extraneous matters, such as nationality, race, gender, religious belief, class, political opinions or who is my friend/enemy.

Emperor Ashoka of the Mauryan Dynasty, who ruled over most of the Indian subcontinent from 268 to 232 BCE, represents the first and most impressive example of Buddhist ethics and values applied in the field of governance and law (Rattini 2019). It is said that his full conversion to Buddhism came in the aftermath of the massacres during a war against the state of Kalinga, which reportedly killed over 100,000 people – including many civilians – and resulted in the deportation of over 150,000 people. Ashoka wrote that he was 'deeply pained by the killing, dying, and deportation that take place when an unconquered country is conquered' (quoted in Rattini 2019).

After his conversion, Ashoka formalised a set of ethical principles derived from Buddhist values in the famous Edicts of Ashoka (Rattini 2019). These edicts represent an inspiring effort to organise the state and government in accordance with the Buddha-Dharma. Here is a short excerpt from the *Kalinga Rock Edicts*, addressed to government administrators:

> All men are my children. What I desire for my own children, and I desire their welfare and happiness both in this world and the next, that I desire for all men .... While being completely law-abiding, some people are imprisoned, treated harshly and even killed without cause, so that many people suffer. Therefore, your aim should be to act with impartiality. It is because of these things – envy, anger, cruelty, hate, indifference, laziness or tiredness – that such a thing [acting with impartiality] does not happen. (Rattini 2019)

The 14 Edicts of Ashoka may be understood as customary rules that had a lasting influence within the Buddhist world. As such, the reign of Ashoka had a profound impact on later Buddhist conceptions of good governance and justice. Even at this early stage in the history of Buddhism, one can find an example of a leader who recognised the importance of treating others impartially, without fear or favour towards characteristics that might otherwise cause division. In order to achieve this, one needs to overcome and transform what is known in the Buddhist literature as the three poisons of the mind: ignorance, greed and hatred.

Likewise, the Buddhist principle of *upekṣā*, which means 'equanimity' but also 'inclusiveness' or 'non-discrimination', invites practitioners to treat all people equally. According to Asanga,[17] we should consider that all beings have been our mother in some past lifetime and, therefore, we should treat all beings in the way we would treat our own mother (Wangyal 2002). This serves as a basis for loving-kindness meditation – which regards friends and foes equally. Thich Nhat Hanh put this understanding into practice by working with US veterans of the Vietnam–USA War. As King recounts:

> It might seem strange that a Vietnamese should offer healing retreats for American veterans, but it is consistent with Nhat Hanh's teaching about the way to deal with suffering .... Veteran Claud Thomas, who was carrying profound psychological wounds from the war, speaks of his shock when he first encountered Nhat Hanh at a retreat. He says he never knew the Vietnamese in any way other than as the enemy. Seeing Nhat Hanh, he suddenly realised that he was not his enemy. And he just started to cry. (King 2009, 82)

Upekṣā means cultivating equanimity in every situation, but it also means maintaining an equal attitude towards everyone. According to the Buddha's teaching, there is no fundamental difference between any humans. Every individual is valued and should be treated fairly and therefore with justice. Moreover, according to Mahāyāna Buddhism, everyone should be treated equally because all have 'Buddha Nature', i.e. the ability to become enlightened. Criteria such as nationality, race, gender, religious belief, class or political opinions are therefore irrelevant.

The principle of neutrality and reflections from SEB

The corollary of impartiality is the principle of neutrality. Both principles denote a level of non-attachment to particular attributes, but the principle of neutrality specifically describes how humanitarian actors should conduct themselves in the face of (1) hostilities/conflict (i.e. military neutrality) and (2) controversies that could limit humanitarian access (i.e. political/racial/religious/ideological neutrality). The OCHA formulation of this principle is as follows:

> Humanitarian actors must not take sides in hostilities or engage in controversies of a political, racial, religious or ideological nature. (United Nations 2012)

As mentioned above, the price for humanitarian actors to be allowed to continue to pursue their objectives during times of armed conflict is that they remain completely out of the fight. In this regard, the principle of neutrality represents an affirmation that humanitarian actors will not engage in any hostile conduct which could jeopardise their protection or access during armed conflict. As a concrete example of how neutrality has been used by those affiliated with the SEB movement during the Vietnam-American War, King claims that:

> Buddhist monks and nuns, dressed in their bright yellow robes and carrying Buddhist flags for visibility, entered into the villages and walked the villagers out, while armies waited on both sides to engage the battle. At other times, monastics helped establish cease-fire lines outside of villages by approaching both sides at considerable personal risk and convincing them to retreat to lines at a distance from the village. (King 2009, 80)

This description bears a striking resemblance to the role of the ICRC in providing protection to civilian evacuees during armed conflict – including by using a distinctive sign to make combatants aware of their presence and intentions. Unlike the red cross emblem, Buddhist flags are not recognised under IHL treaties. Nevertheless, the use of Buddhist flags in this specific context would have informally signalled to combatants that the nuns and monks were not in the fight. Underpinning the ability of both groups to move around the battlefield with as little hindrance as possible and to access affected populations is their neutrality in military affairs – both real and perceived.

One important scriptural touchstone for SEB groups coming from a Mahāyāna tradition is the *Vimalakīrti Nirdeśa Sutra*. This sutra – which likely dates to the first century CE – recounts the story of Vimalakīrti, who is described in the text as having attained a level of spiritual development that surpasses that of many Bodhisattvas – perhaps even being second to the Buddha himself. However, what makes Vimalakīrti all the more remarkable is that he perfects the dharma as a layperson – a wealthy householder – rather than as a monk (Watson 1997).

This text was an important point of reference for the Chinese promoters of *renjian fojiao* from Taixu (Goodell 2008, 105–106) to Hsing Yun and Sheng Yen and, indeed, it is a common touchstone between Humanistic Buddhism in East Asia and SEB in South East Asia and the West.

In his own writing on 'suffering caused by the lack of wisdom', Thich Nhat Hanh quotes some verses from Vimalakīrti's discourse on the Buddha Way – these verses may have some bearing on how SEB groups could approach military neutrality:

> In the time of war
> Raise in yourself the Mind of Compassion
> Help living beings
> Abandon the will to fight
> Wherever there is furious battle
> Use all your might
> To keep both sides' strength equal
> And then step into the conflict to reconcile. (Nhat Hanh 1987, 95)[18]

Moreover, non-violence should be a natural and necessary part of Buddhism, because violence is a product of dualism – i.e. an 'us versus them' ways of thinking. But when we are truly mindful, we realise that all phenomena are interdependent and endlessly interwoven. In Buddhism, particularly in those traditions that gave rise to SEB, there is no such thing as a separate individual. There is no such thing as a separate object, event, or experience, because no part of the world can exist apart from all others. Rather, everything that looks like a separate entity is dependent on, and interwoven with, everything else.

Therefore, from this perspective, taking sides in any kind of conflict is always the consequence of an ignorant state of mind that discriminates between aspects of reality that are ultimately interdependent. In contrast, the Order of Interbeing and other engaged Buddhist groups stand as a contemporary example on how the Buddhist values of non-violence and the recognition of interdependence can be applied to help improve society, especially during times of armed conflict.

In addition to abstaining from taking part in hostilities, the principle of neutrality also obliges humanitarian actors to refrain from becoming involved in controversies of a political, racial, religious or ideological nature. This helps them to gain the trust of the entire population of a country and to maintain their freedom of access – regardless of who is in charge of an area or situation. RC/RC organisations tend to interpret this obligation strictly, while certain NGOs – especially those associated with particular political or religious causes – may apply the principle more liberally. This variability in approach is reflected in how the principle is formulated in the RC/RC and NGO Code of Conduct:

> **Aid will not be used to further a particular political or religious standpoint.** Humanitarian aid will be given according to the need of individuals, families and communities. Notwithstanding the right of [non-governmental humanitarian organisations] to espouse particular political or religious opinions, we affirm that assistance will not be dependent on the adherence of the recipients to those opinions. We will not tie the promise, delivery or distribution of assistance to the embracing or acceptance of a particular political or religious creed. (United Nations 2012)

Since the Code of Conduct relates to disaster relief outside of situations of armed conflict, there is no mention of neutrality in the military sphere. To a certain degree, the wording used in the passage above conflates neutrality with impartiality. Nevertheless, it still urges humanitarian actors to avoid giving the impression that their actions are designed to advance a particular political or religious cause. Indeed, many FBOs, such as Caritas and Islamic Relief, have agreed to follow this principle as it relates to their own operations.[19] It stands to reason that this would not pose a problem for SEB groups either.

In fact, among the Fourteen Mindfulness Trainings formulated by Thich Nhat Hanh that serve as the basis of SEB's engagement, several trainings emphasise the importance of maintaining a non-dogmatic worldview – and refer to the necessity of not taking sides in times of conflict. We draw attention to the first one below which states:

> **The First Mindfulness Training: Openness**
> Aware of the suffering created by fanaticism and intolerance, we are determined not to be idolatrous about or bound to any doctrine, theory, or ideology, *even Buddhist ones*. We are committed to seeing the Buddhist teachings as a guiding means that help us learn to look deeply and develop understanding and compassion. They are not doctrines to fight, kill, or die for. We understand that fanaticism in its many forms is the result of perceiving things in a dualistic or discriminative manner. We will train ourselves to look at everything with openness and the insight of interbeing, in order to transform dogmatism and violence in ourselves and the world. (Nhat Hanh 2012) [emphasis added]

There is an obvious convergence between the principle of neutrality and these mindfulness trainings, which are essentially Buddhist reformulations of ancient values as applied to our time. In both cases, the higher good – seen as the duty to alleviate suffering – supersedes allegiance to a specific sense of belonging such as a political, national, racial, ideological or even religious affiliation.

The Tzu Chi Foundation is an example of a humanitarian FBO based on Taixu's *renjian fojiao* that expressly claims to maintain political neutrality. As such, it has been allowed access to North Korea (King 2009, 6), and Myanmar during military rule (The Economist 2008). Tzu Chi (Hsing 2017, 188–192) and another Taiwanese humanistic Buddhist group, Fo Guang Shan (Johnson 2017), are two of the few Taiwanese organisations that are able to operate in the People's Republic of China. Their presence is tolerated by the authorities because they are not politically active in a way that might challenge the Chinese Communist Party. It should be noted, however, that despite their reputation for neutrality abroad, Tzu Chi and Fo Guang Shan seem to be more politically active within Taiwan.[20]

There are certainly other engaged Buddhist organisations, such as some members of the International Network of Engaged Buddhists, that have a stronger social or ecological agenda and may therefore find it difficult to remain strictly neutral when trying to advocate for social/ecological justice. These groups may regard engaging in potentially politically controversial matters as necessary in order to support the victims of oppression – and marginalised people more generally.

SEB is not a formal, structured movement with a common governance, and many different organisations within the Buddhist world are inspired by its underlying principles. All of them certainly abstain from taking part in hostilities. However, some organisations adhere to strict neutrality in the humanitarian sphere and others take a more activist approach.

As a practical matter, those organisations that follow strict neutrality in the political sphere may have fewer difficulties securing access to affected populations across the entire territory where there is an armed conflict. However, it is important to keep in mind that whilst IHL requires humanitarian actors to maintain absolute neutrality in the *military* sphere, the law does not require such actors to adhere to *political* neutrality as a condition for their protection. Therefore, SEB aid groups that adhere to either strict or activist interpretations of political neutrality represent equally valid expressions of humanitarianism and, indeed, Buddhist humanitarianism.

The principle of independence and further reflections from SEB

On the face of it, one may find it odd for a tradition that emphasises the radical interdependence of all beings to ever embrace 'independence' as a guiding principle. However, it is important to understand the specific meaning of this principle in the context of humanitarian action.

Since National Red Cross and Red Crescent Societies are auxiliaries to their respective governments in the humanitarian field, the original formulation of the principle emphasises the need for these organisations to retain their autonomy so they can act in accordance with the other principles at all times (e.g. a National Red Cross Society should never be obliged to follow a request from government to only give assistance to one ethnic group since that would violate the principle of impartiality). The principle of independence may also be read even more broadly to include *any* undue interference in a humanitarian organisation's work, whether it comes from the government or any other actor. This broader understanding is captured in OCHA's phrasing of the principle:

> Humanitarian action must be autonomous from the political, economic, military or other objectives that any actor may hold with regard to areas where humanitarian action is being implemented. (United Nations 2012)

The wording used in the RC/RC and NGO Code of Conduct reaffirms this idea that humanitarian actors should be free to make their own decisions about how to deliver assistance. In addition, it specifically includes donors in the list of potential actors who may try to steer the course of humanitarian work in a way that serves ulterior purposes.

> **We shall endeavour not to act as instruments of government foreign policy** ... We will never knowingly – or through negligence – allow ourselves, or our employees, to be used to gather information of a political, military or economically sensitive nature for governments or other bodies that may serve purposes other than those which are strictly humanitarian, nor will we act as instruments of foreign policy of donor governments. We will use the assistance we receive to respond to needs and this assistance should not be driven by the need to dispose of donor commodity surpluses, nor by the political interest of any particular donor .... In order to protect our independence we will seek to avoid dependence upon a single funding source. (International Federation of Red Cross and Red Crescent Societies and the ICRC 1994)

This understanding of independence is reflected in Thich Nhat Hanh's Tenth Mindfulness training which states:

> **The Tenth Mindfulness Training: Protecting and Nourishing the Sangha**
> Aware that the essence and aim of a Sangha is the practice of understanding and compassion, we are determined not to use the Buddhist community for personal power or profit, or transform our community into a political instrument. As members of a spiritual community, we should nonetheless take a clear stand against oppression and injustice. We should strive to change the situation, without taking sides in a conflict. We are committed to learning to look with the eyes of interbeing and to see ourselves and others as cells in one Sangha body. As a true cell in the Sangha body, generating mindfulness, concentration, and insight to nourish ourselves and the whole community, each of us is at the same time a cell in the Buddha body. We will actively build brotherhood and sisterhood, flow as a river, and practise to develop the three real powers –

> understanding, love, and cutting through afflictions – to realise collective awakening. (Nhat Hanh 2012)

In addition to this specific instruction from Nhat Hanh to protect the Sangha from instrumentalisation, the general Buddhist predisposition towards non-attachment to views could be seen as encouraging non-attachment to the will of external actors of any stripe.

The practical value of the humanitarian principles for SEB groups

To better understand how SEB groups view the practical utility of the humanitarian principles and their compatibility with SEB generally, the authors approached Somboon Chungprampree, Secretary of the International Network of Engaged Buddhists (INEB), to seek his thoughts on each principle.[21] His response echoed much of what has been mentioned above. INEB sees the principle of humanity as fundamental. Similarly, impartiality is regarded as a principle that must be followed absolutely in all circumstances.

However, Chungprampree indicated that INEB takes a nuanced approach with regard to the principles of neutrality and independence; it views the application of these principles as depending on the particular circumstances prevailing at the time and whether one side or another upholds Buddhist and/or humanitarian values. Like other FBOs and NGOs, certain SEB groups reserve the right to engage in advocacy and protest – and to take sides to support oppressed people, as required. However, a group may adhere to neutrality and independence more strictly if it makes practical and humanitarian sense to do so, for example if it is involved with mediation or peace negotiations. Although some SEB groups may adopt a more liberal understanding of the principles of neutrality and independence than others, it must be said that no SEB group would ever endorse participation in hostilities.

Chungprampree's comments combined with our own analysis of the convergence between the humanitarian principles and SEB values show that it should not be challenging for SEB or other engaged Buddhist groups to publicly adopt the humanitarian principles and to apply them to their ways of working. When working in situations of armed conflict, adherence to these principles, in turn, could help such groups to qualify for certain protections and facilitations under IHL.

For their part, those who promote the humanitarian principles and the NIIHA approach within the humanitarian sector could benefit from a better understanding of how certain humanitarian values are understood in non-Western religions and traditions. It is our hope that this study will help to promote a pluralistic understanding of the roots of the humanitarian principles in order for them to be more universally accepted in practice – by both humanitarian actors and authorities alike.

Conclusion

Considering the humanitarian principles, we can argue that they are highly related to the guiding principles of SEB. They both relate to an ethic of action, leading people to align attention with intention, and intentions with actions. Moreover, the practical ways of working that the principles promote also accord with the way that SEB groups approach humanitarian action. As we have shown, there are even some congruencies between specific formulations of the humanitarian principles and SEB Buddhist teachings.

In conclusion, spreading and deepening the knowledge of fundamental Buddhist values, and supporting the practice of mindfulness and loving-kindness meditation, not solely in a scholarly or ritualistic way, but as a foundation of social engagement, could help foster the understanding of and adherence to IHL in Buddhist populations. The dissemination of such Buddhist values will, in addition, support the action of Buddhist humanitarian workers and FBOs in situations of armed conflict by helping them to uphold the internationally recognised humanitarian principles.

We end with a quote from Shantideva that summarises the Bodhisattva aspirations of SEB:

> With a wish to free all beings
> I shall always go for refuge
> to the Buddha, Dharma and Sangha
> until I reach full enlightenment.
>
> Enthused by wisdom and compassion,
> today in the Buddha's presence
> I generate the Mind for Full Awakening
> for the benefit of all sentient beings.
>
> As long as space endures,
> as long as sentient beings remain,
> until then, may I too remain
> and dispel the miseries of the world. (Shantideva in HH The Dalai Lama 2012, 115–116)

Notes

1. See, for example, King (2009, 1) who considers the broader movement of Engaged Buddhism to transcend any of the established Buddhist sects and states that one can find proponents of Engaged Buddhism in Theravāda, Mahāyāna, Vajrayāna and non-sectarian branches of Buddhism. Some notable

individuals involved in the SEB movement include the founder of the International Network of Engaged Buddhism, Sulak Sivaraksa from Thailand (The Right Livelihood Foundation n.d.); Maha Ghosananda from Cambodia who led many peace pilgrimages known as 'Dhammayietra' (Khmer-Buddhist Educational Assistance Project n.d.); Cheng Yen, the founder of Tzu Chi from Taiwan (Tzu Chi 2014); and Dr. Ahangamage Tudor Ariyaratne, the founder of Sarvodaya in Sri Lanka (Sarvodaya n.d.). These are in addition to Dharma teachers from the Western world, such as Bernie Glassman (Zen Peacemakers n.d.) and Joan Halifax (Upaya Institute and Zen Center n.d.), among others.

2. Yen Pei remembers his encounter with a young Thich Nhat Hanh in his autobiography (Yen Pei 演培 1989, 300–301), where he also writes extensively on his travels and lectures on Humanistic Buddhism in Vietnam, Thailand and Singapore. See also Chia (2020, 91).
3. UNGA Resolution 46/182 established the principles of *humanity*, *impartiality* and *neutrality* as core principles for all humanitarian actors working within the Inter-Agency Standing Committee (IASC) (United Nations 1991).
4. UNGA Resolution 58/114 added *independence* (United Nations 2004).
5. See International Federation of Red Cross and Red Crescent Societies and the ICRC (1994). A full list of the signatories to this Code of Conduct can be found at https://media.ifrc.org/ifrc/who-we-are/the-movement/code-of-conduct/signatories-to-the-code-of-conduct/.
6. Art 71(2), API; Rule 31, CIHL (ICRC n.d.).
7. Art 15, API; Art 9, APII; Rule 25, CIHL (ICRC n.d.).
8. Art 48, API; Art 13(1), APII; Rule 1, CIHL (ICRC n.d.).
9. Art 51(3), API; Art 13(3), APII; Rule 5, CIHL (ICRC n.d.).
10. Art 13(1), API (ICRC n.d.).
11. Art 70, API; Rules 55 and 56, CIHL (ICRC n.d.).
12. Art 71(4), API (ICRC n.d.).
13. Art 70, API; Rule 55, CIHL (ICRC n.d.); (Nicaragua v United States 1986, paras 239-245).
14. SN XXII 86 (Sujatu 2018).
15. SN LVI 11 (Bodhi 2000).
16. GCI Art 12 (ICRC n.d.).
17. Asanga was a fourth-century Buddhist master and philosopher, one of the founders of the Yogacara School of Mahāyāna Buddhism together with his half-brother Vasubandhu.
18. See also chapter 8 of Watson (1997, 101) for an additional translation of the same verses from the *Vimalakīrti Sutra*.
19. Caritas International was one of the original sponsors of the Red Cross and NGO Code of Conduct and recently published a blog on the humanitarian principles, including neutrality for World Humanitarian Day (Caritas 2020). Islamic Relief is a signatory of the Red Cross and NGO Code of Conduct and recently reaffirmed its commitment to neutrality after dismissing a trustee for behaviour which contravened the principles (Islamic Relief 2020).
20. For a critical analysis of these groups' engagement with the Taiwanese government and politics more generally, see Laliberté (2004).
21. Somboon Chungprampree, interview by Andrew Bartles-Smith, 30 October 2020.

Disclosure statement

This article has been supported by the International Committee of the Red Cross (ICRC).

ORCID

Noel Maurer Trew http://orcid.org/0000-0002-2261-8341

Abbreviations

API Additional Protocol I to the Geneva Conventions of 1949 and relating to the Protection of Victims of International Armed Conflicts, 8 June 1977 (accessed from ICRC n.d.)

APII Additional Protocol II to the Geneva Conventions of 1949 and relating to the Protection of Victims of Non-International Armed Conflicts, 8 June 1977 (accessed from ICRC n.d.)

CIHL ICRC Study on Customary IHL (accessed from ICRC n.d.)

FBO faith-based organisation

GCI Geneva Convention I for the Amelioration of the Condition of the Wounded and Sick in Armed Forces in the Field. Geneva, 12 August 1949 (accessed from ICRC n.d.)
IASC UN Interagency Standing Committee
ICRC International Committee of the Red Cross
IGO inter-governmental organisation
IHL international humanitarian law
INEB International Network of Engaged Buddhists
NGO non-governmental organisation
NIIHA neutral, impartial and independent approach to humanitarian action
NSAG non-state armed group
OCHA UN Office for the Coordination of Humanitarian Affairs
RC/RC International Red Cross and Red Crescent Movement
SEB Socially Engaged Buddhism
SN Saṃyukta Nikāya

References

Bodhi, B., trans. 2000. "Setting in Motion the Wheel of the Dhamma Saṃyutta Nikāya." *Sutta Central*. https://suttacentral.net/sn56.11/en/bodhi

Caritas. 2020. *Neutrality, impartiality and independence*. https://www.caritas.lu/en/caritas-news/actualites/neutrality-impartiality-and-independence

Chia, J. M. 2020. *Monks in Motion: Buddhism and Modernity Across the South China Sea*. Oxford: Oxford University Press.

CHS Alliance, Groupe URD and the Sphere Project. 2014. *Core Humanitarian Standard on Quality and Accountability*. https://corehumanitarianstandard.org/files/files/Core%20Humanitarian%20Standard%20-%20English.pdf

DeVido, E. 2009. "The Influence of Chinese Master Taixu." *Journal of Global Buddhism* 10: 413–458.

Eppsteiner, F. 1998. "Editor's Introduction." In *Interbeing: Fourteen Guidelines for Engaged Buddhism*, edited by T. Nhat Hanh, vii. Berkeley: Parallax. https://orderofinterbeing.org/about/our-history/

Geneva Call. 2016. "In Their Words: Perceptions of Armed Non-State Actors on Humanitarian Action." https://reliefweb.int/sites/reliefweb.int/files/resources/WHS_Perception-of-armed-non-State-actors-on-humanitarian-action.pdf

Gleig, A. 2021. "Engaged Buddhism." *Oxford Research Encyclopedia of Religion*. doi:10.1093/acrefore/9780199340378.001.0001/acrefore-9780199340378-e-755.

Goodell, E. 2008. "Taixu's Youth and Years of Romantic Idealism, 1890–1914." *Chung-Hwa Buddhist Journal* 21: 77–121.

HH The Dalai Lama. 2012. *From Here to Enlightenment: An Introduction to Tsong-Kha-Pa's Classic Text the Great Treatise of the Stages of the Path to Enlightenment*. Boston: Snow Lion.

Hsing, Y. 2017. "Social Entrepreneurialism and Social Media in Post–developmental State." In *Taiwan and China: Fitful Embrace*, edited by L. Dittmer, 175–193. Oakland: University of California Press.

ICRC. n.d. *ICRC databases on international humanitarian law*. https://www.icrc.org/en/icrc-databases-international-humanitarian-law

International Federation of Red Cross and Red Crescent Societies and the ICRC. 1994. *Code of Conduct for the International Red Cross and Red Crescent Movement and Non-*

Governmental Organizations in Disaster Relief. https://media.ifrc.org/ifrc/who-we-are/the-movement/code-of-conduct/

Islamic Relief. 2020. *Islamic Relief Worldwide strongly condemns anti-semitic posts and removes trustee.* 24 July. https://www.islamic-relief.org.uk/islamic-relief-worldwide-strongly-condemns-anti-semitic-posts-and-removes-trustee/

Johnson, I. 2017. "Is a Buddhist Group Changing China? Or is China Changing It?" *New York Times*, 24 June. https://www.nytimes.com/2017/06/24/world/asia/china-buddhism-fo-guang-shan.html

Khmer-Buddhist Educational Assistance Project. n.d. *Venerable Preah Maha Ghosananda.* http://www.keap-net.org/about-venerable-maha-ghosananda.html

King, S. B. 2009. *Socially Engaged Buddhism.* Honolulu: University of Hawai'i Press.

Laliberté, A. 2004. *The Politics of Buddhist Organizations in Taiwan, 1989-2003: Safeguard the Faith, Build a Pure Land, Help the Poor.* Oxford: Routledge.

Malkin, J. 2003. "An Interview with Thich Nhat Hanh." *Lion's Roar*, July 1. https://www.lionsroar.com/in-engaged-buddhism-peace-begins-with-you/

Miller, A. 2017. "The Life and Teachings of Sister Chan Khong." *Lion's Roar*, May 8. https://www.lionsroar.com/path-of-peace-the-life-and-teachings-of-sister-chan-khong-may-2012/

Narada Thera, trans. 1978. *The Twin Verses (Yamaka Vagga) of the Dhammapada.* Kuala Lumpur: Buddhist Missionary Society.

Nhat Hanh, T. 1987. *The Miracle of Mindfulness: An Introduction to the Practice of Meditation.* Translated by M. Ho. Boston: Beacon.

Nhat Hanh, T. 2012. "The Fourteen Mindfulness Trainings." *Plum Village Monastery.* https://plumvillage.org/mindfulness-practice/the-14-mindfulness-trainings/

Nhat Hanh, T. 2017. "Discourse on Love." *Plum Village Monastery.* https://plumvillage.org/sutra/discourse-on-love/

Nicaragua v United States. 1986. "1986 ICJ 14." *International Court of Justice*, June 27.

Pictet, J. 1979. *The Fundamental Principles of the Red Cross: Commentary.* Geneva: International Federation of Red Cross and Red Crescent Societies. https://www.ifrc.org/PageFiles/40669/Pictet%20Commentary.pdf

Plum Village Monastery. n.d.a. *The Life Story of Thich Nhat Hanh.* https://plumvillage.org/about/thich-nhat-hanh/biography/

Plum Village Monastery. n.d.b. *The Five Mindfulness Trainings.* https://plumvillage.org/mindfulness-practice/the-5-mindfulness-trainings/

Rattini, K. B. 2019. "'Who Was Ashoka?' The Most Influential Figures of Ancient History." *National Geographic*, April 1. https://www.nationalgeographic.com/culture/people/reference/ashoka/

Sarvodaya. n.d. *Founder.* https://www.sarvodaya.org/founder

Schwendimann, F. 2011. "The Legal Framework of Humanitarian Access in Armed Conflict." *International Review of the Red Cross* 93 (884): 993–1008. doi:10.1017/S1816383112000434.

Shantideva. 2011. *The Way of the Bodhisattva.* Translated by Padmakara Translation Group. Boulder: Shambala.

Sharkey, G. 2017. "Buddhism in a New Key: The Roots and Growth of Engaged Buddhism." *Rangjung Yeshe Institute Symposium.* Kathmandu. https://www.ryi.org/files/documents/symposium/SharkeyRYI2017Symposium.pdf

Sivaraksa, S. 1992. "The First Precept." *Tricycle*, Summer. https://tricycle.org/magazine/first-precept/

Sujatu, B., trans. 2018. "With Anurādha." *Sutta Central.* https://suttacentral.net/sn22.86/en/sujato

The Economist. 2008. "Help with a Bow." 29 May. https://www.economist.com/asia/2008/05/29/help-with-a-bow

The Right Livelihood Foundation. n.d. *Sulak Sivaraksa*. https://www.rightlivelihoodaward.org/laureates/sulak-sivaraksa

Tzu Chi. 2014. *Biography of Dharma Master Cheng Yen*. https://www.tzuchi.org.tw/en/index.php?option=com_content&view=article&id=159&Itemid=198&lang=en

United Nations. 1991. "Strengthening of the Coordination of Humanitarian Emergency Assistance of the United Nations." UNGA Res 46/182, New York. http://www.oas.org/dil/Res_46-182_UN_eng.pdf

United Nations. 2004. "Strengthening of the Coordination of Emergency Humanitarian Assistance of the United Nations." UNGA Res 58/114, New York. https://www.ifrc.org/docs/idrl/I577EN.pdf

United Nations. 2012. "OCHA on Message: Humanitarian Principles." *Office for the Coordination of Humanitarian Affairs*. https://www.unocha.org/sites/dms/Documents/OOM-humanitarianprinciples_eng_June12.pdf

Upaya Institute and Zen Center. n.d. *Roshi Joan Halifax*. https://www.upaya.org/about/roshi/

Valente, M. 2016. "Mindfulness in Times of War: The School of Youth for Social Service." *Leadership for Sustainability*, 2 February. https://eccemarco.wordpress.com/2016/02/02/mindfulness-in-times-of-war-the-school-of-youth-for-social-service/

Wangyal, G. 2002. *The Door of Liberation: Essential Teachings of the Tibetan Buddhist Tradition*. 2nd ed. Somerville: Wisdom.

Watson, B., trans. 1997. *Vimalakirti Sutra*. New York: Columbia University Press.

Yen Pei 演培. 1989. Yige Fanyu Seng de Zibai *一個凡愚僧的自白*. Taipei: Zhengwen.

Zen Peacemakers. n.d. *Bernie Glassman, Zen Master*. https://zenpeacemakers.org/bernie-glassman/

Index

Note: Page numbers followed by "n" denote endnotes.

abhayadāna 113, 330–332, 334–337, 340
act of killing 39, 61, 62, 68, 432
affective change 352–354, 357
ahiṃsā 3, 4, 11, 17, 22, 57, 105–109, 123, 128, 130, 131, 136, 137, 257
Allen, C. 188n33
Ambedkar, B. R. 425
anattā 297, 349–353, 356
anger 33, 34, 65, 82, 160, 290–301, 303, 366, 418; world of 418
appamāda 307, 308, 312–314, 317, 319, 320, 322–326
Appamāda-vagga 308, 313, 318
Appleby, R. S. 303
armed conflict 3–5, 13, 63, 76, 77, 114, 148, 159, 160, 168, 205, 250, 262, 302, 345–347, 435; sexual violence in 345, 346; victims of 32, 159
asātarūpa jātaka 5, 29, 84, 270–277
āsavas 154–156, 158, 163
Ashoka, Emperor 3, 24, 113, 269, 308, 313, 317–319, 323, 326, 433, 434; inscriptions 319–320
assessment 22, 116, 152, 171, 176, 184, 231, 234, 277, 310, 339

bad karma 32, 59, 62, 66, 68, 69, 85, 129–131, 414
battlespace 2, 4, 229, 234, 235, 251
belligerents 9–12, 14, 15, 27–29, 32, 33, 36, 320, 321, 326; intentions of 28, 29, 32
Benesch, O. 244
Berry, Thomas 186n17
bhikkhus 97, 151–156, 161, 162, 291, 296
blockade 84, 259, 260, 263, 272, 276
Bodhicaryāvatāra 295, 297, 298, 301, 429
Bodhisatta/Bodhisattva 68, 69, 80, 81, 84–86, 88, 97, 118, 119, 121, 122, 130, 131, 182, 197, 218, 295, 296, 395, 396, 412, 413
Braboszcz, C. 238
*bra*hmavihārās 290, 300, 301, 304
Buddhaghosa 65, 93, 297, 300, 351
Buddhahood 80, 267, 408, 411–414, 419
Buddhists 2, 5, 12, 21, 22, 26, 29, 31, 37, 39, 58, 81, 88, 111, 120, 154, 208, 241, 321, 393; belligerents 2, 3, 13, 21, 22, 27, 28, 30, 32, 41; combatants 2, 3, 55, 64, 240, 356, 392–394, 400, 402; communities 176, 178, 180, 184, 320, 325, 326, 340, 345, 348, 356; doctrines 6, 18, 207, 332, 335, 343, 345, 356, 357; empirical realism 147–164; ethics 12, 13, 18, 19, 21, 30, 31, 39, 40, 66, 178, 208, 266, 276, 277; *Jātaka* stories 99, 223, 258, 265–267; justification 167, 170, 272; just war thinking 26, 27, 36; law 18, 113, 114, 383; military ordinariate 391, 392; monks 96, 114, 155, 308, 319, 321, 322, 324, 326, 427, 435; non-violence 20, 196; perspective 28, 33, 126, 132, 134, 172, 178, 293, 300, 365, 370, 412, 414; practice, two dimensions of 93–96; principles 2, 4, 6, 25, 161, 168, 208, 346, 348, 412, 415; soldier 4, 105, 106, 124, 136–138, 195, 196, 200, 201, 204, 207, 208; statecraft 13, 22; teachings 9, 10, 37, 39, 40, 78, 110, 293, 312, 321, 326, 348, 349, 392, 394; texts 24, 29, 32, 40, 277, 330, 331, 336, 337, 349, 351; thinking 207; traditions 77, 81, 82, 101, 102, 197, 330, 332, 333, 335, 337–339

cakkavatti 113
Cakkavatti-sīhanāda Sutta 3, 23, 125, 150
Chadha, M. 175
Chakrabarty, Dipesh 378
Charney, Michael 6
Chogye Buddhist Chaplaincy Manual 390–403
Chogye Order 390–392, 402; of Korean Buddhism 6, 391
civilians: advisors 272–274, 276; life 14, 168, 231, 308, 419; objects 14, 31, 63, 131, 168, 230–232, 234, 236, 308; population 13, 14, 67, 84, 85, 168, 174, 176, 230, 231, 263–265, 274, 276; starvation of 261–265, 274, 275, 277
Clausewitz, C. von 209
cognition 170, 171, 173, 174, 179, 183, 184, 238; process of 170, 171, 174, 179, 183, 184
collateral damage 231, 235, 236, 239, 240, 307–312, 314, 321
combatants 4, 28, 34, 35, 65, 160, 161, 163, 213, 215, 217, 219, 220, 222, 223, 236, 346, 354, 355, 370; lives 213–224
common humanity 18, 20, 205, 291, 298, 390, 392, 399, 401, 402
compassion 29, 60, 64, 68, 69, 129, 134, 153, 218, 240, 300, 301, 353, 354, 370, 395, 397, 411, 425, 432
compassionate intentions 130, 134
compassionate killers 69, 70
conflict-related sexual violence (CRSV) 5, 116, 343–350, 356
conflict zone 160, 245, 246, 250
constructed realities 156, 158–160, 164
contemporary failures 39–41
controversies 310–312, 435, 437
Conze, E. 190n51
corruptions 23, 110, 154, 155, 159, 163
Cox, C. 185n3
Crosby, K. 298

David, É. 186n10
death 37, 58, 59, 82, 106, 112, 115, 153, 177, 213, 220, 223, 244, 383, 414
decision-making 237, 239, 272–274, 276, 308, 311, 312, 314, 320, 322, 325, 326
defilements 93, 96, 154, 155, 163, 293, 294, 296, 298, 300, 363–365, 373
Delorme, A. 238
Desbordes, G. 233
Devānāmpriya 87
Dhammasaṅganī 290
Dharmadharmatāvibhāga (DDV) 4, 167, 169–172, 174, 176–180, 182, 183
Dīgha Nikāya 112, 149, 176, 365
dignity of life 409, 410, 412–419
Dinstein, Y. 205
discernment 94, 240, 245, 397, 401
discrimination 15, 168, 170, 179, 184
dosa 91, 95–97, 154, 158, 290, 293, 295, 299, 300

ego 152, 153, 297, 333, 418
empirical realism 4, 148, 149, 151, 153, 161, 162
emptiness 39, 180, 248, 249, 297
enemy 24, 28–30, 38, 59, 66, 70, 122, 131, 185, 217, 219, 220, 235, 399, 402, 414, 419, 434
equanimity 233, 234, 300, 301, 371, 372, 395–397, 431–435
Essential Buddhist Teachings for the Armed Forces (EBTAF) 393–397, 399, 400; conflicting values in 397–398
ethical/ethics 64, 128, 129, 168, 169, 176–178, 204, 206, 208, 267, 270, 386, 387; conduct 33, 81, 107, 173, 176, 178, 180, 181, 208; framework 290, 291, 294, 303; principles 56, 77, 79, 81, 82, 87, 88, 208, 215, 366, 372; soldier 208, 209
ethnic groups 63, 70, 321, 371, 439

fear 113, 117, 118, 131, 132, 134–136, 162, 330–332, 334, 337, 366
fearlessness 113, 122, 330–337, 340; gift of 23, 122, 330–334, 336, 337, 340
fog of war 228–251
Ford, Roshi James 243, 244
forgiveness 5, 81, 290, 292–295, 297, 299, 300, 302
French, S. E. 204
fundamental intelligence 167, 168, 170, 178, 180, 181, 183, 184
fundamental principles 7, 13, 57, 427, 430

gender 6, 273, 344, 348–352, 356, 433, 435
Gethin, R. 59
Gillette, D. 197
Grotius, Hugo 15
guidance 6, 23, 29, 78, 82, 93, 128, 171, 176, 178
Gyeltsen, Lodrö 27

Hagenbach, Peter von 208
Hahusseau, S. 238

Hallisey, Charles 216
heedfulness 30, 31, 308, 312, 313, 317–320, 322, 323, 326
Heirman, A. 60
hell 57, 58, 60–62, 65, 68–70, 124, 125, 245, 247, 413, 414
Holbeche, R. 387n4
horses 62, 84, 113, 118, 119, 331, 401
Hultzsch, E. 177
humanistic Buddhism 425, 426
humanitarian action 7, 351, 431, 433, 438, 439
humanitarian actors 4, 7, 428, 429, 435, 437–439, 441
humanitarian assistance 261, 263, 265, 276, 431, 433
humanitarianism 18, 392, 429, 430, 438
humanitarian principles 76, 81, 416, 425, 427–431, 440, 441
humanitarian workers 148, 153, 160, 163, 164, 339
humanity: principle of 123, 265, 309, 332, 411, 428, 431–433, 440

ideal soldier 196, 197, 207, 208
Ikeda, D. 417–419
impartiality, principle of 433, 439
independence 7, 152, 428–430, 438–440
indigenous ideas 383–386
individual characters 171, 176–179, 181
injury 14, 63, 65, 109, 130, 168, 231, 232, 308, 311, 346
intentional starvation, civilians 5, 257–277
interconnectedness of life 414–416, 419
international armed conflicts 220, 230, 264, 311, 335, 428
International Committee of the Red Cross (ICRC) 56, 195
International Criminal Court (ICC) 264, 273, 345
invariability of life 414

jātakas 27, 28, 80, 214, 215, 217, 218, 220, 221, 267, 271, 272, 275
Jayatilleke, K. N. 98, 99
Jenkins, S. 129
Jerryson, M. 58
Johnson, B. 196
Jones, K. 171, 175
Jung, C. G. 197, 210n10
just war thinking 26, 27, 36

Kafr Qassim 208
Kālacakra-tantra 33, 38
karma 19, 27, 28, 38, 39, 67, 106, 107, 124–127, 161, 332, 333; principle of 161, 353
khanti 5, 82, 84, 289–304, 367
Khantivādī Jātaka 295, 296
kōan introspection 229, 238, 241, 243, 245–250
kōan practice 228–251
Koenig, W. 387n3
Konbaung Dynasty 378, 380, 383
Korean Buddhism 6, 390, 391, 397, 398, 400
Korean War 391
Kosuta, M. 111

Lauterpacht, H. 219
Lederach, J. P. 156
legitimate soldiering 205
Liivoja, R. 204, 205
lineaments 11, 13, 26
loving-kindness 78, 84, 134, 137, 300–302, 353, 354, 395, 425, 431, 432

Maalouf, A. 189
Madhyamaka inquiry 195–209
Mahā-nidāna Sutta 4, 149
Mahāvam 26, 58, 59, 88, 89, 100, 101, 318
Mahāyāna 11, 13, 25–28, 41, 68, 172, 181, 196, 197, 204, 393, 412, 419, 435
Majjhima Nikāya 149, 162, 365, 367
Martens, Fyodor Fyodorovich 281n37
Martens Clause 123, 223, 265
Matsuoka, M. 410
Mayama, A. 416
McMahan, J. 224n1
means of protection 117–119
meditative/meditation 4, 5, 153, 237–239, 300, 325, 350, 352–357; practices 151, 155, 229, 233, 238, 241, 247, 249, 250, 301; techniques 30, 133, 345; training 5, 133, 163, 343, 347, 352, 354–356
military: atrocity 200; chaplaincy institution 391; ethics 11, 33, 123, 239, 268; necessity 3, 6, 29, 31, 32, 131, 205, 258, 259, 324, 331, 332, 392, 397, 400; objectives 14, 84, 131, 133, 168, 230, 231, 259, 264, 339, 411; training 2, 3, 5, 11–13, 20, 33, 34, 40, 41, 355, 356
mind 28, 35, 58, 60, 61, 95, 107, 133, 151, 174, 182, 249, 296, 300, 314, 325, 364, 373, 395, 415

mindfulness 34, 35, 65, 133, 182, 238, 239, 241, 304, 325, 366–368, 372, 437, 439; levels of 325; practice 133, 237, 304, 317, 441; trainings 182, 239, 437
modern warfare 76, 152, 234, 236, 244, 259, 260, 310, 311
monastic *versus* lay ethics 21–22
monks 24, 56, 96, 107, 114–116, 118, 132, 214, 242, 243, 322, 324, 427
Moore, R. 197
moral anchor 247
motive 64, 67, 68, 81, 115, 124, 293
My Lai 208

Nance, R. 185n8, 188n36
neutrality, principle of 429, 435, 437
Nhat Hanh, T. 424
Nichiren Buddhism 408–420
Nitobe, I. 244
Noble Eightfold Path 19, 107, 121, 126, 133, 364, 368, 369, 372, 373
non-combatants 31, 32, 65, 66, 262, 263, 337, 339, 363, 364, 369, 370, 372, 373, 378
noncombatants 232
non-duality 170, 171, 175, 176, 180, 181, 184, 427
non-international armed conflicts 230, 264, 270, 271, 309, 311, 335, 428
non-self 297, 348, 349, 352, 353, 356
non-state space 381, 382, 387
Norman, K. R. 177, 216
nuclear weapons 6, 309, 326, 327, 409, 415–420; abolition of 417, 419; use of 260, 309, 326, 327, 409, 415–417, 419

O'Connor, S. 416
oneness of life 414, 415
openness 102, 432, 437

Pali Canon 12, 61, 111, 118, 121, 148, 149, 153, 158, 162, 312
Pali texts 3, 147–149, 152, 154, 155, 160–163
papañca 4, 156–159, 163
path factor 370, 371
patriotism 207, 244, 392, 402
perception, process of 170, 171, 173–175, 180, 183
Pictet, J. 430
prayers 393, 394, 396–399
precautions, in attack 231–232
precolonial Myanmar royal campaigns 377–387
proportionality 14, 31, 32, 130, 131, 168, 233, 263, 264, 308–311, 320, 326; rule of 230, 231, 234, 308, 310, 311, 314
protection 5, 35, 83, 113, 117, 123, 230, 330–332, 334, 335, 337, 338, 412, 419, 435
Provost, R. 215

Raṭṭhapāla 92, 93
realities 152–154, 156, 157, 159, 163, 179, 180, 183, 248, 344, 345, 427, 431; of conflict 137, 138, 151
reasonable military commander 32, 232, 233, 237, 310, 320, 321; standard 233, 321; test 232, 233
reasonableness 116, 233, 310, 321
reciprocity 128, 174, 215–217, 219, 220, 291; of risk 215–217, 220
relative reality 172, 176
responsibility 126, 263, 265, 332, 334–337, 340, 364–366, 368
restraint 2, 5, 6, 10, 11, 36, 41, 162, 204, 215–217, 220, 314, 367
reverence for life 432
right livelihood 119, 121, 122, 369, 371, 373
right mindfulness 133, 368, 369
risk 29, 30, 70, 205, 213, 215–222, 249
Roy, Kum Rataplan 276
rural administration 380–383
rural warfare 379, 380, 385, 387

Sakka 3, 29, 55, 80, 82, 83, 119, 298, 299, 365, 366
Sakka-sam 82, 83
Sassòli, M. 186n10
Scheible, K. 217
secular mindfulness training 241
self-defence 10, 35, 113, 115, 258
self-regulation 11, 160, 161
Seneviratne, H. L. 59
sentient beings 18, 22, 28, 30, 37, 115, 334, 337, 396, 400, 425
sexual violence 338, 344–351, 369, 371
Shakyamuni Buddha 240, 408, 409, 418
shame 35, 60, 164
Shay, J. 205
siege 258–261, 263–265, 267–273, 276; warfare 5, 257, 259–261, 265, 266, 268–270, 275–277
situational awareness 2, 34, 367, 368
Skilton, A. 298

Socially Engaged Buddhism (SEB) 424–441
Soho, T. 249
Sōka Gakkai 408–413, 415–419
soldier: as responsible individual 196, 203; in social context 205–207
soldiering 21, 119, 120, 123, 197, 204–206, 208; karmic implications of 123–127
South Korean military 390–403
Southwold, Martin 294
sovereign responsibility 334–335
Stanley, Elizabeth 34
starvation 257, 259–265, 269, 270, 276; tactics 260, 264, 268, 271
statecraft 3, 16, 22, 25, 91
state power 81
state space 381, 382
suffering 77, 78, 81, 101, 102, 154, 174, 175, 270, 272, 295, 296, 298, 302, 303, 353, 354, 425, 431, 432
Sugiki, T. 129
surrender 24, 30, 215, 217–223, 259, 262

Taixu, Chinese Buddhist monk 425
targeting 4, 31, 63, 65, 168, 217, 230, 234–236, 250
Tatelman, J. 281
Thera, Nyanaponika 301
Theravāda 12, 22, 60, 62, 133, 337
Tieken, H. 188n32, 188n33
Tissa, Dhanuggaha 214
Trager, F. 387n3
training 2, 19, 33, 162, 163, 173, 174, 179, 181, 182, 239, 243, 244, 325, 398
Treaty on the Prohibition of Nuclear Weapons (TPNW) 417, 419

Ummagga Jātaka 5, 86, 267–270, 272, 275
unrestrained violence 37, 381
unskilfulness, roots of 95, 96
unwholesome behaviours 293–294
upāya-kauśalya 129, 203, 204, 240, 425

Vajrayāna 13, 25, 26, 37, 38, 41
Vajrayāna *Kālacakra-tantra* 27
VanLandigham, R. 204
Varela, F. J. 173
variability of life 413–416
Venturi, F. 140
Vepacitti Sutta 6, 364, 365
victims 27, 32, 157, 230, 299, 302, 344, 348, 350, 417, 438
Victoria, B. D. 244
vinaya 18, 96, 98, 102, 114–116
violence 17, 21–23, 108–111, 137, 148, 150, 151, 159, 218, 257, 338, 339, 378, 380, 382
vulnerable populations 330–340

wachsame Sorge 312
Wakefield, Alex 5
Walzer, M. 220
war: conduct 29–31, 127–132; greater accommodation for 25; restraint in 215–217; thinking 26, 27, 36; tradition 9–13, 15, 25, 28
warfare 5, 106, 111, 121, 129, 215, 217, 219, 222, 259, 262–265, 268, 322, 378, 386, 400, 415; method of 259, 262–265, 267, 269, 277, 413–415; rules of 219
warplanes 394, 398
Wei Chueh 425
Whittemore, L. 236
wholesome behaviours 293–294
Wick, Roshi Gerry 242
Wu, J. 116

Yen, Sheng 425
Yen Pei 425
yodhājīva 58, 124

Zanesco, A. 239
Zen Buddhism 36, 241

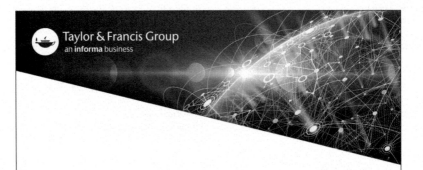